Charles Kennedy Scott needs no introduction to those engaged in the vocal art. At the age of seventy-eight his experience of voice training goes back to the early days of the century; he has been in the front rank of choral conductors since 1904 when he founded the Oriana Madrigal Society. In this encyclopaedic survey his vast experience is placed in the hands of every singer who realises the potentialities of the human voice. It is a book to read and study; even more it is a work to refer to constantly, for it will provide an answer to every technical problem that will, in time, confront the singer and the teacher. It is, in fact, the most comprehensive book on singing ever written in the English language.

Many are concerned at the present decline in the standards of singing. Yet the voice is a common instrument in expressive power. Singing links up quite naturally with everyday movements of the muscular system, such as laughing, sighing, etc.; the tensions applicable to these, delicate or extreme, are the tensions which also govern the voice; there is no break in the system from diaphragmatic to resonantal control by way of the laryngeal or vibratory apparatus and the broad lines of muscular action must be understood before the singer can hope to control the voice. It is, of course, essential that the singer has an ear for beauty of sound and a feeling for the sense that sound conveys.

The weakness of theory is its lack of illustration; how, for instance, can a student *how* to achieve the end in sight.

hat tone-colour ined. But if he it, knows what what modifies ie road to dis- e must be sup- by living ex- ill never teach

THE FUNDAMENTALS
OF SINGING

THE FUNDAMENTALS OF SINGING

AN INQUIRY INTO THE
MECHANICAL AND EXPRESSIVE ASPECTS
OF THE ART

by

CHARLES KENNEDY SCOTT

CASSELL AND COMPANY LTD

LONDON

CASSELL & CO LTD
37/38 St. Andrew's Hill, Queen Victoria Street
London, E.C.4.

and at

31/34 George IV Bridge, Edinburgh
210 Queen Street, Melbourne
26/30 Clarence Street, Sydney
Haddon Hall, City Road, Auckland, N.Z.
1068 Broadview Avenue, Toronto 6
122 East 55th Street, New York 22
Avenida 9 de Julho 1138, São Paulo
Galeria Güemes, Escritorio 518/520 Florida 165, Buenos Aires
Munshi Niketan, behind Kamla Market, Ajmeri Gate, Delhi
Haroon Chambers, South Napier Road, Karachi
15 Graham Road, Ballard Estate, Bombay 1
17 Central Avenue P.O. Dharamtala, Calcutta
P.O. Box 275, Cape Town
P.O. Box 1386, Salisbury, S. Rhodesia
P.O. Box 959, Accra, Gold Coast
25 rue Henri Barbusse, Paris 5e
Islands Brygge 5, Copenhagen

First published 1954

Copyright 1954 by Charles Kennedy Scott

SET IN 10 PT. BASKERVILLE TYPE AND
PRINTED IN GREAT BRITAIN BY
EBENEZER BAYLIS AND SON, LTD., THE
TRINITY PRESS, WORCESTER, AND LONDON
F. 554

"O heart, whose beating blood
was running song"

Swinburne

CONTENTS

PART ONE
(mainly theoretical)

CHAPTER 1. THE VOCAL MECHANISM AND THE WAY IN WHICH IT FUNCTIONS

CHAPTER 2. THE MATERIAL OF SINGING

CHAPTER 3. TONE IN GENERAL

CHAPTER 4. THE RELATION OF BREATH TO TONE

PART TWO
(mainly practical)

CHAPTER 5. PRACTICAL VOWELLING AND ARTICULATION

CHAPTER 6. VOWELS AND CONSONANTS IN PARTICULAR

Preface

In this book I have made an attempt to indicate a path which singers might pursue with advantage. Though written in a prosaic, practical style it is nevertheless intended to lead to the heights where poetry dwells. Fortunately, even technical discussion is not without its excitement.

The keynote of the book is sounded by the words 'tension' and 'resistance', the culture of which alone can give the necessary voice-control, and secure the avoidance of those pitfalls which beset the singer.

Perhaps it is almost hopeless to try to reach unanimity as to vocal procedure. Some twenty or thirty years ago The Society of English Singers had such an end in mind. The intention was to issue a manual, embodying principles deduced from the experience of all members of the Society: principles which might be taken as proved and authoritative. But though there was much pleasant post-prandial talk upon the subject, the manual was never written. Each member had his own view of what was wanted and it seemed impossible to establish a common measure of agreement. If such a manual had appeared it would probably have been the work of a single member of the Society, faintly approved by a majority. The failure did not hinge on taste: whether, for instance, a certain quality of tone were to be preferred to another quality; but simply upon the means necessary to secure tone at all. The Society, there-fore, had very little influence upon the course of English singing. Perhaps it was just as well. In the end we each have to work out things afresh, and, because of it, individual authority may be the safest guide. Vital views seldom proceed from other than a single mind. 'A man is strongest when he stands alone,' said William Tell. At least this is a considerable aspect of the case.

Yet it is obvious that there must be a right answer to everything, provided the question posed is not, in itself, at fault. It would otherwise be a world of 'sound and fury, signifying nothing'. Even in the transcendental sphere we are entitled to believe that realities exist which can be detected by an intuitive process of the spirit, if not by the rational mind. All religions testify to this, though universal assent may be lacking.

In the material sphere, however, where material means are con-cerned, exact knowledge seems possible: for cause and effect are there to check us at every turn. We may not understand what a thing is in itself—we can only accept it, heart to heart, as a sort of

ix

A*

finality—but how it works and what its qualities and characteristics are is quite open to our inspection. In short, we can be reasonably sure about technical matters, provided correct observation has been brought to bear. But it is not as easy as all that. We must not attempt to minimize the difficulties of the case.

What is certain is that some sort of a review of our vocal methods is necessary, and we can at least hope that our present argument is the right one. Doubtless, contradictions will be found in the course of this book, but, on examination and in a fuller context, they may be allowed to be apparent, not real. As here stated, the relationship of means to ends seems clear and consistent, and probably to be relied upon.

It is a pity that we cannot get more guidance from the early practice of singing. In medieval times they must have sung well.[1] These were the days of an almost purely vocal music which made great demands upon the singer; and we cannot suppose that, in the best performance, such demands were not met in a beautiful or, at least, a sufficient way. It was the period of what may be called 'poetical' song, since the music was so bound up with poetry. Later, in the seventeenth and eighteenth centuries, came the splendid epoch of 'instrumental' song, the epoch of *bel canto*, when the voice was developed as an instrument rather than as a vehicle for words 'cloaked' by music. At the present day we are probably closer to the ideals of medieval singing than to those of instrumental song. In serious composition we have reverted to a view which gives equal prominence (if such may be) to the claims of word and note. But we have to reconstruct an effective technique wherewith to deal with it. Strangely enough, we learn next to nothing of the older techniques which were employed when the summits of 'poetical' and 'instrumental' song were undoubtedly reached, and have to turn to the principles of Greek athletics in order to put our vocal principles upon a sound basis.

It would, of course, be ridiculous to assume that these principles are never applied in modern vocal practice, but, as far as I am

---

[1] Though Thomas Morley strongly censures the church singers of his day. In a *Plain and Easy Introduction to Practicall Music* (1597), talking of the motet, he writes: 'The matter is now come to that state that though a song be never so well made and never so aptly applied to the words, yet you shall hardly find singers to express it as it ought to be: for most of our Church men (so they can crie louder in the quier than their fellowes) care for no more; wheras by the contrarie, they ought to study how to vowel and sing cleane, expressing their words with devotion and passion, whereby to draw the hearer as it were in chaines of gold to the consideration of holy things. And this, for the most part, you shal find amongst them, that let them continue never so long in the church, yea, though it were twentie years, they will never study to sing better than they did the first day of their preferment to that place . . . ' Perhaps ideal singing at any time is rare.

aware,[1] they have not been applied systematically, embodied in a theoretical treatise.

There are no schools of singing to-day, in the older sense. Common aims and standards, disseminated largely by oral means, scarcely exist. The nearest approach to them is to be found, as might almost be expected, in the debased form of singing known as 'crooning'. Here we do discern a sort of 'style' spawned over a large part of the globe and entertained by large masses of the civilized race: which leads us to echo the words of Flaubert: 'A mésure que l'humanité ... se perfectionne, l'homme se degrade.' It is true that it does not apply to everyone, but it can scarcely be denied that this phenomenon is a pointer and portent that seems to have a bearing not only upon artistic but political unity.

In itself this particular sort of singing is, of course, not worth noticing, but in relation to singing in general, it cannot be left out of account; for it involves a radical cleavage between professional and popular art which is in the nature of a house divided against itself. In more fortunate times such a cleavage did not exist. There were greater class distinctions, but a similarity of thought and taste yet prevailed. The same results were not achieved by every class. Aristocratic culture was different in degree from that of humble folk. It reached higher ground but it was nevertheless part of the same scene.[2] If we talk about ourselves, it belonged to England; it had been developed by English custom; it bore the English stamp. A village church was a cathedral in miniature; a cottage stool had in it the makings of a coronation chair; a folk-song led up to an ayre or ballet; plain-song, the people's religious song, to a mass, motet or madrigal. There was no exception, no break in the chain from the lowly to the more exalted. Even in the use of words the speech of Chaucer and Shakespeare is but a supreme flowering of common speech. Listen to this:

[1] I have, purposely, read very few modern books on singing, and it may be that others have covered the same ground in a better way. I have preferred, however, to rely mainly on my own experience, and what follows as regards vocal technique in this book has been arrived at, in nearly every case, through first-hand observation and (I hope) good logic. There is, of course, much common property—or what has become so—in a book of this sort. No one makes an entirely fresh start in anything: a fact to be remembered with due humility.

[2] Great art, though it ultimately arises from the people, makes no bid for popularity; advertisement, in the modern sense, is its foe. It is doubtful (as someone wrote, I forget where) whether such art can survive the *full* process of democratization, where everyone is theoretically as good as his neighbour. It is essentially selective, aristocratic; requiring to be removed from 'the world of half-pints and dart-boards'. Blazoned in twelve-inch scarlet letters over a doorway in one of London's busiest streets were the following legends: 'Epstein's "Jacob and the Angel" ', 'The World's Greatest Shocker', 'The Sensation of All time', 'Four and-a-half Tons of Thrills'. Such a vulgar appeal would never have produced the sculpture in question.

> The thing you wot of, milord, were a great trespass towards
> God, a great offence to the world, a great grief to my friends, a
> great shame to myself, and, as I think, a great dishonour to your
> Lordship. . . . Good Lord, that you should seek after so bare and
> country stuff abroad, that have so costly wares at home! . . . then
> were I, poor wench, cast up for hawk's meat, to mine utter
> undoing, and my friends' exceeding grief.[1]

What was it? The reply of a milkmaid, a poor country girl, thus
resisting the discreditable advances of an Elizabethan nobleman.
Such language was common property. Even an ordinary police
notice of the time was couched in rich prose. Everyone enjoyed the
sounding phrase, the grand manner; and in varying degree, all the
other good things of life. There was no absolute division of interests
or values. Nowadays, although democracy has triumphed and all
men are theoretically equal, the nation is essentially in twain. What
seems like unity is in a great degree nothing but a pretence; the
people have lost their birthright for a mess of proletarian pottage.
Popular music and singing shows it as clearly as does any other
aspect of cultural activity. Perhaps it will come right; it is certainly
not right now.

What can be given as a principal characteristic of this state of
things? It is almost ludicrous to simplify it into a single feature, but
it does seem possible to do so; at any rate it is coincident both
physically and mentally with *slackness*. As regards singing and what
is popularly sung, the whole point is in connection with that word.
The technique of crooning depends upon slackness;[2] its purpose also
is to suggest lax emotions in which a minimum of mind is displayed.
This pernicious tendency in popular music has been sensed by the
best of our younger composers and in order to avoid it they have
perhaps over-tensioned their work, to the extent of making it hard
and unsympathetic, thereby eliminating much of romance.

But as popular practice percolates professional practice—the few
can never wholly stand against the many—we find that to-day the
fetish of looseness rules even the best vocal teaching. We see it in
the injunction to 'open your mouth horizontally, not vertically',
delivered under the authority of Dr. Bairstow and Plunket Greene—
the implications of which will be discussed later; we hear it in the
almost universal lack of steady sound and unmistakable vowels—
most vowels are just an approximation through slack shaping; in

[1] Quoted by Virginia Woolf in *The Second Common Reader*. Compare the culture
of this language with modern popular language as shown in the letter quoted on
p. 79; though the sincerity of utterance is probably greater in the second case and,
in a human way, we are infinitely moved by it.

[2] Since writing the above I found the same idea fully developed in Max
Nordau's *Degeneracy*.

flabby, half-wrought articulations; in intonation in which niceties or even exactitudes of pitch are disregarded; and in all the various aspects of rhythm and resonance. And here let us say at once that a singer who cannot keep his voice steady is a bad singer. A boy can hold a steady note; why not a trained vocalist?

Perhaps we lay too much stress on the general habits of a community and the influence that popular taste has on professional taste. But as it was to the good in the past it may well be to the bad now. Whatever the truth of this, the cause of so much indifferent singing, even when devoted to serious song, is precisely the same as that which is responsible for the enormities of present-day popular song, viz., slackness, looseness, or what you will. Relaxation is taught as the guiding principle; or, if not taught, allowed; the claims of tension are ignored—tension in fact is apt to be treated as an unclean thing amidst the loveliness of unfettered expression. Hence results which are patent. Stability, balance, and real freedom go by the wall.

There is of course another side to the picture. When we think of the choirs and competitive festivals in which hundreds of thousands of our singers take part, ought we not to cite *this* as the significant popular movement, and say that all is well? And what of the schools, particularly the secondary schools, which, at the present time, often have the benefit of remarkably competent and devoted music-teachers, and are contributing so much to the raising of musical standards in the country? Such widespread activities certainly command our admiration and rouse our hopes; but unfortunately they do not negative the still more widespread defects of modern singing, nor destroy the validity of the assertion that, in spite of seventy years of free education, the culture of the nation is split in two. The 'haves' and 'have nots' are just as distinct now as ever before; the only difference being that there is an exchange of roles from the creative to the material sphere. I am afraid I am one of those who do not believe that human endeavour can be predicted, any more than can the form and shape of the clouds, or any other natural appearance. In the main the spirit seems to blow where it listeth; the social state is quite incalculable at any particular period.

So much has been hoped from education, but of what kind? We have made a fetish of the word

> *Who having all the substance lost,*
> *Attempts to grasp a name*

as though it were a result to be gained, rather than a means to be adopted. We imagine that education can be effected by a sort of spoon-fed treatment from above; whereas it is an organic process of development from below. We have been trying to stand a pyramid upon its apex. It has not worked. A healthy state of art builds upwards from the people as a whole. It is they who fertilize the flowers of culture. The kind souls who bring art to the masses, without letting them produce their own art in daily life, are almost wasting their time. The possibilities of every age are probably the same but results vary vastly according to the *Zeitgeist*, against which individuals are powerless. No one can engineer a golden age, or prevent an iron one. From such a standpoint individuals need not be subject to blame, though values do not thereby disappear.

What is wrong is, of course, the predominance of the commercial element in modern life. If the modern system had replaced the old in quality, something, though not everything, could be said for it; but it is perfectly clear that what we call commercial as opposed to creative enterprise has not produced the goods. In the fourteenth-century Ming period it is said that Chinese painting became 'not an expression of life but a marketable commodity'. With this went a decline in its power and originality, and a tendency towards artificiality appeared. History repeats itself.

It may be thought that points are touched upon, here and elsewhere, which have nothing to do with singing in the ordinary sense. That may be so, but I conceive singing to be the expression of the whole man and that an important aspect of the singer's art is his attitude towards it; what he desires of it; in short, what his mental and emotional bias is. He need not 'wallow in the immensities' all the time, but he will get precious near to them when he pursues his art *con amore*.

Comparatively few performers have powers of original interpretation, or of what may be called 'rightness' in determining the meaning of a verbal or musical idea—at least I have found it so; but this may easily be due to the temper of the time with its general atrophy of individual creativeness. There is, thus, far too much tendency to rely upon the findings of another, or to copy those findings, parrot-like. The words of Byrd, 'a good teacher and an apt scholar' still sum up an ideal relationship, but the scholar's progress will depend far more on his own aptitudes than on his teacher's ability. I fancy that at present we are inclined to over-rate the value of teaching. One is almost ashamed to add to the millions of text-books which flood the educational market—our forefathers did very well with only a handful. Such books are almost the chief thing in the literature of to-day; certainly, I am informed, the only paying thing in musical publication is school music.

In a former book, *Word and Tone*, published in 1933, much the same ground was covered as here, in a rather different way. An analysis of the relations of breath and tone quality was perhaps its chief concern, whereas in this book tension is discussed more. In both books I have tried to give relaxation its due—relaxation must certainly not be ruled out as an element of vocal technique—but it was implied rather than insisted on in *Word and Tone* and a more balanced statement of tension and relaxation, as of two opposing forces, has now been attempted. So much danger is, however, to be associated with a flabby use of the muscles that we must be very careful as to how far we counsel it.

From a literary point of view it is regrettable that a certain amount of repetition occurs in the following pages. It could not be helped. Sections, treated for the most part as self-contained units, were bound to overlap. Generally, however, when an observation is repeated it is in a different context, and so has a somewhat different significance. In any case, it may serve to drive home what I believe to be an important truth.

My warmest thanks are due to Mrs. Lily Coleridge, Miss Olwen Temple, Miss Eileen Poulter and Miss Shiela Henderson for considerable labour in copying or typing my MS.; to Miss Gladys Todd for kindness in checking the typescript and for grammatical corrections; to Dr. Eva Morton and Dr. S. Taylor Harris for physiological information; to my friend Mr. Hubert J. Foss for his ever-ready advice and help; to Dr. H. Lowery and to Sir Richard Paget, Bart., for radical improvement of some of the more scientific statements in the book (though they are in no wise to be held responsible for any errors of fact that may be observed); and, not least, to Messrs. Cassell and Company for their act of faith in accepting the book for publication. I should here also like to remember valuable criticism from my friend, the late Thomas H. Corfield, Esq.

London,
   May, 1954.

Introductory

WHY DO WE SING?

MUSIC is a very desirable thing—'I cannot but give way to it,' said Pepys, 'whatever my business is.' Pepys, of course, was the amateur *par excellence*; he would not be denied his music at any time. Few, however, can be as frankly indulgent as he was towards what may be only a recreation. But many listen to music, or play, or sing, whenever they get the chance, simply because they want to, without thinking any further about it. To be fond of a thing is the best of all reasons for approaching it.

But there is something more to be said. If we only sing for the pleasure that we get out of it we shall scarcely know what singing means, in a full sense. Is it for what *we* do that singing is so satisfying, or for what *it* does? The questions are not quite the same, though their complete dissociation is perhaps impossible.

We never act from a single motive. Secondary motives group around what we may take to be the only one; many of these we might not care to acknowledge. But setting aside unpleasing ones, such as vainglory, which so easily beset the artist, we recognize others that certainly operate when we sing. We may be moved by scarcely more than a physical impulse—a healthy desire to use our voice and lungs; or by impulses which have more relation to spiritual factors, such as the urge to communicate some thought or feeling—'It is more human to be heard than to hear,' said Dante; or to share some emotion—perhaps the strongest of all impulses, deriving from the very centre of our sympathetic tendencies; or to provide an escape from the world by entering a finer sort of reality. These pressures arise from our deeper selves and come less from instinctive reactions than from the slow broodings of experience. Hopes of a successful professional career may also be a spur, though this will not secure much artistic headway. Apropos of this there is a striking comment by Dame Ethel Smyth in her *Impressions that Remained*. She studied at the Leipzig Conservatorium, and, remarking on the poor standard of the work there, attributed it to the fact that most of the students intended to be teachers and had no other ambition. Dame Ethel was probably right.

The use of our muscles both proceeds from and gives a sense of well-being. We enjoy physical activity provided it is not overdone; then it becomes a pain. Singing, in a large measure, is a form of athletics, in which considerable muscular effort is employed. It involves a high degree of breath control which brings into play some of the strongest muscles of the body. Though requiring the greatest delicacy of muscular adjustment, singing is still dependent upon strength and energy of an extreme kind, and it is as well to underline this. Listless, half-hearted people cannot sing.

Mental activity is likewise a pleasure, and such pleasure is supplied by any form of music. The structure of music is very complex. Rhythmic and tonal analysis show this at once. Great musical edifices such as Byrd's Great Service or Bach's B Minor Mass—to name perhaps the highest peaks of unaccompanied and accompanied song—embody intellectual power and a faculty of organization scarcely credible to the non-musician. The wise Dr. Johnson certainly made a *faux pas* when he said 'that if he had learnt music he should have been afraid he would have done nothing else but play. It was a method of employing the mind without the labour of thinking at all, and with some applause from a man's self.'

The other arts, painting, sculpture, poetry, cannot compete with singing in their all-out activity. Only instrumental playing can, and this not to the same or continuous degree. The subtle accord between body and mind is certainly realized more completely in singing than in any other form of human activity. In games perhaps more physical energy is expended but the æsthetic goal cannot compare with that provided by the combination of poetry and music.

Why do we sing? The couplet:

> *Some sing because they must*
> *. . . Others because they can.*[1]

gives us another answer to the question. But are 'can' and 'must' in such apposition as all that? Here an antithesis is made between skill and impulse; between the singer who at any moment can supply the externals and even the spirit of a song, and one who, like Shelley's skylark,

> *. . . pours forth his full heart*
> *In profuse strains of unpremeditated art.*

It is a pretty but not very sound antithesis because a splendid technique can certainly be used to express spontaneous feeling. Nevertheless it probably remains true that natural impulses tend to cool under the discipline to which the artist must subject himself.

---

[1] I do not remember where I came across this couplet—probably a waggish variant of Tennyson's *I do but sing because I must*
And pipe just as the linnets sing.

A calculable element intervenes and 'first fine careless raptures' give way to something which is more balanced and profound—'Still waters run deep'. The practised artist *knows* what he is doing. The unpractised one is far less aware not only of what he does, but of how he achieves his end.

Thus the impulse to sing is perhaps the greatest with those who make no pretence to the highest standards; with those who sing unconsciously, as the birds sing for the life that is in them. Thought, in a way, goes against the sheer physical delight of singing.[1] You could hardly expect a philosopher to sing, even in his spare moments; nor is poetry packed with reason usually very singable. The best lyrics are those which express emotion in a clear, direct and unequivocal way. But depth is not ruled out thereby.

Doubtless there is a primal urge which never ceases to assert itself, an instinctive joy in creating from which all artistic expression derives—there is joy even in the telling of sorrow; we 'cull solace from the rehearsal of old griefs'. But this urge, this 'must', does not dispose of the situation. Perhaps what is missing is to be found in the foregoing word 'old'. With the mature artist it is not so much an immediate impulse called forth by some experience of the moment—by some sight or sudden reaction to persons or places—it is more a rehearsal of *old* griefs or gladness, 'emotion remembered in tranquillity'. Moreover, in great art whether of composition or executancy, there is always a certain quiet mastery, an objective control in which a good deal of the artist's personal excitability has been shed. Fussiness is exchanged for breadth, the accidental for the general, and there is a tendency towards a reflective rather than an active attitude. Nothing is so difficult as to secure a quality of repose in performance.

[1] There is no doubt that such delight occurs; a sort of overflow of animal spirits passes into song just as it does into speech. People who chatter continuously are generally full of life. On the other hand many dislike singing, not because they dislike song, but because no physical satisfaction attaches to the use of the voice. Sometimes, also—indeed, often—shyness militates against vocal expression. We do not like to wear our heart upon our sleeve if we feel deeply; and this we have to do with singing. Many who are greatly interested in the technical aspects of singing, and, in a private way, are quite competent, still prefer publicly to express themselves more impersonally, upon an instrument. It is verbal significance which is apt to be so embarrassing. A pupil will sing a song in comparative comfort if his thoughts are mainly on the music; but get him to speak the words and he will generally be confused and self-conscious.

Further, the physical delight that singing gives scarcely operates in the same way with instrumental performance. Singing is much more allied to instinctive muscular action; the playing of an instrument is undertaken consciously—it by no means represents the same physical outlet, and is undoubtedly a more detached form of musical expression. To a certain extent this seems to justify us in regarding instrumental as a purer form of art than vocal, and it is a fact that the difficulty of being impersonal in singing is very great. It requires a control that few singers possess, though it is not beyond their powers.

And so, whether we know it or not, the best song and even the manner of its singing, tells of far-off events and is not just a momentary flash of feeling. It has been long in coming to birth; it is more than an outpouring of good spirits. 'Can' and 'must' are slow processes in the singer's endeavour. They are complementary not antagonistic factors, and 'will' must be added before the cycle is complete.

But the worthwhileness of song does not depend upon self-expression, upon the light that it throws upon ourselves. We are not the chief thing, only a vehicle. Song is a voice from the infinite calling up our sense of wonder. We live in the midst of we know not what, we see through a glass darkly; but somehow by the arts of poetry and music we sense the mysteries of existence. Man and his surroundings: these must ever be the theme—human love and passions—prayer and praise—all this, welling up in the midst of nature—the sky, sea and earth, and all that therein is—the daily and seasonal changes that occur in connection with life, growth, decay, death. The magic touch of beauty brings us to the threshold of understanding not only material shapes and colours, but the spirit that is in them. This is the most precious part of art. Thoughts 'that lie too deep for tears' can be found in the simplest strain of song, just as Wordsworth found them in 'the meanest flower that blows'.

We sing because we 'can'; because, like the sculptor or painter, we have so far dominated our chosen medium. To this extent singing is a game of skill, a playing with words and notes, almost for the fun of it. Hence the fine craftsman, the prima donna of the *cadenza* and the *roulade*, the virtuoso who astonishes us by his feats of power and speed. But the craftsman must merge into the visionary before we are satisfied. If he be a composer he must master notes till he can

> *Untwist the cords that tie*
> *The hidden soul of harmony.*

If he be a singer, till the voice tells of something which is beyond sound and yet must take shape in it. Skill and wonderment are the two main impulses which possess the artist. By the first, even when it does not mean much, he moves us to admiration; by the second, even if the tricks of the trade fail, we are turned to large issues.

ARTISTIC VALUE

Dr. Johnson was once asked whether the novels of the day were so poor because they treated love as their theme. 'It is not because they treat, as you call it, about love, but because they treat of nothing that they are despicable,' was his reply, and that is the answer to be given with respect to much so-called art.

An immense amount of it meets us at every turn. It is scarcely worth while talking about, but it is a force to be reckoned with. In terms of thought its contents are almost nil. It is entirely unsatisfying when judged by the test of a rich life. It harps upon trivialities, seldom reaching beyond the bounds of shallow laughter. Ecstasy or tragedy is quite outside its range. In short, it registers nothing with which the serious artist is concerned and through which his work derives its dignity.

It is exceedingly difficult, of course, to appraise the merits of a work of art. Any pronouncement we may make about it is liable to be countered by the old retort, 'De gustibus non est disputandum.' But concerning values there can and must be a good deal of dispute. It seems as if we have no objective standards to back up our æsthetic opinions. But surely we have. We can observe people and things around us, we can know ourselves; we can ask whether such and such a work of art is true to human nature as part of nature; whether, therefore, it is true to nature herself. Does it fill us with something of the respect that we have for a flower or any other natural object? If it does not, if what we are offered has no relation to nature; if in its poetry or music it reveals nothing of even its author's real life, still less of our own life or that of others; if it is a sentimentality, an insincere counterfeit when submitted to the test of reality—as it nearly always is, for instance, when the word 'God' is introduced into a secular song—then surely we have a right to say that such and such a work of art is bad. Others may produce it, others may like it—private and public taste can be deplorable—yet this does not eliminate the truer, deeper values. They have been unperceived by those concerned; that is all. If some can see those values, that is enough to prove them; nor, strangely enough, are they disproved even by those who apparently deny them. It simply means that their minds, as conscious organs, cannot see the wonder of their own being, just as an animal is unaware of its own beauty. 'I never see things like that,' said a lady to whom Turner was showing what, to her, was one of his strangely-coloured pictures. 'Don't you wish you could, madam?' was the artist's reply, and it is applicable here. The trouble is when people have no such wish.

Thus the test of poetry and music is whether it proceeds from life; whether in the words of Emerson it is 'Out of the heart of nature rolled' or derives from untrue, artificial elements. If the former it will enhance life, and make for fine art and artists.[1]

---

[1] 'Pure joy .. culminates ultimately in a deep sentiment of gratitude, in a great and profound sense of reverential wonder at the richness of life. To the wise man

Song is a many-sided thing, as various as nature herself; but, at its best, it is always a true and not a shoddy revelation of some facet of human experience. It must provide for any call that we wish to make upon it: for the more solemn moments of life as well as the lighter ones, for the deeper yearnings and more abiding satisfactions, as well as for those of more passing import. At its best it must minister to what Montague calls 'a boundless release of heart and mind'. These tests apply to all forms of art. Both the song and the singer must be judged by them. Nor are these tests in doubt. Great poets and musicians have shown us the levels at which we should try to work. Our standards fortunately are already supplied.

The Mechanical and the Vital

There is a difference between presentation and interpretation, at least we will distinguish the terms here. In singing a song we can either merely show its form, making clear the words, the time and the intervals of the music—this would be presentation in sound, of little more account than a printed page would be to the eye; or we can show how the words and music strike us. If we remain unmoved by the song, if it arouses no emotion in us which we communicate to our performance of it, we are simply in the realm of the mechanical. A perfectly objective performance of just the symbols and lineaments of the song could as well be undertaken by a machine. If, however, the song has touched us so that we perceive its meaning, to give the meaning we shall have to use phrasing, accent and such fervour as befits the expression. But we shall avoid anything that is unfitting or irrelevant, that does not arise from the nature of the song itself. We shall make use of our physical and emotional powers, as directed by our artistic sense, modelling them to our purposes as a sculptor might model his clay; but we shall never willingly obtrude our personality in the process, so that we focus attention on ourselves. That would be to apply our powers wrongly and false expression would result. This danger is at all times present with performance, and particularly with public performance which in some ways is likely to be best achieved by a performer who likes the limelight. St. Ambrose's warning should be

the real world is infinitely richer than that of fiction or imagination. He lives in the consciousness of his own littleness and narrowness, of his backwardness and his inability to exhaust the resources of life. He sees himself, as one who is too rich, who is overwhelmed and whose power to receive is not equal to the gifts bestowed. His cup is already overflowing, his capacity is exceeded by his possessions. And, in that, he in this way exercises unintentionally an influence as an example, he is a true educator of men in inner spiritual freedom and in the one true happiness.' *Hartmann's Ethics* (Tr. Stanton Coit) II, p. 243.

pondered, even though it referred to church music. 'In chanting,' he said, 'modesty is the first rule.'

True expression is not unfitting or irrelevant; it is implicit in what we are expressing. Every accent, every nuance, is called forth by some feature of the song. 'Architecture,' observes Whitman, 'is what we do to it when we look at it'—a somewhat cryptic saying, but meaning, probably, that only what we see in a thing is, *for us*, the thing itself. In the same way what we do with a song, if it is right doing, shows no more than that we have understood it, seized its significance, though this will be achieved and must be achieved, in our own way. This alone is vital performance, and the ideal at which we should aim.

It is sometimes supposed that expression and interpretation are at variance; that to put 'expression' to a piece is something that is stuck on to it to make it more attractive—so that expression seems to refer to the performer and his particular skill, interpretation to the work that is being performed. To vary what we have already said, expression is but the synchronization or agreement of what we feel with the object of our feeling. This also constitutes interpretation. Thus expression and interpretation are the same thing. Both the piece and the player are required; the song and the singer. 'Live ideas cannot be hung on dead lamp-posts.' Only a mind can interpret.

To interpret an idea, then, it has to be appropriated by the interpreter, to become *his* idea, *his* possession. The values and the enthusiasm that are expressed are his, fired and stimulated by the objective thought with which he is brought into contact. This complete yet modest use of our powers raises the art of the performer to a high level, and if such powers are not used the result is wholly unsatisfactory; but they can only be evoked by adequate ideas. Nine-tenths of popular song at the present day would disgrace the brains of a rabbit. How different was folk-song in which the most vital and lovely traits of human character were reflected! That is why even some simple labour in field or workshop is infinitely more to be respected than the futile exhibitionism which often masquerades as art: for the former serves a useful purpose, the latter none; since based upon either stupidity or pretence it has no ideal content and is devoid of any reality or relationship that would link it up with 'the reason of things'. It is true neither to the seen nor the unseen, to the world of appearance, nor the qualities which that world encloses.

Singing is a revelation of the soul. That it is so is the only reason sufficient to explain why we sing and why we want to sing. There is no art of singing unless this is granted.

xxiii

Secondary Uses of Music

We used the word 'useful' just now. As applied to art, that word needs to be carefully watched; for much of the vulgarity of modern life shows itself in utilitarian tendencies: as when 'separate bathrooms and the use of a private chapel' was advertised by a large up-to-date transatlantic hotel.

William Byrd gave the following among his well-known Reasons 'to perswade everyone to learne to sing': that the exercise of singing 'is delightful to nature, and good to preserve the health of man'; that 'it doth strengthen all parts of the brest and doth open the pipes'; and that 'it is a singular good remedie for a stutting and stammering in the speech'—all of which Reasons are true, but not righteous altogether. Something needed to be added; and Byrd does so in his final Reason—the one that concerns us as artists: 'The better the voyce is, the meeter it is to honour and serve God therewith; and the voyce of man is chiefly to be imployed to that ende'— not a utilitarian end. Allowing for a free interpretation of the word 'God', this Reason could be accepted by any modern singer. Without some such idealistic background very little good can come out of singing or anything else; and most of the great composers and musicians of the past have felt that the main purpose of their work was very much as Byrd states. Other reasons are entirely secondary. They have nothing to do with music as an art, and indeed may very easily lead to its degradation such as by handing it over to the doctor for therapeutic use; to the works-manager to increase the output of his workmen, or (as I believe it was reported) to the zoo-keeper to improve the appetites of the animals under his charge.

Even its consolatory function somehow falls short of what we ask of music. It is not enough that 'killing care and grief of heart' should be assuaged by gentle strains, or that they should charm sleep when the soul is overwrought. Music is something more than 'medicina doloris'. It has such ministering powers, but the artist as such does not lay much store on them, for primarily he is not out to do good to his fellow-men. When people say that music has cheered and helped them, it is a good thing; but it is not *the* thing, because it does not in the least guarantee the value of the music that is so used. To one who needs music to soothe the nerves or distract the mind, almost any music would serve; and to supply such music is not at all the artist's main purpose. That purpose is to create 'a thing of beauty' 'to the glory of God' as Byrd would have said. Then the artist is fully engaged, and with this ideal urge satisfied, his work, according to his creative gifts *may* become of service to man and possibly 'a joy for ever'. It would almost seem as if art resulting from any other motive is suspect; it is certainly so when it is provided as entertainment, which, displacing it from its central enthusiasm, spells decadence and disaster in the long run.

'True for thy truth's sake, for thy strength's sake strong,' was Swinburne's tribute to a brother poet. In this sense 'Art for art's sake' is a perfectly credible though maligned watchword, for it enshrines the idea of absolute values demanding our obeisance; from which values comes the aspiration which is the very life-blood of art.

The beneficent influence of music is unquestionable, but, without wishing to take too austere a view, no form of art can claim æsthetic significance where the mind scarcely operates. There was a recent play of Mr. J. B. Priestley's, *Let the People Sing*, the title of which represents an admirable affirmation of liberty; but the really important point is 'What the people sing' or 'How they sing': in short, what judgment is brought to bear. In approaching art all our critical and intellectual faculties, as well as our receptive ones, must be at the alert, and it is from the use of these critical faculties that the artist probably derives his greatest satisfaction. The artist is not merely a passive pleasurist; he is an active participator in upholding artistic standards. After any work of art a question mark is posed. To accept music as so much delectable sound, to desire it as 'the food of love' (as the Duke did in *Twelfth Night*) or any pabulum which is purely emotional, is largely to misread the nature of music, in its completeness; and to deny the contribution that music demands from us. 'Art for humanity's sake' has temporarily replaced 'Art for art's sake'; but, if understood aright, the latter with all that it implies in critical, impersonal valuation, probably stands for a safer statement of principle. It is very easy to be taken in about 'Humanity'.

An artist must be wholehearted with respect to his work. If he is moved to produce it from, say, a charitable impulse, it will probably be worth very little because his adherence to beauty has been deflected. He cannot serve two masters. He may be kind and charitable in disposition, but this has nothing to do with the immediate production of his art; he may do discreditable things and yet be a fine artist. The sphere of beauty is not the sphere of goodness, though happy it is when goodness, truth and beauty meet. All the artist has to do is to fashion something in the best possible way. That something may be a domestic utensil or as unsubstantial as a dream. The artist may have to take utility into account, but this is just a condition of his work, the direction given, the limits set which channel but do not artistically determine what he is about. Whatever it is, the artist is only concerned with its beauty.

The part of art that matters has no 'use'. A sunset has no 'use', but our heart leaps when we behold it, just as Wordsworth's did at the sight of the dancing daffodils.[1]

Starting from the instinctive conviction that such secondary uses of music as we have referred to are wrong, it may seem as if we are protesting too much, since there is 'applied' art of all kinds apparently to refute the argument. All ritual art is purposeful and there are labour songs and marches and lullabies—delightful to listen to, serving more than a purely musical end. What are we to say about them? We cannot deny the enlivening effect of a spirited march or the help that a sea-shanty gives to a strong and steady pull. Is this to no purpose? Cannot we have both the art and the use? Of course we can, and of course we do. Music undoubtedly has a physically stimulating or calming effect, due to similarities between our bodily movements and its own. That is how music touches us. There must be a nexus. The rocking rhythm of a lullaby or the forceful regularity of a march accord respectively with cradling movements or the steps of soldiers. All musical expression takes place through movement of some sort, whether it be rhythmic, melodic or harmonic. Even so, a lullaby or a march represents illustrative music, rather than music that has been produced for use; and such music if it be good enough, is often enjoyed quite apart from any avowed purpose. Thus beauty rather than use distinguishes it. A mother does not make a beautiful lullaby to put her child to sleep. That may be the ostensible reason but a few random, rhythmic sounds would do that. She makes a lullaby in order to satisfy her love of beauty and because of that the song with which she calms her child is beautiful. In any case all this is very different from using music for an active purpose for which it is not formally related.

---

[1] Another striking passage from *Hartmann's Ethics* (Vol. II, p. 336, Tr. Dr. Stanton Coit) adds point to this view. In a chapter on Radiant Virtue occurs the following:

There are in life remarkable men to whom hearts are attracted as by some secret spell; or perhaps another metaphor fits more closely; in their presence all hearts are opened. No one goes away from them except laden with gifts, yet no one can say what he has received, one only feels that in such men the meaning of life is somehow perceptibly fulfilled, the meaning which one elsewhere seeks in vain. And one feels that in mere communion with them something of this meaning is carried into one's own personality. A stream of light, a splendour, a spiritual grace floods one's life. But one does not comprehend it, one only feels the mystery of it. Comprehension is confined to the sphere of discerned values and of what is serviceable for them. Radiant virtue, however, is of service in no direction. No other values lie behind it. It is only for its own sake, 'a useless virtue'.

Its moral value for him who imparts has no equivalent in the value of the gift. And again that gift has no other value except what is inherent in itself. Hence radiant virtue can never be common to all. And yet the moral wealth of every virtue is somehow related to it, as if it gave to each a meaning. As Nietzsche expresses it in his comparison with gold: 'But tell me, how did gold come to have the highest value? *For this reason, that it is uncommon and of no use and bright and mellow in lustre. It is always radiant.*'

Pure beauty, like pure knowledge, raises itself above practical considerations, and to link it up with well-being, except in a spiritual sense, is, somehow, to besmirch it.

Singing a Physical Matter

But though physical welfare cannot be considered as more than secondary and incidental to the real power of music, it cannot be too strongly insisted that singing is a physical operation, dependent upon muscular exertion. It is, of course, a spiritual activity—of this we have just spoken—at its highest leading nearer than anything else, perhaps, to a manifestation of pure spirit; but this spirit can only be expressed by physical means.

Nor soul helps flesh more now, than flesh helps soul.

We indeed know nothing about music till the senses and the muscular system are brought into play. Tone, rhythm, and all musical attributes have no being, for us, except in relation to our physical organism; so that the first thing to do is to train the muscles to capture and control the elusive thing which music is.

And as with our muscles, so with our senses; they too are of the stuff of music; if not the means, the material. 'Wherefore did he create passions within us, pleasures round about us, but that these, rightly tempered, are the very ingredients of virtue?' wrote Milton. If for 'virtue' we substitute 'music', this quotation serves quite well. Reason is the tempering, controlling factor; and as the same author says a little later, 'reason is but choosing'. Again the region of criticism from which we cannot escape! The soul therefore is 'enabled by our body' according to Donne, and we have to develop and bring into service our bodily powers if, through song, we would pursue the way to music's 'high court celestiall'.

Speech the Basis of Song

An instrument can deal with music, as such, far more easily and effectively than can the voice—even allowing for the achievements of coloratura. But singing has never become wholly identified with purely musical processes, and probably never will. At such periods as it has unduly veered towards them both musical and poetic standards declined; the true glory of song departed. That glory undoubtedly has its origin and being in speech, and we shall be wise never to forget this. The loveliness of song resides largely in the loveliness and variety of speech, of which, with music, it is compounded. Language, that 'miraculous means of mentalizing time and space', brings us into firm touch with the external world—that perhaps is its chief, though not its only function; music rather with the internal spirit, with the qualitative essence of things. Both together, employed simultaneously, offer a vehicle for the complete expression of the beauty and mystery of life such as is impossible in the instrumental sphere alone; but as each sphere, vocal and instrumental, has its own range and limitations, it is not altogether right to compare them, only to distinguish them.

Though music, as some hold, may be the final state to which all the arts ultimately lead, it was almost certainly not the first state. In the beginning of organized thought was the word. It was the word, not music, through which man consciously separated himself from animals, and by which he substituted precise verbal idea for the more or less meaningless cries of beast or bird. Song developed through inflected speech, by which in earliest times collective incantation was made more effective. It was indeed a perfectly natural development which we see in later times happening in Plainsong, which enshrined the ritual of the Christian Church. To begin with, the simplest of inflection was used—as we know by its written signs. Then this was developed into the highly varied and complex Gregorian verbal-musical system which held the key to modern music and has never been surpassed as a fount of pure song. This combined use of words and music has always been characteristic of song, as the natural expression of the human voice, and it probably always will be. To do away with words would eliminate half its strength.

Yet some musicians pretend that words are of no account in vocal music, and that it does not matter whether one hears them or not. Actually one often fails to hear them; but if the words are worth hearing it is a waste of good material and to the discredit of the singer, though the fault is often that of the composer when voices and orchestra are concerned.

The Influence of Words on Music

Words give a subtle shape to the music apart from their poetic beauty. Human means alone can form a word, but a mechanical operation can quite well determine the pitch, length and colour of a note. The constant variation of vowel in song, the nervous articulation of consonants make for a measure of vitality in singing that is quite denied in instrumental playing. One might even be prepared to say that unless the instrumental performer is sensitive to verbal processes and takes his cue from them, he will to some extent be insensitive to the possibilities of instrumental performance;

his playing will otherwise be comparatively rough. Ordinary speech, of course, supplies some of the needful stimulus, but it is not till it is carried further, into really eloquent delivery, that its full influence upon music is exerted.

Speech Values

Few speak (or sing) well naturally. Elocutionary study is needed to show how beautiful words can be. The speech of many of our public men is atrocious; fine emotion is almost incommunicable through it. The music of words is certainly not within their possession; and if it is not they miss much of the grace of life whatever their practical achievement. 'Thy speech bewrayeth thee.' It is not for nothing that we tell a gentleman by his speech. It has the tradition of ages behind it and has a present as well as a past significance of spiritual culture. But the speech of every so-called gentleman is not necessarily beautiful. The untrue, affected speech of many of the so-called upper classes is just as obnoxious in its own way as the boorish accent of those who have been placed in less fortunate ranks of society.

Our Native Tongue Essential

From words, therefore, one may learn, as in no other way, what beautiful instrumental playing may become; but this must happen through our own English tongue. It was a sign of, and perhaps a reason for our relative failure to produce outstanding composers and singers, during the eighteenth century, that our music was then largely divorced from our own language. At that time there were hardly any comings and goings between our poets and musicians; the former showed comparatively little interest in music, and even less understanding of it; and an absurd reliance was placed on foreign musicians and teachers of singing. As if an Italian or a German could ever teach an Englishman adequately. What we need, in order to be singers—it also has vital repercussions in instrumental music—is a sense of English rhythm and English pronunciation, the beauty of which is just as capable of still further development, as of degradation. No foreigner can teach us this, still less can he show us the real meaning and inspiration of English poetry. 'La vérité est dans les nuances'; and we alone can understand the shades and subtleties of our own language, and the truth that is conveyed by them. Allowing that good tone, as an abstract ideal thing, is much the same in every country, it still remains that for us it needs to be approached through the English language and English sensibilities: for there is no reason for its use except to express English feeling. To apply the ideally appropriate tone to an English word and to unify it with its context must be our prime concern. Perhaps the foreigner can teach us how to sing 'out', a thing we are averse to doing; but not how to sing 'in', how to express our inmost being. He can teach us sound but not sense. Yet in approaching a greater vocal sensibility (which is largely the sensibility of words) there is a danger of refining style to such an extent that the tonal power, the muscle and sinew of the voice is weakened.

THE PATTERN OF ELOQUENT SPEECH

Habits of good singing should not be difficult to acquire though, often, singers seem to have a grievous search for them. Some little time ago a Russian lady, already of some standing in the vocal profession, being discontented with her voice, came to me to discuss how she might improve it. I had to tell her that it was very badly produced and warned her (as singing professors generally do) that if she studied with me she would have to begin *de novo*. I thought this would discourage her—I did not much wish her as a pupil— but it had no such effect. 'Oh,' she said, 'zat is nothing; I be at ze beginning six times already!' Such seems to be the fate of very many singers. Perhaps this lady had toured the Continent to find the perfect elixir of vocal tone, whereas it could only really come from her own country and language. Yet, for us, and English singing, the course should be easily set, by the proper patterning of eloquent English speech. *Is* our speech eloquent? Does it really mean anything, or is it just gabble? The verbal pattern is what we must go by; we must check all our singing by it; certainly not in a general way, by the patterns of *singing* which are offered, for most of such singing patterns are but distortions of the nature of speech. Their technical processes are quite incapable of expressing the heights and depths of the human spirit, which (again to underline) represents both the aim and the test of singing.

MUSIC ALSO HAS ITS RIGHTS

So far, in dealing with singing, we seem to have placed a heavy bias on words. But music has its rights, and indeed, even in song, a separate being, if we like to divorce it from words. The two elements are stronger together; being largely of one flesh they complement and fulfil each other, and when associated imprint themselves on the mind as neither would by themselves. This is illustrated by folk-singers who can only sing their song as a whole. They can never remember the tune without the words, or vice versa.

Nevertheless words and music are not indissoluble even in the purest form of recitative. What might be called 'musical elocution' is the *point de départ*, the start and root of singing—so much so that the study of rhetoric might well precede that of music, as it did in the middle ages; but music is the foliation and the flower. The singer must therefore be a musician in the instrumental sphere, quite apart from song: for he has to discover the music in song, as well as to give the words their significance. It should be possible, and indeed it is essential for the singer to be able to make the music of a song beautiful by itself: for, as we have said, music has a message of its own. If words have been well set they will of course supply the main clue to the expression—the singer's task is relatively easy if he has any real sense of words; but even if the words were not there, and only the music remained, he should still be able to make the music presentable. The singer, in short, must be both poet and musician,[1] as he was in troubadour times; or at least capable of thoroughly understanding both poetry and music. The musical portion of many songs such as Handel's 'Largo' to take a well-known example, can, of course, be played instrumentally, without words; and it does not lose much by this treatment: for the connection between words and music is slight. The air is self-sufficing—it is the nature of an air to be so, even though it can serve the purpose of song as well. But the more perfect the fusion of words and music, the less can the two be separated. They have a common life; each is explained by the other. Later we shall refer to this matter again and try to see how the sometimes conflicting aims of music and poetry should be adjusted.

Self-help, etc.

Progress is impossible without aural perception; our own ear must hear, our own imagination must supply the model, our own faculties must decide whether we are approaching it—otherwise we shall never do much, nor will any amount of reading or discussion prevail. Undoubtedly we are helped by others and by outside factors. 'No man liveth to himself.' The traditions we inherit, the general atmosphere in which we move, the teacher who inspires and shows the physical means by which the spirit is made manifest: all this has its influence. But though the position may be illuminated

---

[1] The singer's art is thus a more difficult one than either that of the elocutionist or the instrumentalist, for he combines *both* of these arts. Yet singers on the whole take it far less seriously than do these other practitioners in respect of their arts. Too often the singer is a bad musician and a poor speaker. Ask him even to distinguish the rests in music or to read aloud a poem, or declaim a dramatic piece, and you will see what happens in the majority of cases.

for us, it must be stormed and taken by ourselves. Then it becomes the citadel of our personality, a unique vantage point from which hitherto unviewed prospects can be seen and shown. Even the great Buddha did but 'lead the way'. He offered no salvation. Nor can expensive lessons, or any teacher.

Finally, the artist determines technique, not technique the artist. In the case of a singer, his imagination and sensibility require certain means for their expression, and these means are technical. There is a way to do everything, but the kind of thing that is done will necessitate the particular way of doing it. Thus artistic impulse, artistic standards are the determinants of technical processes. For instance, without an ear for good tone, methods of tone production are bound to be bad. A teacher may know how to patter 'principles' of singing, but their realization is the thing that matters. The 'good teacher' is the fine artist, neither more nor less. That is why one often comes across excellent teachers who know very little about the way they get their results; they teach by admirable instinct, rather than by knowledge, and may even triumph over technical misstatements, cancelling them out in practice. If they knew more they would be still better teachers; but they are infinitely more serviceable to the pupil than the knowing fellow who relies upon catch-words to pull him through. Not every 'good teacher' can produce a good pupil—the 'apt scholar' is part of the bargain; but it is quite certain that anyone who is not an artist, effectively or potentially, never can.

A technical treatise must be concerned in the main with General Principles; their application must be left to individual judgment. To get our general principles right is a great thing; if they are not right, everything is wrong. But at the same time we must remember Blake's thrust at 'Indefinites'. 'He who would do good to another must do it in Minute Particulars'; 'General Good is the plea of the scoundrel, hypocrite and flatterer'; 'For Art and Science cannot exist but in minutely organized Particulars'. This is where the 'apt scholar' comes in. His task is to adjust minute particulars; the teacher's is rather to secure the foundation. Without a mind of his own the scholar will never do much. Even a guide-book has its disadvantages, unless we are in a hurry. Half the pleasure of covering new ground is in what we see for ourselves, the surprises that come, the discoveries we make. When others have blazed the trail, high adventure is discounted, the sense of novelty is dulled, the joy of conquest considerably diminished. Second-hand knowledge may be useful; it is seldom exciting.

PART ONE

(mainly theoretical)

Chapter 1

THE VOCAL MECHANISM
AND THE WAY IN WHICH IT FUNCTIONS

MECHANISM and the way in which it works always presents an interest. The danger is that we forget the object of its use, fixing our attention upon the means by which that object is achieved. Thus, as students of singing, we may get to love what is undoubtedly the fascinating study of our instrument, neglecting the thought which is ultimately to be expressed; or be occupied too largely with technique, with the way in which the instrument is used, rather than the æsthetic appeal towards which that use should be directed.

It is possible to sing well while knowing absolutely nothing of the processes by which it is brought about. The trouble begins when people do not sing well—and hardly anyone does naturally; then it would seem that technical means have to be discussed.

Physiological details of the voice, even of an elementary kind, are sometimes tabooed by singing teachers; not without reason, for it is very easy to go astray. But since the singer is required to have, and can have, conscious control over most parts of the vocal mechanism, he should know what he has to control. That is just common sense. There is no need, however, to go into elaborate anatomy. That is for the doctor in the case of vocal repairs. The singer's chief tool is the ear, not the dissecting knife.

The voice is produced by the vocal mechanism, a machine or instrument made up of our flesh and bone and capable of continuous readjustment, such as is necessary to meet the varied and ever-changing requirements of music and speech. It is worked by our muscular system.

The mechanical basis of singing must be thoroughly recognized. It may be considered under three sections:

1. The separate parts of the instrument.
2. The assembly or integration of the parts.
3. The instrument in use.

SECTION 1: THE VOCAL INSTRUMENT

(a) *The Breathing Apparatus*

This consists of the lungs, with their casing (the thorax, or ribs) and the muscular system which controls the act of breathing. This system comprises the muscles which raise the ribs, and the abdominal

3

muscles, chief amongst which is the diaphragm or muscular wall which divides the lungs from the intestines and upon which the lungs rest.

All this apparatus is capable of great development, and it is not till this has taken place that it is fully serviceable for singing. Ordinary breathing will not do for the singer. Sufficient breath will not be derived from it nor will it give sufficient control of such breath as there is.

In ordinary tidal breathing there is scarcely any tension of the diaphragm or abdomen: the lungs fill and empty almost by their own elasticity with very little muscular help outside them. It is not till great effort is required of the breath that the surrounding muscles come tensely into play. High pressure and full capacity will make a very different call on the muscular system.

The singing breath is also different in principle from the ordinary breath. Ordinary breathing, in which the ribs are scarcely raised, is just an up-and-down, easy cycle of inward and outward breaths. Each expansive effort is followed by collapse. This will not do at all for singing, where there must be no collapse. If collapse happens, i.e., if the chest falls—this at any rate, is the sign of collapse—continuity of effort is lost, and continuity of effort means the continuity of the music, which is essential to good performance. So that what the singer has to do is to develop the capacity and control of the breath, both by general breathing exercises and by exercising separately the muscles that regulate breathing, viz. the chest, back and side muscles; also, particularly, the abdominal muscles. Appropriate exercises will be found in *Word and Tone* referred to in the Preface, but any system of exercises will do. The main thing is the greatest contraction and relaxation of the muscles which are being exercised, for this is what develops them. Deep breathing should often be practised by the singer, at any moment of the day, particularly when walking, or in the fresh air; not only in connection with singing. In the end such breathing becomes a habit which will give a normal breath of perhaps double the capacity of that usually taken.

And just as breathing should be exercised apart from singing, so should the breath muscles be exercised apart from breathing. It is not at all necessary to inhale breath in order to exercise the breathing muscles. It should be possible to expand the chest and ribs to the full without actually breathing—indeed without having any breath at all in the body (this can be secured by keeping the mouth shut and holding the nostrils after expelling all the breath). Unless muscular control of this sort is gained it will be found that the chest is always liable to heave and to collapse, with disastrous results on

4

the singing. For what the singer has to do is to appear never to breathe—in other words to be able to take a breath without disturbing the vocal instrument, i.e., to take and expel the breath from below by the movement of abdominal muscles, not from above by the movement of the chest muscles—at least this should be so as far as possible, and it is almost wholly possible. There must be no apparent labouring of the body in breathing; nor must there be any noise in breath taking.

The base of the lungs is where the main action of the breath occurs. At this point the diaphragm, aided by the abdominal muscles, plays upon the voice like a bow does upon the strings of a violin. The dynamics of expression have their rise here: *crescendo*, *diminuendo*, accent, etc.; also, the steady stream of sound which we call *sostenuto*, and which is perhaps the chief feature of fine singing. There is a parallelism between deep breathing and deep expression.

The centre of all effort, both physical and emotional, seems to be in the abdominal region. Even as regards poetry it was said by A. E. Housman that 'Poetry is a sort of pituitary secretion, like the pearl in an oyster. Its seat is in the pit of the stomach.' The Chinese poet also, according to Lin Yutang, 'ransacks his intestines for a good line of poetry' though Westerners, more politely, ransack their brains.[1] Abdominal activities indeed are now held, by psychologists, to account for our imaginative and intellectual powers: the brain is so to speak energized from the belly, the explanation being that blood feeds the brain, and the brain is most alert when the fullest oxygenation of the blood takes place, which happens with deep breathing.

To return to the difference between the ordinary and the singing breath. With the ordinary breath, as we have said, tension is not

---

[1] A still truer statement, I think, would be: that we should consider the abdominal region as the centre of our emotional life—for physical ardencies seem to be specially situated there; and the head (or brain) as the centre of our intellectual life—where knowledge dwells in cool detachment, where the sense of relationship (as in logic or ordered progression) is established, and from which the will operates. Looked at in this, and I believe the right way, the chest then becomes the link between the emotions and the intellect; between what we feel and the formal aspect of such feeling: both indispensable to artistic expression. But it is not till the chest is *raised*, by tension, that this link or 'gear' is effective, enabling the head to control the emotions, or the emotions to fire the head.

Thus tension is necessary to the complete, inter-related use of our physical and mental powers; and without it neither head nor heart is of much consequence.

The exasperating thing about so much singing is that it has no physical warmth —nothing of what the Welsh call *hwyl*; it is as cold as charity and therefore, whatever it says, it means nothing. It is not that it represents the acme of emotional control, a deliberate checking of emotional outburst (often quite approvable); it is that there is no emotion there to control, and strangely, in the sphere of singing this absence is more associated with women than men—at least that is my experience.

sustained, but with the singing breath there is no relaxation of tension. All the time the rib casing of the lungs is expanded; and this tends to flatten the diaphragm, which, in a state of relaxation, is in a convex shape. The vacuous space thus created automatically fills with air: a full breath has been taken, to expel which the abdomen must contract. Roughly speaking, it is the abdomen which by contraction and expansion—an in and out movement—governs the expulsion and intake of the breath, like a bellows handle—the action of an ordinary garden syringe offers another good parallel; but the expansion of the chest and ribs is constant, though the abdomen moves, and this draws the abdomen in and up, preventing too low or noticeable abdominal movement. Thus—the principle holds in almost every aspect of singing—there is a combined process of expansion and contraction, in which the chest never falls. The singer should feel that the upper chest is continuously supporting some weight, and the support seems to be derived mainly from the abdomen, though there are other factors as well.

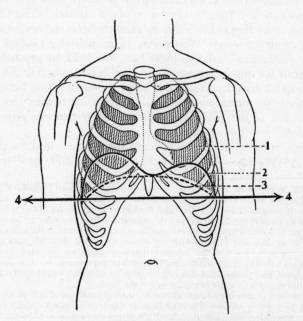

Diagram of the organs of breathing

1. Lungs: shaded part.
2. Diaphragm relaxed: thick line.
3. Diaphragm depressed: dotted line.
4. Maximum rib expansion at this line: sixth intercostal space.

For the singer, then, the practical method of breathing is
(1) ribs out, laterally,
(2) abdomen in and out,
(3) chest up.
If the arms are raised to shoulder height, like the wings of a hovering bird, the chest will be in the proper position. A perfect example of good vocal breathing is given by
(1) standing with left foot forward,
(2) lifting arms vertically above head, palms of hands facing inwards,
(3) raising body on tiptoe,
(4) breathing in and out as deeply as possible.
The strain of all this is felt, where it should be felt, in the abdominal region, and if, *while holding a full breath*, the arms are allowed to drop loosely at the sides, and the soles of the feet to come to ground, the body will seem lightness itself, ready to float upwards like a balloon, whereas in a general way it is heavy and inert. 'Loose and lifted' are the chief watchwards in singing, though a great deal of variation will occur.

This buoyancy of attitude is essential throughout singing though, as there is considerable effort attached to it, it is seldom achieved, except, perhaps, for a moment or two. Much training is required before the singer can command it continuously.[1] Most singing is lamentably lifeless. It shows little power over those features of expression which indicate that the body and mind are fully engaged. When this is so it will invariably be found that the fault lies in the breath, and that the principles just indicated have not been put into practice; in short, that there is quite insufficient use of the breath muscles. The abdomen, particularly, is never in that nervous,

---

[1] The voice if it is to follow 'fancy's flight' must be 'airborne', which, as with an aeroplane, involves continued stress and strain—stress of motive force, strain on the parts of the mechanism; otherwise it will not rise and set out properly upon its course; it will, in short, 'ground'. This 'coming to earth' is a sign of poor singing. Singers hardly ever sustain their voices sufficiently. They, as it were, go up and drop down all the time, from lack of tension. They do not *hold* the sound. In consequence there is no real phrasing, or the expression of an idea, still less of a song as a whole; for this implies continuity, a continuous manifestation of feeling. The ease of that manifestation may of course also imply a certain amount of relaxation. This may be fitting to the expression—one does not want to be as 'tight as a drum' all the time. But tension there must be in some degree—sometimes more, sometimes less, as the situation demands. Highly energetic expression will need great tension—comparatively restful expression much less. Thus tension and relaxation are relative in their application and the fine artist knows how to control and apply such force.
To continue the simile of the aeroplane in regard to relaxation and tension— the action of a heavy plane will involve more stress and strain than that of a light one, just as a heavier weight of tone in the voice will need greater tension to support it than does a lighter weight.

twitching state which is ready to 'touch in' any sort of tone that is required of it.

To be more exact as to where the maximum expansion of the breath takes place; it should occur at a line a little below the breast bone. The ribs should be extended at the sides here to their fullest extent (test it by holding the sides between the thumb and fore-finger!). A 'bulge' will also occur in the fleshy part at the breast bone. This bulge is particularly symptomatic of good vocal breath-ing—the voice may almost be said to be held there. Lower down the abdomen will be contracted: by this process buttressing the whole vocal mechanism and offering a firm base upon which the voice should lie.

And not only the action of the breath, but the influence of the breath is all important. The breath is the sign of everything being right. Particularly is it the sign of concentration both spiritual and physical—the two can hardly be separated; and tonal concentration is impossible without it. If the breath is wrong everything will be wrong: accent, rhythm, tone quality, articulation, whatever is con-cerned in singing. The well-known dictum of Pacchiarotti, a famous Italian teacher, should be taken to heart by every student, 'He who knows how to breathe and how to pronounce knows how to sing.' But pronunciation is largely determined by the breath; the finer and more intense qualities of sound certainly are, for the resonance cavities and articulatory organs do their work at the command of the breath, and are not independent of it. Therefore, 'breathe well, breathe properly' is the supreme counsel for the singer. Think of the breath, practise its development and control without ceasing! More than half the battle of singing is to be gained thereby.

The technique here advocated gives the largest volume and the greatest strength to the breath; but, because it demands much effort it must not be imagined that stiffness of voice will result or a sort of rigor mortis prevail. Far from it. If this sort of breathing is not used, instead of strains being taken at the base of the breath—away from the voice—they will appear in the voice itself. There are inescapable strains; they must be met somewhere; and it can easily happen that by wrong breath adjustment the neck muscles will be wrongly used and 'throaty' tone will result.

Deep control of the breath frees the voice; but the art of breath-ing also consists in varying the level of effort in the breath with corresponding variation in tone quality. This will be shown later in more detail.

What may be called the normal type of right breathing, i.e., the type that is appropriate to average emotional situations, is a developed form of 'panting'. Certain quite natural operations in which the breath is concerned, such as 'sighing', 'retching', 'panting' and 'gargling' are part and parcel of artistic expression, and the singer must know what sort of expression they serve. Natural processes nearly always give us a cue to what we should do when we attempt artificial control.

Right breathing is really stored energy, and any call, however fierce, can be made upon it without disturbing the equilibrium of the voice. The energy is ready, when wanted; whereas, by any other means of breathing, if a sudden call has to be suddenly met, the possible situation is never prepared for, and so the vocal style instead of being quietly assured is just a series of jerky improvisations. A loud *sforzando* or a sustained *pianissimo*—it is all one to the singer who breathes properly; nothing upsets him, for the means are always to hand. And just as an abundance of motive energy is at the disposal of the singer, so also is there a continuous check or curb upon its use. It is always curbed by the muscular tension that is operating; it is always under control; it cannot break away. Thus the singer achieves the power to do as he wills and intends, and not as the vocal mechanism makes him do. He is master in his own house.

It may help the student also to think of vocal breathing as very much like the movement of a piston within its cylinder. The piston action is that of the diaphragm motivated both by its own muscular energies and those of the abdomen; the cylinder is the thorax or rib casing, and effort must be made to expand it to as great a capacity as possible.

In any manufactured machine the cylinder does not vary its size. As regards inhalation and expiration, neither should the vocal cylinder when once expanded and ready for use, unless, to a small degree, it is absolutely obliged. This means, as already noted (though it can hardly be noted too often) the continuous expansion of the chest and ribs.

Finally, there is a further difference between the normal and singing breath as regards breathing in and out. This should be referred to. Normally, we breathe through the nose; in singing it must be through the mouth, because, for one reason, the much quicker intake of breath necessary in singing can then be achieved noiselessly.[1] The channel through the nose is therefore blocked, or nearly so, in singing, the main vent being the mouth. Breath

---

[1] It should be said, however, that noiseless breathing *can* be effected through the nose only; but it takes longer to breathe in this way and therefore, if only for this reason, nasal breathing is useless to the singer. Nevertheless it should be practised, in order to feel what a throatful and mouthful of breath is like; occasionally, also, the singer should see what he can do when he pays no attention at all to the right method of breathing, when he simply lets the breath 'go'. It is wise sometimes *not* to be on one's best behaviour.

recovery is a quite instantaneous process if we breathe through the mouth and keep the chest raised. It has to be instantaneous, for music will not wait upon the singer. Any other way of breathing than that indicated means a fresh start, as it were, whenever a breath is taken: for the chest, which has fallen, has to be raised again. This takes time, which is often not at the singer's disposal. So that when a breath is needed between two phrases, the end of the first phrase may be weakly held, and the beginning of the second may be more or less inaudible: whereas the singer need not have been put about in the least: the music could have carried through with perfect definition, if the technique of breathing had been adequate.

Inhalation and expiration can proceed in three ways:
1. By breathing in and out through nose and mouth;
2. By breathing in and out through the nose only;
3. By breathing in and out through the mouth only.

All three ways should be tried by the singer.

For 1, nose and mouth must be left open;

For 2, the mouth must evidently be shut off;

For 3, the nose must be shut off.

It is important to observe that (2) and (3) may be done at either end of the mouth or nose; as regards the mouth, by the closing of the lips, or the breath orifice at the tonsils and uvula: as regards the nose, by closing the nostrils, or the back entry into the nose. At first the student may find it a little difficult to control the back orifices of the mouth and nose, that is to say, to leave the lips open while breathing only through the nose, or to leave the nostrils open while breathing only through the mouth. But this control should be practised as it is essential to singing. To close off the mouth, the back of the tongue rises and the soft palate falls to meet it; to close off the nose the soft palate rises. All this happens in the region of, and largely through the instrumentality of, the soft palate. Pure open vowelling and tone quality is perhaps chiefly determined at this point, also; it is important that the singer should feel that it is. Roughly speaking, verbal articulation appears to be controlled at the lips, vowel formation at the throat.

To sum up. In singing, the action of the breath is different in every way from what it is in normal life; the breathing apparatus has to work differently (in that expansion is always present) and the breath, after it leaves the larynx, follows a more restricted route than its normal course. These two fundamental differences cannot be too strongly insisted upon. They go to the very root of the singer's art and if they are not mastered the singer will never do much that is worth having. In short, his singing will be just a use of everyday sound, whereas singing is an intensification of such sound and only after this intensification has taken place does the art of singing really begin. This does not mean that singing must appear unnatural or distorted. It has to seem perfectly natural, and to ring as true as ordinary speech.

But for all that it is artificial; its power and passion would be quite impossible if normal processes only were used; this must be made quite clear. The failure of so much singing can assuredly be put down to the inadequate though well-intentioned wish on the part of singers and teachers to be natural, to do 'just what you would naturally do'. But that attitude will not go far. Development is impossible upon those lines, because no 'resistance' is implied or applied in the technical sense, and without it no accumulation of power is possible. It is all too easy to be any good.

Breathing can be looked upon as scarcely more than the operation of a physical mechanism, such as that of the bellows of an organ, and it is largely in this sense that we have treated it here. It is through breath that the voice sounds—breath is the motive force—and it would seem as if all we had to do (or think about) is to discover the best way of using it, that is, the best technical method, so that the best vocal results may be secured. We can thus approach it as a physical science, open to verification; then we are on firm measurable ground all the time.

To approach it mainly from a spiritual angle is to run a risk of high-flown, extravagant statement; at its worst mere flap-doodle, if taken in hand by gushing sentimentalists.

Nevertheless, there *is* a spiritual aspect—there is bound to be where life is concerned—and in Eastern practice breathing takes on a more exalted significance than it does with us. It is considered to be not only a means towards speech or music, but of direct contact with the spiritual realm, where concepts fail, reason has no place, and, in the words of the great Christian mystic St. John of the Cross, 'In order to obtain all, one must abandon all': the final paradox of religion. Here spiritual sensitivity alone counts.

There is little doubt but that, in the East, what may be called pure spirituality (detached from any mental action) has been cultivated to a far greater extent than in the West. We can neither ignore the experiences which are attested, nor despise the processes by which they are attained. They are the fruit of centuries of religious practice. In these processes the breath plays an important part.

Taken as a whole, the West has never laid stress on breathing, as a means of spiritual development—except perhaps in ancient Greece where the culture of the diaphragm (which is practically the culture of the breath) was well understood for its far-reaching effect. This is perhaps why the West, in general, does not seem to attain to the mystical heights of the East—cause and effect is likely to apply here as with everything else. The character of our civilization is more earthbound.

The Buddhist Yogis believe that right breathing is the starting point of, or key to, religious experience and that he who has mastered it gains wisdom, power, insight and also physical perfection and longevity. It is not strange that they should hold this; it has a credible *rationale*: for breath is life. Therefore the better we breathe the more life we shall enjoy, not only physical but spiritual. But, to secure it, aspiration or the search for high spiritual values—a sort of spiritual breathing—must go hand in hand with the physical exercise of the breath. The latter alone will not ensure that which is desired. Neither will the former. It is a complementary process.

Buddhists maintain that breath is not merely a question of chemical action upon the body, providing the necessary oxygenation (and purification) of the blood; but that a much more subtle principle enters with it, which they call *prana*, the etheric, cosmic, vital force from which our highest powers are derived. Western science does not acknowledge it, since it does not register upon any instrument; but again we should be bold to deny that some such principle exists whereby healing, recuperation and indeed all vital energy come to us. The East has a right to its conviction, and its theory may almost be said to be justified by its results.

It is an interesting fact that, in the exercise of breathing, Buddhists counsel that *the chest should be kept high and motionless, both in inhalation and exhalation*, which is, of course, also our own counsel. But it is improbable that vocal considerations entered into their mind. They can scarcely have linked up this advice with the best use of the voice. Their purpose was spiritual not vocal control. The Buddhists and ourselves thus seem to have reached the same conclusion from a quite different method of approach.

To say the least of it, the Eastern view puts breathing upon a high level of thought, embracing as it does the whole of man's activity. Perhaps it is only in the *musical* view that anything like the Eastern view is reached. Can it be wondered at? At its best, does not music lead to the Infinite?

> But if I travel in your companie,
> You know the way to Heaven's door.

Before leaving the subject of the breath a word should be said about deportment with which breathing is clearly connected. Good breathing involves a general straightening-up of the whole body, such as is practised in athletic or military exercises. The right poise roughly means a vertical line from head to foot, the head properly balanced on the spine and the whole body held together by tension. The law of balance in physical movement requires the centre of gravity to be kept exactly and continuously over its base, an impossible achievement except under conditions of tension. This allows the greatest rapidity and force with the least expenditure of energy. And though in singing the body does not move much, the principle is still applicable. Bent shoulders, chest in and abdomen out can never produce good tone, simply because when the body is in that position the muscles are lax and lazy; directly they get properly to work it will be: shoulders back, chest out (with a feeling of strong expansion under the arms and at the shoulder blades), and abdomen in. Then the singer is ready. Nevertheless, there should be no tightness at the shoulders, which (in a general way), with the arms, should be loose. If there is tightness it will probably mean the raising of the shoulders as well; this, in turn, raises the whole thorax, preventing proper lateral expansion. It will also produce wrong tension in the laryngeal and throat muscles which will adversely affect tone.

The physical attitude of the singer shows immediately what his mental and musical attitude is. Generally he has not pulled himself together sufficiently to do anything that is of vital significance. The habits of our forefathers in making children sit up at table and elsewhere were certainly admirable. Sitting well is an excellent preliminary for standing well. Indeed, good sitting and standing and breathing go together. This does not mean that we should never relax; only that we should cultivate the power of alertness and concentration. The way the hands and arms are held is of secondary importance, and at the discretion of the singer, though the pose should be pleasing.

It is not necessary for an artist to be a physical weakling. Great art does not usually arise from weak bodies.

(b) The Vibratory Apparatus

The vibratory apparatus is situated in the larynx, which is a sort of triangular cartilaginous frame to which the vocal cords are attached. The apex of the frame is seen at what is called the Adam's apple in the male throat. The vocal cords are membraneous bands slung between the fore and back part of the larynx. They can either meet completely, closing up the orifice of the throat at the larynx; or separate when breath passes so that there is a slit between them. This slit, as in ordinary respiration, may be wide, or very narrow as in singing. It is generally assumed, and it has been held since the time of Galen (second century), that it is this passage of breath through the vocal cords, under certain conditions of tension, which originates the vocal sound, the theory being that owing to

13

the elasticity of the vocal cords and the pressure of breath behind them, puffs of air escape rhythmically during phonation, the number of puffs per second determining the pitch of the sound which is produced. According to this theory, it is not the vibration of the vocal cords which give the sound—the principle is obviously different from that of a vibrating string such as that of a pianoforte or violin.

That pitch is initiated at the larynx seems also proved by the fact that whispered speech cannot be inflected nor its quality changed, since every vowel is a quality and has a definite oral pitch of its own due to the shape of its cavity. Vowels can be sung at different pitches by the action of the vocal cords, but not otherwise.

This 'puff' theory has been questioned, with a good deal of cogency, by Mr. Ernest C. White in *The Voice Beautiful*, but his findings have not been universally accepted. It still holds the field and it serves perfectly well for whatever explanation of the voice is needed.

Vocal pitch is explained by supposing that a looser and longer section of the cords is concerned in the production of lower notes than it is with higher notes—that is to say, the higher the note the tighter the cords, and shorter the chink through which the breath passes, so that the air 'puffs' come more quickly.

One function of the vocal cords therefore seems to be that they determine the pitch of the voice; another most certainly is that they act as a 'stop' to the breath, either wholly or partially; and *this closure of the glottis*, or slit between the cords, *is an all-important thing as regards tone quality*. The pitch of vocal sound is not under our conscious physical control. All we can do is to mentalize the sound and then sing it; of how we do it we are quite unaware—it just happens as we think it, or more or less so (of this later). But we can consciously control the opening of the vocal cords. If the opening is

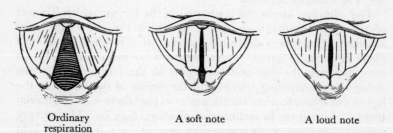

| Ordinary respiration | A soft note | A loud note |

Diagrams of typical adjustments of the cords, showing the scissors-like action by which they are opened and closed; but a host of further adjustments are possible, involving different lateral and longitudinal tensions, affecting pitch and tone-quality.

relatively large and loose, we shall get relatively breathy sound; if it is approximate and tight we shall get telling sound. It is quite easy to feel this loosening and tightening of the laryngeal muscles, and it is important that the singer should be able to feel it, because it is through this process that variation of tone colour takes place; also breath economy.

Looked at in this way, the vocal cords serve as a valve or closure at the top of the windpipe. The valve can be completely closed so as to exclude foreign matter—this was the primitive function of the larynx before it developed into an organ of voice—or to stop any passage of breath; but it can also let a very little breath through—all that is needed for a vocal note. If the valve functions perfectly, hardly any breath passes when a note is sung, so that a single supply of breath lasts for a long time and is quite sufficient for the longest phrase. The sustaining of a long note or phrase, either with steady tone, or with the tone varied expressively, at will, represents a high measure of technical achievement and is one of the greatest *desiderata* of the singer.

I remember once asking Mrs. Kennedy Fraser, the authority on Hebridean folk-song, whether its singers paid any attention to expression as we understand it in cultured performance. She replied, 'No! but they practise breathing and vie with each other as to who can make the breath last longest.' Not a bad principle to work upon!

The compressed nature of the breath acting upon tightly set cords results in firm head tone:[1] a most important phenomenon. It is remarkable how this procedure sends the voice up into the head; it never fails to do so. This may be due to two causes—(1) the strongly fricative effect of the breath upon the cords, which, as it were, releases a shower of upper partials which somehow find their way into the higher regions of the head and the small sinus cavities which are situated there; or (2) that the breath has a directive energy, *after* it has passed the vocal cords, so that it searches out the higher resonances of the voice, by which effectiveness and brilliancy of tone are gained. The first of these causes certainly operates, and I believe that the second does also. For if we take a garden syringe and remove the nozzle, the water which issues will not go far, but with the nozzle on, the water will be sent a considerable distance. The smaller the orifice the greater the carrying-power. It is probably the same with the breath in some measure, and it is clear that it is brought about by muscular contraction. We shall find, so often, that muscular contraction, tightness, if we will—for we need not burke the word—is the secret of so much that is

[1] Categories of tone are discussed later on p. 160 *et sep.*

admirable and vital in singing; at any rate without tightness, properly applied, tone is dull and lifeless.

The vocal cords are of the nature of what are called reeds, like the double reed of the oboe or bassoon. The voice is a reed instrument and the characteristic tone of such an instrument must be discovered by the singer. There is an intense quality about such tone—the French call it *timbre*—which is quite different from the more or less hollow tone of the flute, or the hooty tone which we associate with yodelling or the note of the cuckoo. Every kind of sound is possible to the voice and the singer should be able to make it; but it is not, strictly speaking, singing, till the reedy nature of the voice is drawn upon. Poor singing is invariably without it. Few singers, indeed, achieve true vocal tone, though the vocal instrument is always capable of it; and whether they do or not depends very largely, as we have indicated, upon the use of the vocal cords.

The breath, by the influence of its tensity, in large measure controls the state of the vocal cords, i.e., whether they are slack or tight, but in a very real sense the vocal cords also control the breath and the pressure of which it is capable; and the singer should see, by their approximation and compression, that they do so.

The position of the larynx varies with quality of tone. If a great deal of neck resonance is used the larynx will be low; if an extreme of nasal or head resonance is used, it will be high. Neck tone is also associated with a low breath—nasal tone with a relatively high breath. The whole mechanism, in short, rises or falls together— just as in deep yawning the larynx is low, but in retching or the act of sickness (which is a lifting expulsive movement) the larynx is high.

These relatively opposite movements of the breath (yawning and retching) are in fact the determinants of differences of tone quality: whether the quality shall be full, soft and sympathetic; or thin, hard and mechanical.

(c) *The Resonating Apparatus*

If vocal tone could rely only upon the puffs that come through the vocal cords, it would be very weak and insignificant. These air vibrations need to be strengthened by resonance before they become fully effective, but their potentiality can also be damped out or destroyed by poor resonation (which also tends to put a note out of tune).

Resonance is produced when a cavity, or shaped hollow container of some kind, is superimposed upon a generator or vibrating agency (in this case the vocal cords) and the air in this cavity vibrates in sympathy with the vibration of the generator, reinforcing it, as it is termed.

Resonance therefore implies two things: (1) a resonator, and (2) its connection or coupling with the generator by means of an aperture in the cavity,[1] so setting the enclosed air in motion. When once disturbed the air is not necessarily displaced, but pulsates in and out of the aperture of the cavity, with a sort of jack-in-the-box action, if it could be seen.

It should be said at once, however—and it is important—that sound vibrations, however energized, whether by strings or reed, do not travel from point to point like a train. Breath happens to pass through the vocal cords, though, as has been already remarked, in a very small quantity with good tone; but if the vocal cords had the power of setting themselves in vibration by some interior process, there would still be vocal tone. Sound travels through a sound-wave just as movement travels through the ripples or undulations of water. Actually, in singing, the breath is not projected for more than a yard or two beyond the singer, even with the most energetic use. It is the direction and intensity of the vocal wave which carries the voice over long distances.

(d) Resonance cavities of the vocal instrument

A complex system of cavities determines the reinforcement of vocal sound, so complex indeed, and so subject to alteration that it is occasionally impossible to say to which cavity or its action some type of tone is due. Generally speaking, however, the connection between cavity and tone colour is fairly clear.

Potentially, the cavities concerned are those of

(1) the larynx
(2) the pharynx
(3) the mouth
(4) the nose, consisting of (a) the large general cavity of shell-like formation, divided into two by a central wall, and (b) four smaller cavities on each side of the wall, called the nasal sinuses which communicate with the upper part of the main nasal cavity.

The approximate volumes of these cavities are given by one authority as:

(1) larynx   ..   25 c.c.
(2) pharynx   ..   80 c.c.

---

[1] The condition for resonance is that there should be available two sources of vibration which are in unison, or nearly in unison, with each other. The coupling of these sources, as regards vocal tone, is generally brought about by means of the air passing through an aperture, but it can be effected by any conducting agent. The bony or cartilagenous structure of the mouth may well act in this capacity, ensuring a certain amount of nasal resonance, even though the back passage of the nose is closed.

(3) mouth .. 100 c.c.
(4) nose: (a) main cavity .. 60 c.c.
(b) sinuses .. .. 75 c.c. } =135 c.c.

Even if these figures have to be changed they probably remain relatively true.

From which it will be seen—and this is the important point—that the laryngeal cavities are small; that the mouth is the largest single cavity, the pharynx coming next to it in size; while the nose, if we take its main cavity and attendant sinuses together, contains the largest resonating space.

In a position of rest all these cavities are interlinked and free to take up the vibrations effected by the vocal cords, though, as we shall see, a very important modification of this freedom takes place by the action of the soft palate. The concern of the singer must be to throw open to the voice as much of this resonance as he can, since resonance is power.

A simplified diagram of a cross-section of the head will make the position and shape of these cavities clearer:

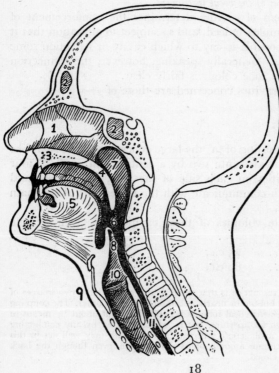

1. Nasal cavity
2. Sinus cavities. There are 8 in all
3. Hard palate
4. Soft palate
5. Tongue
6. Pharynx
7. Naso-pharynx
8. Epiglottis
9. Larynx— Adam's Apple
10. Glottis—vocal cords—at the top of trachea or windpipe
11. Gullet

The pharynx and mouth are subject to great alterations of size and shape by muscular action; on the other hand the structure of the nose remains more or less constant and immovable. The laryngeal mechanism, as we have seen, is open to adjustment and has a very great influence upon tone quality, but whether the relatively small laryngeal cavities have appreciable resonating effect seems to be debatable, as also whether sound is resonated in the windpipe below the larynx, though, strictly, there is no physical reason why it should not be—we certainly do feel the looser, lower vibrations of the voice upon the chest and even further down, though this may be the sympathetic vibration of flesh and bone rather than cavity vibration. Low bourdon sounds appear to come, even, from the abdomen, but as the pitch of the voice rises the feeling of resonance proportionately rises with it, till the highest sounds seem to resound only in the head. Such feelings must be the result of sympathetic resonance of some sort; they are not merely imagined. But the cavities of the pharynx, mouth and nose are nevertheless the main resonators, subject to our control.

To consider the main cavities in rather more detail.

THE PHARYNX

The pharyngeal tube is relatively soft-walled; it runs from the throat to the base of the skull. It may be said to have three divisions, (1) the top division, opening into the nasal cavities, (2) the middle one, into the mouth and (3) the lowest, leading downwards to the larynx. It is within our power to close the top part so that resonation is practically impossible there, but if we do, by an extreme movement of the soft palate, it almost paralyses vocal effort. As regards the lowest part of the pharynx, such is its flexibility that it can be largely reduced or extended—which correspondingly constricts or expands the vocal tone. This expansion, which represents the most important feature of pharyngeal control, is that referred to when we talk of an 'open' throat or neck (though we may also use the term 'open' with respect to the other cavities).

A great deal of the richness and 'body' of the voice hinges upon our power to expand the throat. It is partly secured by a sort of downward pull, or, at any rate, a downward fall of the muscles under the ears at the sides of the neck; also by bringing the jaw and tongue root loosely forward which pouches the throat, much like that of a bird when it is singing.

The throat may be regarded as the reservoir of sound, the nose the spring, and the mouth the conduit (to pursue the analogy of sound with water).

THE MOUTH

Of the three main resonators the mouth is the one that is subject to most change, owing to its capacity for opening and closing, and also to the action of the tongue which can greatly modify the shape of the cavity. These factors, in which the shaping of the lips must also be included, determine the vowels and articulations. Thus it contains the main organs of speech.

The tongue can be a very unruly member in this part of the vocal kingdom, and will arch up when it should lie down, so preventing proper pronunciation; or, and this is what we are chiefly concerned with here, its base or root may be drawn back so as to reduce the cavity of the pharynx at that point, to the detriment of the vocal sound.[1]

The marvellous complexity of singing is illustrated by what is required in the adjustment of the mouth for pitch and vowelling. Every difference of pitch involves some slight alteration of the cavity due to the need of muscular tension or relaxation, high notes requiring more resistant tension than low notes do.[2] This can be observed by looking at the back of the mouth during the emission of the vowel Ah, when its orifice at the tonsils will be seen to draw together slightly and the uvula to rise as relatively higher notes are sounded. And not only is the shape of the mouth and also of the throat altered for each change of pitch; the interior of the mouth is shaped differently for each vowel, so that a double simultaneous process of adjustment takes place when words are sung to music. As with the use of the vocal cords, all these delicate operations are decided more by instinct than the will, though the mechanism which effects them can be consciously strengthened and developed for its purpose.

The influence of the mouth on the lower pharynx, through the tongue root, has been noted; but its influence on the nose is perhaps greater still, owing to the roof of the mouth and particularly to its hinder part called the soft palate. The palatal arch has two distinct divisions; it is bony and hard in front, and soft at the back—hence the 'hard' and 'soft' palates. No movement of the hard palate is possible, but the soft palate can be moved a great deal, and its considerable powers of adjustment make it an exceedingly important factor in singing. As regards tone quality no other part of the vocal

---

[1] What has to be done is to try to get the tongue root away from the *back* wall of the throat and this can be effected either (1) by bringing the tongue forward (which favours brilliant tone) or (2) by letting it fall backward and downward into the loose pouch of the under jaw (which favours dull tone). This last process still leaves the throat open.

[2] Nor must we forget that the breath also changes its position (or level) with each change of pitch. In singing nothing is stationary; except a single note.

mechanism can determine as much. It does this by raising itself in such a way that the opening at the throat becomes of an upright oval 0 instead of a flattened shape $\circ$, and this action, if carried to an extreme can block the nose almost completely, as it does in what may be called a soft-toned Oh. With this particular tone, which is very sympathetic, nasal resonance is practically eliminated. With a loud-toned Oh, however, involving the use of more nasal resonance, it will be found that the raised soft palate is brought a little down and forward, uncovering more of the aperture that leads into the nose. With the bright-toned long vowels Ee, Ay, Ah, Aw, this uncovering always takes place. The characteristic of bright tone, indeed, is the amount of nasal resonance that is included in it. When this amount becomes excessive or too one-sided, we get 'white' tone, *voce bianca*, which, though it is a chief ingredient of good tone, can be ridiculous and ugly, taken by itself. In 'white' tone the back oral orifice is almost closed by the action of the tongue, tonsils and uvula, so that little sound can get into the mouth. In consequence a thin, bleaty sound results, lacking the fullness that would be added to it by the mouth and also the lower pharynx; for with white sounds the larynx is 'set' high, with a corresponding diminishment of pharyngeal throat space. It is the opening of *all* the resonance cavities, combined with concentrated inward tension, that gives the richest sound. This inward tension is responsible for the lifting up of the soft palate, but, in a general way, this need not and actually (I believe) does not block the nose completely; if it does so block it we shall not get the full sonority of the voice. Nevertheless, though tone is engendered in the nose, only a very small amount comes *through* it; just its humming quality, in fact. The main stream of vocal tone must come through the mouth. Vowelling is impossible otherwise. The mouth can be quite shut off at the back by the action of the tongue and soft palate so that only nasal sound can occur; or the nose may be blocked as well, in which case no sound at all can issue. It is, then, as though the whole mechanism were pushed up into the head, jamming the cavity spaces and preventing all ease of movement. Phonation can only be brought about by some release of this rigid condition. What has really stopped the sound in this case is a completely one-way direction of muscular energy. An opposite movement is possible to every movement that we can make. We have the power of contraction and expansion by reason of the dual system of the flexor and extensor muscles. And these muscles can not only work singly but together, so that a balance of forces is achieved between them. When this happens a condition of tensity and freedom is secured; there is no rigidity but there is no laxity—such is the state of all good singing.

In a condition of rest the soft palate with the uvula at the end, falls (as can be seen in the last diagram). This allows the unimpeded passage of breath through the nose, and it is as well to say at once that such a free escape of breath means breathiness and loss of tone. It is contingent upon a slack state of all the muscles, including those of the larynx which offer insufficient resistance to the breath stream and so let it run to waste.

A tense muscular condition, however, tends to raise the soft palate by contraction—the tension of the abdomen must be included in the process. When the abdomen is used energetically it will be found that the soft palate rises and will stay up as long as this tension is exercised, just as it will in the case of sickness when a great deal of expulsive abdominal power (similar to that which is applied to the breath) causes the evacuation of the stomach.

The abdomen should always be at work in singing; if it is, the soft palate will always be raised. This will happen automatically, though the raising can be increased at will; but it *can* and should be done independently of the breath muscles for the sake of practice. As contraction is involved in the raising of the palate all the roof of the mouth will be brought into much the same condition of hardness and this will favour brilliant tone.

Hard surfaces reflect sound better than soft ones do. A room with hard walls, particularly when it is empty, seems to fill with sound in a way that a curtained room never does. Experience in a broadcasting studio will demonstrate the deadening effect of soft surfaces upon the speaking or singing voice. This is why we generally try to direct the voice on to the hard palate behind the upper teeth, because when we do so the tone gains in brilliancy and effectiveness; it tells more, it has more of what the Italians call '*il metallo di voce*' (the metal of the voice) without which tone is dull and soft-cored. This does not mean that extremes of brilliancy have invariably to be sought; tone, if too hard and forward, can even be unpleasant. The use of tone depends upon its purpose, the situation to which it is addressed; in a general way a sympathetic effectiveness is more to be desired than an effectiveness which is devoid of what might be called human quality.

Effectiveness there must be, however, and this is largely connected with the harder surfaces of the resonating cavities, such as are presented by the hard palate, the nose and the higher sinuses which lead from it. It is these surfaces which encourage the high frequencies of tone; the 'upper partials' or 'harmonics' as they are called. The student is probably well aware that the note which we apparently hear contains in reality a whole series of sounds for the most part separately inaudible but which give character and colour

22

to the fundamental note. This series is almost infinite but the most noticeable harmonics are, as for the fundamental bass note C, here given.

When there is a lack of these higher harmonics the tone is dull, when there are plenty of them the tone is bright. Differences of tone colour are brought about by the special prominence of certain of these harmonics. All this can be seen in any elementary book of acoustics though we give it in order to explain the why and wherefore of the management of the voice.

THE NOSE

The nasal cavities consist of (1) what we generally call, *tout court*, the nose, a large cavity of irregular shell-like internal shape extending from the roof of the mouth to the floor of the cranium; and (2) the small sinus cavities, eight in all, which are offshoots of the main cavity. The main nasal cavity obviously plays a most important part in vocal tone; the smaller sinuses are sometimes dismissed as negligible. This cannot be accepted, for highly pitched and piercing sounds can be definitely associated with a feeling of resonance between the eyes, which is where the two frontal sinuses are situated; and it is to be supposed that it is the use of these of which we are then aware. Also we believe that this feeling of 'high-up' sound is needed if we are to develop the full capacity of 'head' tone from which 'point' and lightness of voice so largely proceeds. Mr. Ernest White, whose vocal theory, already mentioned, is of so much interest, goes further than this by asserting that the nasal sinuses are responsible for the actual generation of sound: that is, that they play the role that has always been assigned to the vocal cords. But this does not seem to have a bearing of much importance as regards teaching. All we need say is that, for determining tone quality, and also for overcoming difficulties of pitch, attention may well be given to sinus resonation as far as it can be sensed and controlled. We have already spoken of surface hardness as affecting the higher ranges of harmonics. The hardest surfaces of

23

all are to be found in these sinuses when entirely healthy: and the smallness of these cavities and their apertures may even act, in a special way, towards bringing out the most acute sounds concerned in tone.

The sinuses only develop at puberty, which seems to account for the fluty tone of a boy's voice and more *timbrée* voice of the adult; from which we may also infer that it is these sinus cavities that resonate the higher partials which are present in *timbrée* as compared with fluty tone.

The nasal cavities cannot be altered: there are no movable structures within them. Nasal resonance is therefore constant in quality; it can only resonate one definite area of frequencies. What modifies hard sound is not the nose but the mouth and pharynx. It is the alteration in the size of the oral and pharyngeal cavities which accounts for the difference between M, N and Ng, which we term the nasals. But though nasal sound taken by itself always remains the same if the sound passes freely into the nose, it nevertheless is a chief ingredient of vocal tone, as regards effectiveness of voice perhaps the chief ingredient. It is the main energizer of the tone; clearly the agent that produces most of its *active* quality.

An intriguing theoretical problem arises in connection with nasal resonance. How do vibrations get into the nose when we sing a vowel; and what happens to the breath when they do? But, first of all, are the nasal cavities used in vowelling? Let us be sure about it. We have already indicated our own opinion. It is based upon three very good reasons: (1) we feel sound in the nose; (2) we hear it there; and (3) we know that it must get there if, as we believe it is, the back orifice to the nose is open at all.

The feeling that nasal resonance is included in good tone cannot be fictitious. Such resonance is either there or it is not—the ear can easily judge. A purely nasal sound, like M, must go through the nose, because with it the nostrils are the only vent for the breath. If we sing an M and, while doing so, open the mouth for any vowel, say 'ah', we can hear the M continuing quite distinctly in the vowel: and it becomes even more apparent if we open and close the mouth repeatedly singing, as it were, mahm, mahm, mahm, etc., with special insistence on the M, when the hum seems to merge completely into the vowel, and to become part and parcel of it, the vowel gliding back again into the hum without any break. This hum is the constant element in all vowels, the binding principle.

But how does this nasality in vowelling arise? According to a widely-held theory it is almost impossible for it to operate at all. Mr. A. J. Ellis, whose *Pronunciation for Singers* has become a classic, tells us in that work that 'the slightest degree of opening' between

24

the back of the uvula and the wall of the pharynx during the sound of a vowel 'is unendurable in English, German or Italian singing'. This is equivalent to saying that the entry to the nose, at the back, must be completely blocked. If it is so, nasal resonance could only take place through the roof of the mouth communicating vibration to the nasal cavity; or to the air in the cavity being affected through the nostrils after sound had left the mouth—the nostrils having to be open in either case, since the back aperture would be closed. Some small nasal reinforcement of the vowel might take place by these processes but it would certainly not reach the extent of any full sound in the nose.

Later theory allows that, as we might have expected from what we actually hear, the nasal cavity is not completely closed during vowelling. Nusbaum's experiments with the velar-pharyngeal seal (i.e., the closure effected by the soft palate and the back wall of the pharynx) proved that some or all of the vowels may be sounded without undue nasality while there is an escape of air through the nose, involving an inlet at the back of the nose; and in *The Mechanics of Singing*, by Evetts and Worthington, there is a revealing X-ray picture, clearly showing how what the writers call a normal 'ah' *may* be sung with the soft palate lowered practically as it is in ordinary respiration where there is free interchange between pharynx, mouth and nose. The present author's view is that such a relaxed state of the muscles, though it may give the normal, cannot give the best sound of 'ah'—this belief is substantiated throughout this book—but it seems clear, henceforth, that if all, or even the major portion of the breath stream passes through the mouth, an opening into the nose is not only possible but inevitable with vowelling if nasal resonance is to be made use of, as assuredly, often it must be.

Such diametrically opposed opinions of what actually happens show how difficult physical observation is in singing. Fortunately, however, it does not matter much whether the nose is closed or open. What we have to do as artists is to get sound which will serve our expressive purpose; and the ear will cause the necessary muscular action, even if we imagine that some other action is responsible for it. Still, it is better to have right theory as well as right practice.

But we have not quite disposed of our theoretical difficulties in regard to nasal resonance by allowing that sound in vowelling can and does get into the nose through the back aperture. This, apparently, implies that breath passes through the nose since the nostrils remain open in singing. Yet—and here is the crux—we can shut the nostrils by holding them with the fingers without any, or hardly any, alteration of the sound taking place. It can be easily demonstrated that at that moment no breath *can* pass through the nose. So that we are in this quandary: if we assert that the nose is closed off to vowel sound, as does A. J. Ellis, no difficulty arises as to what happens to the breath, though there certainly is as to what happens with the sound; if, on the other hand, we say that the nasal aperture remains open, then there is difficulty as regards the breath, but none as to the sound.

What is the explanation? It seems to be this: that with vowelling, whether the tone is bright or dull (i.e., nasal or un-nasalized) no breath need pass the nose. It might appear, as we have said, that it would have to—if the rear aperture of the nose is open; the nostrils (the front aperture) by themselves cannot close sufficiently to stop the breath. But, in some way or other, for all that, the breath stream—remember that, in singing, it is very slight—can still be made to come through the mouth.

Later, it will be seen that *both* the foregoing contentions are correct; they must not be considered as mutually exclusive.

As already observed, it is perfectly easy to breathe either through the mouth, or the nose. It is not so easy to understand how we can open both the mouth and nose simultaneously, without letting any breath escape through the latter. We obviously can, however, if we accept the evidence of the ear; and we can test it by holding the nostrils. The most naturally nasalized vowels—Ee, Ay, Aw—best prove it. The nose thus acts as a resonator open at one end (the nasal inlet); or we can close that end, with corresponding influence on the tone. No breath actually passes through such a resonator; the air inside responds to vibration, that is all.

On the other hand we can be sure that, when breath *does* come through the nose, *we get breathy sound* (except with M sounds which are not vowels, since, for them, the mouth is shut). Wastage of tone is always accompanied by this feature of breath escape.

With any clear form of nasal resonance, then, some opening of the back aperture to the nose seems inevitable; in this sense, vowels are (or can be) orinasal, though the term is applied more specifically to certain French vowels of characteristic tone, foreign to our ways of speech, and perhaps, in consequence, a little grating on English ears.[1]

Really unpleasant nasality, however—such as American 'twang' or Cockney 'cut'—is another matter. The French orinasals—heard in the phrase 'M*on* chi*en* br*un* m*ange*'—do strike a fair balance between oral and nasal resonance; American and Cockney do not.

---

[1] All vowels should be practised with *nothing but* nasal resonance, so that they are pocketed in the region of the sinuses about the top of the nose. This gives a very characteristic sound. It is not suggested that it is a pleasing sound, only that it represents an important aspect of tonal control.

These latter accents represent incomplete vocal sound in which oral resonance is starved; the mixture of tone is wrong.

The influence of oral resonance on nasal tone can be observed, particularly with the sound of M, though an M seems to be purely nasal. Singers often fail to get any sonority in M, sometimes even can hardly sound it at all though it can be almost as strong as a vowel. When it is poor and thin, the cause will generally be, that the tongue by rising has blocked the mouth cavity. If the tongue can be kept down, much as it is for 'ah', thereby opening up the front part of the mouth, so that the tone can get right up to the lips (which should be loose), M will immediately sound as it should, rich and full. The lips, of course, are closed for M so that at first sight it seems as if the mouth had no part in the sound; but it has. This brings the mouth into use as a resonator closed at one end, just as we saw that the nose was when the nostrils are held.

We have said that nasality does not differ in kind. The nasal cavities of themselves always give the same sort of sound. But the amount of nasality can vary very considerably. Some vowels have naturally more nasal resonance than others have. What are sometimes called the 'front' vowels, such as Ee and Ay, have a more pronounced nasality than the 'central' ones such as 'Ah': while the minimum of nasality, though it can be varied a great deal, occurs in the 'back' vowels Oh and Oo. This indicates that the opening into the nose is less in the case of the more dull than the brighter vowels, probably owing to a higher blocking action of the soft palate, (produced by the necessary rounding of the mouth) or to a deflection of the tone by other means.

The cultivation of the combined resonance of the mouth and nose is greatly assisted by the practice of the French orinasals. They involve a considerable compression and lifting of the soft palate, together with the opening of both mouth and nose to the sound. Thus, they represent a very concentrated but still open tone. The tendency of these orinasals is towards a superior concentration of vocal control, and every speaker and singer should be able to pronounce them in the way that the French do.

When the breath is well managed, its tension has the effect of lifting the soft palate; it is as though there were two opposite forces at work, thus ↑. At the same time the muscles of the mask of the face, around the nostrils, are pulled down, also acting in a contrary direction to the upward lift of the soft palate, and the nostrils seem to close. A sort of muscular barrier is therefore put up by the mask of the face, which prevents the tone from escaping—running loose as it were. It is much as if a sound-board had been placed there, towards which the tone is directed and from which it is reflected back, gathering power and intensity in the process. This appears to be the explanation of which we are in search (with regard to the possibility of opening the nose without letting the breath escape through it). At the point, or region in question we may have not only an apparent but an actual stop to the breath; it operates with the orinasals as well as with the more usually-recognized forms of vowel.

The backward reflection of tone which we have referred to is very important; it is the antithesis of 'breathiness'. When tone goes through the nose it loses its firmness, its proper texture. 'You cannot sing *out* properly, till you have learned how to sing *in*' is one of the many paradoxes of singing. Nor can you secure searching nasal resonance by any other principle. It favours head tone, by which we generally infer a tone that seems to be placed in the head, to have its being there. Such resonation means the elimination of strained or throaty neck tone, just as proper neck resonance will eliminate harsh nasal tone. Each conditions the other if they are to function properly, and in a normal way, though, at times, extremes of head or neck resonance may be appropriate.

To sum up as regards resonance. What we have to do for the finest sound is to secure as much resonance as possible by opening the cavities and also the apertures which lead to and from them, particularly at the lips, throat and back passage of the nose, always remembering that the right muscular tension will produce a lateral closing of the cavities and apertures bringing them into an up and down shape ( ), different from the relaxed sideways shape, which is ⊂. Perhaps the simplest way of putting this would be to say: contract the orifice at the tonsils, but, behind them, freely open the neck and nose.

We have seen how the resonators govern the quality of the voice. They may (a) reinforce certain frequencies or they may (b) damp them out, absorb or destroy them. With (a) there will be brilliant tone; with (b) dull tone. We should be able to use either at will; but the latter will be more likely *to happen*, from faulty control.

The wonder of the voice as compared with a mechanical instrument is its range of colour—an infinite number of sounds are possible to it and with it an infinite emotional palette. The fine singer can do anything with his voice, not merely sing.

(e) The Articulatory Apparatus

Speech is determined by vowels and consonants. With vowels the voice is relatively unobstructed; it issues more or less freely from the vocal cords. With the consonants a good deal of obstruction afterwards occurs, producing fricative or explosive sound. This consonantal sound is relatively weaker than vowel sound, but it is often of a much higher pitch and so more sharply assertive. Some consonants are momentary in effect and difficult to make audible, particularly at the end of words; others continue their sound, closely approaching the nature of vowels.

We have already discussed those organs responsible for the vowels: the mouth and tongue, which form the vowels, and the nose and pharynx which modify them. The tongue also plays its part in consonantal utterance, the lips and the oral orifice at the back being the other active agencies; they specially obstruct the voice in the shape of the vocals (L,R, etc.), dentals (T, Th, etc.), labials (P, F, etc.), and gutturals (K, G, etc.), to adopt one system of classification.

The nasals (M, N, etc.) are produced by the passive agency of the nose, the lips and tongue supplying such formative action as they require. In a secondary way the teeth, palates, cheeks and jaw are also brought into the articulatory process.

To refer separately to the organs of speech:

THE TONGUE

In speech, most of the control of the movements of the tongue is due primarily to the ear. This is certainly so with the vowels. We wish to sing an Ee or Ay and the tongue assumes the position which will give them. We do not arch the tongue at the front for Ee—and bring its arch a little further back for Ay. We find that this has happened in trying to pronounce these vowels. Nevertheless we can certainly exercise the muscles of the tongue so that they will respond more readily to either looseness or tension, such as we may require.

We have already observed that the tongue should lie quiescent in the mouth for Ah—absolute relaxation will secure this, in which case the tongue will certainly be flat and even a little concave. If we raise the soft palate, which we nearly always have to do in singing, some slight tension is given to the tongue; but this need not cause it to rise. It can still be kept down. It is very apt to rise involuntarily, however, even with experienced singers, who thus fog their vowels by blocking the back of the mouth. There is then insufficient outlet for the tone at this point, and stiffness, as well, damages the quality. A fine open Ah is comparatively rare—largely because the tongue is functioning badly. Till a low, loose position of the tongue can be controlled a perfect Ah is impossible.

The tongue, then, must be relatively immobile for Ah and kindred vowels; but for consonantal articulation it must act with great rapidity. And the more rapidly it moves, the greater will be the tension that is required. With T for instance, the tongue must be firmly held against the hard palate near the teeth until it is thrust away by the breath. With a very strongly articulated 'T' a highly compressed breath is directed to the tongue 'stop' and much tongue resistance is required to meet it.

With L also the tongue presses against the hard palate and if the L is followed by a vowel (as in 'lay' or 'law') a sharp action of the tongue is necessary immediately to reach the vowel.

Lisping and lazy articulation is nearly always due to insufficiently energized tongue action. So that considerable variation as regards tightness or looseness occurs with the use of the tongue.

A great deal of muscular development is necessary before the tongue will do its work properly, 'coining' words (in which it is concerned) with the clearness demanded by the listener to whom they are addressed.

The tip of the tongue scarcely moves in vowelling. It should remain forward, lightly touching the inner surfaces of the lower teeth. Such action of the tongue as is necessary to form the vowels from Ah to Ee is adjusted from the back of the tongue, which moves up and away from the back of the mouth, with consequent increase of pharyngeal space. This latter is a very important point, as a full rich Ay or Ee cannot be pronounced if this forward and depressed movement of the tongue does not take place. The tongue otherwise 'jams' the vowel mechanism instead of 'freeing' it.

One of the features of good vowel technique is this bringing away of the tongue (and lower jaw) from the back of the pharynx (or neck), which secures a feeling of 'pouching' at the throat, much as a bird shows when it warbles. Richness of voice (including richness of articulative sound as well) is mainly due to the proper use of *the back part of the mouth*, and in a general way, the singer should be far more concerned with what he does in this region than in the forward part.

Rapid action of the tongue is necessary to avoid 'mouthing', i.e., the gradual, instead of quasi-instantaneous adoption of the different positions required by the different vowels and consonants. If these changes of position are skilfully made it may result in a little thud or 'percussion' as each change is assumed. When extreme point or clarity has to be given to the expression, this percussion is essential. Liveliness consists in lively movement, not only of pace but of action. Such treatment must therefore be available. On the other hand the expressive quality that is desired may not be of a lively order. The more reflective the style the slower moving it will be, and the less pointed and clear its detail, just as Nature is in her romantic half-lights of dawn or dusk when colour rather than form enthrals us. Appearances in art and nature and the processes by which they are brought about are infinite. The artist has to use the fitting gestures.

Singers should be particularly careful to have the tongue in the right position and the mouth properly opened when a song starts on a vowel or in similar situations. Frequently a vowel is formed after the note has started. This represents a very bad, slovenly style.

THE JAW

The movement of the lower jaw greatly affects tone quality. The jaw can either be brought back—this requires distinct effort; or it can be allowed to fall forward—this loosens the muscles. It is extremely important to recognize these two actions, for they play a great part in determining open (*aperto*) or covered (*chiuso*) tone *v*. p. 160). When the jaw is retracted (as in laughing) it tends to shut off the throat, and to open up nasal resonance; when it falls forward (as when we are seriously inclined) throat resonance is increased, nasal resonance lessened. The one tightens the mechanism, the other slackens it. It is extremely interesting to note the sympathetic action of the breath in regard to these two movements. With the one, the diaphragmatic muscles will contract—the abdomen will be pressed inwards; with the other, the abdomen will loosen and protrude: which is exactly as we might expect, since open, *timbrée* tone is undoubtedly produced by a highly-tensioned condition of the muscles—the vowel Aw is perhaps the best example of this; whereas covered tone is of a looser, easier kind. In short, the breath, with its 'in' and 'out' abdominal movement is a replica of the movement of the jaw.

We thus see that there is scarcely any part of the vocal mechanism which, naturally, works independently of any other part. Good (or faulty) control is generally widespread, not localized.

A sufficient opening of the jaw will give a little concavity—easily felt by the finger—between the jaw socket and ear. This is due, mainly, to the separation of the back teeth which should always have attention.

The looser the jaw the better, but an entirely loose jaw is practically impossible, since any adequate sort of tone has to be *formed*. The long vowels Ee, Ay, Ah (in which the cheeks and lips are not specially concerned) will admit of a looser jaw than Aw, Oh, Oo (which obviously deprive the jaw of its freedom). But, as we have said, tone quality is the chief factor in the situation.

Though the jaw can never be quite free, it is perhaps as well to *think* that it is, and to try to approximate its condition to one of complete relaxation.

The influence of an actual or imagined 'floating' jaw (as it is sometimes termed) is great, probably greater than that of any other single part of the vocal instrument, since that jaw seems to hold within itself most of the movable mechanism. Remember that the mouth should be felt to open at the socket of the jaw, rather than in front (at the lips). This is a sort of corollary to the foregoing. This movement bears on the opening of the orifice leading to the pharynx, and is crucial.

The singer should be able to keep his muscular system in any condition, from that associated with a relaxed state of utter stupidity, to a tense one of great purpose.

THE CHIN

The chin, while not to be poked forward like Mr. Punch's, must still fall forward for loose, easy sound, otherwise constriction of the throat will take place; for tighter, harder qualities of sound it is drawn back, in order to get a better grip at the throat, and to reduce neck resonance. A certain amount of movement is operative in the muscles of the chin though they generally work in combination with those of the lips and cheeks.

THE LIPS

The lips are nervous muscular bands which are brought into use in the formation of many of the vowels and consonants. Their rounded, compressive action is largely responsible for 'Oh' and other vowels generically associated with this. The French language is greatly dependent on pursed lips (shaped much as in whistling) for its special 'accent'.[1] The right pronunciation of sounds like 'ĕŭ' as in 'feu' and the 'ŭ' in 'tu' (so easy to disintegrate into the English Oo) are impossible without great tension of the lips. The German modified 'ü', as in 'müde', is the same vowel as the French 'ŭ'. Whistling needs very tight lips and, as an exercise for the lips (and also the breath), is greatly to be commended.[2] The lips, of course, are capable of great muscular development and such development is required in singing.

[1] A glossary of the pronunciation of foreign languages is given in *Word and Tone*.

[2] The different notes in whistling are produced by different tensions of the lips, which coincide with different shapes of the mouth cavity. These shapes are none other than the oral shapes of different vowels, and the notes sounded in whistling are the resonantal notes of those vowels. Thus, if we whistle the note

and, keeping the shape of the mouth, merely blow through it

(without whistling), we shall hear the vowel Ee (*v.* p. 142 *et seq.*).

With certain consonants also, as the explodents P and B, much lip compression is required, against which the breath is strongly directed, so that a very quick release can be secured.

If these conditions are not complied with a feeble utterance will result, so feeble indeed that the consonants will be quite inaudible; they will have no *flatus* or expressive quality.

The position of the lips has a great deal to do with quality of tone —a smiling position will tend towards bright tone, the rounded one towards dark.[1] If the former is carried to an extreme it will prevent pharyngeal resonance, while the extreme of the rounded position, as in a very pronounced Oh will almost eliminate nasal resonance. These two positions, governing a general shape of the vocal instrument towards the horizontal or the vertical, come into play in all expressive singing. Sometimes if the song is gay, the smiling position will be assumed more or less throughout; the vertical one if the song is sad. All serious attitudes of mind, in fact, are associated with the vertical shape—the horizontal shape can scarcely lead to any deep expression, because it involves a relaxation of the muscles—whereas muscular concentration (which is the counterpart of spiritual concentration) inevitably brings the vertical shape with it.

Another way of looking at the matter and of securing almost the same results as do the smiling or rounded positions, is by considering the action of the upper lip only. If it be raised, showing the upper teeth, the tone will be released to a bright brilliant quality (necessary for emotions of joy, praise, etc.) though such tone will easily tend to get out of hand and become insignificant or silly; if it be depressed so that it covers the upper teeth (bringing the nose downwards with it), the tone will be covered. It is as though the upper lip acted as a shutter, opening or shading the tone at will, much as a shutter or blind will keep the sunlight from flooding a room. If such a shutter is not used, an extreme influx of light might be quite insupportable. At times, perhaps, such an influx is desirable, but in general a more comfortable lighting suits our purpose, and it is the same with the voice. The shaded tone is without doubt the tone that is normally to be used, as it is associated with what might be called average emotional expression, and it is certainly the safest tone to cultivate, because it implies a relaxation in the mechanism foreign to more nasal tone. When the latter is used continuously and to the full, there is apt to be strain, and, through it, the singer is often well on the way to spoiling his voice.

In rounding or pursing the lips care must be taken that they are not drawn inwards but opened outwards like the end of a trumpet —the action of whistling gives the true formation. A very small

[1] See categories of tone, Chap. III, p. 166 *et seq.*

33

C

orifice, of course, occurs in whistling, and this has generally to be enlarged for singing, but the same sort of shape and muscular tension should prevail.

Loose lips undoubtedly favour an open throat, as in a deep drawn sigh; the tightening of the lips may be apt to close or otherwise constrict the throat. One of the difficulties in singing is to overcome this constriction; to procure an open throat with rounded lips. This is particularly necessary when high notes are concerned. If we try to sing a modified ü (see page 319) on a high note, the throat will tend to close and it will be impossible to sing the note at all unless the throat can be opened. Little or no alteration should be allowed in the vowel; but it simply will not sound unless sufficient room is given for it in the neck. This vowel at high pitch provides a very good exercise in vocal management. Indeed it is perhaps the best vowel to practise on in order to appreciate the difficulties involved in tension and to find out how to deal with them.

It should be said that, though rounded lips undoubtedly make for depth and richness of tone, such tone is due rather to the shape of the throat than to the shape of the lips. The rounded lips influence the necessary throat shaping, but the latter can be secured without the action of the lips at all, as may be observed by singing an 'Oh' with the utmost rounding of the lips, and then trying to keep the same sound while relaxing them. Scarcely any of the characteristic quality of the vowel need disappear, though it is probably true to say that strong action of the lips is required to produce 'Oh' in its most intense form. The main thing, however, is the verticality of the throat, not of the lips. The rounded lips certainly help to give the throat its proper shape, to initiate the right process, but the main thing is the deep opening of the throat itself, not the verticality of the lips. When notes get too hard in tone, or too stiff in movement (so that they fail immediately to respond to the touch of the breath, as they often do) a release of the facial muscles to a smiling position will often ease such difficulty.

THE CHEEKS

The cheeks play a considerable part in tone formation. They serve to direct and concentrate the voice, and, in proportion as they do, they will be tightened even to the extent of being drawn in between the teeth, almost forming a dimple. Darkening of tone is associated with tension of the cheeks, brightening with their relaxation. The singer should stretch and contort the face in all directions, quite apart from singing, in order to develop strength in the facial muscles.

TONSILS AND UVULA

The vocal edifice is perhaps more sustained by the tonsils than by anything else. They are called the fauces or pillars of the throat, and only if they are properly erect can the finest tone emerge. What happens at this particular orifice is all-important. If the muscles are weak and sagging here, the tone is likely to be weak and without any real timbre. It is a question whether drastic removal of the tonsils does not affect the voice adversely because it impairs or destroys the muscular support which they give.

Apart from considerations of the general quality of tone, certain vowels depend upon great muscular tension at this point—the vowels Aw and ŏ (as in 'hot') for instance; without this tension their true character cannot be given.

But all the vowels, in proportion as they have vital sound, need some of this tension. Loose tonsils allow the tone to disintegrate, to escape sideways; whereas their function is (in varying degree) to concentrate the tone by bringing them towards each other. This has the further effect both of raising the soft palate and uvula and depressing the root of the tongue, so that the shape of the orifice is ⌂ and not A . It is simply a question of mechanics.

B

There is only a certain width available at A and B. If the tonsils at the sides are drawn in, the curves must be narrowed and the general shape elongated, as in the first diagram.

THE TEETH

Since the teeth are immovably fixed on the jaws, what happens to the jaws must likewise affect the teeth. The main question is therefore: how much should the jaws and teeth be opened? Obviously it will vary a great deal. It must be understood that, since infinitely varied vocal colours have to be dealt with, all actions concerned in singing are subject to great variation. Roughly speaking the front orifice of the mouth blocks the main tonal egress. If therefore a very open effect of tone is needed, the mouth must open considerably, as far as it can without spoiling the sound. Beginners of course, find it difficult to keep the mouth open: they smother the voice in consequence. The rule must be: open the mouth sufficiently to produce the exact vowel that is desired, and open still more according as greater clearness and fullness of tone are needed. For intimate, reflective singing the opening of the mouth will be less than for more public, active pronouncement. Do not champ or bite out notes. As far as possible the mouth should remain still (though open). The teeth must never be tightly approximated. Even for nasals the breath must be allowed to penetrate through the open teeth right out to the lips (which should be loose). To secure open vowels and the proper opening of the jaw, let the back teeth be as far apart as possible.

THE PALATES

Bright, brilliant tone will seem to be directed to the hard palate just behind the front teeth—tone of a gentler quality will tend to recede towards the soft palate. A very 'forward' tone is often desirable, but 'backward' tone must not be ruled out. There is nothing amiss with 'backward' tone provided it is not distorted by wrong muscular action, due to over-tightness or over-looseness (which can be just as great a sin). Indeed, the more human, as contrasted with the more heartless sentiments, can only be expressed by a relatively backward tone.

We have already spoken a good deal about the raising of the soft palate, which obstructs but seldom completely blocks the passage to the nose. With thin, white tone no tension at all is put upon the soft palate; it simply falls 'au naturel', the result being crude uncontrolled nasal resonance with hardly any pharyngeal resonance. The soft palate controls nasal resonance, allowing (by its rise or fall) less or more nasal quality to be mixed into the general tone. Vocal colouring is specially dependent upon its action, which also coincides with pharyngeal action. A raised soft palate and an open pharynx may very well go together; but the tendency of the former is to close the throat.

SECTION 2: THE INTEGRATION OF THE VOCAL INSTRUMENT

Assembly of the Parts

In a state of absolute rest there is the barest connection between the parts of the vocal instrument. It is true that the parts are joined by muscles and ligaments, but they cannot effectively function till they are stiffened and put into working contact. The controlled use of any muscle stiffens it. In principle it is similar to that of a motor car with its engine, gears and transmission. If the engine is not geared to the transmission it revolves uselessly. A 'locking' process has to be introduced; the machine has to be 'set up'.

As regards the voice, the breath (or motive force) has to be coupled with the vocal instrument before it can become operative for the purposes of vocal sound. There are degrees in which this may be done. The connection may be weak or strong. If the former, poor breathy sound will result; if the latter, the sound will be firm and economical. Vocal training is always directed towards developing a powerful breath and an instrument thoroughly capable of resisting it. When these two forces meet, when strength and control are evenly matched, then come the desired fruits of the singer's art.

If we take any mechanical musical instrument such as a piano, flute or trumpet, we see that its structure is exceedingly firm. Both its materials and build are rigid and unyielding. It will break before it will give. The lightest touch or heaviest pressures can be exerted upon it. It can 'take' them all. Why should we expect the human instrument to be different? Why, by adopting the fetish of complete relaxation, should we try to turn our instrument into a jelly? If we succeed in this, and we often do, the results are as, with a little common sense, we might conceive them to be. The application of power is either perfectly impossible, or if power is applied it has to be met in the wrong way. The instrument tightens where it should not, and freedom, which is as important as restraint, can never be achieved. There is no real co-operation of the parts.

What then should be the working principle as to the 'holding' of the voice? Is the vocal instrument, like any other, to be held rigidly all the time, and to the utmost? Should the muscles be stiffened and prepared for a call which may never come? This is going too far, though theoretically it seems logical enough; the mechanical instrument functions upon this basis and the voice is certainly a machine.

What we must say is that the vocal instrument should be keyed up for its expressive purpose. Provided sufficient resistance is forthcoming, that is enough. At one moment it may be less, at another more, according to the situation. But this resistance is not at all dependent on loudness of tone; the softest tone, if it is to be of the greatest intensity, may require all possible power and resistance Perhaps, here, an analogy may help. A bow becomes more and more flexed, i.e., more tightly-drawn, as the archer wishes to send his arrow to greater distances; but, in the first place, it *is* strung up for use.

On the whole we are bound to admit that nothing remains constant and invariable in singing, and that raises the powers of the human voice above those of any mechanical instrument, though mechanical laws have still to be obeyed by the former. Roughly speaking it is the 'attack' of a note that has to be prepared for, and five thousand men (or units of resistance) are not necessary to repel an attack of five, though it were prudent to have some units to the good. The resistance must not give way, that is the real point. Singing must be looked upon as a continual 'attack', though we use the word only in connection with the start of a note from silence. Yet with the holding of a note the same conditions are involved as with its beginning. A good attack is a good continuation; it does not spend itself suddenly—even a smashing *sforzando* need not disintegrate the mechanism. It represents an immediate and perfect adjustment between the resistance of the vocal instrument and the energy which is directed upon it by the breath; and however long the sound is continued, that adjustment must always be present. To start a note well with its proper quality and control, to bring it from silence to sound imperceptibly, without any burst-through or jerk, to vibrate it finely, sensitively, without crudity or coarseness: are among the highest achievements of the singer.

Some singers, particularly in singing German, begin notes with a sort of little 'cough' (when dealing with words starting on a vowel). It is somewhat akin to the 'closed glottis' attack which will be spoken of later. This attack has a significance in breath economy and there is a lesson to be derived from it; but it is to be disallowed entirely for the purposes of artistic expression, perhaps because it is mechanically unsound: there is too much resistance in it, it is uneconomical.

How is the integration of the voice achieved? What causes the instrument to 'lock', to be ready for use?

The answer is *good breathing*.

When we take a full breath such as occurs with yawning (by which act we endeavour to supply a deep demand for air) certain things happen. Without such breathing the neck and head will be loosely joined to the body; the larynx (if we observe it at the Adam's apple) will be high. A full breath, however, will draw the head towards the body and the larynx will almost disappear into the collar bones. A general state of muscular tension will have been introduced throughout the vocal apparatus similar to that which is operating with the breath. The downward pull of the breath (for that is what it amounts to, owing to the use of the abdominal muscles, etc.), will tend to perpendicularize the head, thus, in a sense, raising it; the soft palate will certainly rise in the process, with an opposite movement to that of the breath: the throat will open and expand owing to the descent of the larynx. And as long as this condition of the breath is maintained, so will these conditions persist.

The voice is now 'set' in such a way that the vocal cords, the resonance cavities and the articulatory mechanism function properly. It must therefore be the aim of the singer to preserve this condition of tensity *throughout all breathing*: that is to say both when breathing in *and* breathing out; which although seemingly impossible is really not so. Otherwise there will be a disruption of the instrument at each breath, and, with it, continuity of rhythm and also tone colour will be lost. Effectively the singer would then be supplying himself with a different instrument at each change of breath; at one moment the throat would be open, at the next closed, and other parts of the instrument would alter as well. Anyone who has had experience in this matter will know that this is not a fanciful picture. It can be observed all too frequently, both by the eye and the ear. The falling of the chest at expiration, which even experienced singers exhibit, shows that something like this *must* happen; the change in vowel colour from one syllable to another in a word shows that it does happen. A full, nicely-set vowel will suddenly issue, with a sort of snap or kick, into one which is thin and 'unseated', e.g., lov-*e*th, bivou-*a*c.

Unity of style cannot be maintained unless vowels which have a tendency to a forward and cutting quality (as the ĕ and ă in the foregoing words) are darkened and repressed to the shade of their more full-throated brethren. Then they become just as satisfying in their sound.

The pull of the breath then, accompanied by the continued expansion of the thorax (chest and ribs), is a, indeed *the* vital factor in the proper use of the vocal instrument, by which an open throat is secured and the other resonances of the nose and mouth function in their due measure; the result being not only a balanced tone, but a balanced, easily workable mechanism.

Yet, again, it must be stressed that vocal expression is very variable and that therefore the instrument will vary too in its position and use. It must never be considered as fixed and immovable. The larynx, for instance, though it will always have a tendency to be drawn towards the breath, to become at one with it, nevertheless will submit to varied attractions, as different kinds of expression or different intensities of feeling are brought to bear. It will assume its lowest position only under stress of the deepest emotion—and it will progressively be released from tension as emotion lightens. Inevitably there must be a good deal of unconscious determination about this, but the principle is clear. Also the position of the larynx varies for pitch. Lower notes, involving a looser state of the larynx, will subside into a relatively low laryngeal position: tighter-drawn high notes cause it to rise to a somewhat higher one. For colour, as we have already seen, the larynx certainly changes its position. For lugubrious tones it will be low; for happy, high. But not only the larynx, the *whole vocal mechanism* seems to be lifted up for the latter, depressed for the former, though such depression should never be the result of forcing down the larynx from above; it should always be drawn or sucked down from below.

Forcing down, through wrong muscular action,[1] is often a fault in singing—constricted 'throaty' tone being its sign. Free expansive tone can only be governed from below.

The feeling of a well-set mechanism, ready for the breath to play upon it, is that associated with a condition of panting. In panting there is both tension and freedom. The tension draws the mechanism down, thereby closing the vocal cords, which at the same time are freed by a series of aspirated puffs. The balance is perfect.

If the mechanism is not well-set, if there is insufficient tension to hold the parts together, if the necessary resistance to breath action is not secured, then the vocal machine is in much the same condition as one of Heath Robinson's ramshackle engines; things give way, and *tremolo* or an oscillating, unsteady state of the laryngeal mechanism results. *Tremolo* is the vice of present day singing, and is directly to be associated with unqualified counsels of looseness given to students. Singers should be able to sustain a note quite mechanically, without a quiver. Then, only, is a note in a right condition to receive such impress of emotion as it may be desirable to give to it. Here again breath control is the governing factor.

Further, unless the head and body are properly 'coupled' or 'locked', as we have termed it, the voice will lack sonority because it will be without a base upon which to sound. We have seen how this 'coupling' takes place by the pull of the breath muscles which brings the head towards the body and 'sets' it there. The effect of this upon the voice is much like that of a tuning-fork when it is set upon a table or any other firm resonator. The sound is greatly strengthened. Little sound results when either the voice or tuning fork operates in mid air, so to speak, without any firm contact with another substance. Though the scientific explanation is not quite the same as regards the vocal mechanism and the tuning fork, the effect is the same when this 'coupling' is not secured.

SECTION 3: THE INSTRUMENT IN USE

Mechanical Principles, etc.

> *In shooting at a mark you reach it owing to your strength; you hit it owing to your skill.*
> (The Wisdom of Confucius).

> *As a fletcher straightens his arrow, so the wise man straightens his unsteady mind, which is so hard to control.'*
>
> (The Dhammapada).

Though nature does not ask us to do so before we can sing, it is

---

[1] In physiological parlance, by the use of the sterno-hyoid muscles instead of the sterno-thyroid. These latter are attached to the larynx at their upper ends, and to the breast bone below; and it is the downward pull upon these muscles that we feel when we breathe deeply, thereby stretching them.

as well to try to understand the mechanics of singing. It may help us in later stages of the art, or, at any rate, serve to justify such empirical processes as we have adopted.

So far we have discussed the vocal machine in a state of rest, inoperative from the point of view of singing; then with its parts assembled, ready for use. Now we have to deal with it as a going concern, as a machine in movement.

The movement required of the vocal machine is obvious. The breath is always on the move, the organs of speech likewise. The parts associated with both are continually changing in tension and shape. When sound is 'voiced'—some short-lived consonantal sound is not—the vocal cords vibrate and change their tension with each change of pitch; the tongue and lips move with the consonantal articulations, often very rapidly; alterations of the mouth and tongue occur with each vowel; differences of tone quality involve different resonantal adjustments; and all this is generally determined by or is coincident with different tensions and positions of the breath. Truly a formidable undertaking of co-ordinated movement, though it does not compare with what a coal-heaver has to do in expenditure of energy.

Voice a Unique Instrument

There are peculiarities about the voice and the human machine. Machines of artificial construction which develop power are 'push' machines. They start by pushing some moving part away. The human machine, in company with that of other animals, is a 'pull' machine, acting by the contraction of the muscles. This allows the body to be its own instrument. It is at once the source of power and the mechanism itself. We as it were play upon ourselves, which gives us an intimacy of control over the voice which is denied in the case of other instruments. It is true that the breath plays upon most wind instruments as it does upon the voice. To that extent a similar use is made of our interior energies. But those energies shape the vocal instrument as well, which makes it a very different thing from other sound-producing mechanisms. Thus the voice adjusts itself entirely from within. It is neither fashioned nor energized by outside means as it would have to be if our muscles pushed instead of pulled.

The mechanical methods of living organisms are unique and curious, allowing, by the process of contraction, that mental and physical state which we call concentration, and it is upon this state that so much depends.

Further—the voice is quite unlike any other instrument, for nothing at all is fixed about it. It assumes new positions continually

41

in every part; fixation is only temporary. It is a hundred instruments in one: as many instruments as it exhibits in differences of tone or articulation. It does not add these instruments together, with the verticality of a full-score, like an organ or an orchestra does; it is the same instrument adapting and re-adapting itself in a horizontal way to whatever sound it has to make. Hence its continually changing nature both as an instrument and as a mechanism.

Machines in General, and the Vocal Machine in Particular

All machines work by a motive force acting upon a movable instrument. The machine may be either simple or complex. In the case of the voice it is exceedingly complex: a wonder of muscular adjustment. The requirements of the vocal machine, as indeed in general of all good machines, are that it shall be capable of power and speed, and susceptible to government.

At the outset we have to ask what sort of machine the voice is; what it is required to do. A machine—as apart from an instrument of measurement—is always used to direct energy in some way. In this sense a bow and arrow is a machine directing the human energy which draws the bow in order to project the arrow. Here the energy is suddenly released; it is immediately spent. Anything in the nature of a burst, throw or flick is of this kind. The sustained expenditure of energy, where energy is stored and gradually spent (unless replenished) is in a different category. Of this the steam engine or electric motor are examples; such is also the vocal machine which has to sustain the vibrations of the voice as long as the song lasts.

To secure continuous motive-power is therefore a prime consideration in singing and it is effected through the breath. What is done with such power is a matter of the use of the vocal instrument: the vocal cords, the resonators and the mechanism of vowelling and articulation.

Although there are times when the voice departs from its normal style of *legato* or *sostenuto* by the use of *sforzando* or strong, separated notes (*marcato*, etc.), this exceptional treatment should not exhaust the vocal energy; continuous power should remain. Any and every call that is made upon the voice should leave it fit for service. There need be no failure and in the best singing none occurs. The good singer is always ready to deliver a smashing blow and when this is achieved he is just as ready for a second one. Yet generally the use of his power will be spread more evenly.

Momentary and Continuous Force

There are two ways in which we can apply force: by a sudden

42

impulse, or by continuous pressure. The throwing or hitting of a ball exemplifies the one; the action of a steam engine and, as we shall see, of the voice, the other. With a throw or a hit we can judge the power necessary to reach our objective, and a great deal of skill can be brought to bear towards this end; but it can never be as exact a use of force as the force that is continuously applied. A good golfer can putt his ball so sensitively that he has a good chance of holing it; but if he were to carry his ball from its lie and drop it into the hole he would be absolutely sure that it got there.

To the singer, or any artist, it is not movement which matters—anyone can effect that; it is the control of movement. How far can we control the rate and direction of such movement as we initiate? That is the artistic test. A child can scrawl a pencil mark. It needs the mastery of a Dürer to show what the beauty of a line can be.

When—to take another form of sudden movement—we 'flick' the first finger against the middle one, we can get a great deal of force into the movement; much more than could be given by the muscular action of the fingers themselves. The energy of the whole arm goes into this loose movement; but after movement has been effected no further control is possible till the fingers meet, with a 'thud'. The movement is thus stopped, but it is stopped by external, not internal, means. And the same with any form of 'jerk'.

We sometimes speak of a 'jerked' attack when we burst the glottis open in a 'closed glottis attack'; or of a 'jerked' ending by which operatic tenors often desire to impress their audience—perfectly legitimately—when they attitudinize at the end of a pause note and suddenly stop it with a great show of power. This sort of 'jerk', however, is different from the real jerk. Though considerable energy is accumulated for it, it acts upon a tightly held body (the vocal cords) to which further movement can be given at will; whereas the real 'jerk' acts upon a loosely held body which flies off with the energy in its possession, as it were, and is not open to any further muscular control.

Thus we see that spasmodic applications of energy, though they seem, and undoubtedly are, so effective in their own way, cannot be used in singing; for singing, as indeed all musical performance, is essentially of a sustained nature. Sudden or separated effects, such as *sforzando* or *staccato*, which look as if they were subject to spasmodic action, have to be quite otherwise dealt with. They take their place in a context of sustained tension; as parts of a larger rhythmic whole.

Motive Force
Motive force in a machine can be derived from various sources;

43

from the movement of air or water, from electricity or steam, or from explosion as in a petrol or gas engine. With the voice the motive force is the contained, compressed breath, and the problem is to use this force upon the vocal instrument in such a way that the instrument functions with efficiency and ease. Muscular tension, with appropriate relaxation, will be found to be the key to this.

Tension is the moving principle in muscular action. We move a limb or any other part of the body, just as we do any object outside us, by the tensing or contracting of our muscles. Directly tension takes place energy is developed, and as long as tension lasts that energy is retained ready to be used.

Muscles, of course, can be tightened to no purpose; but there is a purpose in doing so if we care to take advantage of it. By means of such tightening we can do work, or rather by the same effort by which we tighten we can lift and hold weights and bring about movement; and the greater the power of tightening the more weight we can lift and the more movement we can give. In short, the more work we can do in terms of either strength or speed.

The need of the utmost muscular development therefore becomes apparent.

A condition of tension, then, is one of potential energy. We may not wish to use the energy we have developed. There may be obstructions to its use which we have first of all to remove—just as it is necessary to open a valve in an engine before its energy can operate—or the energy may be insufficient for its purpose and more has to be generated.

The point is that muscular tension is the form in which human energy appears, and that singing, in all its aspects, physical, mental or imaginative, depends ultimately upon the capacity for tension.

Signs of Tension

When a muscle is contracted it hardens. It also changes its shape and may thicken and 'bunch up' considerably, through shortening. A muscle has no inherent power of elongating, though it can be stretched by the action of another muscle, or by some outside force.

Sometimes very little seems to happen to the look of a muscle or muscular field, but that does not mean that nothing is happening. With good breathing we should see very little after the initial breath-taking; but we shall hear quickly enough in the vocal sound whether the right state of tension exists in regard to it.

We shall also see, by general signs, whether the singer is 'keyed-up'. It will be apparent in his look. The eye, the set of the face shows it; the stance as well. The attention to the work in hand, the concentration that is brought to bear, also make it abundantly clear. An eager, alert attitude cannot be summoned up if the

44

physical system is relaxed. When the body 'goes to pieces', the mind follows suit.

Resistance

Force is a fundamental, like beauty and truth; and so it is a mystery, virtually indefinable. For our purpose it suffices to regard it as the agency which tends to produce or destroy motion.

Now motion implies the presence of some substance to set in motion; so force, or at any rate perceptible or useful force, cannot exist apart from matter. Put crudely, but with sufficient accuracy, force connotes resistance; it needs something to bite on. Archimedes claimed that he could shift the world if somebody would supply a fulcrum. So, in a sense, force is a sort of Duality, one and indivisible, yet two in one.

Steam can produce or exert force. But when it rises from, say, a boiling saucepan, it simply mingles with the air, manifesting hardly any forceful quality. Yet, with no alteration in its chemical nature, given certain conditions it can move a heavy train. How is this? It is through the advent or introduction of what is called resistance; by the bringing of one power to bear against another, or perhaps we had better say by placing two resistances in contact. The fruit of such a marriage is force, not merely latent energy.

As we have said, the development of force is only made possible by resistance; it has to be gained under duress as it were. There is, in effect, no single force, though we talk as though there were. Force always hunts in couples; conditioned not only by an opposite force but by an equal one. If there were no resistant boiler there could be no pressure of steam. Should the boiler burst such pressure would be dissipated, distributed to outside resistances. If our muscles could not pull upon fixed tendons and against other muscles we should not be able to contract them, thus begetting muscular force.

Paradoxically, then, what in common parlance we call a force is the resultant of two counter forces whose apposition allows it to be generated. We do not create force. Force exists in everything. We can only alter its disposition, the form in which it appears, as when we convert into heat the immense pressure that has turned wood into coal, or, into tractive force the heat energy that has turned water into steam. We can also collect and transfer force—in other words, use it to our own purposes. Finally, however, force escapes us and returns to some state controlled not by us but by the operations of natural law.

We have it in our power, then, to contain or canalize force; as indeed we must for any sort of continuous movement. A rotary engine is a continuously moving machine, so is the voice; both need a continuous supply of force. But force need not be drawn upon. It can be held in readiness, and released only when we wish it. In this case there must be sufficient resistance to prevent its escape; at least an equal amount of resistance must be countered. If such resistance operates, things will then be in a state of equilibrium or quiescence. A locomotive with the steam up, but standing still, is an example of this.

To use the energy that we have stored—itself the result of force and counter-force—it has to be released upon whatever obstacle we desire to move. If this released energy is greater than the resistance that it meets, movement occurs. The energy as it were spills over, is transferred to the moving body; and by so much is the original energy diminished, unless it is replenished, as it must be, for continuous movement. In a tug-of-war we see a sort of catastrophic illustration of this. Great power is developed by the opposite teams. By pulling their hardest they perhaps remain stationary for a time. Then, after give and take, by a tremendous effort one side gains the mastery. Its power is relatively greater and so movement occurs. But at that moment not only is the power of the opposing side lessened, through losing purchase; its own power diminishes, because resistance has diminished. Finally the whole situation comes to grief and there is a general debacle with everyone overbalanced. Such power as there was has been transferred into movement; and the quicker the movement the less power is retained by the opposing teams. They are, in the end, left with practically nothing but their own dead weight, over which they have little or no control.

But this does not mean that movement is necessarily uncontrolled. It is only when resistance has entirely broken down that it is so. If the opposing force is in being, provided there is some measure of constant resistance the rate of movement will also be constant, well in hand.

Thus, movement implies a disturbance of equilibrium, brought about by the opposition of unequal forces and the release of some special concentration of energy. When force is used it ultimately expends itself and becomes part of a general state of equilibrium, just as moving water at last finds its own level; then its movement ceases. And so there is a complex chain of pressures and resistances running through nature; without beginning and without end. As no force is ever lost, so no force is ever created. We may run force to earth, catch it in a moment of crisis, but in doing so we do not destroy it, we only turn it into other channels. Mechanics, however, can only deal with the localized application of force.

Resistance may come from an outside source as far as our muscular action is concerned; we may have to exert our power in moving some object external to ourselves. But *in singing we have to supply our own resistance at all points*: at the diaphragm which controls the breath, at the vocal cords and all the articulating 'stops' without which neither vowels nor consonants could be sounded.

Resistance then is a condition of power; the more resistance the more power and consequently opportunity for work on a larger scale. Resistance is *the* condition of control; the measure of available resistance is the measure of the control of power.

Another aspect of resistance is that of quick recovery. When a hammer hits an anvil possibly a slight impression is made on the surface of both, but they resume their shape instantaneously. If a hammer were to hit a piece of putty, a permanent dent would result; there would be no recovery. Similarly with the vocal instrument and particularly with the vocal cords. If the latter are full of life and are well-set, they immediately recover after any sort of breath impact. Thus they are always ready for work. A poor voice is one which gives and yields like putty. The sound of steel upon steel has 'clang'. The equivalent of this, when the vocal cords are in a high state of elasticity and tension, is 'timbre', 'ring'; in short, metallic tone (*v.* p. 166 *et seq.*). We do not always want the extreme of such tone, but it should be ready, waiting, all the time.

Singing, which is a manifestation of force, cannot escape the laws of blind mechanical forces. It is completely subject to them but it makes these laws serve its own ends which are those of the expression of thought and feeling.

The use of the vocal machine is really the use of the vocal muscles. To what purpose it is used is the matter of art.

Resistance is *not* relaxation. It seems absurd to have to say this; but relaxation is so often accepted as the key word of voice production to the denial of those forces which really do the work.

Application of Tension to the Voice. Breath Pressure. Tension on the Vocal Instrument

Before the voice will sound, the force that has been generated by resistance must be applied. This application takes place by means of the breath which acts as an elastic connecting rod between the parts of the vocal machine which supply the motive force, viz., the abdomen and diaphragm, and those parts which have to be moved in order to produce sound, viz., the vocal cords and the articulatory organs.

The depression of the diaphragm (secured, largely, by the expansion of the ribs) allows air to fill the vacuum so obtained. When, with the lungs in this condition, the vocal cords are approximated, pressure can be put upon the breath by the upward drive of the abdominal muscles upon the diaphragm; and, in proportion as the cords hold or give, so will the breath pressure vary. If the cords give, the expulsion of the breath at different pressures will result in vocal sound of different strength and quality; or, it may be (when pressure is much reduced) in 'flatus', i.e., non-vocal breath sound, only.

The use of the abdominal muscles tends, normally, to close the vocal cords, but the two actions are not necessarily associated; the cords can still be kept open though the abdomen is in a state of tension. However this may be, such force as is available at the diaphragm can be applied to the breath. It then travels up to the vocal instrument in the form of what we call breath pressure, *provided the right resistance is supplied by the vocal cords*. If these are not approximated then, of course, no breath pressure can be exerted. It is the containing of the breath which brings it about. To feel what breath pressure is we have only to close the throat (glottis) and to force the breath upwards against it. As no breath can pass great compression will result.

The analogy of a locomotive is often helpful towards the understanding of vocal action. The thorax or lung casing may well be likened to its boiler; the breath to the steam which can be under high or low pressure just as we desire. We want the largest boiler that we can get; we also want the power of producing the greatest pressure.

As regards lung capacity, the maximum space must be created for the lungs to fill. This is a matter of rib expansion. We must try to raise the ribs as much as we can. Considerable muscular development is needed for this. The process of rib expansion is, of course, naturally associated with the intake of breath, but ordinary breathing is wholly insufficient. This expansive process does not of itself produce breath pressure; it only affects volume of breath. The main source of pressure comes from the action of the diaphragm (the movable base of the lungs, or thoracic cone, as it is sometimes called) which having been depressed by inhalation can now be acted upon strongly by the abdominal muscles, so that it becomes like a piston compressing the breath.

The breath need not always be at the highest pressure. When the breath is forced into the upper part of the chest it will be at a higher pressure than when its force operates lower down. Variations of pressure will be considerable, but as intensity is a more or less constant feature in singing some measure of breath pressure will always go with it.

Opposite powers are at work here: the power of expansion[1] in-

[1] Expansion is apt to be a misleading term. Although we say the chest expands it

48

volved by deep, full breathing, and the power of abdominal con-traction playing upon the diaphragm. The singer should exercise himself in the simultaneous use of these powers by keeping the ribs and chest expanded as much as he can, and at the same time exhaling and inhaling as forcibly as he can by moving the abdomen in and out like a bellows. The ribs should be held at the sides, between the thumb and the forefinger to verify this condition.

The expansion of the thorax, however, is not dependent upon breath taking, though breath taking is dependent upon it. It is a muscular action which can and should be practised with empty lungs, keeping the mouth closed and holding the nose during the process. When this action is thoroughly under control it will be possible to do that most essential thing, keep the chest up, all the time, *throughout* singing. This is not likely to be achieved at once. The continued tension involved cannot be secured unless the muscles are strong and well developed; if they are not strong they will give in. Broadly speaking, strong muscles need never lose their tension; as we have said, they have the power of continuously renewing it. Fatigue of course ultimately steps in and rest is needed, but for considerable periods, as long in fact as is wanted, tension can be maintained. An experienced singer has no real excuse for wilting. It simply means that proper study has not been suggested, or that it has been shirked.

As regards its efficiency, muscular pressure is most quickly directed on to a full breath, and therefore we should always try to keep as much breath as we can in the body, though four-fifths of the contents of the lungs cannot be dispelled even by the most extreme effort. If well managed, it is astonishing how long such a small amount of workable breath will last, and how much can be done with it.

There is still another reason why the singer cannot be excused if he fails in endurance. A great deal of tension of course takes place in singing—tension is the cardinal principle which is advocated—but comparatively little work is done since there is not much actual weight to be shifted, or movement, in physical terms, to be effected. For all that it must not be supposed that singing fails to make a considerable call upon the muscular system. If a prolonged, highly-dramatic situation, or one of tremendous mental strain, has to be dealt with, the singer has to go 'all out', and he may be as thoroughly tired by it as by the most energetic game. It is not all milk and water.

Tension also has to be applied to the articulatory organs. Any-

is brought about by muscular contraction. Muscles never expand by their own interior energies; they always contract. The diaphragm actually contracts when the lungs are filled; it runs counter to and steadies the abdominal pressure.

thing which is fixed or moves (save by its own weight) is subject to tension. Even 'to keep one's mouth shut' is difficult in more ways than one!—for some tension has to be applied to bring it about. The loose jaw falls. This is indeed a way of opening the mouth and a good example of deadweight relaxation.

Nevertheless it will be found that a certain tension *will* take place even with the loosely-open mouth if a *general* high state of tension is prevalent, and a 'high' state of tension means that the breath is pressed into the upper part of the lungs. Lower tensions fall into the lower part.

Much the same principle is at work with any particular sound. An unmistakable Oh, for instance, can be shaped at the back of the mouth, quite loosely, with hardly any rounding of the lips. In this case the breath effort will be low. But with a higher pressure of the breath the mouth will tend to tighten and the lips to round till the fully characteristic Oh shape is firmly determined. With the fixation of any sound there may be high or low tension, which will be found to agree with a high or low tension of the breath.

Degrees of Tension

Power and speed with which mechanics is mainly concerned, may be consuming rather than revealing Deities if they become the only consideration. For both, at their highest, the highest pressures are needed. But lower pressures may well give characteristic and beautiful results in terms of human feeling. We do not always want to be keyed up as though we had to move a mountain or run for our lives.

With the atmosphere there is always a good deal of pressure, but if we look at the barometer from day to day we shall see that pressure varies. It is light when skies are cloudless, heavier when they are overcast. The wind may be calm, or it may be roused to a gentle breeze, or the fury of a storm. Different barometer pressures will be registered in each case. It is the same with the voice. As we have elsewhere remarked, there must always be considerable breath pressure, or at any rate muscular tension. That is a basic condition. But there will be a considerable variation *after* this basic condition is satisfied.

The lower-powered methods of our ancestors led to a more leisurely way of life and probably closer contacts with nature than our higher-powered methods are apt to do; and standardization, the foe of art, follows in the train of power, if power becomes a main quest. There is more in music than power and speed. Moods of soft human sympathies do not accord with hard mechanical efficiency; and different means, different tensions are appropriate to them.

These differences are shown in qualities of tone which open up far more subtle and secret forms of expression than are contained in power or speed. Mechanical forces, it is true, ultimately account for the former, as they do more immediately for the latter; but they are quite in the background of our thoughts when we listen to tone, as tone, and accept it like the aroma of a flower.

Therefore various degrees of muscular tension are necessary. There can be no hard and fast rule; for there is none in the situations with which art has to deal.

Fields of Tension

Sir Arthur Keith, in *Engines of the Human Body*, tells us that 'nearly every one of the muscles of the lower limbs—108 in number—is set going, not all at once, but in a definite and wonderfully regulated order, in the taking of only a single step.'

But we can go further than this and say that muscles do not only work one after another, just as they are wanted; but, sympathetically, in more or less extended fields of tension.

There is hardly ever a purely local action—if by local we mean at the point where a muscle is contracted or where movement actually takes place. What looks like a localized movement, such as even the easy lifting of a finger, influences muscles other than those particularly concerned, and when such an action is extremely pronounced there is no doubt but that it spreads far beyond itself.

This widespread tension can be easily experienced in connection with the breath. With the tension of the abdomen and diaphragm as in deep breathing, the throat will be pulled downwards—the fact has already been noted—and the glottis will have a tendency to close. The muscles of the mouth will also be affected: the soft palate will rise and arch, the palatal walls stiffen. The abdominal action may further extend even to the lower limbs. Indeed when really full breathing occurs the body lifts from the ball of the foot, its weight no longer seems to operate, and something very like floating in space is experienced. This may appear exaggerated, but it is not so.

We are on quite certain ground, however, when we assert that for the smallest action that reaches its most intense form the whole body is brought into play. Homely examples illustrate it. We may have to walk across a sick room when it is imperative to do so without making any noise, or similarly to close the door. In either case we shall find that, to get sufficient control of our action, our muscles will be under tension from head to toe. We have probably all had such an experience, when we have scarcely dared to move. In short the whole muscular system must become a unity if it is to do its more delicate, or most powerful work.

17590

The Centre of Tension

Central effort at the diaphragm is perhaps the most important thing in singing, as it governs the general tension that is essential to a sustained and balanced style. The tension of the diaphragm and abdomen influences the whole of the vocal mechanism, gives it its cue, as it were. Without it everything is lifeless and inert; even the mind cannot function properly since its activities are largely determined by the attitude of the body. Will-power which plays so important a part in what the singer or musical performer does is undoubtedly a (if not *the*) correlative of muscular power.

Not only does the will command tension from the muscles; when the muscles are tensed the will is also strengthened by reflex action. Without will-power the simplest mathematical relationships cannot be realized. Theoretically they may be; practically, never. That is why relationships of time, in performance, are usually so bad, being just approximations without authoritative control. It is the rarest thing to meet beauty in time or rhythm. But beauty of relationship does not come of itself. It comes from the trained will, and the will functions through tension. It is quite an easy matter to say that a unit is made up of two halves. But make it, and see how you will get on! Unaided by his mechanical instruments the greatest mathematician may be but a child compared to an artist who has mental and physical control of mathematical proportions *in his own person*.

Thus the diaphragm is the very centre of the mind as well as of the body, and if its powers are not cultivated, the mind will be weak in will and determinant quality. It has been remarked that one of the great differences between ancient Greek and our modern culture lay in diaphragmatic culture. The Greeks seem to have known the secret of this; we have forgotten it—with obvious results not only on the cult of beauty generally, but even on physical form. The modern woman, particularly, has wide hips. The Greek woman is always portrayed with narrow hips, due to the muscular development of the diaphragm and abdominal regions—and this without doubt was looked upon as the ideal human form in which grace and power were blended. The fat-hipped, sagging bodies of modern times would have been anathema to the Greeks. Woman was something more than a child-bearer to them. Greek Gods and warriors also show the same characteristic.

We are also, of course, in the domain of mental and physical rhythm here—i.e., of movement. The poet's thought is rhythmical. It moves along its appointed path from start to finish; easily, and, one might say, fatally, in its progress. It suffers no jerk or dislocation on the way. Its curve is sure. Similarly with physical rhythm. Beautiful movement of the body is not angular, for this would hold it up; but circular and flowing. With singing too it is the same. Over a long experience the writer has scarcely found one in a hundred singers—this is a favourable estimate—who had any idea of a phrase, i.e., a rhythmic, moving entity. Notes, yes! An idea, a phrase, no! The organic connection between notes (or even words) was unimagined and unrealized. What is the reason? All these people were weak in abdominal action. They had no power of sustained tension at the diaphragm, and with it no power of tension anywhere. In any expressive sense, *thought* was non-existent. Cause and effect seem clear and it is fair to state the matter in these terms.

And if we think that relaxation rather than tension is the main principle of control, when for instance we see the loose hands and arms of the pianist or it may be of the dancer, we have only to observe a little further to disprove it. Those hands and arms, though they may be loose, are held up somewhere; if the body were entirely loose they would simply drop to the sides. Where then are they held up? At the diaphragm. Only if the muscles are there under tension, can the muscles at the extremities be free. Nor could they be free at the extremities if the fingers, hand or arm had to be articulate. Then muscular action could not be avoided; and muscular action means tension. But the main current of action undoubtedly derives from the diaphragm, as was recognized so fully in the past, even to the point of making it a religious factor, and must still be so recognized by any to whom 'know thyself' is a desirable commandment in any full sense.

Stored Energy and its Advantage

Just as the boiler of a locomotive can store its energy, so can the body. In the one case the energy is created by the compressed steam; in the other by the tensed muscles which can communicate their energy to the breath. When movement takes place some of the energy is used, but no movement need take place as long as the energy is countered by sufficient resistance. The closed main valve of the locomotive, or the closed glottis of the voice will afford such resistance and prevent movement and as long as this resistance is forthcoming pressure of steam or breath can be increased. With the opening in due measure of either the steam valve, or the glottis, the locomotive will move, or the voice sound unless other impediments intervene.

But vocal energy need not be controlled at the throat. The breath is not the means of vocal energy, it is only the vehicle. The means are the abdominal muscles and the diaphragm, and these can function strongly even with an open throat. The breath need not be brought into play at all. All that is necessary is for the diaphragm to oppose the abdomen. It is this action which stores vocal energy, and we must be clear that it is not the breath which does so.

Such abdominal and diaphragmatic tension constitutes a reservoir of force like that of steam under pressure in a boiler. This can be drawn off or released for the purpose of movement but if properly regulated very little is used; the remainder is conserved or replenished. The furnace is always at work, supplying fresh steam to the boiler. Heat, produced by chemical changes, is continually renewing muscular force. The sources of energy need not fail save in exceptional circumstances. Thus a reserve of energy is immediately available wherewith to meet any demand of movement.

Since a muscle will respond immediately—a hint from the brain does it—there does not seem much use in storing muscular energy beforehand. Why not apply energy as and where wanted? It seems plausible; but things are not always what they seem.

It is sometimes said that a muscle always 'has its steam up'. But it is not so. It takes time to bring a muscle into operation. Though a muscle can be *told* to function at once, its action is delayed by inertia and by what it has to do. Resistances are present and these have to be overcome gradually till deadweight is converted into live thrust; just as a spring has to be gradually wound, and the heavier the resistance the slower will be the action till the requisite tension is reached.

If, therefore, this tension has already been developed and is there waiting to be used, time is saved and 'attack' is immediate. Nor need the holding of notes ever fail, for they will be sustained by the energy stored through a constant state of tension.

Prepared and fortified in this way, a singer is like a runner crouched for the start of a race, and off the mark at once.

Nervous Impulse

The nerves, which convey from the brain 'the rare elastic fluid' (as Newton imaginatively termed it) that stimulates the muscles, are instantaneous in action. There is no time-lag between the behests of the will and incipient muscular movement. But, as before observed, the full power of a muscle cannot be exerted at once. There is an appreciable delay in the operation.

The nervous system, in artistic matters, counts for perhaps more than brute strength. Strength can be slow and sluggish; that is indeed its tendency.

The man with the bulging muscles is usually not very sharp-witted or lively in action. An excess of muscular development may be a clog.

Highly-strung people, as we call them, respond much more

quickly to nervous stimulus than do lethargic people. Their sails, to a large extent, are already trimmed and tensed.

To be strong is desirable; to be quick is, also. A Nonconformist divine was once characterized as 'a solid and nervous assertor of the truth'; what apter words could describe an artist in whose best work the union of strength and sensitiveness is so apparent.

Principles of Muscular Action

It is said that the most coveted accomplishment of the Jurs (an African tribe) is to be able to move each individual muscle from the forehead downward. Those who achieve it are regarded with great respect by their less skilful brethren, but the price is apparently life-long practice.[1]

It is doubtful, however, whether there is not some exaggeration in this, for, to begin with, it is impossible to use a single muscle. At least two are concerned in any movement, in some, though not necessarily an equal, degree.

Our muscles normally work in a reciprocal or balanced action: the harmonious adjustment of complementary sets of muscles, those which bend our limbs and those which extend them, called the flexors and extensors. They are set up in opposing pairs. When we are at rest no voluntary tension takes place in them. When we wish to contract a flexor muscle, like, say, the biceps in the upper arm—the action of this and its opposing muscle is very easily observed—if the arm does not move, *both* the biceps and the opposing under muscle, the triceps, will be in a condition of equal tension, whatever the tension we exert. If we bend the arm, however, and keep it moving slowly, the under muscle will be found to relax—it must in order to allow the flexion—but directly we stop it the under muscle will again tighten (or the upper muscle slacken) sufficiently to ensure an equal balance of force between the two. Thus, when there is movement the one muscle gives way to the other so that the muscular machine can move—and yet, by its own tension, offers sufficient resistance to steady the action of the other. When we 'lose our balance' it is because we have not learnt or have temporarily forgotten how to control our opposing muscles. A tiny child has not this control and so it stumbles about; and it is worth while noting that the speech organs are so intricate and difficult of adjustment that they were the last to come under man's control. Speech is the supreme glory of our muscular action; but there is obviously no end to the discipline of muscular development and subjection.

[1] Eggleton, *Muscular Tension.*

Voluntary and Involuntary Tension

The tensing of a muscle *while movement is taking place* involves the corresponding slackening of its opponent muscle; and this is true whether high or low tensions are concerned, i.e., whether much or little 'work' is being done. But a muscle, as we have already seen, can contract without producing any movement; a limb can be set at will in any position and different degrees of tension can be applied to its muscles. In this case as long as there is immobility the opponent muscles contract in equal strength so that their forces balance, and only when one of them relaxes or increases its tension (which amounts to the same thing) can movement of the limb take place. Movement must depend upon unequal forces, just as with ordinary kitchen scales. If the weights are equal on either side the scales remain motionless, but begin to move when additional weight is placed on the one side or the other. Equal tensions (or pressures, or forces—for it is all the same thing) mean equilibrium. Only a disturbance of equilibrium produces movement.

If in the attempt to pass from rest to movement the relaxation of an opposing muscle cannot be voluntarily effected, no movement is possible since the balance of forces remains. Fixation then occurs. This happens in abnormal pathological states, produced by certain poisons which hold up voluntary muscular action. But it is not tension which in itself produces fixation. We must get it out of our minds (if it was ever there) that tension is a bad thing, involving rigidity, and that there is some special virtue in looseness. Tension and relaxation are complementary muscular states *in all conditions of movement*. The one follows as the other proceeds. If there is no movement there may be comparatively complete relaxation, but only then. Complete relaxation means death.[1]

Tension and Ease

Easy movement is principally due to balanced movement, as we may observe with a sash window. It does not matter how heavy the window is, provided, through the cord, an equal weight balances it. It will move quite easily whether it is heavy or light, just as equal and opposite muscular tensions of any degree can easily be subjected to movement. If, however, the sash cord breaks, what was perfectly balanced and easy to move, falls with a bang and becomes relatively unmanageable. Its opponent force is then gravity, an outside force, and not an inside one, placed within the mechanism of the window itself.

There are other considerations.

We handicap ourselves by the unskilful use of our muscles, often

[1] There is always some state of tension, or 'tone' as it is termed, in muscles, even though they appear to be entirely relaxed.

working them awkwardly and in a far harder way than we need. We might do things quite easily yet we struggle along as though on a calm day we had all the elements against us. A certain amount of effort is needed to do a certain amount of work; but when more than this is required, through unnecessarily adverse circumstances, there is wastage of effort.

If the parts of a machine do not fit perfectly, if they are badly articulated, friction or delay takes place which interferes with its smooth running. The voice can also have its hold-ups. There can be undue local stiffness, as at the throat when power is wrongly applied; or with the tongue or jaw, which prevents easy co-ordinated action; or parts of the vocal instrument may be strained by bad usage, or worn by the inroads of *anno domini*.

In a general way the muscular system of youth is better balanced and more elastic than that of later age. This can be seen with the skin of oldish persons which takes a comparatively long time to recover its position when stretched or pulled. High notes can usually be attacked more softly and easily by the young than by the old; sound can be better held and hardness of tone is not so likely to be there: though what youth gains in suppleness and control, age does in intellectual and emotional maturity. Moreover, if the voice is well produced it will last a long time, as great singers have made abundantly clear.

But youth, however, does not have it all its own way even in the physical field. It was reported by a contemporary of Michael Angelo that he had seen the sculptor, although then sixty years old and not in robust health, strike more chips from the hardest marble in a quarter of an hour than could be carried off by three young stone-cutters in thrice the time.

The lack of ease is perhaps more largely to be ascribed, throughout life, to lack of skill. People get tied up with their muscles. Muscles will not move through the unskilful balancing of opposing tensions. Sometimes all the muscles are in a state of high tension; at other times opposing muscles must be freed in order to allow easy progress. But the easiest progress is not necessarily right. An agonized Oh will involve very different muscular treatment between antagonist muscles, from that required by a careless, casual 'Ah' which means very little. To deal with every emotional situation we must have the power of tightening muscles to any degree. The 'Marseillaise' with its rousing clarion call will need a higher state of tension than does the mood of Vaughan Williams' 'Silent Noon'; and with higher tension there is more effort.

Ease certainly comes from the use of low tensions, but completely relaxed muscles would produce nothing, except ease. As regards tone, the state would be one of white, bleaty sound, and as regards speech, one of stupid inarticulateness.

One of the most natural examples of ease resulting from balanced tension is afforded by panting, an action to which we have already referred. In panting the breath is held but is immediately susceptible to movement. Its fluttering state proves it to be both poised and free, and gives the almost perfect position for vocal 'point de départ' or, as we often rather inadvisedly call it, 'attack'.

Tension and Power

Energy is of course implicit in every aspect of life and nature. Sometimes, as with water, it only has to be harnessed to whatever use we wish to put it; at other times it has to be converted from one state to another before it is available. Steam is due to the action of heat upon water; muscular tension to changes in the chemical constituents of the muscles. Till these changes have occurred neither the energies of steam nor of the muscles are potential. We talk of summoning up power. This is a true figure of speech. Energy cannot be said to exist in the human body as an effective agent till tension takes place.

Capacity for tension is the measure of available power. Efficiency is dependent upon the way that power is applied, but it is the amount of power that decides the scale of its application. The perfection of a thing is not necessarily a matter of scale but of proportion. Nevertheless large-scale singing has its own particular appeal and for certain situations it cannot be dispensed with. A tiny, though exquisite voice cannot fill a large hall or fight against the forces of an orchestra. The effect of strong men singing, particularly in a male voice chorus, is often impressive in the extreme. The sound seems rock-hewn. There is nothing quite like it in the realm of music, except perhaps a brass band.

It is sometimes thought that speed does not consort with power. It generally does not with the human species, but the statement needs to be qualified. There are advantages in speed which can only be effected by power. A highly-powered motor-car is capable of greater speed than a lower-powered car. Tension is not in itself inimical to speed. It is the adverse tension of opposing weights that checks speed, and as these are removed so speed increases.

We may also think that great power only affects a *fortissimo*. But a *strong pianissimo* is equally dependent upon it. The full intensity of soft singing cannot be realized by weak muscles.

Nevertheless the appeal of power in pure vocal music has never been paramount. Persuasion has counted for far more than shock. It is instrumental music that has developed the *sforzando*. Till vocal music linked up with instrumental in the seventeenth century there was scarcely an occasion for a rough accent. And even now it is the *legato* rather than the strongly-punctuated line which rules with the voice.

Perfect technique is perfect poise.

Tension and Balance

Balance is of the very essence of control—an unbalanced thing is a thing out of control, unsteadied by any counter-force. If we wish to have control of our voices in the highest expressive sense, it can only be achieved by muscular balance which in its turn is achieved by muscular tension. Perfect balance is, of course, equilibrium, the absence of motion, and motion is the disturbance of equilibrium, so that while movement is in progress perfect balance is impossible. Nevertheless the aim of the singer must always be to retain such control of movement that at any time he can return to a state of equilibrium. In short he must never let movement 'run away'—a constant tendency in musical performance.

To refer again to them: ordinary kitchen scales afford an example of balanced tension. If there is an equal weight on either side the arms remain stationary, but when we 'tip the balance' by means of unequal weights, movement takes place. Note (1) that if the weights are very unequal, say 1 lb. on one side and an ounce on the other, the heavier weight will descend sharply and get quite out of hand until it is stopped in its course by meeting resistance; (2) if the weights are equal the slightest touch on either side will induce gentle movement, or if a heavier touch be applied a quicker movement will result; but the balance will always return to its position of equilibrium when the impulse which has been given to it is withdrawn. The action of (1) is as it were a blind force, subject to external control; that of (2) a force having the means of control within itself.

The same principle works with the muscles, which we can balance, at will, by any degree of tension (the equivalent of weight) that we care to apply. We can balance opposing muscles by giving them an equal tension; we disturb that balance by (1) increasing the tension of one of the opponents, (2) decreasing the tension of one, or, what is more likely, (3) increasing the tension of the one and simultaneously decreasing that of the other after the manner of normal muscular action spoken of on page 55. In singing, movement will always be in terms of tone—a 'rest' means the cessation of movement, though not of tension. We have often been advised to 'sing through our rests'; this is what it means. But no movement of tone can take place till the balance of tensions has been disturbed.

In a sense, directly movement starts it is out of hand. By so much as resistance gives way we have lost *immediate* control. When a train is going at full speed the driver has not immediate control of its movement; only a catastrophe could stop the train at once. Just as it has gained its speed gradually, so it must be slowed up—an *accelerando* entails a *ritenuto*. Yet in another sense as long as we determine the *rate* of movement we are entitled to say that we have control of it, even though perfect balance has been upset.

Here, it may be objected, tight and opposite muscular forces ultimately produce rigidity. How, then, can there be ease of action when there is no movement, i.e., when a condition of equilibrium has been reached? The answer of course is (as already indicated): that it is because the opposite forces do not, and in some cases cannot vary, that there is rigidity or an approach to it. Variations of opposing tensions must be possible if real rigidity is to be avoided.

If we start from equal and opposite tensions—which will incidentally give us the most perfect form of 'attack' in singing—and can return to those tensions when we like—we have practically full command over our muscular powers. In the case of the breath where the principle of balance occurs on the largest scale, the contra or balancing forces are the upward pressure of the abdominal muscles, produced by their contraction, following the expansion of the ribs. We can balance these forces in any degree of power or tension that we like; the more power we apply the more work we can do, and the greater variation we can give to that work in terms of power. If initial balance is secured—not mere deadweight balance where there is practically no tension, but tense, live balance permeated by mind and will—we can easily disturb it by applying a little more pressure to the abdomen and at the same time allowing the diaphragm to yield a little. If the diaphragm does not yield, no movement of the breath can of course take place—the expulsive power of the breath depends upon the piston-like action of the diaphragm—but with such breath control everything is easily possible: a swell, an accent, a *staccato* note, any effect which implies a sudden or gradual departure from or return to the condition of tensed equilibrium which was there from the start.

It may here be said that the control of tone is at the same time the control of movement, since movement in music is shown by means of sound, and what affects the one affects the other.

There is another aspect of balance in what we call balanced *tone*. Previously we have referred to balance rather in its connection with movement or rhythm. A word, now, as to how balance affects tone. We are on more difficult ground here, in which subtleties and standards of colour enter, but it is important to try to survey it.

What do we mean by balanced tone? In what does its balance consist, save that we can control it in the speed or power of its issue? What has it to do with *quality*?

Here we are concerned with the kind of tone that arises when the vocal mechanism is in a state of balance. That particular state is, roughly speaking, when the inspiratory and expiratory movements of the breath are of equal strength, and used *simultaneously*; when, in short, we have taken a deep sighing breath and hold it, with the glottis open. At that moment there is no resistance at the vocal cords, so that balance is maintained by the breath muscles only. The full expansion of the ribs at the same time produces the contraction of the diaphragm or abdomen, so that these opposite forces are in equilibrium or balance. Even after this position is reached still more tension can be brought to bear. The sighing process can be carried further till the most intense sigh operates—but an ordinary sigh is sufficient to secure a balance of the singing breath. When more than this takes place, when extreme effort is used, it may tend to hinder mental and emotional activity—particularly as regards the tender emotions—because attention may be directed too much to the muscular effort, absorbing energies which might have been given to the sensibilities and feelings. Emotional states in which physical excitement enters largely—such as those of indignation or anger— require, however, great exertion in the breath muscles.

Directly we begin to use the voice—that is by the closure of the glottis—the extra resistance supplied by the vocal cords calls for more effort from the expulsive muscles of the breath. There is then an upsetting of the balance in which the breath muscles are alone concerned: for breath has to be driven through the vocal cords; but this is not sufficient to disturb the *general* balance of the vocal instrument as long as expansion holds and no collapse takes place—there is still plenty of power in hand.

With a deep full sigh[1] the level of effort or line of greatest expansion is a little below the breast bone (*v.* p. 6). When this is so, certain things happen: the larynx is lowered, the pharynx opens, the mouth shapes itself vertically, and an adequate amount of the sound stream enters the nasal cavity. It is this easy though *held* condition of the voice that gives us what may be called *balanced tone*: a condition in which the ingredients of neck, mouth and nose resonance are in pleasing and, as it were, equal proportions, no one resonance being favoured at the expense of another. With this the tone will be rich and free. It will serve for any ordinary frank

---

[1] A sigh and a yawn involve the same sort of action, but the latter will probably make a greater call upon the breath owing, as it were, to its desperate physical demand.

utterance in which average clarity and feeling enters. It is the best working tone, and may be considered as the normal.

The general balance of the mechanism may, however, be upset by (1) using a higher action of the breath, i.e., compressing the breath more in the upper part of the lungs; or by (2) a lower, more depressed action, in which compression is more in the region of the abdomen. (1) will seem more like a driving out of the breath; (2) like a drinking in.

Further, with (1) the vocal cords will have to approximate more tightly to give the necessary resistance, pharyngeal space will be constricted and the vibratory stream will be strongly directed, almost forced into the nose. In short, the whole level of the voice will rise (needing increased effort) just as the level of the breath has risen. The consequence of all this will be a brightening of the tone, till the acme of harshness is reached. This imposes a considerable strain on the voice owing to the increased resistance that, progressively, has to be secured from the vocal cords. It must not be shirked, but it must not be indulged in to excess. Some of the short vowels (as in 'cot', 'cat', 'cut') if their special character is greatly insisted upon, submit the mechanism to very hard usage. The dramatic situation may, however, require it, and certain valuable aspects of expression are bound up with this particular, and almost brutal treatment.

With (2) (the downward tendency of the voice) the opposite will happen. The level of the breath will be lower than the normal, pressure will be taken off the vocal cords, so that they can function more loosely, the neck will expand, there will be less thrust of sound into the nose, and consequently less metallic ring in the tone. Sober instead of brilliant hues will be favoured; the voice will lose its lustre and appear dull, cavernous, lugubrious. No harm can be done by this type of singing which relieves the throat from strain; but, as with (1), the resultant quality of tone is only suitable for special situations and we soon tire of it. Something is missing from its make-up; the resonances are not fully engaged; the ingredients of the tone are not well-proportioned. We have gone to extremes, whereas it is the middle way that best contents us; the balanced way.

The central effort of the breath, by which the energies of the voice are kept in equilibrium, can be tested by *panting* (as we have indicated elsewhere); and almost as well by *laughing*. Both actions are a series of aspirates. With panting, a tiny amount of breath is drawn in and then pressed out by a sort of *tremolo* action, the glottis remaining open (thus proving the perfect balance of the inspiratory and expiratory muscles during movement); with laughing, breath emerges all the time in a succession of puffs and stops, effected *at* rather than *by* the vocal cords (which exercise very little control as compared with the control of the breath). When the laughing action is done to perfection variations of time and strength can be given to it in quite an amusing way; the control is absolute. The aspirated bubbles of sound can be released slowly or quickly, softly or loudly, exactly as willed. If the breath were not well-balanced the aspirate could not be checked in the way that both panting and laughing entail. With too high a breath insufficient aspirate escapes; with too low, too much. With the high breath, aspiration is throttled; with the low, hindered, though not to the extent of preventing action entirely. The malign, sardonic laugh and the low chuckle arise from them.

Central breathing, however, eases the whole situation; the aspirate is then at its best, ample and free, because everything is in a state of balance. Freedom is certainly hampered, otherwise. It is then as though the weights on either side of an avoirdupois scales were unequal. With equal weights, movement or oscillation can be given to the balance by some outside agency, but the balance will always return to equilibrium of its own accord once the disturbing factor is removed. This is what happens in panting which is a quick in-and-out oscillating movement of the breath, a sort of Jack-in-the-box behaviour. The slightest extra expiratory push or inspiratory pull temporarily disturbs the equilibrium of the breath, but the breath is always ready to return to the position of equilibrium directly the disturbance ceases. Neither the high nor the low breath is in that state of equilibrium.[1] With the high breath, equilibrium is maintained by resistance at the vocal cords; with the low, by resistance at the abdomen. We can feel the glottis close in order to supply resistance as the breath rises, though by a great effort it can

---

[1] Since writing the foregoing I have come across this relevant passage from Havelock Ellis's Essay 'The Philosophy of Conflict': 'It is with the notions of effort and resistance that we have formed our picture of the universe and that Darwin made intelligible—the manner in which we ourselves came to be. It is on the like basis that our spiritual world rests. We create in art on the same plan and with the same materials as the world is created—making greater things, Keats said, than the Creator himself made—and it is precisely in the most fundamental arts, in architecture and dancing, that we find conflict and resistance most definitely embodied. Every pose of the dancer is the achievement of movement in which the maximum of conflicting muscular action is held in the most fluidly harmonious balance. Every soaring arch of the Architect is maintained by an analogous balance of opposing thrusts, without which harmoniously maintained struggle his art, like the creator of the world's art, would collapse in ruins. For in the creation of the forms of art we see, as in the evolution of the forms of animal life, there is no room for violence; conflict and resistance go hand in hand with harmony and balance; we must go very low down in the arts—indeed to the most degraded of all—to find that knock-out blow adored of the militarist.' To which it is necessary to add that the knock-out blow may occasionally find a place in art, as it does in certain catastrophic occurrences of nature.

be kept open; on the other hand it will open more and more as the breath gets lower.

Tension and Speed

As we have already said there is nothing fundamentally prejudicial to speed in tension, by which we mean speed of muscular movement. A muscle or group of muscles can work with intense speed under the highest tension, though it is true to say that the tension of other muscles may, as it were, get in the way. We see this in the articulation of the fingers; where a general tightness of the hand will hinder the separate articulation of the fingers; but the hand itself can develop an enormous speed though it is as tight as a drum. If we tighten the hand and arm and strongly press the tips of the fingers upon a table we can secure a succession of the most rapid taps by slightly (but forcibly) lifting the hand *while pressing all the time*. Without this tension the movement would be much slower; it would have little life in it. This is also interesting as an experiment because it shows how the flexor and extensor muscles can operate with advantage at the same time. Such a principle is at work when the tongue articulates a strong succession of T's.

Muscular response is far quicker when a muscle is tight than when it is slack. A twitch or a jerk—which, with conditions of continued tension is relatively under control—can easily be given to a tightened muscle; and these are very quick forms of movement.

In fact, both for purposes of power and speed tension is an advantage. A boxer's blow at its most effective is not that of a loose swing but is tightly connected to the body by tension so that the whole weight of the body can be brought to bear. This is the punch which counts; a combination of terrific speed and force, though of quite short range.

Another relevant example of quick action through a firm medium is that of a series of, say, ivory balls in close contact. The least touch of the ball at one end of the row will immediately travel to the one at the other end. Had the balls been of softer substance, the given impulse would have been much slower in making itself felt: a clear instance that it is through connected elastic tension, or, as in the above case, compression and restitution, that quick movement is best realized.

It is certainly so in the case of the breath which as we have said can be looked upon as an elastic connecting rod between the diaphragm or energizing force and the vocal cords to which it is applied. The higher the breath pressure the more elastic is this connecting medium and the speedier will be its action. Loose, lower pressures on the other hand will be slower in action, and suited

64

to far more leisurely expression. If clear-cut precision is desired, or a very vital rhythm, the breath must be tightly tensed which is the same thing as compressing it in the higher part of the chest. A high breath indicates relatively high pressure; a low breath, low.

In a general way organisms are built for power or speed. Power is sacrificed to speed[1] and vice versa, or rather such energy as is available is used either to obtain work or speed. If the work done is heavy the movement will be slow, or if the speed is quick the work will be lighter, because it will be dealt with by a different sort of mechanism, say that of a cart horse as compared to a race horse. The former has to be a heavier animal to stand the strain of the heavier weight it has to move. But what prevents it from going quickly is mainly the resistance of the weight of its own body and what it has to do. There is more drag upon its movement. But, as we have seen, given the necessary tension or power, there is no reason why strength and speed should not go together. This is further shown in the action of a big gun when a heavy shell is projected at great speed by a tremendous force. The conditions, however, of this action are so exceptional and the effect of it is so devastating that such a conjunction of power and speed cannot be applied in ordinary affairs, and we have to fall back upon an easier, more comfortable management of force. For all that, strength need not be absurdly slow, nor speed weak. They can be combined to make quite an impressive showing. Heavy voices as a rule do not move quickly, nor have light voices much power. This is in the natural run of things. But heavy voices by proper training might often be much more agile, and light ones be used with a good deal more fervency. A quick Handelian run[2] is quite negotiable by a heavy bass, it need not just lollop along as it often does; nor need a light soprano sing like a child of ten when dealing with grief and anguish.

One of the great difficulties of singing is to give strength to quick

---

[1] The trend of natural evolution is towards speed rather than power; it is the quick moving organism that is likely to survive; and the development of art has certainly been in the direction of lightness, quickness and sensitive control (which is much the same thing). Gothic architecture affords a good example of this principle in its progress from the Norman to the Early English, Decorated and Perpendicular styles in which building materials are continuously fined-out. But the attenuation of mass can perhaps be carried too far, æsthetically. We seem to need for our complete satisfaction both a sense of mass *and* economical structure; or, in other words, some sort of a balance between power and speed if we are to be both impressed and stimulated: the middle way, as always.

[2] We have been reminded by Professor Edward J. Dent (*Mozart's Operas*) that coloratura in the 18th century, and especially in the earlier half of it, was almost invariably heroic in style. This applies to oratorio as well as opera: witness the weighty runs in the Airs of the *Messiah*. Light coloratura is of later date, and has not the significance of the older form.

D

notes. Compared to slow notes they are often hardly audible. They take so little time that if they are to be heard they have to be forced on the ear, so to speak, to be effective. This means a much more energetic use of the muscles than singers usually achieve. Indeed in most cases the strength is not there to do it with.

We are at every turn forced back on the need of muscular development not only for loud but for quick singing. The average singer has to rely upon looseness (indicating less resistance) far more than upon tension for his speed, and with it of course he loses power. To be quick in a forceful way is to be able to spread a *crescendo* or *diminuendo* over a florid passage, varying the tone with as much ease as upon a sustained expressive note; and this is a main sign of accomplished performance.

As resistance, or the counterforce, decreases, so speed increases. A very quick action means that there is relatively little to oppose it —we must never forget the word 'relatively'. The release of energy can be made more or less completely and instantaneously, as in a shout, which represents more or less unchecked movement, and so is of no use in controlled singing. Indeed the tendency to shout is one of the chief faults in singing; it appears in many insidious ways.

In this sense—that of a shout, which is the nearest vocal approach to the jerked throwing of a ball—we may say that speed is inimical to sensitive control. Speed takes charge of the situation; what we gain in speed we lose in control.

Expressive music is slow music; quick music is relatively inexpressive—it is not subject to the touch and nuance that can be given to slow music. The technique of speed is a fine thing, but by its very nature it cannot reach the pains and passions of the soul. Subtleties of feeling need subtleties of control for their expression. We must not allow ourselves to be too astonished by brilliant execution which is so often a cloak for poverty of spirit. The same result in terms of power can be gained by a different combination of resistance and speed: a slow heavy pressure or a quick light pressure may produce the same amount of tone, i.e., do the same amount of work; but the *quality* of tone will vary a great deal. In general with poor resistance we shall get poor quality: a sound which is deficient in upper partials.

Tension and Slow Movement

Music is often called the language of the emotions, and it is so. To try to make music by intellectual processes only, by rule, ingenuity or fabrication, would be like trying to cut a coat without cloth. Feeling is the very stuff of music.

. . . *moonlight and music and feeling are one.*

Art is a state of heightened feeling, and therefore of consciousness and tension raised above the ordinary.[1] Subconscious states are, as their name implies, unconscious and without feeling. Directly we feel we must be conscious of doing so. As preparatory to consciousness, subconscious states have their function. They may represent a process of incubation; but it is not till their fruits appear in the light of day, in full view of the intellective mind, that we know what they are and can be said to possess them. Ideas, images may be formed subconsciously—we really know nothing as to how thought arises—but the moment they are presented to the mind a conscious process intervenes and it is upon this that our critical faculty, also the value of art, ultimately depends. Otherwise we should accept anything that 'comes'.

Emotion is always associated with both mental and physical movement—the word itself indicates movement. What we have to consider is the kind of emotion and movement that serves for artistic expression; whether considerable tensity always enters into it, or whether very low tensions can operate with good result.

One of the older psychologists[2] tells us that an extremely voluminous and copious state of feeling occurs with slow muscular movement, as in 'a sauntering walk, an indolent style, a solemn gesture, a drawling speech, whatever is set down as leisurely, deliberate, dawdling'. And it is recommended as not only a pleasurable state but of importance in our emotional life. It is asserted that there is a close intimacy between the feelings of slow movement and certain powerful emotions, such as awe, solemnity, veneration, and others of a class of mingled tenderness and fear entering into the religious sentiment. Further, that it is precisely because there is so little muscular activity that these emotions are liberated. In other words such a condition favours sensibility and particularly sensibility of this order. If it did, it would upset all our present theory of tension, for we should have to admit slack, slovenly movement for the emotional gain that would ensue. It is probable that there is some confusion here, both in thought and fact. Do feelings of any consequence arise as we approach a passive state but

---

[1] Stimulants and drugs may play an important part in this. Balzac, when at work, constantly drank coffee; Coleridge wrote his *Kubla Khan* under the influence of opium. But in such cases it cannot be assumed that they were unconscious of what they were doing; that their productions were effected sub-consciously, without their knowledge. Rather would it appear that a state of supra-consciousness was present. The intellect was quite as alert, as feeling was acute. If it had been otherwise, if the mind was really 'fuddled', out of commission, there would have been no *Comédie Humaine* and no *Kubla Khan*. Whether artificial stimulus is in the long run desirable is quite another matter.

[2] See Bain: *The Senses and the Intellect.*

little removed from that of slumber? Can they be defined if the mind is half asleep?

Rather would it appear that only very wishy-washy feelings can occur if the muscular system is not taut. To take the instances afore-mentioned. 'A solemn gesture' could never be produced by 'indo-lence'; its importance could not thus be realized. A 'deliberate' act implies will, at its finest issuing in 'majestic instancy': what con-nection has this with 'dawdling'? And as regards 'religious senti-ment' could 'awe, veneration' and the like be expressed with the body in a state of quasi-collapse? Perhaps a sort of pale piety might be possible, but no burning religious conviction, nor the richer hues of devotion and sacrifice. One would like to get worth-while emotion upon such easy terms, but it simply cannot happen. Where is the fallacy?

No one will deny the delights of indolence; it may be nice to 'sit and stare'. Just before sleep and at waking a pleasurable wave will often spread over us, but the mind cannot make much of it. Con-sciousness is not sharpened but dulled. To cast feeling into form another order of activity comes into play. Soothing, passive enjoy-ment has to be exchanged for a brisker state in which tension assuredly enters and dalliance and 'dawdling' disappear. The artist *qua* artist cannot be slack. There are such things as tranquil emotions, but though they may be remembered, they are never expressed in tranquillity. Here, again, concentration is the key to any freely communicable feeling, though certain elements of emotion of a more or less subconscious kind refuse to be com-mandeered in the process; they are beyond our grasp.

A loose-tensed muscular condition *must* produce slow movement, and, with it, emotional states interesting to the psychologist; but a highly-tensed condition *can* also produce it, and this alone concerns the artist. In short, the psychologist is apt to leave *quality* of move-ment out of account. That is where he appears to be wrong. It all hinges upon that, and it represents the solution of the difficulty.

Dancing also shows the true state of affairs very clearly. Ask the dancer to realize the beauty of slow movement by slopping and slouching along. He would tell you that because it is slow his utmost powers of tension are needed and that it is through them that masterly control is secured. Tone also illustrates the principle. A *pianissimo* produced by a lazy use of the muscles will be devoid of intensity and effect.

Muscular laziness has its counterpart in emotional and mental laziness, for body and soul run in harness. A sort of indulgent, dreamy emotion may come from it, but insufficient to produce any-thing more than half-formed thought. It has about as much value as thought which is evoked at spiritualistic seances where the participants are told to be quiet and relax if they would hear words of wisdom from another world. Real spirituality demands more than this; the co-operation of the rational mind is essential.[1]

It would be foolish to limit art to what is straightforward and simple—subtlety must be allowed for. But subtlety need not run counter to clarity. If we take the most atmospheric and moody songs of, say, Debussy—by whom perhaps subtleties of mood are carried further than by anyone else—we still see that there is no vagueness of form. Melody and harmony are absolutely crystallized and comprehensible. A delicate ethereal style is adopted but it is never uncertain in its hold. If it were it would fail as art. Art cannot be defined by messes and smudges, though in recent years a good deal of this sort of thing has appeared under its guise. Much can be suggested without dotting every 'i' or crossing every 't'—full detail need not be insisted on—but logical form there must be, if not merely pleasurable but masterly creative states are to be reached. Vague feeling which is naturally associated with slackness cannot be the subject of art. It can be referred to as something apart, but it cannot be embodied or take shape as an idea.[2]

It is to be remarked that Nature at her calmest does not dispense with tension. When

---

[1] To be set against Bain's assertion is a far truer one of McDougall: 'In attempting to analyse any emotion,' he says, 'we must consider it as experienced and displayed at a high pitch of intensity; for we cannot hope to recognize the elementary qualities and impulses of the primary emotions in complexes of low intensity." Low degrees of intensity do not seem of much use to the psychologist after all, any more than to the artist.

If it be advanced that the religious and even the artistic state is a passive and expectant one—a sort of 'waiting upon the Lord'—in which tension is as far as possible relaxed, it could be answered that that only continues until the idea is conceived. The moment conception takes place, tension begins to operate in accordance with the strength of the emotion and the vividness of the idea—the experience, as A. E. Housman says, being 'generally agitating and exhausting'. As the gestation process advances tension probably increases till at the moment of birth, so to speak, it reaches its zenith, after which, with the *fait accompli*, relaxation is resumed. I think we are entitled to say this about all creative activity, and to refuse to regard it as passive and relaxed *in toto*; also we are entitled to look askance at anything which is produced in an essentially slack condition of either mind or body.

[2] It will be noticed that though we have implied that there is a correspondence between musical form and emotion, we have scarcely attempted to show in what it consists. It is an exceedingly difficult question—much more difficult in the case of music than words, because the objective world is scarcely touched by music.

Some would assert, as does Sir Thomas Beecham in *A Mingled Chime*, that 'music *per se* means nothing,' and that it can be identified with anything according to whim. This may be so as regards things, but not as regards emotion, as Sir Thomas would probably agree. A musical idea has an emotional aura quite particular to itself. Whether we know what that emotion is, can analyse it and name it in all its complexity is quite another matter; though, on broad lines as concerns, say, what is calm or excited, grave or gay, it is clear enough.

The broad sun is sinking down in its tranquillity,

and

The gentleness of heaven is on the sea,

the force of gravity and pressures of all sorts still operate. And we are probably justified in the analogy when we say that in our emotional life, even though its surface is unruffled there is always a similar undertone of tension, provided it concerns feeling which has real significance and is developed to the point of clarity.

There are, of course, technical aspects agreeing with the more dreamy moods in which spirit rather than body dominates. With relatively slow movement a tendency to blur the edges of notes and intervals by *portamento* will occur, just, as at twilight, forms are less distinct, presenting a more romantic aspect; it will also make for less keen articulation, less thrusting, brilliant tone than is required by quick movement. *Portamento* implies a dragging, but not a 'dawdling'; as if there were a weight to be moved that is almost, but not quite, beyond the power of the mover. This is a very important element in expressive performance. It is what determines contact between the performer and what is performed.

Thus, as Bain does, we may recognize three different types of muscular movement: that involved in (1) dead resistance, when tension but no visible movement takes place, (2) slow movement, and (3) quick movement. But he apparently errs in stating that this central type of slow movement is to be specially connected with languor and slackness. It may be so connected, but it need not be. Joy naturally issues in quick movement, sorrow in slow; but deep feeling is implied in both—the feeling of sorrow is perhaps even deeper than that of joy—and, as such, tension must be at the root of it. Tension can only be dispensed with when emotions are not worth registering; if they are too slight or too vague for artistic handling.

Muscular and Musical Speed

What is the connection? It is an intriguing question; one which it is not easy to answer. It would be satisfactory to be able to make a rounded statement that muscular speed agreed at all points with musical speed, in fact that it was its counterpart, that when music moves slower or quicker, the muscles follow suit, backing it up by similar action. But it does not work out like that. We have to be satisfied with something less: roughly speaking, with scarcely more than the fact that as greater muscular movement takes place more life and force is given to the music; not speed, except in general animation.

70

In a sense, though it must not be taken too literally, a note is a 'projection' of energy, just as is a shot from a gun. It is propelled through the glottis, quickly or slowly, according as resistance is offered by the vocal cords. But a tense, firm, loud note may actually move the breath less (i.e., put the breath into movement) than a soft note which is loose and breathy; though a soft note *of the same quality* will not cause as much movement as a loud note. This, however, has nothing to do with *musical* speed. We gain an impression of musical speed from relatively quick notes. Thirty-two demisemiquavers will appear quicker than a semibreve though the same beat determines both, but mere note divisions do not necessarily raise the emotional temperature. Demisemiquavers can be played just as quietly, if slurred, as a semibreve note. The same muscular speed is applicable to both, as can be easily seen in the movement of the violinist's bow. The bowing can last just as long with the quick notes as with the slow ones. Relatively rapid notes are not in themselves a criterion of muscular speed. They may occur in an *adagio* as well as an *allegro*. It is the tempo in which they occur that is the deciding factor.

A quicker tempo signifies greater liveliness than a slower tempo. The reflective character of an *adagio* is obvious, whereas an *allegro* generally expresses a brighter or more forceful mood—more of a dance or march enters into it, more physical appeal; and this will require a more lively action of the breath.

We said just now that it needs no more effort to sing a series of short notes than to sing a long one provided the shorter notes are slurred. But it is otherwise when they are detached, separately articulated. With a long note or a group of slurred notes there is a continuous undisturbed muscular movement, unless an alteration in power, by the use of, say, the swell, takes place, when the muscles which bring it about must move more quickly. But more energy is required when a note is repeated or articulated than when it is slurred, because at that moment there is, as it were, a change of direction or momentum—the movement is pulled up short and turned back—and this has to be met by the use of more muscular force and consequently speed. Notes 'bowed out' by string players are relatively stronger than slurred notes. If very clear playing is desired they must be separtely bowed. The same must happen with the voice. A certain separateness must be given to quick notes if they are to be extremely clear; each note must have a life of its own even though this does not involve complete separation or *staccato*. It must be dealt with by what one might call *marcato-legato*, the equivalent of detached bowing. The use of this, of course, depends on the sense of the music, of which a Handelian 'run', or 'division' passages, are generally typical. Smooth singing is, of course, admirable in its place, but it can be an abomination when it consists of 'slipped', lifeless notes. There must always be a *reason* for slurring notes, such as the organic connection between a dissonance and its resolution, when the resolution seems to arise out of the dissonance like Eve from the side of Adam—though the feminine element must not be accepted entirely as a side issue—it cannot be denied individuality as well as dependence. Relatively quick notes, also, if they are essential, need to be sounded louder than merely decorative notes, i.e., if they are what might be called 'featural' notes, and not merely passing notes. Quick notes, in short, if they mean as much as slow notes, and they often do, require relatively greater energy for their delivery. Any sort of expressive drive will need a corresponding muscular drive. But the matter of slurred or separated notes cannot be entirely disposed of here.

The voice sounds because the resistance of the vocal cords does not completely counter the breath pressure; the vocal cords 'give' a little, so movement takes place. According to Newton's third law, the breath can only develop as much pressure as the vocal cords put up against it. Resistance is eventually determined (1) by their muscular tension, (2) by the glottis opening and (3) to a lesser extent, by what subsequently happens to the breath after it has passed the vocal cords; its meeting with the outside air, articulatory stops, etc. The glottis opening is, of course, largely related to laryngeal tension, and *under the control of the singer*. With a weak control of the glottis, breath pressure must be weak; only a strong control can ensure a strong breath. Therefore at least half the battle of singing hinges on glottal action and the power that we have over it. Degrees and qualities of tone are all determined at the larynx, which must be exercised by 'clicks', 'attacks', etc., till the mastery is gained. That is the lesson the singer has to learn.

It is thus obvious that the rate at which the breath passes the vocal cords, i.e., the breath movement, will be governed by the power of the breath and the resistance of the vocal cords and that both of these factors are interdependent. The more breath used the quicker the muscles have to work to supply it. But we have to beware of thinking that effort means muscular movement: it is generally the very reverse. One of the signs of good singing is the relative *quiet* which accompanies perfect valvular control; indeed quietude and repose of style can be achieved by no other means.[1] Not only that. It is also evident that in proportion as the breath is

---

[1] The greater the artist the less demonstrative he need be. A fine technique is not assured by antics, though a little graceful abandon pleases the eye. The appearance of stiffness must certainly be avoided.

economized the voice can be better sustained. It is not for nothing that *sostenuto* has always been regarded as one of the greatest tests of musical performance: for it can only occur in its most admirable form if the highest muscular tensions operate and are under full control.

The strongest breath pressure is obviously secured when the glottis is completely closed. Then if the glottis is suddenly opened a very hard attack of the voice (called the 'coup de glotte') occurs; but it is so hard as to be unmusical. The perfect *musical* attack is secured when the glottis is slightly open and the vocal cords can gently and immediately respond to the breath. When the glottis is too open wastage of breath occurs, also loss of power since resistance is diminished and breath pressure cannot be developed. The great thing is that, in singing, the breath should escape *as sound*, and not as breath. The breath should, so to speak, be converted into sound. Even with *mezza voce*, in which the glottis opening is wide and resistance is relatively weak, there should be little if any audible escape of breath.

A very quick breath speed with very loose vocal cords, tight vocal cords with slow breath speed, and innumerable gradations of quick and slow breath and tight and loose vocal cords will show how varied is the technique that can be employed.

When we talk of speedy muscular action it must not be supposed that either the muscles or the breath are violently moved except there be sudden collapse, or recovery from it. Great upheavals are not to be observed. With proper control so little breath escapes by the closed larynx that any very obvious movement is impossible.[1] In ordinary breathing the average range of movement of the diaphragm is from one and a half to two inches—when the ribs are kept expanded it is half an inch less; and, as we have already remarked, only about a fifth of the breath is expelled with each expiration—perhaps a pint and a half. Yet breath movement in its own (and very effective) degree is there, and it is by this movement that the art of the singer is specially shown. Resistance is rather the element of strength in singing, speed, that of skill—to apply words of Confucius that are put at the beginning of this section on Vocal Mechanics.

There is, of course, a much greater speed in ordinary tidal breathing than in vocal breathing, simply because there is no resistance; the breath just comes in and goes out with scarcely any let or

[1] It is reported that Rubini, a famous Italian singer, had such breath control that he could hold a note for four minutes without showing any sign of movement. It is also interesting to observe that the great pianist Rubenstein acknowledged that he had learnt more from Rubini than from any other teacher.

D*

hindrance—in this case breath movement is easily discernible. With singing, as the breath has to last much longer, it is bound to be slower in its general action even though a larger amount of breath is taken.

If the same notes are held on the organ with no alteration of the stops, variations of speed do not occur with the wind, nor is there any change of tension; so that, as in its own way the organ is an extremely effective instrument, it may seem unnecessary that any such changes should occur with the voice. But the constancy of motive force in the organ is both its virtue and its defect. Its splendid *sostenuto* is inimitable, an ideal towards which all performers should strive, but it has no *extra* power for dealing with dynamic effects or differences of pitch, and it is easily evident how this engenders lack of clearness in quick notes and how it fails to unravel the complications of confused polyphonic passages. The organ cannot deal with special articulation; its capacity for 'point' is slight. It cannot express the fret and flurry of common life. But in its own field—that of the steady, calm sustaining of notes, and piling them up into great masses of majestic sound, it is of course unsurpassed.

From which it appears that, given only a certain amount of energy, we can utilize it in strength or speed—strength being the equivalent of powerful tone, speed that of a vivacious light style—but not to the highest degree in both; and this is what usually happens. The saving grace is that, in an ordinary way, and for all practical purposes there is a margin of energy sufficient to satisfy the claims of both strength *and* speed in singing if the muscles have been well trained. Great singing is generally associated with a splendid physique, but a small person, of light build, can often make quite a good job of singing in the way of adequate, though perhaps not the greatest sonority.[1]

The upshot of our inquiry seems to be that it is not the relative speed of notes that necessitates increased muscular speed, but the way in which those notes are expressed, the meaning that it is desired to give to them. Emotional drive or physical alertness; conditions which are relatively disturbed or animated: these are the compelling factors—in short what is covered by tempo and expression and not by what we usually term quick notes.

Muscular speed, then, has nothing to do with ordinary time values as such, whether quick or slow—though poorly spaced irresponsible time is doubtless linked up with irregular spasmodic muscular movement. Tension steadies the whole time structure,

---

[1] Caruso is said to have had a chest expansion of twelve inches, and I expect that heavyweights in the vocal world are similarly developed.

which, in the first place must be inspired by ideal proportions, and then implemented by a very pronounced effort of the will.

Tension and Concentration

Tension *is* concentration; it is the act of summoning up our mental and physical powers. Till they are thus mobilized they are un-. awakened, slack and sleepy: totally incapable of combined operations. Before we can *do* anything our muscles have to contract. What was before diffuse and separate, has to be drawn together; squeezed out, as it were, in order to arrive at the essence which is lurking within its loose structure. The blood, actually, is forced from the muscular tissues much more strongly when they are tensed. Concentration raises the blood pressure, increasing the strength and rate of the heart beats. A larger amount of blood is needed to feed the tissues and to repair inroads upon them caused by the extra exertion. In this way, not only is the activity of the muscles secured, but also their growth and development.

We talk of 'getting hold' of something, whether it be by mental or physical grip. To understand a subject, its logic and implications, we have to 'get hold' of it by concentrating the mind; to effect any movement we have to concentrate the body. The greater the task is, the more concentration there must be; and the higher the concentration, the more significant the result. A world of meaning can be put into a single exclamation like Ah or Oh, but only if it is backed by muscular tension, with intense feeling behind it.

Nothing comes of itself without effort. The idea of a song has to be gained through thought; its realization requires the expenditure of will and physical power. All this may seem too strenuous, and, as such, communicate a sense of strain to what should appear unlaboured. Certainly performance should not *appear* to be laboured. But effort must be there. Tremendous calm, a calm 'which may be felt' is only possible through an extreme of tension. Tension is not opposed to calm; it is the very source of it. A loose thing cannot keep steady. It is subject to both internal and external disturbance in a way that a tensed thing never is. Steadiness has to be maintained and it can only be through tension—though it may seem strange to say so. A stretched, as opposed to a slack string will exemplify it.

It may also be objected that there is no need of all this conscious effort. Will not nature do what is wanted of her own accord; must we drive her so hard? Doubtless some sing more or less unconsciously, hardly knowing how they do it, like a typical folk-singer. This may often give more pleasing results than those attained by a so-called trained singer—and it is an excellent beginning. But 'natural' singing will not go very far. Unless nature affords the equivalent of conscious systematic development—which she seldom does—we have to supplement naturally-induced activity by artificially-designed exercise, though this need not be contrary to but only an extension of natural habit, just as a cultured flower is the development of a wild flower. At what precise point in our development this conscious process has to occur if we are to advance beyond a more or less simple, elementary stage in matters of art, it is difficult to affirm. A youngster doesn't need to be taught to walk or talk; he will blunder on by himself quite unconsciously until he does it. But there comes a time, when, if he is to use his limbs in, say, dancing, or his speech in ordered poetry, he will have to know what he is doing. There is, of course, folk dance, and poetry, and music, which we are accustomed to look upon as a sort of wild, unconscious manifestation of art; but it is extremely doubtful how far the unconscious element can be relied on here, since memory plays so large a part. A folk dancer must know the sequence of his steps and positions. This will not come of itself, it must be taught him either by an individual or by the forces of tradition; nor will a folk singer compose a song 'out of the blue', though he may very well not comprehend the features of its structure. It is however something more than the growth of a lily which neither toils nor spins. A certain will towards expression has already entered, though this can be satisfied with comparatively little training. When, however, a more complex art is attempted, as by the addition of several voices (instead of one) and of extended form, a more conscious attitude must intervene, and with it a more conscious training by which to gain control of the various factors. This seems in a large measure to coincide with writing, or the translation of thought and action into corresponding graphic signs. Directly this is achieved we are absolutely detached from the unconscious and then know exactly how we do things, though in the deepest but not cynical sense, we still may not know exactly what we are doing.

Even with natural unconscious singing tension must take place; but, with greater elaboration and range of conscious thought, tension must receive a more sensitive application, and for this training is necessary. Instinctive action can be met by instinctive exercise. Animals in a state of nature do not need what we call training to come to their full powers. The strength of the lion, the speed of the deer, are developed under natural conditions; for conscious thought does not enter into their actions—without language it cannot. The difference between artistic and instinctive action is precisely in thought. Artistic action is the realization of such thought as comes within the domain of art; instinctive action is physical, connected with feelings but not with ideas. Animals can, of course, be

76

bred and trained to do more than they would naturally do, but only because we bring our minds to bear upon it; they do what *we* wish. Purely instinctive action has not the power of such development, though in its way it is very wonderful. The balance and control that animals achieve is often superior to our own but it is not addressed to imaginative ends.

The real difference between instinctive and conscious tension is the intervention of the human mind, with its faculties of concentration. It is because the mind can concentrate that the body functions in ways far removed from instinctive action. *Tension, in the highest sense, is muscular thought.*

How does concentration show itself; what are its results in musical terms? We can certainly see them in tone; in its direction and quality. Tone needs to be shaped and directed, just as all forms of creative activity need shape and direction. The opposite of concentration is diffusion. We may use our tone to little purpose because it is diffuse. Instead of being focussed in such a way as to reach its objective, it may spread around with little effect. We cannot have it both ways. Either it is limited in its area of action, thereby gaining in effectiveness, or let loose with loss of it.

Tone in a very real sense can be 'centred', so that it travels from the mouth in a more or less straight but widening line ⟨====⟩; or it can emerge, as it were, from the sides of the mouth and be diffused without any such directive force, thus: ⤳ ⤳. The

shape of the channel through which the sound comes from the larynx is the determining influence: the orifice at the uvula, the tongue, cheeks and lips all playing their part.

Quality of tone, too, is affected by concentration. The drive of the breath brought about by high tension, the tightness of the vocal cords, and the general drawing together of the vocal mechanism gives tone a bright, penetrative power. Under such conditions it reaches the acme of vocal timbre: the reediness which it ought normally to have. Without such tension tone will be dull, of a loose texture. Of course tone must suit the poetic expression. It must vary. It cannot always be of the most highly concentrated kind— this has already been discussed. But we can be sure that the highest degree of tension will produce the most dominating tone, whereas with lower degrees of tension, tone will tend to subordinate itself, if in competition with that of a more telling quality. We can also be sure that to get the acme of resonance, the most ringing sound, all our physical power is and must be engaged. That is the meaning

77

of such sound; less effort will fail to bring it forth. It was in agony of body and soul that Jesus cried 'Eli, Eli' *with a loud voice.*

The voice can range from the power of a trumpet, as in a splendidly metallic Aw to the sympathetic softness of a fluty Oo. Such an Aw will have firm hard walls indicative of great muscular tension. If the Aw cavity is tightly held like this, with stiff edges to the orifice of the throat, it will respond with a sound which is almost like a loud snore, when the breath (merely) is driven through it. But when the cavity is relaxed hardly any fricative sound can be heard. It is difficult to get other than a relaxed cavity with Oo hence the usually softer quality of this vowel as compared to Aw. If brightness is given to Oo it will be because it has been possible to tighten its cavity.

Concentration is the very reverse of relaxation. They are a difficult pair of opposites which need to be reconciled with the greatest skill.

Tension and Tremolo

If it were only for one thing, the wisdom of modern methods of singing may well be doubted. Now, we scarcely hear a voice that is not tainted by *tremolo*. It has become a widespread disease. Few singers, professional or amateur, are without it; and, once there, it can seldom be eradicated or its depredations repaired.

But it is not only that *tremolo* ruins good voices, it ruins taste as well. Its victims seem to glory in it, or at least to become insensible to its presence; and to a large extent they have carried the public with them.

We should probably object if we were told that we did not see straight; we certainly do not care to hear straight. The popular ear has come to delight not only in sounds which slide from pitch to pitch in a sort of eel-like slime, but to carry uncertainty still further by adding to it a shivering sickness.

The glory of the church organ lies in its absolute hold over tone. An endless note can be held upon it without change in pitch or power. 'The eternal element of calm' is its special province; its achievement that of perfect security. Yet, in the cinema we never hear a steady sound from the organ. We have gone out of our way to travesty its real nature, making the King of Instruments shake like a frightened puppy; and not as a special effect, but all the time. The supposition is that people like it.

And if it be said that only the vulgar masses tolerate this sort of thing, we must in fairness point to so-called cultured singing which for the most part shows exactly the same feature.

What is wrong? Is it a lowering of taste inherent in Democracy itself—for nothing could show a greater degradation of spiritual soundness and intellectual vigour than this modern and ever-present use of *tremolo*? It cannot mean this, or that such a criticism is fatally associated with current political ideals—it should probably be directed to other causes; but it is nevertheless a strange paradox that *popular* music was so much better in aristocratic times, when it should logically have been worse. Democracy will have to justify itself by what it cares for before we can fully accept it; values as well as votes are the test.

But value is not defined by the outward cloak of culture. Sincerity must lie behind anything of worth; and sincerity is no respecter of social position. It can come from the illiterate as well as the literate, and when we get it we know that it is the real thing, the very fount of originality. Crudities do not prevent it from shining through. Who could fail to be touched by this letter from a poor girl in hospital to her sweetheart:[1]

> Dear Alf,
>   I seen you last night in my dream. O my dear I cried at waking up. What a silly girl you been and got. The pain is bad this morning but I laugh at the sollum cloks of the sisters and the sawbones. I can see they think I am booked but they don't know what has befalen between you and me. How could I die and leave my Dear. I spill my medecin this morning thinking of my Dear. Hopeing this finds you well no more now from yours truly Liz.

It is not only the pathetic circumstances of this letter which touch us—the girl died shortly after it was written—but its unconscious beauty: a beauty which in modern terms, is allied to the best folk art.

We seem to have wandered from our particular subject, but we are close to it. *Tremolo* is the very reverse of sincere. It may be that the singer does not wish to delude us by its effect, though by using the tremulant, the cinema organist certainly does. It nevertheless is an effect, and pretends to a significance that it does not possess. It seems like quivering emotion, but it has no roots in feeling. It does not proceed from an emotional impulse. It is wholly different from *vibrato* which it simulates. *Vibrato* is the last touch of feeling when feeling is wrought up, in muscular terms, to its highest point and what might possibly have resulted in rigidity is just relieved from it by an added emotional wave. *Tremolo* needs no such tension. Indeed it results from an absence of it. It means nothing except to remind us of the helpless bleating of a sheep, in significance perhaps the weakest and stupidest sound in nature.

Entire absence of control is of course the real charge that has to

---

[1] Quoted by Walter de la Mare in his anthology on *Love* (Faber & Faber).

be made against *tremolo*. The singer cannot help it; he is entirely at the mercy of a shaky instrument without the power of steadying it. The larynx is untethered. Its muscular cables are not strong enough—they need twisting tighter; and so the larynx casts adrift, so to speak, at the mercy of wind and tide. In other words the vocal instrument is insecure; it cannot resist breath pressure. Resistance can only come from muscular tension; relaxation is the trouble.

How is the voice tethered? Not, as we have so often insisted, by any local application of tension; that is quite insufficient. It must be by the muscular system as a whole; by central tension radiating from the diaphragm and well distributed to every working part. If this is not done the larynx cannot stand the strain. Too much is put upon it. It gives—much as the vocal cords give when they vibrate— and is thereby put into periodic oscillation. This is the main explanation of *tremolo* and it is a perfectly reasonable one; it will not be accepted by the disciples of relaxation who seem quite satisfied with the results they achieve. But whether relaxation is a creed or not—if it is it is a pitiably shaky one—it seems clear that *tremolo* is due to it, and that tension alone can remedy the situation. Tremulous voices, too, have seldom any power of expression. It follows from the same cause, as does blurred unshaped vowelling; and much else.

A singer should not be content till he can sustain a note without a tremor,[1] holding it as steady as a rod. It should also be uniform in strength and quality of tone; in fact mechanically perfect. Then the singer may allow himself the luxury of letting his emotion play upon it.

Vibrato, a legitimate effect which *tremolo* is not, can be abused. It nearly always is in its continuous application. It can develop into a mere trick. It is often quite unnecessary and out of place, particularly with religious music when we want to get away from the personal element which *vibrato* expresses. The words of themselves

---

[1] I have heard children do it in a way which seemed to bring out the whole wonder of the soul. It moved to tears by a sort of natural pathos and far-off beauty, yet it was something more than innocent, though unspoilt. It had even fervour and passion because it was so truly felt, but it was very different from machine-made singing. In one sense, according to Plato, 'of all wild beasts there is none so savage as a boy'; in another (though on rare occasions) we may easily go to children to learn of the vocal kingdom of heaven. The finest choral singing I think I ever heard was from a children's choir of boys and girls—they had scarcely passed the infant stage. This happened at an Isle of Wight Festival. They were trained—if that is the right word, I don't think it is—by an amateur schoolmistress who (when I asked her) could only explain her magic by saying, in a delightfully simple way, 'I love children'; and I hardly know when I have been as moved as I was by a Scotch boy and girl singing songs of their native land in a small Scottish town. It is useless to give further details. A steady note from an adult is so rare that, when one does hear it, it is almost joy unspeakable!

forbid it. When *vibrato* is added to a note it seems to bring it closer to us, taking away its reserve. But in wearing the heart upon the sleeve something of dignity and nobility is lost: a classical statuesque quality—which depends upon a certain coldness and distance.

At the present time very few teachers object to what, in the opinion of the writer, is often a pernicious excess of emotionalism in the performance of old music such as that of Bach, though with later romantic music a greater show of feeling may be desirable.

However this may be, *vibrato* will not spoil tone, as tone. It eases its progress, and even improves its telling power, giving it a lambent, permeating quality. That is perhaps why string players employ it so invariably, though it is said that Joachim was sparing with the effect. Quite recently, also, I was told by a very old friend who knew both Joachim and Piatti, the 'cellist of the Joachim Quartet, that the latter famous player used no *vibrato at any time*, though he was reported to have a specially refined and beautiful tone, superior to that of Joachim. It is quite obvious, then, that notwithstanding weighty modern advice, string players, of even the first rank, can dispense with *vibrato* without loss of tonal beauty. Why, indeed, should they be different from singers?

A true *vibrato* ensures sufficient tension. The whole body and soul go into it. *Tremolo* draws neither on the physical nor emotional powers and so remains nauseating in its nothingness.

We might add that causes of *tremolo* may also be (1) inharmonious adjustment of the resonances of the mouth and neck, which sets up 'beats' or a sort of 'wave' in the sound, or (2) nervous, involuntary twitching of the tongue which seems to be beyond control, but may easily be due to bad breathing and wrong disposition of the vocal instrument.

Another point to note is that if vocal sound has a sufficiency of constant nasal resonance, that is to say, if the sound is directed towards the nasal cavities (whether it be given an open or closed quality—*v.* p. 160 *et seq.*) *tremolo* will almost of a certainty be avoided.

Tension and Pitch

It would seem as if tension, in the sense in which we have used the term, had very little to do with pitch, since although there is tensing of the vocal cords in pitch—pitch depends upon their varying tension—the determination of pitch is an involuntary process. The singer does not know how it happens. But there is another aspect of pitch which is greatly under the control of the singer, and that is 'keeping pitch'. It is difficult to keep perfect pitch without the continual admonition and assistance of an accompanying instrument. Everyone who has had experience of unaccompanied singing knows how liable voices are to flatten. Though intonation may be good at the start of a note, the pitch will very quickly flatten if the voice is not kept up, buttressed up, by conscious tension. This tension is mainly applicable at the base of the breath at the diaphragm and abdomen. Anything like 'sagging' in the abdomen will have its certain results in the flattening of the pitch.[1] Lazy singers can never keep pitch; muscular flabbiness will immediately react upon it. On the other hand (but only on rare occasions) an over-straining upwards may tend to sharpening. The perfect balance, spoken of on p. 59 *et seq.*, between tension and relaxation will alone achieve the desired result.

A moment ago we said that the striking of pitch was involuntary, from which it might be inferred that the start of a note would always be in correct tune. But even here lack of a properly balanced tension may 'queer' the pitch from first to last. Notes may *begin* sharp or flat. This will not be so much from absence of tension but from wrong tension, which in its turn produces a badly balanced resonance. Resonance is clearly accountable for the defect. The tone is not properly 'settled' on the vocal cords, which is much the same thing as saying that it is not properly 'voiced'. It may be blown away from the cords as it often is with the vowel Oo which, with bad production, has a great tendency to go sharp. It is a lack of nasal resonance which produces this, and nasal resonance is largely a matter of control at the cords, which in their turn function at the call and under the influence of the breath. 'Hooty' qualities of tone will go sharp. Choir boys are often champion little hooters.

Tension and Tone Quality

We have already touched upon this matter under Tension and Balance (p. 59), but a little more should be said about it.

The statement that quality of tone depends upon tension is sometimes queried by very intelligent people. They say, 'Surely, if you sing at all there must be tension, and tension of sufficient power.' But they forget *quality of tone*, just as Bain forgot quality of movement (*v.* p. 66 *et seq.*). Apart from kinds of tone, such as those heard in different vowels, there are also qualities of the same vowel, just as a visual colour may be rich or poor in hue, though to be quite correct a different colour is involved with each difference of shade. We feel such vocal colour to be satisfying in its content, or the reverse. It may have or lack depth, body; it may be strong or fail in intensity or penetrative power: indeed, it *will* so fail if it is not backed by adequate muscular effort. How true this is

[1] From which it will be seen how important abdominal exercises are; a sort of sensitive 'squirming' of the abdomen is necessary to 'touch', expression and control.

can be immediately observed in the action of a string player. Why a Kreisler or a Menuhin is supreme is largely because of the superiority of his tone. With it, almost inevitably, goes other expressive virtue. It reaches, as it were, the centre of tonal energy; their tone has greater vitality, greater colour than the average. It 'tells' more. It would stand out against that of a dozen inferior players, completely dominating it. Watch them at work! Watch the concentration of mind and muscle! An extraordinary tension is brought to bear. It can be as clearly seen as its results are heard. Orchestral string players are generally pretty good; but in, say, a concerto, note the movements of the rank and file as compared with those of any great soloist whom they are accompanying. It is a different order of playing, not so much because it is required by the circumstances of the performance, but because the artistry is less. And what happens here happens equally with singing. What the singer does cannot be seen as easily, but the same principle and practice is concerned. No tension, no tone. The quality of the voice, in short, is exactly in proportion to the tension that is applied. Tonal energy reflects muscular energy in every respect. Tone seems so detached from material considerations, so purely spiritual, that we are inclined to forget that it is part and parcel of, or an aspect of, a physical system that corresponds to it at every turn.

We shall discuss later what warrant we have for preferring certain qualities of tone; why one sort of tone is better than another. It is by no means a simple matter. It takes us into the difficult sphere of values. For the moment we will only assert without hesitation, that tonal quality depends upon muscular tension, or its equivalent.

Tension and Rigidity

To hold a heavy weight at arm's length, the arm must be straightened like a rod, its muscles tightened to an extreme degree. A light weight can be held with very little tension. From which we gather that the harder the work that the muscles are put to, the more the muscles must be tensed till a condition of stiffness is reached. We cannot avoid it. We either do the work with stiffened muscles, or give it up by loosening them.

It is the same with the voice. Very heavy work in which great power or animation is present, will require considerable muscular tension, even to the point of stiffness. Light work will make no such call upon the muscles. For instance the raising of the soft palate for tone which is particularly hard and powerful will be associated with a very tense state of the back orifice of the mouth. The firmer things are, the better. But softer qualities of tone will tend towards a loosening of the mouth.

Nevertheless singing cannot be compared to work in which heavy weights have to be shifted. To move the vocal cords is not like moving a sack of coal—singing and coal heaving are rather different —though physical strain is present in each. It is only a question of degree. The actual work in foot pounds required to produce the voice is small, but this does not mean that great power of breath is not there. It is there for the purposes of reserve and control, and the muscles of a singer are probably tensed in the diaphragm in much the same way as a coal-heaver's are. With some singing we may also see throat muscles drawn like whipcord and a general effort almost to the state of bursting; but this represents bad singing in which radiation of tension from the diaphragm (whereby muscular strain is distributed and not localized) is poorly achieved. The voice is forced, not held.

There is something of a reproach about rigidity. But how are we to define rigidity and can we escape it in connection with singing? Is it really as intolerable as it seems? The moment a muscle is tightened, it is on its way to becoming rigid Give it enough work to do and it will become as stiff as a poker. Let us see what nature shows.

A tree has its largely immovable central trunk, which gives off secondary branches of diminishing strength ending in slender twigs. The branches will probably bend to the wind; the twigs still more. All that shows that the greater the strain that has to be met, the more must it be countered by tension. The main tree-trunk cannot help being steadier and stauncher than the easily swayed twig. Such steadiness is natural. But is it the same as stiffness? Yes! If the voice were called upon to take the same relative strain as the tree-trunk—in relation to its own work—then it would have to be just as stiff. It could not avoid it.

What the singer *can* avoid is stiffening when there is no such work to be done; when there is no reason for it. We shall say more about this under 'relaxation'. And we may further add that though muscles are tight and stiff, as long as they *can* be relaxed there is nothing much wrong. Rigidity in the bad sense is stiffening when there is no work to be done, or when it is not commensurate with the work that is being done; and (which is much the same thing) when it represents involuntary tension, a tension which cannot be freed; in short, a tension which does not come under the command of the will. Rigidity in its bad sense thus seems to be the automatic, purposeless form of stiffness, when tension is not amenable to, nor governed by mental control—such mental control being, of course, commensurate with artistic skill.

In view of all this we should perhaps do well to limit the use of the word rigidity by saying that rigidity is when muscles *cannot* move, not when they *do* not.

Tension and Relaxation

Relaxation is not a force—though it is an action, it can do no work; it is only a possible, but by no means invariable condition of the use of force. Its function is to avoid undue drag on movement and so the unnecessary effort which produces strain and stiffness. What we always have to try to get is the greatest rapidity and force with the least expenditure of energy, and, in this, relaxation plays its part at the appropriate time and place. But we must never imagine that tension prevents movement and that tightening in a muscle is the equivalent of stiffness. That we have already seen.

We have so far made a great deal of tension, stressing its vital importance. It is perhaps the main concern of this book. And there can be no doubt that by far the greatest fault in indifferent singing —a fault that is apparent with the majority of singers when they fail to phrase and to point properly—comes from the lack of hold and intensification in their work. But this is not the whole story. A considerable amount of bad singing arises from over-tightening. This tends to rough, hard tone, with an absence of ease and those qualities which charm. The antidote to this is, of course, relaxation. What place should it have in vocal technique? It certainly comes into muscular action in varying degree when the tightening of one muscle is accompanied by the slackening of its opponent. But this seems automatic. We cannot do much about it, or make it a conscious principle of technique.

We have here to distinguish between the instrument and its use.

If we take a wind instrument such as the organ or the flute there is nothing about it which is flabby or relaxed. Every part of an organ is solid and substantial; the flute is made of metal or hard boxwood. Similarly we may be quite sure that the vocal instrument (which is a wind instrument) must be firm in structure if it is to sound well.

But we observe that, though the organ or flute is set up so firmly, certain parts of them are movable. The mechanism is completely free. The transmission from console to pipe in the organ, the keys of the flute, are lightly balanced in order to respond to the touch of the player. They have to move easily. That is the chief function of relaxation in the voice: to allow easy movement of whatever part of the vocal mechanism it is that has to move; or perhaps we had better say to ensure that no unnecessary impediment is placed upon movement.

Relaxation, or a measure of it, has also an effect upon tone quality, but note has already been made of this when discussing Degrees of Tension.

We said a moment ago that the vocal instrument must be firm; and this is so if we take it at any particular moment. It is true that we have counselled that the ribs should be kept expanded.[1] To that extent they are permanently fixed, though breath movement is not. But other fixations are only temporary. Neither vowels, nor consonants when they have settled positions (L, M, N, etc.), are as a rule held for any length of time. They are subject to rapid change, and these changes have to be made as effectively and easily as possible. Undue stiffness will prevent it. But the mechanism cannot be wholly relaxed. As long as movement takes place there must be tightening; no muscular part could otherwise move.

Per se there is nothing sacrosanct in the word relaxation though it seems to be the only word in the technical vocabulary of some vocal practitioners. Tension is never mentioned. Speed and power can get on very well without relaxation in most cases. We have seen how the quickest of all actions is a taut one—a tight string will respond far more quickly than a loosened one. We have also seen how power is built up from tensed muscles, so that the greatest power comes from a close and combined muscular effort. Where, then, does relaxation come in actual technique? What is its exact application?

It is a most difficult question to answer because the claims of tension and relaxation are never constant. They alter at every moment, with each new shade of expression. A greater degree of general tension will mean a lesser degree of relaxation, until at some moments there can be no relaxation at all. We can never say that such and such a muscle must always be relaxed, still less in the case of the whole body. Nevertheless, some general principles are to the point. To begin with:

1. We do not need to tighten a muscle unless it has something *to do*. This is a good working rule. It can be illustrated in breathing, also in vowel formation.

When we raise the ribs by the extensor muscles, there is no need as well to apply the increased tension of the flexors. We *can* do so by expanding and contracting the thoracic muscles at the same time, till a very stiff condition is reached with *both* sets of muscles in hard tension. But the ribs do not keep up any the more for it; it is useless action. All we want and have to do is to raise the ribs, and the extensors working against the weight of the ribs themselves will

---

[1] When, in singing, stiffness is clearly to be seen and heard, it may be wise to practise with a relaxed half-breath or less though the perfect artist can at all times deal satisfactorily with a full breath.

effect this. The flexors need not be brought into play. They can be quite relaxed, and what seems a sort of light, floating condition of the breath will result.

Let us see, also, how relaxation will apply to the vowel Ah.

The tongue has to do a good deal of work in the formation of vowels and consonants, and work always·means tension. Yet there are times when the tongue does not move, when it has to lie quietly in the pit of the mouth. Any tension of the tongue then will probably cause it to rise at the back, which is a very common fault—not many can loosen the tongue completely, particularly at its root—and with it, the series of vowels from Ah to Oo will be mispronounced. The tongue must be relaxed in this case, and as far as possible the jaw muscles must also take part in this relaxation. If the jaw is held stiffly it will probably cause the tongue to stiffen as well; for, by sympathetic action, muscles tend to work in groups.

It is to be remarked, of course, that in these two instances no movement is taking place. The raised ribs and the Ah cavity represent fixed positions. A state of movement would entirely alter the situation. As a corollary to the foregoing we may say that:

2. There is no need to tighten any muscle beyond what is required for the work that it has to do.

If there is a purpose in tightening then obviously we must pursue it[1], as when we store force in the diaphragm and abdominal muscles. But it would be useless to exert the power of the rib muscles beyond the point where the full raising of the ribs has been secured. Similarly we could tighten our cheeks for a round Oh[2] far more than

[1] When a great deal of precision and control is required or any extraordinary happening is taking place, such as a *rallentando*, the tension must be proportionally raised, even in soft singing. A limpid, flexible phrase can allow the release of a certain amount of tension; a precisely-pointed phrase—where the articulation of the words (or notes) must be very exact—will require much more. In short firmness in expression means tightness in tension; ease in expression, loose tension. Thus in Parry's motet 'I know my soul hath power' a typical phrase is:

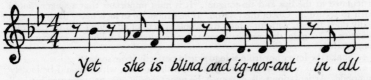

Here a high degree of tension must operate, even though the scale of force is slight. Otherwise it will fail in conviction. Indeed the softest tone may need the highest tension, if tremendous importance or intensity attach to it. An agonized though scarcely audible Oh in which the whole being is concerned, will demand the most complete and tense breath, whereas a less significant Oh can be sung quite loudly with comparatively little expenditure of energy.

[2] It is with the jaw and tongue that over tension is most likely to occur. A quite characteristic Oh can be sung *without* the contraction of the mouth or cheeks, which we generally associate with a round Oh. For this, nothing should be 'set'.

is required for a perfectly characteristic vowel. If you have what you want, that is, the sound you want, it is uneconomical to waste more effort upon it. But tension and quality are so closely related that no hard and fast rule can be laid down.

3. By tightening muscles—certainly the wrong ones—we may prevent the necessary enlargement of a space or cavity, say that of the neck or pharynx which plays so important a part in the development of rich, easy sound. A squeezing process may be introduced instead of an amplifying one. Though here again it is quite possible, and may be advisable, according to the desired expression, to *force* a cavity open to its fullest extent: just as we expand a rubber ring which offers more and more resistance as we pull it open.

4. A graceful note is pleasing in most expressive situations, and this cannot be achieved by stiff, angular methods. Something of an easy curve must enter, which has its parallel in easy muscular movement. Relaxation, in some degree, seems actually allied to this.

There is a great difference, however, between absolute relaxation (which means deadweight) and partial relaxation. This latter is likely to be applicable in singing far more often than is the former, and we must not think that we are all wrong because we are not in the state of a jelly. The occasion to be perfectly loose anywhere will hardly ever arise, and we have to be content with approximations to it. To be loose everywhere is synonymous with complete lunacy.

Something should be said about deadweight in its relation to singing.

There are two forces that the body can use: tension and deadweight.

The mouth should open in a sort of stupid way, with no shaping or tension of the lips. A deep, full, Oh is not debarred thereby. The neck will be quite ready to receive the vowel, and the whole control will come from the breath and a very slight use of muscles in the region of the tongue root (where incidentally, the chief control of the voice should nearly always occur—certainly so as regards vowels and as far as possible as regards consonants, though certain consonants *have* to be articulated at the lips and tip-tongue). It is most important that a singer should learn to secure an Oh in this fashion. If he cannot do so he is never likely to get a really open throat, without which the whole system of vowelling will be radically defective. To gain this requisite muscular freedom the following exercises are commended:

1. Shake the lower jaw from side to side in perfectly loose sockets.

2. Try to talk with the jaw only; not with the tongue, which should be loosely immobile. Articulation will, of course, be poor; mostly only an unformed lisp will result, but no matter.

3. Speak or sing the word 'holy', dealing with the Oh as we have just suggested. See that the vowel y (really 'i' as in 'hit') has the same open throat resonation, which alone will secure a perfectly uniform production of the word. Then take the vowels Oh and i; repeating the pair quickly but clearly: oh-i oh-i oh-i etc., like a continuous note. Only the back of the tongue should operate in this, with an easy 'waggle', again let it be said, the jaw and tongue must be quite loose.

Tension is a lifting, rising force; it is like that of a wound spring striving to discharge its energy. Deadweight is a falling force which is always trying to reach the ground. Before it can be effective it has to be lifted or moved into position, just as the weight of a pile-driver has. There is obviously no muscular tension in deadweight which is simply the force of gravity acting upon any substance.

Deadweight is much used in pianoforte playing but it has by no means the same value in singing. Striking a key is a very different thing from sustaining the voice. After a key is struck nothing further happens to the sound; there is no further need of any sort of pressure. What is wanted is a 'thud' which may be of the utmost strength or delicacy; and this can be achieved in a loose manner by dropping the weight of the hand or arm on to the key in a well-judged way. Hardly any muscular tightening is needed in the process, at least not at the hand or arm; though the weight must be held up somewhere and it actually is, for the most part, in the region of the diaphragm—we can never escape diaphragmatic control.

This relaxation at the extremities allows of a very easy movement of the fingers; much easier than if they were articulated by their own muscular action, for then one finger would impede the other. But, even so, for great loudness or hardness of tone the muscles of the extremities will be found to tighten.

To some extent this principle of deadweight can be applied also to singing, particularly at the head and shoulders. We have already shown its connection with the breath. In a general way there is no need to stiffen the head and shoulders, certainly not to the extent of raising them, for this action brings about bad faults. In the case of the head it elongates the neck, preventing the opening of the pharynx, whereas the shortening and widening of the neck is what is wanted; in the case of the shoulders, raising them brings about a high, shallow, instead of a deep, full action of the breath, because the lungs at the apex have not the same expansive capacity as at the base, and the raised shoulders do not admit of this lower expansion.

Before singing takes place a loose attitude should be adopted. The head should not be stiffly set on the body, but seem to sink loosely into it. The shoulders, arms and hands should likewise feel as if they were so much deadweight, though a *lifted* deadweight. Thus a sort of balance is struck between deadweight and live thrust, with most of the virtues of good performance following in its train.

If a full breath be taken and the arms are held up at right-angles to the body with a minimum of effort, the hands should drop at the wrist quite loosely and the arms be capable of easy movement with freedom at all the joints, so that their action is such as a practised dancer might show in moments of little exertion.[1] Possibly we may be reminded by it of the outstretched wings of a hovering bird; but looks are very often deceptive as to what is actually happening. Grace can quite well be accompanied by tension, and a bird's wings, though apparently so gracefully and easily adjusted either in hovering or flight, are by no means loose. They are in fact quite rigid, though they appear to be as free as the air in which they move.

May this not offer us a simile? Relaxation is the air in which tension moves. We can look upon it like this and thus make peace with both worlds.

There is an amusing rhyme which runs:

> Would you rather be an eagle
> Or a floppy flappy seagull?
> Oh I'd rather be an eagle if I could:
> For a seagull isn't happy
> When he flies so floppy flappy;
> And I'd rather far be happy than be good.

A seagull wouldn't be happy if he flew 'floppy flappy'—indeed he could not do it; neither would a singer be if floppy flappiness was his method of procedure.

In fact, in dealing with relaxation one has to hedge all the time. When we come to be precise about it, as to its when and where, any distinct statement that we have made seems to vanish almost like a dream.

But it is a good general rule to be as easy as we can and to feel that somehow or other muscular tension (which is tight) is pitted *against the force of gravity (which is loose*—at any rate in terms of physical weight it is loose), and that our problem is to combine or secure an adjustment of both these contrary forces till a state of poise and balance is reached between them.

Relaxation is an active feeling—it has to be willed like tension[2]—but, as already observed, it is not a motive force, it can only be a condition of the use of force; and, as it is a 'grounding' not a 'lifting' force, it must never be allowed to take charge of the situation. Its major function seems to be to prevent prohibitive action from muscles which are not concerned in any particular movement, or to allow deadweight to operate when it is an advantage to use this form of power. Even so, in singing, it is perhaps more of a moral

---

[1] It is clear however, that if a heavy weight has to be held up by the hands (this has already been referred to (*v.* p. 83) but it will bear repeating) the muscles of the hand and arm must stiffen. The operations of the voice are entirely consonant with this. Easy situations can be expressed by means of loose tensions; powerful tensions are required at times of great emotional stress, etc.

[2] For practical purposes it may be as well to think of relaxation *as* an effort.

than a physical factor: a state which it is good to imagine we are in, though actually we may be removed from it.

The final counsel and upshot of the matter must be: get the effect you want in the loosest possible way. If it cannot be so achieved then tighten to the necessary extent. Between almost complete looseness and complete tension lies the whole range of expression. Both looseness and tightness are good at their right time and in their right place.

Tension and Rapture

> *Nor peace that grows by Lethe, scentless flower,*
> *There in white languor to decline and cease;*
> *But peace whose names are also rapture, power,*
> *Clear sight, and love, for these are parts of peace.*
>   WILLIAM WATSON

Definitions are notoriously difficult, and they become increasingly so as we move from the material to the spiritual spheres. We know what rapture is (perhaps it would be truer to say we *feel* what rapture is)—a conception of it rises immediately to the mind, for it is a common though, of course, not a constant factor of experience. The 'careless rapture' of youthful exuberance, the spell that natural beauty casts over us, the wonder of human love: all bring it into play on varying levels of intensity; while through the arts, and especially through music, we are absorbed and entranced in ways far removed from those of practical life.

> *. . . Such music sweet*
> *As all their souls in blissful rapture took.*

Rapture seems to be a linking up with the central core of experience. In proportion as we arrive at that we are subject to it. It is associated with the highest degree of love and understanding; it is a form of intense concentration. It is probably what Plato meant by 'the contemplation of beauty absolute', and he records the ascent towards it in a famous passage, though the word 'absolute' immediately brings us into a realm which is past our comprehension.

All pleasurable states contain an element of rapture. Those of the senses cannot be excluded. We may therefore be unwise to make too great a distinction between what may be called bodily and spiritual rapture. Even the Christian Church can include the Song of Solomon amongst its sacred books and can see in it something quite different from what it appears to be to ordinary folk. The Church is right here, though it is not consistent elsewhere; for the limitless is always contained in the limited.

To me the meanest flower that blows can give
Thoughts that do often lie too deep for tears.

When it does so, pleasure melts into perception, the particular into the universal. The experience is different; it is a difference of emphasis, whether we look upon the flower or range the mental world that it opens up. Yet it is not distinct; it is all one.

It seems clear, however, that in our rapturous moments we get away from ourselves, though there may then be an almost boundless expansion of our personality. That is the real significance of rapture: a self-forgetting, not a self-regarding. With most of us there is an ideal urge, an instinct towards externality, a soul that thirsts. Rapture lies in this direction.

From what we have said, one, and probably the more frequent, method of approach to the life of the spirit, lies through formal modes of manifestation and cannot be dissociated from them. A second way claimed by advanced mystics is what might be called the direct approach; the immediate contact of the human soul with the Divine, by-passing phenomenal life. With this, a special mystical sense seems to be involved, though it is worth noticing (as the words of Plotinus, on page 94, and of two great Christian mystics on page 99 testify) that it still expresses itself in very definite concrete images, suggesting that its origin is physical and not purely spiritual. Even such a poem as *The White Peace* of Fiona Macleod seems to enclose a yearning for the visible and to be incapable of detaching itself from it.

It lies not on the sunlit hill
Nor on the sunlit plain:
Nor ever on any running stream
Nor on the unclouded main—

But sometimes through the soul of man,
Slow moving o'er his pain,
The moonlight of a perfect peace
Floods heart and brain.

This direct approach is different from that of Wordsworth who recognized in Nature

. . . the language of the sense,
The author of my purest thoughts, the nurse, the guide,
The guardian of my heart, the soul of all my moral being.

The intermediacy of physical manifestation was necessary to him, as to all artists. Art can only communicate through form. With some, the mystic sense seems roused only by physical contacts; with others, it is claimed to be wholly independent of them. This latter may be the purer form of mysticism, but it is so elusive, so divorced from reason—the extreme mystic is not content till 'the God of reason has been triumphantly dethroned'—that we are bound to be a little chary of accepting it at the valuation of its adepts. It is possible that the failure of much 'modernistic' art lies precisely in the attempt to get into more or less direct contact with an inward spirit, by means divorced from nature, to such an extent that they really transgress her laws and violate her boundaries. The result is no longer valid within the natural order. Its very aim is its undoing. The chastening hand of physical limitation is absent.

It is quite certain, however, that all mystics, whether natural or transcendental, are in search of something beyond the visible, though they may differ from each other as to where that Reality is to be found. The natural mystic would pursue the secret of life through Nature such as he sees around, never losing touch with formal shapes; the transcendental mystic—'the world forgetting and by the world forgot'—looks upon such 'natural' intervention as unnecessary; yet Love actuates both. Essentially, as Plato indicated, rapture seems to be an ideal state of love, a union or communion with Love's very spirit.[1]

Concentration is the key to rapture, great happiness and understanding its special notes, till in religious parlance 'joy unspeakable' is attained. But rapture does not come from the discovery of formal characteristics.

To speak of music. In these days we know so much about music —have dissected and analysed it to such an extent that, in our knowledge of the parts, we are in danger of losing its 'wholeness'; we are apt to see through it instead of abiding within it. In other words, though we cannot do without externals, we fix our attention upon them, passing by the inward mystery.

'Love looks not with the eyes, but with the mind.' How easy it is to speak words or sing notes with no sense of their meaning! But we must not commit the error of thinking that feeling (which is the *sine qua non* of understanding) can dispense with discrimination, if feeling is to be directed upon a worthy object. Though discrimination does not make a lover of art (or anything else), the values of art cannot be maintained without it. The hold of rapture is ir-

---

[1] Sometimes (and quite illogically, though very understandably) we find both the natural and transcendental methods of approach used by the same individual; as it was by St. Francis of Assisi who had quite a pagan reverence for Nature, as his 'Hymn to the Sun' shows, and yet undoubtedly held Christian doctrine. He could bless both the sun and God with a full heart. What matters such inconsistency!

rational, but it is not always wise or fruitful; and this is where discrimination comes in, though in a sense discrimination is inimical to rapture. How can the lover in his passionate admiration be expected to criticize the loved one?—Love is blind. The conundrum must be solved by each one for himself, but the artist solves it every day, for the solution is, indeed, the way to perfection, to the world of beauty that 'ought to be'.

Rapture is generally associated with calm; that of a withdrawn, detached, reflective state—one of inaction. That is supposed to be the especial mood of rapture. But it is not always so, nor is that which is contemplated—the object as it were of rapture—to be thought of as inactive, pervaded with a sort of death-like stillness. Rather is it a centre of intensest light, the core of the living principle. Our 'moving towards' it, however, may be with 'even step, and musing gait' as with Milton's 'pensive nun'; or impetuous, as with the mystic Plotinus who felt himself 'consumed and burning in the very heart of the sun, and poured thence in a flood of light from sphere to sphere.'

'Looks commercing with the skies,' the quiet prayers of the devout, the Dionysian frenzy of a Bacchante, the 'morning stars singing together', all testify to rapture in different ways. But the occasions of rapture are not the occasions of astonishment: they are of 'possession', which is far different. Rapture has nothing to do with *tours de force* or outstanding skill which need not be anything more than external in meaning. The heart may not be reached at all by them. It is the wonder of inward life which seems to constitute the ground of rapture and it is perhaps, as Wordsworth said, when 'our bodily motions are almost suspended' that we are most likely to 'see into the life of things'. But our bodily *state* may be and indeed must be connected with tension;[1] it must be *held*—then the spirit can take its flight. Certainly it is so with the *expression* of rapture in art.

There may seem something almost repulsive in thinking that spiritual matters, especially in their religious form, are in some measure calculable and cultural, linked up with physical control. But just as the mind controls the muscles, so, by reflex action, muscles control the mind. Muscular tension stimulates mental tension; it is its counterpart. And tension, as we have seen elsewhere, is but another word for concentration. Thus instead of a diffuse and wandering attitude, by tension we become centred and concentrated, which is the condition of rapture, and subject to conscious control.

---

[1] Certainly so, if we are to *express* rapture. There is another way of explaining rapture as an *in*pouring which comes when we are in an entirely passive mood, emptied of all physical power. However this may be, I think it is quite clear that tension—the highest tension—is involved in any artistic manifestation of the state in question.

This, as regards music, is, of course, the purpose of muscular tension. It is in its spiritual outcome that the whole meaning of tension resides. There is no use in it otherwise; it is useless for its own sake.

There is nothing new about all this. It is no fresh-fangled theory. It was recognized as true by the ancient Greeks, and it is to this day acknowledged in the religious technique of the East. Moreover, it is an easily verified experience. When people, inspired by appropriate ideas, are in this state of physical tensity at rehearsals or concerts a hush comes over the proceedings, a special at-one-ment takes place, a quality is present, almost a Presence, which makes everything different from what is ordinary; a higher plane, in short, is reached. To the artist it is as near an approach to pure spirit as he is capable of:

> *Music, the greatest good that mortals know,*
> *And all of Heaven we have below.*

Rapture is assuredly bound up with the idea of perfection, which perhaps we are too apt to regard as entirely beyond our reach; so that the extreme mystic, searching for some truer form of experience than he thinks this life is capable of, affects to find it beyond the limits of natural phenomena. But has he really used up this world as a source of mystic joy, following the quest of Vaughan, Smart, or Gerard Manley Hopkins? Till he has he may well be content with the changeful present which nevertheless does seem to establish changeless Law. The order of Nature seems final 'in the least particular'. Law can go no further, though some might venture that Love may.

Can we say that we do not see perfection here and now? Are not the sea and sky ideally beautiful in any mood, and probably the earth would always be too if we did not disfigure it; and even as regards man's works, can we conceive anything more perfect than a fugue of Bach, or a sonnet of Shakespeare? Could such things be better done, and, if they could not, what need we more? We sometimes get out of the difficulty by calling things relatively perfect, and it is not a bad compromise; but that is to delude ourselves, for perfection can never be relative. There are stages of vision; our perceptions rise on a sort of Jacob's ladder of experience and who can tell to where they may ascend; the yearning for some disembodied absolute seems rather like crying for the moon and forgetting the flowers at our feet. It is a vague dream if it is attempted (as it must be) by the negation of our physical powers of tension and our mental powers of discrimination.[1] It is a process that can never

[1] Many, perhaps most, artists would laugh at the idea that they are in a state of bliss (such as we are talking of) while they are at work. They are far too much 'on

be checked, only asserted. Save in the so-called consciousness of the devotee of the higher meditation it cannot exist. He can never tell us about it; it has no terrestrial fruits, because its direction is heavenward and it has abjured phenomena and ruled out material relationships as irrelevant. Such mysticism is not heaven brought to earth, but earth abandoned. We dare not leave earth till the appointed time. As the physicist Maxwell has said in his *Matter and Motion*, 'anyone who tries to imagine a state of mind conscious of knowing the absolute position of a point will ever after be content with relative knowledge.' It may be hazarded that Religion and even Philosophy have made the absolute and the relative too compartmental, destroying a unity which should prevail between them. Can we not consider these categories as complementary, indispensable to each other?—then difficulties seem to vanish; extremes of sense and nonsense are avoided and feeling accommodates itself to reason. In short, the middle way which Art (and Nature herself) follows, is best. Both Art and Nature are tied to formal shapes, but the tie is not a chain holding us in material bondage; it is a cable by which we attach ourselves to the ideal world and bring it close.

the spot', ordering, balancing, arranging what they have to do. They have no time to remove themselves to a seventh heaven of delight. Yet they would be wrong to think that rapture was not included in their frame of mind: for rapture makes art what it is: it is its main and most vital ingredient. What would cause them to deny it (and it is a good instinct to avoid anything that approaches extravagant or insincere assertion) is the fact that they are applying their discriminative sense as artists all the time; and this coolly intellectual process seems to give the lie to anything like irresponsible ecstasy.

We can generally turn to Shakespeare to clear up any point, and in Act III, Sc. IV of *Hamlet* he does so with regard to this particular issue. When the Ghost appears in the scene between Hamlet and his mother, Hamlet says:

> Do you see nothing there?
> Queen: Nothing at all; yet all that is I see.
> Hamlet: Why, look you there! look how it steals away!
> My father, in his habit as he lived!
> Queen: This is the very coinage of your brain:
> This bodiless creation ecstasy
> Is very cunning in.
> Hamlet: Ecstasy!
> My pulse, as yours, doth temperately keep time,
> And makes as healthful music: it is not madness
> That I have utter'd: bring me to the test,
> And I the matter will re-word; which madness
> Would gambol from. . . .

Just as the artist sees the vision, Hamlet had seen the Ghost, though the Queen had not. *That* startling experience was behind and interwoven with his quite collected speech.

Because rapture is governed by reason it does not make it any the less real. The artist has it as much as the most impassioned saint; but he always brings it within the bounds of sense and the senses, limits it by 'fetters of Form' (like Nature herself in her creations), and, if he is wise, never attempts the impossible. Nor does it seem that spiritual sustenance can ever come without the intervention of the rational mind.

96

Beautiful form is not an end in itself, but a vehicle or symbol of something 'far more deeply interfused'. Yet that something is nothing without incarnation, embodiment. In striving for the shadow alone we miss the substance, whereas without the substance there is no shadow. This is not the attitude of the Puritan who tried to make the best of both worlds by 'singing Psalms to hornpipes'; but of somehow preserving the distinction between Psalms and hornpipes while containing these within a single system. Perfection has no sense unless it is used upon something; reality has no significance except in the light of perfection.

'The corn was orient and immortal wheat, which never should be reaped, nor was ever sown. I thought it had stood from everlasting to everlasting.'

The Relative and the Absolute have been the major concern of philosophers from the beginning, and will continue to vex them till the end of time. A few words cannot dispose of this vast subject, but even to think about it carries the mind to the furthest limits of its powers, and it has a close bearing upon art. With the rapturous we reach the summit of technical striving as well as of spiritual search; moreover, rapture is a fact—attendance at any concert will show it, even to the cynical[1]—though our explanation of it may be faulty. As a means only of intellectual interest or pleasurable entertainment music, without rapture, is of little avail.

Summary

The foregoing are some of the principles and implications of tension which must direct the use of the voice: they have been stated extensively to show how dependent singing is upon them.

In all forms of control the *tensed muscles keep contact with the action*. Directly contact is lost, control ceases. In a sense relaxation is a loosening of control and so has to be very carefully dealt with. If the voice is not well held neither will an audience be.

The relations between muscular and musical forces are certainly not easy to understand, yet we ought to try to understand them in order to be sure of our technical ground. It is clear that many good singers know little of the way they sing; for this reason it is doubtful

---

[1] In *The Little Flowers of Saint Francis* the writer tells how, suddenly, there appeared to him (St. Francis) 'an Angel with exceeding great splendour, having a viol in his left hand and in his right the bow; and as St. Francis stood all amazed at the sight of him, the Angel drew the bow across the viol; and straightway St. Francis was ware of such sweet melody that his soul melted away for very sweetness and was lifted up above all bodily feeling: insomuch that, as he afterwards told his companions, he doubted that, if the Angel had drawn the bow a second time across the strings his mind would have left his body for all the utter sweetness thereof.' The naïveté of this account need not at all blind us to its essential truth. It expresses very clearly what rapture is and does, though perhaps it needed an angel to bring it about—a concert violinist might fall short.

E

whether they could be as good teachers as they are executants. Santley made great fun of abdominal breathing, as though the abdomen had no place in the breathing which produced his noble art; but of course he was wrong. The abdominal muscles play a tremendous part in breathing and cannot be left out of account. We have either to say nothing about the technical processes—which is a large and impracticable order—or if we do talk about them try to be sure that they are sound and natural. Conscious art—and great art is so generally—cannot be satisfied with intuitive methods though it is initiated and stimulated by instinct.

We have tried to establish that well-applied tension is at the very root of singing, whether we know it or not: that without tension there is no energy or control. Taut states of mind are also to be associated with taut muscular states; they are dependent on each other.[1] Exactly how far spirit has to be backed by body, functions in connection with it, is perhaps beyond our understanding: but it is certain that even moral qualities, which in the Platonic sense seem so far removed from material considerations, cannot be demonstrated without our physical forces; and it would be possible to maintain[2] that, quite apart from imaginative art, great love, or courage, or endurance are at their best when they are supported, at any rate potentially, by great powers of muscular tension.[3]

What does a great conductor do but galvanize his forces into a

[1] Thought of great cogency and concentration probably depends upon a cerebral organ that is highly wrought, capable of strong yet subtle tensions. And this same organ, physically directed, is used also in the case of the performer or interpreter of such thought; muscular, not only mental tensions, are then brought into play. There is thus a correspondence between muscular and mental states. We may never find out what accounts ultimately for, say, Shakespeare's *Hamlet*, what is its exact relation to nervous and physical forces. . . .

> There are more things in heaven and earth, Horatio,
> Than are dreamt of in our philosophies,

but we can very well assume that such forces enter into the manifestation of *Hamlet* in the highest degree.

In this way, while recognizing the interplay of body and mind, we avoid a deification of brute force. The onus is placed upon mental rather than physical tensions. The mind is the directive influence.

Whence come our thoughts, what fires our action? That is still the question. Who can say?

[2] Diana Watts in *The Renaissance of the Greek Ideal* has done so very convincingly.

[3] There is, of course, difficulty in substantiating such a statement; the unity and interdependence of body and soul is often challenged. But it does seem credible (if we take the *fruits* of the mind into consideration, as exhibited, for instance, in the case of literature) that tension exists with words as with physical effort, and indeed that the quality and force of words can and must be related to such effort.

In *The Eagle and the Dove*, by V. Sackville West, the story of the 16th-century Théresa of Avila has been contrasted with that of her modern namesake St. Thérèse of Lisieux. Two passages, noted by a reviewer in the *New Statesman*, in which the saints describe similar visionary experience shows the difference of their minds: the one strong, sinewy; the other weak, namby-pamby, almost spiritless,

state of higher tension, with obvious results as concerns the performance? What most performers need is not improved detail of expression but a generally improved tension in their work, whereby quickness of action and lightness and sensitiveness of touch—so necessary, for instance, to Mozart's music—is achieved. Ponderous, heavy performance, of which there is so much, is entirely due to absence of tension; it is never as the French say *sur les nerfs*, or capable of being fined-out to a point.

But we may tighten till we are blue in the face: the result may be poor. The inward ear, not the body, must finally decide. In singing it is quality of tone which mainly counts; in another word, pronunciation. The fight is always between things as they are and as we would have them to be; between how we speak and the ideal of speech. Characteristic sound is not necessarily beautiful—Mr. So-and-So's voice may have character—we may be in no doubt that it belongs to him, and to him alone. We may wish that it didn't.

An amusing but very significant fable[1] may well close this section on Tension.

The Harp

'O! O!' cried the harp, as it was being tuned.

'Come, come,' said the harpist. 'You know well enough that if the strings were not taut the music would not be there.'

recalling the decorated texts and cheap religious pictures that a half century ago were frequently to be found in conventual establishments or, indeed, in any pious household.

Here are the words of the high-mettled Spanish Saint:

'I saw in his hand a spear of gold, and at the iron's point there seemed to be a little fire. He appeared to be thrusting it at times into my heart, and to pierce my very entrails; when he drew it out, he seemed to draw them out also, and to leave me all on fire with a great love of God. The pain was so great that it made me moan; and yet so surpassing was the sweetness of this excessive pain that I could not wish to be rid of it,'

and of the meekly submissive, almost childish French one:

'I told the child Jesus not to make use of me as a valuable toy which children are content to look at without touching it, but as a little ball of no price, which He could throw on the ground, kick with His foot, make a hole in, and either leave in a corner or press to His heart if that was agreeable to Him. . . . In Rome, He did make a hole in His little toy; no doubt He wanted to see what was inside it and then, satisfied with His discovery, He let fall His little ball and went to sleep.'

The characters of the writers are clearly displayed in these passages, and we may be certain that their physical traits are also. The catalepsy which affected the Spanish Saint in her early years rather supports than invalidates her highly-wrought muscular powers; whereas 'The Little Flower', as the French Saint was called, was evidently of more fragile make—she died of tuberculosis when she was twenty-three. Nevertheless, when the highest degree of suffering is bravely borne, as it was by both Saints, we cannot discount its quality in order to make it agree with any theory of tension. Intellectually there is no doubt of the superiority of St. Theresa of Avila, but strength of soul is perhaps different from strength of intellect. Mysterious spiritual powers may aid the former. Weakness may show a valiancy that calls not for discussion but for respectful silence.

[1] By Una Hook, inserted by her kind permission.

'Yes,' said the harp, 'but it is very trying to be always at such a strain and almost at breaking point.'

'Well, what do you propose to do about it?'

'O! nothing! There *is* nothing to be done,' said the harp: 'I was only just having a grumble. Screw me up! I wouldn't be heard out of tune for worlds.'

And this fable applies not only to pitch, but to every aspect of music.

Chapter 2

THE MATERIAL OF SINGING

Music and Speech

THE rudiments of pitch and rhythm are, of course, to be found in natural sounds and movement—in the whistling of the wind, the roar of the sea, the heart beat, etc.: exceptionally in a more determinate form—the song of birds. But what we know as speech and music is scarcely suggested in these phenomena, which are almost purely emotional or functional. It is not till the mind enters and consciously selects sounds and regulates rhythm for the purposes of thought that we arrive at speech and music. Both represent a language, i.e., a means of emotional or factual communication, which submits in the case of speech to the laws of syntax and grammar, and in the case of music to those of musical form, though with great variation. Neither speech nor music is unnatural; but both are very far removed from instinctive utterance.

From this it would appear that music came first upon the scene of civilization, since sound is certainly prior to sense. But it is at least arguable that, as already observed, pitch and rhythm as elements of an ordered system developed through the inflexion and rhythm of words. In which case we might consider music as a later manifestation than speech. This seems borne out, too, by the earlier maturity of speech. Poets were using highly expressive language when musicians were scarcely more than fumbling with notes.

It is indeed doubtful whether a purely musical impulse would ever have given us music—whether the language of music would have taken shape without the language of words; and it may be ventured that speech because of its flying start will always tend to be a more advanced medium of expression than music. Certainly we are justified in asserting the tremendous importance of speech in song: an importance that very few singers have any notion of. They 'play upon the larynx' as von Bülow said; the music of speech eludes them and with it the poetry of music.

'The art of singing has within it a great deal that is quite outside the province of music.' Speech, particularly as regards consonants, has no place in pure music. Yet a great deal of the beauty and character of singing, to consider only the audible interest, comes from these foreign elements. We may well say, then, that song represents a more complete vehicle of expression than music alone.

In some respects it does not range so widely, but it searches more deeply. A vocal line (when joined to words) has greater variety, greater subtlety, than an instrumental line.

But the use of consonantal sound is after all scarcely more than a mechanical advantage when considered by itself. It allows a little more articulation of the musical note, i.e., the vowel which is common to both vocal and instrumental utterance, for vowels are but qualities or kinds of sound; music can and does dispense with these articulatory embellishments. A far greater advantage than this derives from the use of words. The shape and structure of words is, of course, largely defined by consonants. But it is the *meaning* of words, not their mechanical form, which adds something that music by itself cannot give and yet amalgamates so wonderfully with the musical meaning. Words are symbols. They bring with them ideas of concrete images and clearly identifiable action. In song it is as though the body had joined the soul, incarnating a single perfection. Song is not merely a simultaneous use of words and music like the combination of gesture and speech. A song *is* words and music: each growing out of each, coalescing organically at almost every turn.

THE SIGNIFICANCE OF SOUND IN GENERAL

Sound has a significance quite apart from its use in words or music. The various sounds of instruments or of language, have a sort of absolute character of their own. 'Cello tone is pathetic; the clarinet, tender, feminine[1]; that of the horn, elegiac; the trumpet, commanding, strident; the trombone, solemn; the bassoon, burlesque; while (in Dryden's words), the flute is 'soft and complaining', the violin 'sharp'. Whether these qualifications completely account for the effect of these sounds upon us does not matter. The point is that some such qualifications are possible and generally recognized. We distinguish also general characteristics in the case of languages. Italian is brilliant, highly coloured; Spanish sombre; German rough; French refined, expressing delicate shades of tone; while the sounds of language may be still further analysed into vowels, each one of which (as we shall indicate later) has its own peculiar timbre.

The infinite variety of vocal sound as well as its close connection with the human personality puts it on a different plane from that of instrumental sound, and it is not strange that vocalists have always enjoyed a privileged position as public performers.

---

[1] Berlioz could even write about it that it seems to evoke 'les femmes aimées, les amantes à l'œil fier, à la passion profonde, que le bruit des armes exalte, qui chantent en combattant, qui couronnent les vainqueurs ou meurent avec les vaincus.'

But perhaps the significance of sound as such is best observed in natural cries, such as an animal will utter when it is angry or afraid, etc. We can generally relate them to some precise emotional disturbance; at least it is to be so related and it will have a constant meaning: the same sound, the same sense.

Natural cries, however, are a very primitive form of expression, though they are never outgrown. They are instinctive, immediate calls or responses, but they do not carry us very far. They are localized in much the same way as physical contacts. In short, they contain no thought. It is the formal element of speech or of music that gives sound its developed significance. By this element it can compass the universe; without it, it is tethered to the particular spot where it happens to be produced.

Thus emotion seems specially to be linked with colour; thought with form. Both are important ingredients in a complete appeal to our faculties; but emotion is relatively elementary in its working—it does not involve the higher intellectual centres. This is why simple souls, to whom form is of little account, nevertheless may respond quite ardently to colour. It is the first thing that attracts. An infant will show its delight in a coloured toy, though it has no understanding of its form; an adult in the glory of the sunset, though he is unimpressed by cloud structure. Educational advance therefore hinges mainly on formal appreciation, though, against it, there may well be emotional loss.

There is something abstract (or abstractible) in form. The form of music can be shown on paper and any form can be transcribed in terms other than itself. Colour can never be. Colour is elemental. We can get no idea of colour save when, in the case of audible colour, we hear it, or of visible colour, see it. Colour cannot be explained, it must be felt.

But though form can be intellectually abstracted from colour, in Nature it is always associated with it. The 'fair forms' of Plato's ideal world are products of the mind. We can imagine them perhaps, arrive at them in cool detachment and by philosophical processes, but we never meet them in actual life. Colour is part of the scheme of things, and sound and colour are inseparable. Music is not to be conceived except in terms of vocal or instrumental colour; nor are words.[1]

Colour vastly modifies the appeal of form. The look of a landscape

---

[1] It is arguable whether we should take the least interest even in the most beautiful building or statue if it were of the purest white and free from shadow. It would be an inhuman abomination. No such thing could possibly occur, however —there is some colour in everything; but the nearer we approach to colourless forms the less they touch us. We are, at any rate, particularly free from any such difficulty with music for colour is the breath of its being.

is quite different under different conditions of light and atmosphere; and so with words and notes. How we colour a formal statement largely determines its sense. 'It isn't wot 'e says, it's the nasty way 'e says it' can almost be taken as a classic statement of this fact with regard to words. It is closely allied to the principles of 'expression', and the 'nasty' (or 'nice') way will be largely a question of colour or vocal timbre. The same words, indeed, can have a diametrically opposite meaning. The simple phrase 'What a lovely day!' for instance, can be made to express the acme of satisfaction or disgust. Yet those words, however used, do serve to fix the situation—they are *about* something; and if they are ambiguous in themselves and only unequivocal when we have spoken them in a particular way, they are nevertheless essential to what we have to say.

Some poets hold—theoretically, at any rate—that beautiful and characteristic sound is the main ingredient in poetry; that the symbolic use of words matters very little; that the 'sense' of poetry is musical rather than verbal. Schelling appears to have supported this view, and later, Holderlein, Novalis and Rimbaud. Their interest was rather in the directly expressive sound of the words which they chose—necessarily, chiefly in the vowels of those words, and in the way such vowels were combined and contrasted—the verbal symbol being thus little more than a pretext for an effect of colour. This, of course, is getting very close to music though poets have always been aware of the significance of colour in words. But music is something more than colour. Rhythm, pitch, intensity, also play their part, and it is primarily from these elements that something akin to musical form arises, even in a poem. To this extent there is music in words but this does not warrant us in believing that the essence of poetry is music, or—and it logically comes to this—that nonsense words and structure are all that the poet requires for the exercise of his art.[1] The evocative quality of a poem lies as much in its objective references as in the feelings which accompany them; in form as much as in colour; and if we wish for form abstracted from symbol we had better go to music

---

[1] It is true that we often meet with nonsense refrains, but they are nearly always *sung* which entirely alters the situation; and even when Lewis Carroll's imaginary monsters 'gyre and gymbal in the wabe' the writer still relies on grammatical structure, or a semblance of it, to hold our attention. Generally, also, nonsense refrains have some sort of form, e.g., 'with a dumble dum dolikin, etc.'

It is also true that words can move as deeply when we have no notion of what they mean; as in the refrain of the Elizabethan song 'Caleno Custare me.' They seem to open up a world of amorous experience; to reach the very heart of it, with its worship of loveliness in the loved one. But here again, we derive our emotion not so much from the words themselves, as from their poetic and musical context, which explains them and gives them significance, so that they seem to gather up and symbolize the whole sensibility of the poem.

straightway. To muddle up the arts—to try to make poetry like music, or music like poetry—is often to do them a disservice, for they cannot develop to the full under such conditions.

The Significance of Vocal Sound

Vocal sound consists of vowels and consonants. Vowels are more or less unimpeded, 'voiced', sound—i.e., derive their vibration from the vocal cords; consonants are the outcome of some obstructive process of nose, throat, tongue or lips, and they may be 'voiced' or 'unvoiced', i.e., be purely breath sounds. Vowels, and, I suppose, also, it would be true to say, consonants, are the audible equivalent of visual colour; but more especially vowels, since consonants are for the most part short-lived.

The general significance of colour has already been noted; also the link that colour has with our emotional life. Colour goes to the root of our being, to its hidden springs. It is the vibrating power which nourishes form. Form without colour, without this emotional quality, is but an empty shape. We cannot exactly specify what a colour means, though we know fairly well how it moves us; but it is quite certain that a meaning could be attached if our knowledge were sufficient. If we are disturbed by colour it is to some purpose.

Instinctive sounds, as we have said, are the outcome of emotion. Both as regards pitch and quality they would indicate (in the case of a human being) what the person felt. Happy sounds would be bright and high pitched; mournful sounds dull and low pitched. Thus the bright-toned vowels Ee and Ay would be uttered in a state of happiness, rather than the dull-toned Oh and Oo. And if we can take our cue from Nature those sounds (or whatever they were) would be perfectly produced; at one with the organism that produced them, apt to their purpose and situation.

But we are obviously a long way off, in conscious art, from the use of these elemental sounds as distinctly representative of emotion. For in words these sounds have been made to serve another function, that of the symbol. Thought, conscious selection, has intervened so that the original meaning of the sound has often disappeared. This is perhaps the penalty of the use of our rational powers. It ousts the natural element. There is a gain but also a loss in the process. A certain dislocation of nature occurs. A sound which was meant to be one thing may now be forced into another service. Nevertheless some of the old associations remain. With music, of course, there is no such problem, except that the sense of the music may run counter to the colour which is used to express it. This frequently happens; a passage may be given to a wrong instrument, a role cast for a wrong voice[1] by the inexpert. We feel how much better things would have been if treated differently.

THE MEANING OF VOWELS

'Vowels are only various voice qualities to which we have given names.' This statement, intended to be authoritative, does not seem to be true. The names we give are not arbitrary though the writing down of them may be—we could agree to put any sort of a sign for a vowel, as is done in the case of different languages.

Vowels are not symbols like words. They *are* the sound which they represent. When we say Ee or Ah, that is the actual sound that the shape of the oral cavity gives us, and we accept the sound as a fact. The sound and the symbol are the same. We could not make the sound of Ee and call it Ah—that is, not phonetically, though we may take an alphabetical symbol, like E or A, and—such are the vagaries of the English language—pronounce it in a variety of ways. With reckless inconsistency, as G. B. Shaw said, we write 'sweet' and 'sweat', and then write 'whet' and 'wheat', just the contrary.[2] But that is another matter. We will not here discuss what the actual sound of Ee (or any other vowel) should be. It may have a multitude of nuances like the colour green, though we recognize a certain 'genus' or family of Ee's as of greens. But to call a particular sound Ee is not like calling a colour green. The writing of Ee, then, is arbitrary but the sound of Ee is not. Hearing Ee is

[1] It is not without reason that the role of the lover is generally given to the tenor, or that of the old man, the father, or the traitor, to a bass. It lies in the natural fitness of things.

[2] As an example of (approximately) phonetic spelling, the following may be quoted:

A BLACKSMITH'S BILL

Sir,—In looking through some old papers, I found the following copy of an old Yorkshire blacksmith's bill that I came across many years ago, and thought your readers might be amused.

			s.	d.
Osarfaday –	–	–	2	6
Ashooinonim	–	–	2	6
Afechinonimom	–	–	1	6
A. –	–	–	0	9
			7	3

The correct reading of the bill is as follows:

			s.	d.
Horse, half a day –	–	–	2	6
Shoeing of him	–	–	2	6
Fetching of him home	–	–	1	6
Hay –	–	–	0	9
			7	3

Letter in *Country Life*.

like seeing what we call green. It is an absolute sound as it were.
This has reference to *direct* expression, not expression via the symbol
of a word. Immediate and symbolical expression are quite different.
Through colour and timbre music appeals to us in the closest
possible way. Sound and colour, as such, are closer to life than any
word can be; yet we *know* these elements less than we know what a
word means. We can discuss the meaning of a word; we cannot
discuss the meaning of colour; we can only *feel* it, as we have said.
In this sense feeling is superior to knowledge; or it is a sort of higher
knowledge.[1]

> *To match and mate*
> *Feeling with knowledge—make as manifest*
> *Soul's work as mind's work, turbulence or rest,*
> *Hates, loves, joys, woes, hopes, fears that rise and sink,*
> *Ceaselessly; passion's transient flit and wink,*
> *A ripple's tinting, or a spume-sheet's spread*
> *Whitening the wave—to strike all this life dead,*
> *Run mercury into a mould like lead,*
> *And henceforth leave the plain result to show*
> *How we feel, hard and fast as what we know—*
> *This were the prize, and is the puzzle!—which*
> *Music essays to solve: and here's the hitch*
> *That baulks her of full triumph else to boast.*

This is Browning's version of the art of music, and it is through
colour, as applied to or coincident with form that, respectively,
'soul's work' and 'mind's work' are achieved.

The need for fine tone is therefore all-important. Why orchestral
concerts are better attended than choral concerts at the present day
is largely because instrumental tone is far better determined than
vocal tone. It is clearer, more highly differentiated. Singers are
content with poor vowels and uncertain tone colour. Yet every
shade of colour that they add to their palette increases the power of
their art. Vocal tone can be as varied as instrumental tone—it can
represent a whole orchestra of colour—then it becomes a glorious
thing; while for sheer beauty the sound of instruments cannot
compare with that of the voice, as Byrd told us centuries ago.

The Character of Vowels

Certain characteristics go with vowels, as with melodies in the
old church modes. Vowels are linked with physical formations that

---

[1] Note, however, that this higher knowledge is not divorced from the senses;
most religions claim a knowledge that is. It is the difference between empirical
and, what Aldous Huxley calls, 'perennial' philosophy.

occur when stimulated by certain emotions—this is their natural basis. To take the long vowels, we may say, without being too dogmatic, that the nature of

Ee: is keen, biting, clear, precise, hard;

Ay: is metallic, commanding, vigorous, telling; and it may have a questioning character as well;

Ah: is free, generous, revealing, happy, contented;

Aw: is noble, firm; it is perhaps the most effective of the vowels in concentrated yet ample sonority;

Oh: is anguished, agonized;

Oo: is soft, sympathetic, veiled; a little brother to Oh.

We are probably not far wrong in these attributes, though people will feel differently about them and each must decide as he pleases.

In the Rosicrucian philosophy speech sounds have definite spiritual attributions. The Rosicrucians claim that there are twenty-two 'sounds of creation' by which the Almighty uttered his fiat. Strangely enough they hold that these sounds were our consonants, not our vowels—on second thoughts, however, it is not so strange, since consonants do represent the active, formative element in speech. From another angle, without implying a divine significance to consonants—though there is no reason why the natural order of things should be at all doubtful of its purpose—Steiner, the founder of anthroposophy ('the wisdom of humanity'), laid down that each vowel had an appropriate movement, 'soul-content' or colour, which he defined; while the tremendous mystical implication of the syllable 'Om' for Buddhists is well known.[1]

All this is not to be disposed of as representing mere convention. To say the least it is an attempt to reach the truth of the significance of vocal sound, and we are entitled to believe that it succeeds in large measure. But whatever the meaning of any particular sound, whatever its correspondence with our own make-up: even on grounds of thoroughly varied artistic material we shall be wise to develop vowel character to the fullest extent.

We thus get a series of what may be called primary colours—roughly comprising our long and short vowels; but as well, such

---

[1] OM is a shortened form of AUM, three distinct sounds which—when pronounced correctly—is supposed to give rise to states of consciousness that induce perceptions different from those that are usual with us. When rightly uttered the three sounds are heard as (1) Ah; (2) U (a sound between Oh and Oo); (3) M (a kind of deep humming, 'which is made to descend gradually into the chest and so appears to originate in the pit of the stomach'—which is where M and indeed all sound of any consequence should come from). The word when a number of devotees utter it in chorus, resembles 'the rolling of thunder in the far distance' and is 'as silence spoken'. For extended information on this sacred symbol and something of the vast doctrine that it enshrines, read Sir Edwin Arnold's *In an Indian Temple* (Oriental Poems).

colours may themselves be 'coloured'. An emotional aura or atmosphere may be given to them, bringing about considerable modification of the raw[1] primary state, almost to the extent of establishing
another vowel, or at any rate of bringing about a mixture or blending of different vowel tone: just as Ee may have (and indeed
generally should have) something of the short vowel ĭ (as in 'him')
in it. Yet Ee and ĭ should nevertheless be recognizable as Ee and ĭ,
even while this process is at work. Of this more later.

Colour is not just *colour*: a vowel that is definite enough to be
labelled. It may be, indeed will be, warm, glowing; or cold, hollow,
dead. In short, the attributes of tone are infinite. The wonder of
it all is clear enough.[2] I remember how my old professor, M. Mailly
of the Brussels Conservatoire, would sometimes hold a chord on a
single stop (generally the 'Cor de Nuit', a fine example of the
'voicing' of Cavaillé-Col) and after listening for some seconds,
exclaim, 'Ah, que c'est beau!' A single chord, a single sound! That
was enough to rouse him to unfeigned ecstasy. He was right.

Vocal sound as arising from the posture of the vocal organs, in
accord with unconscious pantomimic gesture of the limbs and
features as a whole, will be touched upon later.

SELECTION OF MATERIAL

A convenient starting point as regards the selection of vocal
sound is the sound of Uh, heard much as in the word 'glove', if
spoken in a very loose, backward way. Uh has been called the
'neutral' vowel—for it is entirely without character—or, if character
be allowed it, it is one of extreme laziness[3] and want of mentality.

[1] Perhaps some indignity is implied by this adjective but its use is sufficiently
correct.

[2] The more deeply we probe into the nature of sound the more mysterious it
appears. We think of sound as something coming to us from the outside, already
in being, as are all objective things. But sound, as we know it, has no being save
in our own minds. It starts from vibration, from material movement, but it is the
alchemy of the mind that turns it into sound and music. There is no sound save in
ourselves. Thus, a physical cause becomes a spiritual effect; vibration becomes
music. It is the same with the emotion of love. In one, its lowest sense, love is a
physical vibration—an instinctive stimulus of nerve and muscle; in another, it includes our whole mental and moral being, reaching to the very centre of the self.
It is made of 'sighs and tears, faith and service, fantasy, passion, wishes, adoration,
duty, observance, humbleness, patience and impatience, purity, trial, obedience'
so Shakespeare tells us; but its starting point is a far different affair.

[3] Nature is always apt to economize effort; to take the easy way. As regards tone
this can be well observed with children's voices, which, though pleasing, are
seldom clear or open. Children do not work hard enough to secure these characteristics—perhaps because it needs a greater development of muscular system than
they possess. Their vowels are for the most part soft and smothered, and, particularly on high notes, the voice closes in to what is really a sort of hoot. It is of
course owing to the difficulty of tension. Low notes, with everyone, are generally
fairly open—a very little observation will show this—but the higher the note the

There is no control in it. It sings itself. It is the easiest sound to make, and therefore the worst. In fact, it is as much 'the very devil' in singing as was the tritone in medieval composition. When badly sung it represents an extreme condition of slack technique, the reverse of what was advocated in Chapter 1, when tension was insisted upon as the key to good singing.

Professors of singing, to whom relaxation is a fetish, should contemplate the significance of this vowel. Since there is no formation in it, there is no mind; and since there is no tension, no will. It is the very symbol of stupidity, and relates to much bad teaching.

The influence of Uh is to be reckoned with in all vocal endeavour. The human make-up includes an element of laziness, as already observed. When an effort is required we are naturally inclined to attempt it with the minimum expenditure of energy. It is a touch of the old Adam, before he was set to work properly. Thus, with every vowel there will be a tendency to recede to the easiest position of Uh, and to fail in those qualities that a good vowel should have. It is the sign of poor singing, and accounts for 'smothered' tone—a very different thing from 'covered' tone—and for the imperfect 'opening' of vowels.[1]

The English are particularly prone to this fault of speech, which, incidentally, accounts for changes in language as a whole. At the best periods mind and body are alert. That is the hey-day of good speech and song. Then comes slackness and decadence, and with them a far less precise use of the organs and also the structure of speech. Classical Latin altered into French, Italian, Spanish, etc. mainly because people could not be bothered to inflect their nouns and verbs; so they dropped final consonants and syllables, and slurred and elided sounds when it was difficult to pronounce them separately. It is a process that is continually going on. We see it in the sloppy pronunciation of the average American, which makes for the elision of syllables, reducing highly varied speech to what is far more uniform and commonplace. Finally a new American language may possibly emerge. Milton observed the same phenomenon or, at least, tendency, in the 17th century. Of our national pronunciation at that period he wrote that ' . . . we Englishmen, being far northerly, do not open our mouths in the cold air wide enough to grace a

---

greater the tension that is required if it is to be kept open, and so the voice is allowed to fall apart; the concentrated, screwing-up process is abandoned, and a different sort of tone takes place: a sort of Uh tone, much easier to sing but devoid of vitality. It has its virtue in being and seeming more comfortable—but it is at the expense of timbre and definition.

[1] A word of caution is needed here. As will be shown later, there is nothing wrong in the opportune use of 'backward' tone, provided it is properly 'opened'. To which may be added the truth: that unless a vowel is so opened it will not be the intended vowel at all.

southern tongue, but are observed by all other nations to speak exceedingly close and inward so that to smatter Latin with an English mouth is as ill a hearing as low French.' And it all comes down to this 'very devil' of a vowel Uh with its nefarious influence. The fight has always been going on between sloth and action, between energy-saving and energy-spending; and it it is sad to relate that in the matter of the production of speech sounds the first mentioned states have, so far, consistently won, in much the same manner as the 'Gresham' law operates in the matter of currency. Bad money will always turn out good money. The weakening of the various elements of a language alters its shape and form; then things settle down; a fresh start is made, a fresh growth comes, culminating in another classical period, with the inevitable era of decay to follow. It seems useless to try to arrest this natural cycle. Individuals realizing the 'splendour of the prime' will try to retain it as long as possible, and they act as a brake on a too precipitate declension: but, in the end, theirs is a losing battle. What is certain is that the quality of the vowel Uh, *pur sang*, is precisely the quality that spells disintegration in both speech and singing, and that it must be avoided if we are bent on either in their best form.

Nevertheless it must be added that it is perfectly possible to pronounce a *good* Uh, but the shape will not be slack nor its sound lifeless like the *neutral* Uh. It will have to be treated as all other vocal sound if it is to be effective, viz., by tension and concentration (which is the same thing).[1] It is the most backward, lowest-lying vowel of the group of Ah long vowels (which comprises Uh, Ah, I), and therefore will naturally have a comparatively dull tone, as have other low-lying vowels, such as Oh and Oo; but a tense-shaped resonance gives it a certain shimmer and vitality.

Some might consider Uh to be the same as the short vowel 'ŭ' (as in 'lover'), but if pronounced properly with ample pharyngeal resonance—again, good tone *is* good pronunciation—it becomes a long vowel as in the sustained 'love'. Its tendency then will not be to drop down and back but to move forward, approximating itself to Ah. Ah in its turn, if sung well, will veer towards I, and I towards Ee (for that is the diphthongal vowel upon which I ends.[2]). A good vocal habit, particularly as it concerns clear words, tends not only to fall but to rise; a bad one only to fall—as already noted—towards the neutral Uh.

Perhaps it should be said here that any vowel can easily be sung

[1] There is effort in a good Uh, as with Oh. Even the loosest toned Oh will not come of itself, nor will an Uh worth having. Depth must be given to it, and depth has to be gained; lift also, and there is no lift without tension.
[2] In singing and the best speech this sound should be short i (as in 'pit') though *I* is generally noted as Ah+Ee, neither of which vowels it is.

long, or—if it is preferred to put it so—*sustained*, provided plenty of room in the neck (or lower pharynx) is allowed it for vibration. Humanity if it is to develop freely needs *lebensraum*, otherwise its growth will be cramped and distorted; similarly with a vowel. What we are accustomed to call *short* vowels (as in 'kit', 'cat', 'cot') are generally devoid of neck resonance when spoken quickly; but, in singing, it is often necessary to sustain them (on a long note) and this can only be done comfortably by opening the throat. Length of vowel, therefore, is practically coincident with this opening process of the throat, and, by it, the so-called *short* vowels are brought into line with the *long* ones, thus ensuring unity of voice and style.

General Shaping of Vowels

The selection of vowel sounds, then, indicates a departure from the neutral sound of Uh. It is from the position of Uh that the various sounds of the voice begin to take shape. This shaping of the vowels arises from two principal actions:

(1) the raising and advancing of the tongue;
(2) the closing of the lips.

As regards (1):

With the neutral Uh the tongue is completely relaxed and therefore lies flat in the mouth. Starting from this position the tongue can be used so that it partially blocks the mouth. Its tip in a state of rest will touch the back of the lower teeth. If it is brought forward and raised, so that its margin touches the upper molars, the oral cavity for the long vowel Ay is formed. A still further advance of the tongue to what is practically its extreme position will form the cavity for the long vowel Ee. Other vowels in the English system, such as the related short vowels ĕ (gĕt) and ĭ (hĭt) are also formed by the use of the tongue, which as it comes forward is apt to draw

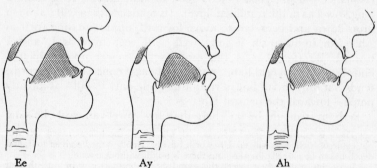

| Ee | Ay | Ah |

Diagram showing approximate positioning of the tongue for Ee, Ay, Ah.

the larynx up with it and so reduce resonation in the throat. Much of the art of singing consists in countering this tendency by maintaining the expansion of the neck throughout vowelling. There is of course less resonance room in the mouth for Ee than for Ay, and much less than for Ah; so that Ee is relatively a thin vowel, and the voice progressively richens as it opens to larger and deeper positions.

The shaded parts of the foregoing represent the tongue and uvula, and it will be noted that the uvula presses against the back of the pharynx (cf. general diagram of the head, p. 18), thus shutting off the naso-pharnyx and preventing escape of breath through the nose—this has great bearing upon the maximum development of tone.[1] The little wavy line at the root of the tongue is the epiglottis,

---

[1] With these diagrams to aid us, it might be well to forestall what will be said under the heading 'Terminology' (p. 160 et seq.), and, by so doing, also perhaps give a more complete answer to the points raised previously in regard to nasal resonance.

The above diagrams, for Ee, Ay and Ah, show the uvula clinging to the back of the pharynx. This completely closes the orifice leading into the nose, damping 'open' tone, and, with it, those aggressive, fiery qualities, characteristic of timbre. In its place attributes of an altogether smoother and more manageable kind emerge, constituting 'covered' tone.

We have the power, however, of withdrawing the uvula from this position—the released uvula will be seen in our diagram for M—which allows the vocal sound to enter the nose, and thus to develop its full power. As already stated tone need not go through the nose, only into it. If the mouth is shut M must emerge at the nostrils. If both mouth and nostrils are shut, then, of course, no movement of breath or sound is possible.

The distinction between subdued and brilliant tone comes about by these two methods of procedure, and this, with intermediate variations, liberates the whole range of vocal colour. It means, in effect, the rejection or admission of M into vowelling, with vastly varied results.

These actions of the uvula are also linked with sympathetic action of the soft palate, which rises when the uvula clings to the pharynx, and falls when the uvula is released; but our argument is clearer if we consider the uvula alone.

In understanding the principles of voice production, half of the perplexity that we have—and it is undoubted—comes from failing to recognize the two main categories of tone; or we tend to alternate them in actual use, temporarily advancing one at the expense of the other, and to forget that both have to be brought under one system, theoretically and practically. Most singers have no idea as to how to set about this; and are, in fact, content with one kind of sound which does duty for every song they sing. This can never stand for 'interpretation'. The tone achieved may be quite beautiful in itself, just as clarinet tone is beautiful; but there are many more 'voices' in an orchestra than the voice of any single type of instrument. The human voice represents a full orchestra of varied sound, with all the colours of the rainbow in it; and only if it is so used can an approach be made to 'poetic' expression.

It is worth observing that we generally use 'covered' (or, as the Italians call it, chiuso) tone in ordinary speech, simply because we have to get over the ground, quickly and easily; if we used 'open' (It. aperto) tone we should have to work much harder, and it would not flow. Although the valleys must often be exalted, it is just as important that the 'rough places be made smooth'. It is largely a question of emotional temperature.

It also needs to be said that the moment we begin to put 'expression' to a note,

or lid of the larynx, which closes off the windpipe when we swallow.

We also show what happens with the nasal M, in the sounding of which breath *must* come through the nose. This occurs also with the other nasals N and ng.

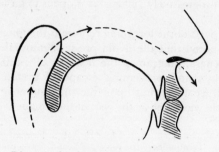

Diagram showing breath action for M etc.

As regards (2):

Again starting from the neutral Uh, while keeping the tongue flat, modifications of vowel can be made by progressively rounding[1] and closing the lips. Thus the first vowel to be formed by this method is the long Aw which is perhaps best associated with Oh and Oo, though it also partakes of the nature of Ah. Then comes Oh with a further closing, and, with still more closing Oo. Intermediate short vowels like ŏ (in ŏn) and ŭ (in ŭp) also occur by this process. With the closure of the lips the larynx tends to lower and there is a slight raising of the base of the tongue: actions the reverse of those brought about by the forward movement of the tongue. This is of importance in vocal production, as the throat expansion induced by this laryngeal movement for Oh and Oo is the means of securing fullness of tone. Brilliancy is to be associated with the metallic-toned Ay and Ee; depth and roundness with the more sombre colouring of Oh and Oo. But the character of the various vowels has already been discussed, and more will be said.

there will be a tendency to stifle it. One can work much too hard in trying to get nasally-opened tone, which will often come of itself, without effort. All one has to do is *really* to open the throat, release the sound, and let it go where it wants to go.

[1] A proviso is necessary here. It is only if these actions are done *vigorously* that the right shape results. Mere flabby rounding and closing will not produce *Aw, Oh* and *Oo*, which require considerable laryngeal and back-throat tension before their character can emerge. This tension at its highest accompanies a tensely-shaped mouth. But the whole range of vowels *can* be sung both with or without a rounded mouth if the throat does its part properly: an important point; but of this more, later.

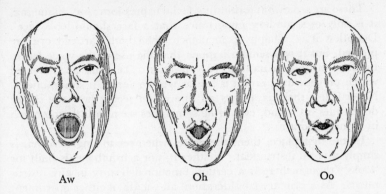

Aw   Oh   Oo

Diagrams of Aw, Oh and Oo in their fully-formed state, showing closure of the lips and drawn-in, elongated shape of the face.

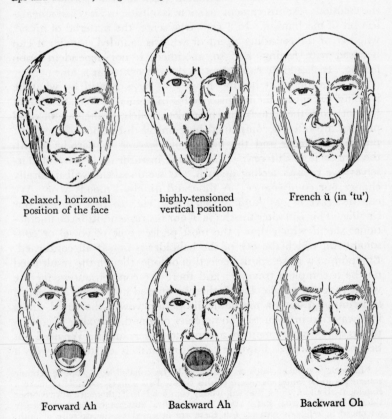

Relaxed, horizontal   highly-tensioned   French ŭ (in 'tu')
position of the face   vertical position

Forward Ah   Backward Ah   Backward Oh

Diagrams of other facial positions

These are somewhat forbidding facial expressions; but, in singing, it is only of secondary importance that a face should look 'nice'. Doubtless it is a happy coincidence when both ear and eye are pleased, but it will seldom happen that the use of the voice leaves the face in quite a natural, easy position. Tensions are involved which prevent this; and it is just as well to accept it straightaway. Nevertheless there is always an interest in seeing how the singer determines his sound, even if he sometimes seems a little too much in earnest about it.

In the first place, then, the voice, when set to sing a vowel, is simply a vocal instrument. Neither it, nor a trombone, is built for 'looks' (though there is a certain functional beauty in any instrument). As a primary consideration, all we ask of either instrument is that it should produce its best and most characteristic sound, which certainly affects us emotionally, but does not proceed from the emotions. An instrument, as such, is outside us; it is just a heartless bit of mechanism. In a very true sense, the material of music, whether of the sounding agent or what is sounded, though it can be used with feeling, and so, modified, is not dependent upon feeling. It should be competent to do its work; that is all.[1]

An instrumentalist hardly shows that he is moved by what he is doing, except by the intensity of his movements. We are content (or not) with the sounds that he makes, which, in the case of wind players, are often accompanied by comical distortions of the face: puffed-out cheeks and the like, easily leading to parody. With the singer it is different. The vocal instrument is part of ourselves; we register feeling upon it. As we do so this will naturally change our countenance. A thousand different moods arise. We can be grave or gay, amiable or angry, etc., so that we 'act' our singing. This will alter the shape of our instrument, its basic unemotional sound which shows the most perfect type of vowel or consonant—in which the eye of the beholder is not at all concerned. Emotion, in a sense, spoils perfection of tone, though the result need not be a complete travesty; and there are compensations, for the whole range of vocal colour is thereby opened up. When emotion is superimposed upon a mechanically perfect vowel, the vowel varies in a way that introduces a complexity of sound, a mixing of colour, that is quite staggering if we attempt to understand it. We need not be unduly alarmed, however. We are unlikely to start off with a

[1] Extreme statements such as this need to be collated with complementary statements to be found elsewhere in this book. It is scarcely possible to make a statement about anything that will wholly commend itself; there are always other sides to it. It is true that certain 'ne plus ultra' statements are dogmatically advanced in religious systems, but these are accepted by the exercise of faith, not reason.

perfect vowel, and at times, freed from ideal restraint, the singer can look as charming as we would wish to see her. Then we shall be delighted by a smiling face, instead of a serious one, and with it will come the muscular release that a smile always brings.

A warning. The energetic use of the lips and cheeks is apt to close the throat, or, perhaps it would be better to say, the orifice of the throat (at the tonsils), for it is the orifice that seems specially affected. This tendency must be counteracted. Strong tensions, i.e., strong contracting movements in any part of the instrument, play upon the throat, as upon everything else; and, when they do so, the orifice has to be *stretched* open; it will not open easily—mere relaxation will not open it (*v.* p. 88). Vocal communication depends upon a clear channel through which the sound can pass. This may be blocked at either end of the mouth. Both the front and back orifices should be fully opened *before* a vowel starts, and should be kept open for a short period *after* it ends; otherwise imperfect, changeful vowelling must result. There must be no gradual opening. Singers find this difficult, because they have seldom developed the muscles of the face and mouth sufficiently to have control of them. They will hold the orifices open for a short time when told to do so, but will as quickly close them, unless continuously reminded. If wrong closure can be avoided, it is certain that the grandest vowels are produced by the highly-tensioned (and seemingly extreme) means indicated in our diagrams. Throughout this book, however, the need for an infinite variety of treatment is stressed. Sometimes shaping must be tremendously purposeful, at others almost nonchalant.

Placing the Voice

Good placing of the voice is good pronunciation, neither more nor less. But there is still something to do after the voice is placed, in the way of vocal emission. It is sometimes believed that a voice should be 'placed' at a certain spot; forward, ringing on the hard palate, or what not. A certain very well-known professor of singing and legitimately honoured in a general way, used to advocate that different notes should ring on different teeth; but of course there is no sense in this. The 'place' of the voice is literally anywhere. There are an infinite number of positions according to the infinitude of colours of which the voice is capable: all of them good in their way, the only proviso being that the colour should fit the occasion.

The placing of the voice naturally groups itself under three headings—

a forward placing,

a midway placing, and

a backward placing,

and these positions may be taken as in reference to the tongue. A forward placing feels that it is near the tongue tip; a midway placing that it is about central on the tongue; and a backward that it is in the region of the tongue root.

Vowels, as we know, are tone qualities and these qualities favour certain positions. Ee, for instance, lies very forward in its untempered state. Oo, at the other extreme, is very low-lying. Thus, the nature of the different vowels, taken generically, demands a different placing; then this generic nature can be modified to a slightly different shade of colour, and this, in its turn, will induce a change of placing. High notes, too, need a different placing from low notes. Easy resonation depends upon it. Roughly speaking, there cannot be a combination of both forward and backward tone. It must be either the one or the other. Everything is and must be in its place, and there is a place for everything. Certain vowels do not take kindly to high notes, and have to be treated very carefully as the pitch rises. The clearest instance of this is the French vowel u (in 'tu'), which is the same as the German modified ü (in 'müde'). If we try to sing it on an upward scale say from we shall find that as we go up, there will be

a feeling of increasing constriction, on account of the tendency of the larynx to rise; till perhaps on the octave, or a little higher, we shall get no sound at all. The voice will stop and pack up. If, however, we can preserve an open throat the vowel can be sung. This of course implies considerable effort, but it produces the desired result.

Language means 'tongueiness', and the word has become a sort of generic term for all kinds of communication just as a race of mutes might call their methods of communication 'handiness', and talk (by gesture) of a 'handiness' of grimace though it would relate to the head; Wordsworth even recognizes Nature as 'the language of the sense'. However this may be, language is largely determined by the tongue.[1] In most of the operations of speech the tongue is

[1] Though this is so, it is nevertheless exceedingly good practice to try to speak without using the tongue at all; letting it lie quite flat and quiescent in the pit of the mouth—as it will do if wholly relaxed. The tongue always has a tendency to automatic nervous action which causes it to rise at the back and block the throat, which thereby prevents the proper pronunciation of the long vowels Ah, Aw, Oh,

called into play. Its position alters for every vowel. Even when it is supposed to lie flat and immobile, as for the series of vowels Ah – Oo, it still accommodates itself to the different sounds; and it is very much concerned with consonantal utterance—there is scarcely a consonant in which the tongue is quiescent. So that, as we have said, it is right that we should group our vowels with reference to the tongue. If we do so, we shall see that tongue positions will give us, in very general terms, three kinds of vowel: front, central and back. Of these, three primary ones are recognized:[1]

Ee, Ah, Oo,

corresponding to the aforementioned tongue positions. From them branch forth the whole series of vowels, extending from the clearest fundamental types to those which register differences so minute as to be barely detected.

To begin, then, with the primaries

Ee – Ah – Oo.

These represent narrow, full, long vowels. Joined to them by a sort of natural affinity are the vowels Ay, Aw and Oh, making the full series of main vowels.

Ee,   Ay – Ah,   Aw – Oh,   Oo.
(peep) (pate) (laugh) (law) (boat) (boot)

Authorities agree that there are two forms of these: narrow and wide.

The foregoing are in the narrow category; what we call short vowels are in the wide. Ee and Oo are considered typical of the narrow form; ĭ (pit) and ŏ (pot) of the wide.

It is a little debatable whether these terms are very clear. One might prefer horizontal $\subset$ and vertical ( ) as indicating shape. What is sure is that the vertical (or in the above terminology, 'wide') shape is produced by a process of contracting the 'narrow'

Oo and their correlative short vowels. Loosening exercise is therefore often essential.

[1] It is curious to note that there is a parallelism between *visual and audible colour*, though perhaps too much should not be made of it. Three primary visual colours are also recognized, red, yellow and blue; other colours are derivative from these. Similarly vowels seem to be grouped in a tripartite way, roughly corresponding to the resonance of nose, mouth and neck. If we take the long vowels, *Ee* and *Ay*, *Ah* and *Aw*, *Oh* and *Oo*, they seem to form three distinct groups. *Ee* and *Ay* are nasal in quality; *Ah* and *Aw* have the characteristics of the completely open mouth; *Oh* and *Oo* of the open neck. Emotionally there may also be said to be a correspondence between this threefold division of visual and audible colour. Red is flaming, fiery—so is the '*Ee*' vowel group *par excellence*; yellow is voluminous, pervasive, life-giving (as in sunlight)—so is the '*Ah*' group; blue is discreet, deep, lacking in luminosity—so is the '*Oh*' group. Perhaps there is more in these correspondences than we are now entitled to admit. Visual and audible colour may ultimately be capable of combination and synchronization in a more certain and scientific way than is possible at present. At any rate the foregoing is of interest.

shape; and that it is quite obvious that it is mechanically impossible for a vowel to be both narrow and wide—⌒ becomes

if the extremities of the arches[1] are brought together, the length of the curve remaining constant. Therefore 'narrow' and 'wide' are to be associated with 'free' and 'contracted'. The free form tends to shallowness of quality, the contracted form to depth; and this is an important distinction because concentrated, 'drawn in' sounds are always those which represent the expressive element in performance.

From these six narrow long vowels, then, are to be derived, by contraction, their related six wide short ones. The contraction seems to take place at the throat and back of the mouth, largely by bringing the faucal pillars (tonsils) closer together, with consequent raising of the soft palate.

Long vowels:

Ee – Ay – Ah – Aw – Oh – Oo

corresponding short vowels:

ĭ – ĕ – ă – ŏ – ŭ – ŏŏ

(kick) – (keg) – (cat) – (cot) – (gut) – (could)

Ee and Ay, being at the extreme end, contract, as they must, towards Oo; Oh and Oo contract in the opposite direction towards Ee, which is the only way open to them to contract; Ah and Aw, being central, contract centrally.

In terms of unvoiced resonantal pitch (which can be heard by just blowing through the cavity concerned) it will be found that the pitch of the long vowels falls, progressively from Ee – Oo, whereas that of the short vowels rises from ĭ – ŏŏ. This shows that the cavities of the long vowels get larger and looser in the above order, but that those of the short vowels get smaller and tighter: an inverse process.

The above are, as it were, the twelve main positions of the voice.

Then all of these long and short vowels can in their turn be placed in front, centrally, or back, though in every case an alteration of position means, strictly, a change of vowel. Or we may simply call it a different shade of the same vowel: for it is easy to recognize the same type of vowel in these three guises.

It is impossible, or at any rate, impracticable here, to give alphabetical or other symbols for all these variants; one must be content to register them in words which contain them, and an approximate list of such words might be:

---

[1] In this case that arch is at the uvula and, below, at the back of the tongue.

Table of 36 English Vowel Positions.

	Ee	ĭ	Ay	ĕ	Ah	ă	Aw	ŏ	Oh	ŭ	Oo	ŏŏ
Front	peep peat feet	pip tip pit	pale tape fate	pet fetch whet	yard pass chaff	pat tap chat	taut thought sought	top pop pot	tote yoke poach	pup touch put (in golf)	poop toot tooth	foot put puss
Central	mere near beer	tilt rill nil	nail lane main	neck lend men	path gnash lack	land ran man	lawn gnaw shawl	loll long gone	roe roll roam	lull lung rush	moon moor sure	look nook shook
Back	green stream glean	give live will	shade drain swathe	dwell tread spread	harm alms draught	brag drag lamb	oil warm mawl	mob shone blob	home moan strove	shrug mug mull	woo'd whose swoon	wool wood hood

These vowels are as I speak them, personally; just as they come in a normal, effortless way, though taking care that the 'voiced' consonants *are* voiced. With greater effort they will tend either to be brought further forward or to recede and thicken. Perhaps owing to a long training in vocal sound, particularly from the musical aspect, my vowels are a little different from those heard in the ordinary run of speech which might suggest a slightly different analysis. I believe that I can discriminate sound quality rather exceptionally; even so, I may be slightly wrong in what I think is the sound of my own voice. Exact observation is most difficult, and, as well, the shade of sounds may vary from moment to moment.

It is most important to realize that advanced vocal expression may almost obliterate the natural qualities of vowels in respect of their volume and colour: such qualities as probably decided choice of sound in primitive word-making. Small vowels (such as Ee or ă) can be enlarged till they become quite voluminous; large vowels can be contracted; brightly coloured vowels, dulled and darkened; and so on. Unification of tone—indispensable to preservation of mood—is bound to bring this about. Grave moods will require the large shapes and sombre colourings of Oh and Oo with every vowel; gay moods, the smaller shapes and brighter colourings of Ee and Ay.

It is not at all easy to decide upon the particular word we want; but we are helped by the facts: that with frontal vowels the mechanism will be inclined to tightness, with backward vowels to looseness. Further, forward positions will be more open in the front of the mouth; backward positions in the neck. And with forward positions the tongue will be raised and advanced; with backward, down and drawn back.

Therefore if we find a shade of vowel falling in with these conditions it is likely to be the one of which we are in search.[1]

As the main six long vowels and their short derivatives are themselves placed either to the front, midway or back, it is evident that if, say, they are to the front, they will only have a further central and back form; or if to the back, a further central and front form, etc., three positions in all. This will give us a total of thirty-six positions, which corresponds to the number listed in Melville Bell's *Visible Speech*, but not quite to the actual vowels. The present method of approach is a little different—it is personal to the author

---

[1] The placing of vowels is, however, a very elusive matter. In a *Poet's Notebook*, the author (Edith Sitwell) contrasts the sound (arising in a poem of Gerard Manley Hopkins), of 'the sharp *u* of "bugle" melting into the softer *u* of "blue" ' in the words 'bugle-blue'. Why should these *u*'s be different? Probably because the *u* in bugle is put between two short, thrusting explodents which drive it from its natural bed (the neck); while in 'blue' it can settle there comfortably and quietly.

—but if not as scientific, it has the merit of symmetry and simplicity —and perhaps can thus be more easily grasped.[1]

Another help in locating these frontal, central or backward vowels is that of placing beside them a consonant which is articulated frontally like P or T, centrally like L, or gutturally like G or B. This has been followed in the preceding table. The truth is that vowels are likely to be tugged in all directions by consonants; perhaps not greatly off their pitch (or place) but sufficiently so as to induce a different shading of their tone. Tight consonants like T or K will tend to tighten the vowels associated with them; loose consonants like L or M to loosen the vowel, with a corresponding influence on the quality. By conscious art, however, we can entirely override what we may call natural pronunciation, and put any vowel where we like; give it, in short, any shade.

The foregoing thirty-six vowels represent our English speech— almost completely. Perhaps a slightly different shading is to be observed in 'bird' and a more forward Ah in the Cockney 'now' (n+ah+oo); also that maid-of-all-work ŭ is subject to more variation than we have allowed for: from the nondescript, lazily-shaped, very backward ŭ in the first vowel of 'again' or the second of 'moment' to a nearly similar, but (to the author) slightly more open sound of the same vowel in 'earth'. Also some might say that the Oh in 'eloquence' is a little more towards ŏ than is given in our table.

The personal pronoun 'I' also may need attention. Its pronunciation is generally given as Ah+Ee, and it certainly is a derivative from Ah, but it may be either of a backward or forward quality. If the former, as in an ordinary pronunciation of the word 'die', it will have a tinge of Uh in it; if the latter, as in 'tie', it will be more of an Ah opened and brought forward. In a *very* forward Ah there may even be a tendency to a whitish quality. 'I' is a very beautiful sound, in any position, but very subtle to catch. It is hardly ever heard to perfection, or in a thoroughly characteristic form, but the vowel occurs so often that it ought to be pronounced well.[2]

What is much more important is the pronunciation of certain foreign vowels that do not come into our list at all, but which the student needs absolutely to master. In a general way our English speech lies more back than French or Italian speech, and also one or two sounds of German speech. Certain sounds of these languages

---

[1] The principle of tension does not seem to be allowed for sufficiently in other systems of vowel mechanism. For instance, the difference between 'pot' and 'long' is largely a matter of relative tightness and looseness. That is where the artist comes in: for he often has to eliminate or modify the tendencies of vowels, making such as are naturally thin and scraggy, full and round.

[2] The student should also read what is said about 'I' in Part 2, p. 305.

are of very small calibre and are brought more to the front than are any English vowels. Two such sounds must be specially noted and studied, those in French 'tu' or its German equivalent modified ü in 'müde', and the eu in French 'feu', or German 'schöne', which is the same. A strong pursing of the lips is required in each case to produce these vowels, which must not fall back into English Oo in the first case or short ŭ in the second. Of these two vowels u (tu) is the farthest forward; eu (feu) slightly more open and back. A position of the lips, as in whistling, will almost give the sound of u; that of eu is very difficult to the Englishman. Other subtleties of vowel are to be heard in the French words 'lune', 'une', 'de', 'veuf', 'un'. They cannot be accommodated to our English vowel system. And what are called the French (four) orinasals are also quite foreign to our own speech. These are to be heard in the sentence 'mon grand chien brun'. Mechanically they are produced by freeing the uvula (letting it fall down and forward) thus allowing the sound stream to enter *both* mouth *and* nose. These orinasals are splendid for developing the sense of nasal sound, and adding to the phonetic armoury of the singer, who should be capable of pronouncing all possible sounds, whether he uses them or not.

We have seen that vowels are modified by (1) consonantal influence. They are also modified by (2) emotional significance.

An alteration of position takes place when we feel the *sense* of words to be different. Thus with the same vowel Ay in the words 'grave' and 'gay' the Ay in 'grave' will be appreciably darker and deeper than the Ay in 'gay'; similarly with the ă in 'sad' and 'happy', or the Ah in 'dark' and 'laugh', etc.

Well-placed notes do not only concern tone but time. Tone and time go together, because both depend upon tension. If tension fail with regard to the one, the tone will lack concentration and that quality which gives timbre and telling power to a note; if it fail with regard to the latter, precision and the absolute point or place of note articulation cannot be established. In other words, tone quality and rhythm are vitally interconnected; they march side by side under the ægis of tension. In this connection it is to be remarked that it is the rarest thing to hear perfectly true time proportions from anyone, because the will is insufficiently engaged. Tension again!

EMOTIONAL COLOURING

Perhaps the best way for the singer to regard the secondary modifications contained in the last Table is as colouring, involving no precision as to placing; just a general movement of the vowels forwards or backwards, according to the expression of the moment.

We need not distinguish these vowels intellectually; we can treat them emotionally scarcely knowing how. Some songs are bright in character; for them a light forward placing will be appropriate; others are sombre and will require a heavier, backward tone. The rationale of the situation is very like that of the play of sunlight upon a scene which at one time will be illuminated by almost dazzling rays, at another almost obscured—it is the same with the mood of the human heart. If it is looked upon in this way, the tone registers an infinite number of shades, merging imperceptibly the one into the other. Vocal tone represents a selection from an infinitude of possible vowels. We have chosen a relatively small number of such vowels, for reasons which will be explained later (on p. 139); but just as the pictorial artist mixes his colours, taking them out of their particular category to suit his own purposes, so does the singer. The former does not necessarily paint with a few pure colours, nor does the singer paint his vocal picture with pure vowels alone, whatever that may mean.

A complete analysis of tone is impossible, just as is an analysis of personality. We may recognize harmonics in each—the salient features—but the sum total will defy understanding. It cannot be got at by science, unless by that finest of scientific instruments, the ear, which, in the process of hearing, analyses sound in a way that no inanimate instrument can. It breaks up sound, but it does not present us with the pieces; it integrates them in an impression. We can hear subtleties that analytical knowledge will totally fail to account for. This is the artist's approach and the deepest penetration comes with it. The scientific approach, in art, is useful perhaps in telling the artist what he ought not to do—describing the intellectual limits of his work, the bounds in which he should operate if he wishes to be understood; it can never tell him what he *can* do. Music, like religion, is about what you don't and cannot understand.

> *Like aught that for its grace may be dear,*
> *And yet dearer for its mystery.*

If it competes with nature, science, though it can do wonders, can only produce *ersatz*. Science may split the atom and even disintegrate the world; but it can never put them together again. It enables us to mass-produce tone, but it is at the expense of quality. We may say there is so little difference between the artificial counterfeit and the real thing, but it is just that little which matters. The debasement of standards of tone quality in these days bears significant witness.[1]

[1] My friend Balfour Gardiner and I were once talking about what made a fine composition—what was its hall-mark, etc. I suggested that there were many

A considerable number of vowels has been listed, but their exact sound is often a matter of dispute among phonologists. It is extremely hard to pin some vowels down. And as any vowel is subject to further modification due to personal make-up or national or local 'accent', the final result is quite outside our grasp. We have to catch our hare before we can cook it—and in the last resort vowel quality refuses to be caught, much less put into the dissecting pot. It is not too much to say that every vowel is unique; it will never be heard again just as it is uttered. And if human means cannot locate it, is quite certain that mechanical means must fail. Hearing itself—how we hear—remains a mystery, and what we hear is ultimately just as mysterious. It seems like a *reductio ad absurdum*. But we have extracted order from chaos by reducing these myriad sounds to a few which can be clearly distinguished. The principle upon which selection has been made will be discussed later.

It is estimated that there are more than a thousand *observed* sounds in human speech. The mind reels before the alphabet or symbols that would be required to record them precisely. Yet all these sounds can be perceived by those who use them. The ear can register what science cannot. Moreover the trained ear can hear differences that the ordinary ear cannot detect. The finest shades of sound are not everybody's business—at least a *conscious* use of them is not. It takes many years for a student to know what he is driving at in the way of tone; and he probably does not fully realize it till by long search or a stroke of luck, he suddenly feels that his aim has been attained.

From the table on page 121, and subsequent comments, we saw how it was possible to keep a vowel (or its genus) while altering its shade. This constitutes the art of colouring the voice; by it the singer shows his skill. The twelve long and short vowels, indeed, may be looked upon as fixed shapes or cavities, absolute constants, capable of being shifted backwards or forwards, and in this way the modification is seen to be additional and not essential to the main process of speech. It is as though tone partook both of an absolute and relative nature. The vowel Oh shows this modification very clearly. It can be made either soft or loud-toned. If the former, it will lie loose and back; if the latter the throat will tighten and the sound will move forward. It comes to this, that a different 'placing' of the voice has been made. If it is placed at the back the tendency of the voice will

compositions, not of absolutely the first rank, or by the greatest masters, which were well worth a hearing, and that there was not so much difference as all that between the best and the not-quite-so-good. His reply was: 'Charles, the difference between these two sorts of work is not the difference between sixpence and a shilling, but between elevenpence-three-farthings and a shilling; it's the farthing that counts!'

be smooth and fluty, if forward rough and reedy; since the backward placing of the voice closes the aperture leading to the nose, whereas the forward placing lowers the uvula and soft palate, and opens it. This is one of the great distinctions between forward and backward tone, of which Ee and Oo are the extreme examples. From Ee to Oo there is a gradual retrogression of nasal tone, and vice versa.

Smoothness of sound is generally speaking a virtue. The English have it, rather than the Latin races whose voices are more forward. But it must not be taken as the only virtue. When emphasis and fire are required harsher, rougher methods are necessary and this can only be achieved with a more forward production. Extreme smoothness, if prolonged, is apt to pall. It is only good *for its purpose*—we have to reiterate these last words over and over again. The 'Oo' sounds of the voice are very smooth—the farther down and back they are, the smoother they are. Nothing is as smooth as a chord on Oo; so that, in choral singing, what we call blend of voice, i.e., when the separate voices merge and unify harmoniously, is best achieved by the general placing of the voice towards Oo. 'Oo' tone is pure flute tone from which the higher harmonics are almost absent—so that the grating effects of these do not emerge. The oboe has a high harmonic formant, as it is termed, i.e., the overtones, which give it its characteristic timbre, lie high: hence the reediness of oboe tone. And lying high they require to be energized more forcibly than lower lying harmonics. Flute and clarinet tone are much more easily produced (or 'blown') than trumpet or oboe tone, just as an Oo is much more easily produced than an Ee. It is smoother, in short. But on the whole smoothness and purity of tone (that of a tuning fork is perhaps the nearest example of an absolutely pure tone since its harmonics die away almost at once, leaving just the fundamental note) is not as interesting as a rougher tone. It does not stimulate in the same way. We tire of it more quickly. And that is why voice production is usually directed forward *all'Italiano*, or in other words, given a nasal flavour. Our English tone is too often harmless and nondescript, lacking in positive character. It may be called 'amiable', the counterpart of a friendly, unaggressive nature. Joined to this amiability is often an over-measure of refinement. We know how that can worry one at times, and long for something that has just a little tendency to break bounds, even to the extent of coarseness. W. H. Mallock, a somewhat old-fashioned writer to the present literary temper, has a sly dig at what amounts to excess of smoothness. In one of his novels he writes: 'Canon Morgan's official voice was one of great refinement; and he read his prayers with a modulation so perfect, that he almost seemed to have arrested them on the way to heaven, in order that his earthly hearers might appreciate their full literary merit.' Excellently touched in! It could scarely be bettered as a warning against being too civilized. The matter with a great deal of church music is that all the life has been ironed out of it. Smooth, insipid, harmonic progressions, such as we find in many Victorian hymns and anthems; smooth rhythms, devoid of strength and incident; and that smooth, mellifluous tone beloved of parsons who really know their trade. There is a kind of refinement that includes power; another that is symptomatic of weakness. One refers to the matter only that students should be on the alert, not to give exact counsel.

REDUCTION OF VOWELS FOR SINGING PURPOSES

Having attempted to distinguish a number of vowels—thirty-six and more—in English speech, we must now proceed to simplify. It is not necessary for the singer to be as exact as all that or to decide that he must place the voice in a different position for each of these vowels. He may do so, and probably will, *but he need not know it.* Placing, to a large extent, is a matter of instinct and unconscious perception rather than of knowledge. Some vowels must be chosen and studied; others can be left to look after themselves.

We have already indicated the line of approach, which recognizes twelve vowels (six long and six short) as generic; and considers other vowel qualities as derived from these or so closely linked as not to demand official recognition. Hardly any addition to these twelve is required for singing in English. The few variants (noted on p. 123) can be used if desired but it is not necessary to do so. The foreign vowels and sounds are another matter. They *must* be differentiated from our English sounds.

A. J. Ellis (a great authority) considers that there are twenty-three spoken vowels included in all the languages in which the singer may have to sing. It is informative to give his list and against it the ten sung substitutes that he proposes.

Spoken Vowels		Sung Substitutes	
beet	Ee ⎫		
bit ⎱	i ⎬	ĭ	(bit)
witty ⎰	⎭		
bait	⎫		
bête (Fr. broad) ⎬—Ay	⎬	ĕ	(bet)
bet	ĕ ⎭		

	Spoken Vowels			Sung Substitutes	
bat		ă	ă	(as in 'ham' broader and deeper than in 'cat')	

ask	(thin)				
lah!	(broader)	}	Ah	(lah)	
lâche	(broadest)				

gnawed		Aw			
nod	}	ŏ	}	Aw	(gnawed)
no (It. ao)					

known		Oh	Oh	(known)	

pool		Oo	}		
pull		ŭ		ŭ	(pull)

jug	(broad)				
herd	(central)	}	u	(cut)	
cut	(thin)				
idea	(deep vanish)				

veuf	(Fr.)	Oe	}		
feu	(Fr.)	eo		oe	(veuf)

vue	(Fr.)	ue	ue	(vue)	

To avoid explanation of the 'glossic' symbols used for these twenty-three vowels I have simplified them to those for our English long and short vowels, but it must be understood that these twenty-three key words do represent twenty-three different sounds, and that because, say, Ah only is written above, it does not mean that it is pronounced the same in the words placed against it, but with somewhat the same variation as in my own table (p. 121).

Nevertheless the ten substitutes that Ellis gives cannot be considered sufficient. Singing is all the richer and better if at any rate our full complement of six long and six short vowels is insisted on, and, as well, the five foreign sounds given in the above list.

It is difficult to see how we can get along without

Ee	and	ĭ
Ay	,,	ĕ
Ah	,,	ă
Aw	,,	ŏ

129

F

Oh and ŭ
Oo   „   o͝o
French   u
and   eu

and, also the vowels I and Er (in 'ice' and 'earth'), both being characteristic and distinct English sounds not contained in the above list, though the former has affinity to Ah and the latter to Uh. This makes sixteen vowels in all instead of the ten to which Ellis would limit the singer. These sixteen must be regarded as fixed and generic, though as well there are a multitude of unfixed variants of these arising from emotional use.

As we have already said, the variety of vowel sounds is infinite, but with the foregoing vowels the singer can make his words quite unmistakable and secure all the basic vowel differentiation that he needs. It is no easy matter, however, to produce even one vowel to the full measure of its glory; much less sixteen.

It is difficult to see upon what principle Ellis advised the use of some of his substitutes, particularly ĭ for Ee and ĕ for Ay, since Ee and Ay and all the naturally thin vowels can be sung broadly and richly, *while still preserving their characteristic sound*, avoiding confusion with ĭ and ĕ. The tendency of singing and even fine speech is to richen and broaden the voice, by making use of neck resonance, which alone can register feeling, emotion and the deeper moods of expression. Even the Frenchman under such circumstances will not say the very forward Ee for instance that he generally uses for 'fil', but will drop it back until it almost, but not quite, reaches the position of ĭ.

There is not the least doubt that singing induces a different mode of speech than that to which we are ordinarily accustomed. It eliminates the accidents of everyday speech in favour of a more sonorous treatment of its own which one might call song-speech. It smooths out differences of pronunciation that exist and should exist in speech. In short it exchanges speech values for musical values. We see this in the singing of a foreign language, for instance. An Englishman can sing French quite well, as well as a Frenchman can; but he cannot speak French like a Frenchman and he never will. An American will often delight us with his singing, though we are by no means enamoured of his speech. One is aware, of course, that foreigners generally make a poor show when singing our language. It is often comical. But that is because they don't usually try to master the English tongue, and especially one or two peculiarities of our speech, such as in the word 'this' with its 'th' and 'ĭ', which vowel is unknown to Frenchmen or Italians except in a very few combinations like Italian 'Ci', 'Gi'. Frenchmen or Italians *could* make as good a job of singing in English as an English singer (who is often quite unintelligible in his own language), though they rarely do. English is not to be despised as a vehicle for song, whatever the foreigner may say. The Frenchman has not our broader ĭ and ŭ which give far richer musical results than Ee or U (as in 'connu') to which he is limited; and he can only show us some very constricted vowels, u ('tu') and eu ('feu') beyond those which we also possess. He may rebel at our consonants and the difficulties that they present, but it is possible to overcome them, sufficiently to ensure good *legato*. He can claim that his method of speech is beautifully clear, precise, forward; but he cannot claim that it is more musical, if by that he means a palette of richer colour.

Long and Short Vowels

A consideration of the nature of long and short vowels throws light on several vocal problems.

We have used the terms 'long' and 'short' with respect to vowels. What do we mean by them? The answer would generally be that the 'long' vowels are those which we naturally sustain in words; the 'short' ones those that we do not dwell upon. Such words as 'caught', 'cart', 'coast', exemplify the former species;[1] 'cat', 'cot', 'cut', the latter. But why do we make these vowels long and short; why do we not sustain or shorten them all alike? We obviously do not in ordinary speech, and there must be a reason for it. This reason is probably to be found in the much more restricted resonance of the so-called short vowels. Taken as a whole, *unless they are specially dealt with*, these vowels are unpleasing. They have a rather nasty aggressiveness; and, as they stand in the rough, are incapable of much 'expression'. When we speak them 'short' we bring them very forward, uttering them sharply and strongly; and in this position they are much more difficult to produce than the long vowels. Their natural habitat is the head; resonance is more distant from the vocal cords, and therefore is not so easily put into vibration. High nasal sound does not sustain comfortably—the prolongation of such sounds requires great physical effort. Therefore we get over such vowels as quickly as we can. There is thus a practical as well as æsthetic reason for their 'shortness'. The art of singing, however, consists largely in making it easy to sustain difficult sounds, and this is always achieved by skilful adjustment of the throat. Throat resonance, as we have indicated, is not natural to 'short' vowels (which by their very shortness drive away from the throat); it has

[1]Though we should observe that the vowels in these words are not of the *same* length.

to be added by the artist, as it were by transcending the natural limitations of his material. But this he can well do.

'Short' vowels are peculiar to English and give a great variety to our speech. There are practically none in the Romance languages, as has been noted. They have a certain hardness of tone which is capable of being carried to the utmost extreme; but in the best and most interesting types of men or things a quality of hardness (veiled or overt) is generally present. It gives a salty contrast to the sweetness that might otherwise prevail. It represents a bony element rather than the softer elements of fat and flesh in speech; of form rather than feeling, owing to the needs of a more precise and compact shape than is required by the long vowels. Take our English word 'Philharmonic' and compare it with its foreign equivalent 'Philharmonia'. The latter word with its long vowels is more ample, but the sparser economy of the former seems (to the writer, at any rate) to be more potent, more full of directness, energy, and durability—in short, to have more character. Perhaps this is insular prejudice; but what is not debatable is the increased differentiation of colour that these short vowels bring, also the increased range of expression that they open up. The long vowels become rather wearisome with their comparatively languid movement and continuous flood of over-lush sound. They never let the light in. The short vowels do, and they, moreover, give a resilience to speech that is all their own. As a means of *staccato* utterance and sharp attack they serve better than the long vowels (which are, as it were, too heavy to bounce and bound) because they are on the whole of smaller calibre and so can be stopped and discontinued more speedily.

The long vowels tend to *legato*; they almost demand to be held—this is recognized in the nomenclature of 'long' and 'short'. But it must not be supposed that the 'short' vowels cannot be 'held' as well as 'long' vowels. If they are properly sung, with the right pharyngeal undertone, they are equally susceptible to *legato*, and of course, the exigencies of song require them to be sustained. It comes to this: that though each type of vowel has a natural tendency towards either 'long' or 'short', the singer's business is generally to obliterate such tendency and make any vowel serve to the full such expressive purpose as the occasion demands. The 'long' vowels have sometimes to be sung in the shortest possible manner, with the cut and sharpness of a 'short' vowel, and the 'short' vowels have to be given the flow and liquidity of the 'long' vowels. In this way unity of vowelling is achieved.

For what might be called general work, the English vowel system is unrivalled; it is 'up to anything'—every mood, every twist of speech. Other languages are far more limited in their possibilities, far less open to the delineation of shades of character; though for sheer ease and *sostenuto* they perhaps compete more favourably than our own. Ease, however, does not cover the whole ground. A touch of difficulty, if it be well overcome (as it can be in this case) adds spice. Let it be repeated: our short vowels *can* be sung so that they are almost, if not quite, the equal of the long vowels. There is no need to apologize for them but rather to give thanks.

To compare the long and short vowels more closely. When vowel shapes are (a) determined by the tongue, the short vowels are the richer, i.e., they open up more deep neck resonance; when (b) determined by the lips the long vowels have a resonantal advantage.

(a)

ĭ (grin) is a more voluminous vowel than Ee (green)
ĕ (met)   ,,   ,,   ,,   ,,   ,, Ay (mate)

(b)

ŏ (cot) cannot be given the amplitude of Aw (caught)
ŭ (cut)   ,,   ,,   ,,   ,,   Oh (coat)
nor ŏŏ (full) given the amplitude of   Oo (fool)
also ă (cat) is not as rich-toned as   Ah (cart)

The upshot of it is that the long vowels are a little more suited to *legato* on the whole, the short vowels to *staccato*; or they can be so suited.

Nevertheless, as we have observed, in ordinary speech the short vowels are spoken abruptly. We do not usually sustain them, unless we wish to invest them with considerable emotion. Such phrases as

'Bats wink in the belfry'

or 'Crickets chirp on the bank'

(in which the vowels are short except the 'ur' in 'chirp'), if casually spoken, would be likely to exhibit just pin-pricks of vowel sound and be very unsatisfying from a musical point of view, which requires a certain breadth of vowel utterance even in *staccato*. The musical ear has to get a sure hold of sound in order to establish clear pitch relationships (which do not exist in speech) and this is, of course, best secured by *legato*; so that it is quite a good plan to think of *staccato* as *legato*, giving a *legato* sense to notes even though they are separated. And herein lies a difference between speech and song. In ordinary speech vowels are rarely sustained. The habit of vocal continuity has to be cultivated in speaking; then it becomes *musical* speech, which speech seldom is. 'Sing as you would speak' has much to commend it as a maxim—art has always to be checked and refreshed by nature; but 'speak as you would sing' is far better advice, or at any rate good additional advice where expressive utterance—art in short—is concerned. We say 'ris'n', 'littl' ' for 'ris-en', 'lit-tle', quite unashamedly, and are even instructed by some authorities to carry over this procedure into singing. But such miserable truncation is absolutely wrong, and we need to be on guard against it. If it is according to nature—everything we do can, of course, be attributed to nature—then we must improve upon nature. The truth is that such speaking is only 'natural' because it is lazy. One need not say 'ris-ĕn', which would make too heavy a second syllable, spoiling the delicate rhythm and balance of the word, but 'ris-ŭn', or something like it, is certainly to be preferred, even in speech, to 'ris'n' which is entirely without dignity or sonority; and the same with regard to 'littl' '. One of the chief desiderata is to get beautiful rhythmic movement into such words and this is secured by light easy endings which nevertheless retain a full measure of vowel sound. The use of the long vowel Ee instead of short ĭ is also another great source of ugliness. How often does one hear 'Ree-joice great-lee', etc.?

Diphthongs

Diphthongs, or double vowels, are very characteristic of English speech. They are scarcely found in the French language, and are used but rarely in Italian. In English, in spite of our consonants, they tend to give the flow of sound that is characteristic of our own tongue, easing and smoothing the general vowel scheme by reason of the subordinate vowel that is included in them. This vowel acts as a link between the more important elements of the vocal sound; and as well focusses the voice when it occurs at the start of the diphthong, as in the word 'you' (=ee+Oo), and when it occurs at the end as in 'I' (=ah+ee), saves it from disintegration.[1]

When it is initial, it acts as a 'take-off' before the voice plunges into the main vowel; when final, as a graceful retirement, the one giving impetus to the sound, the other easing its withdrawal.

We must distinguish between two connected vowels of comparatively equal weight, as in 'a-orta', 'o-asis', and the true diphthong which consists of a main vowel gradually *gliding* into a subordinate one ('I'=Ah+ee), or vice versa ('you'=ee+Oo). In either case it is swiftly touched in as a sort of preliminary 'articulation' or a mere final 'vanish', and must not be dwelt upon.

Diphthongs require to be sung very carefully. The ear must be wide awake to their abuse, ready to detect when a diphthongal

---

[1] In *every* such case where 'ee' is written it should be taken as 'i'. We have only noted it ee to accord with general, but entirely wrong practice.

vowel is unnecessarily added (as it often is);[1] or turned into a more important vowel, thereby drawing undue attention to itself, as in the word 'rejoice', which may often be heard as 'ree-jaw-ees' (or nearly so) with each vowel long instead of 'rĭ-jaw-ĭs' (with the accent on aw) giving the true rhythm of the word. The danger of dwelling too long on the subordinate vowel is always present, particularly when the latter is the second vowel. An amusing example of this possibility appeared in a recent form of serio-comic Cockney adieu: 'good-by-ee!'; but it is not so amusing when trained singers do much the same thing.

When two slurred notes have to be sung to a diphthong another common fault is that of giving the subordinate vowel to the second note. Thus instead of singing

the passage is apt to become something like

in which an obscure 'u' does duty for the 'ar' and 'er' in 'hear' and 'prayer', making what is called a 'murmur' diphthong.

With a diphthongal word ending with a consonant, the fault is still more likely to occur, e.g.,

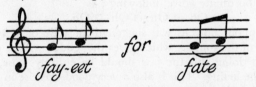

We have remarked upon the tendency of many of our vowels to diphthongal utterance. If we take the usual 'school' series of vowels, A E I O U, only one of these is an approximately pure vowel—the second; and this is perhaps because it lies at the extreme end of vowel production. I and U, must, of course, be regarded as diphthongs, 'Ah+ee' and 'ee+Oo'; but, as well, A if properly

[1] The tendency to make a diphthong of what should be a single sustained vowel is a most frequent cause of poor *legato*: for though diphthongs liquify tone they also close it in, and nothing but a maximum of open positions of the voice will suffice for the best continuity of sound.

sung, will always tend to vanish into ee, and likewise O into oo. And this is a thing that voice trainers should insist upon, as it develops that most necessary factor in a good vocal style, concentration of voice. By this process the voice is kept together, instead of dispersing weakly.

The subordinate diphthongal vowel is nearly always a form of Ee or Oo, with the Ee generally modified to ĭ ('hit') or y ('pity') to make it less prominent and easier to pronounce. As already noted, this modification of the Ee to ĭ is most important.

Though we may write 'Ee – Oo' for 'you', we must not so pronounce it. If we do, the depth of tone in Oo will almost certainly be destroyed or prevented by the thin forward preliminary sound of Ee—and Oo is the vowel that has to be dwelt upon.

Almost at all times what we want is fullness of tone. Ee never gives this, unless the neck is brought into play. Then Ee becomes ĭ, or approximates to it.

Excellent study is to be obtained by putting a preliminary Y (which is almost like a very closed Ee) to all vowels thus making them diphthongal. An exercise like

y.Ee – y.Ee – y.Ee – y.Ee, etc. or
y.Ay – y.Ay – y.Ay – y.Ay, etc.

uttered repeatedly and quickly upon a sustained note will often help to give thrust and direction to a voice which is lacking in those qualities. The Y of course acts as a consonant which momentarily stops the vocal flow, thereby gathering energy for a much more vital release of sound than would otherwise be the case.

The gliding nature of a diphthong is best shown if the main vowel is a deep and broad one, like Oh. Then if this vowel is sung *first*, with the subordinate vowel following , as

Oh – ĭ Oh – ĭ Oh – ĭ Oh

on a continuous note as was suggested for y.Ee or y.Ay, a wavy movement of the tongue, which gives the 'glide', will be easily perceived. In doing this the jaw should be entirely loose, with the tongue alone acting. This is also a very good exercise in relaxation and is much to be commended to students.

The rising of the tongue for i—it will *seem* to take place at the tongue root, right at the back—gives the impression that it is accompanied by a rising of the pitch, even though the note remains constant, much as in this diagram:

Oh – i   Oh – i Oh – i Oh – i Oh

This is due to the fact that as the tongue rises a higher resonantal pitch is involved; also, and this is contingent upon it, the higher harmonics implicit in the vowel Y or Ee give this effect; or perhaps it is just that when a smaller position of the voice proceeds to a larger the latter gives a feeling of greater depth and lower pitch, for the same impression happens even with 'woe' (Oo+Oh), though Oo and Oh are much the same type of sound as regards resonance.

A diphthong thus affords an easy transition from one position of the mechanism to another. That is its use and probably natural function. Hence the liquidity of voice which it favours. It avoids bumping from sound to sound, by reason of the undulating process that we have described.

In any case the counsel must be: do not dwell unduly on the subordinate vowel, and place it at exactly the right time-spot, treating it as a consonant should be treated. If the subordinate vowel is preliminary it should be articulated before the beat, if it is final at the end of the beat: e.g.,

or nearly so. We shall speak more later of the exact pronunciation of I.

There are also triphthongs, to the performance of which the same treatment holds good, e.g.,

taking, therefore, a little longer on the last two vowels 'ee-r' than is needed for the single vowel in 'Ah-ee' (I).

Again, the peculiarity of a diphthong is the glide between the two vowels, not their mere proximity, so that a sort of *portamento* of the sound occurs in respect of vowel quality, just as it occurs in respect of pitch.

A diphthong must be regarded as a monosyllable, in fact as a small organism. Contrast the following words:

137

F*

> Joy
> Joey
> Oyez
> coincide
> coincident.

Only in the first, 'Joy', can the 'oy' be called a real diphthong. 'Joey', though it seems similar, has already a tendency to a bi-syllable. 'Oyez'=Oh+eeAy, and is distinctly bi-syllabic, the diphthong being on the last syllable. In 'co-incide' we feel the Oh and i to be separate, the i becoming like the short vowel ĭ. With 'coincident' we get 'co-in-ci-dent', in which the i, owing to the strong accent on 'in', is rather different from the i in 'coincide', being driven further forward. These are some of the differences and refinements of pronunciation that are often met with in what are ostensibly the same forms of sound.

The scope of this book will seldom allow such detailed analysis, but Alexander J. Ellis's *Pronunciation for Singers*, though published in 1877, still holds first place for the exhaustive information which it gives.

Five true diphthongs are used in English:

Ay–ee[1]	('aim')
Ah–ee	('mine')
Ah–oo	('fowl')
Aw–ee	('foil')
ee–Oo	('feud')

N.B. Oh–ee is only heard in French, as in 'royaume' (kingdom), though the French diphthong is not exactly the same as Oh–ee; and possibly in one German word 'boje' (buoy).)

Or the order of the vowels may be reversed:

ee–Ay	('yea')
ee–Ah	('yard')
oo–Ah	('waft')
ee–Aw	('yawn')
Oo–ee	('weed')

A word more should be said about the final R, which may be a weakened form of the vowel ŭ (as in 'peer'), and so partakes of the nature of a diphthong. Strong vowels followed by this sound are often called 'murmur' diphthongs, though they are not recognized among the true diphthongs in the foregoing list. It is a moot point whether a shade of *trilled* R should be added after the ŭ when it is written in a word like 'peer'. Sometimes there is not time to do so, and then the omission of the 'R' is perfectly correct; at other times,

[1] We have given the usual notation of these diphthongal vowels but *v.* para. 3 next page.

and when it is possible, it seems (to the writer) that there is an advantage in intelligibility to give the slightest final touch of R. Thus 'peer' may be pronounced either 'pĭ+ŭ' or 'pĭ+ŭ+r', as occasion arises.[1] What must not be done is to tack this ŭ vanish on to a word that should not have it: e.g., 'pay+ŭ' should never be said for 'pay', only for 'pair' (=pĕ–ŭ, approximately, with mute R). This adding of a vowel is by no means an unusual habit, particularly after a consonant. Thus 'pair' may easily become 'pĕ+ŭ+r+ŭ' if good watch is not kept on what is happening. It may arise from overanxiety as to the clearness of final consonants, e.g., 'oak-ŭ and -ŭ elm-ŭ' (for 'oak and elm'), but it can never be allowed.

At the risk of over-emphasis (as the matter is so important), it must again be made thoroughly clear that nearly all the faults in diphthongal treatment come from the secondary vowel Ee, as in 'py-een' (pine). If this vowel is taken as Ee it will almost assuredly be dwelt upon unduly. It *must* be sung as ĭ, in which case no trouble is likely to ensue: Final Ee's (as in 'beauty', though they are really ĭ's) must *always* be carefully watched and avoided. Indeed Ee is seldom, if ever, used for a final syllable, and in its raw form has scarcely any place in either speech, or singing.

The vowel ĭ is, especially, the symbol of good, low-lying, 'bedded' tone. An Ah or Ay, with a poor singer, is often pushed to Ee towards the end of its course; in which case the technique of vowelling is almost bound to be faulty throughout. The practice of ĭ is as necessary as that of Ah, and it is a good plan for the student to begin his vocal study on this less expansive, more easily managed vowel; or, perhaps, even better, on French u (in 'tu') so that it buzzes on the almost closed lips, and yet has an open throat behind it.

To conclude (in very colloquial language): Beware of sticking in diphthongs all over the place—a sure sign of poor singing—though a spot of diphthong is, often, such good lubricant to the voice!

VOWEL SELECTION

A very interesting question here emerges. What has decided the choice of our English vowels, and indeed, of the vowels in general use throughout the world?

As regards origin, we must, I think, draw a distinction between instinctive and representative sound. The one arises from an emotional impulse expressing nothing but itself—joy, anger and the like —its manifestation may be quite unconscious; the other is concerned to give a picture of something outside itself (or, it may be, within)—

---

[1] The 'e' in 'peer' is not exactly 'i' as noted, but is a slightly more forward sound, between Ee and i.

it has become a conscious effort of communication. Indeterminate noise characterizes the one; determinate vowels and consonants the other. But it may well happen that there is a relation or overlap between the two—in as much as, in both, an emotional element is concerned.

In their determinate form, vowels can be considered as panto-mimic gestures of the vocal organs, similar to the gestures which we make with our hands to reinforce feelings or ideas. The tongue, sympathetically, rises with the hands (as in Ee) to suggest height; flattens (as in Ah) to suggest calm or spaciousness; tightens (as in Aw) for feelings of grandeur, fear or reverence; combines with the rounded mouth (as in Oh) when pain or deep, inward emotion prevail; and so on, not only with the vowels but with the con-sonants. Every movement of the hands and tongue and mouth—indeed of the whole body—is, from a primitive aspect, a represen-tative movement, by which we express ourselves; these movements, postures, or positions, giving rise to the various types of sound associated with the human voice.[1] There is, obviously, a host of related meanings to a vowel or consonant: for instance Oh, as well, is representative of 'enclosure', Oo still more—language must always be fluid and ambiguous. The point is that vowels and con-sonants were originally expressive, just as animal cries are expres-sive; and that it was not till *homo sapiens* appeared upon the scene that the mind intervened to 'fabricate' words and, through artificial or chance processes, often destroy the real significance of natural sound.[2] What began as representational sound may end by being something quite different: as with the word 'egg', which is now only a symbol but originally meant 'roundness', as in the Latin 'ovum'. We should have to unearth the primitive use of the voice to understand the true signs of language, before, in so many cases, they became dissociated from meaning, through being subject to insensitive, heretical treatment.

Allowing for all this, there is as well a mechanical side, necessarily bound up with the final result. Theoretically an infinite number of vowels are possible, but though this is so, the selection made has probably been dependent upon resonantal shapes that can be clearly defined and differentiated. Too many vowels would not only be difficult to pronounce with certainty, but would sound so like their

---

[1] Those who wish to pursue this matter further can do so by referring to Sir Richard Paget's *Human Speech*, a classic on the subject. A brief but illuminating treatment is also to be found in a book recently published in America, *The Meaning of the Alphabet* by Howard Peachey.

[2] From this it follows that the equivalent of song, in primordial times, is much older than speech; yet I think we are still justified in saying (as on p. 101) that song as we understand it—the combination of words and music—in its *ordered* form, is the outcome of inflected speech, and that speech therefore precedes music.

next-door neighbours that the ear could not distinguish them. As it is, it is difficult for anyone but a practised speaker to make clear the twenty or so vowels we have agreed to use. With most people they are wide of the mark nearly all the time, when judged by a perfectly defined sound; so that age-long experience has shown that it is better to reduce the number of vowels to the manageable proportions that have been decided upon. It still remains, however, that the finest speaking does differentiate far more than poor speaking, and that the test of a good speaker or singer is of how many vowels and of how much vocal colouring he is master. The best artists can exhibit with certainty any shade of sound.

The vowels that we generally use—according to Dr. W. A. Aikin, to whom so much is due for the elucidation of vocal matters—have probably been chosen for their ease of production. As we know, there are three main resonances concerned in any vocal sound: the nose[1] which gives effectiveness to the voice, the neck which gives richness and depth, and the mouth which is the chief articulator and shaper of language.

The cavity of the nose never alters. Its resonance and the sound peculiar to it therefore remain the same. Such differences as we detect in so-called nasal sounds (M, N, ng) are due to changes in the mouth. With M the mouth is closed; with N it is open, and the tongue is raised; with 'ng' the tongue is still further modified. M can also be given varied tone. If there is little room in the mouth, owing to elevation of the tongue, M is thin and poor; with a flat tongue, rich and resonant. The point being that nasal sound *per se* is constant, invariable, like the nasal cavity itself.

With the cavities of the mouth and neck (pharynx) it is different. Both these cavities are subject to differences of shape, either by expansion or contraction, or through the agency of the raised or depressed tongue, or variation in the orifices at the front and back of the mouth. Roughly, the mouth and neck stand for two coupled resonators, which, when superimposed upon the fundamental laryngeal sound, produce what we know as vowel sound. And, as these resonators vary in volume and aperture, so differences of vowel result. In vocal tone all three resonances—mouth, neck, nose[2]— combine in varying degree, but the mouth and neck are alone responsible for vowels as such, and it is these two resonances that have to be harmonized if we are to get easy vowel positions.

A most interesting fact, or at least theory, emerges. It is only when

---

[1] By nose is, of course, meant nasal cavity.

[2] More or less nasal resonance can be used at will by the opening or closing of the back nasal orifice, through the action of the uvula and soft palate. This is a main source of tonal expression.

the relation between neck and mouth (the adjustable resonances) is relatively simple (in numerical terms) that easy vowelling results. As well, the sonority of vowels depends upon such relationship, and *that* is why certain vowels are selected for use—particularly for artistic use—as giving the best and most workable sort of sound. They pass the test of numerical simplicity.

To make this clearer. Each vowel has at least two whispered resonance notes, i.e., notes peculiar to the cavities of the mouth and neck. The one we are most apt to hear, however, is that of the mouth which can be observed by forming the mouth for any vowel and then merely blowing through the cavity (without any laryngeal sound). The cavity of the neck also has its particular sound, which can be heard with a little practice, by tapping the neck. Notes, of course, have a definite number of vibrations associated with their pitch. With easy vowelling it is *likely* to be found that the relation of neck and mouth cavity notes will be represented by a comparatively simple fraction or proportion, just as an easy interval can be so represented. Thus the central vowel Ah if well produced gives the oral resonance note of

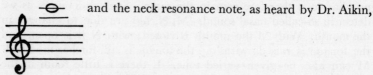

and the neck resonance note, as heard by Dr. Aikin,

is an octave lower, , so that the two sounds are as

2 : 1. With the vowel Ee it is a little different. Here the mouth sound is and the neck sound . But the two resonance sounds are nevertheless in quite a simple ratio (of, practically speaking, 2 : 3—the interval of a fifth).

Dr. Aikin's full vowel table is as follows:

(mouth)

(neck) Oo Oh Aw ŏ(cot) Ah ŭ(cut) ur(her) ă(cat) ĕ(met) Ay ĭ(hit) Ee

in which the upper note indicates the sound given by the cavity of the mouth for the vowel concerned, and the lower note for the neck. But it should be observed that Dr. Aikin was mistaken in the pitch of the higher oral notes. All these should be put up an octave, as we have just done, for the resonances that he gives for Ah and Ee. Later research has shown that Dr. Aikin's resonance notes are subject to considerable variation. The speaking voice, for instance, probably gives very different results from the singing voice, particularly as regards the lower resonance note. Vowel pronunciation differs with each individual, resonance notes are affected by laryngeal pitch, and so on. The matter is extremely complicated. I give Dr. Aikin's 'absolute' table (as regards the male voice) not because it is necessarily exact and unalterable, but to record his contribution to the subject; and show what I believe may still be found to be an underlying truth in the practical politics of singing, viz., that for easy vowelling there is a 'relatively' simple co-ordination of the resonances of the mouth and neck, which the singer generally has to discover by a long course of study and experiment. Dr. Aikin's table represents a very credible statement of the situation, if only because it seems to explain why certain vowels have been chosen for general use; and, also, why some vowels are easier to sing than others. For instance, ă (cat) according to Dr. Aikin's table is associated with the interval of a diminished fifth. This interval, with a ratio of 64 : 45, would account for the undoubted difficulty that the vowel ă nearly always presents in production, particularly on high notes.

One cannot ignore scientific observation, however, in defence of a neat theory (and Dr. Aikin's has been strongly disputed),[1] but I should not be surprised if further investigation of the singing voice —it will be remembered by those who knew Dr. Aikin that his own voice was especially rich in neck tone—proved the truth of his analysis, or, at any rate, of one aspect of the matter.

The point is that the, as it were, current coin of musical thought —pitch relationships (intervals, etc.), time relationships (as they build up in our time system)—has to be simple, based upon the simplest numerical ratios: and it would seem quite as it should be if tone quality, i.e. the relationships of vowel resonance, followed suit.

Extremely recondite relationships may be good for high mathematical reflection, but we are not likely to derive much satisfaction or substance from them. There are limits to the conditions of immediate apprehension—and that is what music calls for. The problem set by music cannot be laboriously calculated. If it takes

---

[1] W. E. Benton says, categorically, that the two principal resonance frequencies 'bear no simple harmonic relation one to another'.

a day to solve a mathematical conundrum, and that only on paper, the mathematician cannot be said to understand it in an artistic sense. Such calculations are of no use for the purposes of musical art which has to make its effect instantaneously. The logic of numbers (or anything appertaining to them) is not the same thing as the *feeling* for numbers. History shows that we have enlarged the bounds of immediate comprehension and are doing so all the time. Trained minds can appreciate note relationships that are quite obscure to the untrained. But it still remains that intellectual, or perhaps we had better say, emotional grasp, when numerical proportions are in question, depends upon a relatively simple basic structure, and that art which ignores this natural limitation is doomed to failure. To try to understand much modern artistic extravagance is not worth the trouble; it has signed its own death warrant. 'Infinite combinations of simply related material' seems to sum up effective products of art. Further, a general impression of a thing is quite different from understanding it. One gets a general impression of noise, but one cannot be said to understand noise. Its contours, shape, consistence, character, etc., are entirely vague, and therefore of no use to music which is based upon the utmost precision of its various factors.

It should be repeated that the resonance notes given in the foregoing table have nothing to do with the notes determined by the vocal cords, except in so far as they reinforce the laryngeal notes. We are here on very difficult ground. How it comes about that the more or less constant resonantal notes associated with a particular vowel can be sympathetically aroused by *any* laryngeal note; still more, how they can *equally* intensify the many fundamentals possible to the vocal cords—it is one of the aims of training to develop an even tone over the whole range of the voice—remains, even now, little short of a mystery. Recent research appears to have confused the issue, rather than elucidated it.

The matter will be further considered. Here we might conclude by saying, also, that it is highly probable that the lack of a simple harmonic co-ordination between the mouth and neck brings about a 'wave' in the emission of a vowel—much as 'beats' arise when the tuning of pianoforte strings is at fault; and that this at its worst in singing—in connection with other factors—becomes a thoroughly ungoverned *tremolo*.

Timbre and Resonance

The relation between mouth and neck, as expounded by Dr. Aikin, seems simple, comprehensible, and in accordance with the sensations of the singer. It has, moreover, a practical value: for when we have decided what whispered note the cavity of the mouth gives for a particular vowel we have only to whisper that note to get the required cavity. Thus if we whisper the note

(or one very near), and retain the cavity that produced it, we shall also have secured the necessary formation of the mouth for the vowel Ah. It is a principle that works, though slight deviations must be allowed for; and it may be considered as theoretically established. As an extra proof, if we try to *whisper* a downward scale *on this same cavity* we shall find that the Ah immediately begins to change into another vowel, till an octave below our first note the vowel will become something like Oh or Oo. Ah simply will not descend in a whisper; and if it rises it will similarly alter, proving that it is to be associated with a particular cavity and resonant note. The note that we hear on blowing through the mouth is, of course, accompanied by another one given by the resonance of the neck which we do not hear so readily. But we can alter our cavity while keeping to the vowel, since a cavity can be enlarged or diminished, giving the same resonantal note, provided its orifice is proportionately enlarged or diminished. This is a most important consideration, for experience shows that in singing a vowel we *have* to adapt its cavity to laryngeal pitch. If we could not do so, it would be impossible to sing the same vowel to different notes.

The particular sound of a vowel used to be considered as arising from the prominence of certain harmonics (*v.* p. 23) in the fundamental sound, i.e., the musical 'note' that we hear. Thus, with flute tone to which the vowel Oo may very well be likened—the second and third harmonics are apt to predominate; with oboe tone corresponding to the reedy vowel Ee—an admixture of high harmonics in great strength is shown. The old idea was that a change of fundamental note did not alter this relative disposition, i.e., that the flute note   would have as its chief

overtones   while   would have in relatively equal strength and prominence,

and so on.

But another theory—the 'formant' theory—has now been developed, according to which vowel or instrumental tone is accounted for by a group of harmonics (called the 'formant') which never alters, no matter the fundamental note that is played or sung. This theory would insist that the characteristic quality of all flute notes (*of whatever pitch*) is determined by the especial presence of or of whatever harmonics are decided upon as

being the ingredients of flute tone as such.

Resonance—or the amplification of an original sound by vibrational response of the air in some cavity like an organ pipe, or sympathetic vibrators of some material like a pianoforte string when, with the dampers up, it resounds to a sung note—is an especial feature of singing. The conundrum

'*Charles the First walked and talked*
An hour after his head was cut off'

is inexplicable in more ways than one without the necessary comma. If our heads were cut off above the larynx and we were still alive after the operation, we yet could utter very little vocal sound. The vocal cords might work but we should neither get vowels nor any strength of voice. Resonance has to be added to the initial vibration from the larynx and this function is fulfilled by the cavities of the nose, neck and mouth, which pick up sound from the larynx, in the shape of either the prime sound or its harmonics, and in so doing give it a quality and strength that would otherwise be lacking. These resonators, in short, superimpose vowels and timbre upon the initial laryngeal note, as well as increasing its power.

We know how this resonance is altered by the position of the tongue, the opening, more or less, of the mouth and throat, or the varied use of the nasal cavities. All this is clear enough. If we do such and such a thing, we get such and such a result. But it is by no means as clear how it happens in obedience to the principles already outlined. The problem is to accord the vibrations of the fundamental laryngeal note and its harmonics with the fundamental notes and harmonics of the vocal cavities associated with a vowel; for the former note may vary considerably while, theoretically, the latter notes do not alter much—if they did the vowel would alter, too.

We have just said fundamental 'notes'. In Dr. Aikin's analysis (*v.* p. 142) one fundamental note is given for the mouth cavity, another for the neck. There is also, of course, a definite, easily-heard note associated with the nose; but as this note does not vary it is omitted—a little unreasonably it would seem—from this particular discussion as to the resonantal nature of vowels.

Sir Richard Paget, that very distinguished investigator, similarly speaks of two main resonances as characteristic of any vowel, and he has established these by many synthetic experiments. Other investigators have arrived at almost the same results as those of Sir Richard, but it will be seen that they are somewhat different from Dr. Aikin's, particularly as regards neck resonance.

Sir Richard's table of resonances is as follows:

He allows, however, that his analysis is relative, not absolute; and further, shows that it is somewhere about the *region* of these notes (rather than upon their fixed pitches) that the 'formants' of the vowels lie. He gives the limits of these regions in a more complete table than the foregoing, which can be referred to elsewhere.[1]

The upshot of the matter is: that a standard pronunciation of any vowel at a particular pitch would be permanently linked with two main resonantal notes, one in the mouth, the other in the neck—the dividing line being where the tongue humps (as for Ee) or, if the tongue is flat, makes an angle with the neck (as for Ah).

If, therefore, these notes are not present in the laryngeal note or its harmonics—i.e., if they cannot be energized or sympathetically respond—the vowel dependent upon them cannot be pronounced.

An instance in support of this theory has been commented upon by other writers. It arises in the opening phrase of Handel's well-known air, 'O sleep, why dost thou leave me?'

[1] Sir Richard Paget, *Human Speech*, pp. 86, 87.

The two resonantal notes for Oh, as given by Sir Richard Paget, are  . But as these are not contained in the

fundamental note or overtones of the first note of the air:

there is no means, at that point, of registering the particular type of Oh for which the resonantal notes stand. So much for the theory, but it is very doubtful if it accords with practice. Singers seldom get a thoroughly good Oh *at any pitch*. This is a fault of technique; it cannot be attributed to an embargo of nature. The required technique is lacking, that is all.

The difficulty of co-ordinating and understanding all the factors of vocal resonance is overwhelming. An oscillograph may record what a certain quality of sound looks like; but though impressive and very interesting, it only shows the high lights of the situation, the most salient features. It bears about as much relation to the reality of tone quality as an X-ray does to the wonders of flesh and bone; at best it is more or less of a blur. How are we to catch the special 'accent' of an individual, or a district, except by the apparatus of the mind? A host of partials arises from any note, though they may be so feeble as to be quite inaudible; and, theoretically, each partial has a galaxy of its own, reminding one of the couplet:

> *Big fleas have little fleas upon their backs to bite 'em,*
> *And little fleas have lesser fleas and so ad infinitum.*

Two resonators or pipes can be put together, and, by getting them to resound, simultaneously, to a note, we hear something like the vowel which depends upon the particular resonances which they give; but it may be questioned whether this does more than touch the fringe of the matter. The myriad degrees and combinations of tension involved in vocal tone are, I think it is justifiable to say, incomprehensible; neither to be analysed nor synthesized; nor, though we should like to, can we trust to the practical use of any such analysis or synthesis in voice production. The personality of a vowel is as unique as any other form of personality.

To return to the Handel example on the previous page. We are

148

in just as bad a theoretical plight, as regards picking up the resonantal notes of Oh, if we sing the B an octave or two octaves lower. An
Oh can be sung, by a man, quite comfortably and unmistakably on
but the harmonics of these

notes do not touch (the notes characteristic at

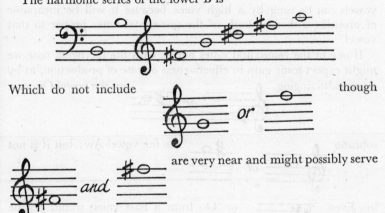

any rate of one kind of Oh, according to Sir Richard Paget).
The harmonic series of the lower B is

Which do not include though

are very near and might possibly serve

for them; or a slight change of vowel might adapt the resonance
to this fundamental laryngeal note.

We know that varieties of a vowel are possible, without departing
too much from its recognizable pronunciation; and each of the
varieties would give a different resonance formula. Perhaps in this
adaptation of resonance we have the secret of good voice production,
but how it is to be brought into the realm of theory it is difficult to
see. It may be solved and *is* solved practically, but that is a far
different thing from understanding it, though there must be a
reason for everything; every result implies a means or cause.

And if we take the notes which follow B in our Handel example,
they are all *above* the lower resonant note of Oh so that

this note is perforce left out of any reckoning with respect to the notes which have to be activated; hence an Oh (which *must* include it) is impossible upon the notes which have to be sung. It is not till we get to the bass note [musical notation] that we can be sure of

activating [musical notation] . There is a snag somewhere.

The lower the laryngeal note, and the higher we go in the harmonic field the more likely are we to find coincidence, but at the same time the available sound becomes weaker and weaker. It seems to come almost to this: that, theoretically, hardly any of the vowels can be sung by a high voice because it will be incapable of arousing either or both of the resonantal notes proper to that vowel.

If one of the resonantal notes agrees with the laryngeal note we might expect some gain in effectiveness or ease of production, as by a contralto singing [musical notation] *or* [musical notation] on the vowel Oo, or a

soprano [musical notation] *or* [musical notation] on the vowel Aw; but it is not

so. Even [musical notation] on Oo from a bass voice would not be

specially sonorous, though [musical notation] *and* [musical notation] the character-

istic resonant notes of Oo, are certainly contained in the harmonic series: [musical notation] Provided the pitch

is comfortable, a vowel is not more easily resonated on one note than another.

We can, of course, turn for reinforcement of the laryngeal note to the nose, whose many shell-like cavities could, between them, probably pick up any sound that came their way; but, here, we are not concerned with this—for nasal resonance can be almost entirely eliminated in vowelling—only with the energizing of the cavities of the mouth and neck which are the cavities that determine the vowels (if we allow that it *is* the mouth and neck which respectively account for the two characteristic resonant notes of a vowel). In this case the resonance of the mouth is perhaps the chief difficulty, for it is especially the volume and orifices—fore and aft—of that cavity which decides a vowel; without the mouth vowels cannot be differentiated at all.

Nor can the overtones of the cavities be of much use to us, except as additional reinforcement to the vowel 'formant', since they are all above the notes which register the vowel.

There is undoubtedly a consensus of agreement as regards the sounds given in Sir Richard's analysis, but it still seems to offer a pretty bleak prospect for the singer (particularly the woman singer) who wishes to sing words intelligibly.

Further, I personally feel that the resonance of the mouth is far more important than that of the neck in determining vowels; as well, it is far more constant. We can change the resonance of the neck almost *ad lib.*, without destroying the basic character of a vowel —i.e., its true genus; and each change will (audibly) give us a different colour, though of what we recognize as the same vowel (even with *falsetto*, when the resonance of the neck is almost entirely foregone). If there were no change of resonance, the quality of the sound would not change. Quite a large stretch of pitch is covered by these resonantal changes in the neck which are only slightly counteracted by variations of aperture.[1]

Another question. To keep a vowel, at whatever pitch, all we have to do logically, is to keep its resonance note. Why cannot we retain the cavities, which give its whispered resonance notes, instead of having to adjust the cavities according to laryngeal pitch? It is impossible. Each different laryngeal note requires some readjustment, because it brings with it some difference of tension. The laryngeal mechanism alters; it tends to become tighter and smaller as the pitch rises, looser and larger as it falls. This, in turn, is communicated to the cavities above. They decrease or increase, and to counteract the change of resonance notes which inevitably follows, the volumes and orifices of the cavities have to be readjusted. Then the same resonance notes can be retained—at least, so runs theory —and the new situation as regards laryngeal pitch is met with-

---

[1] I find that my own neck resonance for Ah is (or can be) much the same as that given by Dr. Aikin; it can even be lower, while still preserving the sound of the vowel. Thus we can verify a vowel well enough under very different conditions. We can scarcely hope to check its subtle emotional variations.

out change of resonant pitch, i.e., without a change of vowel.[1]

Helmholtz showed that a large resonator with a large orifice can have the same pitch as a small resonator with a proportionately smaller orifice, though the larger resonator with the larger orifice will give more sound. These facts, already referred to, are crucially relevant to singing, but the tremendous complication of vocal tone makes it exceedingly difficult to be sure as to their application.

In general, for bright tone, neck resonance is reduced, and compensation must be sought by a larger opening of the mouth; for dull tone this is reversed—the neck opens more, the mouth proportionately closes.

More will be said later about resonance and pitch, but it is clear that if the same vowel and the same quality of vowel is to be maintained throughout the vocal compass, the same resonantal notes must persist; and they can only do so if the cavities are continuously adjusted, in obedience to the principles which have been outlined.

But a dilemma seems to arise in regard to the according of laryngeal with resonantal pitch. Except for slight variations which hardly disturb our recognition of a vowel, we cannot admit any change of its resonance notes, for it is precisely those notes which characterize the vowel. Yet, if we do not alter the resonance notes (which preserve the vowel) in many cases they will be of little or no use to us for the reinforcement of the laryngeal sound; on the other hand, if we do alter them (to get reinforced sound) the vowel will inevitably change.

Variations of resonant pitch, however, though they certainly alter the shade of a vowel, do not necessarily alter its genus. For instance, when the mouth opens progressively to accommodate a rise in laryngeal pitch of the vowel Ah, the whispered note of the cavity may rise from about *8 va* to *8 va* . This does

not prevent the vowel from being accepted as Ah throughout, nor do the very great variations of the same vowel heard with different speakers prevent us from understanding what is meant. We are only baffled when such variations occur in extreme form; when, in short, the vowel changes completely. If with regard to any vowel, the typical posture of the vocal instrument (i.e., the general shape of

---

[1] This is not the same thing as adjusting the mouth for the purposes of whistling; for in this case the oral pitch is altered in order to gain the required note. In the case of an identical vowel at different vocalized pitches the resonant note or notes must not alter, or, theoretically, the vowel would alter, too.

152

the resonators) is maintained, minor variations do not seem to matter.

It may be that we cannot expect, nor do we even desire, absolute consistency in tone quality. The perfectly-kept vowel, with identically the same resonance at all pitches, is probably never to be achieved; and approximations are sufficiently satisfying.

But, in dealing with the two main resonances of vowels, we yet have not disposed of the very intricate matter of vocal tone-quality. We said (on page 103) that 'colour vastly modifies the appeal of form'. It would almost seem as if we had to recognize vowels as tone 'forms': general shapes, which determine the vowels—the 'colour' being derived from the presence or absence of partials lying in a much higher region than the partials which distinguish the special kind of tone which we call a vowel. Or we can say that these latter partials are primary—the ones associated with colour, secondary. What is clear, is that the variability (or 'luminosity' we might call it) of a vowel is not at all the same thing as the vowel itself, which remains constant (or nearly so) under all conditions.

We have further to distinguish tone-quality which derives from the particular instrument responsible for its sound. Thus, not only may the quality (or timbre) of a vowel greatly vary; considerable variation also arises from the kind of voice from which it comes. The same note, say   sung by a soprano, contralto, tenor

or bass, will undoubtedly have peculiarities associated with each type of voice. Though there is a family likeness—the shape, or relation of the parts of the vocal instrument is much the same with all voices—there is also a difference between these voices, as we can easily hear. This difference is to be accounted for by a difference of instrument, registered on what must be a difference in the overtones of each; i.e., by some difference in the 'formant' of the sound, just as it is with the various members of the string family (violin, viola, etc.). In the case of the violin, experiment shows that harmonics in the range approximately 2500 to 5500 cycles per second are generated by the body of the instrument when notes are produced on the strings. It is to these harmonics that *violin tone* (as distinct from viola or 'cello tone) is due, and not merely the series of overtones produced by the vibrating strings: the point being that there is an *initial* difference of sound—and consequently of formant— which comes from the construction of the instrument, quite apart from the *use* that is made of the instrument. Even instruments of the same shape may be different in tone. A Stradivarius violin, owing largely to the wood of which it is made, will have quite a different 'formant' from that of a cheap violin, though the latter may be an ostensibly exact copy of the former. A searching analysis of tone-quality has to reckon not only with the shape, but with the substance (or material) of the instrument which produces it.

Hence it would appear that there are three agencies to be acknowledged in the analysis of vocal tone: (1) That of the nature of the instrument, as such, (2) That of the vowel concerned and (3) That of the 'timbre' or tint of the vowel. Each agency must be held to be 'formative', since it is responsible for some characteristic quality of sound; so that it is not sufficient alone to consider the resonant notes of the mouth and neck in our discussion of the subject.

In a sense a vowel has timbre or quality of sound due to its own make-up, apart from any particular 'shade' that is given to it by the performer. But it is perhaps better to speak of a vowel as a vowel, independent of timbre, reserving this latter term for the degree of luminosity which the vowel may have. We generally call a *timbrée* note one which has a special power of effectiveness or penetration, because high harmonics are present. Dull sounds do not have these harmonics. The light of nasal resonance does not shine upon such sounds—they are relatively ineffective.

A vowel may thus be considered as a generic type of sound, to a large extent *constant*; though, from its character, having more or less telling power in its own right, irrespective of the circumstances of its delivery. Ee and Ay have this power (as we have often observed); Oh and Oo are relatively devoid of it, though it can be given by an almost unnatural use of the vocal mechanism.

It may be advanced that, with a change of vowel, we get what amounts to a change of instrument; and this is so. But there still seems to be a fixed quality of sound in the instrument itself that has to be taken into account, and for which we must postulate a special formant. Every instrument, and every voice has its own 'accent', akin to the personality or nationality of an individual.

To be sure of how and where these three different 'formants' are secured is a difficult matter. The postures of the mouth and throat (and of course the tongue) seem to be wholly responsible for vowelling; timbre is decided largely in the nasal cavities and the sinuses; the characteristic sound of the instrument itself may derive from a subtle inter-relation of all the resonant cavities. But that different formants are implied, different groups of harmonics stimulated, appears incontrovertible. These groups, subject to approximately verifiable experiment, may lie apart, or possibly overlap.

154

As regards the way in which a vowel is pronounced, or an instrument is played, great variation is likely to occur. The formant concerned is, as it were, added to the characteristic and almost unvarying formant of the instrument, or of the vowel, as such. As we have said, a formant of extremely high harmonics is present in the case of brilliant, *timbrée* tone; absent in the case of dull tone. It amounts to the addition (or refusal) of nasal resonance to a vowel; but there does not seem any reason why we should not recognize it as a formative element of vocal tone. It is energized by the laryngeal note in exactly the same way as mouth or neck resonance, and is perhaps the greatest sign of the artistic use of the voice. We know how a good violin player, by the way in which he uses his bow, can vary and beautify the sound of even an indifferent instrument; so can the singer by the way in which he uses his instrument, or 'plays upon his larynx' (again to use von Bülow's depreciatory remark). He can elicit harmonics almost at will, and, in so doing, persuade us of his mastery and poetic power. His instrument becomes something more than an instrument. It is the instrument plus his very soul, though the factors are so intermingled as to be incapable of separation. This is not entirely fanciful.

Involved in this is the capacity that the singer has for (literally) altering the substance of his instrument. He can tension, or harden it; and, if he does so, he will produce a tone in which very high partials are developed. Or, conversely, a relatively loose (or soft) instrument will inevitably react upon the tone quality. The sound will not go into the nose (*v.* also p. 22) and the harmonics which alone can be engendered *there* will fail to be aroused. The tone will be dull in consequence, though it may be quite suitable to the expressive situation. But, to a large extent, the instrument remains the same. Its shape can be the same whether its walls are hard or soft, and with it the formant of the vowel will be constant (or nearly so); so that we can recognize a vowel under vastly different conditions, i.e., under a variety of accents or pronunciations.

To resume: we have considered (1) the part that the type of instrument plays in the production of vocal tone, (2) the type or genus of the vowel that is sung; and (3) the infinitely variable use that can be made of the instrument and vowel. The 'formants' or characteristic series of overtones connected with (1) and (2) will be approximately constant; the series connected with (3) will vary greatly.

Even yet, however, our problem has not been fully envisaged. Besides the resonance of the cavities above the larynx—mouth, neck, nose—there is still another form which I think must be admitted—that of the chest. Undoubtedly, as before noted, the vibration of the deeper vowels Oh and Oo (or of almost any vowel if it is loosely sung) can be felt in the abdominal region. This seems to be due in part, to the vibration of the air below the larynx, more so, perhaps, to the laryngeal sound being transmitted to the harder parts of the thorax—the rib-bones, etc.—in much the same way as a tuning fork transmits its sound to a table or other hard substance, thereby gaining reinforcement. This is in accordance with the fact that the larynx is drawn towards the chest for highly sonorous sound; good breathing in itself brings this about. It represents the contact of the vocal instrument with a sounding board, assuring dark instead of white tone. The possibility of chest resonance has been disputed by various authorities, but it seems reasonable enough to assert it. A great accretion of power does take place when the voice is well in touch with the base of the breath, and we are justified in calling this chest resonance, in the strict sense of the term resonance.

The voice seems able to manage its affairs in a way far ahead of our comprehension. To know why a vowel sounds as it does—wherein its particular quality lies; or why it rings so easily on one note and is toneless on the next: such are for the most part baffling problems. All we can assert is that exactly the same vowel, at exactly the same pitch, will be associated with exactly the same general 'formant' wherever it may lie.

It is the infinite variability of the components, the complexity of their combinations—there even seem to be different ways of doing the same thing (as shown in ventriloquism, or the production of the vowel Oh)—which prevents us from venturing on any precise statement, except as regards certain details. We may follow the rough lines of the argument—the ear is a guide as to that—but how vocal sound picks and chooses its way, amidst the labyrinth of possible paths, remains a mystery.

Part of the physicist's work is to try to find out the ingredients of any composite sound or timbre, also to show with certainty whence they derive and he has achieved much towards this end; the artist's work is to try to produce the sound that satisfies him, and in this he can greatly succeed.[1]

---

[1] Sir Richard Paget (from whose criticism I have much benefited) has given me permission to quote the following from some notes he kindly sent me upon this particular subject:

'It is clear,' he says, 'that the production of the best vowel sounds in singing is a very subtle process depending on unconscious adjustments both of the vocal cords (and their surroundings) and of the unconscious tuning of the resonating cavities through which the sound produced by the vocal cords passes.

'The perfection of these adjustments must depend on initiation by the pupil of a good model—on his cultivation of the necessary critical faculties—and on his capacity for taking the almost infinite pains required to make the whole process automatic!

But it is extremely doubtful whether we shall ever apprehend the make-up of the finer shades of vowelling, and, if we could, the artist would still settle the standards of those shades, and effectively forestall the physicist in every direction. To know as much as we can about everything is desirable—the echo of Goethe's last words 'Mehr licht, mehr licht!' will as well serve for our own longing—but it may yet be necessary to observe that the artist does not understand by way of science, but by way of sympathy.[1]

CLASSIFICATION OF CONSONANTS

Consonants complete the elements of speech. They are the distinguishing feature of words, as vowels are of music; the symbolic character of a word arises from their use. They act as boundaries to the vowel, giving the vowel shape longitudinally and, in the process, intellectual significance by bringing the mind to bear upon what would otherwise be a purely emotional element. The poor articulation of consonants is a sign of mental deficiency; if the brain is not alert neither will be the organs of speech, for their stimulation depends upon whether or not we wish to convey a clear verbal image.

Though it is otherwise with vowels, most people have a fair idea of consonant utterance, otherwise they could not be understood in ordinary conversation. The only consonants which are apt to give real trouble—generally because of physical abnormality—are the trilled R and the sibilant S. Some can never manage to trill an R, while many lisp, either badly or to some extent (if one listens carefully). It is a comparatively easy matter to get good consonant articulation—for one reason because consonants are so short-lived—it is far more difficult to reach a sufficient measure of beauty in a vowel.

Words, as we have said, are determined by consonants, but

'If beyond all these requirements the pupil has, by nature, a well-formed throat and larynx—a good ear for music and the necessary emotional freedom—he may become a good singer.'
The case could not be better put.

[1] I do not suppose that it is, or ever will be claimed that we have a complete knowledge of what might be called the acoustical structure of vocal tone. Much light has been shed upon its mystery, but, as I have said—though I may be wrong —it is doubtful whether the refinements of vocal, or, indeed, any tone can be submitted to final analysis. Many, however, of greatly honoured name, have, in the past, given us an impressive display of physical facts concerning the subject; and we are further indebted to many others, at the present time, who are engaged in very lively quest. To be fair, as well as grateful to these investigators, I should acknowledge that I have contributed nothing, personally, to such experimental, *scientific* research; but perhaps this is already obvious. My interest in the voice has been almost wholly technical and artistic.

beyond this formative function, the expressive value of a consonant is not so much in itself, as in the influence it has on good vowelling. There is, of course, a power to be derived from consonants in, for instance, the emphasis that an explodent consonant can give ('Boy, go back!'), or the rattle of an R (in such a word as 'rage') or the kindly caress of an L (in 'love' or 'lovely')—poets make full use of such possibilities—but, on the whole sustained, heartfelt expression must come from the vowels, if only because they lie much deeper than consonants, and are so much more capable of contacting the springs of feeling. The mechanical impulse, however, which is to be derived from consonants is most important. The nature of a consonant is to delay or 'stop' a vowel and in so doing the vowel gathers impulse and is sped upon its flight with greater force than it would be likely to have if thus unaided. Good articulation of a final consonant, too, helps to keep the vowel on the move; though it cuts both ways: if a vowel has the right life and movement in it, it carries up to the final consonant which it similarly affects. In fact we may be pretty sure that if a vowel is badly sustained the final consonant will have a poor chance of being heard. Good singing is all of a piece, in which both vowel and consonant bear their part. Nevertheless we are not much concerned with quality of tone in a consonant. The 'vocal' consonants L, M and N certainly can be 'toned' well or badly, but in general all we ask of a consonant is that it should be clear and crisp.[1]

Consonants are first classified as unvoiced or voiced. If unvoiced they are simply determined by the organs of articulation; if voiced some laryngeal sound goes with them. Thus F or T are unvoiced consonants, V or D are voiced. The best examples of voiced consonants are to be found in the vocals L, M, N, R. Note that many of the consonants go in pairs, e.g. F (unvoiced), V (voiced); S (unvoiced), Z (voiced), the 'voice' being added to the 'unvoiced' production.

Further classification is into explodents (those consonants which have a complete stoppage of breath before them, and are released with a burst), sibilants (which have a whistling or hissing quality), vocals (which are of a continuant nature, almost like a vowel), and the aspirate H (as heard in 'hop', 'hue', 'which', 'how').

More modern classification has been adopted (with the use of such terms as fricatives and affricatives) but there does not seem much to be gained by it. The classification here given is time-honoured and very clear.

---

[1] This is an under-statement. See what is said about consonantal expression on p. 288.

Classification of Consonants

The organs of articulation chiefly comprise the tongue, lips, teeth and the guttural mechanism which produces the clicking sound of K, or the deeper compressed sounds of B, D, G, th (as in 'they'). Also concerned are movements of related structures like the cheek walls. The soft palate is to be looked upon rather as a deflector, by the operation of which tone can be directed through the mouth, nose or both. The tongue is of primary importance in articulation, as it is in vowelling.

The full list of consonants is as follows:

	(breath)	P	('pay')
	(voiced)	B	('bee')
	(breath)	T	('tea')
Explodents	(voiced)	D	('day')
	(breath)	ch	('chest')
	(voiced)	J	('jest')
	(breath)	K	('key')
	(voiced)	G	('geese')
	(breath)	F	('fee')
	(voiced)	V	('veal')
	(breath)	th	('thief')
Sibilants	(voiced)	dh	('these')
	(breath)	S	('see')
	(voiced)	Z	('zeal')
	(breath)	sh	('she')
	(voiced)	zh	('azure')
		L	('lea')
		N	('knee')
Vocals		ng	('sing')
		M	('me')
		R	('rue')
Aspirates		H	(different placings, in 'heap', 'harm', 'hoe')
		wh	('when', though this is a sort of diphthongal h+oo+ĕ+n).

All these, except ng, may act in an initial capacity ('pay') as well as a final ('ape'), or often both ('pope'); or may be combined in pairs initially or finally, or both ('step', 'pest', 'trust'); or bunched in groups of three ('*strong*', 'drau*ghts*', '*strangle*'); rarely of four ('insti*ncts*').

Chapter 3

TONE IN GENERAL

TERMINOLOGY

THE meaning of certain terms used with singing must here be considered, as well as other important matters.

We have already seen that the difference in vowels is infinite; that they can pass imperceptibly from one to another. Likewise the quality, or shade of a single vowel is subject to limitless variation, though, as with the vowels themselves, we arrest the situation at certain points in order to arrive at relatively clear contrasts. We should get nowhere if we did not do this; the mind would have nothing on which to bite; all would be fluid, slippery. Even so, it is hard to grasp of a certainty the various vowels and the kind of tone which this may display. We attempt to define, rather than define beyond question, and a good deal of misunderstanding is almost bound to exist among practitioners when they begin to talk about the gentle art. Identical terms may connote or be associated with quite different experiences, either from limited knowledge or contending taste. One likes one sort of tone, one another. For instance, in using the terms 'open' (*aperto*) and 'closed' (*chiuso*) with respect to tone, what precise qualities do they designate, by what precise means are they achieved? Can we be sure of recognizing these qualities even in their extreme form, much less in intermediate forms when they blend and mix with other vowels and qualities? Yet the matter can be dealt with in a helpful and sufficiently comprehensible way.

To begin with we distinguish two main divisions of tone:

$$\left.\begin{array}{ll}(1) & \text{relatively tensioned} \\ (2) & \quad,, \qquad \text{relaxed}\end{array}\right\} \text{ tone}$$

The first (1) has a tight mechanism. The breath is more or less under high pressure. This implies a *firming* of the vocal muscles, and the development of what we know as timbre or nasal resonance. The second (2) has a *loose* mechanism. The breath is under a low pressure, and the consequent tone is of a softer kind than that of the first—roughly what we know as *mezza voce* or half voice. In turn these divisions concern what are perhaps the chief aspects of vocal behaviour, (a) the concentration and (b) the position of the voice. Here again we have to observe degrees of concentration and varieties of position—we are never free from complication. But we may be

sure that concentration is linked with tension—the more the tension
the greater the concentration; and that tension and relaxation determine the position of the voice, whether it is, as we say, 'forward' or
'backward'. We may also be sure—and this must never be forgotten
—that all tone is ultimately to be referred to the use of the vocal
valve. This we shall enlarge upon later.

(a) Concentration

If there is a leit-motif in this book, it is expressed by this word. It
will be found that all poor singing lacks concentration. When tone
is insipid, anæmic, sickly, faded, thin, having no power of stimulation, it is because its living properties have somehow become disintegrate. A second-rate picture will show exactly the same
phenomenon in colour. Sometimes one sees a whole room full of
such pictures, not one of which will arrest the attention. Their
colour is lifeless, and that is why we pass them by.[1]

When we feel anything deeply, at that moment our spirit may
be wrung with anguish (as we say) or perhaps is bursting with joy.
In either case it is coincident with tension—a tension of both body
and soul, for the one cannot exist without the other. It is the
principle which tells in art as in life. It was said of a well-known
'cellist that 'to the playing of the smallest note he applied a faith
that would move mountains'. But intense feeling may, of course, be
overdone. A passion can be torn to tatters. How does concentration
apply to tone quality? What effect has it?

We prepare for any effort, and particularly for an exceptional
one, by taking a deep breath. This gathers our vital forces together.
The larynx is pulled down; the muscles tighten, and as they can
only tighten by shortening or compression we at once have the condition of concentration. What was spread and slack becomes drawn

---

[1] 'There is a pale, whitey-brown substance,' says Bagehot in writing to a friend
about So and So's books, 'which people who don't think take for thought, but it
isn't.' The same can be said of colour, when it is wishy-washy, 'whitey-brown', and
therefore totally unsatisfying. It has none of the disturbing, vital quality that
good colour has.

Some words in an article by Mr. P. S. Beales on 'Craftsmanship and Mass
Production' are also very much to the point. He observes that 'Nothing bores or
stales so surely as the continuous use of, and the lifeless and immaculate sameness
of machine-made goods, whether of natural raw materials, or the deadlier and
more devastating synthetics and plastics'—adding that 'The very quality of the
colour of these things is so obviously of the test-tube, and not of the garden or
hedge-row, that we can see quite plainly that they have no "life". When brilliant,
they are crudely garish; subdue them and they have no vibrancy.' How applicable to audible colour if it is produced purely mechanically by a heartless, nonchalant singer! When it is brilliant it is vulgar; when it has no brilliance it is
lifeless, because it has not the necessary concentration, freedom and lift—no
vibrancy, in short.

and taut. This applies to the whole of the instrumental mechanism as well as the breath, and especially to the formation of the mouth, which, as we saw on page 21, tends to alter its natural relaxed shape ◯ to ( ); especially at the back of the mouth where the main control of tone undoubtedly lies. It is by the action of the soft palate, the tonsil walls and the tongue root that the ( ) shape becomes pronounced and operative, not so much by the lips or cheeks, though they can give a final touch. Some action of this sort should generally be present in tone production. It will be, if the singer *feels* his tone. It may be more or less according to the strength of the feeling, but it will be there. If the soft palate is raised, the tonsils will approach, and the mechanism tend to stiffen in that region, as can be heard by simply blowing through the mouth. At its highest tension (or concentration) the breath will, as it were, grate through at the back with considerable friction, since the edges of the orifice will be hard; if they are not so hard a less audible aspirate will emerge.

This technique of concentration is applicable to all the vowels, though it is shown best with the vowels Aw and ŏ which reach their characteristic tone precisely by this means. A concentrated Ah, therefore, will tend to become like an Aw or ŏ, though without reaching these vowels definitively; just as an Ee by the same process will tend towards ĭ, while still remaining a distinct Ee. But in the one case, the Ah will harden in sound; in the other, the Ee will soften.

What really happens is that the Ah has gained more upper partials by this treatment, whereas with the Ee they have been reduced. The voice has moved further forward and more into the head, with Ah; and further back and more into the neck, with Ee. But, *in both cases*, the tone is rounder and deeper and darker. It has been coupled up with the base of the breath and taken on an expressive power that it otherwise could not have.

The looser process, linked with our second and main division of tone, allows the uvula to cling to the back of the pharynx, and, finally, cancels all timbre. As compensation, qualities of ease and softness are induced, such qualities being particularly suited to the fluent delivery of words and notes. *Timbrée* sound has to be forced through the mechanism to its characteristic resonance; the looser sort of sound flows past this resonance. There is little or no resistance, save in the *un*tightened organs themselves; nothing more has been put in the way, no conscious tightening. The result is a type of tone that should be carefully practised as an antidote to tensioned tone, which, if allowed to become habitual, may produce a rigid and altogether unsympathetic style, incapable of flexibility or variation. Loose tone is especially proper to Psalm singing, where laboured utterance would defeat the 'cursive' quality that enables a Psalm to be sung speedily while preserving a sense of dignity and devotion. For liturgical purposes passionate, highly-wrought expression is out of place. The personal factor needs to be suppressed, not stressed. Nasal resonance underlines the dramatic, the 'sturm und drang' of the human situation; whereas religious art in general evades these issues in favour of calm and detachment. Indeed it may be said that, as regards singing appropriate in church, the less we appear to mean what we are singing about the better it will be. *It* must mean a great deal; we scarcely count—a sort of paradox, not easily perceived by the hot-gospeller. The church singer should rely on beauty of rhythm and breadth of phrasing, rather than on vibrant intensity or special points of emphasis. For the most part 'word-painting' is outside his sphere.[1]

The technique of the 'cursive' style is simply this: the breath under very reduced tension, is, as it were, blown up *into the head* through a loose larynx. On its way it catches up and conveys such words as have been coined. There is a minimum of effort throughout. It should be added that *any* kind of tone should always be directed to the head. If it is not it is certain to be lifeless and bad. For secular purposes, too, this technique serves. Much of Lieder singing requires it, when there is no need for the full voice. The full voice cannot be achieved by this method, but quite sufficient tone for ordinary purposes can. A fair *crescendo* up to about *mf* is possible with it. This *is* the principle of *mezza voce* which gives perhaps the most appealing sound that can be made. It can and should have a deep emotional significance. Even a whisper, which is unvoiced, if fervently uttered, can be full of meaning, as it is in a certain passage in Holst's *Hymn of Jesus*, where the composer bids us repeat the words 'Glory be to the Father' in this way; but, unless

[1] It must be owned that one type of what (to me) is supremely religious song does not illustrate what we have here stressed. I refer to those wonderful Negro Spirituals, which, in both words and melody, seem to reach the very core of the religious attitude. These do tell of warm personal feeling, of a childlike love for Jesus, of a heaven (so intensely imagined) which is to come when suffering (like that of the captive Israelites) is over. It is the Bible tale brought to its simplest appeal. There are no reservations, no complications of dogma in these songs, but just a passionate outpouring of the spirit in touching terms of the utmost *beauty*: that is their saving grace, and it is what *emotional* religious song of such a kind hardly ever has. Traditional religious usage gives us something different. It expresses the remote, rather than what is close—attendance at almost any church service shows this, and it is rightly shown: that is its strength, but, in human terms, it is also its weakness. Here a sort of chilly assent appears to take the place of burning conviction, and it does not seem to be a satisfactory substitute. But, if accepted, this is probably quite a wrong interpretation. What we are concerned with is another *level* of experience, in which emotion tends to rarefy as it moves upwards.

there is depth, such whispering would be ineffective. It is always depth that gives supreme significance. The whole body then seems to be concerned, as against merely a part of it—sometimes a very small part. If this latter happens we get what is called white tone, *voce bianca*, the shallowest of vocal sound.

White tone has no richness of colour in it; no mixing of the vowels whereby softer blends are obtained. Ah is Ah and Ee is Ee, etc., and that is about all there is to it. In a sense the clearest and most unmistakable vowels are produced with white tone, because, roughly speaking, mouth resonance only is concerned; the neck is not called upon to play any part. The larynx, if grasped tightly, can easily be felt to rise under these conditions, with consequent closure of the pharynx; and so the blend of tone which the neck supplies is absent. Since there is no interference with the primal quality of the vowel, what we hear is almost painfully clear and obvious, much as might be the effect of the strongest light, which in the end would eliminate visual colour altogether.

> *Life like a dome of many-coloured glass*
> *Stains the white radiance of eternity.*

We need to be a little distant from the blazing centre, before colour can be broken up by the human spectrum. In short, tone needs to be humanized before it can be beautiful to *us*, and it is only humanized when it is, so to speak, taken in by our whole being, and returned, 'stained' in the manifold hues of human experience.

And so we come back to feeling and the physical concentration that arises from it.

White tone at length becomes 'silly' tone, like the bleat of an old ewe; silly, not because the ewe has not a perfect right to bleat in its own way, but because it does not relate to any sound that seems connected with any adequate use of our own brain; and when we do silly things we are likely to suffer for it. With the voice it is certainly so and the use of white tone will strain and wear the laryngeal mechanism, with the probability that sooner or later a visit to the throat specialist will be called for. Nodules may form on the vocal cords as corns do upon the feet, in the end causing great trouble, with perhaps the termination of a singer's career. If the voice is well produced it should last a life-time, otherwise it will fail the owner long before it need. The physical reason for this is that, with white tone, the larynx is high[1] and has been released from

---

[1] It should be made quite clear that if the larynx is too high, white tone will always result, because neck space (which colours tone) is thereby eliminated. But it must not be concluded that the larynx is never to be used in a relatively high position. It will rise with brilliant tone; and be lower with dull tone.

downward muscular tension, capable of resisting the pressure of the breath. The breath pushes it upward and it takes the strain without the help of the tethering, stronger, lower muscles which should hold it in position. It has to work against far too heavy odds and in the end is worn by the struggle.

Ay easily becomes a toneless white ĕ (in 'met') when the mechanism is diffuse and not compact; when in other words, there is a lack of concentration. The only way to correct this is to bring the vowel closer to the breath, to deepen the resonance so that it appears to come more from the chest. We must build in the voice, not let it escape.

When we talk of loose tone (our second main category of tone) it is true that it is different from firm tone. It *is* loose, comparatively if not wholly, as regards the larynx; but it is still subject to concentration. If it were not it would be nearly worthless, the counterpart of the usual tone of a beginner. There seems to be a certain contradiction here. How can 'loose' tone be concentrated? If it were it would not be loose. So the argument seems to run. The answer is that the vocal apparatus is not loose everywhere. One part may be loose, another tight, just as we may clench one hand, leaving the other free. We obviously have the power of localizing tension even when muscles are close together though, as mentioned on page 51, the tendency is for tension to spread, and a great deal of control is needed to prevent it doing so.

We have already seen how, in 'cursive' singing, loose tone can be strongly energized, at a deep level, from the base of the breath. Considerable impulse can be given to it, sufficient to throw it well up into the head, so that it has a fervent, heartfelt quality, though it never becomes fiery, or lustrous as to surface. This is the first sort of concentration applicable to loose tone. Further concentration arises when the resonance cavities are tensioned.

If the mouth is shaped for a thoroughly typical Ah (which can be tested by a whisper) a great deal of tension must be used at the tonsils and soft palate; otherwise an Ah will not be forthcoming —the vowel will be something approaching Uh or Er. The luminosity of a true Ah will be absent. Yet with a perfectly pronounced Ah, involving, as we have said, considerable tension of the mouth, the glottis can be kept open as for *mezza vôce*. Doubtless some of this oral tension is communicated to the larynx and vocal cords—with it one seems to be singing more on the sharp edges of the vocal cords than when there is no such tension; but, in effect, the principle of firm, *timbrée* tone with its close approximation of the vocal cords does not apply. It comes to this: the true, highly-tensioned cavity of Ah can be superimposed upon any degree of tension in the larynx, giving firm or loose tone at will. *What must be maintained, if we wish to sing Ah in either of these ways is the special cavity for Ah.* How we deal with it underneath, at the larynx, is entirely as we decide. We may want a *mezza voce* Ah, or a *timbrée* Ah. With both these types the tension appropriate to the *cavity* of Ah is a *sine qua non.* This fulfils our doctrine that *all good vocal tone must be concentrated in some way or other.* The sheen and shimmer that can be given to *mezza voce* is easily to be heard from a competent singer. Such tone can reach the highest position in the head. On the other hand a lustrous quality may not be wanted—'cursive' singing does not require it; in which case a certain relaxation of the phonatory apparatus takes place resulting in more or less dull tone. The vowels then are not completely intensified or in their most characteristic state; they are modified, mixed with other adjacent vowels, but are still recognizable. Such seems to be the muscular explanation of the different shadings of vowel tone.

Sometimes the terms 'white'[1] and 'dark' are opposed; but this is a mistake. The antithesis should be 'bright' and 'dark', not 'white' and 'dark'. White tone stands altogether apart from decent tonal society. It is colourless, without emotional interest, and in a general way must be ostracized. Perhaps, occasionally, an approach to white sound may be allowed to occur—during some very piteous situation, for instance, or when the bodily powers are presumed almost to have failed; but, as we have said, if the voice is habitually so treated (and it often is) disaster to the mechanism must follow. The antidote to whiteness is always concentration.

Thus omitting 'whiteness' from our usual vocal practice we get the contrasted categories of 'bright' and 'dark', 'clear' and 'covered', 'open' and 'closed' in respect of tone; all of which are compatible with concentration, which 'whiteness' is not.

Brilliancy of tone is obviously a matter of high partials in the sound; and there is no doubt at all but that these are developed

[1] It is difficult to find a word, the true antithesis of 'dark'. 'White', even, does not quite suggest what is wanted. Extreme 'white' tone has no 'body', though 'body', in the most literal sense, can be gradually added to it till it becomes richly satisfying. Perhaps 'disembodied' is our adjective. To begin with, 'white' tone, as we have said, is colourless and silly. 'Whiteness', nevertheless, is a very important attribute of tone, as it is so closely connected with the vowel Ah. 'Whiteness' and 'darkness' in tone can perhaps be best understood by contrasting Ah and Aw—fundamentally different vowels. Ah should be looked upon as proceeding from 'white' tone, Aw from 'dark'. In their most unequivocal form they undoubtedly represent those qualities: Ah coming from a comparatively loose, horizontal technique, Aw from a tightened-in, vertical. It is only by these means that each vowel secures its thoroughly characteristic sound. With Ah a forward production, just at the hard palate, is implied; Aw being gripped (and appearing to be sounded) more at the back, by the tonsils. If there is complete mastery any vowel can of course be sung 'white' or 'dark', according as the typical Ah or Aw process is used.

when the laryngeal mechanism is compressed. The sound will drop away from the head with a loose larynx—it will shoot up into it with a tight one. The best example of this process is seen in the short vowel ŏ (in 'cot'). The distinctive tone of this vowel cannot emerge unless the vocal cords are closely approximated, and a general condition of laryngeal tightness prevails. If it does, the tone will penetrate the sinus cavities—the feeling will be that it is resonating between the eyes—and a hard but exceedingly bright quality of tone will result. If this tense condition is relaxed the sound will appreciably lose in brilliance. There is thus a vital connection between such tension and head tone; and it is capable of application at will. When we want telling tone[1] all we have to do is to tighten; and, *per contra*, to loosen if a less assertive quality is desired. This rule is of the utmost importance, as determining the relative brilliancy or obscurity of vocal tone.

Aw, almost equally with ŏ, can be given a splendidly metallic ring. But any vowel can be highly nasalized by tightening—even the naturally sombre Oh and Oo. Other factors bear upon brilliance, as we shall see, but the chief factor is that of tension.[2] A perfect illustration of the influence of tension upon tone is to be heard in the Ah of the word 'laugh' when we speak or sing it as though we were at the height of convulsive laughter. Up will go the sound into the head. We shall also thereby realize how closely language is connected with emotion. No other vowel would indicate the state that we are in. Its particular quality comes from a natural association of mind and muscle; laughter itself bubbles out of it.

For the more serious and sedate moments of expression (when mechanical precision is not so much in question) a darkening of tone is necessary. This is achieved, once again, by an inward tension or drawing together of the resonating mechanism; so that the face is elongated vertically → ( ) ←, not extended horizontally ← ◯ →. With both bright and dark tone, in so far as it concerns the full voice, the vocal cords are tightly approximated. But with dark tone the larynx is slightly lower than with bright tone, and the tone shifts back, with some blocking of the nose. It must not be allowed to fall back, flabbily; otherwise concentration goes.

[1] The application of bright tone is a matter for the artist and his sense of appropriate colour, but it may be said that anything like a sharp *staccato* or biting attack must be delivered with this sort of tone.

[2] The principle enunciated above goes to the very root of vocal technique. Everything depends upon it, for it represents nothing less than the control of the laryngeal valve which determines breath pressure, breath economy *and* the position and placing of the voice. If the valve works properly one has no need to worry about the placing of the voice: the voice will go just where it is told. One need not say 'I will try to direct the voice to the head, or forward, or backward (or whatever the case may be)'. *It will go there if the valve is used in the right way.*

There is as much concentration in dark as in bright tone. Perhaps one could say that the net amount of tension is about the same in both cases, but the stresses are differently distributed. With bright tone the laryngeal process seems slightly tighter, with dark tone the process above the larynx. The blazing brilliance of tone is sacrificed by the vertical treatment, but a curiously intense, rich colouring takes its places. There is thus a great difference in the quality of bright and dark tone. We must again insist that dark tone is not flabby backward tone, but tone which is kept in its particular place by a strong use of the muscles. It is quite consistent with freedom. The paradox of singing is that tone must be tight before it can (effectively) be loose. No control is possible without concurrent tensity of some kind. The contrast of bright and dark tone can be observed in an Ah when it tends towards ŏ (in 'cot'), or towards Aw (in 'caught') with a tinge of Uh ('cut') in it—it is difficult to be quite sure of these tints. Or we may hear it in a short sharp pronunciation of the word 'debt', as against a very sombre one of the word 'death', when the ĕ will almost become 'ur' as in 'dearth'.

The terms 'clear' and 'covered' denote almost the same thing as 'bright' and 'dark'. Firm tone is presumed in both cases. It is just a question of where it is placed. When the sky is clear, visual colours are brightly differentiated; when it is overcast, they merge and darken. It is the same with the voice. Bright tone has to be cleared of any covering, and this is done by raising the roof of the mouth;[1] a lowered roof darkens and deadens the sound.

Very clear tones are apt to pall, and though the singer must be able to sing with the utmost clarity, it still remains true that most of his work must be done with darkened sound, simply because it means more. Brilliancy has to be sacrificed in order to gain depth.

We have already dealt with the quality of whiteness in tone, which involves, or seems to involve, a sort of 'silly' attitude of mind, as against what might be called a *purposeful*. White tone arises when everything is let go. It represents a misuse of freedom. It is 'open' without the necessary counterpoise of closure.[2] But 'open' tone may be good as well as bad. A properly opened note has a spiritual soaring character, like the arch or pinnacle in building. There is also a resemblance in the shaping of the mouth. A badly closed

---

[1] By so doing, the top part of the head seems to be lifted, just as a lid might be lifted off a closed receptacle. It is mainly the raising of the soft palate which gives this impression, by which action the uvula is drawn away from the back of the pharynx, allowing the sound to enter the nasal cavities. When it rises the soft palate *seems* to block the nose, but the effect is otherwise.

[2] When the vocal tube (or instrument) is shaped by adequate inward pressure, the voice can be used with the utmost freedom—the freer, the better. Not so if it is unconfined—then it will escape without focus, in all directions.

note is earthbound. The word 'open' however, must be carefully considered—particularly so as it may apply either to the throat, mouth or nose—and this may cause confusion.

We talk of an 'open' throat, and this is the most usual association of the word; but the opening of the mouth, in varying degree, is also a pronounced feature of voice production. Equally, tone can be opened into the nose, by which we get 'open' (or *aperto*) sound. In all cases it is a question of bringing the cavity concerned into full play; but this cannot happen with all cavities at the same time. If the throat is opened, that is, given more space by the lowering of the larynx and widening of the pharynx—a fully opened throat seems to expand just under the ears—the process will cut off a good deal of nasal resonance. If the mouth is opened to the full, some diminution of neck space will result, with corresponding influence upon the tone. It is perhaps this opening of the mouth that *seems* to be more in accordance with what we mean when we talk of 'opening' tone: for it is like the action of the 'swell' box in the organ when it opens and allows the sound to come out with greater strength. A *gradual* opening of the mouth is very effective, when a crescendo has to be made to the full force of the voice.[1] In easy singing the mouth need not be opened with any special effort, only when great clarity or strength is required; it is as necessary, at times, for tone to be a little obscure.

In a general way the open *throat* is symptomatic of the best singing. Emotion cannot operate if the throat is closed; warmth and depth of utterance is thereby prevented. Splendidly vibrant tones are always associated with throat resonance, such tones as bespeak eloquence; otherwise all is trivial, or at the most brazenly effective. Emotion narrows with education. We lose the power of primitive animal sounds, which always have an emotional meaning: particularly those of a deep nature, like a roar, or the sound of mooing, which (funny as it may seem) represent ease and *sostenuto* in an exceptional way. Good vocal sound arises similarly from an emotional impulse, having its roots in the abdominal region which ensures an open throat. The reason for our poverty in the deeper ranges of tone quality is probably that the articulatory process (the intellectual process) has largely triumphed over the vowel (the emotional) process. We are the slaves of our civilized development and can no longer, without great practice, make the elementary sounds and noises that were the stock-in-trade of our aboriginal forebears—a very poor squeak suffices to propound, say, a mathematical proposition. We have to remember that we are animals as well as human beings and that our superior humanity is absolutely

[1] But beware! See page 240.

dependent upon its animal origin and cannot forego it without foregoing a large part of the strength of its nature.

It would almost be true to say that we have not produced a complete note till the throat is open; only half a one. A yawn perhaps best gives an open throat—and to retain the mechanism of a yawn without breathiness, during the emission of the breath, should be the aim of the singer. The action of drinking also entails an open throat. If we imagine a quantity of liquid—a glass of water, say—being retained in the throat preparatory to swallowing, it gives us a pretty good idea of the possibilities of throat expansion!

The throat may be taken as the great modifier of vocal sound—through its 'openness' and use emotion is brought to bear, tone darkens and richens, 'expression' operates and is immensely varied.

The opening of the mouth does not so much modify quality as what we might call the 'stature' of tone, as seen in the stunted or fully-developed shape of vowels. The admixture of more or less nasal or neck resonance is what alters quality; the mouth 'exposes' such quality as is already there, and it can give a sort of sheen or gloss to tone, largely by assisting in the forward aspiration of the voice. If the mouth is not opened the voice is dull and smothered. It has a sort of 'matt' surface; its nooks and crannies are unlit. Nor does the full growth of the vowel appear; it is arrested, only half formed and characterized. The sound is there, so to speak, but it has not been sufficiently modelled to make words thoroughly clear. It is therefore largely in respect of clarity of speech that the open mouth is so important. In proportion as the mouth is closed, vowels tend to lose volume and shape; the formative process is not carried to its conclusion—the strength and majesty of speech do not fully emerge; nor can we get the aspirated, eager quality that, in a lovely way, sends the voice about its business of communicating thought. No rule can be given as to how much the mouth should be opened; experiment, and the results obtained must decide. But it may safely be ventured that the habit of opening the mouth sufficiently must be gained by practice. A really open Ah—perhaps the chief goal of the singer—is not likely to come without a good deal of encouragement.

It is perhaps going too far to say that the full opening of the mouth by the jaw and lips does not contribute to some change in tone quality; but its main effect, as we have suggested, seems to be that of enlarging the scale of tone, not of altering the special flavour given to the tone by the varied use of nose and neck.

But whatever kind of tone it is—whether it is *timbrée* or of more sober hue—the mouth must open it out, if words are to be clear. Yet there is a sort of conflict between words and tone. Tone has a tendency to be veiled and backward, in obedience to a desire for sympathetic quality; words on the other hand often need to be opened and brought forward. And it is no easy matter perfectly to adjust these rival pulls.

But it must also be admitted that words can be made clear, provided the throat is well opened; and that in proportion that it is so, a lesser opening of the mouth must occur. If the mouth is fully opened, the throat is to some extent bound to close. This can be felt at the orifice of the throat. When we use backward tone we should in fact consider its orifice as *at the throat*, by the tonsils; and not at the lips. In backward tone the mouth relaxes and in consequence (unless by a sort of unnatural effort) the lips fall towards each other, assuming a closer position; for hard, forward tone, the mouth will tighten, largely because the opening of the lips is imperative. Effectively the orifice is then *at the lips*, not at the throat. But this tightening, as experience shows, prevents the easiest emission of tone. A loose mouth and backward placing are incontestably required if words are to be comfortably pronounced and sustained.

It is perhaps not realized how thin and insignificant vowels generally are when they are sung. In speech, the relatively low pitch of the voice, and, consequently, greater looseness of the mechanism, make for much fuller vowelling. Spoken words can be understood much better than sung words,[1] and this is not only because in singing a certain distortion of the word takes place, since the vowel has often to be artificially prolonged; it is because the vowel itself is nearly certain to be reduced in volume owing to the greater tension (i.e., contraction) required in singing at pitches considerably higher than those of the speaking voice. And as differentiation cannot take place if vowels are undeveloped, the words which contain them will necessarily be ill-defined. In the author's experience blurred words are more often the outcome of poor vowels than of insufficiently articulated consonants; but both, of course, share each other's destiny.

It is through the *nose* that effectiveness of tone comes. The nose is the noise-maker. When we wish to raise our voice as much as possible, we probably shout; and shouting derives its power largely from nasal resonance, that is an open nose. But a shout is just a shapeless mass of sound which for an instant floods all the cavities of the head. It can hardly be associated with a vowel. Nor can it be sustained. A prolonged call such as the sailor's 'Ahoy!' in 'Ship,

[1] As is amusingly shown in this little domestic tale. We had a maid called Emma. Once my wife went into the kitchen and Emma seemed to be saying something to her but my wife could not make out what it was. 'What are you saying, Emma? I am afraid I cannot understand you,' said my wife. 'Please'm, I wasn't saying, I was singing,' was the reply.

ahoy!' has passed beyond the shouting stage into verbal distinctness. A shout in its crudest form is like a magnesium flash—very powerful while it lasts—but its energy is immediately expended. This is because it meets with no continued resistance, or at any rate with insufficient resistance to contain and canalize its energy. It is sound without direction and concentration. Yet it seems to show us how the most powerful sound is to be secured; and what we have to try to do when we wish for such sound is to allow the sound to enter the nose (by way of the back nasal aperture), but also to hold it in check by applying resistance. Such resistance can take place either at the front aperture of the nose (the nostrils) or at the back through the medium of the soft palate. If these resistances are not present the sound runs to waste. It is simply common sense that sound must get into the nose before the nose can properly resound, nevertheless it must not swamp it as with a shout. A shout carries right through the nostrils—this is why its power is so quickly expended. Therefore we have to close the nostrils as far as we can so that the sound may be reflected back from the mask of the face. And we have to regulate the entry of the sound into the nose by means of the uvula and soft palate; giving as much opening to the back aperture as is consistent with the nasality that we wish to have.

In short, we have to open and close, more or less, at the same time, as when a swimmer breasts the water, he tries to open a passage for himself, but gains his power of propulsion precisely from the counter pressure that is around him.

Thus, vocal sound has to be 'boxed' before it is really serviceable. There must be a feeling that it is 'contained' and not allowed to spread to the four winds. A horse will bolt unless checked by a bit; tone will equally do so if it not governed by a backward pull.[1] This is perhaps best observed in the case of high notes. Up to a certain point—about the note with men, and an octave or so

higher with women—tone can be controlled fairly well; with little thought of closure. But above this point it simply refuses to come to heel. It takes charge of the situation and the poor singer is nowhere. It is just a shout, and all the shortcomings of a shout are apparent in it. High notes cannot be sung in such a way. They represent a far greater weight (or tension) than do low notes, and this weight has to be reduced by closure (making the note smaller) or, in other words, by greater resistance. High notes are relatively so

[1] With good production it seems as if the voice were 'held' by the nostrils and contingent muscles; it is the equivalent of the horse's bit.

heavy that they cannot otherwise be sustained. It is a common thing to hear a man's voice 'bellow' at such a pitch, i.e., be too 'open'. On the other hand nature often suggests a remedy—the 'closing' of such tone, because it is so uncomfortable. When that is the case it is apt to be too closed and smothered—there is a sudden change of quality. One of the great difficulties that the singer has to contend with is to bridge over this change from open to closed in such a way that it is unnoticeable. It is always safe to 'sombrer' high notes (as the French say), to give them a duller resonance and to bring this quality of voice downwards; working from high to low notes, rather than the reverse, till control has been secured.[1]

It may be wondered why it is necessary to add any resistance to that which is already present in the normal condition of the walls of the various cavities. Yet more resistance can and must be added; it *will* be, by the *general* process of tension which operates on the muscles when any sort of feeling is expressed—this, indeed, is the main point of our debate. The breath will undergo tension which will be communicated to, or run concurrently with, the tension of the muscles of the nose and mouth, particularly at the back aperture of the latter: in short, a tightening of all the naturally loose membranes will, to some degree, occur. The mouth, for the vowel Ah, for instance, will not open in a loose shapeless way, as though it were a bucket waiting to be filled from the outside instead of a nozzle through which something has to be projected. This would give a sort of bad Uh. Even with the most relaxed tone the cavity will tend to contract, otherwise vowelling would be lifeless and articulation impossible.

In so subtle a mixture as that of tone colour it is hard to be absolutely sure of the ingredients, or of the way in which they are secured; but experience shows that, with regard to them, things happen in much the way that has been outlined. You let the light in (upon tone) by the open nose; you let the tone out through the mouth; and you garnish and beautify tone through the open throat.

(b) Position

The most frequent terminologies as regards position are those of

forward and backward,
outward and inward,
head and chest.

---

[1] It is debatable whether it is absolutely necessary to 'cover' high notes, as some maintain. However it is achieved, it seems possible to get the effect of clear, open, ringing tone from top to bottom of the voice, without the need of any *apparent* change of quality. I believe it is simply a matter of technical competence, though many, perhaps most singers drift into an easily perceived covered tone when they reach relatively high notes.

The first mentioned terms have relevance in a general way to what may be called 'lifted' tone, the second to low-lying tone.

As has been said elsewhere, there is no particular virtue in forward tone. It may serve a certain purpose at a certain time, at moments of exuberance or when it is necessary to be very clear, but it is by no means always to be preferred to backward tone though the latter may seem to be somewhat suspect. A backward sound is not at all the same thing as a smothered sound, in which insufficient play is given to a note; or as a throaty sound, for which wrong muscular action is responsible. What is necessary at all times is spaciousness, adequate egress; but this can occur equally with forward or backward tone. It simply amounts to this; the more tone is 'felt' the more it will have a tendency to be drawn towards the source of feeling which is the abdomen. It is as though the direction of the sound as it leaves the larynx is ↑ or even ↖, rather than ↗ against the teeth and hard palate).

Tone is shot forward by a drive or thrust of the breath, much as the breath gives in the case of retching or sickness—we must not fight shy of this natural expulsive action; it is drawn backwards by a pull of the breath, as in yawning. A very little experiment will show what happens, and observation will make it quite clear that the one action is associated with sound of a sort of forced brilliance, the other with sound subdued to the exigencies of more poetic expression.[1]

---

[1] A Jacobean poet, Sir John Denham (1615–69), gives us almost perfect instruction in good singing when he affectionately commends his favourite river, the Thames, in these words:

> Though deep yet clear,
> Though gentle yet not dull,
> Strong without rage,
> Without o'erflowing full.

The phrase to be specially remembered is 'gentle yet not dull'.

The quality of gentleness, as of mercy, is not strained; but, as its expression involves the greatest beauty of touch, there must be some strain attaching to it: for the most delicate operations require the most control, and they cannot be effected without tension. Gentleness is a very positive virtue; its features will never be shown by a mere absence of effort. If we wish to know what gentleness in music is we have to turn to the supreme exponent, J. S. Bach. He gives us (and allows us to express) a gentleness which is unmatched in the work of any other composer, though certain songs of Richard Strauss illustrate it to an outstanding degree. The latter in 'Meinen Kinde', 'Morgen' and 'Traum durch die Dämmerung' evokes 'twilight and the half-light' and a sort of passionate quiet that only comes from an approach of the gentlest kind; but of dullness there is no trace. A similar approach is necessary in performance. States of rapture are not achieved merely by relaxation, but by relaxation which is borne aloft on the wings of tension till it hovers in the highest realms of spirituality.

In physical terms such singing amounts to this: that the gentlest and lowest-lying tone must nevertheless be lifted, by appropriate breath action, till it is felt loosely vibrating with a sort of *mezza voce*, aspirated quality, in the mask of the face. Only then will it have the vitality that implies an absence of dullness. Real dullness is insufferable at any time.

Such poetic expression will necessarily take an inward direction, which might seem to conflict with an emergence of tone; but it does not. We must remember that tone has very little physical projection in it. We say that it is sent out, and to a very limited extent this is true. By putting the hand in front of the mouth we certainly can feel a slight disturbance of the air, particularly when the orifice of the mouth is small, as with the French 'u'; but it acts for a very short distance when once it has left the body. So little breath is used in singing that it is bound to be so. Whether the voice is forward or backward, therefore, has very little influence on the effectiveness of sound which depends in both cases upon its wave-like quality, not upon an actual projection of the vibratory stream. We cannot detect the movement of sound in any tangible way, only by what we hear. Relatively speaking, nothing alters its position when sound emerges. Sound is simply the oscillation or shivering of the air, which remains *in situ*.

We have already spoken of the reflection of tone by the (closed) mask of the face. This leads to the feeling that somehow the voice is being directed towards the body and not from it. This is always the case with expressive tone. It tries to settle upon the base of the breath, as upon a cushion; to burrow towards the roots of feeling. With the most comfortable sound this is certainly so. Soft sympathetic singing must rely upon this technique. Louder singing requires more pressure and resistance and so is apt to move upwards; but if it is expressive it will not depart much from this downward 'inwardness'. Bright forward tone is almost imperative for *staccato*; the reverse is needed for *legato*. It amounts to the difference between live thrust and dead weight. Notes can perhaps be forced together with a forward tone and made to join, but they will not fuse together: they will always have a separatist tendency.

'Full-throated' is as applicable to human as to bird song. Mr. Vesey-Fitzgerald noted in *A Country Chronicle* that: 'The blackbird has a wonderful ability to turn his golden melody over in his throat, adding yet further richness to vast wealth'; which is both delightful and informative observation. We can learn a good deal from such singing. Another point in connection with full-throatedness (which involves, as we know, a certain 'covering' of sound) is that it is a condition of the blending of voices. This refers, of course, to part-

---

There is an exact parallel, in this connection, between visual and audible colour. Visual colour may be as 'dead' as audible colour, particularly when dull pigments are used; but a painter has the power of making it otherwise. It has been said of Van Gogh's work that 'even the muddy blacks and browns of the *Potato Eaters* glow in that essential manner displayed by very early Cézannes, as well as many murky Rouaults'; and that 'to any painter this luminous quality in the sum of dirty ingredients—blacks, browns, greys—means mastery' (Patrick Heron).

singing but it is not wholly irrelevant to solo-singing, for it is arguable that something is wrong with a voice that will not blend. By far the best blending tone is obtained with the vowel Oo, which harmonizes into lovely soft chording. Oo is the deepest vowel of all, very covered in quality, and resonated almost wholly in the neck, if it is sung easily. Ee on the other hand, is the shallowest vowel of all—and if sung in the usual way refuses to merge with other tone. What has generally to be done, therefore, is to apply the depth of Oo to all vowels, giving a sort of 'mixed' colour to the more strident Ee and Ay, which is the same thing as singing these vowels with an open throat.

'Deep and open'
Is the sign
Of all good tone
That's sung or spoken.

This rhyme should always be present in the singer's mind and especially in the mind of choralists.[1]

Depth and openness in the voice—so necessary if any sort of flow is to be maintained—inevitably take the fire out of tone, exchanging a relatively quiet quality for what was apt to be excited. There is more than a half truth in the assertion that the chief thing to do in singing is to be able to eliminate nasal resonance from the voice. But as one can be so easily misunderstood in this it is perhaps safer to say that the singer must be able to use nasal or neck resonance at will, to the extent almost of excluding one or the other. When he can do so he has practically full command of all the possibilities of vocal colouring.

As to head tone and chest tone: it is mostly a matter of pitch. High notes, by reason of their tighter nature, are resonated more in the head; low notes, because they are looser, seem to be more on the chest. In a man's voice it is quite easy to feel vibration almost as far down as the base of the breath with low, loose, notes. This will gradually tend to disappear as the voice rises. In a lesser degree it is the same with a woman's voice. Thus, vibrations from the larynx can and do find their way down into the body as well as up into the resonance cavities of the head. It is a matter of experience, and this decides it. Whether these chest, or body, vibrations have much

---

[1] I was trying to teach a pupil to get deep tone on Ah and asked her if she were keeping her tongue down. She said she found it difficult. So I suggested that if she tried to draw the tongue root back a little it might help. 'What,' she said, 'must I keep the tongue down and swallow it as well?' 'That is what it almost amounts to,' I had to reply. My counsel was simply a variant upon the Italian precept 'come bere' (like drinking). I am well aware that the French always say that the English 'avalent leurs mots' (swallow their words), but this really amounts to a criticism of our lazy habits of speech as compared with their alertness and precision.

influence upon the actual sound may be open to discussion, but that they occur is undoubted. In this sense we are justified in talking about chest tone. It should further be said that as long as complete looseness can be maintained (our second category of tone is involved here, *v.* p. 160) the vibrations of the voice are sympathetically answered by the body. This indeed, is a sign of the deepest feeling and most profound expression. These very adjectives suggest what actually happens.

There is another sense in which 'chest' tone is used. About the note [musical notation] with women there is often a bad break, when the

voice seems suddenly to alter both mechanically and in quality. The tighter tension of the notes above cannot be carried down across this note which opens in an ungovernable way and as it were drops the sound right through on to the chest. This is apt to be a difficult problem, as are all breaks; and they occur elsewhere—particularly on [musical notation] with women, which is often a very weak note, re-

fusing to sound with any timbre. All such breaks denote failure of the proper tension of the vocal cords, brought about by strain or misuse. With men also there is often trouble on the note [musical notation]

Above this note they will 'close' and then suddenly plump it open in a downward passage. The effect is like coming to a change of voice, which might be called 'chest' voice. Here again it is a matter of skill in dealing with the right tensions.

We must distinguish between *falsetto* and *mezza voce*. Neither employs the full voice that we get with timbrée tone. But whereas *mezza voce* gives the impression of being natural, *falsetto* is a freak tone and seems all wrong. It is not usable except perhaps on very high notes to avoid otherwise insuperable difficulty. It is merely a subterfuge, though it may pass unnoticed if the *falsetto* is soft and can be made to join up with proper tone. It is produced by a compression of the laryngeal mechanism which sends the tone into the head without giving it any real nasal resonance. It is totally devoid of M, having an extreme fluty sound. It is nothing more nor less than a hoot, applicable mostly to high notes outside the normal

177

range of the voice. Swiss 'yodelling' is of this type and it is used amusingly enough in this connection; it is also sanctified to religious use by the adult male alto who is traditionally found in our church and cathedral choirs. But it can never represent full-blooded singing, since the true springs of feeling are not touched by it. Sound has to link up with the base of the breath before this can occur, and *falsetto* does not do this.

All the varying qualities of tone which we have discussed are under the conscious control of the singer, much more so than the vowels themselves. But considered action is quite impossible if the situation is of a momentary kind, which is usually the case. Then the imagination, not reason, takes charge. Of the water-beetle's aquatic progress it was said:

> *If he ever stopped to think*
> *How he did it he would sink.*

And it would be ridiculous to suggest that by taking thought we can adjust muscular action to the fleeting requirements of actual performance.

Finally it should be observed that the different placings of the voice should be well within the control of the singer. A song is a picture in sound. It can never be right unless its colouring is in accordance with the sentiment of the words. The test is not how the singer sings, but how he speaks; the test of elocution in fact. He may sing effectively enough, using his voice like an instrument, but does he use it like a human being? The composer has given him the notes and time of the music. If the singer deals faithfully with these does his responsibility end here? By no means. The crux is with the words and their meaning. Ask him to sing his words and he may 'get away' with a mass of nonsense and absurdity. Ask him to speak them and he will be very likely to give himself away to a ludicrous degree. Almost anyone can detect whether the punctuation, shading, accent, etc., is natural and true to life, or faulty beyond measure. The music will distract our attention from this important matter of the poetry of speech, but we must not allow it to do so. Most singers have a sort of standard, set tone which never varies. It is used for every song, every circumstance. Yet only by endlessly diverse approach can the voice do justice to what is required of it.

Nevertheless tone, merely as 'tone', must not be sneered at. Poetically it may have no intended significance; musically it may have a great deal. Instrumentalists do not worry much about tonal variety, though they may vary their tone unconsciously. But they are much concerned with the effective, telling quality of their tone, and try to develop it as much as they can. A skilful string player

178

will get to the 'nerve' of the note in a way impossible to the novice, who merely 'saws' his fiddle with very little result in terms of strongly-managed sound. For the singer 'tone', as such, is simply a superb concentration of vocal vibration.

The rationale of tone production is simple, logical, consistent. It follows, as we might expect, the course of nature. We act naturally in such and such a way, when compelled by feeling; and this feeling via this action, translates itself into such and such a tone. The concordance between feeling, action, tone is complete. By performing a certain action we get a certain tone and can get no other by this means. We cannot do as we like about tone; empirically follow our own rules of procedure: these are laid down for all time in the 'order of nature', which it is our business to try to understand and follow.

To conclude this somewhat lengthy discussion in a clear, simple way.

We can enumerate eight distinct types of tone, each with its appropriate technique:

1. open ⎫
2. closed ⎬ which are our main categories.

3. ⎫ either of the foregoing made more brilliant or dark accord-
   ⎬ ing as they are modified by a smiling or serious face; that
4. ⎭ is, treated laterally by outward or inward tension:

or

5. ⎫
6. ⎬ the application of *mezza voce* or breath tone to all of the
7. ⎬ above.
8. ⎭

With, of course, as well, a host of intermediate gradations.

IDEAL TONE

We have said already that good tone is good pronunciation—neither more nor less. But what do we mean by 'good'? We have some vague idea, arising from our general experience. But sooner or later we are challenged to be more precise, and have to make an attempt to justify our judgment.

To begin with we recognize two classes of what we call 'good' tone: tone which is fitting, characteristic of a certain situation or person, and tone which seems to have its own beauty, regardless of any particular use to which it is put—ideal tone, in short. There seems to be a sort of antagonism between the two. Characteristic tone glories in local colour; pins itself in a unique way to an individual. Ideal tone strives to wipe out the accidental and personal

in favour of sound which is more or less common to everyone—
something finer and better, which sheds the characteristic in the
process. In a sense it discounts variety, those varied touches which
come from persons or things in their individual aspect, just as
nature makes them. We cannot have it both ways. We may recognize Mr. So-and-so's voice in the dark and, in certain circumstances,
be very glad to hear it; but we might prefer some other sound if we
are bent on the more cultural achievements of art.

So far so good. We can judge pretty well whether tone is 'according to nature', whether it is like what we hear around us, true to a
particular type whatever that may be. But what if we can apply
no such test to it; if we desire it to be not 'according to nature' but,
in a very real sense, to transcend nature?[1]

What is then to be our test? How shall we know what to follow?
Are there any objective criteria to which we can turn for guidance?
'He hath showed us what is good.' How easy it would be if we could
accept authoritative direction of this sort; without demur or question. But where is it to come from in the case of tone? Many assert
that their way is the only way: primitive souls who mistake the
impulses of the subconscious for a direct revelation of Divine will.
Edward Thring, the famous head of Uppingham, was one of these.
His diary refers every incident of his life to the interposition of a

[1] Interesting speculation opens up from this reference to nature. There is
scarcely such a thing as a good natural voice, sufficient to satisfy the utmost
demands of song in the quality of sound. It is strange that it should be so. We
should not think of educating a bird's voice, why that of a human being? If we
could take the natural voice, that could be nature's pattern. We could accept it
at once as our guide, indeed we should not need ever to think about the matter.
How does it arise that we cannot just sing and have done with it, improving the
voice in power and speed, but leaving tone quality to its own devices? Why have
we fallen from natural grace, for it certainly seems as if there had been a fall?
The answer seems to be in the inhibitions and processes of civilization. We
hardly do anything spontaneously now. The mind has intervened too much in the
morals and decorums of community life. In short we are no longer free to do as
nature bids. Language also has arisen to alter natural human sounds and thereby
curbed emotion to such an extent that the voice does not receive its natural
impulse. It no longer proceeds from emotion, it is not 'moved' by this primal
instinctive force, but by the consciously determined will. In other words the
voice has been civilized almost out of existence; and it is only by a process of
education that it can recover its natural glory. We have to learn to be free again,
consciously to let it again become the vehicle of emotion, with the added gain of
intellectual achievement, or, briefly, thought. This, then is the problem; how to
bring about a marriage of thought and emotion in terms of vocal sound. Speech—
perhaps man's greatest conquest—interferes with the easy egress of sound; there
is no such impediment in purely animal (and emotional) sound. The throat does
not close when the lion roars, or the dove coos; nor would man's throat do so when
his voice mirrored his emotion, unless he had to mind the p's and q's of speech.
Emotion liberates, its absence hinders freedom of utterance. Free open resonance
is not likely to occur if we are dominated by the minutiæ of words. In a way, we do
not want to sing words when we are singing, but only sound. This seems to involve
a contradiction of what has been said elsewhere in respect to the deference that
should be paid to speech, but we should not be bound even by our own precepts.

higher power. God is on his side, and if others disagreed they had to bear the brunt of his autocratic displeasure. He was a strong man; his faith was strong; but it led him into all sorts of absurdities. There are hosts like him, inheriting a sort of ancient Jewish or modern Puritan temper which ruled others out of the councils of the Lord. They are not content to say '*If* God be for us, who shall be against us'; they are absolutely sure of His support. An intolerable arrogance goes with such folk. We must be more humble.

Yet we are not left altogether comfortless. We have authority to guide us, even if it is a human and not absolute authority. Further, there are æsthetic and practical tests by which we can be pretty sure of our ground.

By general consent, there have been and are great singers. We fortunately are not at the beginning of vocal technique. Valuable secrets have probably been lost—admirable traditions weakened; but splendid examples of the art of singing are still offered to us by which we may recover standards which in many quarters no longer hold.

We also have the guidance of an inward voice. It would be preposterous not to admit that in the fabric of our being are woven tendencies which press us forward and upward. There are reverse tendencies as well. We know this, and see their fruits. But it does not discountenance the force of the ideal. We may never grasp the ideal;[1] our search for it is relative to our personal powers. It is a will-o'-the-wisp that so often seems to recede as we advance. But we do advance in the process. It seems impossible to deny absolute beauty—or something very like it—when we acknowledge progres-

---

[1] We have to abide by unceasing frustration, in everything. Even in our joys we 'taste nothing purely', says Montaigne, and 'beauty that must die' is the final form of sorrow. Sometimes, in its consequences, frustration reaches tragic heights, as we know; at other times, particularly if we live 'like a log', we may be almost unaware of it. But the fact of frustration implies an ideal state just as a solar eclipse implies the sun. Whether unalloyed bliss (in which frustration would have no place) is possible, or even desirable for us, is another matter.

Ideals exist, but they have to be implemented by the artist, scientist, social worker, etc. That this is so does not discount the force of an ideal, or justify us in regarding ideals as purely the outcome of human expediency and experience. There seem to be not only authoritative and working tests of ideal tone, but a test which is inherent in the very heart of the universe, as in natural law. We discover the standard; in no sense can we be said to create it ourselves. As far as the religious aspect goes, worship, reverence, awe, are the roots of the position. It may be objected that we do not worship natural law, we only try to understand it—*laborare est orare*; but there is something more to it than that. It is curious that even with natural objects, which might be supposed always to represent ideal shapes, we prefer some types to others. We say, for instance, that young kittiwakes are amongst the loveliest birds we know; implying degrees of beauty, even in nature. Whether we are justified in this is another matter. Yet it is so *to us*. There seems to be embedded within us (as we have said) a scale or standard of values, by which, in every aspect, we judge both ourselves and external things.

sive degrees towards it. Nor can we arrogate to ourselves the entire decision of what is beautiful—each one a law unto himself in the matter—because other forms of life have, apparently, no æsthetic sense. We have to recognize objective elements in beauty before which we bow, quite apart from our perception of them; and, in these, norms and standards seem to be concerned. It cannot be a go-as-you-please business. In any case, it is probably better and healthier for us to think that we discover beauty rather than create it; that we are channels rather than fountain heads. There is a categorical appeal with beauty, as Kant found with moral law—however much we may differ in our judgments concerning it.

And, of course, we do differ. We have to allow for fancy—Captain Stratton's or any other.

> *Oh, some are for the lily, and some are for the rose,*
> *But I am for the sugar cane that in Jamaica grows,*
> *For it's that that makes the bonny drink to warm my copper nose,*
> *Says the old, bold mate of Henry Morgan.*

Eastern races prefer a different sort of tone from ours. Even Western people vary in their tastes. In northern Spain a very reedy tone is preferred, similar to that of the reed instruments which compose the orchestral combinations of those parts. Such practice is characteristic and interesting, but different from our own. Who is to decide which tone is best? There is no question of a decision. These preferences have to be accepted and given thanks for. All that we can legitimately demand is that tone *should be the best of its sort*.

But certain considerations still remain. There does seem to be another principle at work which negates these differences; brings them into uniformity. It is that of what may be called common or standard humanity, as represented in the normal constitution of every individual. Feeling, as we have so often said, at its greatest, concerns the whole man. It is not located in any particular or limited part of his anatomy, but spreads from a central source which we know (as the Greeks and others so well knew), in the region of the diaphragm. If, therefore, such complete feeling occur, it must be dealt with by abdominal means; by the deeply controlled breathing of which we have spoken so much. This, of itself, will necessitate a certain type of tone—connected with opened resonances and particularly with the open throat. No other type is possible. An Ah, for instance, if it is to express us to the full must have the fullest and most complete sound possible. Anything less will not serve, nor can anything else *happen*. It will be so. This is the real justification for Western processes, which it would seem must everywhere prevail in the end, simply because the human body is built and must act in that way. Even now such uniformity is very widespread. In obedience to an ideal urge, local differences of pronunciation tend to be ironed out. What we get is vocal and not national tone when the voice is developed as an ideal instrument, or put to ideal use. A good Italian Ah is a good English Ah; 'twang' can have no place with a cultured American singer. In art we are members of the same nationality. And if there are as yet tremendous differences to be observed between East and West—if Western practice has not supplanted Eastern practice—it seems difficult not to believe that this will one day happen. The symbols of Eastern thought may remain, but the sound by which they are made manifest may change for the above-mentioned reasons. Physical and emotional similarities may gradually press towards it. A universal language is perhaps a far-off dream—it can hardly be imagined that differences of verbal symbolism will cease to exist—but just as visible colour is pretty much the same all over the world, so the audible colour of the various languages may tend to approximate. There is not such a difference, say, between the colour of an Indian scene and of an English one, as between the sound of Indian and English music.

But whether this is straying into very debatable land or not, there can be no question of what a beautiful Ah is. Its ideal form—or rather, that it has an ideal form—is scarcely likely to be contested, though it may be exceedingly difficult to arrive at it.

There is a final, absolute quality in a vowel, that places it outside human frailty. The ideal vowel is just *it*, as essentially perfect as a circle, or numbers. And if it be objected that little human interest attached to such perfection, we must reply that without it there would be no human interest at all: for it is upon such norms, such fixed assurances, that human interest revolves (however much they are varied by circumstance). The shades of a vowel are infinite. We saw this in previous discussion. We saw in our table on page 121 that, at the least, we have to recognize a forward, central and backward position of every vowel. The sound of Ah could be either that in the words 'pass', 'laugh', or 'harm'. They are all good sounds. The first is a little more nasal than the others, the last more voluminous and less nasal, the central one a sort of balance between the two. On the score of preference the forward sound might be preferred at all times; or the more backward one. Certainly each is good upon occasion. Which, therefore, is the ideal Ah, for there can be only one?

It is contained in the generic central form. This is the pure Ah—the others are accidental modifications, brought about by what is really functional or emotional disturbance, though this is never sufficient to remove it entirely from the parent stem. When we come closely to examine those various forms of Ah we see that the variant qualities are not those of a pure Ah. If we take the forward, fully-opened mouth position of Ah (giving the largest measure of nasal resonance) we find that it is not quite Ah but has a flavour of ă (or perhaps ŏ) in it; while the backward, fully opened throat has a tinge of ŭ. The purest, perhaps we might call it the absolute form of Ah is the central one *which cannot be referred to any sound other than itself*. We thus seem justified in saying that there is an ideal Ah, however much we have striven against the pronouncement—for ideals are nowadays by no means fashionable philosophy. The best of its sort *is* the ideal—and it eliminates all other kinds.[1] Identity is established by difference. It is because things are different from one another that we know what they are. When everything foreign to an element has been removed—we are in the presence of that element, and only then; it has been isolated, as the chemist says. And this is applicable to the whole vowelling system. A backward Ee is a combination of Ee + ĭ without entirely becoming the latter vowel; a backward Ay of Ay + ĕ. Very forward and backward shadings in general represent 'mixed' tone, a subtle adjustment of the generic vowel with another. When a vowel is completely *itself*, there is nothing further to be done; we are at journey's end. Can it ever happen? Sufficiently so. Doubtless differences of physique will prevent an entirely consistent solution. In a sense there must always be relative attainment. But our common make-up ensures that we can get very near to the mark if we try; we can see the goal even if we cannot quite reach it, which is a very different thing from saying that there is no goal, or that we can make our own goal.

Whether we call this ultimate final form 'beautiful' does not matter—some may think it too perfect to be beautiful—but with it we have possibly succeeded in attaining a state like the Buddhist Nirvana where human judgments cease to operate, simply because there is no further field for them.

We are thus out to attain an absolute control of an absolute quality. Needless to say we usually have to be satisfied with rough-and-ready approximations.[2]

---

[1] In a sense, of course, every vocal colour has an absolute quality. It is that and no other. It may be generic, as a pure Ah; or a mixture, as with other modifications of Ah; but such as it is, it is the best of its sort whether one wills it or not. The only *perfect* colour, however, is the colour which is *unmixed*, and that implies a process of selection in accordance with what can only be said to be an ideal standard.

[2] Perhaps we have to admit that there will always be some subtle, unanalysable personal quality in a voice however near it gets to ideal purity: to that extent ideal tone *is* never reached, and we have to be content with a relative form of it. But it still remains that it can approximate so closely to an absolute form, that for practical purposes we can call it perfect.

All this may seem academical and not in the least practical. But very important practical considerations are linked with it; none other than styles proper to personal and impersonal art.

Art can be directed towards or away from the individual. If the former, it will express particularities of person or place; if the latter, rather those universal properties or principles which have their own being apart from any special manifestations in which they are concerned. They are what may be called the constants of existence— unvarying as the laws of nature, entirely independent of our whim and caprice. Such would be an ideal vowel. A certain abstract quality attaches itself to this. It is no longer the personal, but the super-personal: something bigger than ourselves, partaking a vaster life; allowing us to be raised to our fullest stature. It involves a sacrifice of detail. The mind cannot fix upon the broadest and most minute aspects of anything at the same time; but the sum is greater than the part.

> *There is a soul above the soul of each,*
> *A mightier soul, which yet to each belongs;*
> *There is a sound made of all human speech,*
> *And numerous as the concourse of all songs.*

It is something like this which proclaims the grandeur of religion which places what we call the sacred apart from the secular. It is the note of Greek sculpture with its abstract treatment of the human form in which an idea is envisaged rather than a fact; it is that of primitive painting before the skill of the painter allowed him to get too close to reality; and of polyphonic music—the music of Palestrina and Byrd—before the resources of melody, harmony and orchestral colour were opened up sufficiently to express subtleties of personal emotion (and also the trivialities that so often accompany it). The relative breadth, calm and aloofness of religious art may not be approved; we may have no use for 'cool, Attic shapes', preferring a more stimulating encounter, but they have to be reckoned with; they cannot be airily set aside. Adequate religious art does tell us things that other art fails in; and if we wish to pursue it we have to do so by sinking individual turns and traits of expression and establishing a style in which they hardly count, as happened in medieval times when it was hardly possible to know who built a church or cathedral, composed a mass or motet, or was responsible for the still more ancient strains of Gregorian song.

Some such reasoning as this appears to be relevant in deciding what ideal tone and its significance really is.

The 'grave and stadie' aspect of religious expression was, of course, observed long ago by Thomas Morley, and this has to do largely with rhythm—the kind of movement which the composer uses; but gravity and steadiness are also features of ideal tone. Gravity is associated with breadth, and tone only reaches the full measure of its volume and powers when it (i.e., the vowel) is ideally shaped, and this in its turn guarantees steadiness: for the tension and control implied in the one fulfils the necessary conditions in the other. Emotional disturbance (*vibrato*, etc.) which is quite proper and necessary in 'personal' art is generally quite out of place in 'impersonal' art: for impersonal art should direct our thoughts away from any particular individual with his private concerns—its function is to lead us to broader, higher ground. Thus, if we are required to sing in the first person, as in the exceedingly beautiful phrase:

JOHN MUNDY.

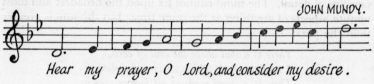

Hear my prayer, O Lord, and consider my desire.

it must be applicable to humanity at large. The singer voices the words not only for himself but for everyone, just as a priest speaks for the congregation. His personality is not wanted, it would be an intrusion. Priest and singer must be a type, not a person. Therefore we must have perfect tone in this phrase, perfect *sostenuto*, and such 'expression' as we use must be determined by the sense of the words and music, in all its breadth, and not by any fret, caprice (or infirmity) of our own. Sometimes, after morning prayer on the wireless one hears a hymn tune and variation played by strings, *vibrato* and *espressivo*, a nauseating experience; in which the dignity of religious art is utterly lost sight of. If we cannot give such a dignity to work of this kind, let us at any rate cease to apply the paints and pomades of artificial civilization to it; better no expression at all, than such misplaced attempts. Religious art at its best is never a matter of petty personal pronouncement—but is after the manner of liturgies, depersonalized by tradition and broadened by common use. But let it not be thought that 'common' means 'ordinary' or that the religious style is an easy one; it is the most difficult of styles both in rhythmic and tonal control and nothing but ideal vowelling will serve for it.

We have discussed the test of authority in regard to tone perfection, also the ideal test (that is implicit in our very being) to which we give instinctive allegiance. The third test is the practical one. What is required of good tone—what are the conditions that ensure it; how does good tone work, in short? We may be pretty sure that the best tone will best satisfy technical processes; that it will be mechanically perfect.

As Rosalind's virtues could hardly be encompassed—there seemed no end to them—so it is difficult to speak of all the qualities of good tone; but these are perhaps the most obvious.

Good tone

1. presents an unyielding front—it is consistent, solid—can extend a melodic line firmly, or build up an entirely safe harmonious structure;

2. is strong-sounding—gives the impression of power and sonority, even in *pianissimo*;

3. is capable of the utmost *nuance*—commands the 'swell', so that a well proportioned gradation from pp to ff is possible,

4. possesses tonal energy; has that vital, *timbrée* quality which alone will define words and notes clearly;

5. is able to darken bright, open sound, while preserving richness of colour;

6. is capable of a perfect *legato*;

7. or of *staccato*, *marcato*, and any sort of accent;

8. can move at any speed;

9. and with absolute ease in a smooth, liquid flow, with no hitch or roughness in vibration;

10. is so poised that a perfect 'touch' upon it is possible; that the demarcation between silence and sound can scarcely be detected.

If, by these tests, we criticize the singing that we generally hear, we find that as regards

1. tone is wavering, perforated, discontinuous, seldom approaching the firmness of instrumental sound;

2. the majority of voices are just pip-squeak affairs, or shall we say, more poetically, somewhat like 'the earliest pipe of half-awakened birds', negligible in authority, without any real grip of the situation;

3. a pliable, varying line of tone is absent, though something like it may do duty from sheer lack of control;

4. the tone is without resonance in any complete sense and therefore incapable of 'feeling' or expression;

5. most voices have only one quality of tone at command—their own natural quality—the modification of tonal quality in any certain way is outside their power;

6. how rare is a good *legato* which links up notes in an indissoluble way, so that one note is almost part and parcel of another!—there is generally some sort of spiritual hiatus

187

between one note and the next though the sound may not actually stop;

7. emphasis, or power of assertion is usually very weak;

8. extremes of speed both slow and fast are not often within the capacity of the singer;

9. one is seldom satisfied by grace of movement which combines tension and abandon;

10. a very rare accomplishment.

These defects may, of course, be due to lack of training and experience—one cannot expect a finished artist in the early stages of study; but they are often due to faulty principles of technique which disregard mechanical law. The principles that are applied would never produce what is wanted. Ease, effectiveness, point, power, speed, volume, etc., depend upon the conditions outlined in Chapter I, Section 3, of this book; and when these conditions are fulfilled not only will the movement of tone be assured, but its quality, also. Qualitative characteristics of sound are effectiveness, richness, and exact vowelling (i.e., colour) none of which can happen save by the best use of the vocal instrument, which in its turn gives the highest measure of these things—in other words, ideal quality. If the very acme of perfection is not reached—if a relative standard still operates—it nevertheless, as we have said, may approach perfection so nearly as to suffice for it. Certain human achievement seems about as good as it can be. Even a god could scarcely improve upon a Bach fugue or any of the recognized masterpieces of music—such is the inevitability of their structure. They disclose the hidden soul of harmony—a sort of objective truth that does not seem subject to man's fallibility. And it is the same with tone. The best tone reaches a level upon which the personal note is not heard.

The line of demarcation between the sacred and secular is, however, not clearly marked. Some[1] refuse to admit it at all. But this is surely to deny all categories and standards. There *is* something different between the sacred and secular, though it raises confusing arguments. Ideal tone is certainly applicable to ideal situations; but what are such situations, how are we to know them? Perhaps they are best judged by means of words, though a musical counterpart must be possible. A phrase such as 'Ubi caritas et amor, ubi Deus est' or its more familiar equivalent 'God is Love' as compared with the opening words of Grieg's song 'Ich liebe Dich' gives us the cue. The one is entirely objective, the other subjective; the one moves away from us—it is centrifugal, as it were; the other is self-centred, bound up with personal emotion; the one is a greatly calm state-

[1] Even Schweitzer in his study of J. S. Bach.

ment, having its place within us, perhaps, but equally, far above and beyond us; the other has no significance save that which is given to it by the throb of passion.

Or take the words

> O death, where is thy sting?
> O grave, where is thy victory?

and see them side by side with those of Shakespeare's lyric

> Fear no more the heat o' the sun
> Nor the furious winter's rages;
> Thou thy worldly task hast done,
> Home art gone, and ta'en thy wages.

They are not parallel in thought—but the styles may be legitimately compared. The Biblical words, though expressing triumphant conviction, nevertheless seem beyond the range of individual feeling—theirs is a broad question with the universals 'death' and 'grave' in full command; with the Shakespeare, though something of a universal element is present, there is also intermixed a tender, sympathetic, personal understanding—the address is to someone we have known and loved, and now shall see no more. The two attitudes are different and, if carried to an extreme, we have on the one hand, for example, the impressive objective style of the world's liturgies, and on the other the moody, introspective style of romantic verse. It can be seen at once that the application of tone colour to these contrasted styles cannot be the same.

There is much intermediate ground where the universal and individual notes mingle; where something of grandeur is lost, but something of sympathy or pathos is gained; when the remote is still suggested, though a certain nearness discounts its mystery; where the massive content of the abstract is somewhat sacrificed to images that are of smaller, more familiar and concrete significance.

The poetry of Henry Vaughan and George Herbert offers examples of the type that is midway between the sacred (in its most imposing form) and the secular styles.

> Sweet day, so cool, so calm, so bright,
> The bridal of the earth and sky,
> The dew shall weep thy fall tonight;
> For thou must die.

> Sweet rose, who here, angry and brave,
> Bids the rash gazer wipe his eye,
> Thy root is even in its grave,
> And thou must die.

Sweet spring, full of sweet days and roses,
A box where sweets compacted lie,
My music shows ye have your closes,
All, all must die.

Only a sweet and virtuous soul,
Like seasoned timber, never gives;
But, though the whole world turn to coal,
Then chiefly lives.

This poem of George Herbert has very obviously one foot on earth, the other in heaven; and it is to be remarked that an ethical or moral note is almost inseparable from the style. The serious import would otherwise fail in stress. In such words the loveliness of earth is seen, somehow, *sub specie aeternitatis*; it is not only loveliness but something more, which links up with a sense of the ideal as an objective reality. Nevertheless, it is not the highest expression of the religious attitude, stamped with the authentic seal of sacred literature.

The great abstract pronouncement, whether it be in terms of Deity, or of universals

'To mercy, pity, peace and love,
All pray in their distress,'

hardly engages one's emotions, or only the specifically religious ones of awe, wonder and the like (which really still personal expression). As performers, all we have to do is to present such pronouncement in the clearest form, without comment or any show of feeling in the ordinary sense. It is the music and the words which matter; devoid of colour, glamour, atmosphere, or anything which relates it to ourselves, or our daily surroundings. For the moment we are withdrawn from these things; the vision dominates; light, not heat, emerges; the perception is intellectual rather than emotional, formal rather than expressive.[1]

To conclude. The better a thing is done the more impersonal it

---

[1] Certain aspects of the Christian religion relate us to the personal and therefore stimulate personal reaction. The figures of Christ and His Mother for the most part appear as persons. An 'Ave Maria' or 'Jesu, Dulcis Memoria' therefore cannot be sung in a quite impersonal way, though an attempt may be made to do so in deference to ecclesiastical propriety; but one then feels that something is amiss and that a quasi-secular carol rather than true sacred song strikes the more intimate, religious note that personality requires. The fact of personality seems to open up a decline of quality in religious practice, and it often ends in sentimentality and emotional excess. Buddhism with its insistence on the impersonal steers clear of this. When tone is veiled or unsteady it is quite incapable of the clarity and dignity peculiar to thought of this sort; capricious ill-regulated time is also against it. The matter cannot be further pursued.

becomes, the less does it seem to be associated with the doer. In other words it approximates more to an ideal condition. We are individually recognized by our faults, not so much by our virtues.

CHARACTERISTIC TONE

We have tried to speak of what we have called ideal tone, and found that it did not depend upon circumstance, which might modify it; that it was constant in its quality because all impurity had been eliminated, or, at any rate, that was the aim of its control.

Characteristic tone demands something different: that it should be true to a particular situation, linking up with local habit and specific individuals. Particularity rather than normality is stressed; diversity rather than uniformity.

Culture is not all gain. It tends to bring things to a dead level, to destroy natural raciness—nevertheless the full measure of human development cannot be achieved without it, for it adds an intellectual to an instinctive power by which alone the possibilities of nature can be realized. What is wanted is that these achievements shall be applied in the right way, to glorify nature not to travesty her. What passes as culture is often an enervation of natural power, not its strengthening, and we have to return to the fount of nature, almost forgetting civilization, to see where we have gone astray. Thus the voices of simple folk—sailors, fishermen, labourers of all kinds—may give us tone which is essentially stronger than the educated tone of those classes who have submitted to the process of education; but educated tone *can* be strong, not only in power but in significance—and if it is it will be capable of ideal as well as characteristic application.

There is something ridiculous in refined tone being used for what one might call 'rough' songs, as seen in those of the student and folk type. The whole spirit of the song is against it. Ordinary sentiments of jollity or vigour are much better dealt with by a sort of coarse, countrified, manly tone, whose force has not been too fined down. But it is otherwise with ideal sentiments which are the result of culture. As always, tone must be fitted to circumstance.

If the singer is a *dramatis persona* he must sing his part. It is only when what he is expressing lies in a world of beauty, so to speak, outside himself that he can fulfil an ideal role. If the poet makes use of local speech, as Hardy does in 'The Homecoming' and other poems, the singer must follow suit. His singing amounts to nonsense unless he does this. Therefore he should have command of different accents and shades of tone for his own language as much as for a foreign language. To speak Hamlet's words with a boorish accent would be just as bad as to speak country homespun with a silky sound. You can talk about a countryman with the utmost refinement of speech, but if, through you, it is he who is talking, you must adopt his manner.

An Irish or Scotch song cannot be sung with an English accent. It must be true to type. The utmost command of colour is therefore necessary: a thousand qualities of the same vowel. But it is highly probable that unless ideal tone is mastered, characteristic kinds of tone will not be available; just as a well-controlled *rubato* depends upon an absolute hold of strict time. A good *rubato* is just as hard to manage as strictly proportioned movement; indeed, in its own way it is just as perfectly proportioned as the latter. Similarly, characteristic tone is as sure in its control as the purest of sound.

Experience shows that the average singer is generally incapable of using his voice in any but the way that is natural to him or in which he has been trained. There is no capacity for colour or the alteration of the same genus of tone. It is *his* voice, not *a* voice that can be used for any purpose. This is not art, it is just singing—a very different thing. Characteristic or 'character' singing is a difficult affair, and as such is, in a general way, to be undertaken only by soloists. Combined voices have to use a more conventional tone, to gain uniformity.

A singer may not like to degrade his tone: to sing badly, in fact—as he may have to do if he wants properly to impersonate certain characters. The Witches in Verdi's *Macbeth*—to give a specially good instance—cannot sing with 'beautiful' tone; they have to make their tone almost as ugly as it can be. Alas, for poor professors of singing and their nicely-brought-up pupils! One can only say again that it is as difficult to sing really badly as to sing really well; or, at any rate, to know *how* to sing really badly.

It might appear as if 'characteristic sound' applies only to words; and there is much truth in this, for it is, in the main, founded upon local habits of speech. Music seems to be above local considerations; to have a sort of ideal quality of its own, independent of time and place. Yet since music is expressive, it also must show signs of its cultural origin. There are undoubtedly rough as well as cultured types of music; and different types of tone are applicable to them. This, however, need not be discussed here, since the voice is seldom used purely as a vehicle for music. Words nearly always give the clue. In this the singer is much more fortunate than the instrumental player; and there is very little excuse if the former fails to follow the verbal lead, not only in sense but in shape and form and accent of the word-phrase. Sometimes compromise is necessary between words and music; often song will tend to give a broader sweep to words than they would have by themselves—though this amounts to scarcely more than asserting the music of words. But speech is undoubtedly the dominating factor in song.

'Characteristic' tone of the uneducated, simpler sort, is mostly comprised under the term 'dialect' which represents a departure from 'received' pronunciation—though what the standard of such pronunciation is or should be opens up a veritable hornet's nest. Perhaps what we have said about 'ideal' tone does, however, elucidate the matter, and it is probable that 'pure' tone, i.e., pure vowelling, will be conceded as at any rate a possibility—and a desirable possibility; also that tone which fails to meet this aim is either bad tone or of the nature of dialect. From this point of view dialect (in as far as it fails to conform to pure tone, whatever that may be) is a falling from grace. It is not pure tone. The great artist may have control of the purest tone and deliberately exchange it, for the moment, for tone which is less pure—to dialect in short. Yet it is obvious that occasions for the display of full-blooded dialect—or outlandish tone of any sort—are very limited. Art is not very concerned with such matters; its ideal nature precludes that. A tinge of roughness or awkwardness may be good in song or opera, but it seldom appears to an extreme or fully-truthful degree. There is not much room for it in the works of the great masters of song, though in folk-song and the like it may often be appropriate enough.

It is probably in its comic and amusing aspect that characteristic singing is especially valuable; the serious aspect can seldom be satisfied by it. When, in the well-known nursery song 'Who killed Cock Robin?' the animals one by one proffer their services for the obsequies of Cock Robin, it would be very tame indeed if the same sort of voice were used for each. Half the fun of the song is to characterize each animal by appropriate tone, and this inevitably means some sort of distortion of the best vocal procedure; but such distortion could not be suffered in, say, Mozart's *Requiem*, though it is an absurd comparison.

George Bernard Shaw, when serving on a committee composed of English and Americans, said that he realized the impossibility of deciding upon a standard for the pronunciation of even such a limited vocabulary as 'yes' and 'no'. He afterwards wrote that the only criterion of speech which any man could adopt was to make certain that his listeners secured the impression that he was intelligent and educated. But this would not necessarily guarantee a constant individual pronunciation. Upon different occasions pronunciation of the same words varies. Easy-going speech would have a different colour from speech used at formal functions.

This is true enough. We can observe it in our own voices. When we have on our best clothes we talk rather differently from when we are in our lounge suits. But we probably do not depart greatly from our normal habits at any time: habits that have been developed by the circumstances of our life and upbringing, or by the efforts we have made to improve our pronunciation.

And it is not only our own speech which varies. Everyone pronounces a little differently from his neighbour, even if they have submitted to a similar training. Sometimes variation takes place to a ridiculous degree. Not only 'quot homines, tot sententiae' but 'tot voces'. In educated circles of the Church we get almost as many varieties of 'God' as there are vowels—'Gŏd', 'Găd', 'Gŭd', and other variants are frequently exhibited. Or it may be that euphony requires an adjustment of pronunciation. Thus in the phrase

'Goes down the garden singing'

the 'the' would be pronounced differently from what it would be in

'To hear the alleys ringing'

In the former the 'e' would be soft (much as in 'earth') in the latter harder (much as in 'thee'). The position of a word relative to its neighbours may easily modify its sound; just as different consonants will influence the same vowel to different qualities (*v.* p. 123).

Variation is to be found, too, according to locality. The southerner in England says 'pŏŏt' (as in 'good') for 'put', the northerner 'pŭt' (almost as in 'cut'); while pronunciation of place names varies even in the place itself. Some call Romsey (in Hampshire) 'Rŭmsey', others 'Rŏmsey'. These are major variations. Slight variations exist everywhere, so slight that they can scarcely be analysed.

To the average American our general pronunciation of English sounds seems affected; to the Englishman American pronunciation sounds unpleasing. But it is worth while saying that when the American is taught singing his 'accent has to be changed; and the same is also true, to a large extent, when the Englishman submits to the process. So that there does seem to be a sort of norm of good sound that we instinctively respect. The tendency of cultured speech is undoubtedly towards uniformity—*pace* Mr. J. B. Priestley when he says that the only accents he dislikes are those 'of people who have run a long way from their local accent, to something that came out of a cheap tin can'. There is, of course, no need to run in this direction at all; the fount of pure tone as well as a weaker wash of artificial speech is open to us. Mr. Priestley is right in rejecting what may be called a poor exchange, but he is wrong when he seems to approve of all kinds of local accent. It depends upon where this accent comes from. If from large towns or industrial centres, where tone is largely determined by its power to cut through the noise of traffic or machinery—being shorn of those influences which will cause it to merge with and approximate to the sounds that inanimate nature herself makes—it is not likely to have much to commend it. Cockney, for instance, is scarcely a thing of beauty. The truth is that when the voice has been divorced from the open air and natural pursuits it loses even its human quality, and itself takes on something of the sound of an unfeeling machine. Dialects from the countryside are on the whole good; those from towns more or less bad.

It cannot be conceded that this is a wishful interpretation of the facts. The best tone is probably a golden mean between a too-thin quality and a too-thick quality in which both over- and under-educated sounds are eliminated.

It might also be noted that even backward, boorish speech has its forward perversities: such as the pronunciation 'pĕth' or 'paeth' for 'pahth' ('path'), when the low position of the tongue is sacrificed just as it is in the over-refined pronunciation 'beŏ' or 'bayŏ' for 'beeur' ('beer'). It is probably the low position of the tongue which guarantees all good vowelling, including the ŏ and all the short vowels. If the tongue is relatively high, vowels can only be sounded in the most 'heady', constricted way. The same is true, as we know, of the nasal sound of M.

What are we to say of all this mix-up? Who is to decide upon the standard—like the French Academy does? Why should we prefer the word 'God' to be pronounced 'Gŏd', and shudder when we hear it as 'Gŭd'? It is a very difficult question, perhaps incapable of solution (except empirically, by some central authority) as Bernard Shaw found.[1] Accepted pronunciation varies, too, over the centuries. The Elizabethans did not pronounce as we do. We say 'thŭnder' (or do we?); they said 'thoonder'—using a much broader vowel.

The same breadth and backwardness is to be found in all dialect speech. Dialect does not move forward as does the Oxford accent, unless this too is to be counted as dialect. Dialect is of the soil, not the mind; it is quite content with its lowly state, preferring it to higher cerebral accomplishment. Generally speaking, strong 'voiced' consonants are used rather than their weak 'breath' counterparts; and so in the Dorset dialect, the backward V takes the place of forward F, Z appears for S, G for K; or, as regards vowels,

[1] It is not enough to say that the ŏ in 'God' is the traditional vowel, accepted over the centuries. Other languages have other sounds in 'Deus', 'Dieu', etc. The Saxon ŏ however, does seem to meet the case in a rather remarkable fashion; for this vowel is the most concentrated of any vowel, the veritable 'centre of intensest light' in terms of sound. Perhaps this is why we prefer it.

'en' replaces 'ing', and the lower-lying oo, u: as in the second of these two lines from the Dorset poet, William Barnes:

> *High over head the white rimm'd clouds went on,*
> *Wi' woone a-comen up, vor woone a-gone.*

If Oo, the deepest vowel of the voice, can be put in, it is, as in 'hwome' (dialect for "home'), or 'mwoan' (for 'moan')—the 'w' standing for Oo.

How different is the direction of the cultured or quasi-cultured voice! It frankly gives up the advantage of an open throat, and is satisfied with resonance that extends scarcely beyond the limits of the mouth, so that we get a plethora of the vowel ŏ in its most disagreeable form. Whenever it can be brought into a final syllable it is, regardless of right vowelling—'mother' becomes 'mŏthŏ' (instead of 'mŭther'), 'culture' becomes 'culchah' (which is almost the same as 'culchŏ')—the differentiation between the final vowel in 'mother' ('er' or 'ur') and the final one in 'culture' ('e+oor' or 'eur') being quite lost sight of. In its own way this little vowel ŏ is extremely important, as we shall see later—but its abuse is degenerate and dreadful. The long vowel Oh has also to submit to this 'advanced' treatment and for it we often hear 'ow' (as in 'town') instead of its deep round sound, and there are other bad variants tolerated not only by gutter-snipes but by grave professors. The intellectualizing process serves speech well enough for a certain time, as long as it runs hand-in-hand with emotion; but at length it forges too far ahead, forgets its needful partner and gets stranded like a boat borne by the tide up a beach and there left high and dry.

The following verse by Miss Ruth Duffin, (who, I trust, will not object to my reprinting it here), pillories the main faults of modern speech. It is entitled 'A Petition from the Letter R to the B.B.C.'[1] and was intended, at the time, to cloak a protest against microphonic abuse, and particularly against a gentleman who pronounced 'leopard' 'leppid' in a travel talk.

> *O culcha'd rulahs of the aia,*
> *Listen to my humble praya!*
> *There was a time when I knew my place,*
> *But lately I have fallen from grace.*
> *You hurry me from pieh to pillah,*
> *And then transf' me to a villar.*
> *From heah and theah I'm forced to paht*
> *Till Asiah takes me to her heaht.*
> *I used to be alive in modern*
> *But now I find it rhymes with sodden.*

---

[1] Quoted some time ago, in an *Observer* article by St. John Ervine.

Seven and Severn are alike
To those who speak upon the mike
(Rophone), which is the modden patte'n
Of speech to all except the slatte'n.
Ah oh! my tempah is not tepid
When I am banished from the leppid,
And you may feel my angah bu'n
When I am ousted from Trahe'ne,
And awdahed shahply to connect
Idear-of, aw to effect
A marriage between lawr and awdah
Of which I hate to be reco'dah.
I cannot beah to heah of waw.
It irritates me maw and maw.
Anathemar on him who slays
His native tongue in suchlike ways!
Lawds of Culchah, lend an eah
And my sad petition heah.
Rescue me from this disgrace
And I shall be, aw neah aw fah,
Your slave the Letter R or Ah.

The tendency of cultured speech is, then, to thin out; to become more forward in placing; and (by inevitable weakening of its emotional basis) to lose the rich rusticity of folk-speech. Perfect speech would try to keep this natural richness of sound, while making it more open and communicative. But without the necessary feeling openness turns to whiteness; communicativeness to mere gush. What was fed upon the satisfying pastures of rural experience, becomes starved and attenuated on the stony wastes of towns. Barnes believed that 'the beautiful in art is the result of an unmistaken working in men in accordance with the beautiful in nature'. This belief is shared by many. We need to live with nature, to be continually reminded of her beauty; or we get 'out of tune'. And natural beauty as regards the voice is to be found in simple dialect. Barnes affirmed that Dorset dialect was 'purer and more regular than that which has been adopted as the national speech'; and, in essential, he was right. Strong speech comes from the country—not the townsman—this is the first stage; in a middle stage, at probably the best period, speech becomes both strong and skilled, owing to conscious development; finally it emerges as mere skill. Then, by catastrophe or upheaval of some sort, the cycle is repeated. We might expect the best speech from small cultured communities, where a happy blend of town and country prevails. The London of Elizabethan times must have supplied it; the London of to-day certainly does not.

We have spoken of 'ideal' tone in contradistinction to 'characteristic' tone; but though the latter is evolved unconsciously we shall never arrive at the former merely by taking thought. The ideal pattern (which I think we are bound to postulate) can only be discovered through its physical shape. As this shape is gradually determined, so will the ideal, in correspondence with it, become clear. It is through matter that we see what mind is.

Dialect is not tolerable in cultured singing. We feel that it is wrong and have to ask ourselves why we so feel it; can we justify the feeling? The question has already been answered at some length (on p. 193) but it may be added that the best pronunciation also probably derives from considerateness towards our fellows; it is a sympathetic, kindly way of approach; a sign of good manners, which rougher forms of speech cannot indicate. Rough speech may be sincere, but it is also slightly repellent. It lacks the grace and smoothness—not necessarily to be associated with 'smooth nothings' —which make for the easiest form of social intercourse, whether at home or abroad; and to a certain extent this represents its failure. Moreover, such speech is technically imperfect. It lacks ring. It does not make the most of itself. A well-produced voice has twice the sound of a badly-produced voice, and (to a certain extent, again) the dialect voice is badly produced.

Both from the expressive and effective points of view dialect tone has to be criticized; on the other hand the virtues of dialect are also clear. It is not the mere substitution of a dialect vowel for a 'received' one that can be counted a fault—Aw+ĭ for I+ĭ (first personal pronoun) is a perfectly good exchange. It is that the dialect placing will generally be found to arise from a relatively lazy emission of the tone.[1] Theoretically, it would be quite possible— once the change of vowel has been allowed for—to improve and refine dialect vowels till they become as good as educated vowels; but then they would lose the particular character that made them dialect. This character, I think we are bound to admit, represents an imperfection of ideal beauty, though it interests as do all characteristic things.[2] But we cannot interpret ideal situations through it. We should not tolerate Palestrina, for instance, being sung with a Lancashire burr, simply because we should not get the right spiritual

---

[1] This is equally true, in the opposite direction, of over-civilized speech.

[2] It is quite certain that dialect will never exhibit a beautiful, open Ah; nor, for the matter of that, will *any* speaker or singer exhibit it, till it has been secured by a long course of study. The English Ah is nearly always quite wide of the mark; the Italian Ah is by nature much nearer to it, because Italians speak better than we do.

expression from it; it could give us a rich earthly quality, scarcely a heavenly one. In proportion as art becomes universalized, dialect disappears. The effort is, then, to determine an ideal speech, free of local taint. But this does not mean insipidity. As we have said, the strongest human emotion can be expressed through ideal speech, and when it is so there is an increase, not a decrease, in dignity and nobility. Universality should be a bigger thing than particularity. Just as the Greeks desired to do away with the individual actor by the wearing of masks, so it is often necessary to do away with the individual singer by reducing his personal pronunciation to a minimum, and endeavour to produce a voice (or *la voix* as the French would say) which, as far as possible, does not seem to be his private possession.[1] And vagaries of accent surely do tend to disappear, once a serious study of the voice takes place, particularly if it is influenced by music.

There is a sort of deformity in tone which must not be associated with dialect. Dialect is more than individual utterance. It is a tint or tinge that covers the voice of a district or community.[2] It is *their* way of speech. It may not be perfectly educated speech, but it is not deformed speech in any but the most limited sense. There are distortions of speech, however, which seem too far removed from the normal to be regarded as anything but monstrous; just as there are distortions and deformities of the body. They are not merely variants of the normal—they are abnormalities. They strike one immediately as wrong, as definite faults of voice, which will be discussed later. Dialect does not appear like this. In a way it may satisfy us better than does refined sound. It does not come from peculiar people, but from those who are very sane and strong. You can easily mimic the peculiar—this will be in the nature of a comic turn; less easily the characteristic; the ideal will defy your fun—you cannot mimic it—it will consume you, bring you to its own image, before this takes place. A talent for mimicry is necessary if the peculiar and the characteristic is to be shown. Those who have developed the best form of speech often find it difficult to unbend into variants of it. A foreign language doesn't trouble them, for this is entirely different from their own, and therefore far easier to

[1] There is such a thing as impersonal emotion—an abstract expression of emotion, reflecting only that contained in the song—and in which the performer's personal contribution is eliminated, or reduced to a minimum. Tennyson suggests something of this sort when he speaks of Maud as being 'neither courtly nor kind .... but a voice.' It might perhaps be called cosmic emotion.

[2] It is almost impossible to analyse it in terms of mechanism, or to deal with it by the rules of singing. It comes from habit. Unless you grow into it, from childhood, you will never quite get it. The mind has no more control of it than over the vibration of the vocal cords as regards pitch. It can be imagined, willed; but not understood.

fix. Perhaps we must be content if the singer sings his own language well, together with Italian, French and German.[1] This list of languages can be, and sometimes is, extended, but most song seldom requires it. Nevertheless the 'compleat singer' can adjust himself to dialect and characteristic tone with ease, though it is too much to hope for the gifts of a Ruth Draper in such matters. But the capacity for the varied colouring of accepted pronunciation—that is, to be able to sing vowels in a forward, central or backward position, has to be within a competent singer's grasp.

To conclude. Dialect is the very root of the matter as regards good tone; but it is too slow in movement, too slack in concentration to serve all or indeed the highest purposes of vocal art. It has to be delivered with far greater intensity, but by this treatment it loses some of the characteristic colouring, some of the softer, *mezzo* shades of dawn and dusk, in favour of a colouring more to be associated with the clearer light of day. It thus, to a greater degree, enters the realm of intellectual clarity, becoming less characteristic, but more universalized.

[1] Latin is also necessary, but Church Latin is pronounced just as is Italian.

Chapter 4

THE RELATION OF BREATH TO TONE

TYPES OF BREATHING

THERE is nothing esoteric about good breathing. Anyone can breathe properly if they will only take their cue from two natural actions, yawning and retching. With the first we take in as much breath as we can, with the second we expel it as strongly as we can. Anything further consists in developing these two actions, not in superseding them. No one has either great volume or power of breath to begin with, whereas much of both is needed in singing. To a large extent, then, we are required to improve upon the ordinary processes of nature, bringing skill to bear; but, as with everything else in regard to singing, we only do what it is natural for us to do as human beings, and go wrong when we depart from nature's ways.[1]

It is obvious that at times we shall need all the breath that we can store; also that we shall have to use it as powerfully as possible —other uses of the breath we have already discussed; they need not be referred to here.

We never exhale all our breath—nothing like it, in fact, though it may appear so. With each expiration we lose a small amount of breath at the top of the lungs and at each inspiration we regain it at the base of the lungs, through the descent of the diaphragm. This latter action can be effected so quickly that there is almost a continuous expulsion of breath, if we so wish it. It is equally within our power to make the expulsive action last for a long time. Both these actions, if carried out to perfection, require a control that only comes from years of practice.

There is, thus, an intake and output of breath in the completed cycle of breathing, and stress may be laid on either the one or the other. If the former we shall be mainly occupied with downward expansion, if the latter with upward compulsion. In other words, we may attempt to keep the base of the lungs filled as long as we

---

[1] *Yet nature is made better by no mean,*
But nature makes that mean: so o'er that art
Which you say adds to nature, is an art
That nature makes. . . .

           Winter's Tale.

For virtue is nothing other than nature carried to its highest perfection.
          Cicero, de Legibus, Bk. I.

H*

can—this will release the muscles of the neck; or to expel it as energetically as possible, which will tighten the muscles of the neck. In both cases, *provided there is continued intensity of action*, the vocal mechanism will be 'set' for the production of sound, i.e., the vocal cords will be in such a state that they function rightly as a valve of control for breath emission. If there is no continued intensity of action, neither will the breath hold, nor the vocal cords be ready to vibrate in any musical sense.

Two types of breathing are involved here: (1) the 'yawning' and (2) the 'retching' type (for the sake of politeness we call it this, but it is simply how the breath acts when we are sick). With (1) the effort is to preserve the deep inhalation of a yawn; with (2) to give exhalation the greatest pressure that we can. If our attitude is towards (1) the diaphragm will be more depressed and the abdomen protrude more, though it will still be drawn in; if towards (2) the diaphragm will be raised more and the abdomen strongly contracted. With (1) what we may call the 'level' of the breath is low, since it is distributed rather at the base of the lungs; with (2) it is high, since it is compressed rather at the apex. In short, with a comparatively low breath pressure the breath will be low; with a high pressure, high. Further, since a low pressure does not need as tight a valve—i.e., as tightly approximated vocal cords—as a high pressure, low breath pressure will mean a loose vocal mechanism, and high pressure a tight one.

Perfect co-ordination between breath action and the state of the vocal instrument is thus indicated. It has a logical connection such as we might expect. Nevertheless it is *possible* for the vocal cords to be tight, and the breath loose and low. This is indeed not only *a* but almost *the* method of bad singing, in which case distortion of tone—throatiness, etc.—is bound to occur, since strains are put upon the mechanism unnaturally and to no good purpose.

It comes to this, then: that when the breath level is low the vocal instrument will also be low-lying; when it is high it will tend to lift the instrument with it. The larynx will fall with deep breathing and the throat will open; with high breathing the larynx will rise and the throat close.

Types of Tone

The effect of this on the sound is easily heard. With the low breath it falls from the nasal cavities, coming, as it were, to rest in the open throat; with the high breath it is lifted into the nasal cavities but at the expense of throat resonance, since the throat tends to close.

Thus, tone will be easier and of a darker shade with a low breath, and tighter and of a more brilliant quality with a high breath.

This appears to be incontrovertible and its implementation shows the great variety of tone that is opened up by these muscular variations. There is no such thing as 'vocal tone'—if by that we mean one particular tone; there are thousands of sorts of tone, each one of them linked to its own emotional state.

We have therefore two main types of tone corresponding to the two main types of breath. These naturally link up with 'breath' and 'firm' tone,[1] but not in a hard and fast way. It is the action of the larynx which finally determines the situation, though it will generally be influenced by the position of the breath.

Breath and Firm Tone

All tone may be sung with a less or greater degree of resistance at the vocal cords. If there is but slight resistance we get 'breath' tone; if resistance is strong, 'firm' tone. Breath tone has a natural affinity with the low-lying breath, and firm tone with a raised breath—since a low, deep breath action tends to loosen the larynx, whereas a high action tends to jam it.

To make the voice 'breath-tight' is one of the chief aims of the singer because the maximum of power is thereby achieved. When wastage of breath occurs, tone diminishes in strength, but it may still be quite beautiful. Breath or *mezza voce* tone is the most poetic of all, for with it hardness has disappeared.[2]

Ŏ (in 'hot') has the hardest texture of all vowels; or can have it, by literally squeezing the breath out of the tone. Scarcely any breath need be used with it. It affords the outstanding example of breath economy. But it can also be sung in a *mezza voce* way; in which case some aspirate must be present. Just as we write 'Ah' so we should have to write 'ŏh' for this softer type of ŏ sound.

Going from breath into firm tone should be practised by a gradual approximation of the vocal cords with corresponding breath tension. Thus:

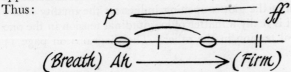

(Breath) Ah ———→ (Firm)

[1] Corresponding to the main categories of tone 'relaxed' and 'tensioned' discussed on p. 160 *et seq*. The matter is so fundamental, that further reference to it from a slightly different angle may not be amiss.

[2] This is not entirely true, though it seems so. In vital *mezza voce*, there is a core of hardness as with all good tone. That is to say, concentration can still operate, and this must involve tightening of some sort. Further discussion of the matter will be found on p. 166.

or on a succession of vowels:

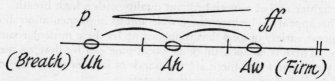

(Breath) Uh   Ah   Aw (Firm)

The breath tone must be gently aspirated and then strengthened till it becomes hard and metallic. Also proceed in reverse, from firm to breath tone. If carried to an extreme—and it sometimes has to be—the action involved in the foregoing *crescendo* is as though the voice were being gradually 'twisted' up, until it stops with a strong glottal jerk.

It will be obvious that as more breath has to be used for breath tone, the breath will not last as long for it as for firm tone; but it will last long enough, sufficient to cover an average phrase. Also, breath tone cannot be developed as strongly as firm tone; but here again, breath tone need not be *pianissimo*—it can respond to considerable dynamic expression.

It may be asked, is there not some contradiction between the tightening of the vocal cords for pitch and their loosening for *mezza voce*? How can both happen at the same time? The answer is that the glottis works independently of the vocal cords. The cords may tighten but the opening between them may be extended, and it is this opening that constitutes breath tone. Perhaps it would be wiser to connect breath tone with a loosening of the larynx as a whole, and firm tone with a compression of the larynx. At any rate the general feeling of breath or of firm tone is of loosening or compression *at* the vocal cords; that is to say, the valve which they constitute is enlarged or contracted according as we wish more or less breath to issue through it.

Though we have no conscious control of pitch tensions, we certainly have of the varying degrees of laryngeal compression. Strictly speaking, the degree of tension of the cords determines pitch; the form of the glottis opening influences the quality of the vocal sound. It is really a matter of longitudinal tension in the one case, and lateral tension in the other. The diagrams on page 14 make this clear.

BALANCE AND DIAPHRAGMATIC CONTROL

All muscular movement radiates from the diaphragm. The least twitch of the fingers registers in that region though it may not be felt consciously. But if the fists are tightly clenched, it will be immediately obvious that the effort is backed up, if indeed it does not originate—it is a moot point—at the diaphragm. This is best perceived by making a sharp, sudden movement of the foregoing (as at a word of command) and then holding the tension involved at its strongest. The equivalent of this important fact is registered in all good singing. If the necessary diaphragmatic effort is not made, and is not continuously present, the voice will be poorly sustained; it will be relatively raucous in tone, without charm or smoothness; in short, it will be devoid of expressive beauty. The lower the breath effort, the more round, rich, mellow and covered will the tone be; the higher the effort, the rougher and more aggressive the tone. It is largely a matter of opening the throat, and of the use of those means which secure it. All tone is good if it is willed, and adapted to the occasion. Nevertheless the most pleasing tone is undoubtedly produced by the breath at a low level, largely because production is then almost effortless. The tone almost sings itself. A recognition of this, if it has not been acted on before, will, in a quite remarkable way, change a singer's style, revealing qualities of tone and expression absent till that moment. It will also affect *portamento*, since the poise and buoyancy that diaphragmatic action gives prevents any sort of 'sticky' treatment in the taking of intervals. Notes are easily lifted, or easily fall; they 'float' lightly to their objective, instead of laboriously reaching it. So that *portamento*, though present in sufficient degree, never obtrudes. It is scarcely known to be there.

We have implied the word 'balance' in the previous paragraph and have often used it in the course of this book. But what do we really mean by it? It is not altogether easy to answer.

Balance is a state of rest, an absence of movement—equilibrium in short. The smooth surface of water indicates this state; when it is ruffled the balance has been upset. A slight force will thoroughly disturb shallow water but have little effect on a mighty mass, such as the sea. Equilibrium can be maintained under quite different conditions. Scales, for instance, can be balanced by an ounce on either side, or a pound, or a ton, if they will stand the strain. But what is this equilibrium as regards the voice; what equal and opposing forces are concerned? Is it the equilibrium inherent in the forces which control the breath, or of the breath pitted against the vocal instrument?

It seems clear that there may be an equilibrium of the breath muscles alone whether they are in a state of small or great tension. Though great tension of the diaphragm and abdomen will tend to close the glottis—this may be easily felt—it may be maintained with a fairly open glottis. This, however, will not produce any pressure of breath; it represents only a potential amount of stored energy, in a state of rest. Breath pressure does not begin to operate effectively till the glottis is closed, or partially closed, offering the necessary resistance to pressure; or if some stop, elsewhere (such as at the lips), is placed against the breath strain. Then pressure can be developed and its use controlled. The use of this pressure is the disturbing factor, in singing; its movement produces the movement of tone. Where, then, does balance in tone come in: for tone is by its very nature a disbalance of vocal forces? The answer, I think, is: that good singing, just as it should always come from a state of perfect balance, tends to return to this state, once the disturbing factor is stayed; and even during disturbance there should be an inherent tendency towards rest. It should aim at equilibrium, though it is momentarily deflected from it.

We have several times stated the problem in terms of 'dead' weight *versus* 'live' thrust, illustrating it by the lifting of an entirely loose arm, the looseness of which persists even though it is lifted. What is the equivalent of this relation of forces in the voice and what effect has it upon tone quality?

The force of gravity continually exerts itself upon our bodies. It accounts for our weight which we have to move if we wish to get about. We are wise to use this force when we can: a force which is always striving to come to a state of rest.

As regards the vocal instrument (by which we mean the vibrating mechanism situate in the larynx and the resonance cavities of the head—the general weight of the head, in short) there is no doubt that it will have a tendency to fall if it is left to itself and not lifted by tension, such as by the raising of the shoulders, etc.[1] The resonance cavities have certainly to be adjusted, according to the exigencies of vowelling and tone quality; but, notwithstanding, a large degree of looseness or dead weight can be allowed to the muscular material which forms their shape; so that, as already observed, a state of rest is always the ultimate objective, and such tensions as have to be used are thought of as temporary disturbance.

There are different degrees of balance, according as they are associated with light or heavy weights (as in the case of an ounce or a pound), or, what is the same thing, with slight or strong tensions. But balance *is* balance, no matter the weights or tensions involved, and movement is easy under all conditions provided it starts from a state of balance and has, as we have said, the power within itself to return to such a state. Nevertheless, strong muscular tensions are necessary in the vocal mechanism when very loud tone or quick movement has to be dealt with. Indeed to sing loudly and quickly

---

[1] The head, shoulders and arms should generally be loose.

is one of the chief aims of the vocalist, and the most difficult to implement. When do we hear the tremendous airs of Handel like 'Rejoice Greatly' from the *Messiah*, or the operatic *furibondo* for contralto voice, with the power and speed which should be given to them?[1] A certain stiffness, therefore, is present in such singing which may hamper movement unless at the same time balance is preserved or, at any rate, sought. The same danger is encountered in loud, quick pianoforte playing, where, unless the weight of the hand and arm is taken advantage of, the fingers will get tied up and refuse to serve. There is little danger of this, however, if only light tensions operate, the required work being done mainly by the natural resistance that the muscles, etc., afford, when in a state of comparative relaxation.

The head, etc., will have a natural tendency to settle down upon the trunk of the body, the body itself upon the ground, etc. This downward pressure is always present. What we have to do is to balance it by tensional 'lift'; to, as it were, remove the force of gravity for our own ends; using it, but not letting it function in the way it wants to, which is to reach this equilibrium above the earth, with and within our own bodies.[2]

If, as regards singing, we play with the force of gravity, we shall find that the lower jaw will loosen at the sockets, the mouth and tongue will fall down and forward, the muscles under the ears will be free; in short, that the throat will open and, with it, the sound; a really open Ah will be possible without taint of Aw, and all vowels, provided this loose condition is maintained, will be free, expansive, and reach a perfection that will be denied under any other conditions. Crabbed sounds, which never spread their wings, will almost certainly come from any other policy. What we have to do is to use the breath *against* this state of things, to apply pressure upon the vocal instrument without closing the relaxed tubes. There will come a time when great pressure will bring some counter closing with it, in obedience to the needs of resistance. *But pressure can be put upon a quite loose instrument*; and the student should practise

---

[1] Baroque art, of which Handel is the great exponent in music, has been summed up as 'movement imparted into mass'. This is what we nearly always get with Handel's 'runs': massive movement. To treat them lightly is usually to travesty their nature. Handel's short notes are as important as his long ones. They are not so much decorative as essential: hence the strength of Handel's style.

[2] Tension in a very real sense *is* lift. If we wish to raise the body, by going on tiptoe, we can only do so by tension, the main effort of which is taken at the diaphragm. Then the body is poised in a far different way from when we are on the soles of our feet. Exactly the same sort of tension lifts tone, preventing it from being, as it were, flat-footed, without the capacity to rise; it also tends towards light, thin tone of small calibre. As this tension is reduced (by a greater measure of relaxation) so tone spreads and thickens. Such tension also gives the voice its *holding* power, much as a screw holds the more firmly as you turn it.

incessantly till he can get a sufficiency of sound in this way. This type of tone has not the characteristics of completely *firm* tone, but it need not be 'breathy', only aspirated. In other words, it is *mezza voce* in quality, with a range of force from sound that is barely audible, to quite a satisfying strength. For it the level of breath is low. If higher levels are attempted, greater pressure is brought to bear, with consequent tightening of the mechanism. The great thing in 'breath' tone is to let the voice lie easily, as upon a soft cushion at the base of the breath. Then the sound will be soft in texture, gentle, reposeful; having qualities of loveliness (and lovableness) that can be gained in no other way. But we must not suppose that *only* this low level of the breath is applicable to breath tone. Higher levels can be brought to bear, even the highest, which will develop its intensity, carrying it more and more into the head. The tone then tends to be whiter, more purposeful, but can still be of a particular beauty.[1]

There is a whole range of song that requires treatment which only 'breath' tone can supply. The delicacies and refinements of the Elizabethan Ayre, for instance, depend upon it. It is not till we come to later music that the full batteries of the voice need to be brought to bear. Compare Purcell's bass air, 'Arise, ye subterranean winds' with almost anything of the sixteenth century or before, to see what a difference the rise of dramatic music made to the art of singing. There is scarcely room for a really loud note in a song of John Dowland or other writers of the period; but with 'Arise, ye subterranean winds' the whole force of nature (as it were) has to be unleashed.

Again (and again) let it be said that it is not relaxation, complete relaxation and nothing but relaxation that is wanted, but relaxation in a state of balance with a lifting force: the balance of freedom, by constraint. To insist upon relaxation alone is utterly wrong; it is equally wrong to insist only upon tension, though on the whole the latter will produce better results than the former, if they are considered apart. Certainly the singer will never get to the heart of expression without tension, or be able to immerse himself in what he is doing. This is seen perhaps most noticeably in dealing with the time element in music. For good time and rhythm depend upon will-power, upon the throb and measurement that the will alone can control, and the will in its turn is utterly dependent upon diaphragmatic tension. How often must we say this! It should represent the constant refrain of all training and teaching.

We often see pupils, and indeed singers who have passed that stage, letting the chest collapse immediately they start a note. This

[1] See also what is said on pp. 166–7 about this matter.

is a hopeless way of doing things. Breath must be energized from the bottom of the lungs, not the top. It must likewise be replenished at the bottom, for there is its greatest capacity, not at the top where its capacity is least. If this is not done, there is dislocation (at each breath) between the breath and the laryngeal mechanism. In effect the singer will be trying to play upon an untethered instrument, which of course must yield overblown, hooty tone.[1]

EMOTION AND PUNCTUATION

Emotion is the prime ingredient of song. Its seat, as of almost everything else, is at the diaphragm, or thereabouts. Emotion expresses itself in colour and, when adequately considered, emotional impulse accounts not only for colour, but alone directs the singer as to the colour that he should use. If he is not *moved* to express a song aright, to enter into the thought of the poet and the composer, his tone will probably be quite inappropriate. He may prove that he has a good voice, but not that he can 'act' or 'paint' with it. Singers seldom have a capacity for vocal colour, or seldom show it. One sort of sound does duty for everything. The result to the listener is little more than cold print is to the reader. The symbols of the song are presented, the words and notes may be clear but their meaning is negligible. Meaning has to be supplied as in the case of the printed word. This is really the job of the performer. He should tell us what the song is about, not leaving it to our imagination, though, of course, the listener is equally at the mercy of his own understanding.

Emotionally, we may wish sound to go on for ever. It is *legato* that fills our souls—that is why the music of Delius, almost above all other, is in this respect so satisfying. But a compromise has to be made with the intellect. Intellectually, we have to cut sound into bits or fragments, to bring it within the measure of our understanding. No stops, no sense.

---

[1] I have noticed that *at a distance*, one can distinguish the absence of timbre more clearly than close at hand. Hootiness seems intensified the further away one is from the voice—the lack of piercing quality is then very apparent—which is what one might expect. Types of tone, fairly suitable for intimate situations and close range, have little value when it comes to impressing a far-off listener. Then the need of concentration is apparent, just as it is with any sort of projectile—and the voice, after all, is a mechanical projection. It is the relatively small bore which sends the bullet furthest.

There are two main faults in singing: hootiness and throatiness. The former is too much in the head without being properly connected with the vocal cords; we may say it is unvocalized. The latter is too little in the head; it is chained to its point of origin, so that it cannot rise freely into the head resonances. Of the two, hootiness is the mere frequent fault. Very few voices are free from at least a suspicion of it.

It is astonishing to what an extent punctuation is usually absent from verbal (and musical) delivery. It is imperative to connect words or notes, when they have an organic nexus; it is stupid to run them on, when commas, etc., are applicable. The art of the *cæsura* is the art of understanding. A subconscious (or conscious) feeling for the smallest grammatical divisions ('motifs' in music) is a sign of the finest interpretation. If we take the words:

Arise/shine/for/Thy light/is come

they divide as indicated. The knife of the intellect dissects the phrase at such points by an inevitable process. These divisions have to be shown in some way. It would be easy to overdo punctuation of this sort—the phrase as a whole has to be thought of—but if it is not, in full detail, at the back of the performer's mind, his sense of the phrase will be at fault.

In the matter of education it has been said that 'Punctuation is more important than spelling'; and Ben Jonson, who, in Elizabethan times, left behind notes or rough materials for an English grammar, began them by asserting that 'Grammar is the art of true and well speaking a language: the writing is but an accident.' Such speaking (or rhetoric) with its implied punctuation has to be carried into song; with certain reservations as to the overriding power that must be allowed to music—at times, even, sound may be more important than sense.

It is obvious that a phrase is not 'put together' by constructing it of its parts.[1] We first of all have something to say before it can take form. We construe it simultaneously, though it may be subject to second thoughts. Analysis does not account for form; form accounts for analysis—otherwise the cart goes before the horse. That is to say, a phrase or idea is an emotional expression of some sort. One needs to insist on this. Even the barest statement involves feeling and has its counterpart in tonal quality. When a high degree of feeling is aroused—and it is generally the function of art to effect this—more vivid colours emerge because of greater muscular tensions.

We are *moved* towards lovely phrasing, intelligent delivery or whatever it is. It is an affair of the heart not the mind, except in so far as the mind is the servant of the heart. Some mysterious, primitive urge is present in every truly creative action; we need not even be aware of the ingredients of that act.[2] Even such a calculable

---

[1] Any more than an action is brought about by dealing separately with its component factors. Animals have no need of conscious analysis to perform almost miraculous feats of muscular control, nor of special training.

[2] It is very difficult rightly to assess the part consciousness plays in the produc-

thing as time is dependent, musically, upon feeling for its realization. It is not enough to know that so many crotchets, etc., go to a semi-breve, or what time signatures mean; though the reading of notes involves recognition, and ordered movement in performance can be developed and disciplined by more acute comparison of note values. The mind comes in in all matters of measurement, logic, relationship; but as a checking, rather than as a creative agent. Many singers have no *feeling* for time, or for tone; and so the mainspring of their work is absent, or so weak that it fails to awake any living response.

In extremely pregnant words, the Christian Church speaks of the 'knowledge and love of God'. Are not these words fundamentally synonymous? Is there any *real* knowledge without love? Is it not love that precisely constitutes knowledge? It is the same with art as with religion. When Thomas Morley tells the Elizabethan composer that he must possess himself with 'an amorous humour' if his work is to prove admirable, he is saying just the same thing. Emotion is at the root of understanding, and it is by emotion that we do things if they are to be of consequence.

Throughout this book we have used the word 'emotion' rather than 'passion'. The general connotation of 'emotion' is that it is more lyrical, diffused, sustained, than what we understand by 'passion'. 'Passion', with its tendency to sudden 'bursts' rather than steady 'drive', seems to have more reference to the dramatic. Nevertheless 'passion' has the greater weight and historical warrant.

tion of art. Its function seems to be to amend or criticize something already produced. Before we can be conscious of a thing it must be there. 'I have noticed,' said Raphael to Leonardo da Vinci, 'that when one paints one should think of nothing: everything then comes better.' Mozart gave a similar account of musical composition. We often call folk song an unconscious manifestation and an art song (like one of Schubert's) conscious. But is there any difference in the way such song comes about? The only difference may be that the folk singer is unaware of the structure of his song, whereas Schubert was aware of the structure of his.

In poetry, Paul Valéry distinguishes between *le vers donné* (which seems to come from an outside source) and *le vers calculé* (in which almost an act of will is implied). But the will need not rule out the unconscious element. It may select from it, delaying the final result; it can never replace it. Calculation (or choice) may represent a flash of inspiration, even though it is momentary and not continuous as in a purely spontaneous process. Consciousness, knowledge, what you will, seems to be a sort of final blessing that man possesses—allowing him to contemplate what he (or nature) has made, but which is not ultimately responsible for any truly creative act. We must, I think, beware of asserting the supremacy of mind over feeling, as we are inclined to do, or of denying the motive force of the latter.

In teaching one has to be conscious of what one is doing—in simpler words 'to know one's job'; even so, unless enthusiastic impulse goes with it, it will not be of much avail. A good lesson is really an adventure in which all one's capacities of mind and feeling are brought into play. To impart knowledge coldly, or simply as an affair of memory, is an impotent proceeding. Performance *of any sort*, in fact, requires an emotional approach.

'Hamlet,' says Mr. Gilbert Hudson,[1] 'asks the play-actor to deliver a "passionate"—not an "emotional"—speech; talks of the "passion" of the scene, and admires the actors' ability to shed tears and look distracted, in a fiction, in a *dream* of *passion*.' Emotion seems a weaker brand of this essence, and we shall be wise not to forget the older word.

We can do no better than take a lesson from an account of two famous singers given in Castiglioni's *The Book of the Courtyer* (trans. T. Hoby, 1561). It praises 'the manner of singing that Bidon useth, which is so artificial, cunning, vehement, stirred, and such sundrie melodies that the spirits of the hearers move all and are inflamed, and so listing a man would weene they were lift up into heaven. And no lesse doth our Marchetto Cara move in his singing, but with a more soft harmony, that by a delectable way and full of mourning sweetness maketh tender and perceth the mind, and sweetly imprinteth in it a passion full of great delite.' This tells of the real thing, and, if we have it not, there will be no commerce with the sun, the temperature of our work will be chill, our sound dead (needing to be raised, in every sense). And it is the breath, as ever, which decides the situation. Strong breathing is the sign of strong feeling.

A soul that labours and lives,
An emotion, a strenuous breath.

These words but reflect different aspects of essentially similar experience.

BREATH AND PITCH

Just as when the voice rises in resonance—i.e., makes use of more nasal sound—so when it rises in pitch does it require a higher breath. The reason is clear. The vocal cords have to tighten in both cases—for greater brilliancy and for higher notes—and therefore need more energizing, which can only be supplied by greater breath pressure. And, as we know, breath pressure can only be increased by a stronger concentration of breath in the upper part of the lungs, which is the equivalent of a higher breath level.

Experiment has shown that with tones of medium pitch the pressure of air in the windpipe is equal to that of a column of mercury of 160 mm.; with high pitch 920 mm.; with very high pitch 9,165 mm.; in whispering it may fall as low as that represented by 30 mm. of water. Variations of pitch and quality[2] have therefore to be met with very great variations of breath pressure; and, though

[1] *Terms and Topics of Elocution.*
[2] Whispering is but *mezza voce* carried to an extreme.

the art of singing may consist in so modifying valvular control (at the vocal cords) that pressure can be eased and lightened, it still remains that changes of pressure do occur and that the singer must be able to deal with them. There must be nothing like stiffness in breath control but an infinitely elastic use of the breath. This needs saying. So many singers just 'stay put' after they have taken breath, particularly a deep breath. An active, nervous element is lacking, which can instantaneously touch in an accent, give a 'swell', adjust varieties of tone force, or exhibit those innumerable signs of life which are the marks of good performance. The base of the breath should be like a boiling cauldron, 'on the work', ready to energize; seldom still. There should be a capacity for blowing the breath upon the vocal cords, giving it continuous *movement*. This is specially necessary in *mezza voce*. All of which shows the immense need of breath sensitivity.

As regards articulation, one has only to listen to the ardent utterance of a good operatic singer to realize what an expressive power goes with it. The calmer waters of lyrical singing do not ordinarily produce in it anything like the same degree, yet fine articulation is just as important there. Pressure (and drive) of the breath is the key to articulation, as to all else.

To sum up. The breath is subject to varying levels and pressures. If a low position of the breath is used, the pressure will be relatively low; if high, it will indicate more pressure, or perhaps we should say the possibility of more pressure, for the energy stored at either a high or a low level need not be actually used, as a soft note can be sung with a high breath, or a loud note with a low breath, though the softest and most easily vibrated notes are associated with a low breath, and the loudest (but less amenable) ones with a high.

Tone quality is also influenced by breath position. Low position, with less pressure, will naturally give a less forced and brilliant tone than high positions, with greater pressure; and we have just seen how pitch is affected.

Much of the art of singing consists in being able to use the resources and variations which the breath affords.

Generally speaking, we shall use the breath better if we stand than if we sit, because to keep an erect position the abdominal muscles have to be brought into play, whereas in sitting those muscles (and indeed *all* muscles) are apt to be relaxed. In standing we are therefore somewhat on the way towards right breath control, but much more has to be done before we are in the state that we should be. On the other hand, even in sitting, the abdominal muscles *can* be made to act properly from a singing point of view. We have to will it more, that is all. It was not for nothing that our grandparents made us sit up straight, though the present generation regards it as an unnecessary display of authority. This matter is particularly relevant to choir singing. The best work will usually be done standing, though we all like to 'take it easy'.

Breathing ought to be cultivated quite apart from singing, till the breath muscles are as strong as they can become. To do this, the fullest expansion should be given to the chest, ribs, etc.—by taking the deepest possible breath—and, *while this expansion is kept*, the contracting muscles should also be brought to bear in the most energetic way; so that both expansion and contraction operates simultaneously. A great feeling of power, particularly at the sides, under the armpits and at the shoulder blades, is thus engendered; and this will stand the singer in good stead, whether it is used or not at any given moment. In the most complete sense athletics and singing go together.

Many singers are not even aware that they have muscles in the abdominal region, and have never *consciously* used them. Till one *is* conscious of muscular tension, it is probable that the muscles concerned are more or less inoperative.

PART TWO
(mainly practical)

Chapter 5

PRACTICAL VOWELLING AND ARTICULATION

FEATURES OF VOWELLING

General Remarks: Mind and Mechanism

WHEN all is said and done as to the use of the vocal mechanism, it remains true that the imagination and sense of what is required must be brought into play; and that the process of assuring good tone is a double one: of desire and of doing, each acting upon the other. By the mind or imagination alone good tone could never be secured—in fact it would be impossible exactly to imagine what is wanted—the artistic 'conscience' will not suggest it; neither will trying to use and hold the mechanism in the right way. Good tone will only come *by endeavouring to produce it,* and the perception (or the imagination) of good tone also comes like this. It is very doubtful if anyone who has not been through the mill, that is, who cannot himself make the sounds that are wanted, will even be able to discriminate such sounds. The old tale of it not being necessary to be able to lay an egg in order to know what the taste of it is like, is not relevant, though it is a useful refuge for critical incompetence. If you are going to be an *expert* egg taster you must have tasted many an egg. Therefore it can be said that a fine sense of the tone of vowels can only come when you have heard many varieties; and further, that this sense is increased when you have personally succeeded in producing such tone. It is common experience that pupils simply do not recognize or appreciate the vowel quality that the professor may pattern, till they can produce it themselves. Then all is clear.[1]

[1] Even with a long experience of tonal *nuance*, the author lately found that he had considerable difficulty in catching the diphthong 'wy' in the Welsh word 'hwyl'—a very expressive word, by the way, indicating fervency of emotion, without which performance is a dead thing, though it is easily abused by the overzealous. In this particular case it was not only the difficulty of copying the sound (patterned for him by a Welshman), but, evidently, of hearing its particular shade. It was quite clear that the author did *not* hear it properly at first—the nearest he could get was something like hooil—and that it was only after he had succeeded in (more or less) reproducing the sound correctly *that he did hear it.* It is doubtful whether we really understand (or are fully conscious of) anything that has not entered into our minds through nervous or emotional muscular tensions. Many hold the view that we must be able to do a thing (actively) before we can thoroughly understand it. Knowledge is not experience; or rather the only knowledge which is any use *is* experience. And even if a less circumscribed view is held, we have sharply to distinguish, as do philosophers, between two kinds of knowledge: that which *is,* and that which is *about.*

Shaping of the Voice, Cavity Formation

'I go to prepare a place for you.' No heavenly note will come unless the cavity is ready to receive it. This refers chiefly to the mouth. Without straining similitude too far, it may be said that the nose, mouth and neck, in vocal practice, are the equivalent of colour, shape and mass in substantial things. Nasal resonance gives those sparkles of light which illuminate the tonal situation; the shape of the tone seems to be decided by the mouth; the neck gives the tone whatever mass or weight is desired. The idea of substance as well as shape in the voice is stimulating and important. Singing should seem like the guiding of a stream of solid or at least liquid sound along the bends and channels of the vocal instrument. Further, most singing is too indeterminate to be anything more than a mere solution of tone (or music); it never crystallizes, or takes shape in any complete way.

With firm enclosing walls the voice can be directed to an objective ahead of it; without them, it issues to the right and left, escapes and wastes through the sides of the mouth, instead of being projected centrally. In short, it has no straightforward character. Forcefulness or penetration is impossible; it is diffuse, weak. What is lacking is, of course, concentration, and concentration is synonymous with shape. Within the limits of such shape there must be ease, as much ease as can be secured; ease and shape are interdependent; what may be called 'spread' sound will never give controlled ease.

If the cavity is right, the sound will be right. The sound, as it were, has only to take possession of it. The perfect cavity makes the perfect vowel. But it must be prepared well beforehand. When a vowel follows a consonant, the vowel cavity should, if possible, be already there; as, in most cases, it can be. Otherwise 'mouthing' or gradualness of vowel must ensue, with consequent lack of definition. It is often difficult to know what a vowel is meant to be. If the throat is kept open and the soft palate raised the singer is well on the way towards the formation of any vowel cavity; the quickest of actions is possible after this when the formation of the cavity has to be a little delayed owing, let us say, to a very forward consonant like T or S (which raises the tongue root) having to precede a very backward vowel like Oh or Oo (in which the tongue root is low).

But not only must the movable cavities (the mouth and neck), be already shaped, if possible, *before* they are used for the particular vowel for which they are wanted. : they must also be held unchangably during the emission of the sound. This is seldom done. 'To vowel and sing cleane' throughout the full length of a note represents high technical control. Just as the intended vowel often does not put in an appearance till an appreciable time after it should, so is it apt to disintegrate and change colour before its appointed end. It is not mere pedantry to insist that this should be avoided. It should be avoided because nobility of style, breadth of utterance, splendour, *sostenuto* and much else are damaged or destroyed when the vowel (or its cavity, which is the same thing) does not hold throughout its course. If a full meed of tone is not given, it is, moreover, unlikely that a full meed of time will be given. The length of a note depends upon the same sort of 'hold' as does its consistent quality. Nevertheless the artist sometimes transgresses the strict letter of the law, deliberately blurring and softening the extremities of a vowel and its note for poetic purposes. The student, however, had better first secure mechanical perfection before he begins to vary it to gain more expressive, personal ends.

A certain amount of tension—sometimes very great tension—has to accompany the shaping of a good cavity. It is no good thinking that a cavity can be held quite loosely. Any sort of 'hold' precludes that. At certain moments of great insistence there will be considerable hardness in the cavity walls. This can easily be felt with a highly characteristic Aw or Oh. As long as a cavity holds, the breath can play quite freely upon the vocal cords and through the vocal instrument. When it does not hold, some degree of wrongful strain must ensue. The problem is to oppose the necessary resistance at the proper place; which is largely supplied by the right shaping of the cavities. When this is done the vocal instrument will be able to take any shock; any power which is applied will not disturb it. Then either serene or agitated utterance can be easily expressed. The whole vocal system hangs together. If one part of it is badly used or ill-adjusted it will affect all the other parts.

As the cavities harden, tone will harden too. A metallic ring cannot come from a soft cavity, nor fully sympathetic sound from a hard one; but at all times some tension will be present. It is useless to tell the student to relax completely. Looseness and tightness are equally bad in singing, unless they are balanced. With looseness the voice is allowed to go anywhere; with tightness, nowhere. What is wanted are wide open channels through which the voice can flow, strongly banked and surrounded. Again the throat, mouth and lips may be thought of as a rubber ring to be enlarged as much as possible. The more the ring is stretched, the tighter does it become.[1] But the art of singing is like the Christian religion: it offers no detailed code of conduct; it simply teaches the right fundamentals and leaves the devotee to apply these according to his own artistic conscience.

---

[1] A good principle to have in mind, however, is that of a *loose lift* of the voice—the looseness guaranteeing ease, the lift sufficient tension (which will always keep the note up, in the head). This is really the principle of poise.

If a wind player can keep a steady sustained note and a singer cannot, the reason for it must be in the shaping and holding of the vocal instrument: for the instrumentalist's and the singer's breath power is potentially the same. The state of the vocal instrument—whether it is as firmly set up as a mechanical instrument, such as a piano or flute—is, of course, largely influenced by the state of the breath muscles; but if these are functioning properly there is no reason why the sound of the voice should not be as satisfactory as the sound of a mechanical instrument. Much more so. Again:

Hold your cavity and you hold your note; and the corollary of this: the cavity *is* the note.

Full Vowelling

In singing nothing is quite as it seems; contradictions abound. The reason for this is that two opposite principles have to be combined: tension and relaxation. In one sense singing is an attempt to bring the naturally diffuse tone of the voice into a smaller compass—to contract the vocal mechanism and the sound as much as possible; in another sense to enlarge the mechanism and sound. There must definitely be a feeling that, in varying degree, the tone is being held together; just as the fingers have to close upon any object that we wish to handle. If we have to deal very forcibly with the situation, if the material to be controlled is recalcitrant, then our grip must be tight; if it submits more easily to what we want, then our grip can loosen. The point is that some sense of contraction will always be present when work has to be done; and that when much work has to be done, when great effort is required, the sense of contraction will be greater. So that soft notes will seem of larger calibre than loud ones.

With this preliminary understanding, the larger we can get our vowels—or vowel cavities (which is the same thing)—the better. How is this to be achieved?

It is evident that the nasal cavity cannot alter its shape. All we can do with regard to its use is to let more or less of the sound stream into it, thereby increasing or decreasing nasal resonance. But, and here is another paradox, the sound must always be lifted up into the head, *whether nasal resonance is drawn upon or not.*

The cavities that can be modified as to size, are those of the mouth and neck; particularly, in the case of full vowelling, the mouth: because room in the mouth will also largely guarantee room in the neck.

The situation hinges upon the tongue and tongue root. In Ah, Aw, Oh, the tongue, as we know, should be flat; any arching of it destroys or prevents the true character of these vowels. But the depression of the tongue can be carried further than the limits of mere relaxed flatness. Particularly at the back the tongue can be drawn deep into the pocket of the jaw. How far this can be done can easily be felt by placing the thumbs under the jaw. This is the movement that is principally responsible for increasing space. And with it, as it were in contrary motion, the soft palate will arch, thereby securing the largest amount of mouth space. Further the depression of the back of the tongue opens out the lower pharynx more, though perhaps a little more opening can still be given to the pharynx under the ears; or apparently in that region, in rough terms.

But we must not forget that all these operations are connected with deep breathing. It is perhaps possible to use the muscles concerned, if great control has been gained, without stimulus from the breath muscles, but there is no doubt that co-operation of the complete physique is a great help in gaining the required end.

Here we are back again at the open throat which the pupil often finds difficulty in securing. A very sure indication of what a really open throat is can be seen (and sensed) in the process of yawning. Natural movements such as yawning, or panting, or laughing, always show us what we should do to sing well. In them the principles of breath power, breath economy, are clearly demonstrated; and with them the right condition of the vocal instrument above the larynx. We can never improve upon these natural techniques; all we can do is to have them thoroughly at command, strengthening the muscles towards the desired end. It is good practice to yawn to the utmost before every phrase, and to attempt to keep the position thereby gained throughout the whole of the phrase. By this means poor tone will instantly gain in depth, richness and freedom; instead of being starved of resonance space it will become *bien nourri*, as the French say. Note that with a yawn the breath muscles at the abdomen are felt to be strongly in operation, and it is this combination of the breath and vocal instrument which produces the state of which we are in search.

Elsewhere we have spoken of thin vowelling; of tiny vocal sounds that scarcely count. A noble voice is always a big full voice, though capable of reduction in scale. Voices need not be as insignificant as they generally are; particularly female voices. Men, of course, start with an advantage over women as regards the size of the vocal organs, so that there is all the more need to effect a remedy, by proper procedure, in the case of the latter.

Full vowelling is very much the same as open vowelling, though white sound must not be countenanced in this. If vowel positions are opened as much as possible—if the mouth and throat are fully enlarged—the resultant *will* be dark sound, because open resonators depend upon a deep pull of the breath, and with this white sound cannot arise. Open vowelling secures the full development of the voice; otherwise the voice is smothered, shut, or half-formed; 'smothered' sound is quite a different thing from 'covered' sound (*v.* p. 168). Fine singing is largely dependent upon the *room* that is given to a note; but of room rigorously shaped. Meagre sounds are always those starved of resonance space. If such space is not ample, words and music will be insufficiently embodied; to the extent that the listener cannot follow them. This is especially the case in rapid passages. There is nothing for the ear to catch hold of. The sound is too light to satisfy, too ill-shaped to be clear. A certain weight of sound is always necessary; mere wiry tenuity does not suffice. There is no real eloquence without volume and openness; nor can vowels be differentiated. Two qualities are specially necessary in a good vowel. A vowel must *tell*; it must have tone; i.e., make a noise such as a resined bow gets from a violin.[1] Secondly, it must be quite distinct from its neighbours. Without openness of position one vowel will be very like another, particularly the long and short vowel correlatives, such as Ee and ĭ, Ay and ĕ. The short vowels, indeed, can hardly be sounded at higher pitches without ample neck and oral space. When they get it they are as rich and fine-sounding as the long vowels. It should be possible to distinguish every vowel given on p. 128 *et seq*. Each vowel is a personality in its own right; and can be made so. The blurred sound one generally hears gives no idea of this; nor can it, without the necessary openness. If a vowel is not properly 'opened' it will be much the same thing as when a

---

[1] Though smoothness is a sign of good tone, a little roughness should be included in it. But it should be remembered that a very *timbrée* quality will never give the impression of repose, or paint a truly placid picture; it is too excited, too energized for that. Quietness in song can only come through the use of tone in which nasal resonance is much, indeed, sometimes wholly, reduced. On the other hand, clear light rhythmic patter as in 'Oh dear, what can the matter be' (arranged Arnold Bax *Collingnon Repertoire*) and the Gilbert and Sullivan examples, must have telling nasal tone. This seems to involve a contradiction with what was said above, but in reality there is none. Before tone can be covered or darkened *there must be tone*; just as the eclipse of light presupposes light in being. This vocal light is associated with the nose. It is by means of nasal resonance that it is brought about. Complete vocal tone is nasal and there is indeed *no* vocal tone without nasality. It is that which gives it the particular quality that we call 'vocal'. Let it never be forgotten that the voice is of the nature of a double reed and not a sort of flute-blowing. Therefore *nasal sound must be cultivated first of all* before the varieties and modifications of it are attempted. Dull, unnasalized tone should always have the power of returning to bright nasal tone at will; just as movement should have the power of returning to rest. That is to say, the right tension or the immediate capacity for the right tension should always be there; ready waiting, so to speak—waiting for the turn of the screw. When this is so, the full palette of vocal colour is at the disposal of the singer; from tones of brazen intensity to those of 'dryad twilight'.

foreigner says 'plĭs' for 'please'; but even the comparatively thin Ee can be developed till it has a full sound. When this happens it will have an open throat as if for ĭ, but nevertheless Ee and ĭ must be clearly differentiated—by slight movement at the back of the tongue.

Vowels have to be exhibited, exposed; almost (with effort) turned inside out. If they are not, all line drawing goes; words and music become just a harmonic mess. This example from a Morley *Canzonet* (a 6):

Hark, Alle — lu — — — — ia !

is hopelessly ineffective if, at the start, an open Ah is not used; it simply will not 'register', or 'appear' as an individual entity when the other voices are singing—you will never know that it is there. A haze of sound is not detailed sound.

In full vowelling, then, the paradox must always be recognized, that it is necessary to contract the voice as much as possible before it can be enlarged profitably. In bad singing the 'bore' of the voice is often quite unmanageable, particularly on high notes. It is a mechanical truism—most things in this book are truisms though they are forgotten—that thrust and direction of a force is increased when it is relatively confined. The old blunderbuss is a comparatively innocuous weapon beside the modern rifle.

The Englishman seldom opens his vowels properly, or has any idea of lustrous tone.

It comes to this: that the right state and shape of the throat is determined, literally, by gripping or holding the sound at the throat, as in a thoroughly good Aw sound, or in a characteristic Cockney Oi, though it must not be taken that these sounds cover all the *desiderata* of vocal tone. This grip or contraction influences the proper adjustment of the vocal cords, giving the necessary valvular resistance. Such adjustment is fundamental and more or less constant if effective tone is to result. Directly this adjustment 'gives', the tone goes, because nasal resonance goes with it. Above this point, i.e., above this point of 'hold', the various oral vowel positions are superimposed. *They* alter; the 'hold' of the vocal cords, roughly speaking, does not. If it does, some form of 'hootiness' ensues—the antithesis of proper vocal tone.

Hold of Voice

At the risk of over-emphasis—for it is so important to get this in mind—singing is almost entirely a matter of (1) how we hold, and (2) where we put our instrument, i.e., the level or position of the instrument (which, of course, is the laryngeal mechanism). If it is not held rightly, we shall probably get cavernous or throaty tone; and the same may happen if we fail to put or place it right. Take the word 'earth' (approximately=ŭrth with a tendency to 'er'), a very difficult vowel to sing with depth and tone. If the right compression or hold is not present, the vowel will have no 'lift' or head ring about it—it will be dead in timbre; if the place of the note is wrong— if it is too highly placed—it will be too thin, lacking in depth and richness. Yet it must be achieved without the slightest push or undue effort; with mechanical perfection. As an exercise, sing the phrase 'where on earth?' *on any note, getting the right sonority.*

The voice will slip from the leash, i.e., the proper hold, at once, if it gets half a chance. It is very easy to let this inward tensing go. We are all prone to slackness. A momentary effort is possible to most of us, but continued effort is quite another matter. Ask a singer to keep his mouth pursed or rounded. He will do so for a few seconds, then the mouth will generally 'give', though he may be unaware that this has happened; frequently, also, with a beginner, the muscles will tremble. Few can be trusted never to relax, particularly where an imponderable like the voice is concerned. If we are given some weight to hold, we shall probably hold it, to the limit of our strength, as long as is required. But to hold a note seems different, nor are the muscles concerned in a general way sufficiently trained to this end. We are so often frightened to use muscular effort at all with the voice. Yet it is obvious that the term 'hold' means just the same whatever is 'held'—and that tension alone can effect it.

The voice is not only held *together*, it is held *up* by tension. Without the requisite tension the voice, literally, falls to the ground by a sort of gravitational process. The lowest notes of basses have frequently a tendency to flatness. These notes are so easy to sound that they are apt to be sung carelessly, too loosely; whereas as much tension is needed for low notes as for high, in the cause of proper hold. This hold throughout the voice induces a tensed vertical, instead of a relaxed horizontal shape of the vocal instrument. A similar movement occurs when the lips and mouth are firmly rounded for the vowel Oh. This latter effort also has the effect of drawing the throat together. It is this drawing together of the throat that is the main consideration. The mouth can be relaxed if the throat is kept tightened. As already observed a good Oh *can* be sung without any rounding of the lips, but never without a rounding or inward compression of the throat.[1] So much for the 'holding' of the voice—which is completely analogous to the actions of 'clawing', 'pinching' or 'gripping', though, if these seem monstrous terms as applied to vocal procedure, we can camouflage them by talking about 'concentration'.

As to the height or position of the larynx, this will vary, largely as the height of the breath effort varies. We shall discuss this more fully later. At the moment we need only repeat that a high larynx tends to bright, even white tone, a low larynx to sombre tone; and that in general the larynx should be low—simply because feeling can only be expressed through such a position. If the larynx is high the voice will be associated with nothing but the head. There will be no complete physical sound, no sound in which the whole human personality is engaged. In terms of tone the result is quite insignificant. For religious song—plain-song and the like—only a low position of the larynx will ensure the amplitude and flow that such song needs, for only then can the throat function to the full, thereby ensuring continuous sound. The rolling, onward periods of plain-song are otherwise impossible; they will have no undertone.

The higher we get in the scale of resonance, i.e., towards brilliancy, the higher will the larynx be. This is because the tongue will tend to move forward and bring the laryngeal mechanism with it. But there are limits to this: the limits of sonorous as opposed to silly tone.

Further, there is a certain position of the larynx, to be found by experience, which, by reason of its perfect adjustment, seems to give the easiest tonal emission. In this position (regardless of any particular expressive quality) the sound functions almost automatically; hardly any effort being needed to set and keep it in vibration. A great deal of singing should be of this nature; a sort of *son ordinaire* of no particular flavour, *which seems to be without conscious tension of either breath or the vocal instrument.*

There should be a potential *crescendo* in every note. The important thing is not so much what you do with the beginning of a note, but with its end. Sometimes, of course, a *diminuendo* must occur in notes in feminine groups ⌒ > or cadences; but this is

subject to the will—it does not happen from want of technical con-

---

[1] For practical purposes we must recognize two orifices of the mouth, those of the front and back. For loose, backward singing the back orifice has to be used; for tight, forward singing the front orifice (the lips). This, as already noted, can be tested by an Oh vowel which, if soft-toned, can be formed entirely by the contraction of the back orifice (the tonsils, palatal arch, etc.), just as a ventriloquist forms it, without any obvious use of the lips.

I

trol—in this case the tone does not peter out by chance. Therefore, unless there is good reason for a *diminuendo*, notes should be *steadily held*, even to the extent of a little *crescendo* at the end. Indeed a point—and a good point—is made by operatic singers, at times of great emotional stress, of, as it were, twisting the tail of a note at its conclusion, throwing it off with a full-blooded gesture; accenting it, in fact, with a special concentration of sound. It is a very effective way of doing things. It appeals to the gallery, as we know; but it is a perfectly rightful and masterly appeal. An anæmic ending has nothing to commend it. It is just a confession of physical defeat.

Build of Voice

The voice can be built either upwards or downwards. It is probably best to consider it as *developing* downwards; starting, as regards the sound, from the nasal cavities which give a potent though thin sound, and proceeding to greater dimensions, by bringing neck resonance into play. Viewed in this way, the ideal voice would appear to be very much like a spear head   coming to a sharp

point at the top and filling out towards the lobes, as occasion requires; it being understood that the 'point' or the capacity for 'point' is always there, however full the sound is. Thus the same sum total of resonance volume would give us shapes such as   or

according as much or little resonance is used in the nose,

or in the neck. If much is used in the nose there will be proportionally less in the neck, and vice versa. This is entirely true to what actually happens. A very brilliant nasal tone cannot have full neck tone, while full neck tone will be comparatively dull in quality. But *all* tone, brilliant or dull, must appear to come to a point; to be lifted into the head. There is something wrong about what we may call 'snub-nosed' tone which may be pictured as   with its

proper point cut off   . Such tone will be flat and lifeless, not merely dull.

226

The best way of thinking of tone, as we have said, is as building downward from the nose. This is the hard, efficient, instrumental way. But from the point of view of emotional growth, tone may be considered as building upwards from the base of the breath. The softer, more sympathetic aspects of tone are derived from that region, where the emotions have their seat. Of the two, the 'downward' way is technically the safer way, since it guarantees the right hold and position of the voice; the upward way, though more human in its approach, may easily degenerate into flabby treatment, by losing sight of the fact that the voice is an instrument with (in one sense) a quite heartless role to play. Thus it is probably better to be instrumentally right, before trying to touch the chords of emotion; rather than to begin from an emotional urge, and from there proceed to build up a good instrument. In other words, tone, *qua* tone, apart from emotional significance, is the thing to cultivate—and there is such a thing as beautiful objective tone—a sort of property common to all tone, however we may apply it, or modify it to suit individual artistic purposes. Some may feel that emotion should regulate the instrument, rather than the instrument the emotion; that emotion and instrument, in the case of the voice, are not divisible, but one. To which one can only reply that this is not so with any other mechanical instrument, which has its own fixed form before we begin to play upon it. Doubtless æsthetic choice goes to the making of a good instrument. A 'feeling' for beautiful colour must be there before we get the tone that we want. But it is an incomplete emotional appeal, which can be satisfied in a more or less mechanical way, by what the instrument does; not so much as by what we do to the instrument.

As regards tone, the vocal instrument is required to produce different vowels, with as perfect a pronunciation as we can manage; but little more is implied in this than perfect mechanical control, clear shaping and the like. The springs of emotion are scarcely drawn upon—never with any conscious certainty—till they are touched by an idea, some mental picture of a human situation which moves us; this, of course, is to be found in either lyrical or dramatic song. Then tone is, or can be, used in a truly emotional sense; otherwise its production is largely a matter of accordance with a pattern, to be achieved by scarcely more than intellectual means. But it is extremely important that instrumental control should be gained by the singer, in the 'downward' way (for that is the instrumental way); otherwise its further expansion into emotional control is not likely to be of much account. It is just as well to know your trade before you aspire to be an artist.

At the Paris Conservatoire in 1905, it was decreed that singers during their first year should study only *l'émission de la voix*, or what we should call tone production. Songs were not to be attempted till after that. Such strict 'preliminary' can perhaps be carried too far, and the author, while advocating great attention to the purely instrumental side of singing, particularly in the early days of a student's career, would nevertheless at the same time allow the practice of songs. Though the emotional faculty cannot be relied upon to gain technical ends, it can stimulate their pursuit. Finally, a sort of balance between the 'downward' and 'upward' way is struck, and the emotions are expressed through a perfect instrument.

Once good nasal resonance is achieved—and it cannot be achieved till there is a certain opening of the throat, the actual use of nasal resonance can be 'according to taste'. Nasal resonance is something like a condiment which imparts flavour to the solid aspects of tone. In a way it is better to have too little than too much of it. Emotion seldom requires an all-in allowance unless 'full brass' is called for.[1]

---

[1] It was said (p. 24) that nasal sound is the chief ingredient of tone—certainly the most effective ingredient—yet it is here counselled that we should be chary of its use. How are we to harmonize these apparently conflicting statements?

The answer is twofold: (1) We want different amounts of nasal resonance according to the idea that we are impressing; and (2) technical purposes—the easy emission of notes—require sometimes that nasal tone should be considerably modified, e.g. on the higher notes of the voice. A first condition of the control of the vocal instrument is that the larynx must be kept relatively low. As the voice rises increased pressure is put upon the larynx and at length generally about

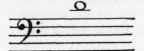

'the great break' with men, and an octave or so higher with the so-called 'head notes' of women, this pressure forces the larynx upward (unless something is done about it), with the result that the tone over-floods the nose through the raising of the soft palate and the consequent unstopping of the back entry into the nose, as in shouting. Control then disappears, as there is no resistance; the tone simply runs amok. Therefore at this point more resistance must be applied; resistance must be increased, in short, as the voice rises. This resistance is gained by greater breath pressure and a more considerable closing of the nose, which progressively cuts off the nasal resonance.

It will also be said (p. 246) that the singer should attempt to get the same true vowel at all pitches, and further that this could be done. How then, are we to secure this, if, as the voice rises, less nasal resonance can be brought into play? To this the answer must be: that no vowel guarantees a consistent tone *at any pitch*. We have it in our power to alter the *shade* of any vowel. We can make a vowel bright or dull at will while still keeping the genus or true nature of the vowel, so that it is absolutely recognizable as the vowel in question and is heard as no other. Thus the assertion that Oh is singable at any pitch is quite justified. It can be sung; but neither it, nor any other vowel, will have quite the same shade of sound at high pitches, that it has on low. If we hold, rigorously, that every change of colour denotes a new vowel, then perhaps special pleading has been advanced in the foregoing; but if we hold, as seems possible, that a vowel is determined essentially by mouth shape, then, if this is constant, we have the right to say that the

Covering of Tone

A few more words as to this are perhaps necessary. The term 'cover' as applied to the voice may very well be taken to mean what it does in a usual way, viz., 'to clothe'. All natural objects have an outer covering of some sort. Bark covers the wood of the tree; skin covers flesh, and so on. Protection is needed; the voice has to be protected also; an uncovered sound is rough, raw, naked, almost indecent. It hits the ear instead of caressing it; it is brutal, not persuasive. It stands out; it will not blend in a general picture. It lacks, in short, the atmosphere, the surround, by which its crudity is tamed and tempered. Only covered sound can come within the orbit of our affections, and most art is within such an orbit. An occasional outburst may be necessary, but in a general way we could not live in any degree of comfort with sound which is, so to speak, 'bared to the bone'.

We have said that uncovered sound will not blend; neither will it flow. Its elements stand out starkly, note by note; viciously self-assertive, never moving in an easy stream. It is impossible to sing recitative or any run of words, as in Psalmody, except with covered tone; otherwise the words will just click and clack along. What is the reason for this? What is covered tone?

Perhaps a word we used a moment ago will give us the clue: the word 'raw'. Tone that is forced or is allowed to go its own way is raw; it has an edge to it; it has not been brought to heel. Fully-nasalized tone is usually of such a nature. When, by contraction of the resonance chambers, a certain constraint is put upon the sound its quality alters. The rough edge is rounded off; shrillness is softened; notes and words are, as it were, pressed together instead

---

accidental tone of a vowel may vary (through varied use of nose and throat resonance) without the integrity of the vowel itself being affected. That the use of the accessory resonances of the nose and throat is *not* constant throughout vowelling is proved by the fact that the 'Ee' type of vowel favours nose resonance, and the 'Oo' type, neck resonance. Thus for the different vowels and the different pitches of those vowels nose and neck resonance is variable: but mouth resonance may be said to be invariable.

It may seem an extreme statement to say that, in a general way, we want less not more nasal resonance; but the required parallel may be found in normal organ tone. A preponderance of blaring reeds completely does away with decencies of sound. Diapason tone has always been recognized as the ideal foundation of organ tone. It is from this tone that the organ derives, or should derive, its characteristic dignity and sobriety. Over-blown reeds, or flue tone which approximates to them, destroy the rich, round, mellow colouring that the organ should have—and did have in older times, before the advent of cheap-sounding cinema and even church organs. There is also such a thing as cheap vocal tone in which vulgar reedy effects are preferred. Nevertheless it should be fully recognized that for certain occasions and with certain languages, particularly French, tone *has* to be highly nasalized; further, that if dull tone is used *it must never degenerate into hootiness*.

of having a separatist tendency.[1] The tone, in short, becomes more amenable in every way, yet not to the extent of taking the life out of it. There is still plenty of life there; but it is controlled, not riotous. The physical explanation of this is somewhat difficult: because, as we have seen elsewhere, when a 'closing in' process is applied to resonation (by bringing the tonsils together and so raising the soft palate) the usual effect (if this action is carried far enough) is precisely to bring the uvula away from the back of the throat, thus allowing the sound to enter the nose. This results in brilliant colouring; whereas 'covering' implies that this brilliancy is relatively subdued. On the other hand, we know that it is the lack of lateral tension which allows the soft palate to fall, and the uvula to block nasal sound.[2] How is it then that inward tension can still produce 'covered' tone? The answer, I think, is, that, with covered tone (of any intensity) lateral pressure is applied more at the neck and tongue root, than at the soft palate and uvula; it takes place lower down. Thus, we get a depressed or 'lowered' use of the mechanism, instead of a 'lifted' use, and, in proportion as this happens, nasal ring is reduced. If the soft palate were raised as high as possible we should be bound to get fully-opened tone. With 'covering' it is evident that this does *not* happen, and the reason seems to be as suggested. One can test this by singing any vowel 'open' or 'closed'. With the former we feel that lateral tension is higher than it is with the latter; and, if this is correctly observed, practice fortunately accords with theory. So far, this technical point (which is of considerable practical value) has not been made.

One knows that the voice generally has to be 'thrown back' on high notes. If this is not done, particularly with hard-toned vowels (Ee, ŏ, etc.), the notes will probably 'crack' and be quite incapable of *sostenuto*. What perhaps one does not realize is that *this throwing back of the voice actually throws back the uvula,* so that the uvula clings to the back wall of the pharynx, by which process we get the necessary 'covered' tone.

Further, just as chords blend best with covered tone (such as that of Oo, *par excellence*), so do the sequent notes and vowels of an individual (or solo) voice 'blend' by a similar use of covered sound. Absolutely 'open' sound will scarcely ever give the impression of a unified voice, or of a voice which really 'holds together'.

---

[1] Without absurd comparison, 'covered' notes are very much like sardines in a tin, which are softened by the oil and pack easily into place. Fill the tin with nails and this could not be done. The equivalent of bringing hard, 'open' notes together, in the attempt to blend and weld them, would be something like this.

[2] Beginners seldom, if ever, have the capacity fully to uncover tone; the sound they get is mostly of a dull, unresonant kind, because their powers of tension are weak.

When tone is not properly covered it often has a curious quality best described as 'glassy'; there is a thin, hard brittleness about it which is liable to fracture at any moment. It has no roots; sound associated with it reminds one of the seed which fell upon stony ground. Covered sound alone has body and permanence. Other observations on this matter (pp. 160-79) should be collated with the foregoing.

Opening of Tone

Considerable has been said about this on page 221, and we need add here only that the opening of tone—or the resonance cavities, which is the same thing—in no wise conflicts with the principle of covering tone; except to this extent, that a complete *laisser aller* would result in shouting and the like, which prevents anything like sustained or controlled sound. Directly control is put upon a sound it 'covers' to a more or less extent. But we must avoid making any quite definite or inelastic pronouncement upon the subject, since variation is bound to take place, according to the expressive situation. Within the limits of what amounts to the vertical hold of the instrument, as much 'opening' as possible should be given to the sound, particularly by means of the cavity of the mouth. The nasal cavity, as we have said, is to be opened 'according to taste' and circumstance; the neck the same. The point is that the opening of the mouth must be vertical and not horizontal. The smiling position of the mouth is a horizontal one, and tone coming through it finally degenerates into stupid, silly tone, if it is not associated with sufficient general tension. True happiness or joy are serious manifestations, not to be confounded with the inanities of the flapper; and whiteness or utterly-released tone is just as foreign to joy (of any account) as it is to sorrow. The face can well show a smile, however, if the back of the mouth and laryngeal mechanism have the right muscular concentration; but to think that tone is to be completely associated with the 'let-go' of a smile seems to be an utter mistake and at variance with all the processes of vocal control. Perhaps we can and should distinguish between a smile and a laugh. A smile, though a sort of tenth-cousin to a laugh, is a very poor affair, expressively—one has only to look at the usual run of 'society' or 'professional' photographs to see that. It hardly engages emotion or the physique. A laugh, however, is a different matter—we 'split our sides' with a laugh. We feel it at the base of the breath. We are 'all-in' with it. A smile, like a rustle on the water, may be beautiful enough in a small way, in some soft, transitory passage; but it can never satisfy a lengthy or important mood of happiness— that is, if the physical attributes of a smile are adhered to.

Unless it is properly 'opened' we simply do not know what a vowel is.[1] With the buds of flowers it is much the same. It is not till they unfold that most of us could say for certain what species they belong to. In choral singing it is extremely noticeable how this works. Words become clear at once with open sound; with smothered sound they are nearly indistinguishable. But 'smothered' is not 'covered' sound; nor 'open' sound necessarily 'white'.

Ease of Vowelling

A low position of the tone is one of ease; a high, one of strain. The low lets the voice lie as on a couch; the high forces it upwards —with corresponding quality of tone colour in either case: rich, full, sympathetic in the one; thin, bony, cartilaginous in the other. Neither is right or wrong. Their respective use must be governed by the needs of the situation, though as an easy, sympathetic touch is generally the more desirable, the soft-toned sound may be advanced as the more normal, and hard tone a departure from it. But the singer must have both at command.

What is sure, however, is that a lovely flow of words depends upon a low position of the voice, and that this is a rare phenomenon. Most singing has a sort of percussive quality in it, where the syllables are tapped out rather than issue in or on a stream of sound. No *idea* can possibly be expressed in this way, for the essence of an idea is motion, rhythm, a rise and fall of sense and sound, an undulation, what you will of this order. Exclamatory, dramatic interjections are another matter. But whether the syllables of a phrase are sustained (*legato*) or separated (*staccato*), the principle of continuity must underlie them. *Staccato is legato*, and *legato*, *staccato*; both *legato* and *staccato* are different facets of the same ryhthmic impulse. In another book I have given a diagram of what is meant by this and it may be repeated here, in relation not only to *legato* and *staccato*, but to *crescendo* and *diminuendo*:

The shaded portions represent the part of the sustained note which might be taken away (not sounded) in *staccato*. The mind, however,

[1] It is notorious how badly the Englishman speaks. 'Ils avalent leurs mots' ('they swallow their words'), the French say of us. Even Milton, in his *Essay on Education*, had to counsel that the speech of youth should be 'fashioned to a distinct and clear pronunciation, as near as may be to the Italian', adding quaintly, 'for we English-men, being far northerly, do not open our mouths in the cold air wide enough to grace a southern tongue, but are observed by all other nations to speak exceedingly close and inward; so that to smatter Latin with an English mouth is as ill a hearing as low French.'

fills up these blanks, by reason of the symmetry which prevails. The notes lead on to one another. In writing, the passage might run:

Fine v. Forced Vowelling

Not only can one animate a note, one can kill it, destroying all beauty of vibration. It is the perfectly resonated and perfectly regulated vibration which counts. This is to be heard in all good tone; it is the control of tone by the master hand. Good vibration is very much like the smooth running of a machine, which gathers impetus as it goes. Bad vibration is jerky running, when the force that impels it is applied spasmodically, and checks to the movement are continually present: as with bowing on a stringed instrument when it produces a scratchy noise. With the voice it is a matter of steady breath control.

Imperfect resonation is another cause of ugly sound. Good resonation reinforces sound, bad resonation spoils it. We must remember that three resonators are concerned: the nose, the mouth and neck. If they do not harmonize, by reason of bad shape-adjust-ment, or overblown, forced vowelling which develops out-of-tune upper partials, then the tone suffers. For instance the short vowels as in 'cat', 'cot', 'cut', are apt to fail in sonority. This is because the right relation of the mouth to the neck cavity has not been found. A good singer will make these vowels sound as strong as a more easily adjusted long vowel. And it is *sound* that we want, all the time, for music is composed of sound. The greatest singers have splendidly resonated voices. A wealth of sound is at their command, not so much because of a superior vocal organ, but because they know how to use it. It may be exceedingly difficult to determine where faults of sound lie—the resonating system is so subtle and complicated, and for the most part we cannot see what is going on —but it is not at all difficult to hear when a note is full of easy, unforced tone; effective, telling and perfectly pitched.

With so many voices the surface is, as it were, pitted or pocked, indicating that the vocal mechanism is not working well. The machine is indifferently constructed and poorly run. The conse-quence is that it is deficient in carrying power.

Vocal tone can be, and generally is, much finer than the tone of a musical instrument; the vibration is finer. I once heard a choir

I*

singing from the steps of St. Paul's Cathedral, accompanied by one of the Guards' bands. I was standing at the bottom of Ludgate Hill. Whereas the choir was quite audible, the band could hardly be heard from that distance. It seems very probable that it was because of a superiority of vibration in the voices. Yet when I came closer to St. Paul's the band *seemed* louder than the choir.

Did not William Byrd tell us some centuries ago that 'There is not any musick of instruments whatsoever, comparable to that which is made of the voyces of men, where the voyces are good, and the same well sorted and ordered'. And whoever has heard music played on strings, and the same music sung unaccompanied (as can be heard in the case of Delius' two wordless part-songs 'To be sung on a summer night on the water', arranged for strings), can hardly fail to endorse Byrd's dictum. Compared with vocal tone, that, even of strings—which gives the nearest approach to it—is relatively coarse.

Differentiation of Vowels

However it may be elsewhere—and the Latin countries are certainly ahead of us in clear speech—in England a really open vowel is scarcely ever used. Most vowels that one hears are truncated, half-formed. They may just pass muster, but the regiment to which they belong is barely recognizable. For artistic purposes they fail utterly. Do not let us delude ourselves by thinking that we can use any brand of vowel that we may like or have the habit of using. There may be fifty different kinds of Ah, but there is only one fully-defined Ah, completely significant of its beauty and character; the others are personal or local variants, all more or less wrong, judged by an ideal standard. It is almost impossible, for instance, to get English singers to sing the Ah in the word 'Sanctus' of the Mass with a really open quality that seems to reach to the highest heavens in its acclaim. Similarly with all vowels. A good vowel gives the impression of being wafted freely upon the air, not tightly tethered to its place of origin.

The wrongness of a vowel can seldom be discovered fully, unless it is sustained in song. In speech, syllables pass before us so quickly that only a highly trained ear can, in any detail, detect impurities and imperfections of sound. We know more or less by the context what the speaker means to say; and the consonants are a guide to the situation. But in singing, the guide is rather the vowel, the musical portion of the word, since it bears the brunt of the expression. The energy, life and openness of a good vowel also gives a superior definition to the consonants; vowels and consonants rise and fall together in the *scale of significance*.

It is the opening of a vowel which determines almost the whole matter of its purity and perfection.

The interest of singing lies very largely in the variety of its colouring, i.e., in the varied vowels which the singer has at his disposal. He paints his vocal pictures with such colour, just as an orchestral picture is painted with the sounds of the different instruments in the orchestra.[1] The different vowels have each the individuality of a different instrument, and when that individuality is stressed to the full, the full glory of vocal sound appears; but only then. This represents the emotional, æsthetic appeal. The intellectual appeal of clarity is equally at the mercy of fully-differentiated vowelling. It is absolutely important that the listener should be clear both as to the notes and words that are sung to him; if he is in any doubt about them the singer has failed in his task. What we all wish is to be able to understand what we hear. That is the first consideration, before there can be any talk of expression.

The rationale of 'expression' is by no means easy to fathom. There is something of a mystery about it. Is 'expression' part and parcel of the musical or verbal idea, inseparable from it as are the notes and note values; or is it due to the reaction of the performer: his view, in short, of what he is contemplating? I think we must accept this latter explanation. An artistic idea, or any idea, for the matter of that, is static, invariable; a mould wherein we may pour our feelings, or perhaps it would be truer to say, a form whereby our feelings are aroused. There is no expression in an art form; it is we who give it expression. Just as words stimulate the most varied interpretation —if they did not, interpretation would not exist—so do notes. To one they mean one thing; to another, another. Yet such variation is not a nightmare of contradiction. We are kept on our course by the central idea. It is, as it were, an object which we approach from different angles and directions according to our personal nature. An idea is a symbol, larger than any one of its possible interpretations; the greater the idea, the vaster its orbit of significance, the more its power to arouse thought: different thought, but always relevant.

An idea, then, is cold, abstract; its warmth comes from us. It is a stimulus towards expression; it is not expression itself.

What are the abstract qualities of words or music; what *is* music, what *are* words, apart from us: for it is here that clarity and precision—the very groundwork of art—come in? We can observe

---

[1] Lately, on the halls, an entertaining 'orchestra' of voices appeared, which gave a very fair account of almost all the orchestral instruments: showing the adaptability of vocal tone. Truly the voice is a 'wondrous machine'—perhaps the most wonderful if we consider how music and speech come from it.

these qualities under those very convenient divisions: time, tone and tune. The time of a note is precise, mathematical, absolute; ideally it admits of no variation. The tone of the ideal vowel is just that of perfect pronunciation, independent of emotional utterance. Tune consists fundamentally in a succession of exact intervals. These three unvarying aspects of an idea, in terms of sound, constitute its objective form; they are what belongs to *it*; it has nothing to do with us. It is not till we appropriate that form, take it to ourselves, that modification occurs. In obedience to our feeling, to the dictates of 'expression' we alter strict time by hurrying or slowing, *rubato*, or whatever it may be; or we alter vowel pronunciation according to our mood, the mood suggested by the idea which is confronting us; or we alter exact pitch to give greater expressive force to the note. Nothing of this is foreign to the nature of the idea. The idea evokes all this. But in a very true sense it is a departure from the ideal form of the idea. Finally, it becomes *our* idea; before, it was *an* idea.

Thus, the accidental is our own special contribution as interpreters. Our role is to translate ideal shapes into human realities which bear our varied imprint. Everything seems to come from those ideal shapes and to resolve back into them when they are put into terms of an idea. Though the composer feels emotionally, when he creates his music, yet he cannot notate it in that form. He is bound to eliminate those subtly varied factors of time, tune and tone that *his* emotional urge dictates, and to record those factors in ideally perfect proportions, which seem outside and beyond the breath of life, but which have the power of rousing life afresh directly we behold them. It is not a confession of defeat that we have to fall back upon apparently dead symbols to record our feelings; it shows that behind the accidental there is something in the nature of objective law which rules even our most vagrant emotion if it is to be subject to the discipline of art.

The point of all this is to show that art depends upon curves and proportions of an ideal kind; that mechanical precision is the very basis of art and that (as regards vowels) vowels have to be completely differentiated and perfectly pronounced before we can vary them (in obedience to emotional impulse) with any degree of mastery. Further, a 'pull-back' towards precise proportions should be inherent in any departure from them.

Unification of Vowels

The voice is required to do what no other instrument is required to do, viz., to unify different sounds or vowel qualities so that they appear to come *from the same instrument*, i.e., with unity of type or style.

With the organ or orchestra you add or superimpose different qualities of sound; with the voice, what amounts to these different qualities come consecutively, with each change of vowel in words. Unity under these conditions is one of the great problems of a singer. Vowels are apt to pop out of the tonal picture which should be thoroughly harmonized; unless they are carefully dealt with. For instance the upstart vowel Ee with its cutting tone will easily break away from the position of more amenable vowels like Oo and Oh, if it follows them, as in this phrase:

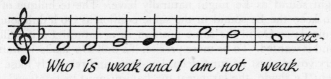

Who is weak and I am not weak

Here the diphthong vowel Ee in 'weak' (Oo+Ee+k) will tend to shoot forward. In consequence the appropriate backward Oo resonance of the phrase as a whole will be disturbed, and the gravity of the expression lost. Or this:

HANDEL

Come to me soothing sleep

where on the underlined vowels the same thing is likely to happen, with the quiet beauty of the phrase destroyed.[1] So that what has

[1] Again we must underline the need of closing the back of the nose for most vocal sound with the exception of sound which is determined by nasality (m, n, ng and the French orinasals). In a general way sufficient brilliance can be given to a note even though there is this check to full nasal resonance, while really 'comfortable' sound can be gained by no other means. The pressure of the uvula against the back wall of the pharynx is the factor that achieves this closure. Directly this particular movement of the uvula is released the voice enters the nose with a more or less amount of sharp, cutting quality. Certain it is that an atmosphere of 'poetry' is incompatible with excess of nasal tone, which may be right for aggressive or dramatic action, but cannot serve sensitive moods of contemplation. For instance it would be impossible to sing a setting of Blake's 'Dream Valley' (such as that by Roger Quilter) with any but this closed-off, veiled tone, which at the same time eliminates the obvious. There would be no 'Dream' about it, no 'floating' of the music upon the stream of remembrance, no 'darkened valley' or 'silent melancholy'; in short, no transport to the 'mists of the spirit'. The words may well be given in full as an example of a poetic issue which may often confront the singer; the same composer's setting of Tennyson's 'Now sleeps the crimson petal' is another example; or, in a different, heavier vein, Schubert's 'Der Wanderer'.

Dream Valley

Memory, hither come,
And tune your merry notes;

237

to be done is to keep the same position of the voice for all vowels when a mood persists. If the mood is bright, all vowels have to be bright; if sombre, all vowels must be sombre. The tendency of vowels is to differ not only in colour but in hue. If we take the long vowels Ee, Ay, Ah, Aw, Oh, Oo, those around Ee will have a bright tendency, those around Oo a dull tendency. The good singer will eliminate this natural disposition when required to do so, by giving Ee the same sort of sound as its extreme fellow at the other end, viz., Oo; or (it may be) giving Oo the same sort of bright sound as Ee might naturally have. The technique of this is to keep the Ee sound in the same position as Oo if dull sound is required; or Oo in the same position as a natural Ee if brilliant sound is wanted. To be more precise, if a dull Oo shade is wanted, every vowel must be sung deep, low-lying and relatively loose; if a bright Ee shade, the laryngeal mechanism must be tightened, thus raising the soft palate and at the same time lifting the tone more into the head, where brilliant sounds are resonated.

In a general way the difficulty is not to get bright (and often thin) sounds, but rich, deep, dull sounds. This exercise is therefore recommended:

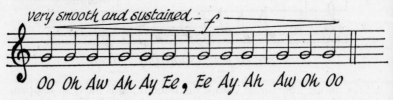

Starting from a deep soft-toned Oo proceed through all the long vowels and back again without any change of neck resonance. Ay and Ee are the dangerous, undisciplined members of society.

Vowel Quality

Good tone will always have a hard core, no matter how soft the

> And, while upon the wind
> Your music floats,
> I'll pore upon the stream,
> Where sighing lovers dream,
> And fish for fancies as they pass
> Within the watery glass.
>
> I'll drink of the clear stream,
> And hear the linnet's song;
> And there I'll lie and dream
> The day along:
> And, when night comes, I'll go
> To places fit for woe,
> Walking along the darken'd valley
> With silent Melancholy.

surface may be. Remarkably wise singing counsel was given us by Professor Sir Walter Raleigh when he said, as regards the speaking of poetry, 'You must teach people a pronunciation harder and clearer than is needed for daily speech. Then let them soften the edges to taste. . . . It is a kind of personal scale of expression, enormously varied.' This contains almost all the 'law and the prophets'. Whatever else is added is just a sort of radiation or development of this central doctrine. It is just the 'iron hand in the velvet glove', in another form.

Perhaps the two most important things in tone are strength and sympathy; a close, compressed, concentrated quality, as of tightly twisted cord, combined with a pleasing 'feel' that yields to the touch. A loose voice, like a loose skein of hemp, has no strength in it, no holding power; nor will weakness ever display a lovely appearance.

When this concentrated treatment prevails the voice will be dark and full of colour; anæmic, white sounds cannot function. Lack of 'darkness'—of tone, in short—is always due to letting the voice rise from its proper 'bedding'; and this principle of keeping the voice down must be observed whether we wish tone to be bright or dull.

The genus, or essential character of a vowel is determined by the mouth, by the position of the tongue, the opening of the cavity and the shape of the front or back orifice at the lips and throat. The nose adds colour, the neck volume; but neither nasal nor neck resonance are absolutely necessary to a vowel: that is to say, a vowel can be perfectly pronounced by the mouth alone, though in singing this never happens since the three resonances cannot be wholly divided from each other. A whispered, almost soundless vowel proves, however, that it is possible. It is important to recall these facts because they show how vowels can be bright or dull, have timbre or be devoid of it, without losing their integrity; they only begin to lose it when their particular shape or position in the mouth alters.

Nasal sound is *small* sound; to increase its stature the neck must be brought into play.

It does not need a whole song to show the mettle of the voice; a single note will do.

Percussion of the Voice

The advantage of the pianoforte as an instrument is that it responds immediately to the touch. At once we have the note and pitch, without ambiguity, whenever we strike the key. Pianoforte sound is not well sustained, but it is admirably precise at the start; and it is at the start where percussion tells. Something of this process should be apparent with the voice, which often fails in percussive, instaneous effect, though it is not always right to use this effect in its most extreme form. What happens in most singing is that consonants are too slack to be smartly articulated, or that the vowel cavity is either not prepared *before* it is wanted or assumes its shape in a sluggish way. In other words, the process is one of gradualness; the sound is 'mouthed'.

'Speak the speech, I pray you, as I pronounced it to you, trippingly on the tongue: but if you mouth it, as many of our players do, I had as lief the towncrier spoke my lines.' So said Hamlet to the Players, and more that followed in the way of instruction should be taken to heart by any who speak or sing.

It is important to draw a firm distinction between 'mouthing' and 'modelling'; the two are often confused. Without modelling, i.e., a keen action of the lips and cheeks (in which elements of speed and compression are at work) complete verbal definition is impossible. It is true that a great deal can be done when *apparently* the lips and cheeks are immobile, but, unless they are brought into play, at some point or other in speech failure will occur, particularly with the labial and tip-tongue consonants f, p, s, etc., whether 'voiced' into v, b, z, etc., or not. Further, if inward modelling does not take place, vowels will be shallow and lack volume. Volume can only be gained by this inward 'up and down' process, as is best seen with Oh, to which, by this means, a tremendous cavity can be given: for it has its effect upon the throat as well as upon the mouth. An Oh cavity can be formed (sufficient to make a distinguishable Oh) without the use of lips and cheeks, but the full character of Oh cannot thus emerge. This treatment also prevents rough, coarse tone. Nothing is as soft and beautiful as a well-produced Oh (*v.* also pp. 313–4).

Another point. If sound is modelled well at the forward orifice (the lips, etc.) and is thus held *continuously*, also (and this will happen almost automatically) if this is backed up by strong diaphragmatic tension, the throat can be kept relatively free. One has only, as it were, *to blow through* the throat to get the required sound.

'Mouthing' is quite different from all this. It is purely a jaw action, like 'chewing' and 'champing' which represent quite useless actions for singing purposes. In all this we should take example from the French. Modelling at the lips is their method of speech, and they are probably the finest speakers in the world.

The main thing is the holding of tone at the extremities of the vocal instrument (the lips and diaphragm). One need not bother much about the vocal cords, if this is done.

When, by sudden impact, breath is forced upon a firm hard surface, or into a sharply-defined cavity, a sort of aspirated shock ensues, which can or need not be accompanied by vocal sound—it can be heard in a whisper. This is the equivalent of the meeting of two solid bodies as in instrumental percussion, such as that of the drum stick upon the drum, or the hammer upon the strings of the pianoforte. But if the breath is not keen in movement, nor directed upon a steady, fixed surface, no such shock will occur. The sound will be indeterminate, at any rate at the start, lacking the little 'ping' or 'thud' that can be given to it by the proper means.

In a general way singing should be

(1) tense
(2) quick } in movement
(3) ample

though it is evident that the degree of these characteristics must vary according to circumstance. For percussive effects, however, tensity and speed are essential; the one depends upon the other. Without tensity movement cannot be quick, since it will have no initial impulse; and slow movements will never produce what we are here in search of, either in regard to vowels or consonants.

But it is generally when a vowel follows a consonant that the presence and absence of percussion is most noticeable. A vowel alone does not show it to the same extent except through the use of the closed glottis, or 'jerked' attack, which brings about exceptional initial definition; this attack, however, owing to its rather brutal nature, is not allowable in the best English singing.[1] It is the sharp passage of a well-compressed consonant into the clear vowel that is mostly associated with percussion. If it is done very quickly, the separation or release of the articulatory organs in itself produces 'flatus' or aspiratory 'kick' of the breath, after which the breath proceeds to take charge of the vowel cavity with a further sense of percussion. What happens with both consonants and vowels is that the air rushes in to fill the vacuum that has been suddenly created, and this makes the percussive noise that we are speaking of.

The utmost clarity is obtained by percussion, with its clean-cut edge of sound. If the effect is not used the singer is always liable to be misunderstood with regard to his words, and to lose point and emphasis of style. Certain it is that all lively expression—percussion is specially associated with *staccato*—must be dealt with by percussive means, by 'direct action' in short. Gradual, slow movements of the mouth and tongue are the reverse of vital, and bound to be doubtful in definition. To know what a vowel is, only when a note is half through is to put an undue strain upon the listener's attention, and often entirely fail to capture it. Nevertheless, we do not always wish to be confronted with perfect clearness which may be too

---

[1] It is, however, excellent, used in moderation, as a gymnastic of the voice.

mechanical for our purpose. Some blurring of the sound lends poetry to the situation, as does a softened outline in a picture. A persuasive rather than a percussive touch may be wanted. In certain conditions we refuse to be hurried, or driven into clear-cut situations. Notes can be taken a little under pitch at the start, vowels a little indistinctly, the perfect time-spot may be accelerated or delayed: all this involves some modification of perfect 'attack'. But as a basis of operations precise control is required in all aspects of performance; the extent of departure from it is for the artist to decide. What must never happen is that irregularities come of themselves; from a want of, not the exercise of, control.

Timbre, Nasality, Shading

English tone is devoid of *timbre* if compared with the tone of the Latin races, i.e., it lacks nasal ring, and the vitality and brilliance that go with it. There is a penetrating, piercing quality in a *timbrée* note that makes for effectiveness; it 'gets there', whereas a dull note is apt to remain at the place of its origin. The dull note may be the more 'homely' note—that is perhaps why the English, who think so much in terms of 'home', prefer it; but for wandering afield and for adventurous, dramatic issues only the brilliant note will serve. The essence of brilliance is, of course, concentration; which engenders the spark of tonal light. Tone is, as it were, raised to incandescence by concentration; as when the sun's rays are caught by a prism and focussed into greater power. Tension focusses tone—we saw this on p. 77. Loose tensions give dull tone; strong tensions, *timbrée* tone. There is something of the clang of metal in good tone, or at any rate, in tone which is very active and wide-awake. The Italians call this clang *il metallo di voce*—the equivalent of the French *timbre*.

In *Word and Tone* I quoted a passage by the French writer and critic, Legouvé. It is so to the point that I venture to repeat it here. He says:

Certain particular gifts are necessary if speech is to possess colour. The first of these is metal in the voice. He who has it not will never shine as a colourist. The metal may be gold, silver, or brass; each has its individual characteristic. A golden voice is the most brilliant; a silvery voice has the most charm; a brassy voice has the most power. But one of these three characteristics is essential. A voice without metallic ring is like teeth without enamel; they may be sound and healthy, but they are not brilliant. . . . In speech there are several colours—a bright, ringing quality; one soft and veiled. The bright, strident hues of purple and gold in a picture may produce a masterpiece of gorgeous colouring; so, in a different manner, may the harmonious juxtaposition of greys, lilacs, and browns on a canvas by

Veronese, Rubens or Delacroix. Last of all is the velvety voice. This is worthless if not allied with one of the three others. In order that the velvet may possess value it must be reinforced with 'metal'. A velvety voice is merely one of cotton.

But just as we should not care to be assailed continually by the blare of trumpets, so, in an extreme 'brassy' form, the voice would soon pall; it would be too stimulating, too exciting—we could not dream in its midst, and it is of dreams more than of action that poetry speaks. Nevertheless, as Legouvé tells us, there are degrees of timbre, i.e., of nasality, and probably some tinge of it should always be present in tone, and will be, if the right concentration is brought to bear; for the voice will then be lifted up to the 'ceiling' (the roof of the mouth and raised hard palate) where the shining surfaces of tone scintillate, and will not sink into the depths where dullness and final effacement awaits it. Thus we may proceed from the 'glad notes of daybreak' to the sombre ones of night without losing such rays as are needed to illuminate *any* situation.

The shading of tone, therefore, though in a sense at variance with timbre, is not entirely inconsistent with it. The colour can still be luminous, reflecting not absorbing the light, even if it does not catch its full glare.

Timbre—again it should be affirmed—is to be associated with compression of the vocal mechanism, particularly in the region of the larynx. This compression literally lifts tone up into the nasal region where timbre has its place. Timbre is, as it were, the 'juice' of tone—and we get this, much as we would squeeze the juice from fruit, due provision being made for other necessary factors. It has already been gathered, perhaps, that tone can be viewed mechanically as the outcome of two forces, a falling force (or dead, loose weight), and a contracting force, which is alive, tense. This may be shown in a simple diagram, which should always be in the singer's mind: $\rightarrow \downarrow \leftarrow$. The falling force is best exemplified in the vowel Uh (dull), the loosest vowel of the voice; the contracting force in the vowels Aw or ŏ. But an Uh if it is to be of real tonal value must also have a tendency to Aw, or a vowel with some similar inward pressure; and an Aw if it is to feel free and easily workable still needs a touch of Uh in it. In short, a balanced voice is the resultant of both falling and inward pressures; and, according as *timbrée* or less *timbrée* tone is desired, so will the inward $\rightarrow \leftarrow$ or the falling $\downarrow$ movement predominate, i.e., tightness or looseness of the muscular mechanism. 'Down' and 'in' are the key words which open all the mysteries of singing, since they represent the vertical and lateral forces which together produce the finest sound. Without lateral tension timbre is impossible; without vertical, ease. The control of tone should range from between the eyes—the highest level of vowelling—to the lowest level which is in the region of the abdomen; though, as we have said, these extremes of level cannot operate at one and the same time.

Vowels and Pitch

The subject has already been partly discussed, but as it is particularly important it needs further consideration. Some of the chief difficulties of singing are concerned with it. Over and over again the singer finds that he does not know how to 'get' a note, in spite of lengthy training; or, having succeeded in getting it, that it no longer represents the vowel that he wishes to sing; or that ease of production fails at high pitches, effectiveness of tone at low pitches. He becomes aware of breaks and registers which interfere with the even flow of his voice; and, in short, is quite unhappy with his vocal procedure.

A *whispered* vowel has an absolute pitch, or (it would be truer to say) *seems* to have an absolute pitch. In reality it is a compound of two or three simultaneously pronounced musical whispers; but it is the note given by the mouth that we particularly hear. This note affords a way of establishing the correct pronunciation of any vowel. When the resonantal note of the mouth cavity alters, the vowel associated with it alters. In other words, any departure from this whispered pitch inevitably means a change of vowel.

But, by a wonder of nature, this need not happen with a vowel *when it is sung*. A sung vowel is not tethered to any particular note. It can range more or less freely throughout the vocal compass, provided the resonators adapt themselves to the changes of pitch.

We have nevertheless to ask whether *exactly* the same vowel can be sung at all pitches, or whether a vowel has a natural tendency to alter as it is sung to a higher or a lower note. Further, does a slight alteration of a vowel—for it will amount to no more than that—prevent its recognition as the intended vowel?

It is unwise to draw any hard and fast conclusions as to what can or cannot be done with the voice. At times of great emotional disturbance the voice is capable of a considerable extension of its normal powers. Not only is the range of the voice greater—this applies mainly to high notes; vowels can be clearly defined at pitches usually prohibitive. Such deeds of valour do not necessarily offend. They sound well; they are right enough. Our powers of tension have increased and they are better applied; that is all. A good singer, moreover, can do things which an indifferent singer finds utterly impossible. The good singer has found out the way; the indifferent singer has not.

It is noticeable, too, that vowels are truer and clearer at all pitches when highly nasalized tone is used—a fact exploited by music-hall and comic characters—though vowels *can* be made quite recognizable with hardly any nasal ring.

There is also a kind of vowelling which by sheer brute force can be made to sound fairly correctly at extreme pitches; but at the expense of ease, towards which fine muscular movement is always bent.

The difficulty of singing high notes easily and effectively is known to all teachers and students. Low notes of the voice also give trouble in regard to effective resonation. As the voice goes up it cannot bear the heavy *weight* of tone of a more central note; as it goes down, the *width* of tone has to be lessened or there will be a loss of focus and *timbre*, also—and it is common—a tendency to bad intonation.

There is no doubt that words on high notes are far more distinct—particularly as regards soft singing—when a light rather than a heavy tone is used. Such a passage as this, from a madrigal of Weelkes (1597)

is an unintelligible mess when sung with thick tone, but clarifies immediately with thin tone, i.e., tone in which neck resonance is greatly reduced.

We may go even further and say that the finest tone is, literally, the 'finest' tone, in which only the edges of the vocal cords seem to be involved. It can easily be observed that poor singers never 'get their voices up'. They always make use of thick tone, as though their cords were of leather, rather than of a highly elastic or very thin metallic substance. The consequence is that their voice never reaches the higher resonances, and is without sensitivity. All is clumsy, and the result, as well, may be flatness. If it be objected that we have to make do with the cords that nature has given us, the reply is that every bit of our muscular system can be improved —the vocal cords being no exception.

Scientists tell us that the same vowel cannot be sung throughout the vocal range; to which, in some measure, observation forces us to agree.

If we try to sing an Ah, for instance, to these notes

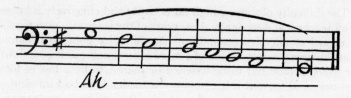

using the same cavity throughout, we shall inevitably end up on a vowel different from the one on which we started, though we can to some extent correct the difference by an increase of breath pressure. But there is no need to keep to the same cavity. A progressive opening of the mouth and strengthening of the breath *will* give us the same Ah. Keeping a true vowel when the pitch goes down is difficult, but scarcely impossible. Allowing for slight inconsistency, the ear will accept what is offered as—to all intents and purposes—a similar sort of sound.

When the pitch goes up a vowel is more likely to alter, but, even so, it would be rash to assert that it *must* alter, or to what extent. We dare not trust the scientist too implicitly when he demonstrates the bounds of the singer's art. For the time being science seems to lag behind practice. The practitioner can easily go one better than the scientist. This is as it should be; for if art were to be limited by knowledge (unless gained by the artist himself) it would be in a bad way. We had thus better take our stand on the ground of practical mechanics rather than that of theoretical acoustics; the former gives us quite sufficient foothold.

There is an original quality of sound produced by the laryngeal mechanism before it is taken in hand by the resonators. Not only that. The formation of a vowel sound appears to be assisted by the vocal cords, inasmuch as they produce a note weak or rich in harmonics: a phenomenon observed by Professor Oscar Russell, and in accordance with what we know of laryngeal compression and its effect on tone quality (*v.* p. 167).

But singing does not arise till resonation by the mouth, neck and nose takes place; the process of fine singing is very largely that of the skilful adjustment of these resonators to laryngeal pitch, and its object: to sing any vowel (as far as possible) at any pitch. The singer cannot be excused if he uses a sort of nondescript 'instrumental' instead of a 'verbal' sound, though the claims of the voice *as an instrument* have fully to be recognized; speech is not everything in singing.

Central notes are easier than extreme notes to couple with a correct vowel. But I think we do not know enough about resonantal selection and adaptation to say that such and such a sound *cannot* be sung through sheer acoustical impossibility at any particular pitch. And even if it happens to be true, there is always something quite near to the perfect pronunciation of any vowel which can be used for that vowel, without fear of mistake regarding its identity.

I have always had difficulty in getting resounding high notes from sopranos, such as one heard from Tetrazzini—notes which seemed to be made of hard boxwood—particularly in *staccato* effects. This is about the only difficulty I have met with. But, as in the case of Tetrazzini and others—Kirsten Flagstad, for instance—it is possible to overcome it, and to give a full meed of brilliance, power and climax in the top part of the voice. Here we are speaking of tone in general; whether exact vowels can be preserved by sopranos on their highest notes is another matter. But brilliancy is naturally connected with Ee, Ay, etc., and if brilliancy can be achieved on high soprano notes it seems likely that a very good idea of these and other vowels can also be given at the same pitch, though modification may be necessary. The great singers of the eighteenth and nineteenth centuries knew nothing about 'formants' and the limitations apparently arising from them; but probably they were able to produce the required sounds, i.e., to adapt their resonators in such a way as to sing with consistent quality throughout their vocal range. Sudden failures of pronunciation or of strength—'breaks' of any sort—would never have been allowed in a perfect artist.[1] I do not see why vowel consistency should be less possible with the voice than upon an organ stop or any other mechanical instrument. Doubtless, in every case there are slight differences of colour according to the pitch of notes—the lowest notes of a flute are rather different in sound from the highest notes; but we recognize all of them as flute sound. They preserve a unity which we should expect

[1] A pretty problem is posed by the fact that if on the gramophone a song is lowered in its recorded pitch by an alteration of speed, the vowels change in accordance. Lowering the pitch alters the vowel. Similarly the raising of the recorded pitch of a song must alter vowels. In Mozart's time the level of agreed pitch was three-quarters of a tone lower than it is now; and in earlier periods even down to a minor third lower. Were the vowels of those times different from ours or have we to adjust our vowels to suit the altered conditions of pitch? The student should amuse himself by trying to find the answer, or demonstrate that the question is absurd. He will be all the wiser afterwards.

from the same instrument of unvarying shape and material.[1] The particular tone of the flute is the equivalent of a vowel. Is it likely that the voice, with far superior powers of adaptation as an instrument, must fail to achieve what its humbler sister can so well accomplish?

Conversational speech demands a maximum of clarity with a minimum of effort. When the voice rises above or falls below the level where this is established, greater strains are put upon it if ease and effectiveness are to be secured. The speaking voice has nothing like the range of the singing voice; because it has nothing like the tension. When we speak, we scarcely cover more than an octave of sound; when we sing, it may be through two octaves and more. This seems to imply that different techniques are applicable to speech and song. In what does it consist? When does speech become 'music', instead of being merely 'musical'?

We can speak words without audible phonation; indeed, to do so clearly is a very good exercise in verbal intensity. Such whispering will remain around certain pitches: those of the whispered resonances of its vowels. These pitches can be extended a little—a note or two up or down—by energetic action, but they are scarcely subject to variation. This whispering process is essentially that of speech.

Rudimentary song begins with the phonation of whispered sound. When *voice* is added we can immediately extend the compass of the sound. We can 'raise' or 'lower' our voices according to the exigencies of emotional speech. If we raise them the tone will become more brilliant and telling; if we lower them, more sympathetic and subdued. This certainly gives us a cue to the natural behaviour of the voice which not only reacts in tone quality to changes of pitch, but rises or falls according to different states of emotion. It would be incongruous to recite 'Full fathom five thy father lies' in a squeaky voice, or to say 'My heart is like a singing bird' as if it came from underground; and, in song, the composer would see that this does not happen, though the singer may still do dreadful deeds in the matter of unsuitable tone-colour, placing his voice where it would not naturally be placed if his emotion were sincere and gave him the right stimulus. All this is very evident in speech where we observe at once whether things are right or wrong;

---

[1] We should not forget that it is the *totality* of resonance that governs tone-quality. In the case of the voice this includes the characteristic harmonics produced in the mouth, throat and nose; by the material of the instrument (whether it is hard or soft); by special treatment of the larynx and vocal cords; and by the way in which all these agencies are combined and related. A very complicated issue is thus presented which it is impossible fully to analyse or to reproduce in other than its own terms, i.e., the exact mechanism of the voice itself. We can have a rough idea of what is happening, but never a complete one in which all the factors are brought under observation.

but it is less clear when words are joined to music, and become subservient to *its* melodic progress.

The relation between pitch and emotion is of great interest, for it includes the problem of how it is that a vowel which has a fixed whispered resonance pitch—uniquely its own—can still be made to sound at other pitches in obedience to the call of music or varied states of feeling.

Even with ordinary speech, however, we do not keep to any particular note or notes. Speech is fluid, not fixed. Its general position may be high or low, but the passage from syllable to syllable is relatively slow and sliding—very subtle in its movement. By degrees as we approach music, more definite pitches are registered, until we 'monotone' on a certain note and extend our control of sustained sound over a much larger range; in short, apply words to melody, as in a song.

Having to keep the same vowel over greatly varied pitch *is quite an unnatural proceeding*—an art in fact—called forth not by words, but by music. Any vowel has to serve for this purpose: as in singing a solfège.

Speaking, in a technical sense, has nothing to do with music, only with the adjustment of the resonance cavities, and the articulation of the vocal organs. Both speech and music can get along very well without each other; music can be made by the voice, apart from speech. They can combine, but their point of origin is different. Speaking is the art of laryngeal to cavity adjustment; singing, of cavity to laryngeal. Different techniques are implied, different orders of precedence. In the one case the pitch adapts itself to the vowel, in the other the vowel to the pitch. That is to say, a spoken vowel, if no strain is put upon it, will naturally take the pitch of its oral resonator—for instance the word 'son' will be spoken about the note, _____ or 'green' about the note _____ —though,

as we have said, once a vowel is phonated it *can* be raised or lowered in pitch; but a sung vowel *has* to accommodate itself to the pitch of the vocal cords, which means that, by some method or other, its resonant pitch or pitches must be made to agree with the harmonics of the fundamental note, otherwise its 'formant' cannot be awakened.

We are on very difficult ground here, as indicated in the previous section *Timbre and Resonance* (pp. 144-57) and shall perhaps be more sure of our way if, as before suggested, we attempt to cover it on mechanical, rather than acoustical principles.

The need of reducing the scale of rising notes has been recognized in many systems of voice culture which have established it in what have been termed 'registers' ('chest', 'middle' and 'head')—the lowest register making use of the full length of the vocal cords, the middle register of much less, and the highest register of only a small portion; at least so it runs theoretically, but the problem may be viewed somewhat differently, and it is perhaps better to understand it as a reduction or tapering of the piping of the voice, in other words, as a gradual contraction of the resonance cavities for the better safeguarding of the tone, which may well include a contraction of the larynx and consequent shortening of the glottal chink.

Much of the difficulty of vowelling lies in the application of the right resistance around the resonating cavities. If resistance is not present on the higher notes on Ah, for instance, shouting results; i.e., there is no control of the emission. It is much the same with all vowels though it is not so apparent with the small-bore vowels such as Ee or Oo, because their formation supplies a certain natural resistance. The first cause of trouble on high notes, then, is lack of resistance, or 'surround' whereby the sound seems to fly off in all directions, without point, focus or concentration.

The second cause of trouble is lack of neck space. We have before remarked, in talking of the vowel ü (German), or u (French) that it simply will not sound on the higher notes unless it has increased room in which to vibrate. The breath pressure produces such laryngeal constriction that it has to be loosened and this can only come with a greater opening of the throat. Relaxation always goes with an open throat.[1]

The two great needs on high notes, then, are increased resistance (or contraction—much as a spire gradually tapers) in the case of the looser vowels; and increased neck space (or relaxation) in the case of the tighter vowels; though resistance never operates to the exclusion of relaxation, and vice versa[2]—a proportion of each

[1] It would seem as if this larger cavity applied to ü would necessarily lower the resonant pitch of the neck, so that the vowel could not be sounded; and that, instead, we should get something like the cavity required for Oo which gives a pitch about five semitones lower than that required for ü. But—by virtue of the Helmholtz Resonator principle—the larger cavity will give the higher note, if its orifice, i.e., the opening leading to the mouth is sufficiently enlarged. Nevertheless, we can hardly avoid the conclusion that, as there is undoubtedly a change of vowel quality when neck space is increased, *some* modification of the 'formant' must take place, though it need not mean a complete alteration of the vowel, only of its secondary characteristics.

[2] There seems a contradiction here, as these are two antagonistic qualities. But it can be solved if we remember the principle of balance or equilibrium. It is clearly put in Indian philosophy which notes three qualities of matter: *tamar*, the lowest of the Trinity—which may be translated as inertia; *rajas*, the second— being force, activity, motion; and *sattva*, the third—the quality of balance or harmony which unifies the two others. Such an analysis recognizes the necessity

will always be present. How does this affect vowel quality? Let us take the extreme long vowels Ee and Oo in their average placing, neither far forward nor back. In both these there is considerable tension or resistance brought about by the high raising of the back of the tongue for Ee and the close rounding of the lips and back orifice of the mouth for Oo. But in nature, they are fundamentally different. With Ee (unless it is modified) the throat is relatively closed; with Oo it is open, and these tendencies will be accentuated as the pitch rises and more pressure is put upon the breath. Ee (as with ü) will be squeezed out of existence; Oo will become too cavernous. If therefore we want to be able to sing something like these vowels, sufficient for the purposes of identification on high notes—we certainly do not want to alter their quality too much if it can be avoided—we must open the throat for Ee and close it somewhat for Oo. In the case of Ee, this will give us something like ĭ (the short vowel in 'give'); in the case of Oo (to gain resistance) to something like ŏŏ (the short vowel in 'good'). This overcomes the difficulty of high notes with these vowels; it is the same with the French vowel u (as in 'tu'), or indeed with any of the very 'close' vowels. Observe that ĭ gives a darker sound than Ee, since it is further down and back; and ŏŏ a brighter sound than Oo, since it is further forward. Observe also, that the posture or shape of the forward vowel Ee is maintained by the mouth and tongue, the inessential throat representing, mainly, the modifying process; that of Oo is determined by the throat, and so the mouth, in this case, represents the factor that can be changed without fundamentally altering the vowel. All this will happen quite naturally with these vowels.

Similarly Ay will tend to change to ĕ (a larger vowel) and Oh to Oo (a smaller vowel) as the voice rises, but it would be absurd to think that a recognizable Oh cannot be sung at all pitches, or indeed that any vowel needs such 'doctoring' as completely to distort it. 'Lawve' for 'lŭv' (love) would be quite inadmissible though it is not unheard even in select circles.

The larger vowels Ah and Aw require much the same solution. A broad Ah cannot be carried up the scale. It will get completely out of hand. If its brilliant Ah quality is to be maintained it will have to be closed at the throat and brought further forward. It is very difficult—indeed almost impossible—to sing the Ah in 'dark', high up, if this word is given its naturally sombre character—but the

of relaxation (or *tamar*) if a true state of balance is to be attained. Effort and ease are the twin sisters of all beauty of movement. This amounts to much the same thing as 'dead-weight, lifted', which the singer should generally have in mind as a main principle of his vocal conduct.

251

tighter and more forward Ah in 'laugh'—such as befits laughter—is quite easy to sing on high notes.

Aw, though in a sense a contracted vowel (it gains its metallic 'ring' from this), is, yet, too large to deal with comfortably on high notes and must be still further contracted towards ŏ (gŏt).

If exceedingly bright tone is wanted Ah may also be given a touch of ŏ, but in this case the throat may have to be opened a little more to make the production easy.

Oh and Oo have a deep, open throat, with, in consequence, a recession of the tone. Though naturally 'drawn in' they will have to be contracted still more as the voice rises, not only to keep control, but so that their dullish sound does not lose all its 'life'.

Strangely enough, as we have already said, a process of contraction or tapering—or what seems like it—has generally to be adopted for lower as well as for higher notes—much as in this diagram

where the middle width represents the central region of the voice. When the voice goes downwards, just as when it goes up, it tends to become 'white', and to lose its rich, full, central tone. It is as difficult to keep a low note as a high note *down*; the larynx will always want to rise; on high notes from too much tension, on low notes from too little. The singer must be very careful to secure sufficient downward tension on low notes, by breath compression. In this way the voice will be equalized and unified throughout its range, its natural loosening at lower pitches will be counteracted and flatness avoided. What we really have to get are contraction and concentration in the over-loose positions of the voice—whether these are due to pitch or to the nature of the vowel itself—or room and relaxation in the over-tight positions; otherwise control is bound to suffer.

It comes to this: that vowels have to be modified to exclude 'whiteness' and over-tightness, when these are encouraged by pitch. The exact tinge of tone which will do this can be allowed almost to look after itself, once the attempt is made properly to darken the voice and to secure a sufficiently open throat. It is scarcely more than another aspect of the modification of vowels for 'colour', or rather 'shade', discussed on p. 124; not a full change of vowel. The singer should never lose sight of the vowel that he *intends* to sing, even if he does not quite sing it.

The 'darkening', or holding-together of the voice is the chief clue to control.[1] Releasing the voice after a certain point—letting it

[1] Difficulties of terminology enter here. 'Darkening' is not quite the same thing

'go'—is a sign of unskilled singing. One can hear it in church, on the high notes of hymns when sung by a really exuberant congregation. This point is reached—it is especially noticeable with men—on or about the 'great break'[1] of the voice where danger is encountered which must be met by a considerable difference of muscular tension. It is thoroughly recognized that here a 'closing' process must occur. Santley said[2] that he began it about

though it did not fully operate till   and with most

men singers who know their job the same can be observed. It is generally best to work downwards over the break, starting from a note or sound that is thoroughly 'closed' or drawn-together, and endeavouring to use the same mechanism in descending. The over-open sound should never be forced upward. 'Closing', however, does not necessarily take the 'ring' out of tone; on the contrary, as the mechanism is contracted the voice brightens. When brilliant tone dulls it is generally (probably always) because the mechanism 'gives' allowing the voice to fall back.

It is always a good plan in voice training to begin on high or relatively high notes, where the voice by a sort of instinct of self-preservation naturally 'closes', and to try to keep this closure as the voice descends. It will not be entirely possible; but the influence that it has is good. Or it may be that some particular note gives an

as 'Dulling'; a considerable amount of nasal resonance may still enter into a 'Dark' sound.

[1] It is curious how the great break of the voice occurs about

with both men and women. It almost seems to indicate that a woman's voice is an extension of a man's, and that a woman's voice does not, so to speak, start off again in its own right. For this main break is at the top of a man's voice (where emission is difficult) but at the bottom of the woman's (where emission is easy) and so it does not *seem* to have anything to do with tension in the sense in which we are here discussing it. It is a bad patch which must be got over somehow, and that is all we can say about it. Woman seems to have inherited man's bad qualities, without having deserved them. Man's fault is explicable; woman's isn't.

[2] To Mr. Frederick Austin.

especially good 'ring'; if that is so, it should be taken as a type of what the singer should aim at elsewhere. The test of a cavity is whether you can sing softly and tonefully in it; whether it will respond to the slightest touch.

As the voice goes up, then, the calibre (or bore) of the piping must decrease, or seem to decrease, by contraction. Vowels, particularly Ah (the central orb of the system), will modify their sound accordingly. Just how much the voice can approach an open fully-nasalized Ah on top notes, must be found by experiment in going from, say, a closed Oh to a more open Ah position. Owing to failure of control the mechanism will warn, 'thus far and no further', and this will show to what degree the necessary modification of the vowel must be retained.[1] A rise of pitch is naturally accompanied by a brightening of the tone (v. p. 248), and when possible we should study to ensure it. Brightening means contraction. After a certain point it happens that we are liable to give up the ghost, owing to difficulties of laryngeal tension, and allow the voice impotently to fall down and back, with a complete alteration of tone quality. It cannot be too strongly stated, that what accounts for 'tone'—'firm' tone as we have called it elsewhere—is precisely the approximation of the vocal cords. If they do not approximate, 'hooting' and such like (the very antithesis of tone) results: the vocal control, as it were, being shifted from the cords to the resonators, resulting in 'blown' instead of 'vibrated' sound. Even with 'breath' or *mezza voce* tone, there needs to be a degree of approximation, or it will be 'breathy', instead of silvery and shimmering. Some artists secure very beautiful effects by suitably contrasting firm and breath tone, not because they *have* to do so for reasons of pitch, but for expressive reasons. Even when, on high, soft notes, pitch, almost willy-nilly, decides the matter, the relaxation of tension whereby *timbrée* tone yields to a sort of *falsetto* is not entirely to be deprecated, as it may help to get over a difficult passage, such as the famous *melisma* in the St. Matthew Passion which the Evangelist has to sing when Peter denies Christ:

And he went out, and wept —————— bit ~ ~ terly

Here the high B, unless forced, can scarcely be sung with *timbrée*

---

[1] Theoretically, if the muscles were strong enough, fully-nasalized tone might be secured from top to bottom of the voice, though what has been said as to 'scale' of piping still holds good.

tone, but a transition from firm to *falsetto* at this point, can yet be so skilfully managed, that we are hardly aware of an absolute change of quality, though, of course, such it is.

It is reported that Caruso practised ascending scales beginning on Ah, passing through Oh and then to Uh; which is not exactly in conformity with our principles, but was probably adopted to secure an open throat, somewhat at the expense of brilliancy of tone. The tendency of a full-throated Ah will be towards Uh. When the tendency is towards ă or ŏ, the sound will be more potent, but less ample.

It is difficult to be exact as to vowel quality on top notes: to know quite what the shade of vowel is that you want and *can* sing. It should not be far from the pure vowel, but it will be slightly different from it. A sort of nondescript sound on top notes is inadmissible; or such sound as completely travesties the vowel which appears in the word which has to be sung. Some would have it that at extreme ranges verbal definition should rely chiefly upon consonants, and that vowel purity can be neglected; but this is a needless confession of defeat. It is clear that vowel distortion, if carried too far, must mean verbal distortion. On low notes, for instance, 'than' may often be heard as 'then', 'shall' as 'shell', making nonsense of the words. No one would pretend that it is not more difficult to get true, or sufficiently true vowels at extreme pitches than at a central pitch: the singer's business, if he can, is to make it appear easy. We have also to admit that the play of 'colour' is inevitably lessened on high notes, owing to reduced freedom. 'Colour' is brought about by modification of tension, and it is obvious that when notes are 'keyed up', as they have to be at high pitches, they cannot be greatly relaxed, or they will 'fall down', and that would be the end of pitch, colour and everything.

Alexander Ellis, years ago, offered an illuminating remark when he said that vowels originally were framed for speech, not song—i.e., that they were selected for use in the middle part of the voice. Often, therefore, they are not well adapted to different circumstances, as when Ee has to be sung at a very low pitch, or Oo at a very high pitch, etc. Other vowels, or modifications of our present ones might have been chosen if the level of speech had been other than it is.

We seem, then, to have secured some vital points of technique with regard to high notes: that the brilliant vowels (Ee, Ay, etc.) require more and more neck room as they go up, that they must be resonated further back, that they must become more 'covered' in quality, i.e., that, in a general way, less nasal ring must be given to them; and that the dull vowels (Oo, Oh, etc.) require more resistance as they rise in pitch, must be brought further forward, become brighter in quality, and be given increased nasal ring.

But, with all vowels, it is necessary to avoid too much nasality on the highest notes, because this disturbs ease of production. The whole question is one of ease *and* definition, and the careful give and take between these two factors.

'Dark' tone is a balanced tone, full of colour, generally rich in harmonics; 'white' tone is colourless, the result of 'harmonic' poverty; with very brilliant tone high harmonics are forced and accentuated; with dull tone low harmonics prevail. The gradual 'covering' of tone is brought about by the gradual elimination of its high harmonics, which are developed most of all in the nose.

It must be understood that breath action plays a great part in this modifying process, because it is the breath which ultimately is responsible for muscular tension and relaxation. Slight muscular movements may perhaps *seem* localized at the place of movement, though even with them a connection with the diaphragm could be traced; with strong movements there is no doubt whatever as to their point of origin—it can be felt abdominally. With an open Ah or Uh the breath is relatively loose—particularly if the vowels tend to be white.[1] With a well-shaped Oh the tension at the base of the breath is very considerable. Any strong shaping of the mouth, etc., needs to be backed up by tension of the breath. We have therefore, in this, the condition of 'darkening' the sound: for it involves a contraction of the vocal instrument.

If we observe the formation of the face for an Oh (the most expressive of all the vowels, for it suggests the greatest amount of 'feeling'), we find that the upper lip is brought well down, like a shutter, over the top teeth, and we also find great tension of the breath in the region of the diaphragm and abdomen. This gives us our cue towards any requisite 'covering' of sound. As long as the upper lip is down, and the breath acts in this way, a sound cannot escape or run loose; it is pinned, as it were, by the resistance of the lip and nostrils, and, further, is held by the breath pull. Experiment will show that all difficulty of 'cover', even with an Ah, can thus be solved. Per contra, the release of the upper lip to a smiling position releases and opens the sound.

Both bright and dull tone—it is important thoroughly to recognize these two types—are affected by pitch, though differently. On high notes bright tone seems to come further forward, to be directed horizontally towards the hard palate or mask of the

---

[1] It is quite easy to observe the level at which the breath acts. With white sound the breath effort, or what there is of it, is felt to be high up in the chest; but breathe deeply, and at once the sound is of a darker quality.

face →; dull tone increasingly follows the vertical line of the pharynx ↑ emerging, as it were, through the top of the head. If we had to do with only one type or shade of tone the matter could be stated with greater precision; its variability prevents us from being quite dogmatic: for we may wish to ease and cover bright tone at high pitches, or tighten and brighten dull tone, in which case the technique must change.

The matter of 'Vowels and Pitch' is not without difficulty. We have endeavoured to answer the questions it raises, and have found that vowels change their colour according to pitch, because of changes in the vocal instrument, forced by differences of muscular tension. These changes take place mainly at the back of the mouth, at or near the laryngeal mechanism. Strictly speaking, the slightest change of pitch registers a change of the vowel concerned, since a slightly different tension operates modifying the vowel cavity. But the singer, by his art, can still give a very fair representation of any vowel throughout the compass of his voice, sufficient to preserve it from being mistaken for another vowel. The exact shade of any vowel which arises from these variations of tension is however most elusive. It is scarcely to be stated in terms of a fixed sound. The most one can say is that there will be a *tendency* towards Aw or ŏ when a tightening of the mechanism is required, as for extremes of pitch or brilliant tones; or a *tendency* towards ŭ, when a loosening of the mechanism is wanted, as for increased neck space or dull tone.

Resistance and room are the determinants of the vocal situation; but they run counter to each other unless harmonized and balanced by right breath action. When that balance is achieved everything is easy.

To review our findings.

The problem is to keep the same, or much the same, resonance, as the voice rises or falls; i.e., to keep the same vowel, as far as possible. We have seen that more resistance is needed as the pitch goes up or down (*v.* p. 352); this holds good for both bright or dull tone. The feeling with the one, is that the voice is brought forward, the cavities assuming a more or less horizontal smiling position ⊃; with the other, that the voice is tipped back, the cavities being vertically elongated ( ).

If bright Ah is contrasted with sombre Oh, it will be found that both, to increase their volume, have to submit to more tension, Ah, in the mouth, Oh in the neck. Such tension appears to be, and actually is a process of contraction: the outward pressure, due to the enlargement of the cavity, requiring to be countered by inward pressure. In other words, space, in this case, is secured by stretching (which involves tension), not by relaxation—increased breath ten-

K

sion being coincident with it. But there is a limit to bright tone on high notes. When the larynx gets too high and the back orifice too constricted, neck resonance (essential to vowelling) is cut off, and relief has to be sought in opening the orifice and increasing neck space, as with Ee and Ay which must tend towards ĭ and ĕ on high notes.

There is also a limit to dull tone. When the larynx is too low and the back orifice too slack, neck resonance is over-stressed; and control, i.e., resistance, has to be regained by compression, i.e., closing the back orifice and reducing neck space.

In the one case the brilliancy of the tone will be somewhat lessened; in the other, the dullness.

Roughly the procedure, *at extreme pitches*, is for a long vowel to be given something of the character of its corresponding short vowel—which amounts to a contrary movement from the one to the other.

This seems to be the rationale of the matter. In tabulated form it would stand thus:

	front orifice	oral cavity	larynx	back orifice	neck cavity
Brilliant tone	opens	enlarges	rises	shuts	reduces
Dull tone	shuts	reduces	falls	opens	enlarges

it being understood that this represents a progressive tendency as the voice rises or falls from what might be called its normal central position, in which the cavities have their maximum of relaxation.

These solutions are mechanical solutions, imposed by the mechanical situation and the need for control. It is possible that some other improvement or easing of the situation may be preferred; some slightly different shading. Each singer probably solves the question in his own way. But *something* must happen; some modification of a vowel in respect of pitch must be made. We must beware of establishing hard and fast rules. Vocal colour is so subtle and various that it cannot be engineered with perfect precision. Much must be left to the imagination, by which results will be unconsciously secured.

The student is not likely to be able to disregard the practice of vowel modification. He will probably find that good pronunciation at extreme pitches is by no means child's play and that some principles are needed to guide him. If that is so, what we have said may be helpful. Some singers, however, instinctively do the right thing and are untroubled by difficulties of pitch and pronunciation. They may even not realize that they alter their vowels as they go up or down. To sing comfortably is more than half a guarantee that they are singing correctly. Much talk about it may often serve to make a technical process more difficult than it really is.

Starting and Ending Notes

How the voice is brought on and taken off gives the best indication of the art of the singer. Not only the first note, but every note that is sung submits to a process of start and finish. A song is a series of such incidents and the way in which they are carried out determines in a large measure the beauty of the performance as well as its style and aptness. If the performance is cold, the 'attack' of the notes will show it; if it is expansive, warm-hearted, it will be shown in the far different approach that the singer makes to his notes. It is within the power of the performer to suggest either a blow or a benediction in his handling of tone.

Quality of approach, too, is almost if not quite the same thing as quality of *vibration*. Loveliness of tone, which by its regularity soothes rather than stimulates, permeates rather than pierces, cannot come from a rough beginning. It makes all the difference whether you have to take a sledge-hammer to open a door, or whether the door is so balanced that it will move with the slightest touch. Of course, you may not want to open the door if there are burglars about, but, when you do want to open it, the more easily it will move, the better. It is interesting to observe that a great thinker like Aristotle placed the highest value upon 'touch' as a sign of culture. In most cases, therefore, it is better to use the word 'touch' rather than 'attack' for the way in which it is desirable to begin a note. We have to refer to harsher methods—these have their uses—but art as a whole is more concerned with persuasion than with pounding; civilization goes with sympathy, not with brute force.

It is said that the Navajo Indians look upon 'breath' and 'sound' as very much the same thing. With them the notion of breath, as the manifestation of life, contains the notion of sound—'moaned breath'. It is as though sound were actually in the breath, not only activated by it. It is a beautiful idea. Primitive people may be nearer to truth than are the sophisticated. Who can say when sound, or anything, begins or, for the matter of that, ends? We lose sight of a bird as it flies from us into the distance, yet we know it is still there. Similarly, the mind, through hearing, registers something which we call sound, but it may be there all the time, only awaiting the circumstance to embody it, to bring it to our sense perception. It is almost a Platonic conception. At any rate with the finest of 'touches' there is no sharp dividing line between breath and sound; and it is the business of the singer to try to erase any such line as far as he can. Breath should merge imperceptibly into sound and sound into breath. This seldom happens. Very few singers show such vocal command. Either the instrument is stiff and insensitive, or badly poised (which is much the same thing); or the breath plays upon it by fits and starts. Whatever the cause, the sound comes on with a burst or a click, and generally a little late. Its rough entry draws attention; it does not 'weave' into the musical fabric but is like some outstanding knot of thread. In a word it represents bad workmanship, preventing those subtle adjustments and diffusions by which the real artist is shown. On the other hand a good 'touch' opens up qualities of expression undreamt of in the philosophy of the average singer. The deeply 'moaned' or 'crooned' sound is that which the singer should try to build upon. Almost all vocal virtue is within it, for this sound has the finest 'touch'.

Without at all advocating 'breathy' singing—i.e., where there is an obvious wastage of breath—there is no doubt that a certain admixture of breath in tone is necessary to the act of vocal 'touch'.[1] Tight, hard sound cannot consort with touch. The aspirate is the oil of singing. The voice will not run smoothly till it is aspirated. The aspirate forms, as it were, an elastic pad between the joints of the vocal machine, allaying friction or jamming. The whole of the mechanism is eased thereby, and sympathetic qualities are also released. We are back again at the 'moaned breath' of our Indian friends.

There is an opposite way of looking at the matter. We can think of touch as operating from above, like the touch of the hand upon the pianoforte, in a downward movement; not from below, in an upward movement from the base of the breath, as with moaning. It is thus often good to imagine a note as gently alighting upon the vocal cords, like a bird coming to earth, the whole muscular system waiting, as it were, to receive it; keyed in expectation. The descent

---

[1] When we sing a characteristic ŏ ('cot') we are literally squeezing the aspirate out of the tone. The result is the most economical use of the breath. But the tone will be hard, though tremendously telling; and to make it start it has to be driven— it will not be coaxed. For a more sympathetic sound, some aspirate must be used.

We write A*h* for Ah and it is not without reason that we do so. The 'h'—both as final touch and constant factor—represents just that quality that Ah possesses so supremely; the quality of free emergence which seems to allow it to contain all the most desirable features of vocal tone, whether from an audible or technical stand-point; so that Ah is generally considered the singer's vowel par excellence. The aspirate can, of course, be reduced or increased with corresponding variation from what may be called the normal tone of the vowel.

is such that there is no shock. This is a variant of the idea of dead-weight as regards the voice. It is valuable in its power of suggestion. In a sense vocal sound has weight; it is for ever trying to make contact with the base of the breath. Certainly the muscles concerned (in as far as they are loose) have a tendency to fall; only they are not permitted the fullest measure of relaxation. The vocal cords stop that; they bar the way.

Elsewhere I have likened touch to a *point* of contact. It is the point which matters. It might be shown in a diagram:

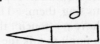

The louder the note the more quickly does the point expand into it: ♩ or even ♩ but the point is always there,

representing the emergence of the sound from silence.

If 'touch' is involved, either end of the note has such a vanishing point ♩ . We take leave with just as much delicacy as

we enter. Such is the touch that will register the slightest breath of emotion, or usher in a full volume of free sound. Touch (in this sense) involves, therefore, a series of miniature swells: $< < <$. But we must be careful to avoid anything like an impression of 'pumping' notes, by prolonging the act of touch beyond due limits, or letting notes progress in this fashion: $<> <> <>$. A thoroughly bad style is typified by this, because it isolates individual notes; they are not really related; there is no dynamic proportion, no principle of direction which organizes them into a phrase; they do not 'carry through'.[1] 'Pumping' is a very common fault, not only with singers but with instrumentalists. String players often fail to sustain their notes to the bitter end. Dignity, nobility of expression and much else go by the board when this quasi-emotional slobbering takes place. Whatever happens in the way of 'swell' at the beginning of a note, its end as a rule should not weaken.

The most beautiful tone is soft tone, for to it the best touch has been applied. From which it follows that as sound is reduced in

---

[1] Nevertheless, the swell, or what the Italians called the 'mezza di voce' is the *sine qua non* of all 'expression'. Without the faculty of swelling and diminishing a note or phrase $< >$ everything is lifeless.

force, so does its quality improve. This is borne out by experience. When sound is scarcely audible rough humans are dismissed; fairies and the 'lordly folk' come to take their place. Music, indeed, can be distilled of all sound and, in some strange way, it still remains. 'Heard melodies are sweet, but those unheard are sweeter.'

The difficulty of singing lies in dealing with fixed notes and time values. This induces (almost inevitably) fixation of mind and mechanism. The singer becomes stiff and unnatural. Words which he would have spoken quite well lose their sense when he attempts to sing them. Their flow is broken, their accents are false; they have no 'touch', they are without expression. It is interesting to get a pupil to talk the words of his song at the place and about the pace at which he would have sung them while the accompaniment is being played, in a sort of *'sprech-gesang'*. How different the result generally is from what it would have been if he had tried to fit the words to the notes. Truth and freedom of speech must be recovered in song, for it will surely be lost for a period. The factor of this freedom is undoubtedly the factor of touch: the supreme sign of control.

Clumsy methods of singing will never produce 'fine' tone—i.e., tone capable of being fined down to a point. Only from such tone can lightness come. One talks of a string player playing with a single hair of the bow. It is much the same thing as singing upon the very edge of the vocal cords, not with coarse thick tone, but with tone which will immediately respond. This should be within the capacity of the singer. It is no use employing a delicate touch upon an instrument that refuses to sound. There is such a thing as a beautiful instrument as well as a beautiful touch. The former is probably a gift. Oldish voices, particularly if they have been badly used, have often very little power of response. With the best will in the world they will not 'play'.

Every virtue has its danger. That of easy vibration is an absence of precision.

So far we have spoken of sympathetic touch, represented by $<$. Where the affections are concerned this is the only touch that will serve. Tenderness must be expressed by a scarcely-daring approach; and as love, from which tenderness springs, is the ruling emotion in life, a large proportion of art shows this quality. In song, particularly, this is so. Three-quarters of lyrical poetry concern love. Ruskin even asserted, that tenderness is not only the characteristic of a large proportion of art, but of the greatest art. But it can be seen that an excess of emotion can easily arise in this way, together with an absence of that control of form which we associate with 'classical' treatment. The blurred outline, the poor proportion: all such things come from insufficient intellectual application. This latter represents the stern, critical aspect of art and it is for ever at war with the tender aspect.

Classical art is cut with the sharpest of implements. Its definition is uncompromising. Its formal bias has little use for 'touch'. Just as from the 'ping' of a plucked instrument like the harpsichord our attention is directed to form rather than feeling—it is the neat, highly wrought structure of harpsichord music, its discretion of statement, that specially delights us—so, in an opposite way, the softer hammer-blow of the pianoforte tends to romantic, emotional effect. Art, by its dependence on form, has of course at all times a classical bearing, and by its feeling a romantic—all art shows a fusion of both aspects—but the stress of the one or the other differs, and when it so differs it is largely a matter of touch, or perhaps it would be truer to say of an *absence* of touch in the former case.

So that we get another sort of initial impulse to a note, which can be more truly described as 'attack'. It may be represented by ⌐ in which 'touch' (indicated by the dotted lines) is omitted. It is obvious that this attack is somewhat heartless. It implies a sudden impact. Its nature is aggressive, forceful, emphatic. It is allied to a 'jerk' or 'smash'. But it has its uses in clean definition. It is a necessary antidote to sentimentality, as in *staccato*. Singers are particularly prone to sloppy style because the voice is naturally inclined to *legato*. As a rule singers are inexact and undecided. Few can take a lead. They have little sense of a 'point' of time because their instrument has no mechanism which stimulates or enforces it. Keyed instruments have. Training in 'attack' is therefore as necessary as in 'touch'.

The most vital form of attack is (1) the 'closed glottis' or *coup de glotte* attack. In this the vocal cords are tightly approximated so that the breath can concentrate strongly against them. As long as the cords hold no breath can escape. When, however, the breath pressure exceeds the resistance that is put up by the cords, the breath suddenly bursts through with an explosive action like a cough,[1] only deeper set. There is *no* wastage of breath with this form of attack. The maximum power is obtained with the least *expenditure* of force. But wastage may easily occur *after* the breath has passed the cords. The cords may then slacken far too much by the resistance

---

[1] We know that words often exhibit the sound that expresses their meaning—probably the original form of a word always did. This is shown in the word 'laugh', its particular shade of Ah being actually produced by rippling laughter. Similarly with the word 'cough'. When we cough we sound the vowel ŏ, which, so often in this book, has been indicated as of the very essence of tone, since it proceeds from the perfect adjustment of the vocal cords (*v.* pp. 14–15). The great teacher of singing, the second Manuel Garcia, advocated, for certain purposes, the starting of a note by an action akin to a slight cough, and by this he must have intended the vowel ŏ, as coughing is always accompanied by this vowel.

being entirely overcome, the defence, as it were, giving up the contest and retiring in disorder. To make the most of the situation resistance must be strongly maintained after the position has been carried—as when a soldier clicks his heels and *keeps them there*. The singer should try to continue with the same concentrated tone that comes at the moment of attack. If he does this he will find that as a technical exercise the closed glottis attack may be of great value, leading to the maximum output of tone. But only as a technical exercise. The procedure is too rough and forced for anything like sensitivity of expression. It can hardly ever be used in artistic expression, only for muscular training; and of course it is only applicable when a word starts with a vowel, as in Debussy's part-song, 'Yver, vous n'estes qu'un villain', when a distinct 'bite' on the first word is so appropriate.

Cases for its effective use are however very rare.

(2) The normal attack is termed the 'clear' attack. With this attack the vocal cords are approximated, but less tightly than with the 'closed' attack, so that the 'shock' of the glottis is not pronounced. The different forms of attack are ruled by tension. With the greatest tension the breath has to burst through the vocal cords as with the closed glottis attack. With somewhat less tension the breath can issue without sudden irruption, though the cords are still held firmly and there is little or no breath wastage. This represents the 'clear'[1] attack. With a further, though not complete release of tension—for this would entirely destroy phonation—there

[1] Sometimes called the 'open' attack, in contradistinction to the 'closed' glottis attack; but a really open glottis provides an aspirate and therefore perhaps this term had better not be used. Both the 'clear' and 'breath' attack depend on a certain closure of the glottis if there is to be an economical output of voice. What determines all forms of attack is the degree of tension of the vocal cords and laryngeal apparatus.

We may remark here that there is a sort of contradiction between closed *tone* and a closed *mechanism*. By closed tone we are apt to understand a covered and generally loose tone; but the more brilliant tones are most certainly produced by a closing or drawing together of the larnygeal mechanism—in particular of the vocal cords, which, as we know, are the supreme governors of the voice. Thus a paradox is involved which may easily confuse when we begin to talk about qualities of tone and the means by which we achieve them.

Strangely enough too, when the voice is allowed to go loose—that is to have insufficient tension or contraction applied to it—the tendency of the voice will be to sharpen, whereas one would have thought it would flatten. The reason is that with the loose tone—particularly if power is used upon it—the voice may be blown up and away in a sort of hoot. Hooty tone always goes sharp—especially with Oo—

is a limited wastage of breath, hence what is called (3) the 'breath' or '*mezza voce*' attack, though 'touch' is more applicable to this particular form of initial impulse. There is thus a progressively softening influence over tone as tension of the vocal cords decreases, from the hard, almost purely mechanical process of the closed glottis attack, through the more amenable but still powerful stroke of the 'clear' attack, to the delicate and infinitely beautiful adjustment of the 'breath' attack. In the end, of course, by the release of the tension, the vocal cords cannot vibrate at all, or rather the necessary breath puffs cannot be emitted so that only the comparatively soundless aspirate (H) results. As always the middle way, which is the clear way, is that which best serves for normal expression, the tightly 'closed' and loosely held 'breath' forms being reserved for special circumstances. We have said before that the 'closed' attack is almost outside the pale of pleasurable effect, but 'breath' attack is frequently appropriate when 'atmosphere' has to be suggested or a dreamy mood defined. *Mezza voce*, indeed, may colour the whole song and it is perhaps the chief tonal feature of modern romantic song, which, since the nineteenth century, has set out specially to reveal emotion of an intensely intimate, personal kind. Brahms' 'Feldeinsamkeit' is a very good example of this subjective approach, and represents a large proportion of Lieder. Older song has a beauty proper to itself. It relies less on personality and the personal reaction of the singer. It is consequently more independent of tone colour, or such colour as is given by subtle, varied feeling. Practically any medium of colour is sufficient to indicate its objective nature. A *bel canto* song can be 'sung' by almost any instrument. Or we may say that romantic song lives in a *milieu* of sympathy. Its warmly vibrant life is evoked by communion with its surroundings— just as a note upon the pianoforte, when the dampers are lifted, vibrates with its fellows, gathering in under- and over-tones external to its own. It brings Nature into the picture to a far greater degree, extending the range of human experience, chiefly perhaps in the direction of colour. When poets and composers were more or less restricted to themes of human relationships, as they were in earlier times, these could be expressed without much reference to colour.[1]

whereas the tighter tone brings the voice down firmly on the breath, preventing hootiness.

[1] Though where there is sound there must always be *some* colour, and thought cannot be entirely self-contained :

> Man is all symmetry, full of proportions,
> And all to all the world besides ;
> Each part may call the farthest, brother :
> For head with foot hath private amity,
> And both with moons and tides.

All thought has outside correspondence.

K*

It sufficed that thoughts were presented with order and grace and proportion, that they had beauty of form, in short; because this is the beauty that specially satisfies the mind. But with an extension of man's consciousness to natural beauty, colour which is indispensable from it, takes on a more essential function, and this is reflected in the colourings 'rich and strange' of romantic song and romantic music generally. Such colourings are undoubtedly effected in special degree, as regards the voice, by *mezza voce* (or varieties of 'breath' tone); at any rate the tonal palette is greatly extended by it. Thus the colder and less emotional 'clear' attack is usually more appropriate to older forms of song, whereas 'breath' or *mezza voce* touch has greater place in the performance of romantic song.

All kinds of voice-approach, whether 'closed', 'clear' or 'breath' are, as we know, a matter of resistance. If the cords are tightly approximated a hard, speedy 'attack' results: if loosely, a soft, gradual 'touch'. With the former the breath will be under high pressure, from the resistance which is put up against it; with the latter much less breath tension operates, in fact tension is scarcely apparent. The level of the breath rises and falls accordingly, from a concentration in the higher regions of the lungs (the chest) for brilliant tone, to a dispersal in the lower regions (the base of the lungs), for more or less dull tone. Some vowels favour tight 'attack', e.g., Aw or ŏ; some loose 'touch' e.g., Oh or Oo. A fully characteristic Aw is almost impossible with a loose glottis, and, in reverse, an Oh or Oo with a tight one. Every vowel has its own particular requirements as regards tension. Some vowels are naturally hard, some soft. It is the business of the singer to unify them as far as he can.

Put in another form, energetic 'attacks' depend upon preliminary concentration. Notes which are subject to them stand

> '. . . *like greyhounds in the slips,*
> *Straining upon the start* . . .'

Relatively quiet 'touches' have no such initial strain.[1]

The end of a note is as important and revealing as the beginning. If 'touch' is involved, a note should not only arise out of the breath

---

[1] Notice that when the voice is subject to 'touch' the lower jaw will fall downwards and be perfectly loose at the sockets, also the mouth will not open much. For 'attacks' the mouth opens more to bring the voice forward; this will diminish neck space. A soft touch can only be brought to perfection if there is plenty of room in the neck. The more the mouth is opened the less the throat is likely to be, and vice versa. Opening the mouth too much and at all times can become a bad habit, as it is apt to over-tighten and constrict the neck. Singers who invariably sing with a very open mouth will generally be found to have hard, rough voices and to be deficient in easy movement.

but disappear into it, without any sharply dividing line in either case. Breath should merge into sound, and sound into breath quite imperceptibly. This is the supreme test of control. Anyone can bring his voice on with a bump. But a 'touch' can never happen unless the vowel is formed before the breath is brought to bear upon it, and retains its shape not only during the emission of sound but after the sound has ceased. The vowel is there all the time, so to speak, ready waiting for the 'touch' which will bring to life, and it is still in potential being when life has been withdrawn. It is not quite the same with an 'attack'. Its relation to the breath is far less intimate. It does not make friends with the breath, it makes war with it; hence the sudden impact, and the sudden 'stop' which seems to completely cut off any further projection of the note. It annihilates it. We cannot imagine its existence beyond this particular point. Such an ending is the equivalent of the 'closed glottis' attack in reverse. By bringing the voice up on its haunches, as it were, it gives a show of great authority, particularly when led up to by a strong *crescendo*; or it may be thought of as a 'twisting off' of the vowel by the application of the utmost resistance to, and compression of, the breath. At this final moment very brilliant, powerful tone results. It is as though one said 'Ah!' (with a very explosive 'h') in a tone of the greatest disgust and reproof. Singers out for effect often use this form of ending.

Marcato, sforzando, spiccato, staccato, etc.; all these are species of attack, and it is very necessary to be master of them, even though they are of an instrumental rather than a vocal nature. Words seldom require more than a *mezzo staccato* treatment; for, save in interjections, they do not naturally detach themselves from each other. Fluidity is the general characteristic of language. Still, the voice *is* a musical instrument as well as a vehicle for words and we must make the most of its possibilities. Besides, it all tends to technical mastery.

Such phrases as these must be sung *mezzo staccato*:

Smiling meadows seem to say   *etc~*   come, ye wantons here to play

Taken by themselves the words would never be spoken like this. When set to music they are uttered differently. Music influences the delivery of words, in a sense dominating them, and, of course, musical timing is not at all the same thing as verbal timing.

The sharpest form of *staccato* is practically a closed glottis attack as can be seen by singing the following:

O O O etc--
(as in "cot")

Variants of closed and clear attack should be practised thus, with the notes cleanly sung, and the penultimate bar of *legato* devoid of undue 'slide'.:

on Ah . . . or any bright vowel.

A warning against over-tension must be given. *Marcato* needs such an accumulation of energy that the singer may get himself tied up and be unable to expend it. A loose 'fling' of tone is often needed for *marcato* effects so that the voice may reach the nasal cavities without hindrance. Otherwise full sonority is checked. The equivalent of this action is the 'jerk' which is associated with the throwing of, say, a cricket ball, or the flicking of the fingers (*v.* p. 43), when a very lively though loose impulse is given to the muscular movement. If the words of this opening phrase from an air of Bach

Bass

a-wake, a-wake!

are not properly 'released', they fail utterly in force and effect; they are simply stifled.

An attack implies a 'stop' of some sort and attacks are, therefore, not confined to the glottis. Consonants also imply 'stops' of the breath, so that the principle of attack must also be conceded to them. Some consonants hold up the breath as completely as it is held in a 'closed glottis' attack, e.g., the 'explodent' consonants P, T, K, etc., in which the sudden burst through of the breath is accompanied by a touch of highly-compressed momentary flatus: p^h, t^h, k^h. If, however, this flatus is continued it means that the consonantal mechanism has gone to pieces, just as the vowel mechanism goes when a note is 'breathy'. Consonantal attack is often as defective as vowel attack, giving no impression of spirited delivery. When this is so it is impossible to get a light, clear, forward utterance such as is needed for the little Elizabethan ayre:

Phyllis was a fair maid, be-loved of Cory--don

The *staccato*, however, must not be overdone, or the grace of the song will suffer.

To develop this particular style it is a good plan to sing this (or any other tune) with the syllable 'ping' to each note, till the required attack is achieved.

The equivalent of *pizzicato* can only be produced by strong breath pressure and compression right at the tongue tip; this alone will send the sound up into the head sinuses where it must be resonated. It is an effect which can scarcely be had with a large vowel such as Ah, or with a loose initial consonant such as 'l', e.g., with the syllable 'la'. The short vowels and closed consonants are best fitted for this treatment as with the syllable 'ti' or 'ping' already given. Then only can the necessary point and precision be reached. It is very important to secure what might be called this 'direct action' of the voice which is an antidote to all kinds of roundabout utterance.

The frankly aspirated attack should be practised in the form of a light-hearted laugh[1] and also of a deep chuckle, with the notes just bubbling out:

etc.
up and down
the scale.

Ha ha ha etc~ (but the 'ah' not too open)

though this is rather in the nature of consonantal than vowel attack.

Very often an aspiration of *legato* notes, as Gigli does it, is of great advantage to note definition. We must not be afraid of the 'intrusive H'[2] if it serves a purpose. If for

[1] There is nothing better than a laugh to demonstrate balance and control of voice. If the singer can laugh to order, at all degrees of pitch, speed and force, there is nothing much the matter with his technique.

[2] A lot of nonsense is talked about the 'intrusive H', which, after all, is only a form of attack, subject, in itself, to considerable variation—from a quite breathy treatment, to one in which there is hardly any escape of breath, but is more like the

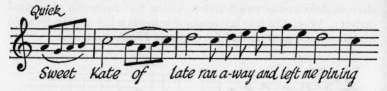

Sweet Kate of late ran a-way and left me pining

we sing 'Sweeheeheeheet Kate ohohohof late', in such a way that we are hardly aware of the addition of an aspirate, it will be all to the good.

Notes have an individual life of their own, which consonantal treatment accentuates. It is seldom that a note slips out, as it were, from its predecessor, as in this binary grouping:

Don Giovanni ~ MOZART.

From the same tenor air from which the above is taken we get another good instance of the necessary use of the aspirate in *quasi-legato*:

e de(h)l be(h)l ci-glio

If the second and fourth semiquavers are not aspirated the passage tends to become

e del bel ci-glio

'tongueing', which wind-instrument players bring to bear on quick notes; also it has an obvious affinity to the little 'thud' that takes place in rapid whistling. It seems to come more from an oscillation of the vocal cords, than from a distinct push of breath on and through each note; but it is a particularly difficult movement to analyse. Certain it is, that ordinary *legato* treatment, in which notes 'slide' into each other, without any 'stop' or articulation (such as is given by a consonant) is an impossible technique for dealing with quick notes on the same vowel. Something has to be done about it, and some form of 'intrusive H' seems the answer.

phrased in groups of two semiquavers instead of an even group of

with every note articulated in its own right.

Slurring, however, is nearly always required in Plain-song; its sweeping neums and phrases can be rendered in no other way. The same is true of almost any song in which words are the dominating factor.

Also, a fairly quick series of 'clear' attacks without an aspirate affords good but difficult exercise.

Here the notes must be separated.

Further, practise repetition of a *sustained* note:

In this there is no separation of notes—only a series of pressures. Such a pressure, with the tiniest touch of aspirate, is often required in phrasing old music, as in the following:

in order to secure a repeated note without any breaking of the *legato*.

In all matters of vocal attack and release and, indeed, in singing as a whole, the mechanism must not 'give'. The breath should always play upon a steady instrument, just as the pianist plays upon the steady stringed frame of a pianoforte.

There must be no heaving of the chest, chewing with the jaw, or any other sign of movement than may possibly occur at the larynx; even here, movement should be scarcely seen.

Portamento on Vowels and Consonants

When a note is separated from its fellows by *staccato* or a rest, written or implied, there must be a fresh impulse of breath, in other words, a fresh attack. Something of the sort, even in *legato*, also happens, though it is not so clearly seen. If breath pressure were continuous in strength throughout a series of notes, we should have the *passage* from note to note as loud and obvious as the notes themselves. This would draw undue attention to what after all is a point of transition, of secondary importance to the fixed notes which go to the construction of the melody and harmony—of the music, in short. Nevertheless, complete separation of the notes would be at variance with *legato* treatment. Some nexus must be shown, if notes are to be joined; some connection cannot be avoided. The art of connecting notes is the art of *portamento*.

Grave faults of style may result from an exaggerated use of *portamento*, as we know full well, not only from singers but, more disastrously, from instrumentalists who in jazz bands and elsewhere debase the public taste, not because they are technically incompetent, but because they are completely lacking in artistic conscience.

Portamento is shown when the wind rises and falls in pitch, or in a similar process with the voice. It is a good exercise for the singer to move up and down from the lowest note of his voice to the highest without waiting on any intermediate note, varying the strength of the sound, *ad. lib.*:

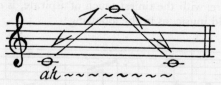

as in the above, or according to compass. This develops ease and freedom, but of course it represents an overdoing of *portamento*. It is all *portamento*, in fact.

Directly notes appear upon the scene, *portamento* takes second place, and it must then be modified to allow of the clear supremacy of the fixed sounds. Thus, as we have said, there cannot be the same breath pressure on *portamento* as on the notes. Breath pressure can be either less, the same, or more. It must be less. When it is the same it is bad; when it is more it is an abomination.

The smaller the interval, the less likely is *portamento* to be abused, for the movement from note to note is quicker with smaller than with larger intervals. With large intervals great care must be taken to avoid whooping and scooping up to the higher note. The reason for this is that higher notes need greater breath pressure than lower notes, hence a tendency to force *portemento* in reaching them. Thus  will probably not suffer from

over-slurring; but easily may. The singer

should practise large intervals such as is in

or

till he can sing them fluently and cleanly by means of the necessary breath adjustment.

Portamento must be relatively rapid: it must not take up too much time. Thus, in both strength and length *portamento* must be quite subordinate to the written notes.

Portamento has of course to do with *legato* and it is therefore most applicable to a group of notes on the same vowel. But it can be used when notes are articulated and even separated by consonants. Thus, when liquids and continuants (L, M, N, R) are concerned, as in the glide can be

effected in this way: (a)  by going

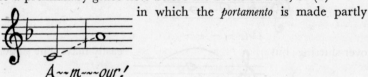

to a preliminary grace note before the accented note, or (b)

 in which the *portamento* is made partly

on the vowel and partly on the consonant. (a) of course is more emphatic than (b). If a closed or stopped consonant were involved as in 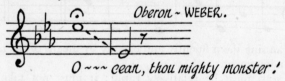 the method, if used, would

have to be as at (a); (b) would be quite wrong.

The foregoing examples concern a large rising interval in which there is always a danger of 'scooping'. Descending intervals are more easily managed because the breath pressure relaxes for the second note. Thus, with

portamento is certainly appropriate, and gives little difficulty, provided the voice is dark and deep in tone.

In the aria 'Per pieta' from Mozart's *Così fan tutte* this tremendous interval is encountered:

but the descent is easy enough. If it were an ascent it would be

274

another matter, and few singers could be trusted to undertake the journey successfully.

The *portamento* in downward intervals can be more prolonged than in upward intervals.

Good taste enters very largely into the use of *portamento* and how to use it is the test of the artist. Some singers avoid *portamento* simply because they have not the power to do otherwise. Such singers will generally be found to have hard, incalcitrant voices, totally at variance with supple movement. They hack and hew out their notes; they do not let them 'run'. Notes will naturally coalesce if they are free to do so. On the other hand, slurring and slipping of an undisciplined kind is just as bad as a lack of fluidity. In broad terms the difference between the amateur and the professional is that the former lets his notes tumble into place, the latter puts them there: each note is intended to be just where it is and the progress from one to another is thoroughly controlled.

Portamento will be most concerned with *cantabile*, which, as the term implies, derives from song and is therefore closely related to verbal utterance. When the tendency of note treatment is towards *marcato*—an instrumental feature, *portamento* will be progressively inappropriate. Then clean, clear delivery must be sought.

There is thus infinite gradation in the use of *portamento*, from a strong clinging to the slightest connection of note with note. Finally, according to the needs of performance, *portamento* or any suspicion of it must be completely eliminated.

It must never be forgotten that *portamento* is a grace, an embellishment, and not an essential—its presence must never be insisted upon; yet it will be contained in any spacious flow of sound—percussive taps do not achieve this.

Portamento is peculiar to slide instruments like the trombone, to stringed instruments when it is allowed by a change of position upon the finger-board, and to the voice which has gradually to tune up or down, though it can do so in a way that appears almost instantaneous. Instruments with fixed sounds like the pianoforte, or holed instruments like the flute or oboe, cannot join their notes by *portamento*. In their case the energizing force of the breath can be maintained at constant pressure. They lose the delicacy of note contact which *portamento* brings, but gain somewhat in a stauncher *sostenuto*.

Portamento should be considered as an emotional effect. It indicates great sensibility on the part of the performer. It registers minute shades of feeling and an affection for notes that remove them entirely from the category of the mechanical. But again, the greatest discretion must be used with regard to it.

FEATURES OF ARTICULATION

Function of Consonants

When vocal sound overflows into a sort of ineffective wash, as it easily may, it is generally coincident with lack of articulation. Just as consonants confine the vowels in a word—giving the word form and allowing it symbolical meaning—so, in actual performance the articulatory organs give shape and direction to the vowel flow, imparting to the music much more meaning than it would otherwise have, because they offer boundaries without which there is no shape (or sense).

Poor articulation or, indeed, poor definition of any kind, is a sign of mental deficiency, if habitual and not 'put on'. What may be called intellectual quality—the quality that the discriminating mind gives—shows itself in definition; to be clear is half the battle. When this quality is absent we may get an emotional appeal—just as a crooner will articulate 'little' as 'lil' when he wishes to be endearing. But the result is simply maudlin. It has lost its form, its intellectual quality; and is therefore on the lowest rung of expression.

Vowels represent a condition of stability; and, on the whole, consonants one of short, sharp movement. Vowels should, if possible, remain constant from start to finish; but consonants (with the exception of those which approximate to vocal sounds—L, R and the nasals) are defined by their articulation and disappear from the scene at once.

Energetic Delivery

As they are so short lived, consonants need to be greatly energized if they are to be fully audible and effective. Further: this energy can only come from compression, not relaxation. In this consonants are different from vowels whose beauty and character often depend upon a loose, easy treatment. Consonants, as we know, really involve the breaking down of the barriers or stops set up by the lips and tongue in front of the breath stream; and it is not till the breath pressure has collected strongly behind these barriers, that anything like adequate consonantal delivery can take place. With the explodents P, T and K, and their 'voiced' equivalents B, D and G, this is clear enough, as the name 'explodent' implies. It is evident that the greater the charge, or compression, behind the lips for P, the tip tongue for T, and the back of the tongue for K, the greater will be the power of articulation. Similarly, for 'flated' sounds such as F, S, or 'voiced' as V, Z, and for continuants like L, R and the nasal M (which have something of the nature of vowels), nothing much will come of them if they are, so to speak, left to themselves. A vowel, then, can often be sung well with very little expenditure of energy; a consonant seldom can. Nevertheless, a good deal of variety is possible even with consonantal utterance. Consonants, like vowels, can be brought forward or taken back; or (comparatively) be strongly or loosely energized. According to these variations, they will be high or low-pitched, shrill or soft in sound.

Perhaps the most important factor in consonantal clarity is the quick movement of the articulatory organs, independent of the extra speed that can be given to them by breath pressure which forces the movement to increased action. Most people have little muscular development in the lips, tongue and cheeks. The muscles concerned are flabby; they have not the power of working strongly and smartly, (though lack of nervous temperament is, of course, also at fault). It is necessary therefore to secure this development by facial exercise: by stretching and contorting the face in all directions, till the muscles are stimulated, awakened and ready for use. Ordinary speech does not bring this about. What will serve in conversation will not serve for speech in a large hall, and particularly, for speech in song, when the vowel attracts the attention by reason of its prolongation at the expense of the consonant. Consonants have to be exaggerated in song if words are to be clear; increased speed and amplitude have to be given to them. The organs of articulation, in short, have to work much harder. Nevertheless this has to be done without too great a display of violence. Consonants must be telling, but they must not spit and splutter in an exaggerated way, particularly if they involve anything in the nature of a hiss, though, in my experience, this is unlikely to happen—quite the reverse, even with an S. The difficulty of combining clear consonants with easy vowelling is considerable; but it can be overcome. An exercise recommended by Miss Marjorie Gullan is warmly to be endorsed. She terms it the 'lipping' exercise and gives it as follows: 'Imagine you are in a room where someone is asleep and where you may not move or speak for fear of waking the sleeper. There is, however, someone else at the extreme end of the room to whom you must give a message, and give it without any mistake as to meaning. To do so you must summon up all your force of breath, direct it to the very front of the lips, and manage to convey what you wish to say practically by means of mouth shape and movement alone.'

If the words of every song were to be practised like this much ambiguity of utterance would disappear. It is obvious that if you can make yourself clear without any sound, you will be doubly clear when sound is added.

This particular exercise is not sufficient however. It represents the shaping of vowels and consonants—especially the vowels—but not articulation to the necessary extent.[1] The adequate articulation of consonants depends upon speed of movement, and this speed can only be secured by great tension. Speed, as we know, is sometimes guaranteed by looseness—actions in the nature of a 'flick' show this—but as we also know (p. 64 *et seq.*) speed may be linked with strong continuous tension, and the action of most consonants is of this sort when it is a question of repetition or quick consonantal delivery—patter and the like. Lip and tip-tongue articulations, such as P, T, Ch, M and N, certainly do, while the same even holds good with the mid-tongue one of L and the back-tongue ones of K, G, etc. In short, all voluntary movement must be well tensed; on the other hand when movement has to be 'involuntary', such as that of R, looseness is essential. An R cannot be trilled if there is any tightness of the tongue. It is when articulation consists in the *pressing together* of the vocal members that great tension is required. Without it, a P or T, for instance, is more or less ineffective; while if a series of these articulations occurs, tension to a high degree must be maintained throughout. The time-honoured 'twister', 'Peter Piper picked a peck of pickled pepper', etc., is as good an illustration of the process as can be given. Considerable practice of these words is recommended, till they can be articulated quickly and energetically. The lips should be tightly compressed all the time, and this compression should be coincident with great breath compression which backs up the tension of the lips and brings about the short sharp explosions in the front of the mouth which are the feature of this patter. The short vowels ĕ and ĭ used in nearly every word of 'Peter Piper' also help this explosive frontal treatment, and, if properly spoken, they issue in sharp little snaps of sound. If this passage is articulated to perfection and repeated the lips will be quite tired, showing almost as much evidence of use as those of a trumpet or trombone player. This is the sort of thing to which singers and elocutionists should apply themselves. They seldom do; in consequence their facial muscles are largely undeveloped and only capable of slow movement.

Timing of Consonants

Not only do consonants define sense in words—a vowel hardly ever does, except in such cases as I, Oh and a very few utterances of this sort—they supply the formal boundaries of words as well. They give words shape; they fix their time limit. There is an art

---

[1]Full articulation produces 'flated' sound, which is by no means silent; and many of the consonants are, of course, 'voiced'.

in timing consonants in performance. Where do they come in the time structure? To get a perfectly placed consonant is far from easy, quite apart from its successful articulation. Yet it has an exact point of delivery. This is the rule:

> Consonants come *before* the note or beat to which they are attached;
> Vowels come *upon* the note or beat.

Thus:

should be sung

which seems very complicated in notation, but can be rendered easily enough once the habit of rightly-placed articulation is gained. To begin with, it needs careful practice.

Sometimes when the note to which a word is sung is contained in the next harmony, or when the same harmony persists, a composer will carry on the word thus:

in which case the final consonant should be sounded *on* the first beat. The initial consonant, however, should still be sounded before the beat.

We have often been advised—by Plunket Greene and others—to 'sing through our rests'. We should also say: 'sing through the consonants'; make music with them. Associate them for the most part with a particular note, the note on which the vowel they are joined to is sounded. This means that, when it can, the sound of an initial consonant forestalls the vowel note. Thus

if meticulously noted, would appear as

or something very like it.

It is possible, however, for a good deal of blurring to take place (according to expressive requirements) while remaining within the bounds of artistic discretion. Mechanical exactitude, though a necessary preliminary virtue, is not always a final one. But the principle as to the placing of consonants always holds; though that, as to the note on which they are sounded, may vary.

Length of Consonant Sound

What time should be given to consonants? For how long should they be sounded? It will depend upon the *tempo* and spirit of the music, upon the dramatic emphasis that the words require, upon the *legato* or *staccato* that is necessary, etc. In Polyphemus' 'I rage, I melt, I burn', in the recitative before the air 'O ruddier than the Cherry' (*Acis and Galatea*), the 'r' in 'rage' can be greatly prolonged and the other consonants pronounced with tremendous vigour. The whole of this recitative and air must be sung on a giant-like scale. This takes time. Giants do not move like rabbits. Again no absolute rule is possible, but the general one 'prolong the consonants' (particularly the vocal ones) as much as possible can usually be followed, with advantage to clarity and sense. The great thing is to be clear; after that you can demonstrate what other weapons you have in your armoury of 'expression'.

Consonants and Vowel Percussion

Well-articulated consonants can obviously give stress and 'attack' to words, and end them with a sort of twist or snap; but further than this they make for 'percussion' in the vowels (see also p. 239). The compression and quick release of the consonent into the vowel—provided the vowel cavity is already formed, or formed instantaneously and not gradually—gives a sort of initial 'ping' to the vowel, greatly adding to the life of the word or syllable by bringing it immediately on the scene. This sort of treatment is associated far more often with instrumental than vocal performance; but there is no reason why a singer should not gain the same power of 'directness' as an instrumentalist does. Singing is usually very weak in this element, largely owing to insufficient development of muscular tension.

Vowels and consonants may be looked upon as bricks and cement. See that the 'cement' strongly binds the vocal edifice!

Doubling of Consonants

A difficulty may arise when two consonants come together, particularly two explodents as in 'pepper', 'potter', etc. Should they both be articulated? Some authorities say that it is sufficient to articulate only the second consonant, bringing the articulatory organs sharply together for the first consonant, but not releasing any flatus;[1] in short, not giving the first consonant a full articulation.

Other authorities, including Sir Charles Santley (whose enunciation was superb), have advised the clear articulation of all double consonants in English, just as the Italians do with their double consonants. In a general way I am also in favour of this doubling of consonantal sound; but it must not be exalted into a strict rule. It would be absurd to double the 't' in such a word as 'pretty'; likewise in 'buff', 'nett' or 'gross', though the case is somewhat different with these latter words, in which the double letter is simply a matter of orthography, not of sound. With liquids or continuants like L and M doubling should certainly occur. 'Fel-low' should have a double 'l' ('fel-low' not 'fe-low', though no vowel should be heard after the first 'l'; it must not be 'fele-low'—of this danger of speech, more later—it is only a *pressure* on the second 'l' that is wanted); similarly with 'hum-ming', neither 'hum-ing' nor hu-ming' suffices. The first syllable not only needs an ending, the second has to be sent about its business with a fresh consonantal impulse. Such a word as 'mil-lion' *is* invariably given with a double 'l'. Thus *within a word* the practice may be either to double the consonant, or avoid this as occasion requires. For very distinct utterance, doubling is good; where the word is thoroughly clear without it, or where it seems pedantic to insist on doubling, it need not be insisted on. Thus, there seem to be three possible ways of treating doubled consonants in a word:

 1. In the case of continuants (whether voiced or not), by a pressure on the sustained consonant, e.g., 'col-lie', 'jif-fy',

---

[1] Though there *will* be a touch of flatus (or breath noise) with any sudden closing or opening of the lips, etc.

though another element crops up in such words, where the second syllable is weak; if is weak, then very little pressure is advisable; if it is strong, as in 'col-lide', then more pressure is necessary. Compare, carefully, 'col-lie' and 'collide'. In any case two distinct syllables are required. Contrast also 'whol-ly' with 'ho-ly'. With 'whol-ly' the *two* syllables should be far more evident than with 'ho-ly', which seems almost to flow on in one syllable.

2. In the case of two explodents ('stop' consonants) the first is formed by bringing the articulatory organs together, only, without any release of final flatus; the second consonant has the flatus natural to it: e.g., 'pret-ty' is 'pret-t^{h}y' not 'pret^h-t^{h}y'.

3. A vowel may be (and often is) tacked on to the first consonant, e.g., as in 'ăkŭ-kawrd' for 'ac-cord' but this is 'bad manners' in speaking and should be scrupulously avoided, though it is done in a misguided attempt to gain definition. It is however much more likely to happen in the case of two different consonants as in 'ac-cept', by saying 'ăkŭ-sĕpt^h', but this is not a true example of 'doubling'.

When two words are concerned, less latitude is allowable with adjacent consonants of the same kind. The final consonant should usually be kept distinct and separate from the following initial one. Thus, in the sentence:

'Like to hurt tree: trunk cut, bark torn, sap killed'
the two 't's' and 'k's' should undoubtedly be fully articulated. But in 'take care!' it might be possible to omit the complete pronunciation of the first 'k', though if stern admonition is to be expressed, both 'k's' should and probably would be sounded. It seems to be a question of avoiding affectation and exaggeration while guaranteeing the utmost significance.

When a comma intervenes between two similar consonants, a cæsura should definitely be made, as with 'd' and 't' in 'Ted, dolt, told, debt'.

Never tack a final consonant on to an initial vowel of the next word, e.g.,

'Oak and elm', not 'o-kan-delm'; or

'A-di-tup' for 'add it up'.

On the other hand—and there seems to be a contradiction here—one would not sing

it is   but   *i ~ t'is*

yet we should divide  as it stands, and not as

 . Obviously very fine considerations of sound-

flow and intellectual sense are involved in these matters, though the rule that separate words—not so much separate syllables—must be separately pronounced, generally holds good.

Words of two syllables are apt to be spoken as words of one syllable. Avoid 'reel' for 're-al', 'rite' for 'ri-ot', etc. In short, beware of elisions; they are always a snare for the poor speaker and have accounted for much degradation of language. Present-day single final syllables like 'sion' used to be bisyllabic in Elizabethan times when 'pa-shen' (passion) was 'pas-si-on', set to three notes of music, as in

JOHN DOWLAND

(If my complaints) could pas-si-ons move

or our 'righ-chus' (righteous) was trisyllabic 'righ-ty-us'.

A further word on the explosive consonants may not be amiss; their action should be thoroughly understood, because difficulties as to 'doubling' will most likely derive from them.

The articulation of a closed consonant is effected by:

(1) tightly contacting the organs concerned,
(2) sharply separating them.

When these actions are done with breath pressure behind them, a 'flatus', or tiny explosion, will be heard both when contact *and* separation takes place—though what we call the 'articulation' is associated with the latter action, as it makes the greater noise. In the case of explodents between two words, e.g., 'Bob barks', the smart approximation of the lips is, in itself, almost sufficient clearly to define the first B—then comes a short silence—only for the second B are the lips separated, releasing the 'flatus', or little puff of air, which completes the consonant, leaving us in no doubt that B is concerned. This way of indicating two closed consonants between words is therefore generally sufficient, and it nearly always is when the consonants occur medially.

A very good illustration of this particular procedure is to be heard with the first three syllables of 'Hip-pip-pip-hooray!' We should never think of saying either

hi-pi-pi

or   hip-pip-pip

with all p's fully articulated—which would be far too much of a business.

The natural way is:

hi(p)-pi(p)-pip,

which is enough to define every 'p'.

If, however, instead of the previous phrase 'Bob barks', we had to say 'Bob, bark!' The comma would necessitate the full doubling of the B's, with flatus after each, thus 'Bob^h, b^{h}ark!'—the small h standing for the flatus.

As a musical example of the need for the complete articulation of two explodents between words, the following, from the soprano air, 'Softly sighs', from Weber's *Freischütz*, may be given—the words are, of course, an English translation:

It will probably be conceded that for 'what terrors' each 't' requires full articulation. By this the phrase becomes more highly wrought, and a greater degree of emotional stress is suggested. The slight gap between the consonants is not to be deplored, even though the sense of the phrase is *legato*, but welcomed in the interests of the expression.

Clearness of Speech

Consonants, as we have said, can be over-articulated, but they are unlikely to be if they are linked up properly with their vowels—for they are hardly ever used as interjections or appear apart from vowels. If initial they should be looked upon as preparing the vowel; if final, as issuing from it. There should be no hiatus such as 'hu-sh' (hush), or 're-st' (rest), where the 'sh' and 'st' are disjoined from the vowel. In this case the final consonants would be too obvious, and indeed, ridiculous. But with the proper 'glide' or connection almost any amount of energy can be given to their emission. Again: consonants and vowels stand and fall together; a similar impulse controls both.

Clearness of speech is therefore obtained by vowels *and* consonants; they should be regarded as part and parcel of each other, as they are, quite obviously, in the case of nasal sounds. Timbre consists in an M running through every vowel, though different degrees of nasality may operate. Conversely, there is a vowel underneath every nasal sound, and the more vowel, or its equivalent, there is, the better the consonant (M, N, ng). As to whether consonants play a greater part in verbal definition than do vowels: it is a moot point. Most people would say that the consonants do; just as in writing we can generally distinguish a word by a sort of consonantal shorthand, e.g., env'n'm'd, obl'g'd, t'g'th'r, c'nf'd'nt, L'd N'ls'n. In some cases a word can be still more abbreviated without losing its identity, e.g., m'v'ts (movements), d'l'g't (diligent).

Nevertheless, I now feel[1] that vowels clarify words more than consonants do; not when seen in writing, but when heard in song. Because we can identify a written word by only its consonants, it does not follow that we can do so when we only hear it. Further, consonants are always uniform in sound, though they may fail in sufficient articulation; but vowels vary enormously—they are seldom pronounced as they are meant to be. Therefore, though the consonants may be right, the vowels may mislead us. If vowels are not exact and defined beyond fear of mistake, words cannot be clear, however clear the consonants may be. It is the fully-open vowel (not its smothered travesty) that really distinguishes good speaking, or, perhaps it would be better to say, good singing. Vowels, too, specially engage our hearing. It is the vowels which make music and the music of speech; for it is upon them that we dwell. The ticks and touches of the consonants scarcely count beside them. As well, in colloquial speech (or in writing) the consonants follow each other so quickly that it is often possible to know what word is implied, without either hearing or seeing the vowels; but in singing the consonants are not close together—as regards verbal organization they cannot be taken in at a glance, so to speak. They may, indeed, be so distant from each other that all sense of their relationship is lost. The vowel alone gives the link—often it is a very long link—and it must be very strong and well made to do what is wanted. Hence the need of pure, clear vowels. It is the vowel, too, which carries along the impulse which is necessary to energize final consonants. Final consonants are often inaudible, because energy flags almost from the start of the preceding vowel. There is no force with which to energize them. A well-formed *open* vowel, however, guarantees this energy throughout its course and up to the following consonant; it could not otherwise be main-

---

[1] In *Word and Tone* I did not.

tained as a well-formed vowel. The process of 'opening', in short, guarantees both vowel and consonant. Therefore I think we may well assert that vowels rather than consonants are the more important feature of words, in singing.

Weak Verbal Endings with L, M, N, R

It is sometimes difficult to know how to treat weak verbal endings involving the continuants L, M, N, R, as in 'symbol', 'serum', 'pardon', 'fever'. In speech an uncertain, indistinct vowel generally goes with these endings, but, as we have said elsewhere, sung vowels should be made as rich and distinct as possible. The same vowel sound is used for them all, though it may be written in a variety of ways: thus 'um' in 'serum' is the same as 'om', 'am', 'em' in 'wisdom', 'Adam', 'Salem', or in 'potion' or 'taken' with 'n' as the final consonant. Occasionally, no vowel appears at all in the spelling before the final consonant, e.g., 'prism', 'trouble'. What vowel should we use for these endings? Should it be like the ŭ in 'dumb' or ĕ in 'pen'? Neither. The ŭ is too dark and heavy; the ĕ too lively to give the soft effacement necessary to a weak ending. The vowel to be used is midway between ŭ and ĕ, produced by pronouncing the former vowel with a slight raising of the back of the tongue; this is the vowel we want, though it can hardly be noted by our alphabet. It is not heard in the strong 'um' of 'umbrage' or the strong 'en' of 'entity', but takes a middle and quite musical course peculiar to itself.

What we do *not* want is to hear these weak terminations *without a vowel*: 'po-shn' (potion), 'sym-bl' (symbol), etc.; or with so little vowel as to be quite negligible from a musical point of view. When singers do this sort of thing—it often occurs—they place the final consonant, instead of the vowel we have been talking about, on the note concerned. With 'symbol', for instance, they sing

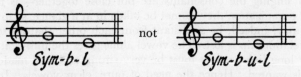

as it should be. The continuants, of course, lend themselves to this misuse, because they are very like vowels. The point is that notes should never be sung to a consonant. Consonants have to be fitted in, but they are not part of the musical picture in any essential way, though they embellish it; nor is a vowel, at any time, part of consonantal utterance. Singers should again be reminded that a vowel should never be tacked on to a consonant in an over-zealous endeavour to gain definition. 'That-uh man-uh' (for 'that man'), *et sim.* is quite impermissible.

Sounding of Consonants

It is more difficult to sound consonants than vowels; a greater barrier or resistance has to be overcome in a much shorter time, and, as they are further from the breath than vowels, they cannot be so effectively or easily controlled. More energy has therefore to be expended upon them. A sharp, upward thrust of the diaphragm—induced by, or coupled with, a contraction of the abdomen—is often required to articulate consonants successfully; particularly with the mute finals P, T, K, their voiced equivalents B, D, G, and un-accommodating groups of initial or final consonants as in 'Theodore Thickthorn thrust thistles through the thick of his thumb.'

When, however, a quiet, smooth verbal delivery is wanted, consonant articulation must be weakened proportionately; it is for pointed, emphatic effects that it must be strong.

The consonants which are most likely to be missing from speech are final D, S and Z.

With regard to final D, its characteristic compressed laryngeal sound is not sufficient to make it clear when it ends a word, and we have to break our rule of not allowing any vowel sound after a final consonant. It is only when we add a *slight* touch of vowel that we can hear the D in such a passage as this:

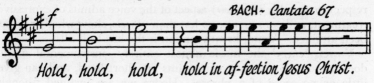

BACH - *Cantata 67*

Hold, hold, hold, hold in af-fection Jesus Christ.

And at all times with a more or less degree of force, this treatment must occur. D is the most difficult of final consonants.

With initial D it is otherwise, because either a vowel or (generally) an R succeeds it, in which case a vowel or its equivalent *is* there to do what is wanted in ensuring definition.

Final S and Z are often conspicuous by their absence. Far from being too prominently sounded, they are seldom sufficiently to be heard in singing. It is obvious that an overcharge of sibilants may be very unpleasant; but this is not likely to happen, though, from sheer laziness the hiss may be too prolonged. Since either S or Z is the sign of the plural they occur very frequently in speech, and must be adequately dealt with.

If words are not well articulated, it is a sure sign that they mean little or nothing to the singer.

Expression in Consonants

To complete the foregoing discussion we must extend it and roundly assert that, in spite of previous remarks, consonants are in every respect, within their limits, just as expressive as vowels. So far we have only spoken of the need of clearness in their articulation—giving them more or less vigour in the process; and of their function in affording a good 'take on' or 'off' of vowels. Such are, of course, features of expression, and a great deal of consonantal significance is derived from it (indicating different states of mental and physical energy). But consonants are open to something more. Not only can they vary in strength, but often in length; and also (strange though it seem) in pitch and tone quality. In short, they can be 'coloured', by being brought forward or sounded in a backward position, which gives them a higher or lower pitch, and consequently a different colour. These effects are largely due to the closing or opening of the resonance cavities which lie behind or in front of the articulation. For instance, 'S' may have a sharp or subdued flatus, according as it is dealt with at the very tip of the tongue or further back, by strong or weak breath pressure—if the former it will give a higher note than with the latter; and even a tip tongue explodent such as 'T' can be hardened or softened in the same way to suit the emotional situation. When this hardening or softening takes place, at the same time the harmonics associated with these states will vary, which is exactly what happens with respect to vowels. Thus *every* aspect of the voice admits of expressive treatment, and consonants, no less than vowels, show whether it has been attained. Again, breath tension is the key to it all.

Vowels 'carry' the music almost entirely—instrumental music does without consonants; consonants are short-lived, and can give little or no sense of a phrase. Hence we are inclined, though wrongly, to relate 'expression' only to vowels. But, as we have seen, they can still partake of all the essentials of expression, and have certain qualities in their own right, which are very valuable components in the sum total of expressive effect.

Chapter 6

VOWELS AND CONSONANTS IN PARTICULAR

VOWELS IN PARTICULAR

Introductory

CORRECT vowelling is far more important in song than in speech.

It frequently happens that one cannot make head or tail of a singer's words. What *is* he talking about?[1] Vowels are not defined. There seems to be a general vowel—little more than that—running through the sound, and as it is rather through the vowels than the consonants that words are made clear—at least that is the opinion of some of us—we are in a poor way of understanding. Consonants of course, matter; but, if vowels are bad, consonants are not likely to be good. Moreover, a vowel may be much prolonged either on a single note or in a cadenza, etc., such as,

from "Fae ut portem" Stabat Mater~ ROSSINI

and we lose our bearings very easily if it is an incorrect vowel, and, further, weakens before a final consonant—in this case the 'm' of the syllable 'rem' which comes on the last note (F #) of the phrase. Very great care should be taken with delayed final consonants, so that they are distinctly heard.

If we are outside a room and the door is shut, we shall not see anything that is inside the room. Often we cannot see inside a vowel cavity. Its content is shut in; the tone is smothered; the furniture of the voice is not 'on view'. Vowels need to be 'exposed'; to be 'open', in short, before we can distinguish them. This is not difficult with white sound, but it is otherwise with sound of a deep, rich, coloured quality. Then a great deal of art is called for.

[1] We might imagine that the initial fault would lie in defective speech. It often does, but not always. Frequently words are much more clearly defined in song than when they are spoken. I have noticed this when singers come from places where indistinct speech is common, scarcely to be understood by anyone foreign to the district. I have in mind certain pupils from Wales, whose ordinary speech is just a jumble of sound, but which changes directly they sing: vowels become relatively correct, and articulation is such that no ambiguity arises in regard to the words. Which seems to indicate that singing may be a cure for slovenly speech, just as it was said by Byrd to be for 'stutting and stammering'.

L

The need for the control of thin, 'sheet-of-paper' tone must again be stressed. It is the last thing that singers usually achieve though it comes first in importance. Without it vowels will never be clear and open, and really admirable part-singing of Madrigals and the like will be impossible.[1] To sing a light Madrigal such as 'Flora gave me fairest flowers' (Wilbye)—to name one of the best known examples— with tone suitable to the hearty conviviality of, say, 'Here's a health unto his Majesty' (Savile), is to travesty the situation. Weight can easily be added to lightness; it is far more difficult to reduce weight. This, indeed, is perhaps *the* main problem in singing, and even a naturally weighty voice has to demonstrate that it has been solved.

A relevant example from Weelkes has already been given on p. 245; another from the same composer may be noted as the matter is of such consequence:

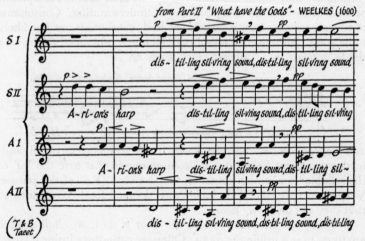

Anything approaching thick, heavy tone—*be it ever so soft*—will utterly fail to give clarity to this passage.

We talk of 'voice building', but the vocal edifice is ours from the start. All we have to do is to inhabit it, to gain entry. Yet this is not so easy; it is a laborious task. When accomplished, we look on to the outside world from its upper chambers; from its lower, into ourselves, and, just as awareness of external things comes first, that of self later, so should the higher resonances which secure the objective 'facts' of song—the shape and form—be our first concern; then, the lower resonances which search states of feeling. Which is

---

[1] In the whole course of my career I have never heard a Madrigal sung in a way that has completely satisfied me as regards tone. Such a delight may still come!

further justification for our dictum that the singer should make sure of the 'point' of his tone (so that his vocal calligraphy may be clear), before he proceeds to amplify it by giving it a broader base.

Under previous headings we have discussed the different shadings (or colourings) that the same vowel may have: how tone may be

open   (aperto)
closed   (chiuso)
or
mezza voce   (breath tone)

These are the three main variations that take place, in which the first (open) is determined by tight approximation of the vocal cords, the second (closed) by considerably less tension, the third (mezza voce) by a minimum of resistance. It is almost entirely a matter of how the vocal cords operate. Here, we will not pursue this aspect, only that of the differentiation of the various vowels; so that they are fully contrasted with one another. This can happen under very wide differences of manifestation. Whether a vowel is sung with open, closed or mezza voce quality, it is still possible for it to be recognized as that particular vowel, and no other.

The singer should therefore study to contrast such vowels as may be easily confused, because there is so little change in their formation. Nevertheless, the minute changes involved can be developed till they have the effect of very big changes; till in fact each vowel emerges as a personality and not as a sort of nondescript sound which it is impossible to symbolize with any precision. We talk glibly as if, by the very fact of speaking, we could do such things; but we are far from achieving it without the greatest care and practice. We may know what a speaker says from the consonants, the context (principally), and some (often very meagre) sort of likeness to the vowel that is meant. But analyse it and we find gross departure from perfectly defined speech. It is a joy to listen to pure vowels, and a joy to produce them. The physical pleasure, even, that is associated with good tone, the exhilaration of ringing resonance, the thrill of discovery, the sense of conquest (as though a new world were opened up), the knowledge that what we are doing is 'just right'—clearly to be felt and heard—is a great experience which may come suddenly (by some stroke of good fortune), or slowly (which is more likely), by infinite perseverance. Even so, nature has the final say; her gifts cannot be taken by storm.

A very few exercises are sufficient for vowel study—just as it was in the case of the famous singer Farinelli, whose master Porpora put all that were required on a single sheet of paper—at least so the well-known story goes. Sustained notes to begin with in the middle of the voice; then three notes in a similar position:

291

In the major key (a) for the bright vowels Ee, Ay, etc.; in the minor (b) for the darker, heavier vowels, Aw, Oh, Oo, etc.

Then some extension of pitch on scales and arpeggios, giving the major formula (a) to the bright vowels and the minor (b) to the darker ones as before.

Ah may also be sung to

legato and staccato on the same breath, though it will be found that a really short staccato is difficult with a relatively loose Ah, and that a tighter form approaching ŏ had better be substituted for it.

Finally two octaves should be attempted, both with scales and arpeggios:

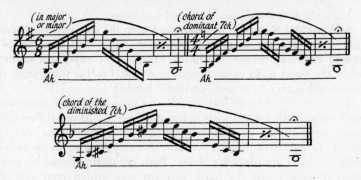

and, to complete the basic musical material of singing, the chromatic scale may be practised in groups of threes and fours, for an octave, in the middle of the voice:

also, such technical study ought to end with the trill, rhythmed as follows:

and starting on the note above, similarly:

etc.

Vary the foregoing, also, in speed and power.

Solfèges and songs can be attempted from the start, at the discretion of the teacher as regards difficulty. This will considerably extend Porpora's recipe. Technical exercises are important as they allow the pupil to focus on quality and skill, but the inspiration of music and poetry is, as well, certainly needed.

The contrasts of vowel (which follow a little later), are concerned with minor rather than with major differences. Major differences occur with all the long vowels, though similarities must also be noted. Ee and Ay are much the same in quality, owing to the raised tongue which accounts for them. Both are distinguished by their nasal resonance and the hard, brilliant tone which characterizes them. Oh and Oo, which employ a mechanism peculiar to themselves, are also allied in character. Their tone is of a dull, sombre kind, opening up great depths of expression. Ah and Aw are more or less laws unto themselves, having a sonority which has little or relatively little in common, either with each other or with the Ee or Oo group of sounds; nor can short ŏŏ (good) be readily associated with any other vowel.

But, though Ee and Ay, and Oh and Oo are similar in a certain way, they are also different. There is, indeed, a wide difference between them. An Ee is not like an Ay—it could never be mistaken for it; nor is Oh like Oo. These vowels, as all long vowels, represent generic differences; they could not be interchanged without destroying the groundwork of speech. To say 'green' for 'grain', or 'dome' for 'doom' would be entirely to mislead.

There is, however, far less difference between some of the long vowels and their short vowel correlatives, as they are called.

Ee	and	ĭ
Ay	„	ĕ
· Ah	„	ă
Aw	„	ŏ

are very much the same in structure, and, at a pinch could replace each other not only in singing but in speech. Actually, we often hear, particularly in local usage, something like 'geehlt' for 'gilt', 'hayed' for 'head', 'hahth' for 'hath', 'Gawd' for 'God', etc. Nevertheless we should be giving up a considerable source of variety if we allowed this sort of thing in received speech, where a certain sound should be that sound and nothing else—though we generally have to put up with tiny peculiarities, almost inseparable from person or place.[1]

[1] The other day I was telephoning to a friend I had not seen for years. We each recognized the other's voice. It struck me as very wonderful that this could happen; that a person—one of millions—could be identified by an invisible wave of sound,

The glory of the English language is precisely in the variety of its sounds, leading to the largest vocabulary of any language.

Uh, Ah and I (personal pronoun) are also very much alike and may well be taken as variant members of an Ah group of vowels. At any rate this is a practical way of dealing with the matter.

We have thus accounted for all the long and short vowels, noting the measure of their differences, and implying that, as these differences decrease, become less noticeable, the more they need to be defined.

Still more minute contrasts have to be made clear, though perhaps they represent rather a change of shade than of vowel. Such are those between

dull-toned and bright-toned Oh
(the equivalents of Italian closed (chiuso) O—as in 'amore' (ahmohray) and open (aperto) O—as in 'gloria,' in which the O is nearly Aw);

between

the weak 'vanish' of 'en' and strong 'en'
(the first heard in 'garden', the second in 'end');

between

'ur' and 'er'
(as in the two syllables of the word 'murder'),

and, which is almost the same, between the vowel in

'err' and that in 'earth'.

It is very difficult to detect what the nature of some vowels really is; one can hardly pin it down. The vowels we have just noticed are very elusive; so is short ŏŏ ('good') if prolonged, and the diphthong ow (in 'loud'). We can perhaps, pronounce them in a word well enough, while scarcely knowing what it is that we do pronounce, or being able to extract them without distortion from their surroundings.

However, it is only fair to say, as regards final 'el', 'em', 'en', 'er', that, according to Ellis, the precise vowel which these syllables embody had not, in his day, been satisfactorily established; nor are we certain of it now, though we shall not be far wrong if we take it as a thin, forward ŭ, obtained by advancing the tongue, and opening the mouth a little more than is required for a fuller sound of ŭ.

Further, emotion introduces all sorts of subtle changes in a vowel while it remains quite recognizable; that is to say, preserves its characteristic formation. The resonantal mechanism scarcely moves; the height of the tongue and orifice of the lips, which account

as surely as by a fingerprint. How can the scientist ever hope to analyse such subtle differences as are here implied, though he can transmit and reproduce them (which is also wonderful).

for the major differences in vowels, remain almost constant. Such changes must be left to chance; to determination upon the spur of the moment. They cannot be engineered consciously, nor systematized in writing. The most we can do is to secure an *un*emotional vowel which represents the normal form of its type, leaving accidental colouring to passing fancy.

There are four ways by which small, though clear differences of vowelling may be effected:

(1) depressing the root of the tongue (which opens the throat), as for all darkening of sound;
(2) bringing the tongue slightly forward (while keeping the throat open), as in going from ĭ to Ee;
(3) dropping the lower jaw (which opens the mouth more) as with
Ah to ă
and with the sequence
Uh – Ah – I;
(4) tightening the back of the mouth (which gives it a more vertical shape) as with
Aw to ŏ

Or it may be that these movements are combined. With

Uh – Ah – I

all seem to operate. The open throat is very pronounced with Uh; then the tongue progressively comes a little up and forward and the mouth opens for Ah and I; while at the same time these movements induce a slight tightening of the mechanism.

Though the short vowels ă, ŏ, ŭ (in 'cat', 'cot', 'cut') are not at all similar in structure, their contrast is recommended for study. They are difficult vowels to fix, and it is perhaps still more difficult to make them consecutively clear.

Exceedingly fine pronunciation is a very subtle matter, governed by accent, context and many other factors. We are obliged to rough out our vowels into a dozen or so, but the fine speaker multiplies these several times over. With singing it is not quite the same. Fewer vowels serve the singer; but there is still room for much variation in these, particularly when he is dealing with dramatic situations.

The Contrast of Ee *and* ĭ.

Ee, by nature, is a very cutting vowel. It is apt to be resonated only in the nose. But this will not do. It must certainly have nasal quality, but it has to be tempered by the use of neck resonance. It is better to proceed by way of ĭ—a more agreeable vowel—and then to alter the position of ĭ toward Ee by a slight forward movement of the tongue which should give us the Ee of which we are in search. The open throat, which goes with ĭ must be retained for Ee—this is most important. The tendency is always to reduce and alter the neck resonance, which, incidentally, destroys unity of vowelling. If the right procedure is adopted Ee can be clearly contrasted with ĭ *while remaining as rich and full as ĭ*. It is a pity to forego this differentiation (as some authorities counsel) in favour of the use of ĭ for both Ee and ĭ; besides it may lead to confusion, as with words like 'grin' and 'green' which have to be distinguished.

ĭ has of course a covered quality, that is why it is so much more pleasing than Ee when this vowel is sung in what may be called its raw state; it is also deeper and consequently looser. A raw Ee will not work easily; really fluid movement is impossible with it. Try such an exercise as the following on this type of Ee:

then with a good ĭ, noting the smoother progress of the latter. This smoothness has to be kept with Ee; large intervals best show up the situation. A badly 'bedded' Ee is likely to have a perforated instead of continuous sound. It will vibrate in fits and starts. Or it will only sustain by forced vibration, implying the expenditure of much more energy than is necessary. Very little force is wanted in an average note on any vowel, if it is rightly balanced and 'set'. A good vowel almost sings itself. There is no need to get red in the face about it, or show tight bulging muscles in the neck, except under special circumstances when tremendous effort is called for. The aim of the singer, then, must be to make Ee musical at all pitches, and to reduce its natural 'edge' while taking advantage of the timbre which is encouraged by its thin formation. Its very thinness makes Ee an easy vowel to control—certainly ĭ is very easy; many find that this latter vowel is best suited to the demonstration of a musical phrase. It comes to hand at once, as by a natural process of selection. It also seems to be the most widely-used vowel in the English language.

The student should therefore strive to contrast Ee and ĭ in the aforesaid way, by, say, the following exercise:

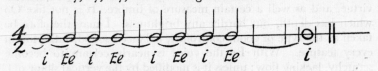

on any comfortable note, linking the vowels in continuous fashion.

Contrasted words can also be spoken and sung, e.g.:

ĭ   Ee

297

grin	–	green
din	–	dean
bit	–	beat
bid	–	bead
dip	–	deep
fit	–	feet
	etc.	

N.B. The short vowel is put first; *it* must be the point of departure.

Ee is a most important vowel, since (together with Ay) it is so brilliant, *timbrée* and telling. Its blatant character has to be modified, as we have shown, but even after this is done it still has an outstanding degree of nasal sonority, and shows where the voice should in a general way be placed if clear notes are to be forthcoming. A good example of the need of a telling Ee and Ay quality is to be seen in the opening phrase of the 'Qui sedes' of the *B Minor Mass*.

Qui se——————————des

The tone here must be something like that of an oboe, though duly tempered towards ĭ and ĕ (for the vowel Ay in 'sedes'). The breath has to have a certain 'lift' in it, if the nasal cavities are properly to be reached. Just as cynicism is required to give a cutting edge to life, so something of an edge must be given to all tone or at least must be potentially present. Such an edge is supplied especially in the vowel Ee. Nevertheless, the *formative* quality of ĭ must further be stressed. People who habitually sing Ee for ĭ—and there are many—usually have no 'body' to their voices. Even if the tone is not unpleasantly nasal it still remains thin and quite unsuited to the deeper aspects of expression. Heartfelt emotion, pathos, tragedy, can never be suggested by it. With ĭ the vowel is shaped as it should be, vertically; Ee is of a horizontal nature. This verticality must, in general, be preserved in all vowelling. Ĭ has this virtue, and as well a certain measure of timbre. It is not like Oo which has depth, but hardly any brightness. Ĭ may therefore be taken as the type of good, controlled, balanced sound, satisfying in every feature. With Ee the voice is nearly certain to become scratchy, lacking flow; unless it is modified by the vertical shape of ĭ.

If a voice is very backward (simply through incapacity to place it elsewhere),[1] 'y' prefixed to a vowel, as in the words 'Ye' and

[1] *Art* has no use for what merely happens, whether it is good or bad (one is

298

'Yea', will often help to bring it forward. 'Y' is a very thin forward sound, and just as ĭ tends to open up the backward resonances, so 'y' serves to open the forward ones. Nevertheless 'y' should be regarded as a variant of ĭ, and not given a hard Ee pronunciation.

The action of the back of the tongue is all important with Ee and ĭ. It must be loose, able to oscillate freely, and *entirely independent* of any other action. If it is not so, constriction of the throat and of the vocal instrument takes place.

One aim of singing seems to be that of not allowing the position of consonants to interfere with, or determine the position of vowels. Distinct consonants are often apt to spoil vowelling. Their nature mostly, is to close the mechanism; the nature of a good vowel is to open it. Rich, neck sound, such as one gets with ĭ, is almost the antithesis of frontal articulation, and it is very difficult to combine the two. That is why singers with the best tone often have the worst articulation. If we sing the word 'with' we shall probably find that we shall get good throat resonance throughout, because the 'w' and the 'th' (which represent Oo and dh) are themselves low-lying sounds; therefore the vowel ĭ is not likely to be displaced from that position. But with the word 'in'—and this often happens—the 'n' tends to push the vowel into the nose; the ĭ may easily become a sort of Ee—at any rate it will be likely to lose richness. Thus, consonants may greatly influence the sound of vowels and it is the singer's business to prevent it when it runs counter to the effect he wishes to produce.

Soft, unassertive finals must be carefully watched. The 'ly' in 'lovely', for instance, often has an aggressive sound of Ee (or nearly Ee) which draws attention to what should be a weak syllable.

Sir Hubert Parry's *Welsh Lullaby* begins with the word 'Sleep' on a long held note, similarly the well-known air 'O sleep' of Handel, from *Semele*. The atmosphere of either would be quite spoilt if a rasping instead of a soothing sound were to be given to it. The same thing applies to the word 'me' in the *Messiah* air 'Come Unto Me'. The need of vowel modification is thus seen to be very necessary. It represents the colouring of vocal tone according to the emotional mood, and it is from Ee and ĭ, and Ay and ĕ, that we learn best how to do it, for these are the vowels that are most susceptible to modification and call for it most.

Again, we have to learn not only how to put sound into the nose, but how to take it away from the nose, otherwise we shall be in

inclined to add) though this is perhaps a little too severe. 'Beauty *does* matter,' even if it cannot be credited to the artist, as such. A beautiful voice, like the wondrous gate of Chaucer's Dream Palace, is

'. . . *by aventure*
wrought, as often as by cure.'

trouble all the time and our singing will be harsh and vulgar. But it must be noted (again in the words of Alexander Ellis) with regard to nasal sound, that 'resonance *in* the nose can be nearly as effective as resonance *through* the nose', and that for vowelling we generally have to close the nose off, though passage through must be permitted in the case of the strictly nasal sounds (M, N, ng) and the French orinasals (*v.* pp. 24, 114).

To recapitulate. In the production of *both* Ee and ĭ, an agreeable quality should be maintained by keeping the throat well open. Ee must be as musical as ĭ; but kept quite distinct from ĭ.

The Contrast of Ay and ĕ

Ay is a vowel of very much the same type as Ee. Both have considerable nasal resonance, from which they get their special character. But Ay is a larger vowel than Ee—it has more mouth space; therefore it is rather more imposing in effect. Both are naturally hard and brilliant in sound, as is the case with all tone which has its habitat in the nose; both have to submit to some check of this natural quality, save in exceptional circumstances, when stridency is called for. The actual pronunciation of Ay and Ee is due to the position of the tongue; high up at the back for Ee, a little lower, but not much for Ay—one need not go into further details. The main thing to observe is that, with this relatively high position of the tongue, throat resonance is reduced, and has to be increased if the tone of these vowels is to become rich and round. As with Ee, some modification of the natural sound of Ay has to be made before it is fit for service. Fortunately the vowel ĕ (as in 'met') comes to our aid. Ĕ, of course, can be pronounced in a bleating way, without neck resonance, but, at its best, it must make use of an open throat.

The root of the tongue will then be drawn down and away from the back of the pharynx, giving the required resonance space in that region; by so doing the sound of ĕ will be full and mellow.

If the neck cavity of ĕ is maintained during the singing of Ay, Ay will take on a similar quality; though, as with Ee and ĭ, Ay and ĕ can be kept quite distinct. There is nothing disagreeable with Ay, if treated in this fashion; there may very easily be if it is not.

A crude Ay, just as a crude Ee, will refuse to *move*; it will have no fluidity, and as well be very difficult to vibrate. In such a passage as

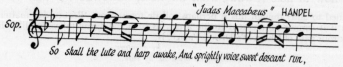

"*Judas Maccabæus*" HANDEL

Sop.

So shall the lute and harp awake, And sprightly voice sweet descant run,

the Ay on the high G is almost impossible unless the tone is allowed to lie comfortably down and back. Nor will another florid passage from the same air, on the word 'strains', run as a 'sweet descant' should, if it is not modified in the same way.

In the pure strains

A tap 'running' regularly (perhaps through the agency of an anti-splash contraption), not in fits and starts, is an ideal example of how notes *should* 'run'.

Ay (and Ee) are specially prone to forced, intermittent sound, though this can be got over in the way suggested, when their progress will be as smooth as that of an Oo.

Weak, final syllables with ĕ, as in 'lov-eth' and 'lov-ed' need watching just as do those with ĭ. They will have an almost invariable tendency to rise and become too prominent. Too great a difference, however, in tone force must not be made between accented and unaccented syllables, or the unity of the musical phrase will suffer. Blobs of sound do not constitute a phrase. Instrumental players generally hold their notes and give them superior individual value than singers are inclined to do. Accented and unaccented syllables are a source of great interest in speech and also in song, but the principle must not be abused. The English language is particularly associated with strong and weak syllables, and a considerable sense of *music* is necessary to prevent snappy, spasmodic utterance in delivery. Somehow or other the quality of *melody* has to be applied even in speech. With the Latin languages, especially French, there is no such danger of lineal weakness, as they are far more even in sound.

In practising the contrast of Ay and ĕ, the same procedure should be adopted as for Ee and ĭ. Get the right cavity for ĕ and then try to pocket Ay in it; that is to say, do not alter the neck resonance of ĕ when you sing Ay. The complete independence of the back of the tongue must again be stressed. A very slight movement at that place will produce the difference between Ay and ĕ. This movement should be repeatedly and quickly performed, so that there is a rapid but perfectly clear alternation of these two vowels.

They occur in such words as

ĕ		Ay
met	–	mate
knell	–	nail
pen	–	pain

shed	–	shade
sex	–	sakes
less	–	lace

which should be spoken and then sung in any way that seems best. Keep the fullness of ĕ in both vowels—the normal voice should be full. Remember that the deeper the position of a sound, the deeper the position of the breath. The level of the breath corresponds, as it were, with the resonance level.

Thin, scratchy, ill-sustained tone will generally be found to coincide with (1) bad resonance on Ee and Ay, (2) bad management of the diphthong I (=Ah+Ee) in which the final Ee is similarly concerned, and (3) poor sound on the nasals M and N (especially). In each case it amounts to the removal of the sound from the neck, or, in other words, wrong closure of the throat. The remedy is always to sing

Ĭ for Ee
and
Ĕ for Ay

till the voice acquires the *habit* of keeping down. When it is properly set in the saddle and does not bump off it, then the *modified* Ĭ and Ĕ should be used for Ee and Ay, in the manner already indicated.

The Contrast of Uh, Ah and I

These vowels form a progressive series. The extreme ones may be said to be variants of central Ah, though they are not generally treated as such. With all these the tongue is depressed, concave; though it rises slightly from Uh to I, as the mouth gradually opens, which it should.

Uh.—Uh is the most backward sound; it is also the loosest. When no effort is made to produce the voice this is the sound that arises. For this reason it is called the neutral vowel, and it may easily lack shape. Unless it is caught up, drawn together by an inward, concentrating process, it will have no purpose or direction, nor develop those overtones which indicate 'life'. This is a most important observation, for it goes to the root of what we have been driving at throughout this book: the need of tension as the agent of definition (and every other virtue). Uh in its primitive, thoroughly relaxed state is 'without form and void', it represents merely chaotic sound, useless till it is shaped and modelled, and has the impress of mind put upon it. We have called this sound Uh—to be polite; but in reality it is nondescript, nameless. Uh is, of course, the same as the short vowel ŭ, but it can be, and often is, treated as a long vowel. It upsets the validity of such nomenclature. All vowels are long whenever it suits the purpose of the musical setting; and when the short vowels are prolonged *in the right way* they are as rich and full as the long vowels, and generally easier to sing.

Uh (or nearly Uh) should be used for Ah when a deep surge of sound is wanted. Students will often sing a clear Ah (approaching ă) for the first diphthong syllable of Schubert's 'Aufgethelt':

Rau·schen·der sturm , brau·sen·der Wald.

Unless the 'Au' is taken almost as 'Uh and oo' we shall not get what is wanted. When an Ah is dark, deep and covered it will veer towards Uh; when it is exceedingly clear and forward, towards ŏ. It is a matter of relaxation and the open throat; or the opposite process.

It should be noted that vowels which have a backward placing tend to coalesce into an indeterminate sound, if we are not very careful to keep them distinct. Uh is certainly the type of this backward sound; indeed it is a sort of 'blue pigeon' type towards which every vowel will more or less revert unless its 'strain' is rigorously preserved.

But the very looseness of Uh, though bad if carried to an extreme, has an essential function: for it supplies the counterweight to the tension that has to overcome it. It is the inert force against which the force of tension has to be exerted, thus ensuring a state of lively balance. In artistic economy there are limits to the force of inertia. As emotional stress operates, so must tension be brought to bear. But in as far as inertia can be used, it should be. It is a waste not to do so; it guarantees against stiffness and economizes power.

The cultivation of relaxation is almost as much of an art as that of tension. We find it difficult to relax to the full; some involuntary twitch is usually present. So that the class of sound represented by Uh—mumbling, rumbling, moaning, groaning, fall within it—is a very important one. It relates to the softer forms of expression,

> *Jen has a sweet voice,*
> *Low like the south wind;*

as well as to the mightier roar of troubled things.

Uh tends to comfortable sound; it is the antidote to hardness and harshness. 'Speak *comfortably* to Jerusalem.' The singer should remember these words (from the opening tenor recitative of the *Messiah*). The Uh in 'comfort' is the precise vowel upon which we do speak most comfortably. In all cases of tightness or strain of voice, Uh should be sung for Ah, till a cure has been effected. There are many valid forms of Ah—as of any vowel. Uh, or nearly Uh—it must not be like the *short* hard vowel in 'cut'—will always be understood for Ah, though it is very different in sound; but its dull quality may easily go flat in pitch, unless proper breath action is taken to prevent it.

Ah.—The gradual opening of the mouth, while retaining the pharyngeal position of Uh, will bring the sound to Ah. Ah is the great central vowel. It is slightly more tensed than Uh, owing to its more forward placing; but it is very full in tone. Its boundaries are wide, and, because of this, it easily disintegrates; whereas an Ee, which is closely confined, seldom does. Tension at the vocal cords, and in the walls of the oral cavity, is essential, but Ah does not easily submit to control without losing the quality that makes this vowel so eloquent and expressive of satisfaction. It is the most expansive of the vowels, at its best full of golden radiance, but this is vitiated by any admixture of Aw. At its purest, Ah is neither like Uh nor Aw. If it is like Uh it loses its brilliance, if like Aw its characteristic freedom. But, inevitably, it *will* become like Aw or ŏ, if it is sung *staccato*; otherwise there is insufficient resistance to take the stab of the breath. It is an entirely happy vowel; the sun shines upon it through clear skies. Directly the sky darkens we return to the shade of Uh. One could hardly upbraid with Ah; its benevolence would 'always be breaking through'. It would have to be near ă or ŏ before it could suggest any sort of venom.

We are always in search of an *open* Ah. But Ah may become too open; it may lose depth in the process of rising towards the light. A good Ah, like everything else, is only free within limits; when those limits are removed it escapes in all directions. It needs to be 'buttoned up', as every other vowel, or it will flap impotently, like a loose sail, when the breath blows upon it; in other words, be toneless, through lack of resistance. It is the most difficult of vowels to intensify, and it is only by as it were 'twisting' it—like whipcord is twisted from loose hemp—that a really loud Ah can be achieved. Then it can be shattering in its intensity.

Ah easily degenerates into a shout, by losing contact with the base of the breath.

The opening of the mouth is more pronounced with Ah than with any other vowel except I; and this opening is apt to reduce throat resonance to such an extent that the sound loses the *undertone* that must be given to it. This is particularly the case as the voice rises, when the increased pressure of the breath may drive the voice off its proper 'seat'. High notes on any vowel involve this danger, but Ah is most liable to succumb to it. An indication of the character of Ah may be seen in its symbol AH.[1] Certain other vowels are also written, very properly, with a final aspirate (e.g., Uh, Oh). This implies a generosity of sound which the harder-toned vowels (e.g., Ee, Aw, ŏ) do not have. These start and come off with a click or some effect of tightly-closed glottis; the whole progress of their tone, is in fact, tight. Ah, of course, can be treated in the same way, and it is often necessary to practise a severely economical use of its sound; but, by nature, it is not niggardly with its favours. Yet Ah must not be breathy; the aspirate must be an influence, not an intrusion.

Perhaps (what I think we are entitled to call) the 'emotions' of sighing and laughing are what chiefly distinguish Ah. A heartfelt sigh naturally expresses itself in this vowel, likewise carefree laughter. Both represent a liberation of feeling, a cry of sadness or of gladness; a stirring of the depths, or a rise, like bubbles, to the surface. The aspirate is part of the expression, indeed essential to it. For a sigh the H is especially prominent at the end of the vowel—AH; for a laugh at the beginning—HA. But we are thus speaking of the addition or precedence of a consonant. Throughout there is an admixture of H which denotes emotional outpouring—the aspirate may be called 'the breath' of emotion, its living sign.

When Ah truly 'lives' it has something of the quality of a flame. It is warm, and warmth frees; just as coal, when it burns, releases its gaseous content, whereas, when cold, it has no such power.

As already advised there is nothing like a series of jolly 'ha ha's,' thrown well up into the head, to discover nasal ring and what is meant by balanced tension. It is not possible to get a perfectly pure Ah in either a very frontal or backward position; only a central position will define it. But a slight admixture of another quality will not prevent it being accepted as Ah.

I.—This vowel is the third of the triad of Ah's. Uh, Ah and I are very much alike, but they should be carefully contrasted. The I we are considering is the long vowel that we pronounce for the personal pronoun, not the short vowel of 'him'. By reason of what it stands for it is a very important vowel. The whole personality is, or can be expressed by it, if we are masters of the sound. It must therefore have depth as well as openness. I is further forward than central Ah. There is a general progress of backward Uh to forward I, through central Ah. This is effected mainly by the gradual opening of the mouth, which brings with it some slight adjustment of the tongue in a forward lifting movement. It is as though the sound were being

[1] Though other symbols are sometimes used for it.

tipped or shovelled forward. As with Ah, a distinct touch of aspirate runs through I. It might fairly be written Ih. Ah is very often used for I, but with I the little diphthongal 'vanish' of Ee shows that it is different from Ah. Ah can be quitted without any such diphthong; I cannot. I must, of course, never degenerate into Aw+Ee, though this, too, is a common fault with the uncultured. Ah has far more affinity with I than it has with ă—the vowel that is usually coupled with it. This is why we have taken Uh, Ah and I together, though fully recognizing that each has its own particular quality.

Nevertheless, for the singer, these three vowels are inter-change-able. They can be considered as different forms of Ah. Ah, at one moment, or in a certain circumstance (as with a very faithful expression of the word 'dark'), might be pronounced as Uh; at another moment (as with the word 'bright') it might take the place of I. With this there would be no confusion of speech. The singer would be quite well understood. From which we see that consider-able variation can be allowed in the pronunciation of a vowel before it ceases to be accepted as the vowel in question. The application of 'colour' in singing depends upon this principle.[1]

We should be careful that the back of the tongue does not rise much when I is sung, or the ensuing tone will be white.

It is sometimes recommended that Ah should always be sung for I, but this is a mistake. I is a definite colour which often may be suitably used, and it would be a pity to forego it. The student should therefore practise to contrast these three vowels, but he will find it more difficult to sing I than to speak it, as ordinary speech does not call for the same richness of sound as singing, and the more backward movement of the voice which singing involves is apt to prevent the forward opening required by I.

The following words are suitable for contrast:

Uh	Ah	I
but	baa	buy

[1] Conversely, there is no doubt that fewer vowels are needed in singing than in speech, and the question may be asked, 'Why?' It is a matter of sonority. Ordinary speech is dealt with in the front of the mouth; it is dominated to a far greater degree than in singing by the articulation of consonants, the variety of which influences a great variety of vowels. Singing takes place more at the back of the mouth, its tendency is towards the production of fine vowels, which largely depends upon the use of an open throat.

The throat is a far more constant factor than the mouth with its capacity for different positions of the tongue and lips; and so, with singing, vowels tend to become less varied but richer in sound. The musical quality of the voice is stressed, rather than verbal clarity. Fortunately, a great deal of simplification can operate in vowelling without losing the sense of words. Closely allied vowels—as in 'tough', 'cut', or 'heed', 'idea'—may be reduced to a single vowel, while the words themselves are still taken for what they are meant to be.

cut	cart	kite
fun	farm	fine
huff	half	hive
hut	heart	height
luck	lark	like
must	mast	mice
duck	dark	dyke
luff	laugh	life

Exercises can easily be devised upon them, or upon the vowels that they contain.

The Contrast of Er and Uh

The contrast of Er and Ur has been touched upon (on p. 295), but, as observed, this is a minute contrast and can almost be disregarded. The contrast between Er and Uh is more important and fundamental.

Er is one of our sixteen main vowels (*v.* p. 130) and must be looked upon as a long vowel; also, as quite distinct from any of the others. Yet it has a close relationship to Uh, as may be gathered from its equivalent spelling Ur, so much so that it could almost be included in the foregoing tripartite group Uh – Ah – I.

If Er is oscillated with Uh, it will be found that though the tongue is depressed at its root and drawn back for Uh, for Er it is raised a little and brought forward. It is as though Uh had been advanced to the tongue tip. This slight added tension gives it a firmer, closer quality. than Uh, and makes for superior control. The vowel is also specially dark and rich in sound.

Ellis allows the substitution of Uh for Er in singing, but this is a pity, and quite unnecessary. It does show however that he looked upon these vowels as first cousins.

The following are contrasted words which should be spoken and also sung (on the same note, or different notes).

Er (or Ur)	ŭ
blurt	blood
bird	bud
herd	hut
curd	cut
learn	luck
myrrh	mud
sir	sun
dearth	doth
shirt	shut

The Contrast of Aw and ŏ

Aw.—Aw is perhaps the noblest of the vowels. It does not persuade; it can scarcely be 'touched'. It commands. The sinews of the voice have to be strung up tightly for it, so that it is fit for battle, fit for attack. Its sound is of metal, like a trumpet's. If its brilliant, piercing quality is softened, it is no longer Aw; but Uh or some softer vowel. Its character has gone.

This essential hardness of Aw—a hardness that will make it ring through all other vocal tone—is produced precisely by a hardening of the instrument; in other words by great tension. For it the vocal cords are strongly approximated; the pillars of the voice (the tonsils) are straightened and brought together; the soft palate is tightened and therefore raised; the walls of the mouth (cheeks, etc.), are firmly set up; and the lips shaped with the utmost energy. The effect of all this is to produce a powerful resistance which needs to be overcome by powerful breath pressure. Vibration therefore has to be coerced. An Aw will not 'sing itself'. Hence the force of Aw.

Aw, with its short correlative ŏ, is the supreme *tone-former*,[1] by reason of its concentrated character. A hooty quality is excluded by its adjustment. It gathers loose sound together, compresses it, twists it into a highly tensile state, like whipcord, in contrast with the slack hemp of which it is made. It is only by a process of tightening and compression that the core of tone is reached. Such a process represents 'tone', and in a greater or lesser degree it must always be present in tone production. We saw this with the central vowel Uh in its inadmissible state (*v.* p. 109 *et seq.*). Even *mezza voce* has to be vitalized in this way.

Tone has to be brought into the smallest possible compass if it is to be at its most effective; in other words, focussed. Spreading tone is ineffective. The larger the shape of a vowel, the more must it be drawn in, the more must the resistance of its cavity be accentuated; otherwise shouting and bellowing results.

With Aw it may well be said that the power of its tension equals the power of its tone. For any steady, 'straight' tone there must be a steady mechanism, and this is achieved by tightening it up. The possession of a thoroughly characteristic Aw is therefore indispensable to the singer. It is an antidote to the looser sounds which we

---

[1] I am convinced that it is mainly by the influence of Aw and ŏ that the voice steadies, centralizes and reaches its full stature, but great care has to be exercised in regard to the practice of these vowels. At any sign of unusual, and particularly of local strain, singing should cease for the time being; the strength needed—and considerable strength *is* needed—must be developed gradually. Local strain, however, is not likely to occur if effort is properly distributed over the whole muscular system, chiefly through the agency of tension at the base of the lungs. If all this is safeguarded there is nothing that the voice cannot stand; the roughest treatment can come its way. Indeed it *must* be able to stand it, or the singer has gently to be relegated to the ranks of the second-rate.

have often been obliged to counsel, since singing embraces all modes of feeling.

As Aw needs such tension it is obvious that a considerable effort of both mind and muscle has to be directed upon its achievement. Aw has to be '*willed*' more than other vowels; it tends to discipline the *whole* of the singer's attitude towards purposeful tone.

Contraction of the back orifice of the mouth always has the effect of sending tone up into the nose, and so we find a great development of nasal resonance with Aw. The hardness and brilliance of this vowel has already been noted; it is tremendously potent and 'telling'. It is somewhat similar to tone produced by metal strings of the violin and 'cello. Their 'tang' is peculiar to Aw, and must generally be present in its sound, though, at the expense of its true quality, it can be avoided by relaxation. As noted in the earlier part of this book, force does not become effective till it is confined. That is why the superior confinement of Aw produces such forceful tone.

Ŏ.—The glory of Aw lies not only in its concentration, but in its volume. It is an imposing vowel, of far larger calibre than Ee or Oo, for instance. For it the tongue is flat—flatter even than for Ah. The back of the pharynx can be best seen if the mouth is shaped for Aw. Ŏ is still more highly concentrated, and therefore of rather smaller shape. With ŏ the soft palate is thrust more into the head—the tongue rises a little in consequences—and the back of the mouth is still more constricted. The breath, of course, helps to maintain this taut and high position of the mechanism by a strong upward pressure.[1] The result of all this is a lifting of the tone into the highest possible position in the head. An ŏ, at its most characteristic, seems to be (and probably is) resonated between the eyes, or (if the explanation is preferred) in the sinus cavities which are situated there.

Ŏ gives the very essence of vocal sound, but, as with other concentrated things, it needs careful use and handling, or there may be some strain of voice till sufficient muscular strength has been developed in order to deal with the extreme tension that is required of the instrument. On the other hand, the singer will probably not be *able* to form this vowel till he has such strength, though he may pronounce it aright *in speech*. Even this, however, is unlikely. Most of us *never* succeed in shaping ŏ, because of the difficulty involved, or, if it is momentarily achieved, the necessary tension is almost certain to be relaxed when an attempt is made to sustain it.

Such an exercise, therefore, as

[1] The connection between the breath and soft palate is very much like that of a rod or 'sticker' which pushes up the palate as the breath rises.

ŏ , ŏ , ŏ , ŏ , ŏ —

is greatly to the point. It is something of the same thing as the exercises for 'attack' given on p. 268. The quavers should be sung *staccatissimo*. This will be impossible without a high degree of breath pressure and general tension; but with it a real ŏ may result. The crux comes in the sustaining of the final note. This note should have just the same quality as the short notes. A similar exercise should be adopted for all vowels if there is difficulty in pronouncing them properly. The sudden 'rap' or 'jab' will often place the sound where it should be placed, and with this sound in mind the singer can then proceed to try to sustain it. He will often find that he cannot do so. Short notes (or words) have to be chipped and chiselled out, with sharply defined edges. Neither singers nor players like to make the effort that is required for these clean little 'bull's-eyes' (as Sir Charles Villiers Stanford used to call them). The consequence is that their performance is apt to be lacking in style and precision; it needs tidying up. And even if *legato* notes are in question, to have power over smart *staccato* will give them a far more 'accomplished' progress. All this has great reference to the technique of ŏ.

If I wished to propose a test for a good singer I think I should ask him to sing the vowel ŏ. If he could pass it adequately, sustaining the exact sound free of all diffuseness, then I should know that he would be capable of singing *any* vowel clearly and effectively. Without the more or less persistent influence of ŏ, the voice will be lazy, and backward (in the worst sense), and we shall get such a pronunciation as 'mur-sy' for 'mercy'. Voices must be made of wire, not wool. That is to say—as Sir Walter Raleigh told us—there is a central hardness in a good note, however soft its surround may be. Ŏ has with it a 'snotty', 'snorty' quality which is the counterpart of this hardness, and it must not be vetoed because we may think it a little hard and unrefined.

A good example of the need of an ŏ quality in the expression of all firm, brilliant statements is to be found in Cantata 35, Bach, for alto voice. The second aria opens with the passage:

Gott hat al ~ ~ ~ ~ ~ ~ ~ ~ ~ ~ ~ les wohl ge·macht,

The main vowel in this is Ah. If it is not drawn together as for the ŏ in 'Gott' it will have no penetrative power. It simply will not be heard. We shall lose sight of the semiquavers before they have gone very far; whereas, if we tighten the mechanism as the phrase proceeds, the tone will brighten and we shall hear every note. Certain phrases have to be *driven* home; they will not go, with sufficient life, of their own accord. True, in this case, the sort of Ah that is required is a mixture of Ah and ŏ; or what amounts to the same, a tendency (and more than that) of Ah towards ŏ. If a loud Ah had to be sustained with a *crescendo*

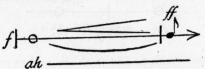

it would be necessary to end it almost upon ŏ by a sort of 'screwing up' process:

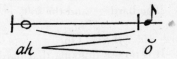

otherwise sufficient power could not be put upon it. In other words, almost all tone veers towards ŏ when its force has to be increased, by reason of the need for concentration and resistance.

Aw and ŏ afford splendid 'glottal' exercise. These vowels best develop the muscles of the larynx, etc.; as do the guttural consonants K and G.

The following words contain Aw and ŏ and should be contrasted in various ways; also the vowels alone.

Aw	ŏ
jaw	jot
caught	cot
gnaw	not
wrought	rot
yaw	yacht
dawn	don
fawned	fond
clawed	clod

Again, it should be stressed that it is by retaining the shape and flavour of ŏ that Ah (indeed, almost all tone) gets its timbre. Practice should therefore be directed to pronouncing a perfect ŏ, with its highly concentrated and characteristically hard sound, and then proceeding to Ah by the slightest change of the cavity till the tone of Ah is much like that of ŏ, certainly having kinship with it.

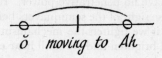

ŏ moving to Ah

On the other hand it is equally important to stress the kinship of Uh to Ah if ease and sympathetic quality is desired. Ah must then proceed from, and largely retain the cavity of Uh.

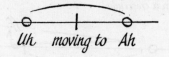

Uh moving to Ah

Ŏ and Uh may (with perfect truth) be said to represent the two great categories of vocal colour.

The brilliant and the dull

The clear   and the veiled

The hard   and the soft, etc.

The Contrast of Hard- and Soft-toned Oh

Hard-toned Oh.—It is no use thinking that hard and sympathetic tone can go together. They cannot. Hard tone can be loosened and sympathetic tone tightened, but this causes a modification of the one towards the other, with a loss of the hard or soft sound which characterizes them. Nevertheless an attempt should be made to effect a transition, so that soft tone merges gradually into hard, and vice versa. Much skill is involved in this. Both sorts of quality have their place in singing. At one moment the one is required, at another the other. We have often stressed the need of a sympathetic touch, of the softer *mezza voce* tones which indicate the more human side of expression. But there is an objective side which is concerned with clean delineation, with firm outlines; with form, in short, and not with emotion. It is in the service of ideal, detached attributes—in a sense, of words and notes in their own right—that hard tone has its value and must be cultivated.

The contrast of hard and soft-toned Oh is rather a contrast of quality than a difference of vowel. Some slight difference of vowel is always involved with a difference of quality, but it need not be sufficient to bring about what we recognize as a *change* of vowel. This matter has already been discussed.

Hard-toned Oh is produced in just the same way as hard-toned Aw or ŏ: by a tightening of the instrument, particularly at the back orifice of the mouth. But in reality the whole instrument is involved.

The vocal cords may be looked upon as the prime engineers of hard tone in as much as they represent the first great obstruction to the breath stream. This obstruction may be strong or weak; whatever its degree, it influences, or accords with, all those other obstructions which go to the making of tone in all its varied manifestations. If it is strong it will bring the voice forward and induce much play of nasal resonance. In this procedure the tonsil 'pillars' of the voice play an important part. Sound is only kept up—that is to say, resonated in the head—by the tensing of these pillars which, like the pillars of a building, prevent the structure from falling. The roof of the mouth is thus raised and we get a sort of dome into which the sound may be said to rise.

The muscles of the lips and cheeks are especially developed by singing Oh; so are those at the back of the mouth and the throat. At its greatest tension the face is stretched up and down, the lips are rounded and open outwards like the bell of a trumpet; this gives Oh, and the hard tone of which we are speaking—tension and hardness always go together. Thereby *tone* is enclosed in the strongest possible way, and also enlarged by the stretching process. There is a tremendous feeling of 'cavity' with Oh—a large solid body seems to occupy the mouth and throat. The pronounced rotundity of Oh shows the singer what volume means in tone formation, and how resistance relates to strength; no other vowel does this to the same extent. A different sort of Oh is to be heard in soft-toned Oh.

Soft-toned Oh represents sound of a very beautiful kind; from which all hardness has been removed. It comes softly, sympathetically, as a sort of low moaning, such as these last two words would suggest; to other words it gives special loveliness—'roses', for instance, seems to have the fragrance of the flower itself.

With this Oh the tensions of hard-toned Oh have been eased, the muscles relaxed. This allows the sound to fall further back and to reach its natural depth: for Oh, in its expressive sense, is a very deep vowel. There is a certain artificiality in the higher hard-toned form, which prevents it from being taken as the true type of Oh. The soft-toned Oh lies, with the utmost comfort, in the throat; the throat opens to receive it. Yet the very drawing down of the voice, from its deep breath attraction, models and moulds the sound, controls its cavity, so that it is not in the least like relaxed Uh. A good Oh (of this sort) is the most manageable of all the vowels; capable of the most expression, of displaying the finest shades of feeling.

So sensitive and delicate is the touch that can be used upon it, that it is like painting with a camel's hair brush, whereas stiff bristles would be required for coarser colours.

This tone stands for what may be called 'introvert tone'; its movement and direction is inward, 'come bere'.[1] It is always seeking contact with the seat of feeling, obtaining its sustenance there. For this reason it is not only the most manageable but the most expressive of vowels. It 'means' more than any other vowel; it searches the whole being, revealing profundities of emotion beyond that attainable by Ah, with which it alone can be compared. An agonized Oh is the most intense sound that the voice can utter, nor does it depend on being loud; what counts is its preparation by the whole physique. Mere breath will display its power; a soundless Oh is even more significant than a sounded one. Ah scarcely goes beyond personal joy; Oh is chiefly linked with pain and anguish, which states, it would be generally conceded, 'move' us most of all. In every sense Oh is a 'great' vowel—withdrawn from the glitter of nasal resonance, it opens into those darker regions where, vocally, the vaster issues of life are deliberated.

As we saw, hard-toned Oh depends upon the greatest tension of the instrument, which gives Oh more than a tinge of Aw; at times even, it may be forced into Aw. With the release of hard into soft-toned Oh, the lips need, indeed *should* not be used in the formation of the vowel. This formation can be effected at the back of the mouth (*v.* p. 34). If the lips are rounded, tightening at the back will occur, and the Oh will not fall into its proper place. It is only for the hard-toned quality that the lips should be brought into play.

In the singing of Latin, one often meets with thin, scraggy tone. 'Agnus', for instance, is pronounced 'Ă-nyus' instead of 'Ah-nyoos'. To secure rich, full vowelling, it is a good plan to think of the voice as being slung low in the neck (as from shoulder to shoulder) in the position of Oh; this too, is absolutely necessary for smooth singing. The hard and soft forms of Oh admirably exemplify the two great divisions of vocal colour: the clear and the overcast. The singer should become master of this contrast, which he may effect either abruptly

oh (bright), oh (dull), oh (bright), oh (dull)

or gradually

oh (dull) going to (bright)

and vice versa.

---

[1] To sing 'come bere' (like drinking) was well-known advice in the classical period of Italian songs.

It has been said elsewhere that the tongue is flat for Ah, Aw, Oh, Oo. This is roughly true, but not quite. The most depressed position of the tongue is with the deepest vowel of the voice, Oo; Oh runs it very close. There is a slight lifting for Aw and Ah; but the degree of lift is very different from that required by Ay and Ee.

The Contrast of Oo and ŏŏ

Oo.—Long Oo brings us to the deepest sound in the voice; its connection with the lowest position of the breath can easily be observed. It is not for nothing that the opening words of the Psalm 'De profundis clamavi' have Oo for their main vowel. It plumbs the depths of the spirit, just as it might those of the earth. In such a case little distinction can be made between the spiritual and the material. But though Oo is deeper than Oh it has not the volume of Oh; it is altogether a smaller vowel, nor has it as much 'tone' as Oh—very little kick or 'devil' can be given to it. It can therefore hardly compete with the other vowels, and it is very difficult to bring it into line with them. In loud passages it is apt to disappear, or to fail in emphasis when force is required. Its quality is soothing, not strident. If one had to say 'You brute!' in any but a playful way, one could hardly do it.

As with Oh, a hard or soft tone may be given to Oo. It is again a matter of tension. But it is less easy to harden Oo than Oh. Its nature, like that of Oh, somewhat rebels against the treatment. Just as essentially soft sound has to be prevented from going into the nose, so has hard sound to be prevented from going into the throat. The danger with the latter is that it tends to throttle. With hard Oo considerable effort has to be made to keep the throat sufficiently open. The back of the tongue will want to rise, and, if it does so, Oo may easily degenerate into a hoot, i.e., a sound which has lost contact with the vocal cords—in other words, is not properly 'voiced'. Such sound will almost inevitably sharpen. Oo is the vowel as to the intonation of which one has to be most careful. Nasalized sounds will generally keep in tune.

The technique of Oo is almost the same as that of Oh, only it is a little closer, upon a smaller scale. In its soft form Oo is a very important vowel. It shows what has to be done to tone to take away its 'vice', its (what may be called) anti-social qualities. It is the blending vowel *par excellence*; its formation guards it from aggression. That is why boys' voices are mostly trained upon Oo, and its flavour given to every vowel—sometimes with debatable and even disastrous results. What is wanted in voice production is more the influence of Oo than its omnipresent sound; the steadiness that the Oo position gives, its guarded character.

Not only does Oo show how 'horizontal' unity may be developed in vowelling, so that vowels consort with one another and do not lord it or domineer; it also shows how 'vertical' unity may be attained; how, in harmonies, voices can be made to fuse and balance. A very simple experiment will constitute a perfect object lesson. Get a choir or a few voices to sing a four-part chord on any vowel they like. The effect will probably be very rough. Then on Oo. The sound will almost inevitably become soft and smooth, and much more beautiful in its appeal. Or take a part-song with words, and note how poorly it will be sustained and dealt with, in comparison with the singing of it on Oo, without words. This is because the technique of Oo is not applied. It really amounts to neglect of the vertical, 'up and down' position of the voice, without which cultured qualities of song cannot be attained.

The movement of soft Oo, through the other long vowels, to Ee should be practised; till the depth and softness of Oo can be given to every vowel.

Thus:

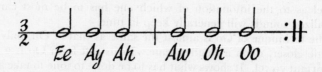

In this the low level of the voice should not change. If it does, a different quality or character of tone is bound to occur; the unity of the sound is destroyed. Serene, solemn tone—such as is required for, say, the *Stabat Mater* of Palestrina, and most church music—a tone that is as dispassionate as a boy's voice and has none of the excitement that nasal resonance gives, derives from this treatment; but it is not easily achieved by the adult singer.

Contrariwise one should proceed from the full brilliance of Ee, giving this to all the vowels.

Here a high level of the voice (and breath) must be used, in accordance with principles stressed repeatedly throughout this book.

For normal tone a middle course is advisable; and it is a good rule to try to get, in every vowel, as much of the brilliance of Ee and the roundness of Oo as possible; that is to say, to merge the two extremes of sound representing brilliance and depth, though not to do so to

316

the extent of altering, fundamentally, the pronunciation of the vowel.

Long Oo, when hardened, becomes, practically, the short vowel ŏŏ (as in 'good').

Oŏ.—The short vowel correlative of Oo has much the same kind of sound as Oo, but is not tunnelled so deeply into the body. It is brought a little more to the fore by a forward movement of the tongue—much as ĭ is brought to Ee by a similar process; but, with it, care must be taken that the back of the tongue does not rise. The general feeling of the vowel is that it is more or less breathed and directed into the mask of the face. With long Oo, in its harder form with pursed lips, it also seems as if the breath was being blown on to and through the lips. Any such tightened action of the lips brings the voice to that place, concentrates the effort there. That is why it is so good to sing in French, because of its much-accentuated lip action. It is almost impossible to be 'throaty' with French, though its general sound is by no means as rich as the more guttural German. French for this reason also is a very *timbrée* language. Soft-toned Oo, on the other hand does not seem to be on the lips, which, for it, are loose; the sensation of the sound is that it is sunk in the throat.

It is almost impossible to get a really hard, *timbrée* ŏŏ, just as it is with Oo. Its naturally soft quality will always prevail. Still it can be hardened a little, in the usual way: by tightening the instrument. If the lips are kept tight, as it were by a band round them, also the back orifice of the mouth, some hardening will occur; but it does not amount to much, and the vowel is so lacking in amplitude that it scarcely fits in with full vowelling. Perhaps because of its small shape, also because of its elusive character—one can never quite fix it, or be sure of it, apart from a word—it is not greatly used in speech. But, like other difficult pronunciations, it should be practised both by itself and in contrast with its nearest relation—in this case, Oo.

Woo'd (verb 'to woo') and wood
may be considered examples of the softer, slacker form of these vowels; and

noon	nook
pool	pull

of the harder tighter forms. Choice, however, is limited; and it is difficult to find words suggestive of the desired *colour*. The singer will have to experiment mainly with the vowels themselves.

One should add that if the tight, rounded-lip form of Oo is used, then short ŏŏ will be shaped by a depression of the back of the tongue, i.e., a widening of the throat; if the loose-lipped backward form of Oo is used, then the ŏŏ will want bringing a little forward by a reverse process. It is not easy to give exact instruction for the formation of vowels, because it depends on what sort of a vowel you start from.[1] The general principle (often stressed) is that the throat widens in going to a larger vowel or to a darker quality, and narrows when a smaller vowel or brighter quality is in question.

The Contrast of Oh *and* Ou (*or* ow)
should be studied, as in

though	thou
boat	bout
no	now

The latter vowel is of course a diphthong (=roughly Ah+oo), but in reality it can scarcely be fixed with any assurance. What is certain is that the Ah must not be too thin and forward, or anything like ŏ; but a full Ah, in which case the 'vanish' oo will look after itself sufficiently well.

The Contrast of ă – ŏ – ŭ
It is convenient—at least I find it so—to contrast these three short vowels, as in the words

cat, cot, cut

They group naturally together, being variants of the Ah family. In their short, snappy form they can be pronounced fairly well; but they are not easy to sing with good tone. This matter has already been discussed.

The French orinasals ŏn, ăn, ĕn *and* ŭn (*v.* p. 112)
should be carefully studied. They are heard at the end of the words

mon grand chien brun

and are especially serviceable for developing nasal tone, also for their influence as regards modelling and controlling the voice. They may be said to derive from the long vowels Oh, Ah, Ee, Uh, and, in France, are taught in connection with them and practised thus:

Oh-ŏn, Oh-ŏn, Oh-ŏn, etc.
Ah-ăn, Ah-ăn, etc.
Ee-ĕn, Ee-ĕn, etc.
Uh-ŭn, etc.

[1] The truth is, that vowelling is almost as unconscious an operation as pitching a note. People pronounce well, not because they know how to do it, but, for the most part, because they copy the pronunciation of others. If they are brought up in a good tradition of speech they will follow that tradition; to get out of a bad one is almost impossible.

Example rather than precept counts in speech; the gradual accustoming of the ear to a certain sort of sound. Broad rules can be given, such as the right action of the breath, the position of the larynx and so on, but the adjustment of the resonating cavities can hardly be prescribed.

It is not a bad plan to put our little friend Y before the above, to assist in the right drive and placing:

Yoh-ŏn

Yah-ăn

etc.

The orinasals are strange sounds to English ears, and require to be patterned before they can be pronounced. They are, of course, nothing like the terminations in 'gong', 'pang', 'sing', 'rung'.

The French vowels u *and* eu, *as in* '*tu*', '*feu*', should be mastered. They are practically the same as German modified u and o, heard in the words

müde, schön.

As they also are different from any English vowel, they need to be patterned by an expert. Eu (Fr.) or ö (German) is a most difficult sound for an Englishman—who generally objects to using his lips for the purpose of pronunciation.[1]

The vowel u (Fr.) is especially good for training the voice, for bringing sound well forward and at the same time opening the throat. With it also the lips present a barrier to the breath, which has to be overcome by considerable breath pressure. Every student should go through a course of this vowel.

The foregoing are some of the chief distinctions in vowel sound that have to be made.

To turn now to:

CONSONANTS IN PARTICULAR

Introductory

There is a constant struggle going on between articulation and vowelling. Consonants are generally formed in the front of the mouth, vowels at the back; and they only run together in proper harness after much breaking in. We can deal with articulation at the expense of vowelling, or vice versa; but to get full use of both vowels and consonants as they occur in verbal sequence, to preserve continuous as well as detailed sound in the management of words, is no easy matter. To say 'this and that' with clear articulation and full tone is an example of the difficulty. Here the consonants, with the exception of the D, are all tip-tongue—and even D is a voiced variant of T. This tends to bring the vowels into the same forward position. As such the result is entirely unsatisfactory as sound. Ĭ and ă, as we know, are naturally thin vowels. They have to be amplified before they are fit for singing. This amplification

[1] The more the singer can accustom himself to the control of strange and difficult sounds, the better will be his singing. He ought to sing in foreign languages as a matter of course.

319

takes place in the throat, right away from the tongue-tip, and thus the sound has to travel backwards and forwards, from consonant to vowel, over a distance which we are apt to try to reduce unless we are very expert. In consequence a foreigner (and even an Englishman) is apt to say 'theeze' for 'this'. It is by no means impossible to keep an open throat while articulation is going on. This, of course, is the secret of good singing—but it is not likely to be effected without prolonged study.

Consonants do not need to be discussed as closely as vowels, though, as we have seen, both can be coloured in much the same way. But, perhaps, the outstanding factor in their treatment is that of force. They can be dealt with more or less vigorously. This is where taste comes in. To spit and splutter consonants in a quiet passage would be to destroy its effect; not to emphasize them when their expressive power is deliberately sought would be equally foolish. The poet himself will largely suggest what we ought to do. He will probably reserve his hard vowels and consonants for highly dramatic moments, and lean towards softer vowels and consonants when he wishes a gentler, more lyrical mood to prevail.

Thus, Kent's outburst, in *King Lear*:

> *—Revoke thy gift;*
> *or, whilst I can vent clamour from my throat,*
> *I'll tell thee thou dost evil.*

is schemed, particularly in the second line, in syllables that almost have to be hacked out—each is full of explosive, pent-up passion. Neither the vowels nor consonants flow of themselves, as they seem to do in:

> *And flights of angels sing thee to thy rest!*
>
> (Hamlet)

or:

> *O, it came o'er my ear like the sweet sound,*
> *That breathes upon a bank of violets,*
> *Stealing, and giving odour. . . .*
>
> (Twelfth Night)

An analysis of the sounds used in these passages will show how it is that they produce their special effect and require easy or energetic delivery.

Or compare the envenomed agony of Othello's:

> *Arise, black vengeance, from thy hollow cell!*
> *Yield up, O love, thy crown and hearted throne*
> *To tyrannous hate! Swell, bosom, with thy fraught,*
> *For 'tis of aspics' tongues!*

320

with the pathos of his repentant, final words:

> —*of one whose subdued eyes,*
> *Albeit unused to the melting mood,*
> *Drop tears as fast as the Arabian trees*
> *Their medicinal gum.* . . .

to see the part that not only vowels but consonants[1] play in the subtleties of verbal expression.

At times words are purposely disjointed, at other times they merge like the notes of a sustained melody.

> *'Tis not enough no harshness gives offence,*
> *The sound must seem an echo to the sense :*
> *Soft is the strain when Zephyr gently blows,*
> *And the smooth stream in smoother numbers flows ;*
> *But when loud surges lash the sounding shore,*
> *The hoarse, rough verse should like the torrent roar ;*
> *When Ajax strives some rock's rash weight to throw,*
> *The line too labours, and the words move slow ;*
> *Not so when swift Camilla scours the plain,*
> *Flies o'er th' unbending corn, and skims along the main.*

The singer should give heed to these words of Pope; they are as apt to his as to poetic endeavour. What the poet is required to do, he has to do, if he claims to be an interpreter of song.[2]

Music reflects words in its pointing and phrasing. *Legato, marcato, staccato*—all is proper to it—and we must not mind if consonants break up the perfect continuity of sound. An everlasting *legato* would be wearisome in the extreme, though it is certainly implied in any organic relationship of either words or notes. A phrase means that its elements are fused with one another. The sense of such a fusing can however be given even if the elements are not actually in contact. Words and notes can be made to 'carry on', though the sound is broken up. Logical progression is not destroyed when a consonant intervenes or a note is not held to the end. *What must be constant is the sostenuto of the breath.* It is this which symbolizes

---

[1] The difficulty of finely-modelled speech is shown in the central part of this word, which so easily becomes 'consnants', with the vowel omitted.

[2] Though sound is the special concern of the musician, he understands its *finesse* and possibilities, I think, far less than does the poet; it is not brought home to him to anything like the same extent. When the aural sense is fed only upon music, it can scarcely respond to the delicate palpitations of words, their flavour and fragrance, their urgencies and hesitations, their colour, placing, and all those manifold but mostly elusive qualities that go to the making of poetry. They are heard by a poetic ear; it is seldom that the musician's is attuned to catch them. How wonderful singing would be, if it combined, in equal measure, the essential properties both of words and notes.

M

the phrase and really holds it together. So we must not be too hard on consonants; or look upon them as an unmitigated nuisance, merely to be tolerated. On the contrary, a welcome variety comes from their use. They are a great source of expression, not only in their mechanical aspect, but in emotional significance.

Nevertheless, it is seldom that consonants have the main appeal, because they cannot sufficiently delineate music—vowels must be relied upon for that—and so, in a general way, articulation must not be overdone, to the detriment of vowel sound. They can be so fiercely attacked that they absorb the attention of the listener, which should be directed to other matters. But, in as far as they contribute to sound and sense, consonants are good.

Sound, sound—always sound![1] In every aspect of singing this is what is wanted. To develop power over *sound*, to secure splendid vibration is the aim of all vocal study. Whether it is loud or soft, we must feel that sound satisfies and stirs us. This applies to the sound of consonants as well as to that of vowels. Consonants are not anti-musical; we can make music with them as well as with vowels—at least to a degree.

As well, consonants have a technical function. By their means vowels gain in energy and direction. A vowel derives impetus from its obstruction at the vocal cords; it almost doubles it by the further obstructions it meets with in the shape of consonants. These have a sort of delaying action by which vocal sound 'gathers' and intensifies, till it is sped on its way by an increase of pressure which bursts its barriers. In lively singing the advantage of consonants is obvious. Because of them a song can be far more alive than any instrumental piece. But the singer must be alive in the first place.

The whistlings and the buzzings and the trillings of consonants also give 'life' to song. Here again their use should be more in the nature of an influence than an intrusion. They release a mass of tiny, high-pitched sounds, and these undoubtedly help to give brilliancy to the voice. The technique of vowelling helps the production of consonants, as that of consonants helps vowelling. Vowels back up the sound of consonants; at least, the cavities associated with them do. An M for instance has twice the usual sonority if the cavities of the mouth and throat are thoroughly opened underneath it. This is true of almost every voiced consonant. It is particularly necessary that the power of 'voicing sound'—of, as it were, 'digging it in'—should be applied to the quick 'patter' delivery of syllables. But again, if the resonance cavities are not opened, little sound will result; we shall scarcely hear what is going on.

Consonants shape the outline of words, giving them form and

[1] Almost the equivalent of Rossini's 'Voce, voce, voce!'

structure. To this is added what they do in regard to the significance of speech. A word *means* something by reason of its consonants. It brings us into particular relation with objects and enables us to understand ourselves. Vowels cannot do this. A vocalize does not carry us as far as words and music; if it did, great composers would write vocalizes for the voice, not songs. They seem satisfied to think that a song is superior to a 'song without words'; and so the writing of vocalizes is generally left to secondary composers. If, therefore, words are used in singing they must offer some advantage, but only on condition that they are made clear; 'You are a singer, I will say for you' is Peter's sly remark in *Romeo and Juliet*. The situation is eternally the same. I am not sure whether we ought not to tell a singer always to 'say', and not to 'sing'. This means that their vowels must be true; their consonants distinct.

To make consonants distinct requires considerable effort. A vowel, in most cases, will 'sound' more easily than a consonant; breath can be looser for it. This can be verified by singing, first, by saying the vowel 'i', and then placing the closed consonant T after it. The vowel can be sung with little or no effort; when the consonant comes there will be a twitch and a 'lift' at the base of the breath, otherwise insufficient articulation will be given. In short, more breath pressure is generally needed for consonants than for vowels. Some consonants approximate to vowels: the 'vocals' L, M, N. These can be sounded fairly easily. But the explodents P, B, T, C, etc., and even the vocal R will not work unless much energy is applied; at least, they will not be sufficiently heard at a distance, while such a word as 'acts', still more the word 'instincts', will generally defy the speaker or singer and be replaced by 'axe', 'instinks'. With half-hearted treatment consonants are almost inaudible.

Anything like a full development of the 'stopped' nature of consonants is seldom to be met with. They are 'let go' loosely; and therefore ineffectively. For the purpose of practice the breath should be concentrated behind the 'stop', till almost bursting-point is reached; then the consonant should be sharply released. But *the tension of the abdominal muscles should continue after the articulation has occurred*, just as it should with vowelling. As long as vowelling or articulation is going on, there should be no cessation of abdominal tension. For instance, in the series of final articulations

whether sung (or, indeed, spoken) *legato* or *staccato*, the intensity of the breath action is constant. The voice does not 'go to pieces' after each sullable, or 'pop', like a blown-up paper bag. In short only *one* highly-tensed breath is used for a succession of notes in a phrase. When this is the case energy is immediately available for either vowelling or articulation and the whole of the vocal instrument is 'toned-up' to meet whatever strain is put upon it. Some poets demand almost superhuman efforts in consonant articulation. As in this, and what follows it, from a setting by Julius Harrison of one of Browning's Cavalier Songs:

Kent~ish Sir Byng, etc

If taken at the proper power and pace, the physical energy required is tremendous. Browning is perhaps the most outstanding exponent of consonantal use in poetry, and, it is worth saying that, as well, he is one of the most intellectual of poets. We have remarked before on the formative, intellectual function of consonants.

Articulation in speech does not need quite as much care as articulation in song; because more energy is available for it. In speech the vowels are relatively short; in song they are much longer. This not only distracts the singer's attention from the consonants, but leaves him with less strength to cope with them. Therefore we have not only to say that true vowels are more important in singing than in speech (*v.* p. 289), but that, in singing, it is more difficult to ensure clear consonants. All the way round, the art of singing, being less natural to us, requires greater application than the art of speech; so that standards of professional speaking are on the whole much higher than those of professional singing, judged only on the score of verbal clarity.

To discuss some of the principal features of articulation.

Voiced and Unvoiced Consonants

With the exception of the aspirate H, the vocal cords play no part in the *formation* of consonants. Consonants are formed by various parts of the instrument above the larynx; by the lips, tongue, and the back of the mouth, which offer impediments to the breath stream. But sound is *added* to consonants, simultaneously, by the vocal cords. Such consonants are called 'voiced' consonants. This added, underlying sound is in the nature of a vowel, but it is

a very indeterminate vowel—a sort of rumble more than a recognizable sound. It is the basic sound of M—the nearest approach to it
being, perhaps, French eu (boeuf) or German modified o (boëcke),
which is the sound one gets after the consonantal barrier has been
removed. Any vowel can of course be made to follow a consonant;
but only the sound just indicated is part of the consonant itself.
This sound must not be confused with a vowel sound which is often
tacked on to a consonant by indifferent singers—thus,

eat may become ea-tuh
age ,, ,, a-juh, etc.

Consonants are thus divided into two main classes: 'voiced' and
'unvoiced', though the unvoiced should come first; for it is the unvoiced form that determines the voiced. 'Voice', as we have said,
is simply added to the unvoiced sound, which, as its name implies,
is not musical or singable in the strict sense. Distinct pitch, however,
can be given to unvoiced sounds. We can hiss a tune on S, or blow
one on F; which shows that other factors, besides those of the vocal
cords, operate in pitch definition. This has a bearing upon the
extremely complicated matter of vocal resonance, also upon vocal
theory; but we had better leave it, as it is not of much practical
importance, though, as we know, vowel exactitude may be tested
by whispered resonance (v. p. 145).

The 'voicing' of such consonants as L, M, N, R, is not difficult.
Their continued sound almost allows them to be taken as vowels.
A very fair idea of music can be had by humming, which is an effect
often used for the purpose of accompaniment, though generally
irritating and unsatisfactory. There is also a continuant quality in
the sibilants, V, dh (as in 'thee'), Z, zh (as in 'vision') and even in
the explodent J; which makes these articulations relatively easy to
produce. It is otherwise with the explodents B, D, G, when heavily
voiced. The sound then given to them is so confined at the larynx,
and necessarily of such short duration, that it is very hard to articulate them properly. Half the time they are not given their full
sound, but are represented by a backward version of their *unvoiced*
correlatives, P, T, K, using more oral space. This serves well
enough for *initial* articulation. A difference can be made between
T and D without any 'voicing' as in the words 'toe' and 'doe'. But
we must not pretend that this sort of D is 'voiced'; nor can the same
force be given to the articulation as when it is (what is called)
'imploded', i.e., given the particular 'thud' that it has when the
vocal cords are made to sound with it. The same holds good with
G, as in 'goal', and also with B, as in 'bowl', though a slight voicing
is likely to occur with B. In their capacity as finals, however, B,
D, and G can hardly be recognized unless they are voiced; they

will be too weak in definition and liable to be taken as P, T, and K. Doubtless a certain amount of 'kick' can be given to B, D, G if we flate them sharply and strongly as buh, duh, guh—where the uh is simply breath; but it is more likely to result in a real tacked-on vowel; as gle-buh ('glebe'), bod-uh ('bode'), do-guh ('dog'), and we certainly have not 'voiced' them in this way. It is difficult to come to a cast-iron conclusion on this matter—to know exactly what to do to make these consonants clear. I am inclined to treat a final D —always a source of trouble—by adding, exceptionally, just a touch (or more) of final vowel, as I suggested on p. 287.

What is certain is that audibly voiced, i.e., 'imploded' B, D, and G, should be practised, after which they can perhaps be left to look after themselves. A snippet of tune such as

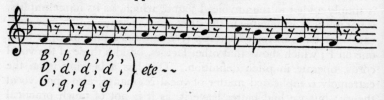

may be sung to the *laryngeal* sound of these consonants; but we must be sure that it is only this sound, and that it does not go into M. It is a sort of throttled 'grunt' that can only last a second or less.

Breath Consonants

These, as their name implies, are unvoiced. A secondary form of aspirate goes with them—a little escape of breath. P is one of these consonants. For if the lips are held together, more or less tightly according to circumstances, a small amount of breath is compressed behind them—again, more or less strongly according to circumstances; then the lips separate sharply, and a short puff or 'flatus' of breath is emitted, like a minute explosion. Hence P is called an 'explodent' consonant. Why the breath does not continue to escape is (1) because the vocal cords close immediately after the puff, or (2) because the process passes on, almost instantaneously, towards another element of speech, as in the words 'pay', 'ply'. What is heard with P might roughly be written 'ph'—the small 'h' indicating the sharp flatus which finishes the consonant, though there are more accurate ways of noting it. It is very important, however, that this 'h' should not be prolonged, or altered in character, as it will be if the general tension of the voice loosens. Then it might turn into a full aspirate, coming through the open glottis, making 'pay' into 'p-hay' with an 'h' as in 'phase'; and 'ply' into 'p-lhy' in a similar way: which would be entirely wrong. Yet, something of this is what happens when voices are over-aspirated, or an excess of 'gush' is present in speech.

It is perfectly obvious that some sort of noise must be made after a consonantal closure of this sort, if we are fully to know what the consonant represents. Merely to shut the lips tells us very little. The complete action is the closure and the little succeeding puff. The lips can of course be made to close with a thud and open with a 'pop', if we use them very energetically. But no basic application of the breath is concerned in this; it is not a movement of speech. Speech movements are carried along by basic, i.e., diaphragmatic breath action; they move onwards in continuous progress, save for such stops as the sense requires. In other words articulation has to be backed up by the breath; it is not at any time sufficiently activated by only the articulatory organs. The tiny 'puff' that we are speaking of may be hardly, or extremely, audible. In most cases, perhaps, we shall not know that it is there. But, when very clear articulation is needed, considerable power must be put into it. This will 'tell' especially when it appears in a final consonant, or before a rest or cæsura of some kind—particularly if it is in the nature of an exclamation, 'Help!' 'Stop!' Then we certainly shall hear the effect; exactly to what extent is a matter for the artist to determine.

We may take it, then, that such flatus should be present in the articulation of all closed consonants, breath or voiced. The only time it can be omitted is when such consonants are doubled, and a very smooth effect is desired; as in this passage:

(1)
If, however, a more individual treatment of the word were wanted, as in

(2)
it would be better to put the lips and mouth into position for the first P, completing the articulation for the second P. In writing it might appear:

$$ha(p) - - - - p^hy$$

In (1) scarcely more breath pressure would be needed for the consonant than for the vowel; in (2) rather more 'fillip' would have to be applied.

The closed breath consonants are:

P
T
Ch ('chest')
K.

All these must be articulated as we have shown.

The remaining breath consonants are

F
Th ('thief')
S
Sh ('she')
H

though H must come in for special attention, later. Unlike the closed consonants (with the exception of Ch),[1] those in the latter group are all 'continuants', i.e., their sound can be prolonged. This, of course, means that while they are sounding, the glottis is open, whereas it is only so momentarily for the closed consonants. The sudden action of the 'closed' variety has to be developed by study. This should not be neglected. Generally speaking, 'mouthing' and such-like evidence of poor technique will be its sign. Rapid successions of all the breath consonants should be practised, as in the following:

This exercise should also be whistled—the breath consonants

[1] Ch is certainly an 'explodent', but it is also of a 'sibilant' nature. Its use, instead of 'tu' must be avoided: thus 'nay-ture', not 'naychure', certainly not 'naycher', for 'nature'; nor must its voiced form be used for 'du': 'verdure', not 'verjure'. Hisses and buzzes, particularly, should never be substituted for other forms of consonants.

have considerable affinity with whistling. Observe, how on the lowest notes, when articulating or whistling the above, the mouth will be shaped as for the vowel 'er' ('purse'), and gradually tend towards the shape for Ee ('peace') as the pitch rises. This leads to

Division of Syllables

How should we divide words, or syllables in a word? The two words, 'It is', are again convenient to give us a clue. The words are clearly separate; should we make them so in singing? Should it be

(a)

with the 't' disconnected from the 'i' in 'is'? or

(b)

with the 't' connected with 'i'? or

(c)

with the 't' put into position on the first note and sounded on the second—making a sort of double 't' of it, though only one is heard?

The last (c) seems the proper way; (b) would be quite wrong; and it would be almost impossible to use (a) unless great emphasis had to be given to the words 'It' or 'is' as in phrases '*It* is the essential' or 'It *is* the fact'. Though we scarcely acknowledge it, the process of (c) is on a par with French 'liaison', as in 'reste ici!' where the 't' would be joined on to the 'i' of the next word, (res(t) – – th 'ici); which avoids the sudden 'pull up' which would otherwise occur, and is used in the interests of fluency.

We thus seem to see that consonants tend to gather round a following vowel, particularly if it is accented. This is especially so with words of several syllables, such as 'hearken' (obviously derivable from 'hear') and 'protected' (from 'protect'); so that if we divided the syllables *in writing* we should have to note them 'heark-en', 'protect-ed'. But we should not sing them in this way.

They would have to be sung either as

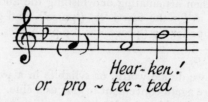

Hear- ken!
or pro ~ tec ~ ted

introducing the flatus after each of the closed consonants; or, better still (as we saw with (c)), in 'it is' as

Hear(k)-ken!
pro (t) ~ tec (t) ~ ted

if we wish to clamp the syllables together in the most secure way.

A vowel acts as the sort of nucleus of a syllable. If it can, it couples up with a preceding consonant, as in the foregoing examples, and collects a final consonant to complete the organism; or a bunch of consonants may be concerned at either end of the syllable.

If we spoke the syllables of the words 'great attraction' separately and very distinctly, we should probably say:

great a-ttrac-tion

but in quick sequence they might easily become

grea(t)-ta(t)-tra(c)-ction

in which the words would be joined, and the syllables made to connect as much as possible. But we could hardly, under any circumstances, say 'grea(t)-t'actions' for 'great actions'—one of the reasons being that the accent falls on the second syllable in 'attraction', but on the first in 'action', so that the latter word would be almost unrecognizable by so doing. Nor must we put in an 'r' after a vowel in order to fill up a possible gap in the sound. Such an urge often introduces an 'r' between two vowels, as in 'Maria(r) is ill'.

If it were necessary to take a breath during such a word as 'trusting', owing to its appearance in a florid passage, or because it had to be sustained for a long time, it might be done by dividing the word between the two central consonants 'trus-ting' or 'trust-ting'; but not 'tru-sting' which would give too much weight to the second syllable, and forego a satisfactory ending for the first syllable.

Even though a double consonant were written, however, as in 'struggling', one would not repeat the 'g', 'strug-gling', but divide the word, 'strug-ling', because of the difficulty of starting the second syllable with 'gl'.

The rule for dividing syllabled words seems to be: 'connect an accented vowel with a preceding consonant, if possible, but avoid doing so with a preceding unaccented vowel.' Thus, 're-ply' ('reply'), but not 'den-y' ('deny'); but if the syllables have to be divided either for an intervening breath, or (what is more likely) for underlying different notes, it would be better, in both cases, to prepare the consonant 're(p)-ply', 'de(n)-ny' at the end of the first syllable, articulating it, i.e., giving it flatus, at the beginning of the second, in the way we have already spoken of

re(p) ~ply
de(n) ~ny

From what has been said, it will be seen that the elements of speech are rightly connected or disconnected according to accent, flow, sense, and—perhaps mainly—the call for beautiful movement in sound. To escape faults by overlapping sounds which should be separated, or, gratuitously, putting in sounds which are out of place, involves a very watchful ear; otherwise mispronunciations and illiteracies may easily occur.

The subject of glides—the movement from consonant to vowel (and vice versa), or from consonant to consonant, is, however, very extensive, and it is impossible thoroughly to explore it here.

Preliminary and Final Articulations

We must not imagine that articulation will look after itself, or that articulation in singing is the same thing as articulation in speech. Reasons for this have already been given.

Preliminary articulations are more likely to be attended to than final articulations, particularly if they precede an accented syllable. A final consonant does not seem to have any dynamic function. Italian does without final consonants, hence the fluidity of the language; hence also, the suavity and grace of Italian song, which is very marked in comparison with the song of other nations. Vowels tend towards music, consonants towards words. The preponderance of vowels and the relative absence of consonants in

Italian has therefore had its effect in securing beauty of sound rather than significance of speech in Italian song; and we turn to English and German, with their abundance of consonants, to give us the alliance of great poetry with music, in what have undoubtedly been the supreme manifestations of song—the Elizabethan Ayre and Romantic Lieder. Once a word is sent on its flight, largely by means of the 'spring' that a consonant (or consonants) give it, it can come to earth quite well upon a vowel and perhaps in some circumstances is all the better for avoiding a bump. But a consonant does give precision to a verbal ending; it rounds off and completes a word. One hardly knows how to stop a vowel, it wants to go on and on, and seems to, even when it has been silenced. So that, formally, there is an advantage in a final consonant; it sets a limit to vowel sound, it gives it shape. Singers often feel a need for a more decided finish than a vowel can supply, and at the end of a note give their voice a 'twist', which serves the purpose of a consonant (*v.* p. 267); also if a word begins with a vowel they are inclined to 'click' it, if they wish to be very exact. This latter treatment should seldom be used with English, but with German it is constantly applied.

Though consonants interfere with restful qualities of expression, they certainly make for vigour. This is shown most of all in the German language, which is capable of such extraordinary emphasis. English, also abounding in consonants, is a gentleman's language beside German—largely owing to the more guttural placing of the latter.[1] This placing favours the deepest expression—one recognizes the superior qualities of German for emotional utterance—and it also gives greater *weight* than the more forward placing of English and the Latin languages; so that, with German, we get both weight and impulse, from the delaying action of its consonants, in outstanding form.

We may possibly be able to hear a consonant close at hand, even if it is feebly articulated; in a large hall it may be quite inaudible unless its sound is exaggerated. There is so little sound in most consonants that we cannot expect it to be otherwise, even allowing for the piercing quality that some consonants have. In quick singing there is no doubt about this. It takes time to make any sound tell, and, when there is very little time, clear articulation can only come from heightened purpose. Even in slow singing there is a danger that final consonants will be poorly sounded: for the preced-

---

[1] People are too often told to speak or sing 'upon the lips', as though that were the only place where the voice should be dealt with. Training on these lines may account for the fact that so many present day actors can hardly be heard. If, like the Germans, we would use our throats more, we might get better results. 'Trippingly upon the tongue' may be all very well, if we want the voice to 'trip', but it will not do if a stronger, sturdier gait is wanted.

ing vowel may easily exhaust the energy that is required for them, and absorb the attention in such a way as to make the singer forget that there is still something to be done before his work is complete. The truth is that vowels and consonants are part and parcel of the same sustained impulse; this we have repeatedly stressed. Consonants are not just stuck on at the beginning or end of a vowel; both are compounded in the sound stream[1] and are of equal, if different, importance. The whole principle of words is contained in this statement; there is no word without a consonant, nor is a vowel sufficient unto itself in matters of speech. If we do not wish to have anything to do with words we can turn to music, though the world of music would be a strange world taken by itself, and it is doubtful whether for long we should be satisfied with it.

One problem, then, is to secure a union of vowels and consonants, in such a way that they strengthen each other. The consonant must give energy to the vowel, the vowel must do the same to the consonant: each one passing on the life that is in it. In matter-of-fact terms, consonants must be well articulated, vowels well sustained.

The following exercises are advisable:

Simple Preliminary Articulations

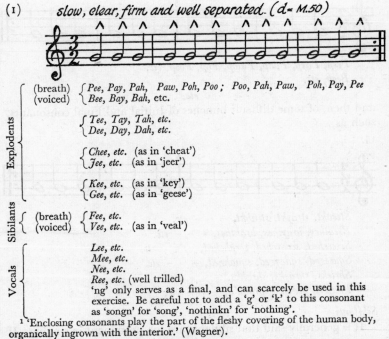

(1) *slow, clear, firm and well separated.* ($\bullet$ = M.50)

Explodents

- (breath) { Pee, Pay, Pah, Paw, Poh, Poo ; Poo, Pah, Paw, Poh, Pay, Pee
- (voiced) { Bee, Bay, Bah, etc.

{ Tee, Tay, Tah, etc.
{ Dee, Day, Dah, etc.

{ Chee, etc. (as in 'cheat')
{ Jee, etc. (as in 'jeer')

{ Kee, etc. (as in 'key')
{ Gee, etc. (as in 'geese')

Sibilants

- (breath) { Fee, etc.
- (voiced) { Vee, etc. (as in 'veal')

Vocals

Lee, etc.
Mee, etc.
Nee, etc.
Ree, etc. (well trilled)
'ng' only serves as a final, and can scarcely be used in this exercise. Be careful not to add a 'g' or 'k' to this consonant as 'songn' for 'song', 'nothinkn' for 'nothing'.

[1] 'Enclosing consonants play the part of the fleshy covering of the human body, organically ingrown with the interior.' (Wagner).

Aspirates { *Hee, etc.*

In this the greatest energy should be applied to the articulations; only *one* sustained breath should be used for every two bars; the breath pressure should be strong and constant, the articulations should not disturb it.

Then make the exercise one of

(2)   Simple Final Articulations

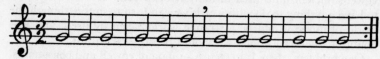

Eep, Ayp, Ahp, Awp, Ohp, Oop; Oop, Ohp, Awp, Ahp, Ayp, Eep
Eeb, etc.
Eet, etc.
Eed, etc.

                              etc.
Then of both Initial and Final Articulations
(3)

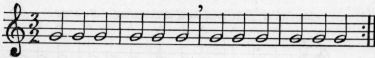

Peep, Payp, Pahp, Pawp, Pop, Poop, etc.
Beep, etc.

                              etc.
and then, of some difficult bunches of Initial and Final consonants, such as
(4)

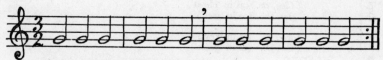

Streakt, straykt, strahkt, − − − etc.
Breathes, braythes, brahthes, − − − etc.
Screeched, scrayched, scrahched, − − − etc.
Squeezed, squayzed, squahzed, − − − etc.
Shrieks, shrayks, shrahks, − − − etc.
Preen'd, prayn'd, prahn'd, − − − etc.

Sibilants

It is generally said that sibilants are too prominent in singing. If they were that would be a good reason for subduing them. But my own experience is that of all consonants they are least likely to be heard; or if this is going too far, that they are often not heard when they should be.[1] Poets, like Tennyson, sometimes take pains 'to smuggle sibilants out of their verse', but when they put them in, as does Sir Walter Raleigh (the Elizabethan, not the Sir Walter quoted on p. 239) in such a phrase as

> *Heav'n, the judicious sharp spectator is,*
> *That sits and marks what we have done amiss*

on in this, from Osme's Song by another Elizabethan, George Darley

> *Fruits delicious*
> *For who wishes*

it is for a purpose, and we must attend to them properly. The flavour of such passages lies precisely in the S's. We either have to ignore the character of the English language, or revel in it.

In our list of sibilants we have included F, V, Th and Dh, though perhaps the term would commonly be taken to refer to the hissing and buzzing sounds of S, Z, Sh, and Zh. All these sounds, however, resemble each other in being produced by a continuous movement of the breath on the lips, teeth or tongue tip. These forward obstructions are present whether the sound is voiced or unvoiced. But, if we wish it, we can distinguish F, V, Th and Dh by calling them 'fricatives' rather than sibilants, as there is some difference in effect—the word explains itself.

A great deal of lisping takes place, though many people would be very vexed if they were told that they lisp. Lisping happens because the lips are loose and the point of the tongue is not held stiff enough to form the narrow channel behind the top teeth through which the breath must be driven. This channel can be altered considerably without losing the character of a hiss. The tongue-tip may be either relatively low or high, giving softer or more piercing qualities of S, largely because of the need of less or more breath pressure. But there comes a point where, by the lifting of the tongue, the breath becomes entirely blocked, or, by its dropping, its stiffness cannot be maintained—then its channelling will fail and the S will go into lisping Th. Nevertheless lisping as a vocal exercise has its uses. It is quite a good plan to try to talk without any movement of the tongue: this is what lisping amounts to. So that, if we lisp, the

---

[1] What may easily happen, though, is that they are *sustained* far too long and so we get the 'hissing' effect that is often complained of. The fault is likely to be much accentuated when many voices are concerned, as in a choir.

looseness of the tongue is assured; the tongue, then, *must* lie inactive, in the pit of the mouth, and we thereby become conscious of the tongue being in this state. Involuntary raising of the tongue is coincident with, and accounts for most of the faults of singing. All kinds of stifled, throttled sounds are due to it. The back of the tongue blocks the passage of the voice, and because of the wrong tightening which goes with it, the throat cannot be opened. Tongue tightness is also responsible for scooping up to high notes. The voice has to struggle upwards; it is, as it were, held by the coat-tails all the time; it can only float upwards through a comparatively loose mechanism of which the loose tongue is especially the sign. Even with perfectly clear speech we can with advantage imagine that we are lisping, so that we may be inclined to loosen the tongue and open the throat as much as we can. From a musical point of view S may be a very unpleasant noise, too sharp and cutting to amalgamate with the general run of vocal sound. But, as we have said, it can be softened;[1] and if it is shortened as well to the greatest possible extent, it is not likely to sound amiss. It is at the end of words that the singer will be inclined to prolong S unduly.

But there is at least as much danger in omitting the articulation of S, as in prolonging it. It needs a certain effort to stiffen the tongue and drive the breath through the very narrow groove by which it has to pass. This effort is not made.

Often a speaker or singer cannot sound frontal articulations, including not only the labials (P, F, etc.) but all the tip-tongued formations (S, T, Ch, etc.). When this is so the fault can be cured almost immediately by *pursing the lips*, after the manner of French speech. In any case, such consonants will not be perfect till this is done, because full resistance to the breath force which generates them can only be secured in this way.

Laziness is the cause of bad articulation; it is so in the case of S.[2]

---

[1] It is interesting to note the natural pronunciation of the two sibilants in our alphabet C and S. We say CEe, but ĕS; the reason being that C is used as a hard, momentary sound, S as a soft continuant. They represent two opposed forms of speech. If we are bent on a sharply-sounded S (i.e. C), we shall have to close the organs of speech completely in order to get sufficient energy for its articulation, after which a vowel easily follows. A vowel cannot be put *before* it without conscious effort. But with a soft S, and indeed all continuants, the throat is not closed at the start, so that a certain amount of vowel tends to escape just as the organs are drawing together for the sound. To put a vowel *after* a soft S is relatively difficult. From which we see that easy speech comes when the vocal organs work harmoniously together in passing from vowel to consonant and vice versa; difficulties of speech when they do not. With the former, movement of the mechanism is reduced to a minimum; with the latter it is accentuated. Thus the words 'cease!', 'west' can be easily spoken; 'set' and 'east' with greater difficulty. Observe also that easy speech tends to be soft-sounding; difficult speech hard-sounding.

[2] 'There is one class of phonetic dangers—which are neither more or less than

S and T, with their correlatives Z and D, are, as we have said, likely to be the least articulate of the consonants—particularly when they end a word,[1] though the afore-mentioned tendency to prolong S has also to be reckoned with. The voiced form of S, which occurs so frequently in plurals, must be carefully watched. More effort is required to 'voice' a consonant than to leave it in its 'breath' form, and instead of Z we are very inclined to say S. But it should also be noted that any consonant whether voiced or unvoiced is easier to sound the nearer it is to the base of the breath; it is the same with vowels. The easiest sounding vowels are undoubtedly Oo and Oh, which are the lowest-lying. Thus if Z is sounded in a very forward way, at about the position of S, it is difficult to vibrate; but if it is taken well back, as though the vocal cords only were concerned, it will vibrate easily and be much more musical in sound. This latter fact should be remembered. All consonants, with the exception of the 'vocals', are apt to be irritating interruptions of the more satisfying vocal sound. It needs all the art of the singer to get over this, and one way certainly is, by taking consonants well back.[2] This reduces the necessary breath pressure, amplifies the sound (such as it is) and lessens friction; so that flated or hissing noises are thereby softened, and their value, as evidence of life (somewhat analogous to the ever-present, though often unperceived, noises of nature) reaches its right proportion.

Plurals of course are sometimes S, sometimes Z, as in 'cats', 'cads' —note how 't' glides most easily on to S, 'd' on to Z—which it is must be made thoroughly clear. In the case of a double S within a word, one had better be omitted; as in the conglomeration of sibilants

HANDEL ~ *Judas Maccabaeus.*

in the pure strains of Jes ~~ se's son

the result of laziness. Every letter requires more or less muscular exertion. There is a manly, sharp and definite articulation, and there is an effeminate, vague and indistinct utterance. The one requires a will, the other is a mere *laisser aller*. The principal cause of phonetic degeneracy in language is when people shrink from the effort of articulating each consonant and vowel; when they attempt to economize their breath and their muscular energy.' Max Muller, *Lectures on the Science of Language*. Quoted also in Piunket Greene's 'Interpretation in Song', which so admirably discusses the more æsthetic aspects of the art of singing.

[1] Final V is also very apt to fail; one seldom hears the full pronunciation of the little word 'of'.

[2] Which is the same thing as giving them more resonance room.

which should be rendered

of Je~~~ se'z son (or perhaps si'z)

The Z will have to be pronounced, to distinguish it from the following S; but as there is so little time in which to do it, it is difficult to deal with. Where two words are concerned the S and Z will generally have to be doubled, as in 'this sheep', 'those zanies'. A little of S goes a long way; but it must be S.

Vocals

These consonants comprise

L
M
N
NG
R

The first (L) is what is called a 'lateral consonant'; the last (R) is a trilled one; the remaining three are nasals. L, in which the tongue presses against the palate, but so that the breath can pass by its sides, is the nearest approach to a vowel sound that there is. But it is still not sufficiently resonant to dwell upon; and, when it forms a syllable by itself, *if it has to be sustained*, we must put a vowel before it, singing

li(t)--tul
da(b)--buld

for 'little', 'dabbled'; never

li(t)--tl
da(b)--bl--d

Being of so vocal a nature, L makes for great liquidity in singing; full advantage should be taken of this. The tongue must of course be adapted to the sound, but it must still be loose enough to allow its sides to flutter slightly. As we have observed elsewhere, the sound of consonants varies according to the tension of the obstacle that they present. This tension modifies the resonance that is behind. Thus, a tight L will have a small, forward resonance, a loose L a large, more backward one. Whether the one or other is appropriate is a matter of circumstance.

The Welsh 'll' should be attempted by singers, since they may be called upon to sing Welsh folk-songs. It is the only Welsh consonant that offers difficulty to the Englishman, and it is usually inadequately overcome. He tends to say Thl (the Th as in 'thin') for the double l, which is by no means the characteristic pronunciation. Ll is a flated form of L, the breath being as it were blown through the L formation. But there is apparently a difference of opinion as to whether the breath passes both sides or only one side of the tongue. Perhaps we can accept the authority of William Salisbury who, in the oldest English book on Welsh pronunciation (1567), quaintly asserts that:

'The Welsh ll is spoken the tongue bowed by a lyttle to the roufe of the mouth, and with that somewhat extendying it selfe betwyxt the fore teeth the lyppes not touching together but leaning open as it were for a wyndow the right wyke of the mouth for to breathe out wyth a thycke aspirated spirite the same ll. But and if ye wyll have the very Welsh sound of thys letter, geue care to a Welshma' when he speaketh culltell, whych betokeneth a knyfe in Englysh: or ellyll a ghoste!'[1]

Here the one-sided form of ll is insisted on, and apparently many Welshmen agree that this is right.

In the 'Fa la' refrains of Elizabethan Ballets a very quick movement of the tongue is needed, also a *staccato* treatment of the notes. L is the principal ingredient. It has to be kept going all the time and a short release and recoil of the tongue will give all the vowel that is wanted. The vowel on the *staccato* notes must be Uh and not the altogether too cumbersome Ah, as written:

The phrase

Fa   la la la la la la la la   la

---

[1] Quoted by Ellis in his *Pronunciation for Singers*. It is too good not to insert here also.

would therefore be sung

Fah luhl luhl luhl luhl luhl luhl luhl luhl lah

with the shortest touch of Uh for each of the quavers, otherwise it
is nothing but a continued L. This sort of thing affords excellent
practice and should be applied to repeated notes, scales, etc.

M, N and NG are predominantly nasal in sound. The importance
of M as an ingredient of 'tone' has been insisted on throughout this
book. A rich, full-sounding M must therefore be gained. This will
largely depend upon the resonance space in the mouth. If the
tongue blocks up the mouth, M will be 'peekit', as the Scots say;
if the tongue is out of the way, as for Ah, the M will be much more
musical. The lips for M must be loose, and barely closed. Much
the same principles as regards resonance apply to N, save that, of
course, the lips are open and that the action of the tongue makes
for a smaller oral cavity than that for M. Whereas for M the
sensation is that of having a big bag of air in the front of the mouth,
for N the attempt must be made to have this bag at the back of the
mouth.

Final N should not be dwelt upon. A vowel will always precede
it; a note should be sustained on this.

Thus[1]

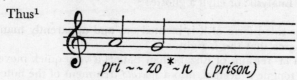

*pri ~~ zo *~n (prison)*

The same applies to M, even though no vowel is written, as in
'prism', which should be sung

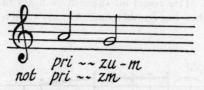

pri ~~ zu - m
not pri ~~ zm

Ng is never an initial in English. It may occur medially between
vowels as in 'singer', or finally as in 'sing'. Be careful not to put
K for G, e.g. 'think' (for 'thing'); nor to add on another G, as
'songguh' for 'song'. Ng is not as resonant as M or N; there is still

---

[1] This vowel may be taken almost as ŭ, if preferred.

more reason than with these latter for not prolonging its sound, and for using the preceding vowel when the syllable Ng has to be sustained.

Thus

R can be trilled (1) with the tip of the tongue, or (2) the uvula. The English do it in the former way; the French, in colloquial speech, the latter way, though, where the purest French is spoken, as at the *Théâtre Français*, uvular 'r' is, or was considered a fault, and disallowed. It is often found difficult to trill an R, but the action for it must be acquired—R is such a constant element in English speech. The 'flapping' or 'fluttering' of the tip of the tongue, which produces it, cannot be effected by voluntary action, only by blowing the breath strongly against a loose tongue, held in almost the same position as for S. This explanation, however, will scarcely serve to secure an R. A better way is to purse the lips and try to say 'purruh' or 'burruh' repeatedly, when the compression of the breath for P or B almost guarantees the required movement of the tongue-tip if *it is kept loose*.

Practise it thus:

(or with B instead of P) till the trill can be continued for the whole of the last note. The first four notes should only have a touch of R, immediately after which the tightly closed lips for P should be resumed.

Finally, it should be possible to sing a whole phrase on R. R should be trilled considerably at the beginning of words (though not as much in English as in Italian). How much will depend upon the word and its emphasis. A very advanced position of the consonant increases the difficulty of trilling it. 'Wretch' may want a good deal of trilling; 'rest', much less.

Final R is said not to occur in English, except as a permissive trill. When R is written at the end of a word, as in 'ear', 'o'er', it is generally replaced by 'murmured' u, which is apt to be a rather indeterminate vowel; but a single 'flutter' or R *may* be added. It is a matter of taste (and time), though anything like a northern 'burr' must be avoided. 'Ear' and 'o'er' are really diphthongs, though they have become single syllable words; their bi-syllable derivation is obvious—'Ee-ur', 'Oh-er'. The last syllable is mostly written as 'er'. When 'ur' is used an e generally follows, as in 'pure' —though this word, of course, includes a triphthong, 'ee-oo-er'. But whether a diphthong or triphthong is involved, the pronunciation of 'er' and 'ur' remains the same, i.e., murmured 'u' or 'ur' (with the slightest of trills). 'Ear' could therefore be 'Ee-u' or 'Ee-ur'; but 'Ee-rie' would have to be 'Ee-u-ri', with **a** trilled R.

'Our', like 'ear' and 'o'er', is, now, compressed into a single syllable. The older writers of English verse treated it as two syllables, 'ow-ur', but it is really a triphthong, with three distinct vowels, 'ow-oo-ur'. Even if we do not sound the R there are still three vowels, 'ow-oo-u', which go to the formation of the word. The vowels in diphthongs and triphthongs should be practised slowly and clearly—'Ee-ur', 'Ow-oo-ur', etc.—as a preparation to their being merged into a monosyllable. If analysed such syllables will be found often to contain very shady specimens of the vowels which should be there.

A slight difference may and often should be made between 'ur' and 'er', as we indicated (on p. 295) in the case of the word 'murder', where, though the vowel in each syllable is substantially the same, a broader version of it seems to be required for the accent.

In ancient usage the final R of 'ur' and 'er' was trilled, so that its omission, now, in favour of simply the vowel u, represents a degeneration, or at least a change of speech; but the fact that R was there does give countenance to a preference for final R, if we care to use it—and some do—though it must be in moderation. It is perhaps better to reserve the use of final R for its occurrence in the last word of a phrase, e.g., 'We sing, and praise Thy power', where, in this particular case, it certainly adds force—there is not much 'power' in an obscure 'ur', which, by itself, gives a weak ending. But, even if final R occurs *at any point* in a strong pronouncement, it may be good to trill it.[1] The speed with which words

[1] An interesting example of this is to be found in Thomas Morley's Ballet 'Fire, fire!' (1597). It begins

and is usually printed thus. But 'Fire' had originally two syllables: 'Fy-er', and,

follow one another, also influences our decision.

A great many, perhaps the majority, of the faults of speech concern the letter R. It is only after Ee, Ay, Oh, Oo (or their short vowel equivalents) that we can drop R in favour of murmured u. After Ah or Aw we must certainly pronounce it, being careful not to say 'Ah' for 'Are', 'Aht' for 'Art', 'Waw' for 'War', etc. Nor must we omit the R in such final combinations as 'ard', 'erd', saying 'sluggahd' for 'sluggard', 'rewawd' for 'reward', 'shepahd' for 'shepherd'. 'Ard' is nearly always pronounced 'erd', but whether it is the one (as in 'race-card') or the other (as in the foregoing words) the R is likely to be left out and Ah called in to take the place of the 'ar' or 'er'. This has already been referred to in the pronunciation of 'brother', often heard as 'brothah', 'brothaw', or even 'brothŏ', which latter is the acme of affectation.[1] The usual pronunciation of 'brother' is 'bru-thu' (more correctly written 'bru-dhu') but a final R *is* allowed—a single curl of the tongue suffices in this latter case.

We must not put in an R to bridge over two vowels, an example of this fault was given in the phrase 'Maria(r) is ill'; though when it occurs in its own right as in 'For ever' the R *may* be joined to the following vowel—but not in an exaggerated way. If we do not do this, an unpleasant 'hiatus' or gap occurs; which seems pedantic and wrong. From which it will be seen that R has considerable importance both in its use and abuse.

Though not exactly connected with R, here is perhaps the place to refer to the word 'the' which may have two different pronunciations of the vowel concerned, one of which is the same as the vowel in 'ur' or 'er'. 'The' may be pronounced either as 'Thee' (or perhaps 'Thi'), or as 'Thu' (very like the last syllable of 'brother'). Foreigners find it difficult to know when to use the one or other

it is necessary so to sing it; also strongly to trill the 'r' (which represents the second syllable) if the requisite excitement is to be maintained. 'Fi u' would be absurd. The passage should really be noted

Fy-er, fy~~~~ er my heart!

[1] I find that I have a tendency, myself, to put Aw for Oh (and even Oo) in many words, e.g. 'pawt' for 'pohrt' ('port') 'shawrly' for 'shoorly' ('surely') a very pregnant word in the Bible. This is probably because a more lilting sonority is obtained with Aw. On the other hand, Aw is sometimes rightly used for Oh: 'Lohrd' '(Lord)' is not generally distinguished from 'Lawd' ('Laud') for instance—both words can be pronounced 'Lawd', though a touch of R in 'Lord' makes it more complete.

pronunciation; or to understand why in

the first 'the' is practically 'thee', the second 'thu'. Yet these
pronunciations come quite naturally, the reason being that the
voice does not like shifting from back to front, or vice versa, when
it can avoid it. 'Eye' in 'eyes' is a forward sound, therefore the
voice prefers a forward 'the' before it; 'bl' in 'blind' is a comparatively backward consonantal combination so that the 'the' which
precedes it is best taken in its backward form.[1] It will be found that
such vowel modification continually occurs in speech, in obedience
to the foregoing principle. One can scarcely pin any vowel down
to an exact pronunciation, since circumstances tend so much to
alter it.

The Aspirate

By this term we usually understand the consonant H, which is
produced by breath being driven through the open glottis; i.e., the
opening between the vocal cords when they are not tightly approximated. Under certain conditions of tension we hear this
process taking place; there is an audible emission of unvoiced
breath. But breath sounds need not be blown from the lungs; they
can come from the mouth only, without any diaphragmatic movement, as the consonant Ch ('cheese') or the 'flatus' which happens
with P or T. Nevertheless, these aspirates are so short-lived that
they are of secondary importance. The more recognized form of
aspirate is H, for only H will give a continuous flow of breath,
either in its own right, or by way of what we know as the breath
consonants F, S, Sh,[2] etc. It is true that the output and intake of
breath can be made audible. Even in ordinary respiration, if it is
a little quicker or more energetic than usual, we can hear the
friction of the air against various parts of the vocal structure—
particularly at the larynx as it goes in and out. But as—unlike an
Eastern pipe instrument, which is played by *sucking* the air through
it—the voice does not use inhalation for the purposes of tone: we
must rule out inward aspirating and rely only on the outward
aspirate for vocal sound, though audible breath-taking—a sort of

---

[1] Smoothness is a main sign of good speech; difficult changes of vocal position
being negotiated in such a way that they pass unnoticed.
[2] Which is the sound that Ch has when it is sustained.

'catch' in the voice, difficult to explain—may be occasionally fitting and of dramatic effect in singing. H, then, is the sound that we get when breath is expelled through the glottis without any resultant 'tone', and when it does not meet with any specially-placed obstacle on its way to the outer air.

But there are great differences of quality in H, just as there are with vowels, and, indeed, all other kinds of vocal sound. These qualities are the qualities of 'whispered' vowels. In passing through the mouth H disturbs the air which is there. This air is always tuned to some resonantal note, according as the mouth is shaped for one or other of the vowels, and the aspirate takes on both the quality of the vowel and the note that is associated with it (*v.* p. 145). What the vowel and the note is, is decided by tension. H, therefore, has a note, and by this very fact, a quality; and both note and quality may vary a great deal. We have just said that the pitch and quality of H are decided by tension. As a corollary, the power of sustaining H is decided in the same way. It is important to work this out, as it shows us why some vowels are more capable of *sostenuto* than others, and how at least one test of a good vowel is whether it will sustain.

With ordinary breathing, in which the laryngeal mechanism is almost entirely relaxed, both inspiration and expiration are of short duration. The breath does not 'last', it 'goes' at once. One of the aims of singing is to draw in breath as quickly as possible, but to let it out, or rather drive it out, as slowly as possible. This is why ordinary breathing will not do for singing; it is neither quick enough in inspiratory action, nor slow enough in expiratory. This is accounted for by the relaxed conditions which accompany it. It is not till they have been tightened up that the requisite control is obtained. The vowel that we get with ordinary breathing is the neutral vowel Uh of which we have so often spoken. It is precisely when the 'vocal' mechanism is in position for this vowel, *in its wrong state*, that we cannot sustain H. The channel through which the breath has to pass is then too loose and flat to give any control, it must be relatively tight and vertical before that can happen. Even so, the cavity of Uh cannot be tightened a great deal, so that, with it, the breath is emitted too freely. It is not till we get to the far tighter cavity of Aw that we can do what we like with H, making it last almost as long as a vowel. We thus see that the control of H is practically the same thing as the control of tone, and it is not surprising, since it is by the breath that the voice is energized. If there is an excess of aspirate, tone will be wasted; if there is an insufficiency it will be hard.

Nevertheless we do not want the same sort of tone all the time.

345

There is room for the greatest variety. Tone is but voiced breath, and the breath may permeate it in varied degree.[1] The more free the breath stream, the looser and softer will be the tone; the more controlled, the tighter and harder. Some vowels are of a more aspirated nature than others: Oh than Ay for instance. We should never think of writing an h after Ay, but we do so in the case of Oh. It follows that Oh is a relatively soft vowel, Ay relatively hard.

But however free a vowel is, it must be controlled by some degree of inward tension at the larynx and of the vocal instrument as a whole: identically the same process as that of controlling H.

Much or little breath can be allowed through the vocal cords. If too much, it will be quickly expended; but, as the vocal cords are gradually approximated, so will breath be economized. With a whispered vowel, breath is driven through the cavity of that vowel with greater freedom than it could if the aspirate were voiced—voice puts still more control upon the breath. But, as we have seen, the shaping of a cavity does affect breath control, i.e., the control of H, though the supreme measure of control does not come till the glottis is sufficiently closed to produce tone without any suspicion of aspirate. Then the 'stop' of the breath is complete, or as complete as it can be, without denying the breath passage altogether. We can of course expel the breath, with the glottis wide open, through the semblance of a vowel cavity, i.e., form the cavity to *a certain extent*, independently of breath action, and then simply blow through it; but this represents scarcely more than blowing through the position of neutral Uh. With it we do not hear the very characteristic friction—a sort of cartilaginous sound—that we get when vowels are properly shaped with the requisite degree of tension. And—this is the point—no control of the breath is possible under these conditions; the breath comes out with a rush, it cannot be sustained or gradually emitted. If, however, we use a *fully formed* cavity—say that of Ah or Aw—we shall find that this *does* act as a control of the breath, but that, if we relax the cavity, the breath will escape.

A vital point in voice production is, therefore, the adequate shaping of the vowel cavities by means of the necessary tension. Again we must say 'tension is control', and that the various factors in voice production are related and interdependent.

What we call H is an audible sound; this inevitably turns it into a distinct consonant. But breath may emerge inaudibly, or with only the slightest of sound; so that it can hardly be called H. When

---

[1] 'Voice' is only *added to* breath sound; it has nothing to do with vowel formation. Vowels can be whispered or voiced. They remain just the same in either case. So that a good deal of vocal practice can be done by whispering; quite apart from singing.

we 'touch' a note there is scarcely any sign of aspirate with it, or there should not be. It is the perfectly smooth passage from breath into sound that constitutes 'touch'. But, as we know, H may burst through the closed glottis with a sort of cough ('the *coup de glotte*') ; a much more energetic proceeding. These are extreme forms of initial aspirate, with, of course, intermediate variations. Similarly breath may be audible at the end of a vowel, or it may be heard more or less gently, as with a sigh of 'Ah', or be roughly added. In short, consonants as well as vowels are subject to a relatively quiet or vehement treatment. The words 'horrid!' or 'halt!' would have quite a different initial aspirate from that in the word 'happy'. These matters have been dealt with under attack and release (pp. 259-72).

An important form of aspirate—it must be accredited as such, though it is not strictly H—is the audible passage of breath through almost closed lips. This sound is now written 'wh', as in 'which', 'while', 'whistle', etc.; but the ancient orthography was 'hw', indicating a true aspirate. Its derivation is Anglo-Saxon—the original spelling of the afore-mentioned words was 'hwich', hwile', 'hwistle'. Since the Norman Conquest there has always been a tendency to drop this initial H, from there being no H in French, the language of the ruling race. But the full pronunciation of 'hw', should be insisted on, as it is a virile sound; moreover, if we do not pronounce it, there is nothing to show the difference between 'which' and 'witch', or 'while' and 'wile', etc. When H begins a written word it should nearly always be pronounced. There are a few exceptions ('hour', 'honour', etc.) ; but in a general way to leave out initial H puts a very bad mark against the speaker's upbringing. More than this, the singer should make the most of H and its derivative flated sounds ('hw', 'ph', etc.) as, in a very special way, they all tend to loosen and ease the voice; the impulse that they supply is so free that it is an invaluable aid to good production.

The aspirate enters very largely into 'expression'. It shows the singer's attitude—whether he is hard or soft-hearted, sensitive or unfeeling; by its absence or presence it defines emotional situations, determines brilliant or subdued colouring; links up, in short, with almost every aspect of technical control, being part and parcel of all vocal sound. It is therefore not a mere consonant, one item in the material of song; 'Mother of Song' would be a more apt designation.

We must also recognize that there is much more expression in an aspirated (or breath) sound than in firm sound. The fact of having to show emotion without sound gives the communication an intensity that diminishes with the increase of audible vibration. Schubert's

'Death and the Maiden' shows this very clearly. When the maiden perceives the figure of Death, after his silent approach, she draws back in an agony of fear, scarcely able to question his errand:

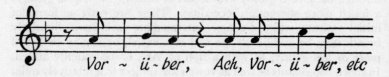

If her words are sung with full *timbrée* tone (no matter how softly) the result will be as nothing, wholly without significance; in proportion as they are animated with breath so will they gain in rightness of effect.

Nevertheless, although the aspirate is so important—in a large measure it determines quality of tone—it is the amount of it that, on the other hand, leads to so many faults in singing. We can all hear them when a voice is 'breathy'. It is precisely because it is so that its control is defective. The valvular mechanism is not functioning properly. Hard tone, which is almost synonymous with 'tone' as such, is not aspirated—one has almost entirely to avoid aspiration in order to get it. An aspirated tone is bound to be a soft tone, or at any rate a tone lacking in timbre and brilliancy. A 'breathy' sound, of course, is essentially ineffective and must not be confused with true *mezza voce* which in its own way is full of 'tone' because considerable tension is attached to it. A singer will often try to get tone by forcing the breath against what is insufficient resistance at the vocal cords. The result is bound to be bad. The cure for this, and much else, may lie merely in the attempt to eliminate breathiness; in fact, all breath that does not convert into intensified tone.

Breath sound is essentially 'personal' sound; the firmer types of sound have a more 'objective' purpose.

Chapter 7

INTONATION

THE singer shows his art as much by tune as by tone. He must become *intonation conscious*. Most singers scarcely give it a thought, because up to a point they can get along fairly well with very little trouble; but their intonation will never be really admirable unless it is a matter of critical concern. An artist should be conscious of everything he does (or doesn't do). However his emotions may be engaged, his brain, as the controlling agent, should be 'packed in ice', as Lord Kitchener's was said to be during his Sudanese campaign. The artist calculates his effects quite coldly, though he may contemplate them with considerable feeling.

There is nothing more lovely and satisfying than a perfectly tuned chord; it is a gem in itself.

A soloist can get away with quite faulty work; it is not till notes are put together in chords that errors of intonation strike to the full. Perhaps it is too much to say that 'For this, for everything, we are out of tune', but the fetish that singers sing naturally in tune must be exploded. That theirs is the perfect untempered scale of sound which they reach by a sort of instinctive propriety is only a sort of half truth. Most singers do *not* sing in tune, though perhaps they find it easier to approximate to it than do instrumentalists, like string players, who also have to make their own pitch. A beginner in singing will produce much better intonation than a beginner on the violin for instance. It is not till much later in his career that the latter can be trusted to please our ears with the right 'concordance of sweet sound'.

A choir, by some curious power of combination, will often seem to sing in tune—by no means always; but take a single singer from each part and they will seldom be above reproach as regards the intonation of even a major chord, or anything else.

As we have implied, intonation is a fine art; it is only secured after great pains and an acute training of the ear, which generally needs to be assisted by an outside critic who is himself capable of detecting impurities of pitch. As well ask a pianoforte tuner at once to be master of the subtleties of his profession, as to expect an untrained singer or player to know what is wrong when they attempt to tune *their* instrument. Here again, it is only in the *doing*, in the conscious struggle for right adjustment, that perception comes.

349

We have said elsewhere that good tune is a matter of good resonance; if this is not achieved notes *cannot* be sung in tune.

Though good intonation needs training of the ear, it is perhaps not so much a matter of a good ear as of a good mechanism. The fact of imagining a perfectly pitched note by no means guarantees its production; a good ear may be entirely unsuspected in the results that are actually achieved. Many think, quite honestly, that they are performing in tune; it is for others to tell them, with equal candour, that they are not.

It is absolutely necessary to be able to 'keep pitch', i.e., to leave off at the same pitch at which we began, a thing much more easily accomplished by children than by adults who so often have developed bad vocal habits. But, even if achieved, this does not guarantee the position in detail. We may end up on the right note and yet, during the course of our wanderings, pitch notes badly. Some notes may be consistently out of tune—through faulty hold or resonance—though the general pitch may be sustained. At the extremes of the voice intonation is often bad. Strangely enough, with men especially, low notes (which are relatively easy to sing as compared with high notes) often tend to be out of tune; they will go flat. This is owing to a lack of inward tension; the tone spreads and disintegrates; it is not kept up by the compressed 'hold' that we have often referred to. High notes also are a danger. With them the need for increased tension may produce shrillness, sharpness, screeching,[1] and the like from a too-closed throat; or, on the other hand, flatness will occur from sheer inability to use sufficient physical tension. These faults, which are matters of poor technique, are to be disposed of by singing in the proper way.

The 'proper way' will also include the capacity for *sostenuto*. If a note is imperfectly 'held' it will sag in pitch. Any physical condition —often the outcome of being tired, or of a close or stuffy room—in which the body is not up to its job, will almost certainly react un-favourably upon the intonation; for much the same reason that a note on the piano tends to fall in pitch after it is struck, because the disturbing force which caused the string to vibrate is not continued. Piano tone lacks the power of a possible *crescendo*; if the voice also does it cannot be kept up.

But there are other faults of intonation connected with the direct-ing ear rather than with the use of the instrument.

[1] Screeching, or something like it, is a very common fault. Modern composers (Beethoven, Wagner and others) have often used the voice so brutally that it is almost impossible to deal with it by pleasing means. Bad singing, of course, is also responsible. We feel, unless we are tonally demoralized, that such singing is wrong; and it is wrong because it suggests pain and not pleasure. It is not absurd to suppose that art should please.

What we call perfect tuning refers to the intervals which are selected: intervals which we seem to select naturally, though in practice by no means always sing them. The reason for this selection is probably, indeed assuredly, that the mind is prone to deal with the simplest mathematical relations if it can, rather than with difficult ones. We instinctively choose the simple relations as the basis of our tonal operations, or, in other words, for our 'scale' (*v.* also p. 143): the perfect fifth 3:2, the perfect fourth 4:3, the major second 9:8, the major sixth 5:3. These simple relations give us an important difference between the major and the minor second; in the key of C, between what we are accustomed to call the full tones

of and This differ-

ence should be recognized in actual practice. The interval C to D (major tone) should be slightly larger than the interval D to E (minor tone), and relatively so for all scales. The ear should be able to detect this difference and it should be carefully put into effect in singing. This is one source of bad intonation. Another source is the half tones between the 3rd and 4th, and 7th and 8th degrees of the scale and

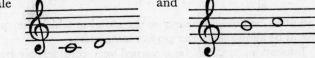

which are seldom sung small enough particularly in descending passages. Going up, the thrusting character of the 3rd and 7th degrees will probably ensure the right pitch. A good practical rule of intonation is: sing your intervals large going up and small coming down; this tends to preserve the general pitch. But of course the thing is to sing in tune and not to rely upon 'tips' of this sort.

The truth is that there are pitfalls at all times, whether the notes ascend or descend. It may even be that the greater difficulty will be found in ascending: for, though it is usual to *over*-tighten the mechanism as the voice rises, it is also quite common for the singer to fail in sufficient tension on high notes, with flattening as a result. Insufficient tension on low notes has already been commented on with respect to pitch. Tension and pitch go together, as do tension and tone quality. Properly applied tension is the controlling factor in all aspects of performance.

Although perfect tuning is to be commended, it by no means follows that it is always to be practised, any more than is a perfectly pure vowel. It will depend upon the kind of song that we have to deal with. The purest intervals lack life and ring, especially those of the perfect fourth and fifth, if they are tuned to their exact mathematical ratio. For acoustical reasons the clash of overtones is somewhat missing from them; they are inclined to hollowness, just as flute tone is. If, therefore, a bright aspect has to be given to the music, a *slight* imperfection of tuning will probably assure it; just as equal temperament, with its slightly false intervals, livens up the general effect. But if a sombre colouring is wanted, then more perfect intervals will tend that way.

Expressive tuning continually invites a modification or adjustment of perfect pitch. Flat descending notes, particularly of a chromatic nature, such as

and sharp ascending notes, such as

can often be brought nearer to the sound to which they point than would be allowable under perfect intonation.

Intonation, too, will be governed very considerably by whether the emphasis is placed upon harmonic or melodic elements. Subordinate harmonies must conform to more rigid rule than is required of a dominating melody. If a melody is to stand out, it may be quite an artistic proceeding to indicate it by individualities of pitch as well as of power and colour. Perfect tuning and expressive tuning may be often at variance; yet underneath expressive tuning must be the power of strict conformity, just as underneath *rubato* must be the power of strict time. Without a perfect norm to which to relate it, all departure therefrom loses its significance. The norm pitch must be clearly apparent, otherwise all is chaos.

It is obvious, however, that very little latitude can be allowed for the niceties of 'expressive' intonation. A little sharpening or flattening of a note may improve its pitch flavour, but if we are aware that it is sharp or flat the virtue of the treatment is lost. It must always appear to be in the tonal picture, in spite of variation.

Involuntary sharpness and flatness are both due to lack of laryngeal tensing. If the voice is relaxed too much, that is, if it has insufficient grip and hold at the larynx—it will fall into the neutral vowel (Uh) position, and, at its worst go flat, simply because relaxation is not balanced by tension.[1] This will apply particularly to the naturally bright-toned vowels, Ee, Ay, Ah, Aw, etc. The dull-toned vowels, Oh and Oo, etc., will go sharp if they are not firmed up by tension, i.e., if they are not 'voiced' properly. Any sort of a hoot will tend to sharpen.

It is worth noting that dull tone, if contrasted with bright, will appear flat. Harmonies, therefore, should be dealt with by much the same sort of tone quality if they are to seem in tune. This also is a reason for a uniform tone of voice in phrasing. If different *shades* of colour are used consecutively it may well give the idea of bad intonation.

---

[1] I find that in my own teaching I am apt, for a period, to over-stress tension, and then to over-stress relaxation; whereas the middle way should always be adopted; tension balanced by relaxation and vice versa—no single principle should be run to death.

It is the same in performance. For certain songs, soft, relatively dull tone is appropriate; for others, hard, brilliant tone. If only one type of tone is practised, the singer will never be a 'compleat singer'. Vocal control is a difficult matter. The singer's craft is always up against a head wind. Unless he tacks to and fro across it, approaching his objective from different directions in turn, he will sooner or later founder upon the soft shoals of relaxation, or the hard rocks of tension.

Chapter 8

THE INSTRUMENTAL SIDE OF SINGING

THE instrumental side of singing has two main aspects: (1) *bel canto*, and (2) *fioritura*. *Bel canto* is the perfect sustaining of the vocal line in its melodious sense; quite apart from the words, though words convey the sound. It is the appeal of musical rather than verbal beauty; of melody, in short.

In much song, particularly song of the older Italian type, in which Handel is included and also to a large extent even the Germanic Bach, the words could be dispensed with and the result remain musically satisfying. The solo part could be played upon an instrument, as we often hear in the case of Handel's famous *Largo*—originally the contralto aria 'Ombra mai fu'—which is as apt for a violin as for a voice, scarcely to be distinguished in nature from Bach's almost equally famous instrumental 'Air on the G String'.

It is perhaps too much to say that in the Handel aria the words are of no account whatsoever, at least they are in accord with the spirit of the music; but it is clear that they are not indispensable to an elucidation of the *form* of the music, which may be said to be the test of true song. In such song words and music are so fused that the rhythm, shape and accent of both are faithfully paralleled, or as nearly so as may be. This happens in plain-song, recitative and most prose forms of song.

The nearer song approaches an Air in definite metrical structure, the more it becomes self-supporting as *music*. But, by the very fact of its musical significance it places an obligation of *instrumental* effectiveness upon the singer. He can 'get away' with nothing less than sheerly beautiful melodic expression, and this will be found to consist largely in the power of perfect *legato*, much as a violinist gathers a phrase of notes under a single impulse of the bow. It is the high-water mark of fine singing, of *bel canto*; which holds the attention of the listener because the notes are held.

The difficulty of *legato* has already been stressed. Good instrumental players always reproach singers for their lack of *sostenuto*, or *legato*, which is the same thing. Where a mass of singers is concerned the situation is often guaranteed by a general effort: one singer holds the sound, when another fails to do so. But with solo voices (either singly, or in combination), lack of *legato* is usually quite obvious. The harmony, as adumbrated by a vocal quartet,

354

for instance, is hardly ever to be compared to that by a quartet, say, of strings. In the case of singing there is, of course, some excuse. Singing is not continuous vowelling, as instrumental sound may be said to be. With words, consonants intervene to break up the vocal line. But, even so, *legato* is possible, or at any rate the illusion of *legato*, in which notes are dovetailed rather than merely brought into contact. The art of *legato* consists in a 'run through' of sound, representing the continuity of an idea; *portamento*, too, is almost bound to be involved, if there are to be no holes or hiatuses.

The second aspect of the instrumental side of singing is that of *fioritura*, or florid treatment. It is the art of agility as applied to vocal notes. Singers, particularly at the present day when this art is not cultivated to the same extent as in the past, are usually deficient in florid technique. One has only to listen to a performance of the *Messiah* to substantiate this statement. Basses lollop along the triplets in 'Why do the nations':

The first triplet of notes in each group of six may be audible; the last three notes seldom are. Or, in the tenor air, 'He shall break them', the runs on 'like a potter's vessel' are seldom staunchly delivered or hammered home at the required speed; the 'rod of iron' is missing. 'Rejoice greatly', though usually more in the soprano grasp as regards definition, is generally sung so lightly that it fails utterly in 'grand style'. To secure speed *and* force is perhaps as difficult as to secure a good *legato*. But it can and should be accomplished by the finished singer. The splendour of a clear, *weighty* run is hardly attempted nowadays. The tremendous physical effort that is needed perhaps accounts for this (*v.* p. 65), but failure has to be chronicled unless this effort is surmounted.

The singer has indeed much to contend with in gaining an adequate technique. He has to be a good instrumentalist with his voice, to be as capable of power, speed and *sostenuto* as the instrumental player; and as well he has problems of verbal understanding and tone colouring that the instrumental player is quite absolved from. He must, in short, be an actor and an instrumentalist rolled into one.

Something should be said about the *raison d'être* of florid passages. They occur even in the relatively austere forms of plain-song. When words fail to express elation of spirit to the full, music alone is drawn upon to supply her special powers. Thus, when the heart o'erflows with joy to such an extent that the cramping element of words needs to be abandoned, we get the 'jubilus' in plain-song, which is a word-less musical phrase of florid character, soaring and falling as the spirit moves. These 'jubilations' or melismas are perhaps the finest examples of *fioritura*, since they are utterly melodious, as free as air, and never degenerate into an unmeaning display of scales or arpeggios.

But, at its best, even later floridity is *expressive*. It must not be sneeringly dismissed as mere formalism, the relic of an insensitive age. Purcell and Bach decorate their melody in terms of the utmost beauty. What could be more apt than this

with its final upsurge of exuberance; and the less subtle sequential 'runs' of Handel have a sturdy value all their own. In 'Why do the nations', for instance, the clash and turmoil of opposing peoples is driven home with tremendous force in the florid sections; they supply, as it were, a musical commentary to the situation. The objective statement is in the words, the heart of the matter is in the musical 'divisions'; this is the function of *fioritura*. But vigour need not always dominate; grace can play its part. *Fioritura*, in fact, can be the vehicle of any emotion. Even Handel (following the poet's thought) asks for melancholy in the bird song from *Il Penseroso*.

Two technical points should be mentioned:

When notes pass before us very quickly they are apt not to register, unless clearly illuminated. In other words, bright tone is generally applicable to rapid passages, though softer shadings may be re-quired.

Also, it needs skill to get sound out of a very short note; a note may be too short to be heard.

Chapter 9

VERBAL FLOW

STACCATO 'seasons' singing; *legato* is the staple fare. The way in which words follow one another, whether they are badly or well joined, and more than this, whether they are part of the same impulse of sound, is therefore of primary importance.

It is not so difficult to link notes; it is very difficult to link words. Consonants come in to disturb the vowel flow; even changes of vowel do. When singing a phrase upon a single vowel—Ah or what not—the same formation of the voice throughout offers little disturbing feature of readjustment. With a change of vowel there is a change of formation in which all the resonating cavities are concerned—mouth, neck, nose—and to get a smooth ordering of this change needs skill. The change from Oo to Ee, for instance, involves a complete *volte face* of the 'instrument', from a resonance which gives a relatively subdued quality, to one the quality of which is bright and blaring. At any rate, these contradictory qualities are likely to be stressed if the vowels are allowed to sound as they please, according to their natural habit, without artificial modification. Art is needed to unify the one with the other, roughly achieved by getting the same neck adjustments; then they will run together, driven as it were by the same hand, or at least flow on in sequence without hitch.

The addition of consonants, in words, further complicates the situation, for there is often a complete stop to the sound when a consonant comes; at other times some worrying alteration of its course. One consonant, say T, will be articulated in the front of the mouth, another, say K, at the back; or the tongue will be shaped for S and have to be reshaped for L. All this has to be done with ease and speed of movement, before there can be anything like satisfactory continuity.

Nevertheless, in the main, the problem resolves itself into continuity of *vowel* sound. If this is guaranteed, the consonants will not unduly interfere with verbal flow.

What we have to do then, is to try to deal with every vowel in much the same place, allowing as little shifting as possible of the general position of the voice. The voice may be placed to the fore or at the back; wherever it is, all vowels must concur in the positioning. The forward position of an unmodified Ee may determine that of the other vowels. In this case there will be little neck resonance,

357

and the tone of every vowel will be relatively bright; or the backward position of Oo may dominate, when the tone will be less luminous.

The important point to note here, however, is that the bright Ee position will make the movement of the sound difficult; there will be a sort of forced progress, in which the steps will be taken almost by fits and starts. With the duller Oo position sound will be smooth, and its outpouring attended with little or no strain.

The effect of vocal placing upon the egress of the voice is much discussed throughout this book, so at the moment we need not pursue the matter. A relatively backward position of the voice may therefore be taken as a *sine qua non* if we wish to give the best, or indeed, anything like an adequate illustration of verbal flow. It amounts to an open throat, used, as far as possible, with every kind of vocal 'sound'. Consonants as well as vowels profit by the 'undertone' that the open throat affords; even frontal consonants can be coupled with it. Thus, a *reservoir* of sound is supplied, which is always there to be drawn upon. Sound has not to be freshly fabricated for each element of speech. It waits for release, it does not press for it; the material is immediately at hand wherewith to model vowels and consonants in an effortless way.

It is scarcely necessary to add that beautiful speech has a sort of enveloping quality, as of a soft garment. It is not hammered home, or roughly thrown at the listeners—on occasion it may have to be, but we soon get tired of a disconnected, 'snappy' style. Verbal ideas are characterized by a linking, not a breaking up of words; while the nature of music is towards union, harmony, not separateness. We can scarcely conceive of a *staccato* 'melody'. The cumulative effect of connected sound, such as the wind and sea give us, is nearly always what is wanted. That alone fills the ear, and towards it music seems ever to strive.

To get an easy flow of words at any pitch and speed is therefore of great importance. Beauty of sound and movement derives largely from it. Spoken words tend to liquefy by means of diphthongs, glides and such like *portamento* effects, which counteract, smooth over, the separating influence of consonants.

In speaking we generally say what we have to say with a minimum of effort. We must aim at this in singing. It is when the tongue stiffens, the jaw is more or less locked, etc., that the trouble begins; and it is very apt to begin when the voice is required to develop from speech into song, with its artificial prolongation of the vowels and its more intense articulation of the consonants. Speech seldom stays upon a fixed note, though the best speech preserves a general level of pitch, suited to its subject. Poor speech has very little hold of anything like sustained pitch; good speech undoubtedly has—it is musically inclined, though it never becomes 'sing-song'. This indefiniteness stimulates an easy progress of sound, and this must be preserved as far as possible when definite notes and time values are imposed upon the spoken word.

Psalmody offers the best line of approach to what we are in search of. There is nothing like it to develop suppleness of speech in song. We should do a great deal of this sort of practice, singing the Psalms, in Latin preferably, and to the Gregorian Tones; as in the following to the 7th Tone:

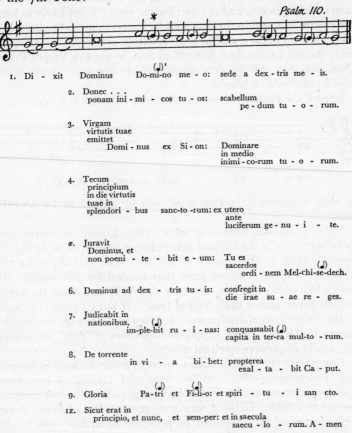

Psalm 110.

1. Di - xit Dominus Do-mi-no me - o: sede a dex - tris me - is.

2. Donec . . . ponam ini - mi - cos tu - os: scabellum
     pe - dum tu - o - rum.

3. Virgam
    virtutis tuae
    emittet
    Domi - nus ex Si - on: Dominare
     in medio
     inimi - co-rum tu - o - rum.

4. Tecum
    principium
    in die virtutis
    tuae in
    splendori - bus sanc-to -rum: ex utero
     ante
     luciferum ge - nu - i - te.

5. Juravit
    Dominus, et
    non poeni - te - bit e - um: Tu es
     sacerdos
     ordi - nem Mel-chi-se-dech.

6. Dominus ad dex - tris tu - is: confregit in
     die irae su - ae re - ges.

7. Judicabit in
    nationibus,
    im-ple-bit ru - i - nas: conquassabit
     capita in ter-ra mul-to - rum.

8. De torrente
    in vi - a bi - bet: propterea
     exal - ta - bit Ca - put.

9. Gloria Pa-tri et Fi-li-o: et spiri - tu - i san cto.

12. Sicut erat in
     principio, et nunc, et sem-per: et in saecula
     saecu - lo - rum. A - men

¹ The crotchets are interpolated for the extra syllables. The above is written in ordinary notes but the singer should learn the old Plain Song notation; This, however, is not difficult. Two little books—Parts 1 and 2 of *Plain Song for Schools* (Rushworth and Dreaper, Liverpool)—are strongly to be recommended as giving the student plenty of material for practice; telling him all that he needs to know about the subject.

Or we may sing the Psalms in English, to Gregorians, using a good Psalter, preferably the one edited by Dr. J. H. Arnold (Novello).

Latin, however, specially lends itself to fluency, and to rich, full vowelling, so that the singer will be wise to become thoroughly acquainted with the sounds of the language, even if he cannot quite grasp the sense. Its influence on his voice will be wholly advantageous, while plain-song opens up such wonderful musical experience, that he is bound to be glad if he decides to explore it.

At first he will find it hard to sing the words as they should be sung: fairly quickly, and *at sight*: for the singer is not likely to know the Psalms in Latin in the way that he knows them in English. If he takes all the Psalms it *will* be sight reading, practically speaking, for him; though he can limit himself, at first, to the five Vesper Psalms (Nos. 109–113) till he gets accustomed to the style. Some expert help is, of course, advisable.

Even if the Psalms are sung to this very simple formula:

Dixit Dominus
Domino   me-o: sede a dextris me-is.

or only monotoned, 'verbal flow' will be gained as by no other means.

There is another form of quick wording, known as 'patter' often to be met with in the Gilbert and Sullivan operas, or as in Figaro's opening song in the Barber of Seville. The technique for this, however, is quite different from that needed for plain-song. It is associated with energetic, not easy delivery; and must be termed 'verbal drive' rather than 'verbal flow'. It has its place, of course, in the singer's vocal equipment—it is a very necessary accomplishment—but it can never supply the qualities of 'flow', or produce any really impressive spiritual effect.

Comparatively toneless voices—that is, voices lacking in intensity and penetration—often exhibit delightful facility of movement. Children, for instance, seem able to sing with a fluency generally denied to adults. Gaining tone may mean a loss of flow. A very high degree of art is needed to preserve an artless aspect. Artlessness naturally associates with ease; ease with relatively slight power. Directly power is developed, tightness begins to operate, and it is very difficult to overcome its possibly adverse influence. Bright voices, which reflect higher states of tension than dull voices, will be far less likely than their humbler sisters to master a fluent style.

In the attempt to gain brightness—voice training is largely concerned with such a quest—precious qualities of truth and simplicity are often lost, and they must be found again before the singer can thoroughly please us. 'Except ye become as little children——'!

One of the chief features of speech and music is stress, without which there is no sense; for some words and notes are more important than their neighbours, and, unless by appropriate means, we show that they are so, the thought that they embody is entirely equivocal.

Stress can be effected in three ways:

    (1) by quantity
    (2) „ quality
    (3) „ pitch

with

    (1) the significant syllable or note is relatively prolonged;
    (2) dynamic accent is generally applied, though there are other ways of varying quality;
    (3) stress is shown by a difference of pitch, usually to a higher, but sometimes to a lower level.

If stress is not actually realized by one or other of these methods it has to be imagined, before we understand what the words or notes are about—as with performance on the organ, which scarcely admits of dynamic accent.

Perhaps the least used of these forms of accent is the accent of quantity, the most subtle of the three. Even in present-day English it is important; it was all-important in ancient, classical speech. One of the chief signs of beautiful delivery is the prolongation of the main vowel in predominant words. Poor speaking seldom exhibits it. In musical performance, also, note prolongation is a highly significant element, particularly when the movement is slow, as in adagios. When effected it of course to some extent destroys or modifies exact time proportions, but only in the interest of a superior principle, that of essential meaning. In recitation, prolongation can be applied without reserve, save the reserve of good taste; even in words to measured music, considerable latitude as regards the length of written notes is justified. A flowing phrase is scarcely possible unless it moves forward from stress to stress, or urges towards an objective.

N*

Chapter 10

FUSION OF WORDS AND MUSIC

> *. . . Lydian airs*
> *Married to immortal verse,*
> *Such as the meeting soul may pierce.*

WHATEVER is the case with music, words do not allow any suspicion of nonsense; they immediately bring the situation into one of intelligibility, where meaning and the laws of grammatical structure rule. We know too much about words, in the course of our everyday life, to be fooled by their delivery, unless we abrogate our powers of criticism entirely; or, though we have ears, still do not hear. Unfortunately this latter condition seems often to prevail. We accept stupidities of speech in a song—dislocations, false accents, etc.—without a murmur.

We should judge a singer far more hardly than we do, both in his interest and ours. To give words the finished expression of which they are capable is more than we can expect from even a good singer, if by that we mean one who has a certain control of his vocal organs; but at least he should satisfy us by making his words clear and in a general way avoiding distortion of their sense.

With music, as regards phrasing, we are perhaps on more perilous ground than we are with words. For we are not as familiar with the language of music as with the language of speech. Words are the current coin of communication, notes are not. If we fail to use words aright, we soon get into practical trouble; with notes we can escape disaster. We are not even likely to be found out when we commit a blunder of emphasis, though both music and words are often capable of varied meaning, according to the accent which we could give them. The same notes and words could be phrased to very different effect, as in:

The point is, that without accent the phrases are ambiguous, without sense.

In some ways music is more clearly defined than speech. Time values and the pitch of notes are fixed. The instrumental player has not to modulate his instrument like the speaker, nor determine his pace and progress. Primarily this is done for him by the composer, though on the higher levels of performance, adjustment and modification of the basic facts of notation will certainly be required of him. But as long as he plays his notes correctly we shall know what he is up to, and may indeed prefer to interpret the sense of the music according to our own powers of expression. This can actually happen. It is a well-known phenomenon that we do 'tick off' a succession of exactly similar notes into twos or threes; *we* give them order and form, though no hint of it is apparent in what we hear. The same is undoubtedly true of nuance; *we* supply it imaginatively in case of need, as indeed we may have to do with organ music, when the level of sound is constant. There is a subjective element in expression—the listener can put things to rights even when they are presented inadequately or wrongly; but he does not like to have to make too much of this sort of effort.[1] However this may be, the singer will probably offer a far better idea of the music than of the words, and he should be asked to equalize the significance of the two factors. Can this be done? Broadly, I think it can, even though we are dealing with the fusion of two developed and separate arts. Even in a song language does not determine the *sense* of music, though it may influence musical accent. The sense of music is not the sense of words. Each has a terrain which the other can never occupy, a characteristic method of utterance; but this is not to say that they cannot live harmoniously together without violent antagonism or disagreement. Let us consider some of their points of contact.

We often talk about the 'music of speech', or of someone having a 'musical' voice—and we are right in doing so. We are also right if we speak of the 'language of music', indicating by this not merely that music has a structure similar in many ways to that of speech, but that somehow speech has entered into the formation of music, influencing it, even determining it to a very considerable extent. There is common ground between notes and words before we attempt to fuse them into song. If there is no music in a singer's words, in the way that he *speaks* them, he will bring very little music to bear when he sings them: for, as we have said, music is implicit in speech; it cannot be absent in the one and present in the other.

[1] There is an appreciable fraction of time, during which the mind registers what it hears; and, in this, we can correct what we hear to our own ideal image (or understanding), such as it is. A poor, halting speaker who has no notion of saying what he has to say in the best way, may nevertheless impress us, though only partially by his own effort. *We* have to discover what he is driving at, which we can only do by putting his words into the right expressive shape, otherwise he may simply annoy us.

There are certain *qualities* which we recognize as musical, of which words and notes are merely the vehicle: the sensitive approach, which, to gain admittance, knocks gently at the door of the spirit—entrance seldom comes by storm; the feeling for beauty of tone; for beauty of movement—subject to the slightest impulsion; for poise and balance—without which movement must be jerky, spasmodic, never gracious; for undulation, rise and subsidence, tension and release; for the right accent, the right groupings; for all that will show you your way, with a smile, when you ask: these are some of the qualities inherent in the music of words. Perhaps they can be reduced to the main ones of 'sympathy' and 'order'. In the best speech, even of a prose nature, there is an evenness, a symmetry, a spacing, which brings it very close to poetic metre.

It may be held that such a definition of music is too limited. Music has a far wider range than that of charm (certainly a main outcome of the foregoing qualities), or of the faculty of soothing the savage breast. Even savagery must come under its expressive dominion, in an all-embracing, full-scale grasp of life. We could scarcely quarrel with this. Yet savagery and song somehow do not seem to mix. Their contiguity is not often apparent, nor likely to be. Nearly all song that we know is 'musical' in the sense that we have outlined. The lyrical impulse does not work in harsh, rough ways, whatever the dramatic one may do. Indeed art, like civilization, inclines to set aside the fierce and brutal; it cannot wholly reject it, but it seldom selects it for attention.

If we accept the criteria that we have adopted, we must say, therefore, that not only is song 'musical', but speech is also. In these particular elements (which seem to give the exhalation of music, its very note and temper) we see that there is not the slightest difference between words and notes. They *use* the same vocal material, tone; and in the same way—good tone is just good pronunciation, as we have often remarked. But, though the use of tone in words probably preceded its use in music, I think we can say that, now, by a sort of inverse process, a speaker is not likely to reach supremely good pronunciation unless his voice has been developed through song. We are sometimes told that song is good speech applied to music— in a considerable sense, it is—but it might be better to aver that music applied to speech is the truer sequence of events, and that it is the influence of music that produces good speech. It is for this reason that the beauty of Shakespeare's words so seldom emerges in a performance of his plays. The discipline of the voice both as regards rhythm and tone in a purely musical sense, apart from words, is not sufficiently undertaken by actors.

If we further pursue the similarity of music with words, we shall see that both can have the same dynamic stress as in the following[1]:

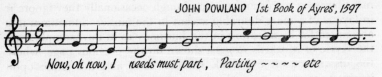

JOHN DOWLAND 1st Book of Ayres, 1597

Now, oh now, I needs must part, Parting ~ ~ ~ ~ etc

Here the stresses of words and notes coincide, but the result is apt to be rather mechanical and humdrum owing to its 'regularity'; particularly if the stresses are exaggerated.

Further, fully developed vocal sound is never heard in ordinary conversation, nor can it be attained by speech alone. If an ordinary spoken vowel is to be called 'natural', then (as a pupil of mine once said), the vowel that we are bent upon securing must be called 'supernatural', and I do not think that this can come about save by the agency of song, through which the muscles concerned strengthen to their full capacity, and the resonance cavities—particularly the cavity of the neck—grow to the required shape and stature. The result is *very different* from that which the speaking voice alone can secure. It seems of another breed, though its natural origin can of course be detected. The principle of growth must be underlined. We seldom hear a perfectly shaped vowel—giving the sound peculiar to it and to no other vowel. Most vowels are just 'half-breeds'. Oh, for instance, might generally be anything; it nearly always is, when the pitch is raised above that of the normal speaking voice. The truth is that there is a sort of embryo stage in vowel formation when, as in the human foetus, there is no decision of structure—it is a more or less unrecognizable blob or mass. Then it develops most wonderfully into a highly distinctive organism, ready to appear as such at the appointed time. This happens with any natural growth. We cannot expect a vowel to be completely formed without a process of gestation, requiring infinite care and purpose.

e ~ le ~ ~ i ~ son   etc ~

[1] The tune of this ayre was known as *The Frog Galliard.*

The general practice of song composers is to secure stress agreement between words and music, though occasionally they ignore it in favour of a more desirable accent in the music. Sometimes it is accounted for by a feature in the harmony as in the example from the Kyrie of Mozart's *Requiem* shown on the previous page, where the dissonance on the weak syllable 'son', and the pause upon it, causes a strong musical accent which is quite at variance with the natural accentuation of the word 'eleison'.

Or musical considerations may demand a different accentual treatment of the same words. Thus, in the following:

The Lord is a man of war, The Lord, the Lord is a man of war.

the word 'is', in the first phrase, is naturally unaccented; in the second phrase, owing to rhythmic change of the music, it certainly needs accent.

We must beware in song, of invariably associating dynamic stress with relative length or height of note. Generally the three go together, as in:

Ungeduld, Schubert

Dein ist mein Herz, dein ist mein Herz und sol-les e~~wig, ewig etc

but they may not, and then verbal stress must prevail, unless other (particularly harmonic) considerations arise.[1]

Thus, in these examples from Dowland:

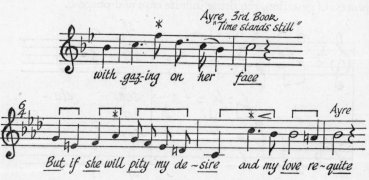

with gaz-ing on her face

But if she will pity my de~sire and my love re~quite

[1] The subject of accentuation is too large to treat thoroughly here.

We may be inclined to accent the notes marked *, but we must not do so, nor is there any compelling need why we should; in fact a great deal of lightness goes out of singing if we rigidly follow our natural instinct to associate a rise and fall of voice with *crescendo* and *diminuendo* or a relatively long note with an accent.

In this example also from Dowland, we see that the most important word in the phrase is given to the shortest note:

The whole matter of accent in song (according to present methods) is often turned topsy-turvy by the Elizabethans, who cannot lightly be dismissed as having no sense of the English language or of music.

And what are we to do with such a problem as this?

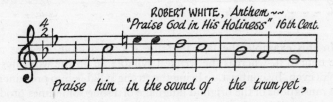

Musically, it would be quite possible to accent it metrically, just as it is barred in 4/2 time: thus,

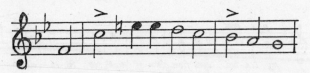

and words could be put to it in agreement with such an accentual scheme—such words as 'O Lord let thy mercy shine on us', though the result would be a little crabbed and angular. Further, it would seem quite right to accent the note C on the first beat of bar one, since this note is higher than F.

When, however, we put the right words to it, we see that the verbal accents are:

'*Praise* Him in the *sound* of the *trumpet*': which will give us a

367

totally different sense in the music. The phrase then becomes, quite clearly:

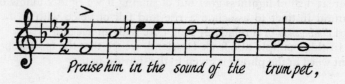

which is frankly in triple time, and is of a much superior rhythmic beauty.

Without the verbal association this would never have struck us.

In plain-song we often find many more notes given to a weak syllable than to a strong one, but this does not mean that this syllable should be stressed, or that the melismatic treatment of such a syllable should occupy the attention to the exclusion of less decorated but stronger syllables.

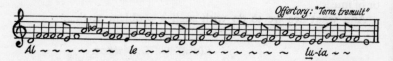

In this example the fact that the strong syllable 'lu' has only one note to it, whereas the weakest syllable 'le' in the word has 25, serves even, by contrast, to bring the strong syllable into prominence.

Translations of the original language of a song sometimes produce great absurdities of accentuation, but they must be put down to the incompetence of the translator. Thus one translation of Schubert's 'Du bist die Ruh' gives us for the culminating phrase:

Compared with the original words (placed underneath) it will be seen how atrociously the music fits the English substitute. Further comment is unnecessary.

Another source of trouble is when a composer sets a language with which he is not on full 'speaking terms', which is often the case with Handel, especially in his recitatives. Singers, even in the *Messiah* wrestle with such impossible passages as:

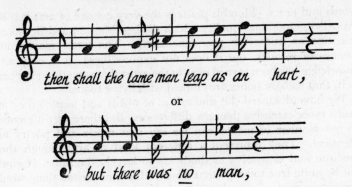

then shall the lame man leap as an hart,

or

but there was no man,

though, if they were slightly altered, they would be quite singable, and no one would be harmed. A composer, however, does not usually err in giving false verbal accents. It is the way we deal with his work which is often amiss.

To return to our argument respecting similarities of speech to music.

Similarity is also to be seen in what may be called the 'logic' of words and notes. Both are gathered into phrases which make an intelligible pronouncement. Within those phrases words and notes are connected, they are in relationship; they progress towards a climax, recede from it; they constitute an idea, in which the notes function very much like the parts of speech do with words.

A note upon a light up-beat can stand for an indefinite article; an appoggiatura for an adjective or a qualifying word; the equivalent of a noun has a longer and stronger note, the chief stress of the musical phrase is (or might be) an active verb wherein is collected the main energy of the expression, and so on. The parallel between words and notes in this respect is very close indeed. The comparative weight of words is the same as the weight of notes; some notes, just as words, are loud or soft, prolonged or fleeting, according to the sense and grammatical function. That is why they can so comfortably run together in harness; but the relative importance of words or notes, viewed as parts of speech, must not be too pronounced in performance, or phrasing will be fussy and over-detailed. A good 'style' equalizes the constituents of phrase; broadly overarches them in favour of the phrase as a whole. This unifying quality is musical rather than verbal. Notes of course do not symbolize material things as do words, but the 'logic' of words is not material or symbolical; it can well be looked upon as *musical* in its ordered, inevitable, progressive movement.

It is hardly necessary to speak of 'mood' as being common to both words and notes. Mood is perhaps the very essence of art; it is the evocative, emotional quality which distinguishes an artistic from a scientific or utilitarian pronouncement. The latter may arouse feelings of wonder, but it does not express them. It is only after knowledge has been turned over to the artist that something happens to it, that its bare bones are clothed with living tissue.

We have discussed the similarities of words and music; they are much more extensive than the differences. But there *are* differences. By no manner of means can we say that music and poetry are identical. They represent a different kind of art, though their medium and expressive methods are so largely the same. It would not be quite true to assert that if words had not existed there would have been no music, or that if music had not played its part, words, in a poetic sense, would have been quite insignificant; but it would be very nearly true. Yet it still remains that music and poetry *are* complete in themselves; that they have founded autonomous empires and do not need to be linked in order to function. Modern instrumental music and poetry show that. On the whole, modern poets know nothing and care very little about music; whereas a Shakespeare was surprisingly conversant with musical technicalities —even musicians go to him to be illumined about their art. That music and poetry are now self-supporting is due—particularly as regards music—to the great extension of their expressive means. Since instruments began to be constructed, and the dance developed, the divergent process has slowly been making way; though, for all that, we must not assume that no further convergence is possible. As long as ritual words are used, or lovers unburden their hearts in verse, song will be with us, as it always has been, from unrecorded time.

Homer is said to have sung his poetry to the lyre. This need not be taken merely as a legend, since reciting to music was common in ancient Greece; the dramatic power of Greek tragedy was largely sustained by musical resources. In the middle ages poetry and music were in frequent, indeed, almost constant, alliance. Very little reading was done; people could not read. They talked of course. But on set occasions, when something more than informal speech was wanted, music was called upon to give force to the pronouncement. Rousing narrative verse would be sung; this helped its remembrance, as it did in the case of all traditional verse.

Lyrical verse required music, though epic verse or large-scale poems increasingly dispensed with it. Dante insisted that lyrical verse could not stand by itself. For him the action of the lyrical poet *had* to be supplemented by that of the musician. Nowadays lyrics are written without any such proviso, though the word 'lyric' implies a musical setting. The association of words and music was even closer in Elizabethan times. Then a mass of verse appeared which resulted in that wonderful flowering of English song—the Lutenist Ayre—which in its 'short measures' proved that 'life can perfect be'. Elizabethan verse was also used by our Madrigalists. But though Madrigals and Ayres were termed 'Songes' indiscriminately, what we know as accompanied solo song—the forerunner of the songs of Schubert and Brahms—was the Ayre and not the Madrigal. Nevertheless the quasi-instrumental rhythm of the Ayre was a potent factor in disturbing the balance that had hitherto existed between words and music, tilting it upon the side of the latter.

Henceforth in song, the poet's office was to be less valued than the musician's. Since the sixteenth century, poetry and music have more and more dwelt apart, and to-day we have to lament (with A. H. Bullen) that poets give us little 'immortal verse' that calls for music.

In consequence our song writers tend to return to medieval poetry or to the Elizabethan lyric for inspiration.

The true vocal style—that is a style in which words and music contributed equally to the general effect, neither the one nor the other being the predominant partner—is best exemplified in plainsong and medieval polyphony.

It is not necessary to consider the contrapuntal aspect of polyphony, only that of a single part or voice—one part reflects the practice of the other parts.

Plain-song undoubtedly started from the spoken word. It represented heightened speech, giving an added dignity to the words of Holy Writ or the Church liturgy; it allowed words to travel better in a large building.

By degrees very simple verbal inflexion was extended into wider sweeps of melody and more ornate forms, those of 'melismatic' chant. But its verbal origin was never lost sight of, or its vocal style confused with instrumental style, as happened almost consistently after the sixteenth century. When the instrumental dance, with its regular barring, became the basis of composition, or, at any rate, served as one of its chief elements, the purely vocal style was doomed, since words, even in metrical verse, refuse to be treated according to the rigid accentual pattern of the dance, and also are spiritually at variance with *marcato* which applied so obviously to the livelier forms of dance.

Speech, unless in exceptional circumstances, is flowing, not marked or *staccato*; and this, its character, is reflected absolutely in the melody of plain-song.

There are no separated or suddenly-emphasized notes in plain-song. In it everything is smooth, as befits its name, *Cantus Planus*.[1] Nor, even in the hymns of plain-song, which are cast in regular metre, do we find a metrical *musical* pattern. Any metrical suggestion is eliminated; irregular prose structure is the rule. Occasionally when only one note is given to a syllable something very near a metrical melody arises, as with the sequence, *Lauda Sion*.

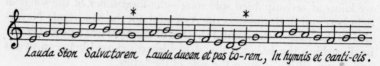

Lauda Sion Salvatorem Lauda ducem et pas to-rem, In hymnis et canti-cis.

But it will be observed how the strict metre is broken at points marked *; and, in performance, a rhythmical swing and freedom of movement prevails, which cannot be brought into line with the measured progress of modern music. In more fluid examples we are still further off from anything like a metrical system, as can be seen in the opening strain of the Offertory:

Laetentur Coeli.

lae ~ ~ ten-tur   coe ~ ~ ~ ~ ~ ~ ~ ~ ~ ~ ~ ~ li etc

Polyphonic melody, which issued from plain-song and remained continuously associated with it, shows the same feature of prose rhythm, i.e., a succession of irregular groups: an 'imaginative mixture' of notes, as H. G. Wooldridge calls it, though the notes themselves are always even, never jerky. In this instrumentally accompanied 'Song' of Byrd the rhythm is clearly 'free'.

From Virgins womb this day, this day   did spring etc

Its style is paralleled in all the music of the polyphonic period. In the 'Ayres' of Dowland we often see an overlap of polyphonic and instrumental rhythm; but most of the composers of 'Ayres' were frankly on the side of metrical rhythm; their methods constituted a rebellion against the older 'prose' dispensation. When we reach such things as 'Above Him stood the Seraphim', with its dotted notes:

[1] Some would not accept this interpretation of the word 'planus'.

we know that the old order has passed, or is about to pass; that, in short, speech rhythm has been superseded by rhythm proper to instruments.

Instrumental rhythm, as will be immediately perceived, is still further accentuated in the following phrases: as

and a little later we get the cheap absurdities of Italian opera, which, as in this,

represent the nadir of song, since in them the ways of speech are for the most part entirely travestied, and, for the matter of that, the ways of music, too.

True verbal *melos* is to a large extent uneventful as regards rhythm. The notes move evenly as words do in speech; so that we can sing the words without feeling that they are pulling in an opposite direction to that of the music, or that striking rhythmic features are forcibly claiming our attention. The effect, in short, is a combined effect: a contribution by both partners to a general purpose—two in one, and one in two. This is borne out by the attitude of the folk singer, who can never think of his words apart from the tune. 'Celui qui perd ses mots, perd son air' is a Breton proverb, underlining not only the equality of words and music, but the conviction, apparently, that folk singers have in all countries, that the words and music in folk song are part and parcel of one another.

The association of words and music tells in various ways. There is not the slightest doubt that we remember the words of a poem far better when they are set to music; and also remember music better when it is accompanied by words. Each reinforces the appeal of the other, and tends to fix it in our minds; we are much more impressed by the dual attack upon our attention.

In the German Chorale words and music were powerfully united. People were thoroughly familiar with these 'Geistliche Lieder'. The melody would recall the words; the words the melody. Bach's Chorale Preludes, in which only the melody appears, were not just music to their hearers; they would remind them of the words, and bring the strength or comfort which the words gave. *We* hear these Preludes as beautiful pieces of music, scarcely more. But, though Bach might treat only the chorale melody for instrumental purposes, he never used the words in a separate sense. If but one line of a verse of a Chorale was inscribed in the libretto of a cantata, he immediately quoted the phrase of the Chorale which went with it, suspending his own music at that point. To him the association of the words with their traditional melody was inviolable, whether the words were imagined, or actually present. The compositions of those times, in which a Chorale is used, must have meant much more to the Germans than they can possibly mean to us.

Cecil Sharp tells us that the following metrical formulæ are, perhaps, especially characteristic of the English folk tune:

which is what we might expect with the closest correspondence between words and notes. There is of course much variation, but it never approaches the foregoing Handel or Boyce examples. And when as in the song, 'Riding down to Portsmouth' a rhythmical form such as this appears:

it is so irregular that its fluidity is not impaired, and it can do service
in much the same way as a more regular type of folk song melody.

In recent times instrumental rhythm has prevailed, but latterly
a more delicate adjustment of the claims of words and music has
been attempted. Holst, in his four Medieval Songs for voice and
violin, returned to something very akin to plain-song; and, among
others, Benjamin Dale, Vaughan Williams, and, more recently,
Benjamin Britten and Gerald Finzi, have all shown that a metrical
structure does not always satisfy them when they have to deal with
words. Increasingly I think, though not of course entirely, we
shall use the older rhythmic methods to express not only verbal
subtleties, but the very nature of speech in its flow and sequence
even after it has submitted to metre. Here is Holst's solution of the
problem:

He came all so still Where His mo-ther was As dew in A-pril that fal-leth on grass:

There is no need to analyse it except to say that the hint of lilt
and metre in bars 4 and 5 gives warmth and charm to the expression,
but that this, strictly speaking, is rather a musical than a verbal
effect.

If we have any feeling for words, we shall *not* treat them in the way
that Beethoven does in the Finale of the Ninth Symphony, an
example followed in much choral music of his period and later. It is
no longer singing, but a shattering of the voice. The only way to
perform it and the like, effectively, is by something like sledge-
hammering each syllable in a style utterly at variance with the
style of words. The grandness of its conception may have compelled Beethoven to 'write it in the rock' or 'grave it in brass with
adamantine pen', but it would have been better if he had shown
more sympathy with his material.

Sixteenth-century composers also ask occasionally for such
martellato treatment. Jannequin does in his four-part Chanson 'La
Battaille de Marignon'; only, in this, it is not a question of words but
of picturing realistically the sounds of war—trumpet calls, cannon
shots, etc.—on syllables (Pom, Zim Zim, etc.) which represent
them. In much the same way it is perfectly legitimate and indeed
necessary to express Brahms' 'Der Schmied'; but here again we are

in the realm of musical illustration, which has very little to do with a feeling for poetry as such.

As we have said, the Tudors, particularly the Elizabethans, produced a mass of lyrics which were intended to be sung. These lyrics were in many cases cast in avowedly musical form. The words did not determine that form, the form impressed itself upon the words which were written in obedience to it, just as Burns and Moore often set an existing tune to words. The Elizabethan poet, however, was far more meticulous than later writers in the correspondence of the words to the notes; he was closer in touch with music. Since the music of an 'Ayre' did not change—it was the same for each verse— the smallest detail of verbal punctuation would often be repeated. Not only that, where a stanza consists of several sections, 'the sentiment of each section is paralleled in succeeding stanzas'.[1]

One of the best known songs of Dowland gives a good example of such structural correspondence:

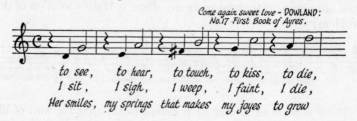

Come again sweet love - DOWLAND:
No.17 First Book of Ayres.

to see,   to hear,   to touch,   to kiss,   to die,
I sit,   I sigh,   I weep,   I faint,   I die,
Her smiles, my springs that makes my joyes to grow

The rhythmic nature of words and music, though it agrees in so much, is nevertheless very different. Words *move* differently to notes. Notes are *strictly* proportioned; words, in their time values, are not. The structure of music is built upon rigid intervals and time; words are far more free, and, in consequence, far more subtle in inflexion and movement. Though the general run of words may be more or less regularly measured—it usually is in the best speech— the detail is infinitely varied, owing to continual variation in the strength and length of vowels, due to their position, interaction, and to the influence of consonants.

These points can be verified by really capable reading of the Psalms, which, owing to their comparatively short phrases specially lend themselves to the observation of verbal rhythm. If we take the first verse of the 2nd Psalm:

/*Why* do the / *hea*then so / *fu*riously rage to/*ge*ther; and / *why* do the / *peo*ple i/*ma*gine a vain / *thing*?

[1] *Music and Poetry of the English Renaissance*, Bruce Pattison, which should be read by anyone interested in the subject.

we could almost bar it metrically in the way we have done; likewise with other verses.[1] There is a certain regular throb about it, which is seldom interfered with. It is not as regular as it would be with a purely musical phrase, but it is still sufficiently regular to give a sense of order—much as with 'dog-tooth' moulding in Norman architecture, where V's were cut upon arch stones of approximately the same width, but taken much as they came to hand, without being exactly similar.

The effect of this is of a free symmetry, without its being mechanically perfect. Nature herself works in this way, without exact repetition; as is so well demonstrated in the honeycomb formation of the Giant's Causeway—in which no two of the millions of hexagons which comprise it are quite the same. For this reason the rhythm of speech is, as we have said, more delicately adjusted than that of music. It often is disordered—badly so, with incapable speakers—but it need not be. Analysis is very difficult, because of the subtlety of the procedure, but in the last degree I think it will be found that the rhythm of speech is based upon a strict *musical* norm, to which it may be referred, and by which its departure therefrom is both perceived and justified.

To yoke words with music is something like putting them in a strait jacket. It cramps their rhythmic freedom—distorts their natural flow. If we *speak* the words 'Hope of my heart' well, in easy sequence, their rhythm will seem beautifully right, though absolutely elusive. It will be nothing like this:

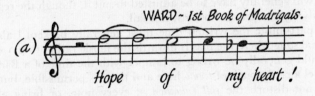

WARD - 1st Book of Madrigals.

(a) Hope of my heart!

but tend towards

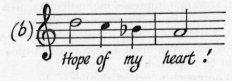

(b) Hope of my heart!

In the original, as with (a) the note for 'of' is far too long, though the phrase is part of a very lovely musical passage. Even if it were noted as at (b) the verbal rhythm would still lose something by being

---

[1] Landor says that 'good prose . . . is only an extension of metres'.

so exactly measured. A compromise between verbal and musical rhythm is therefore inevitable. Neither words nor music can be quite true to themselves when they are combined. Words certainly cannot be. Music has the whip hand since its notes are of fixed length and pitch, though even they are subject to flexible use, particularly in certain classes of solo song, when the control of the words predominates. The Germans call this sort of song, *Sprech Gesang*, and, in it, naturalness of speech must be aimed at.

Cyril Scott's charming little song, 'Don't come in, Sir, please', is an example. If we take its last 'refrain' line:

we should have to sing it something like

which looks dreadful in notation, but sounds right.

Whenever talking has to be suggested, the length of the written notes will generally have to be adjusted to suit it, though the regular underlying musical throb must not fail.

In part-music the written time must generally be kept,[1] also in classical song where the bias is towards the music rather than words. It would generally be wrong to tamper with the time of a Bach or Handel air. A touch of *tenuto* here and there is permissible, but this must not disturb the *full valuation* of every note, or bring about dotted note effects that are unwarranted. It is the formal perfection of the classical style that impresses us; in that it represents supreme control, constancy, safety—the reverse of the erratic. *Bel canto* song—for this is what such song is called—the *Messiah* airs are of such a kind—is conceived upon a basis of exact time proportions, and these must be respected.

The nearest approach to verbal rhythm is obtained in recitative, where melodious interest is reduced to a minimum. Bach recitatives often conclude with a passage of *Arioso*, in which music comes to

---

[1] Such a part-song as Elgar's 'Owls' however comes very near to *Sprech Gesang* and is largely subject to it. It is very difficult to sing convincingly.

the fore, to the disadvantage of the natural movement of the words; but at other times in such recitatives he generally gives a quaver (occasionally divided into semiquavers) to each syllable, and, by this method, allows an almost unfettered delivery of the verbal text. In adapting the English 'Authorized' version of the Gospel to the *St. Matthew Passion*, certain editors have completely travestied Bach's intentions and style—turning what was a smooth, dignified and almost free *melos*—ideally suited to recitative—into fussy snatches of timed melody, ill-according with the nature of speech.[1] Thus, the 'Evangelist' can recite his phrase almost as he would speak it, with Bach's noting:

Bist du der Ju-den Kö-nig? Je-sus a-ber sprach zu ihm:

but with the English words forced into an uneasy alliance with the deranged notes, the whole thing is stiff and wrong:

Art thou the King of the Jews? And Jesus said unto him:

The vexed and so far insoluble question of English chanting could easily be adjusted if it were agreed (1) that one syllable should go to one note of the same denomination (unless very exceptionally), and (2) that triples should be used whenever they were necessary. One of the reasons—indeed the main reason—for the flexibility and good carriage of Elizabethan verbal setting, is precisely the way in which triples were introduced whenever the text naturally suggested them. Without here pursuing the matter further, even the comparative stiffness of the Anglican chant (as regards the music) can be avoided by the aforementioned means, and beauty of rhythm substituted: as with this—to take Wesley's chant to the 121st Psalm:

I will lift up mine eyes un-to the hills from whence cometh my help; even from the Lord, who hath made hea-ven and earth

---

[1] One hesitates to give this advice to singers (as, by trying to conform to it, they may make confusion worse confounded), but, in general, time values in recitative should be ruthlessly modified in favour of natural declamation whereby right verbal rhythm is safeguarded.

What could be simpler or more satisfying? There is no down-beat 'bump' to this—the bane of all bad rhythm—or torture of our language. It works.[1]

The singing of quick words or 'patter' (generally based on even notes) can also be achieved with a considerable approximation to speech. Yet, while allowing that the rhythm peculiar to words has, for the most part, to be surrendered in song, it still remains that, on balance, both words and music inspire each other, raising each other to a higher power. The musical significance given to a word quite apart from its accentual or elocutional quality; the prolongation of its vowels, flowering into melody; the increased glow, breadth, consistency, 'presence' that words have when joined to music, more than make amends for a certain loss of their naturalness. And as regards the notes, there is no doubt but that words tend to articulate them in a far finer way than music by itself would ever do. On the whole the compromise, in song, between words and music, is advantageous to both. Words give up most, but gain more than they lose; music is entirely[2] the gainer, by the superior modelling of its material; also—though this may be open to question—by its association with the more definite emotional purpose of the words; by the character that words give to the music.[3]

Some may say that the indefiniteness of music is the measure of its unique appeal; that words bind its wings, arrest its flight. The author does not thus feel it; he is not conscious that words offer any check to his musical faculty. On the contrary, they render it more acute. Verbal thought helps musical performance. It gives the key to the expression, suggests *tempo* and much else. There is hardly any excuse for failing to make a song convincing when the words are there to tell the singer what to do.

---

[1] I hope, shortly, to 'point' the whole book of Psalms in this way with a view to publication (C.K.S.). An extended Preface to it is already written.

[2] One does not forget that consonants may distort *legato*. It is the singers' business to see that they do not. Words of course do alter the 'run' of musical sound. A *legato* phrase with words is not the same thing as a phrase without them. But because it is different it is not necessarily less good. The difference can be most easily demonstrated by first singing a 'solfeggio' in the usual way, on the vowel Ah, then putting tonic sol-fa syllables to the notes (though it must be admitted that these syllables have no final consonants and that in them we only have to cope with *one* initial consonant). With different syllables also, the difficulty of continuous sound is increased, because of the changing of the vowels—instrumental performance (as on the flute or violin), makes use of only one vowel or its equivalent. But, by skill, the difficulties both of consonants and changing vowels can be overcome, and a good *legato* achieved. We do not grumble at the lack of *sostenuto* on the pianoforte or harpsichord. What we may well object to (when it happens), is poor dynamic relationship between the notes; in other words, poor phrasing. The fault is when words or notes do not *lead on and into* each other, or give this impression; and for this a perfect sustaining of the sound is not necessary.

[3] In connection with this, a passage from Burney's *History of Music* is very much

We are not to infer from this, however, that at all times music would be improved by the addition of words. That would be absurd. A song is quite different from instrumental music. In the finest songs the musical detail corresponds with the verbal detail, the *raison d'être* of the music is, indeed, the words. With instrumental music this is not so. It is conceived as music, and to put words to it is not only superfluous, but impertinent. Occasionally, at children's lectures, an instrumental phrase, such as the subject from one of Bach's 48 Preludes and Fugues, is saddled with words in the attempt to make it better understood; but it brings in an element of flippancy that is completely out of accord with musical thought. Though we need not say, like Jessica, that we can 'never be merry' when we hear sweet music, we should not play the fool with it. We must learn to *think* musically as well as verbally, and not go about the former on crutches, unless we are completely crippled.

There *is*, of course, such a natural correspondence between music and poetry that they can be conceived apart and yet be brought together, suitably enough. But this only applies to the simplest of strophic forms: the equivalent of a 'tune' in music. In this case the connection is loose; scarcely more than parallelism is involved, not fusion. As the bonds strengthen, the music 'fits' the words better, 'clokes' them, as the Elizabethans would have said—with greater care. Their shape and sense is indicated more faithfully, though not servilely, each preserves an individuality which accords with the other; imagination plays upon both. Poetic values are transmuted into musical, not merely added to the latter.

Many instrumental tunes have had words set to them—Burns, and Moore (in his Irish melodies) wrote hundreds of lyrics upon this principle. Here the *point de départ* is the music. But the song-writer generally proceeds in the opposite way. He sets his music to the words and, if he pursues the path just outlined, what he writes, finally, will have no *raison d'être* apart from the words; not only its existence, but its explanation will lie in them. This is song at its highest.

To imagine a poet putting words to a Beethoven Sonata is to show the absurdity of such an attempt; it is no less absurd for a dancer to put steps to it. But a poet could very well write verses upon the plan of a simple tune. Whether Dowland fitted the tune to the point. Talking of Rubinelli's singing of Handel's 'Return, O God of Hosts' he says:

'I missed several apoggiaturas which I remember Mrs. Cibber to have intro-duced, who learned to sing the air from the composer himself; and who, though her voice was a thread, and her knowledge of music very inconsiderable [she was of course a tragic actress first and foremost—C.K.S.], yet, *from her intelligence of the words*, and native feeling, she sang this admirable supplication in a more touching manner than the finest opera singer I ever heard attempt it.'

of the 'Frog Galliard' (a traditional dance tune) to the words, or whether the poet fitted his words to the tune does not matter—precedence is of little or no account in such a case—but it is of very much account in such a developed song as Schubert's 'Erlkönig', even though a pianoforte piece was made of it by Liszt. And song writing gets even further away from the purely instrumental in, say, Wolf's 'Der Genesene an Die Hoffnung', and many another of his songs—which seems to show that there is a sort of central ground where poetry and music meet and lose their separate identity. At the extremes each may exist apart:

$$\text{Music} \quad .. \quad .. \quad \left\{ \begin{matrix} \text{music} \\ \text{poetry} \end{matrix} \right\} \quad .. \quad .. \quad \text{poetry.}$$

Also, at these extremes music *may* be put to poetry, or poetry to music; in which case the fusion is incomplete and it may resolve into its elements again while allowing each to retain its self-supporting quality. But when the fusion is complete, neither music nor poetry can escape from the other without loss: for each tends, as we have said, to raise the other to a higher power, by reason of mutual illumination. The poetry gives the sense of the music, the music reveals the spirit of the poetry. The fact that the very important principle of 'association' may have been brought into operation, so that the music and poetry can scarcely be thought of apart from each other, does not mean that they are organically and irrevocably knit. This view does not find favour with everyone. W. J. Turner (no mean poet, and as well of considerable repute as a musical critic) said in an essay (in *Music and Life*), 'a poem is a completed thing: it is a finished creation to which nothing can be added and from which nothing can be taken away. . . . The value of the song is entirely musical. The composer can do nothing, absolutely nothing, for the poet. To imagine that he can is to imagine that you can interpret a sculptor's rude figure by dressing it in an appropriate costume.'[1] This is scarcely borne out by experience. It may be true of poetry which is so involved and recondite that we have as much as we can do to find out what it is all about; if music were joined to it, it would not assist our comprehension, only hinder it. Poetry must *lead* us somewhere, evoke a condition above and beyond that of the intellect, before it calls for music. When that condition —an emotional one—is reached, then poetry and music go hand in hand together. The simplest words may (and generally do) touch us most deeply; lyric poetry is of this kind—it is *musical*.

If words can suggest music, then a song can be made of them. Any welling up of the emotions will have a musical import. 'The Lord

[1] Also quoted in Cecil Gray's *History of Music*.

is my Shepherd, I shall not want', 'Calm was the day, and through the trembling air', 'Stern daughter of the voice of God'—such words as these have musical implications; an emotional aura surrounds them.

In strophic song, it is this aura upon which the composer particularly depends for his expression; not so much upon the scrupulousness of his declamation. It is clear that when several verses go to the same melody, there must be times when the form and spirit of the words is in disagreement with that of the music; unless the poet and composer write with the most perfect understanding of what is required—as did the Elizabethans. Brahms maintained that the strophic song was the highest achievement of the song-composer's invention, beside which the declamatory song is 'child's play'. His dictum is obviously weighty. It is possible that the strophic song,[1] with its supreme concern for melody, is more difficult to compose successfully, because it is a sort of concentrated essence of musical invention—'melody is music's battle cry', said Schumann—and perhaps depends upon inspiration to a greater degree than 'through composed' song, which is apt to be 'concocted'. The latter can scarcely have the 'sweep' of the former; its details are settled more consciously. But this only means that strophic song is more *musical*, not that it is superior as a combination of words and music. Nor must we necessarily assume that a great composer cannot be inspired to a great combination of the two arts of poetry and music. Wolf achieved it, or came very near to it; and even if he takes rank below Schubert or Brahms (which some would not admit) it by no means follows that a better composer, say Schubert or Brahms, could not have dealt with a complete, inseparable fusion of words and music in as satisfying a way, musically, as that offered by the less organic style of these latter composers. The truth is that there are various degrees and approaches to a fully developed song, taken in its composite sense. Though they have a strophic basis, Schumann's 'Mondnacht' or 'Fruhlingsnacht' are nothing like strophic song in its simplest, quasi-folk-song form; but there is surely no failure in them. Poetic and musical agreement could perhaps be taken further, as in Wolf's 'Der Genesene'; but what was a success with these more advanced songs of Schumann need not necessarily be denied to the song of Wolf or its equivalent—that is to say the closest connection of words and music, amounting to an equal distribution of this interest, can still allow *both* to function at their highest. We must accept the good where we find it, in all its different guises of significance. In one song the bias of interest may be towards music,

---

[1] A large proportion of song is strophic, or based, in some degrees upon a repetition of the music which goes to the first verse of the words.

in another towards poetry; in still another there may be a more equal distribution of interest. We may be charmed and satisfied by each, and are rather unwise if we have any *parti-pris* in the matter. Moreover the resources of music are almost inexhaustible. Allowing that detailed verbal illustration is apt to disturb musical continuity —words differ so much in meaning, contiguous thoughts may dart in opposite directions[1]—music, while handling them, may still preserve a unity, if not by melodic flow, at least by means of symphonic development, though the simultaneous use of both is possible. The songs of Schubert show this, where a motif is developed in the accompaniment, against a predominant melody in the voice part. Such processes may be more calculated than those of naive melody taken by itself; but a reasoned treatment is seldom absent from conscious art. Did not Beethoven repeatedly alter first thoughts even of his melodies, while composition as a whole implies a still greater use of criticism and selection, neither of which is contrary to an ideal result? It merely means a *slow* instead of a *quick* working of the spontaneous principle, though this may seem a contradiction in terms. The end which is achieved may be the more desirable from the intervention of reason. After all, the processes of inspiration *are* rational.

If Mr. Turner was correct in his statement that music adds nothing to words, song is a ridiculous affair from start to finish: a sheer waste of time on the part of the composer and singer. The poet, moreover, should have strongly objected to the superfluous accompaniment of music to his verse. Yet it does not seem that he has often done so. He may have gone his own way, particularly in modern times, but unless lyricism is expressly excluded from a poet's aim— in which case he sacrifices the very nature of poetry—it would seem that there must always be verse which calls for music, and that Mr. Turner was rather belittling his own beautiful verse when he would have kept it from the embraces of the sister art. Both poetry and music can fulfil the law of their own being apart from each other, but they can also quite well fulfil it hand in hand—though in a different way from when they are bent entirely upon their own business.

It is strange how Mr. Turner's idea is shared. Cecil Gray further remarks in his *History of Music* that 'practically all Moussorgsky's music is set to words', adding 'it would be a mistake to imagine that

---

[1] It is however, mostly in dramatic song, that this will occur, owing to the clash of characters. Lyric song is generally in a single emotional vein, in which violent contrast is avoided. We like to sustain a mood; this is what music can do so wonderfully, and till we are replete with it, do not want to change it. Repeated change is exasperating; this is why an Air—or something which approaches it in unified, sustained feeling—is almost a necessity in opera. The mind needs lyrical repose.

they are in any way responsible for the intrinsic quality of the emotion which his operas and songs arouse in the listeners. It is latent in the music itself, and repeated experience conclusively shows that it can be as powerfully, though naturally more vaguely expressed, by those who have not any knowledge of the text as by those who have.' Which one may beg leave to doubt. To do so would be to give up the whole rationale of song. In the case of opera, even if the text is not understood, gesture and *mise-en-scène* still offer a clue to what is being sung. Further, in Moussorgsky's case, the musical coat *was* cut according to the cloth, or rather according to the verbal body which it was required to clothe; not only that, to the verbal spirit which it attempted to elucidate. The result to a great degree, may be self-sufficing, since each art separately—music and poetry—contain ample to interest us. But surely it cannot be conceded that something superior, something more complete, does not happen when they are combined, as they were intended to be.

The song writer does not mean that the skin of his song should be sloughed off when he has completed it; or if he prefer to think of his music as the kernel and core of the work, that it should shed its sheath, like a butterfly, before it starts on its winged way. The body is no worse for being clothed, nor is a coat the worse for being well fitted; it remains a good coat just as music may be good music when fitted to words. The truth surely is that a new manifestation, a new form of appearance, occurs when a garment is placed upon the body, or music is set to verse; the result is neither the vesture nor what it clothes, but the combined effect of both. The body is indispensable to its covering; the covering to the body; the two go together. Song, therefore, is neither poetry, nor music; but both. This is the answer I think, to Mr. Turner's remark about clothing a statue.

It may be that the process of song precludes an entirely reasonable use of words. Music is more remote than speech. It tells of far-off, not immediate things. It carries words with it into regions where factual truth scarcely matters. A composer could set a page of Bradshaw. After it were done we should not care much whether a train left London at five o'clock or five-thirty; yet we might possibly be interested in the music. When, however, words themselves transport us emotionally in much the same way as music does, we are very glad of their company. Each partner reinforces the appeal of the other. Who can separate the words from the music in 'Du bist die Ruh'? How should we feel the utter repose that is contemplated, if the words were not there to guide us, or the music to show us its very meaning? It is a double appeal. It has been said that Schubert's 'greatest strength as a song writer lies in his astonishing

385

O

and uncanny power of hitting upon a melodic phrase so suited to the poem that it is henceforth impossible for us to imagine any other conceivable setting of it, or to think of the one without thinking of the other'.[1] This is something more than mere association, as of a hymn tune to the usual words which go with it; it is elucidation in the deepest sense, a closer searching of the issue. And as well the expressive situation is magnified. Fine speech as we have already said, is distinguished by the prolongation of the vowels; the speaker lingers upon them, makes them last as long as he can, or as long as it is fitting. Such speech is musical: for vowels rather than consonants belong to music. In song, vowels are still further lengthened; the words are entirely caught up in the stream of music. This is secured by an increase of motive force which not only affects the vowels but the consonants, so that the words mean more. Thus singing is not only more intense than speech, it is spread over a longer period of time; and therefore a poem gains in importance when it is sung—it is more of a set piece. In singing, a rapturous quality can be maintained—an elevation, poise, suspension—that is quite beyond the powers of speech. No wonder that a song holds the attention even when it is poorly sung. No wonder that a song is everybody's pleasure, when music or words by themselves fail to move.

But though words and music seem to have an almost magnetic urge towards each other, it is useless to deny that disquieting problems arise from their association. Is union so inevitable? Does it amount to what we have conceived it to be? Has *force majeure* never to be used to effect it?

We are confronted at the outset by the extremely disconcerting fact that, if a singer can pronounce a foreign language well, even without understanding a word, he can interpret a foreign song with considerable success, provided he gives a satisfactory interpretation of the music. This often happens. It would thus appear that the words are not of much consequence, as regards their meaning at any rate; and that once they have inspired and fertilized the music they can be set aside as of little or no account.[2] It is also doubtful whether good pronunciation is not an entirely musical matter; it certainly is, primarily. When we pronounce well, do we care very much for the sense of the words? Are we not endeavouring to get a *musical* tone, and in securing it have we not reached the heart of the word in most cases? These arguments seem plausible enough, but they by no means cover the whole ground. The sense of words does count, not only in their performance—a host of expressive

---

[1] Mr. Cecil Gray again.
[2] This is in conformity with Cecil Gray's dictum as regards Moussorgsky (p. 384).

touches come from them—but in heightening the general appeal of song.

We have already referred to the question of verbal and musical rhythm, and have had to admit that there is a great difference between the two. Verbal rhythm is more or less free even when it operates in metrical form; its details are not strictly proportionate. Two syllables seldom take the time of one in an exact sense, in the same way that two quavers go to a crotchet. In musical rhythm exact proportions are necessary to our understanding. We should soon be at sea if they were not so; and the horizontal combination of parts would be an impossibility upon any other principle. The structure would topple over into chaos. Though we may talk about 'contrapuntal' rhythm in verse, it is in reality nothing like counterpoint in music. It is merely a more or less recognised departure from an ideal rhythmic standard: the equivalent of strict time in music, but which seldom operates in the case of words unless they degenerate into sing-song.

That words seldom do measure up correctly is precisely the factor that distinguishes verbal from musical rhythm; and thereby prevents utter comradeship. Words can afford to be less trim in time, because their *sense* allows us to grasp them. In their delivery musical significance has also to be considered, but it must not be pushed too far or it becomes too musical, and the genius of words is destroyed. Combined with music, however, words are, and have to be, treated differently; compromise is essential.

Nor can we quite successfully explain the use of the same music to different words, as in a succession of verses in strophic song. The bond does not seem very great when this can happen. Certainly music is put to the words, but a thousand substitutions could be made, leaving the situation very much the same. We may prefer a particular setting of a song, but that there can be variants rather disturbs our equanimity. How far *is* music the counterpart of poetry? How closely is the meaning of a poem reflected in the meaning of the music—this, after all, is the true test—when so much difference in the music can be entertained, and no single version specially accredited?

This appears in its most flagrant form when a composer, successfully enough, puts totally different words to music which he had previously composed for other words. Bach and Handel frequently did this sort of thing. The 'Agnus Dei' of the *B Minor Mass* went originally to a text beginning 'Ach, bleibet doch mein liebster Leben'; the chorus 'Unto us a Child is born', in the *Messiah*, was first cast as an Italian love duet; while Chorales and hymn tunes shift their verbal ground *ad lib.*, one of the most remarkable cases being that of the famous *St. Matthew Passion* Chorale which went to almost ribald secular verses in its earliest form. Allowing that there can be apt transference of words, it still remains that it can only be effected upon the basis of a more or less loose agreement between the sister arts. But perhaps its very looseness is its strength, as in most working forms of accommodation. Rigid ties snap; elastic ones give. It would be possible to establish that the vital thing in combining words and music is not so much the perfect correspondence of text and notes but the similarity of sentiment that each conveys. If that is maintained a great deal of freedom may occur in its application. A contradiction of sentiment would immediately strike us: a happy strain of words could not be put to a sad strain of music, or nobility coupled with triviality; but varied expressions of similar emotion can mate. We do not expect more than that, any more than we expect a husband and wife to be of identically the same pattern—it may still be quite a pleasure to see them together. Faults of accent, like downright quarrelling, of course, cannot be tolerated.

Perhaps the real answer to this particular problem lies in the fact that the meaning of words is so elastic and uncertain. Words have no exact meaning.[1] The simplest verbal phrase would need a volume of explanation before we could know what was in our minds in regard to its use, and even then we should not be sure of it. We have to *feel* words in much the same way as we do music; and the fluid nature of this feeling, which we can only sense but never wholly understand, allows a comparatively free combination of words and music, provided, as we have said, that a general sentiment is not violated.

In short, we are not shocked by a change of words to the same music, unless, by long habit we have come to regard certain music as the rightful, inalienable companion of certain words; but this is quite another matter, though it is by no means to be set aside as of little moment.

Another disquieting thought is that indifferent words are often set to fine music. What are we to say about this? It seems to indicate that music goes its own gait unhampered by the quality of the poetry that may accompany it; that it is more or less independent of the words, receiving little inspiration from them, and, consequently (as so many assert), that the words do not matter at all. If we are satisfied with the music, that is enough. But supposing it were the other way about: that we had to stomach poor music for the sake of fine poetry. Should we say then—if we were lovers of poetry—that the music did not matter? We can, of course, deny the good of song altogether, preferring to have our music and poetry

---

[1] 'It is in the nature of words to mean many things.' Virginia Woolf.

unmixed—entirely apart. As long, however, as song is a recognized form of art, we are surely right in insisting that both its elements should pass muster; and, if one of them does not, we *do* mind. Unspeakable words (or mediocre music) can only 'make the judicious grieve'. The appeal of a song which completely satisfies us must be greater than that of one in which we find fault in part.

We must admit, then, that words, nearly always, *have* to adapt themselves to music in the matter of 'timing', i.e., the length of time given to syllables, etc.—to that extent there is a lack of agreement; but they *can* adapt themselves comfortably enough—certainly so as regards accentuation—to the mechanical structure of the music, and also to its spiritual content. Our confidence in the perfect correspondence of words and music may have been a little shaken by this discussion—the poet's assertion that 'music and sweet poetry' 'needs must' agree cannot be accepted as wholly true; but we get very near to complete agreement in recitative or a free *melos* such as Holst uses in his *Four Medieval Songs* (*v.* p. 375) and, on the whole, the situation is by no means as bad as it may appear.

There are progressive stages in which music can be brought to the service of words. As we have seen, words are essentially free in time and inflexion, music is fixed in those respects. Those fixed musical attributes can gradually be imposed on words. Metrical verse is not at all the same thing as metrical music; it hardly ever has the regularity of the latter. It is only when it is actually joined to music that it takes on a dancing quality. Nor do words, in a general way, stay upon a particular note. It is very easy to perceive a marginal line between words and music in respect of pitch; the wayward 'up and downness' of speech is quite different from the melodious movement of note to note. In short, time and pitch are regularized in music; not in speech.

As music gains ground when it is combined with words, more and more of the specific character of speech is relinquished. To begin with, it may only be a case of monotoning words. This is the first thrall. It substitutes a fixed for an uncertain note, but may very well leave verbal rhythm intact. The reciting note in Psalmody is the easiest form of musical fetter that words can submit to, the medial and final cadences of a Psalm tone decide a closer bond:

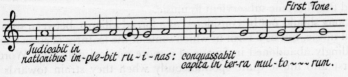

First Tone.

Judicabit in nationibus im-ple-bit ru-i-nas: conquassabit capita in ter-ra mul-to~~~rum.

In this it will be observed that the cadences slow up the movement of the voice and introduce a degree of note measurement; their melodic significance is clear. When unison develops into part-writing the words are still further fettered; a stricter measurement of the music takes place, with which the words must comply. But, in the medieval Motet, even when verse was substituted for the more usual Biblical or liturgical prose, the music nevertheless retained much of the prose nature of speech. At that time music was not in the ascendant; it was undoubtedly the handmaid of words, and, if the words were omitted, the music by itself could hardly have proved satisfactory. Yet, from relatively early times, we do find vocal music transferred to instruments, and Elizabethan composers, in some cases, certainly designated their madrigals as 'apt for viols *or* voices'.

From the seventeenth century, however, music took charge of the situation and assumed paramount importance; its general style was instrumental. The difference between the *melos* of this Kyrie of Palestrina:

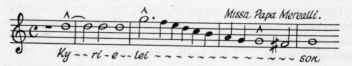

and this of Bach:

is shown by the accents (marked ∧). The irregularity of the one, and regularity of the other is clear.

In the nineteenth century the Romantic song writers were inspired by a greater respect for poetry, though instrumental habits of composition still lingered with them. Now we have again learnt how more equitably to adjust the respective claims of words and music. The struggle has always been between fixity and freedom. Words, *qua* words or *qua* spoken words, will not be bound to a procrustean bed of metrical rhythm. If it is attempted, their naturalness goes, and they become subservient to music.

Song should not be considered as a forced alliance between words and music, but as a form in which some of the features of speech are willingly abandoned in favour of a more musical delivery. Words burst into music quite spontaneously when they strain towards a higher emotional expression; this only music can supply. Then they become musical words in the true sense, not merely in the sense of being delivered with a 'musical' voice, but of being projected whole-heartedly into the form of music, though without losing those particular significances that make them words. We can imagine that words may be used purely for their emotional appeal: sound without sense (as we conceive it in language).[1]

If that is so—and it has been advocated as a main principle and distinction of poetry—we are as well off without them, for we can immediately soar into music without their aid, and are better served if we do. The point is that, in song, words retain their identity as words even when they adopt those features of pitch and rhythm that characterize music. They lose something of their spoken nature—a very valuable something; but they gain in amplification, glow, intensity. Song, in a sense, coarsens speech, but it carries further than speech, fills larger spaces. The rhythm of music is also bolder than the rhythm of words. It has a stronger flow; it is more consistent, more cohesive.

But because of it, the sung word is held in a certain bondage. It cannot move so easily; register such fine shades of feeling. When notes cling closest together, as in good *legato* and *portamento*, they are not so susceptible to detailed action, as are words in more loosely-knit speech. Hence, in song, breadth is more noticeable than subtlety.

In illustration of this, and also of the generally superior claim that music has in matters of expression, we may take the following phrase:

O love-ly fish-er mai-den

---

[1] But we should be wrong entirely to disassociate sound and sense; even at all. Sound never 'signifies nothing'. Every change of vocal shape and tension has a corresponding change of meaning. But it is certainly true that we may give the wrong significance to sound. The word 'God' for instance, is quite inadequate to express the majesty of the Creator, or the idea of Fatherly love. As a conventional symbol it may be understood—as an expressive sound it fails. The superiority for its special purpose, of the word 'Jehovah' (say) to that of 'God' is very obvious. Not only vowels but consonants are *directly expressive* serving far more than the differentiations of language. Doubtless a great deal of confusion has arisen in the course of the development of language; the original (and true) sense of vocal sound has in many, perhaps most cases, been separated from its rightful significance, but each and every sound has its particular meaning. One sound touches us in one way, another in another, till the whole gamut of our emotions has been covered; more than this: till the whole universe finds its counterpart in the various sounds inherent in words. We cannot afford to dispense with the power of words, with their symbolical sense (allied to our rational nature) their faculties of remembrance and association, and their immediate appeal to the emotions (which is none other than their musical appeal).

The tendency in speech, is considerably to weaken the final syllables of these words, so that, when sung, the phrase is apt to become

O love-ly fish-er   mai-den

This completely destroys the *musical* phrase, which needs a broad treatment such as this:[1]

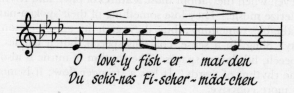

O love-ly fish - er ~ mai-den
Du schö-nes Fi-scher~mäd-chen

The important thing to note is that weak syllables, in speech, often have to be strengthened, in song, to approximately the same weight as the strong syllables. Undue weakening of syllables is a sure sign of merely colloquial speech.

A well-balanced spoken word can quiver like an aspen leaf, it will respond with infinite sensitivity to the slightest touch of the breath. The sung word is bound to be steadier; a greater measure of control is put upon it. One might almost say that the methods of notes are masculine in their firmness and precision; those of words, feminine, in their more nervous adjustment. To the performer this is abundantly clear. He has only to sing a musical phrase, and then, separately, speak the words that may perchance go with it—the foregoing example will serve for the purpose. He will notice the more continuous effort required by the one, and the less constant effort by the other. And he will be bound to acknowledge that the stronger sweep of song is achieved at some loss of the beauty of speech. Nevertheless poets (*pace* Mr. Turner) have, on the whole, welcomed this sacrifice as leading, in song, to a higher, or at any rate, more complete, form of expression.

In his *Apologie for Poetrie* Sir Philip Sidney said that the poet 'cometh with words set in delightful proportion, either accompanied with or prepared for the well-enchanting skill of music'. The final expression, at least in the case of lyric verse, was to be that of song;

---

[1] The apex of a 'swell' generally, or very often, comes on the up-beat, or its equivalent.

not a mere parallelism of words and music, or an 'underlaying' of the music with words—what might be called the 'worded note'—but the absorption of words into music, whereby the two are as one.[1] That his words suffer some sort of 'sea-change' the poet knows full well; but he is content to allow the ministrations of the musician, in the deeper knowledge that the latter's art will not destroy the meaning of his own work—its literary significance—only elevate it into a region where it is transfigured by the Orpheus-like 'enchantment' that music alone can give. In song we get the best of the worlds of speech and music: the one keeping us firmly planted on earth by the 'material' connotation of words, the other casting as it were a heavenly spell upon us by the more spiritual nature of its appeal. We may rebel against the definite symbolism of words, seeking to escape from it by whole-hearted subjection to music. On the other hand, we not only may be, but are, grateful for the 'local habitation and the name' which words bring. Both these urges are contained in our make-up, both are satisfied in song. The art of song is, therefore, a very special one, not to be confused either with that of poetry or of music; but combining the two in a way allowed only to these closely related manifestations of the arts of sound—'the sister and the brother'.

There can be little doubt that words have influenced musical form. The feminine endings characteristic of polyphonic music in all probability are due to the influence of the Latin language with which it was mainly associated. The endings of words and phrases in Latin are almost invariably trochaic or weak, as in 'Pa*ter*', 'Domi*nus*', 'exalta*bit*'; whereas English is rather an iambic language, as in '*be*gone', '*mis*trust', '*de*feat'. The iambic foot is the most common in English verse, and is the normal foot in our verse plays. Blank verse, if regular, has five iambic feet in a line: ten syllables in all, with the accent on the even numbers. The consequence of this is that the polyphonic cadence is generally a 'falling' cadence and this persisted till, in England, the vernacular became the ruling tongue, when a heavier 'rising' cadence was developed. With the Latin, cadential interest was centred on the movement from supertonic to tonic (or final), as in plain-song:

[1] '*His heart in me keeps him and me in one,*
My heart in him, his thoughts and senses guides" etc.
Sir Philip Sidney.

O*

With English, it shifted rather to the movement from leading note to tonic:

though harmonic considerations also largely entered.

On the other hand music undoubtedly affects the expression of words, especially in the way that they are sung; whether *legato* or *staccato*. Verbal thought does not seem to have anything to do with *staccato*, or next to nothing; and, when *staccato* is used with words, we may safely say that violence is done to them. We are enjoying, in short, a purely musical effect, as in:

Or in things like:

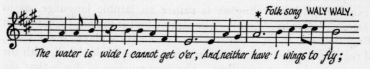

we tolerate the unnatural prolongation of the word 'have' in the interests of musical symmetry. In skilful composition the accents of words and music need never clash. If they do, as in the last example, the musical accent should generally prevail. But we must be very careful, before discarding verbal accent in favour of musical, that the verbal accent is really out of place and the music cannot adjust itself to it. Thus in hosts of madrigalian passages like the following:

the musical accent seems utterly at variance with the verbal. But it is not so, and one of the chief accomplishments in the art of singing is to be able to touch in verbal accent anywhere, no matter the length, pitch or place of a note. We are apt to be hide-bound in regard to what are generally looked upon as the strong and weak beats of a bar. This sort of mechanical accenting, which is more prevalent than we may care to admit, must be utterly disregarded unless there is good reason to observe it. In the foregoing example it will be seen that the accent, both verbal and musical, can come on any beat. When a song is well sung, the singer first of all attends to the words. As far as possible he speaks them according to their nature and natural accent. He projects them into the accompanying music, at the same time being fully aware of the music as such and endeavouring to express *it* according to *its* nature. If he thinks only of the music, his performance may be musical, but a relative failure as song, for a clue is missing; if only of the words, half the interest goes. Nevertheless, though the approach to all types of song must be through the words, it does not mean that they always claim the main attention. Declamatory song—in which an immediate situation is dealt with, and action is the ruling feature—depends more on verbal than musical delivery. The singer has to make the words ring true at all costs, and so the general style of declamatory song is *puntato*, or *con forza*. A supreme example of this style is Iago's 'Credo' in Verdi's 'Othello'. Lyrical song, on the other hand, is essentially ideal, remote, meditative. It generally subordinates the verbal to the musical interests as the finer medium of expression. *Arioso*, *cantabile*, are therefore its distinguishing features. There may be touches of melody in declamatory song; seldom, if ever, long stretches of it, for this would be a contradiction of its nature; whereas melody is the very soul of lyricism. The declamatory and lyrical styles are usually contrasted in a recitative with its following air, as in the recitative 'Thus saith the Lord' and air 'But who may abide' from the *Messiah*. Here, it is quite easy to distinguish the tremendous emphasis given to the words of a Person, that of the Godhead, in the recitative; as against the more musical significance of the reflective and almost impersonal matter which follows in the air.

But what is spoken is not always declamatory, nor what is sung always lyrical. Even when speech predominates, it can be so combined with a melodious quality—as nearly always in Bach's recitatives—that the declamatory element is much reduced, and sometimes, in lyrical song, conversational words enter in such a way as to bring the expression within sight of declamatory utterance. The singer has to decide upon the relative claims of the words and the music; decide how far he must dramatize his words, or indulge his musical sense. In so doing, it does not mean that he forgoes either the music or the words; only that, in favour of the one or the other, he allows the bias of expression to flow in its natural direction. A good composer, by the disposition of his notes, will generally make it quite clear what the singer should do, and so will the poet—for *his* words will move towards the condition of music when they demand lyrical treatment, and away from it, when they underline more personal and dramatic elements. Strictly, perhaps, one should associate declamatory style with the more impassioned moments of speech, when words have to be driven home, and their meaning enforced by extreme articulation.

An elocutionary bias can be given to song, either in recitative or air, *without* the assertive treatment that issues in pronounced *marcato*. On the whole a recitative will demand more pointed expression than an air, but it can and often does approximate to the more usual *flow* of speech. To admit that words always require to be hammered out noisily in order to bring them to the fore, would be to abrogate the position we have so constantly maintained: that *legato* is the natural way of speech; though, as well, we might also say that it is the natural way of music, and that both words and music submit to *staccato* only for special purposes of emphasis and expression.

In this example of Mozart recitative it will be seen that it is considerably removed from an extreme declamatory style. The words, however, are the main thing; the slight musical accompaniment shows that:

Le Nozze di Figaro

È Su-san-na non vien! So-non-sio-sa di sa - per come il conte ac-col-se la proposta.

How far verbal accent should dominate musical accent, is a matter of artistic judgment. But it is clear that words *are* at all times extremely important, and that the singer must be as sympathetic to poetry as he is to music. This is seldom the case. A sense of poetry and of the significance of words is hardly ever to be found with singers. They 'get away' with their work largely on the strength of their musical, not poetic resources.[1] It should scarcely be neces-

---

[1] Recently I asked two quite good vocalists—I will not call them 'singers'

sary to stress the importance of both words and music when they are combined, or refuse countenance to the idea that words do not matter, and can be discarded once the composer has used them to serve his purpose. Yet in practice, this is what the singer so often maintains.

It is hard to say exactly wherein the power of song lies. We have seen that words, in their emotional aspect, are attracted towards music; also that the formal structure of words and music is very similar. The marriage of both is almost inevitable. When such a union takes place, the result is not merely the addition of the two factors, but a fusion which produces a new thing. No one can pretend that two beings in love are the same as when no such emotion engages them. There is a mutual stirring that alters the personality of each. Love may not be always a lasting miracle. It may break up into its elements and combine into a fresh phenomenon:

> *Oh, when I was in love with you,*
> *Then I was clean and brave,*
> *And miles around the wonder grew*
> *How well I did behave.*

> *And now the fancy passes by,*
> *And nothing will remain,*
> *And miles around they'll say that I*
> *Am quite myself again.*[1]

just as words and music may separate and enter into new combinations. But while it lasts, in the setting of a particular poem, something does happen to both the music and the poetry. The wonder may pass by, the poem may be appropriated by another composer—but fortunately, that wonder once achieved, is enshrined for always in the written masterpieces of song and can be recaptured.

because that term includes the power of elocution—to *read* some of the recitatives of Bach's *St. John Passion*. In the particular numbers tried, one took the part of the Evangelist, the other of Jesus. Neither of them could characterize the part, or give anything of the quality of the fine, sustained speech befitting the situation. The reading was entirely trivial; the words of Jesus might have been spoken by a Cockney coster—how could they have been *sung* adequately? By the grace of the music some approach would be made to dignity of expression; but the result would be almost negligible. The voice of Jesus, with its calm, beauty and benignity, could not issue from such a spoken background; nor could the tale that is told by the Evangelist impress in the slightest by speech, little more than colloquial, which never rose to the height of the subject. A setting of the Passion is dramatic-oratorio, drama without action; and if the dramatis personæ are just sawdust figures, there can be no convincing performance.

[1] A. E. Housman, *A Shropshire Lad*. By permission of the Society of Authors and Messrs. Jonathan Cape Ltd., publishers of A. E. Housman's Collected Poems.

Song is as old as the hills, and it will endure—'the thread that runs from end to end of the story'[1]—after they are made low. Before time was, 'the morning stars sang together', and we can imagine that *they* will never cease their song, though the human voice is stilled.

[1] Sir Hubert Parry. *The Art of Music.*

Chapter 11

GESTURE

Gesture is concerned with words, rather than music, to which it applies mainly in the physical manifestation of the dance. In general, words have a physical significance, they suggest objects and their movement; whereas music seldom does. Its link with objective reality is slight in comparison; it dwells rather in the spiritual than the material sphere. Gesture, therefore, which is an art of movement, is especially stimulated by words.

Its further application to singing is obvious. In opera it is essential, and on the concert platform it cannot wholly be avoided if the singer responds to the sense of his song. Yet we should at once say that very little gesture should be used with the recitation or singing of most lyrical poetry, though how little or how much cannot be decided by rule.[1] One singer may almost dispense with it and yet hold our attention completely; the singing of another may be improved by some show of 'action'. What must not happen is that such action is irrelevant or distracting. To try to captivate an audience by a put-on smirk, or set, wooden positions that mean nothing, is entirely wrong. Looks and movement must at any rate *appear* to be spontaneous and natural, arising from, and appropriate to circumstance; in which case they will combine and vary in a thousand ways under the impulse of the imagination. Sometimes the 'rhythm' element will be specially suggested (as by nigger

---

[1] Folk song is the ancestral type of all secular song. In regard to it, Cecil Sharp, in his *English Folk Song*, tells us that the traditional way of singing it is as follows:

'During its performance the eyes (of the singer) are closed, the head is upraised, and a rigid expression of countenance maintained until the song is finished. A short pause follows the conclusion, and then the singer relaxes his attitude and repeats in his ordinary voice the last line of the song, or its title. This is the invariable ritual on formal occasions. Its apparent unconcern does not proceed from any lack of appreciation.' The folk singer at such times, indeed, does what every singer might do; dispenses with gesture altogether, even to the extent of facial expression; perhaps to the advantage of his song, as a song. At any rate, it is a very characteristic method of approach. But, the author adds: 'On *in*formal occasions, by his own fireside' for instance, he may get 'quite excited when he is singing a song that moves him, and rise from his chair and gesticulate and, perhaps, beat the table to enforce the rhythm of the tune': which shows that there is another side to the question, and that song, under certain conditions, naturally spills over into gesture. The union between song and dance as in primitive ritual, or the Balletta of the 14th century (which developed into the Elizabethan Ballet or Fa la) also demonstrates the same tendency. So that, even according to unsophisticated practice, no hard and fast rule can be laid down for either the avoidance or use of movement with song.

minstrels when they 'sway' to their song); more often the 'expression'; but always sparingly. Far better too little than too much. Rhythmic 'action', however, will generally relate to comparatively simple or comic situations. The more searching and serious the order of thought, the less does it need to be supplemented by action; obviously this applies, in greatest measure, to religious thought.

Before action takes place the body should be in a condition of ease and repose. A certain amount of tension is necessary to stance. To keep an upright balance, muscles have to be brought into play; but with a minimum of effort. When standing, the head, shoulders and arms should usually be loose. This is required not only for graceful carriage, but for technical reasons connected with singing. A stiff attitude is combative and repellent; a pliant one is friendly. Fidgety, unmeaning movements only irritate the beholder.

A singer gains by looking well on the stage or platform. Some achieve this naturally, others can certainly improve their appearance. The position of the arms needs consideration; for these are the most mobile parts of our anatomy, and, unlike legs, are not disposed of in the act of standing. They remain free, and we often do not know what to do with them. Whether the hands should be clasped together, or fall by the side of the body; whether one arm should be bent and brought across the body, or a symmetrical treatment be preferred, is a matter of taste. But it is not a matter of taste if the body tilts to one side, or one shoulder is held lower than the other, or we stand with the feet apart (women often offend in this), or do anything by which balance is disagreeably upset when it is supposed to be static. In short, all defects of poise and elegance should be remedied.

To some extent posture entails movement as a preliminary; it might be called stabilized gesture, as of a bird caught on the wing. Proceeding from which we come to actual movement, i.e., the passage from one point of rest to another—though movement itself is made up of innumerable postures such as we perceive in a 'slow motion' picture. In opera, as we have said, gesture is part of the business; an indispensable means of dramatic expression; an art by itself. With concert singing it has to be approached very warily, though for the singer to appear entirely unmoved by what he is singing can be as distracting as if he uses too much movement. We resent an apparent lack of interest, unless indeed it is adopted for a humorous purpose; and singing can be quite ineffective (when we are looking at the singer) if some sign of the meaning of the song is not registered at least on his countenance. To sing Moussorgsky's 'The Flea' without turning a proverbial hair would be just as unnatural as to submit, similarly, to the attentions of that particular insect. If the laugh of the singer were not as evident to the eye as to the ear it would be absurd; but it would be just as absurd to 'act' Schubert's 'Litany'.

Strictly speaking, gesture is an addition to song, it is not integral to it. The singer should aim at singing so well that he can persuade his audience purely by vocal means, as though he were not seen;[1] though if he can use action without spoiling the appeal of the song he is entitled to do so.

Where two or more people are concerned in a dramatic situation action is inevitable. The give and take of dialogue cannot be conducted as though it were a soliloquy. Lyric song, however, is always individual. The singer generally 'acts' it in the theatre of the mind; but let there be no mistake it *is* acted, even in thought. When such thought is reminiscent or contemplative, as most often it is, it does not press towards external action; but it 'moves' the singer for all that, and he is almost bound to convey this inward movement by *some* outward show. Lyric song can very well occur in opera, as in operatic airs. A large proportion of song is of this order, when almost all that is needed of the singer, physically, is that he should display a state of pensiveness or absorption. On the other hand, descriptive songs may invite a modicum of gesture; and, where a song is clearly dramatic, as Purcell's 'From Rosy Bowers', which depicts a lady distracted with love, in various kinds of madness—'sullenly mad; mirthfully mad; melancholy mad; fantastically mad; stark mad' (according to the directions of the poet)—the corresponding physical state must be suggested, but always with discretion. Gesture must never be overdone to the detriment of the main purpose of song, which is to express feeling, of whatever kind, through the arts of sound. The words and music of a song constitute a sufficient expression of what the poet and composer have to say, though it can be further enhanced by discreet action.

At the present day the English are undemonstrative; they make little use of gesture in conversation, so that they are more inclined than some of their continental neighbours to discard it when singing. It was different in the time of Shakespeare when (it would appear) we were emotionally expressive and unreserved to a degree which would now be considered extremely un-English; so that custom, as

---

[1] Gesture, quite apart from words, is a very powerful means of expression; instantaneously, silently, surely, reaching the very core of the emotional situation—a glance can reveal the innermost depths of the heart.

Words are but gesture transferred to speech, and they must be considered a such. The vocal organs are organs of gesture (*v.* p. 140); therefore, in as far as they perform this function, there is no *need* to reinforce their gesture by further visible movement. This is perhaps the real reason—it is certainly *a* reason—why the singer can and should rely mainly upon his particular form of gesture: that of speech, embodied in song.

well as propriety, probably decides the amount of gesture that we can tolerate.

It comes to this: the singer must show that he is full of his work, not indifferent to it; and, if his enthusiasm impels some further physical demonstration, nothing much can be said against it, provided it is sincere. Reticence, however, is never amiss; judgment is always necessary.

The eye catches the slightest change of attitude. Small, subtle signs of movement serve greater purposes than exaggerated ones which distract without convincing. We can see at a glance what a singer is up to; whether he means what he is singing about. If he appear dull and vacant, his singing will follow suit. Some show of life there *must* be. It is hardly possible to hide our emotional reactions, except by a quite unnatural *tour de force*; and it may be remarked that an intelligent face provides, in itself, a considerable amount of interest, not wholly irrelevant to any matter in hand.

Earlier, we spoke of the rhythmic 'swaying' indulged in by nigger minstrels. Metrical, and even prose music, is permeated with the spirit of the dance. 'Swaying' is a form of it, almost the vital sign; and only if a singer has this urge will he understand what rhythmic movement really is. Great conductors show it, in fact every great performer; though it may be more imagined than operative. At base, this is the spirit accountable, even, for the realization of time proportions. The practical politics of measured time is 'action'; the mind only comes in to compare and check the measurements.

As well, the singer has problems of movement mechanically connected with the production of his voice, just as an instrumentalist has them in connection with the playing of his instrument. This is a different thing from movement which arises from 'expression'. It is unavoidable, and we cannot object to it, though it should be reduced as much as possible, and never degenerate into 'exhibitionism'.[1] There is a best stance for singing—all posture may be said to be arrested movement; there has to be breathing, though good singers show little or no evidence of it; vowels and consonants have to be continuously readjusted, etc. Expressive movement is superimposed upon all this, but there is no difficulty in distinguishing it from technically-imposed movement. Both, however, often agree; and if they do not—as, for instance, when the vowel Oh, with its natural tendency towards a rounded mouth, appears in a phrase where a smile is appropriate—a sufficient technique will

---

[1] To see 'the works' of an artistic performance is in no sense helpful to our enjoyment of it. The means are only of importance to the practitioner; the listener is concerned with the result, which is far more mysterious and, consequently, impressive, when he does not know how it comes about.

enable the singer to make the countenance correspond to the spiritual expression; that is to say, use a smiling or serious face no matter the vowel that he is called upon to sing.

But, in a general way, differences of emotional tension will be registered in clearly apparent differences of physical tension; the relation between mind and body cannot be disregarded. Grave tone will be forthcoming from a serious face; gay from a smiling one. Contradictions will occur; but, on the whole, the unity of mechanism with meaning will be *seen* to operate.

To sum up. Pose and gesture should start from repose. Relaxation (as far as possible) should go with action. Reduce gesture to a minimum, and, when you do use it, see that it enhances your singing and does not run counter to, or compete against it. All we have to consider is whether the expression of the song is improved or weakened by a show of facial or bodily movement, the song being always our first concern.

Chapter 12

ODDS AND ENDS[1]

VERY soft notes are apt to be ineffective unless spirit is put into them. Spirit is breath.

§

There are two ways in which we can move anything: (1) by pushing, (2) by dragging. With (1) the direction is up or forward; with (2) down or backward. With (1)—as regards singing—the force of gravity has to be continuously overcome; with (2) the force of gravity is used. There is more strength used to push than to pull; the weight of the body counts more in the latter. Pushed notes are therefore tighter, more tensed—things are very apt to go wrong with them; notes which fall towards the base of the breath (with due safeguards as to merely lazy action) are altogether easier to produce. Both principles have their uses and special emotional significances.

§

The singer is always between the devil and the deep sea; the devil of hard, telling tone (so suitable to certain effects), and the deep sea of the profundities of tone. In a sense these two types are quite contrary, but if they cannot be dealt with at will, the singer will lack full control of his mechanism, unable to steer a purposeful, central course, avoiding exaggerated, extreme deviation.

§

Certain sounds *drop* into place; others have to be put in place.

§

Notes must be properly 'housed'. If you kick them out of the neck, generally they will not sound; strangled, inhibited tone may result.

§

Mechanically, the problem is to sing loudly and quickly; spiritually, to sing softly and slowly. Few singers show, or have the power of expressing simple *humanity*, which perhaps can be taken as the 'mother' spirit—strangely enough men seem to possess this

[1] For half a century I have been in the habit of jotting down points that have arisen when teaching or training singers. Some of these points have already been incorporated in the foregoing pages, but I think a gleaning from the remainder may be of interest and tend to complete my argument. There is no sort of logic in the arrangement of the paragraphs.

more than women. This is not a mere opinion, nor unjustified. Ask a singer to sing a lullaby such as the old 'Coventry Carol', and hear what he or she makes of it. In most cases it will be devoid of tenderness, full of forced, worried, uncalled-for accent; in short, nothing like we desire to hear, and recognize as right, when we do hear it. The mechanical production of the voice, though a necessary factor, does not produce this sort of thing, which comes from something quite other—from the heart. Any capacity for an objective realization of notes and time values—of the printed note and word—is as nothing beside it. The *singer* shows it—it comes from himself, himself alone; it is his character, his whole affectionate system.

§

Some seem to be impersonal because they have no feeling; or at any rate show none. It represents just a void or vacuum of expression. The only valid impersonality is the control of personality to broad issues.

§

The trouble with many singers is that they have no integrated mental and physical personality; their head and their belly do not work in unison. They have, in short, no capacity for 'expression'. 'Expression', strictly speaking, is impossible till the belly is brought into play. A mental sense of music by itself is impotent. Indeed, without risking much exaggeration, we might go further and say, that there is no mental sense without a corresponding physical sense. As has been said elsewhere we cannot *imagine* a vowel, unless we can embody it physically. We may *try* to imagine the tone we wish to get, but shall never completely succeed in mentalizing it till we have the power to shape it.

§

There is no such thing as a short vowel in singing; that is to say the snappy, tight sound that usually comes when we speak such words as 'cot', 'cat', 'cut'. Singing does away with these almost entirely, even in short *staccato*; substituting sounds which are eased and richened by the use of an open throat. Thus 'cot' will (or may) become a sort of ŏ+Aw; cat, ă+Ah; cut, almost Uh itself. However the resultant vowel is analysed—and it is difficult to say what it really is—it will certainly not be hard in the spoken sense. To get a good, perfectly recognized vowel it has to be opened. As regards the mouth, this can be done at the back or front of the mouth—one or the other is absolutely necessary. In the former case the mechanism will be opened backwards, by a sort of drawing back, falling movement of the jaw and tongue; in the latter case by a forward and rather *tensed* movement, which lifts the larnyx somewhat. Smooth easy tone is the characteristic of the former; a more *timbrée*, lively quality, of the latter.

§

There is a certain lustre with an open vowel that is never secured by an untrained voice. To get this into such quiet words as 'rest' or 'love' indicates a high degree of vocal control.

§

Ordinary speech is scarcely more than communicative, seldom selective in the choice of words. A poet chooses his words for their sound as well as for their sense. Their sound goes a long way towards indicating what he wishes to say.

§

Thou shalt break them with a rod of iron,
Thou shalt dash them in pieces like a potter's vessel.

Were ever words better chosen? No *cantabile* here, but a ruthless hammering of hard, short vowels, quite devoid of friendly connection. The temper of the passage is so inflexible, the tension so highly wrought, that, to save themselves from utter rigidity, the words almost *have* to burst asunder.

§

Notes must always 'cling' loosely to the vocal cords, much as a horseman by his own weight—if it is allowed to operate—clings to his saddle. Singers are so apt to bump notes off their seats, with resultant incapacity for *legato* or any easy quick movement of notes.

§

Staccato needs great energy, as can be tested by a performance of, say, Strauss' song 'Schlagende Herze', with its 'Kling Klang' etc., syllables. Shortness of note is always accompanied by nasality. Tension drives the voice into the head. But this is not at all at variance with lightness; on the contrary. The voice can be used in the lightest way with the strongest tension. It will have a resistance that loose, low-lying sound can never have. A loose skein of hemp will fall inertly if dropped; if tightly compressed, it will rebound. It then has life and spring. The use of nasal sound undoubtedly makes for liveliness of action, as well as timbre.

§

The 'veiling' of tone is like pulling down a shutter at the nose.

§

Sound always wants to push its way *through* the nose, particularly in a *crescendo*. This must not be permitted. A feeling must be gained that the sound issues through the mouth. This is a firm principle of technique.

§

Provided that the vocal instrument is held firmly, with the cavities properly shaped and tensed, singing can be automatic and almost effortless.

§

Be careful that the vowel ă does not become ĕ: 'and' not 'end', 'shall' not 'shell'. It is sometimes difficult to secure a dark ă.

§

The voice should 'engage' gradually, as a screw, which starts its work easily, then increases its tightness till it grips finally with full power. This is just simple mechanics.

§

The perfectly balanced breath, upon which the voice can lie, as it were, motionless, is a combination of the retching and yawning breath; their opposition, in fact. Tone and tensity are quite dependent upon that basic foundation. If the retching movement predominates too much, strained, pushed tone results; if the yawning movement, breathy, flabby tone.

§

To get control of the necessary muscular action the singer should do this exercise:
1. Strain the breath upwards, as in sickness, then while holding this position
2. Endeavour to yawn as deeply as possible.
                                    or
the reverse process:
1. Yawn deeply
2. Use the retching muscles strongly against it.
Do this repeatedly.

§

It may help the singer to think of his notes as solid entities, resting on the closed cords as on a table set to receive and sustain them; they must never be allowed as it were to fall through the cords. Gargling, by which the gargle is kept from going down the throat, is a good example of this process. This is by no means a mere figure of speech, but a practical observation.

§

Let the voice go downwards till it, so to speak, reaches the bottom

407

of the breath stream; in much the same way a good touch upon the pianoforte reaches the key 'bed'.

§

The 'touch' on the voice is secured by breath attraction, the 'hit' (*sf*) by breath thrust. The one is inward, the other outward.

§

Wide is the gate which leads to destruction; it is the strait and narrow path which must be kept in singing, as in everything else. Essentially, control is limitation.

§

Poor, slack tone will often blend the best, just as a lot of unassertive people will make the most amenable crowd. This is not the ideal of fusion, however, in tone or anything else; the idea is that of a disciplined combination of lively elements.

§

The following letter which appeared in the *Sunday Times* some years ago, is worth more than momentary consideration. I trust the writer will not object to its inclusion here.

Sir,

I am a teacher of French of some 30 years standing. With every year that passes I find it harder and harder to obtain correct articulation of sounds. In recent years I have insisted on 'jaw exercise'—opening and closing of the jaws as rapidly as possibly—before beginning actual speech training.

Nobody could stand in front of my classes and be other than appalled at the terrrible disuse into which the jaw muscles of some 50 per cent of the students have fallen. It has to be seen to be believed. It is perfectly true that some of the smaller boys and girls find it difficult to move their jaws at other than a snail pace!

The sight of the students eating their school dinner is painful to me; in many cases there is the slightest movement and nothing more. I often wonder what is the cause of this state of things; there are times when I feel like accusing the nation of being far too 'proper'! Heartiness of speech, heartiness in eating are derided. However that may be, the fact that the muscles of the jaws are little exercised cannot be gainsaid. Does not Mr. James Agate reproach our actors and actresses with mumbling? Lack of muscle, Mr. Agate, lack of muscle!

Yours, etc.

Holywell, N. Wales.   NEMO.

§

'One word from me, and Winks does just as he pleases.'
This comical remark was made to me by an Irishman whose duty

408

it was to take out an unmanageable little terrier, 'Winkie', for his daily run. Our vocal conduct is often like Winkie's. We tell our muscles to do one thing and they promptly do another. The mere fact of thinking about a muscle tends to make it twitch and contract, when we may want it to do the very reverse. This is particularly the case with that 'unruly member', the tongue. We may wish it to lie flat, in the pit of the mouth, as for Ah. Up it will go, though it might have been amenable enough if we had desired nothing of it. There is another reason for its frequent contrariness. The necessary tightening of adjacent muscles, as in the larynx during phonation, is apt to spread to the tongue as well, giving it quite the wrong shape. We *can* keep the tongue down by tension, but the usual effect of tension is to make the tongue rise. Relaxation, on the other hand, tends towards inertness and the flattening of the tongue. To some extent most of us are tongue-tied, though we may chatter nineteen to the dozen all day long. Our tongues are generally much too slow in movement. and do not secure a sufficiently defined oral cavity. Hence to a large extent thin sound and poor articulation.

§

It must never be forgotten that white tone—which easily resounds in the nasal cavities and gives 'noise'—is the basis of the finer and more expressive tone which lies deeper, and is darker and more covered. Good tone is simply bad white tone, humanized. Fundamentally it cannot be done without, just as our spiritual nature cannot be divorced from our physical brute nature. If we omit crude nasal 'noise'—just such a noise as is made by the shouting street urchin—we omit the essence of vocal sound.

§

The consonant M, which nature gives us—we have no hand in its formation—has already been referred to as the 'stuff' of vocal tone. It is interesting to observe that, in a much wider sense, it is also used in words which represent a primary element of existence from which differentiation arises, e.g., the word 'mother'—nearly every language has an initial M for this word—or the word 'motion' and kindred words; special *kinds* of motion are designated by other consonants.

§

As long as a singer has the bar and mechanically measured notes (for which, of course, the composer is responsible), to guide him, he can give some idea of the rhythmic qualities of his song; but without these measurements he often makes a sorry show of rhythm. The natural rhythm of words in recitative is the real rhythmic test:

what, in short, can be done with words in a musical phrase when there is no, or scarcely any, clue to note length or accent, as in plain-song. It is then that the real capacities of the singer show themselves, whether what is done is pretence, determined by factors from without, or issues from an inner rhythmic conviction.

§

A good note should be sharp and not snub-nosed; tiptoed not flat-footed. We have to sharpen a pencil before it is fit for service; we run upon our toes, not our heels.

§

Beautiful tone is like a person sleeping upon a bed. The sleeper is relaxed, with all the comfort and ease of sleep, but the bed upon which he rests is firm and staunch. By 'relaxation' in singing many would include the 'bed' as well as the 'sleeper', in which case 'down will come baby, cradle and all!'

§

Do not make the breath govern the vocal cords, but the vocal cords the breath.

§

In itself, beautiful tone is expression. What we generally call 'expression' is hardly needed with it.

§

A perfect note scarcely seems to have vibration, it is so smooth, so wedded with and woven into the surrounding air. It does not fret you or grate upon you; it envelops you without your being aware of what is causing it, like a spiritual presence.

§

A note comes from where you *feel* it. If you feel it at the base of the breath it will come from there, and you will open your throat at the same time.

§

You must 'kill' a note in order that it shall live.

§

A good note should be like a parachute coming to earth; it should open as it descends and settles on the breath.

§

Just as refuelling is required for any expenditure of mechanical energy, so vowels need to be continually renewed.

§

An effective, 'telling' note can be sung quite well in a fairly high-lying position; but a 'touching' one can only come from an open, low-lying position.

§

There is the beauty of the earth, but the heavens are over it; a good note also has its 'heavenly arch'.

§

By music words are lifted into a rarer atmosphere, but at the same time lose something of their definite character and special ways of expression. Just as the earth is more varied than the heavens, so are words more varied than notes because of their material significance. In song, this variety has to a certain extent to be surrendered in favour of the more general appeal of the music. We give up detail in order to secure more breadth.

§

It is possible to be profoundly musical and yet not to relate music to any specific object or even emotion. Some always wish to explain music, or connect it with something else; when they hear a piece of music it immediately suggests something in words. Music, of course, touches our emotional life, but we need not in the least understand how it is so, or what it means in terms of another form of expression. Nevertheless there *is* a very close link between words and music, both physically and spiritually, and this is the justification of song.

§

The 'swelling' of individual sounds, without relation to the phrase as a whole, is just as symptomatic of emotional disease as are swellings of an inflammatory and unhealthy condition in the human body. Many performers, particularly string players, do not seem able to sustain a note without sentimentalizing it in this way. They have no sense of line.

§

A 'touching' performance naturally depends upon touch; upon the way that the performer *approaches* his material. If touch is absent singing will never move us; it will have no sympathetic beauty.

§

Popular sayings nearly always 'hit the nail on the head' and when we are told that a man 'puts no stomach' into his work we are given exactly the right reason for it being of poor quality. It applies to singing most thoroughly. If a singer does not use his stomach or,

411

more correctly, belly muscles he will never have either good tone or good rhythm.

§

If the tension 'gives' between notes there can be no true *legato*. The notes may seem to be sustained, with some sort of continuous sound between them—but this is not *legato*. *Legato* is not only tension but a tendency towards *increased* tension. That is the only way notes are bound to one another, the only way that *espressivo* happens and *portamento* is brought to bear.

§

The distinguishing feature of music is vowel; that of words, is consonant.

§

Music is fluid not fixed; it is the movement of stone after it is carved; the winged element; life itself.

§

After breath taking, or a cæsura or rest of any kind, there must generally be a stress, indicating a new lease of life. This is an important structural point in performance. The capital letter placed at the beginning of lines in poetry stands for much the same thing.

§

Everything tends towards equilibrium. If a bottle of chalky water is allowed to settle, the chalk will eventually precipitate itself to the bottom. This is what should happen with the voice. It should tend to 'settle', and, if it does so, vowels will be clear and open.

§

Though there is an English, French, Italian and German language, there is only one *singing* language. The loveliest sounds have no nationality.

§

It is quite clear that interpretation, which aims at expressing the true feeling of a song—or at any rate the feeling which arises in oneself with regard to it—must be concerned with tone colour, the particular shade or quality which alone can suggest it. Mere notes, effected by a sort of standardized technique, are quite inadequate; such a process is pattern-making, not a revelation of spirit.

§

Ritualistic, religious art, though it ultimately depends on sincerity and the personal will, is not art because of that. The orgies of a revivalist meeting have nothing to do with art. Art does not begin till the critical faculty has been brought to bear; till a search for beauty as well as truth has been initiated.

§

Though, fundamentally, a voice needs to be hard (or to have an immediate capacity for hardness), it must generally be softened by warmth and feeling.

§

Tonal continuity is a sort of lambent flame, burning up the notes of a phrase as it goes along.

§

G. M. Nicholson says that the starling 'has a consuming love for hearing his own voice'. So has many a singer, and why not? Unless he pleases himself he is not likely to please others, though it does not invariably happen that he does the latter.

§

'Expression' is the sign of understanding. The only expression worth having is what you put in yourself. If you cannot supply it, *without expression marks,* the music means nothing to you.

§

Nor do I think it a matter of little moment whether the language of a people be vitiated or refined . . . I believe, rather, that when the vernacular becomes irregular and depraved, there will follow the people's ruin or their degradation. For what do terms used without skill or meaning, which are at once corrupt and misapplied, denote but a people listless, supine, and ripe for servitude?
English trans. from one of Milton's Latin letters.

To which may be added the fact that the fall of Greece and Rome *was* accompanied by the debasement of their language: classical Latin, for instance, turned, through a process of sheer laziness, into the Romance languages of Italian, French and Spanish, which, in their turn, by slow degrees, were again raised to classical perfection.

§

The theory of moral and intellectual education ultimately resides in the fact that we are all built to much the same pattern, and have much the same possibilities of development.

§

It may be noted that there is a sort of antagonism between rhythm and expression—if by expression we mean, as, in a chief sense, we

413

must, 'feeling' in a note or phrase which realizes itself in a *crescendo* or 'swell'. To *feel* a note is to develop it; to cause it to take root and grow. Now this growth of sound is accompanied necessarily by increased tension which is apt to tie up movement, preventing its easy flow. And so we get a paradoxical situation in which an urge of sound tends to retard speed, and a slackening of sound to quicken the movement. Effectively this is what we note in performance: that quick movement does not favour expression, and that expression is at its highest in slow movement.

§

The general, unconscious tension, always present in the living body, is, or may be, sufficient to deal with the softest vocal sound; i.e., the vocal mechanism may be relatively loose, and still (up to a point) adequately tensed. This, however, applies rather to vowels than to consonants. To get clear consonants, more breath pressure is required than for soft, sympathetic vowels. So that, on the whole, a certain amount of extra tension, when words are in question, cannot be dispensed with even in very soft singing.

I think we should be very careful how far we pursue the matter of tonal analysis—or rather of the way in which we pursue it. Art is a matter of feeling, and there is a grave danger nowadays of substituting intellect for feeling in art; in other words, of adopting a scientific attitude for an emotional one. I doubt very much whether the scientific analysis of tone serves the singer very much. It is interesting with a graphic electrical record of tone, to see with some precision what are the overtones (and their relative power) that go with any particular sound-quality. But the quality itself can never be produced by any such process, nor can the *mixture* of tone (or resonance) be deduced from it. The proportions and dispositions of tone are much too elusive for that. The ear, stimulated by the right attitude and feeling, alone can tell us what is wanted. This sufficed in the great days; and it suffices now. It is the training of feeling (controlled intellectually) that matters; not scientific analysis. In a very true sense (as it seems to me) the scientist is a foe of art; and if many scientists have artistic inclinations (as they undoubtedly have) it is not because of their science, but because of the artist in them.

§

A work of art is always greater than any performance can be. More is implied in a Shakespeare play than can ever be expressed. The complete sound picture will never be given of a Beethoven symphony. An ideal will never be manifested in its ideal shape; that

414

is to say, the symbol will always contain more than any or all of its realizations. And so our expression of any song or piece will be to a certain extent imperfect. Its formal beauty will be marred by faults; its spiritual beauty will be missed and misunderstood in very much. At best it is only *our* idea of the symbol that we shall manifest. Expression in the sense of which we are talking is what we *do* to a poem or a song when we perform it; it shows what we see in it. If we see merely formal beauty—beautiful proportions and juxta-positions—our performance will be cold and uncoloured; if it fires our imagination and evokes correspondence with our emotional nature it will be warm and charged with colour. By the way, what a blessing it is that poets do not put expression marks to their words!

§

All vocal 'colour' has a quality of darkness in it; incandescence has no colour, such as we understand it.

§

A necessary part of *mezza voce* tone is its sheen or lustre; without it *mezza voce* is ineffective as it has no little body. It has to gain in quality what it loses in weight. 'Slumbrous light' gives a very good idea of what most *mezza voce* should be.

§

The magic of 'atmosphere' is easily dissipated by crudity of colour (which nearly always concerns the vowels Ee and Ay); and it comes from the skilful covering of notes, together with the capacity to keep the higher partials in them.

§

It has been said that ethics is a science of limits, so is voice production.

§

It is important that the voice should not only be drawn together, towards a vital centre, but should also radiate from it, like light from the sun.

§

In a sense the pursuit of the ideal is apt to standardize and check the inexhaustible variety of reality. This must be guarded against, by a sort of fight between the two. What we should lose if personality were not allowed for, and did not persist in having its say!

§

Do not force notes, feed them! A poor singer says 'off you go' to his notes and syllables, the good one 'come here, come here!'

415

Expression always consists in a 'digging in' of tone, though it emerges as 'lifted' sound. The sign of a swell < >, with its divergent and convergent lines, is a picture of the process.

§

Interpretation is always a kind of pretence, dependent upon the mastery of the tricks of the trade. This can be reduced to an almost mechanical art, a sort of 'shorthand of emotion or feeling' as someone has observed; but it is then as spurious as it is limited, because it has little or no relevance to meaning or situation. Imagination is never really summoned by it; one can see through it at a glance. It is worth nothing as a revelation of character. Most instrumental interpretation is as bad as singing in its ill-considered gush.

§

Recently she has become interested in poetry, particularly Shelley and Keats, and can recite the 'Ode to a Grecian Urn' with the same feeling she puts into 'I'm Dreaming of a White Christmas.'

From the Daily Express.

§

When thought takes the place of feeling, things go astray. It is difficult to feel too much, it is very easy to think too much.

§

Make the most of syllables, avoid elisions.
The f *e a* lty life pays its rightful kings.

T. R. Lowell.

Commands all light, all infl *u e* nce, all fate.

Wordsworth.

On the other hand, make as little as possible of secondary diphthonged vowels, e.g., 'He *ur* my *ee* pray *ur*' for 'Hear my prayer', etc.

§

The development of the diaphragm is essential to physical fitness. Borotra, the famous tennis champion, says that he always exercises his diaphragmatic muscles for a quarter of an hour every morning, and gives this as the reason why, at fifty-one, he can beat younger men of half his age.

§

One is bound to admit that expressionless voices are generally the best produced and the most trustworthy. They rely for effect upon a fine mechanical technique; they are not distracted by verbal niceties. But those niceties are still the aim and end of singing. It takes words and music to make a song. The best soprano I have ever known was pitiably weak in recitative. Her *sostenuto* was strong and effective, everything was clear; yet she was quite at sea when she could not rely upon musical elements. It showed that she had no sense of words, and that her elocutionary resources were almost nil; *vox et præterea nihil.*

§

It must be emphasized that vowels are *colour*, and that one paints one's vocal picture with colour. It is not the use of vowels in words as *symbols* that matters (in this sense), though the associative element in words is very important; it is their emotional significance which shows the true inwardness of speech. From end to end beautiful pronunciation, beautiful colour, is the main factor in poetic expression.

§

In a sense the voice should 'trail clouds of glory' *after* it, rather than, as it were, send out sparks *before* it. For the latter would tend to be over-excited whereas the supreme quality of calm can only come with the former method.

§

'All music is what awakes in you when you are reminded by the instruments' (Whitman). The only good of music, or any other art, is that it allows us to express ourselves.

§

Emotion is a human thing, a stirring of our being. It cannot be looked upon as contained in any object, whether that object be one of material form, or immaterial idea. Emotion is something that *we* supply, it is not intrinsically in things outside us. There is no emotion in music save what we give to it.

§

The distinction between composer and performer should not be overstressed. All the composer gives us or can give us is the bare notes, the bare facts of his art. It is the performer's business to vitalize and clothe them.

§

The great secret of expression is, in the first place, to put none in. A paradox, but try to eliminate the accidents and misfortunes of 'expression', and you will see what is meant.

§

The progress of language in every department, accompanying

417

P

and representing the advance of the race is, in the art of speaking as in other arts, on the whole, from the grosser to the more refined, from the physical to the moral and intellectual, from the material to the formal. But we must never lose sight of its lowly origins (which represented action) and allow language to become passive, without life and vigour. The very forms of our speech are active. Our auxiliaries of tense and mode all go back traceably to words of physical meaning—as *have* to 'seize', *may* to 'be strong or great', *shall* to 'be under penalty', and so on; likewise, *of* comes from the comparatively physical 'off', and *for* from 'be*fore, fore*ward'; *right* means etymologically 'straight' and *wrong* means 'twisted'; *spirit* is 'blowing', *intellect* a 'picking out among', *understanding* a 'getting beneath'. And, when this is so, it is unwise to move in too rare an atmosphere of detachment or believe that we can cut adrift in this life from the iron bonds that hold us to the earth. If we do, the danger is that we shall attenuate speech and lose its strong content. This the artist can never afford to do, whatever direction the saint or sage or philosopher elects to follow. To feel the *force* of a verb, the *quality* of an adjective, the *content* of a noun, and even the connective physical vigour of a preposition is a *sine qua non* for admirable declamation or song.

§

Really *open* tone—i.e., tone of the utmost clarity, purity (and metallic ring)—seems to demand a straight passage from the vocal cords to the exit. It is the bend in the instrument, the turning of the corner, where it occurs at the back of the mouth ⌐→ that prohibits this clarity, fogging the tone, or at any rate modifying it; as it were placing a stopper or plug at a point where the channel should be entirely free and unblocked. If we imagine—and, indeed, cause the tone to be unimpeded, by straightening the piping, as far as possible—almost making it a continuation of the vertical piping of the pharynx—we get 'clear', not 'atmospheric', tone and a directness of attack, an instantaneous registration of sound, hardly ever achieved, but perfectly obvious when it is. An *open* 'Ah', produced without let or hindrance, and, in fact, openness of vowelling as a whole, seems to be dependent on the principle here outlined—or it feels as if it were. How often do we hear a perfectly open Ah, as in such words as 'heart', 'laugh', 'sanctus' (Latin), etc., unless it is 'white', when of course it is bad, devoid of expressive power?

§

Even a soft attack should 'strike fire' instantaneously.

§

Until we can sing Ah properly we shall never get tone which at all times will sustain effectively; it will 'go to pieces' on the larger, freer positions of the voice. Because it is relatively so free a good Ah shows tonal control as nothing else.

§

In one sense a piece of music is continuous; in another by no means so, but a series of completely-formed and separate pieces joined together.

§

Be alive and it will cover a multitude of sins.

§

Imperfection born of perfection is the nature of art. In regard to their calligraphy the Chinese say that a square should never be a perfect square but should be higher on one side than the other, and that two symmetrical parts should never be exactly similar in size and position. They call this 'shih' or 'posture', representing beauty of momentum.

§

With the best singing there is a sort of diaphragmatic *agony*. This alone gives meaning to words, highly wrought definition, and that intense quality (even with the softest sound) which betokens that we are using our full powers.

§

To the author a song generally means something to him in relation to his own life; it has a sort of ritual significance. The point must not be stretched too far, but, unless we can deal with art in this sense, of what good is it to us? Merely to survey a work of art, because you think someone else might be interested, does not seem to have adequate purpose.

§

Perform nothing that you do not believe in personally.

§

The artist tries to understand life, to be at one 'with the reason of things', only to know finally that he is baffled in the attempt; hence a terrible background of sadness is always present in his work. '. . . in the very temple of Delight veiled Melancholy has her sovran shrine.'

§

The two main elements with which the singer has to deal in song

419

are declamation and melodiousness. Without declamation there is
no sense, without melody no music.

§

In song we have to consider:

    a.   the tonic accents of the words and

    b.   the undulation, or rise and fall of the complete phrase; a
        detailed within an overarching expression, as in the
        following:

where the tonic accents (underlined) should be indicated (though
not extravagantly,) by the 'swell' stresses, noted at (a) while the
general undulation of the phrase, noted at (b), should also be suggested. The combination of words and music produces many
problems of accenting; we must never forget that vocal expression
is a two-fold process.

§

It is much more difficult to sing with no expression whatever, 'as
cold as stone', than with, at any rate, the semblance of expression
in which variations of force and speed occur. The following is a
good example of the need for it. It is from Handel's opera
'Rodelinda', where Bertarido, the king, supposed to be dead,
returns and contemplates the tomb that has been falsely erected to
his memory.

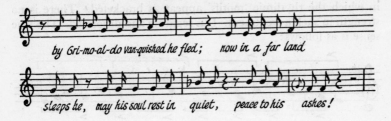

by Gri-mo-al-do van-quished he fled; now in a far land

sleeps he, may his soul rest in quiet, peace to his ashes!

§

The sign of whether a verbal or musical phrase has been understood appears largely in the accenting.

§

The 'time-spot': that fatal moment when something happens, a coming and going *at the same instant*. The artist knows how to place this moment. The finer the artist the more inevitably does he articulate his work; it could happen at no other point of time.

§

Accents are like a series of explosions which propel the music; not necessarily loud explosions, but sufficient to produce the desired effect. They may even be a sort of gradual accumulation and discharge of energy in the nature of a swell ($<\ >$).

§

A contralto air from Handel's 'Hercules' illustrates the difficulty of 'voicing' quick syllables. Its opening phrase runs:

See, the dreadful sisters rise, Their baneful presence shakes the skies!

If the throat closes the syllables will become almost inaudible, or are likely to be so feebly resonated that the sound, particularly on the lower notes, will be insufficient to satisfy the demands of force and clarity.

The phrase also affords a good example of an important rhythmic consideration. It easily becomes:

in which the rhythmic 'motifs' appear as bracketed. There is no strength in such a treatment. It is separate and disjointed. The true sense is as follows:

which rivets the notes soundly together—'cross-riveted' would be the better term. This means that the verbal accent is on the down-beat, but the musical on the up-beat. To satisfy both these accents *marcato* is therefore essential to every note:

See the dreadful sis·ters rise

Nothing less will serve. Even an *sf* on the lower notes would not be amiss; it would certainly show the rhythmic structure. The import-ance of the 'up' beat is here recognized. Bad performance is nearly always of a 'down' beat kind. The life of a phrase is in its 'lift'.

§

The beat is not merely a 'tick-off' or measurement of time; it should also be looked upon as the generating power of rhythm, as a step (such as we take in walking) from which movement springs. If this is clearly seen, 'time-beating' becomes an absurdity in any musical sense.

§

Beauty is expressed in movement, quite as much as in nuance.

§

Vibrato denies the element of *distance*. It brings expression within the realm of the particular and accidental. It is of the essence of time in a restricted immediate sense, not of timelessness. With it we cannot move in the regions of the spacious, the eternal; music is then close to us. The mysterious, the really impressive is never close.

§

Dr. Parker, the famous preacher of the City Temple, was offering up a prayer, when a commotion arose in the congregation. He stopped and asked what was the matter. "A man won't remove his hat,' was the indignant reply. 'Is that all?' said the doctor. 'Let be, let be, there's nothing in it!' and forthwith proceeded with the service.

'There's nothing in it,' is often applicable to our singing.

§

The more you put into music, the slower you can take it. According to Wagner the extremes of *tempo* are reached when the melodic or rhythmic element predominates to the exclusion of the other. Those who have heard the percussion orchestras of the South African natives at almost any of the Rand mines will realize the extent to which this is true. The speed and almost demoniac fury with which they assert the rhythm, the excitement of it all, is immense. It can be done because the melodic interest is relatively poor. There is no need to wait on the notes; the effect comes from the rain of percussion accents, driven home without respite.

§

There are two sorts of *agilità*, the expressive and the *bravura*. We must be able to get expression through a *series* of quick notes as well as through a single note. The quick sections of the 'Queen of the Night' airs in the Magic Flute are not just showy, heartless exercises in velocity; they can be made to accord with, or reflect, the dramatic situation with more than bird-like joyousness.

§

In a way any fool can sing quickly. It is the slow things, the slow movements, that tax the resources both of composers and performers.

§

We must distinguish between 'flow' which is superficial, and which is as of deep waters. The one may move as quickly as the other, even more quickly—the movement is there; but the strength and the significance is far less—weight is lacking. It is obviously far more difficult to move a heavy than a light weight, and to keep it on the move—a flow of deep full tone needs great effort and control, but its greater emotional power is incontestable.

§

No vowel will 'open' unless we *make* it open. Mere relaxation will not do it; management (which is the same as effort) is required. The Englishman never opens a vowel naturally, as an Italian does; in some way or other he smothers it—quite a different thing from darkening or covering it. Our own language is quite as susceptible to clear sound as Italian, though Milton's reason for our failure is probably quite valid (*v.* p. 110). Every English vowel must be 'opened' as far as possible, not only for distinct speech, but because, without it, the colour of the voice is confused and muddy. A lovely picture cannot be painted with dirty, indeterminate colours.

§

The first requisite in singing a song is that its words should be clearly understood. So said an old theoretician. How simple, yet how wise; and how often transgressed by singers who have not the ghost of an idea of the meaning of either the words or the music of their song. This is evident from the way they sing; with false stresses, rhythmic indecision, inept colouring, and all the signs of *mis*understanding, which it is useless for them to deny. The same thing may be said of speakers, clerical or other. So much so that it often appears that a so-called unbeliever, through his imagination, knows far better what he is talking about than the so-called believer. The truth of the imagination is generally to be preferred to what may be called credal truth.

§

It was said of an actress[1] that:

'She takes hold of the dramatist's conception, absorbs it, and then gives it out again recreated in terms of her own personality and delighted imagination, so that you get the two-fold joy of one fine talent superimposed upon another.' At its best, this is what happens with the singer and his song.

§

Keeping the attention of an audience is not arrived at by any supernatural power, such as magic or even mesmerism, but simply by holding notes well. It is an affair of tension, as its name implies; of good *sostenuto*, in short. If the voice is pinned down properly, the listener is likewise affected.

§

When the soft palate is raised too high and the sound is not only concentrated but unduly constricted by cutting it off from the throat so that it cannot be eased and amplified, we get what may be called 'haw-haw' tone. It is the defect of the quality of concentration, the carrying of it to extremes; thus defeating its own ends.

§

Drivelling words, in the end, mean drivelling music. Music and poetry rise and fall together.

§

[1] By James Agate.

'Be not anxious how . . . or what ye shall say: for the Holy Spirit shall teach you in that very hour what ye ought to say.' The value of spontaneity cannot be underrated.

§

If the main principles of singing are mastered, detail will almost solve itself.

§

Phrasing is the movement of thought.

§

There is an expressive power in breath-taking. The intense, audible 'catch' in the breath, the sob, the sigh, are of great value when used at the right time; they need cultivation as much as any other aspect of singing.

§

I think we must distinguish between what may be called natural expression—the expression inherent in the very sound of a word, and emotional expression which may pass all bounds of decency, as it often does in hot-gospelling and such-like unbridled effusion. It was said that Whitfield, the preacher, could subdue his congregation by the utterance of a single word—the blessed word, 'Mesopotamia'. But the word itself could have sufficient meaning even without the personal instrumentality of the speaker. Again let it be said that *sound has its own significance.* In very many cases all we have to do (or little more) is to pronounce clearly, having developed vowel quality to the full and given ample articulation to our consonants— in itself a high achievement. The result will be quite satisfying, and there is no need to pump out our own feeling upon it. A perfectly objective presentation has a very healthy value of its own; it is often more capable of impressing, than a messy outpouring of personality.

§

If you work too hard on a note you are very apt to inhibit it, to (as it were) hang on to its coat-tails. To hit the target—somewhere in the region of the hard palate—the note has to fly off freely from the mechanism.

§

Telling tone comes more from the way the instrument is held—the relative position of the various parts—than from the power that is used upon it. If the factors are properly co-ordinated the effort required for even a loud note is not particularly great.

§

We may know about a thing, but the thing itself remains a mystery.

§

A good attack is as touchy a business as threading a needle—the slightest error, and the sound will not come through properly.

§

The voice is essentially the instrument of humanity. Objective nature links itself rather with the sounds of other instruments. It is through the voice that our emotions and aspirations are expressed. These therefore give us the criterion of of vocal sound and determine its kind and quality. There is no other criterion. A voice is to be judged by its human appeal, in the broadest sense. At its best the singer's art represents the endeavour to express fine poetry intensified by music.

§

Punctuation is the saving grace of passion; it makes sense of it, gives it coherence, prevents it from running amuck.

§

Brilliant, *timbrée* tone is the only tone which will clearly demonstrate the reedy nature of the voice. It is the *point de départ*, the perfect vocal state, towards which our supreme effort must be bent. Covered tone comes from it, as when light is shaded. Light is never extinguished, nor can it be. The amount of luminosity behind tone defines its quality. All colours are forms of light.

§

Colour is sensual; line is sense.

§

We have just said that there is no darkness without light. To which should be added that there is no openness without closure. Nothing exists except in terms and by reason of its contrary. How can there be openness, an open sound, unless there is something to define and limit it? which is to say that these contraries or opposites are not separate from each other, but condition each other *at one and the same time,* just as one force is conditioned by another. A deep philosophical truth is embedded here. The practical politics of this—did not Ruskin say that the voice afforded a perfect example of political economy?—is, that true freedom of sound is only possible when constraint goes with it. The finer the constraint, the more glorious the freedom; each plays upon its opposite. The most intense tone is produced by the strongest inward tension fighting the strongest outward expansion. Constriction or chaos can only come if each is taken by itself. Absolute relaxation is nonsense.

§

Extraneous Aids to Voice Production

(1) To get looseness *and* the requisite tension : the lifting and moving of the arms at right angles to the body with the hands hanging like dead weight. This indicates exactly what is wanted in the matter of balanced tension and relaxation. As the weight to be moved increases , i.e., in case of louder, firmer sound or greater vitality of utterance so must more tension be exercised.

(2) To get sound in the mask of the face: place hands, stiffly, each side of nose, as it were boxing and centralizing the sound there by this means.

(3) To get concentration of tone and the right verticality of the mouth : press cheeks in between teeth with fore-fingers.

(4) To get an open throat: hold back of neck (spine) with hands, feeling tension of muscles at that place. This, as it were, tends to get the back of the pharynx away from the front and so open the pharyngeal tube.

(5) To increase lift of breath: standing on tiptoe will often help in this.

(6) To ensure a truly expressive tone: use the left hand while singing, as a violinist might for *vibrato*. This tensioned throb will draw the mechanism together. Indeed, the whole body will, so to speak, converge upon the vocal cords, so that they become the focus of its energy.

Again it must be stressed that vocal technique is a physical matter in its mechanical aspect. How the body and muscles are used determines tone quality.

§

Gymnastics of the glottis, repeated throat 'clicks' of all sorts— k's, g's, etc.—should be practised, quite apart from singing. Vocal control is largely dependent upon this particular form of action.

Watch an acrobat at a circus. We marvel at the strength and beauty of his movements. But is there any difference, fundamentally, between such movements and those that a singer is required to make? The ordinary person is as far off the artistry of the one as of the other, and for precisely the same reason : that he has not learnt the necessary muscular control.

§

It is astonishing how with the music of the old masters, even the most unpractised ear can detect a wrong note: such a note does not *seem* right. It contradicts what is expected—it is illogical, against the nature and sense of the music. With much modern music any note will do—notes never appear wrong, because they are never right—or, shall we say, in proportion as they are not right (and according to the nature of music) we have no sense of wrongness. The nature of music may perhaps be defined by our sense of a *wrong* note.

§

Notes have to be bottled like champagne before they become sparkling and effervescent. It is the confinement, the limitation of sound which gives it life.

§

Provided you throw the voice into the head, you can start it from any depth you like, with corresponding modification of the tone. The important thing is not where the sound comes from, but where it goes to.

§

Heraclitus averred that strife was the parent of all things. Resistance is a sort of strife, the strife of opposing forces and it certainly seems as if both technical and spiritual perfection in performance depended upon it.

§

An exclamation, more than anything, shows up the indifferent singer. It must be natural; any artificiality spoils it. Thus:

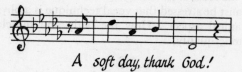

A soft day, thank God!

contains almost the whole difficulty of this particular song of Stanford.

§

If you sing Aw when you intend to sing Ah, the Aw is bound to be bad, though, in itself, Aw is a perfectly good vowel—a matter of purpose.

§

Quality of tone and the means that secure it are one and the same thing; they cannot be divorced. Much hinges on this twofold truth.

§

428

'Be still and know that I am God.' The hardest thing in singing or indeed in performance of any kind is to express calm, unruffled by any hint of passion or excitement.

§

Theories are of no use unless they are acted upon; they are not even true till they are found to work. 'Truth is a whole situation of thought and person; it is the map *and* the traveller making the journey.' (H. J. Blackham).

§

'Honneur ne cherche, fidèle je suis.'

This grand old motto may be commended to the singer or indeed to anyone who aspires to a public career. It represents the supreme test of integrity. We transgress the purity of such an affirmation a dozen times a day—the artist is specially tempted to do so—but it will always remain to look us in the face and to say to us 'Well, or ill done!' according as we have been true or false to its principle.

§

'Every virtue has its possible defect: that of tension, unless counteracted, may induce hard tone and restricted resonance.'

Index

433   R